IRISH MINSTRELS
AND
MUSICIANS

IRISH MINSTRELS

AND

MUSICIANS

WITH NUMEROUS DISSERTATIONS ON RELATED SUBJECTS

BY

CAPT. FRANCIS O'NEILL

WITH A NEW INTRODUCTION BY

BARRY O'NEILL

 NORWOOD EDITIONS • DARBY, PA. • 1973

This reprint first published in the United States
of America 1973 by Norwood Editions, 842 Main St.
Darby, Pennsylvania 19023

Library of Congress Cataloging in Publication Data

O'Neill, Francis, 1849-
Irish minstrels and musicians.

Bibliography: p.
1. Minstrels.   2. Musicians, Irish.   I. Title.
ML287.05   1972   781.7'415

Library of Congress Catalog Card Number
72-9366
ISBN 0-88305-494-9

We are grateful to the Gertrude Kistler Memorial Library, Rosemont, Pa.
for making available to Norwood Editions the copy
from which this reprint edition was produced.

Manufactured in the United States of America

Introduction to the Reprint Edition

The core of *Irish Minstrels and Musicians* is the biographies of the traditional musicians. The dissertations on related subjects include histories of the harp and pipes, and samples of Irish folk tunes and texts. Drawn mostly from other publications in O'Neill's five hundred volume collection of Hiberniana, they make interesting reading but lack the systematic presentation and evaluation of evidence which is the mark of the scholar. This was inevitable for one without library facilities and the stimulation and criticism of his colleagues, working five thousand miles away from Ireland's shores. But as a storyteller, a chronicler of the musicians themselves, O'Neill excels. His language is flowing and eloquent. His enthusiasm for his subject is obvious. He seems to be living in the world of the wandering minstrels a century earlier, and one wonders how he was able to manage the police department of a large American city.

The titled sketches include 191 Uilleann pipers, 54 fiddlers, 38 harpers, 19 pipemakers, 12 fluters, 10 warpipers, 8 music collectors, one accordion player, and one ceili band. No players of the concertina, banjo or tinwhistle are mentioned. These numbers certainly are not intended to reflect the relative sizes of each population. Rather, they show Captain O'Neill's attitude as to which instruments are properly traditional ones.

The emphasis on pipers resulted from his conviction that their race would soon be extinct, an understandable view in the light of the history of the Irish harp. When the last of the wandering harpers died in the early 1800's, the traditional style of playing was lost. Artificial respiration in the form of revival societies, harp schools, and stipends for harpers proved ineffective. The class of wealthy Irish gentry had disappeared leaving their harpers without a source of livelihood.

At the turn of the twentieth century, one hundred years later, W. H. Grattan Flood made the assessment that there were scarcely a dozen good pipers left in Ireland. Unlike the harp which had made its niche with the upper class, the pipes had entertained gentleman and countryman alike. But the famine had sobered the mood of the rural people. General poverty and the opposition of a large sector of the clergy to dance and group merriment had made the vocation of the wandering pipers an unremunerative one, synonymous with that of the pauper.

It is remarkable that Captain O'Neill should try to wage a programme of revival from the midwestern United States, and even more remarkable that his efforts have had significant impact. Born in 1849 in the family home which still stands at Tralibane, Co. Cork, he travelled the world as a seaman before coming to America in 1866. He gained a position on the Chicago police force in 1873. Within a month he was shot by a fleeing burglar, but his tenacity in the encounter gained him the first in a series of promotions. From 1901 until his retirement in 1905 he held the highest post of all, general superintendent of police. Throughout his tenure he sought out and hired the finest Irish musicians, assuring them of stable and socially respectable jobs on the police force, with adequate time to pursue their music.

O'Neill's Music of Ireland, a collection of 1850 dance tunes and airs, was published in 1903. In 1907 *O'Neill's Dance Music of Ireland, 1001 Gems of Irish Melody* appeared, similar to the 1903 work, but with some alterations in the dance tunes, and without the airs. These books have since become the main printed tune references for traditional musicians. In the early twenties he published *O'Neill's Irish Music* and *Waifs and Strays of Gaelic Melody,* each containing 400 tunes arranged for piano by his niece, Selena O'Neill. Captain O'Neill tells the story of his collecting experiences in *Irish Folk Music: A Fascinating Hobby,* 1910, also reprinted in 1973 by Norwood Editions in its Folklore Series.

The completion of *Irish Minstrels and Musicians* in 1913 was as much a part of the Captain's revival effort as his collection of tunes for publication and the hiring of musicians for the Chicago police department. Drawing on a large repertoire of laudatory phrases, he extols the musicianship of his heroes of the past and present. No contemporary fiddler or piper could miss the point. The tradition of the bards, the king's harpers, the travelling pipers welcome in every cottage— that heritage is now in his hands. Chapters on "Reverend Musicians," "Dancing, a Legitimate Amusement" are included to combat the stifling effect of clerical opposition. A chapter on "Gentleman Pipers" strikes at the notion that pipering is the occupation of beggars.

Irish Minstrels and Musicians was a financial failure. This seems odd considering that the census of 1910 counted over 4,000,000 Irish-born or first generation in America. The price of the book was $2.50. Certainly the American Irish are no less conscious of their national origins than other ethnic groups. While the American Irish continued to define themselves as a community, they abandoned many of the national traits of their homeland. Only a few valued the traditional culture of language or musicianship. Facing poverty and bigotry by the established, the community's aim was social and financial respectability. The Irish-American press reflected these concerns. It emphasized the gaining of nationhood for Ireland and the contributions of noted Irishmen to the United States. Irish-Americans should be regarded as full and equal citizens, was its message as it stressed those aspects in which the two countries were alike. This, however, did not include the tradition of itinerant musicianship and crossroads dancing. Search the output of Irish-American journalists, authors, and political leaders of O'Neill's time for descriptions of rural life back home, and O'Neill's work stands out almost alone, marking the strong-mindedness and sense of self of its author.

The monetary failure of the project must be blamed partly on the Captain himself who seems to have felt obliged to forward a complimentary autographed copy to most of the people mentioned in the work.

In any case O'Neill's publishing activities cost him several thousand dollars. His embitterment at cultural apathy, revealed in the closing paragraphs of the present volume, lasted until his death in 1936. We wish he could have known that the demise of his beloved music was not imminent, that his own efforts were partly responsible for its preservation.

In 1972, traditional music and the pipes in particular are being pursued by the young not with a sentiment of nostalgia or duty to their ancestors but with fanatical fervour. The *Fleadh Ceoil* festival of traditional music of August, 1972, was attended by 1400 players and tens of thousands of spectators. *Na Piobairí Uilleann,* a society for Irish pipers formed in 1968, lists almost 200 pipers in its membership. In America and England, Irish music is being taken up by persons of all ethnic backgrounds.

This could not have developed without a store of traditional musicians, and it is likely that *Irish Minstrels and Musicians* bolstered the determination of these artists during the darker days of the twenties, thirties and forties. In a new society, bearers of a folk tradition come to regard their art as worthless and foolish. I have found skilled pipers and fiddlers who simply laid down their instruments forever, for want of encouragement. What more effective way to combat this dejection than the publication of an honour roll of names, origins, and personal histories. I have visited musicians who had never seen this book but drew pride from mere knowledge of its existence.

While we learn many of the idiosyncracies of the players, details of their instrumental technique are sparse and vague. Jimmy O'Brien "produced combinations and turns by a dextrous movement of the bottom of the chanter on his knee." John McFadden, the fiddler had an "airy style of playing" with "crispness" and "rhythmic swing." This is more regrettable in view of the present trend of local styles to fuse into one or two eclectic styles. Disc and cylinder recordings of O'Neill's pipers show many different fashions of playing, some of which are not currently represented. What a varied garden of techniques must have flourished in the early nineteenth century. It is a frequent situation that those writing from personal knowledge develop unstated rules dividing what ought to be published from what ought not. As these rules are not explicit they are not subject to critical scrutiny and we are left wishing the writer was still available for questioning.

The descriptions of pipering and pipemaking in America are of special interest as cases of a rural art attempting to adapt to an urban environment. In O'Neill's opinion the finest uilleann pipers were to be found on his side of the Atlantic. A number of their phonograph recordings remain and, even to the ear of a beginner, a distinctive American style is evident—fast reels with plentiful ornamentation, staccato fingering, the ends of phrases chopped off to give the sensation of hurtling onwards, the use of the regulators in a varied and syncopated way. It evolved for use on the stage of the variety hall and in vaudeville, and was designed to catch the attention of listeners of any ethnic origin, not relax them in an entertainment lasting for hours. Patsy Touhey of Galway, Boston and the Bronx was the outstanding practitioner of this style. Michael Anderson of Sligo and New York, Michael Carney of Mayo and Brooklyn, Tom Ennis of Chicago are gone, but in the present day the style is continued by Tom Busby of Fermanagh and New York, Andy Conroy and Paddy Lavin, both of Roscommon and New York. Evidence of its origin points to John Eagan of Galway and New York, the teacher of Anderson and Touhey, and Billy Taylor of Cavan, Louth and Philadelphia. But this is conjecture for these two players died in the last century.

An Irish-American style of pipemaking originated by the Taylor brothers of Philadelphia is exemplified in the instruments of the members of the Chicago Irish Music Club (p. 479) and in some of the photographs of the American professionals Barney Delaney (p. 311), Thomas Kerrigan (p. 262), Patsy Touhey (p. 314), and Eddy Joyce (p. 264). For contrast the older style can be seen in the hands of John Wayland (p. 331), Robert Thompson (p. 277), and Shane O'Neill (p. 269). The keys of Taylor's regulators are formed as wide slabs, silver or nickel-plated, in contrast to the brass, teardrop shapes of the older style keys. The top of the bass regulator is folded and lies back down along the side of the stock. The bodies of the chanter and regulators are often squared blocks of ebony. Four or five regulators are not uncommon—in general a more lavish and massive style of pipes in response to the taste and greater wealth of the Irish-American players, their stationary lifestyle, and the variability of the American climate.

The Taylors worked on Euclid and Race Streets in Philadelphia. Billy Taylor was a short man, light-haired and competent on many instruments. His death occurred in 1892. His younger brother Charles, said to have been the real mechanic, died in 1893. Their fashion of pipemaking has been pursued by Michael Anderson of Sligo and New York, Patsy Brown of Boston, Edward Boyle, Robert Hutton and Conner of Wilmington, Delaware, Ned and Tom Crowley of Roscommon and New York, Patrick Hennelly of Chicago, Edward Brennan of Philadelphia, Michael Carney of Brooklyn, and Richard L. O'Mealy of Belfast.

Taylor's most extravagant models may be seen in the hands of Nicholas Burke (p. 280) and John Beatty (p. 479). The former is fashioned of ivory, while the latter is fitted with a double chanter, two bores, two reeds in a single piece of wood. An extra regulator is provided to give three low notes. The most unusual feature is the design of the two middle regulators, each of which contains four separate bores, reeds and tuning pins, each regulator key activating a separate chamber with its own reed. Beatty's set, alleged to have cost him $500 in the 1880's, could sound fifteen different reeds at one time, with the co-operation of his friends. These pipes are today owned and skilfully played by Joe Shannon, a Chicago fireman. Their craftsmanship is perfect and they have survived the years in untarnished condition, but no wandering minstrel could afford to buy or have the endurance to carry this mass of ebony and metal. Surely Taylor and those he inspired belie the assertion that America is one of the few nations without its own distinctive species of bagpipe.

For several years I have been compiling the personal histories of Irish-American pipers with the intention of publishing a sequel to this book. Frequently I have come upon the memory of Captain O'Neill's heroes, but always there were signs of its ultimate disappearance. Thomas Kerrigan's grandson knew of his grandfather's fame, but Kerrigan's great grandson did not. The widow of Barney Delaney's grandson knew his name and occupation but was unaware that he was musically inclined, let alone that he was, in O'Neill's opinion, the greatest living player of music for dancers. Hopefully this republication of *Irish Minstrels and Musicians* will inspire others to record the history of all types of Irish music before it is forgotten.

I am grateful to Brendan Breathnach of Dublin, Karl Partridge of Belfast, Sean Reid of Ennis, Co. Clare, Tom Standeven of Haddonfield, New Jersey, and Gail Kendall of Ann Arbor, Michigan, for information and ideas used in this introduction.

BARRY O'NEILL

Department of Psychology
University of Michigan
Ann Arbor, Michigan
November, 1972.

CAPT. FRANCIS O'NEILL

IRISH MINSTRELS

AND

MUSICIANS

WITH NUMEROUS DISSERTATIONS
ON RELATED SUBJECTS

BY

CAPT. FRANCIS O'NEILL

AUTHOR OF "IRISH FOLK MUSIC: A FASCINATING HOBBY"

COMPILER OF "THE MUSIC OF IRELAND," "THE DANCE MUSIC
OF IRELAND," "O'NEILL'S IRISH MUSIC FOR PIANO OR
VIOLIN," "POPULAR SELECTIONS FROM THE DANCE
MUSIC OF IRELAND, HARMONIZED"

PROFUSELY ILLUSTRATED

"Oh ; native music beyond comparing
The sweetest far on the ear that falls
Thy gentle numbers the heart remembers
Thy strains enchain us in tender thralls"

CHICAGO
THE REGAN PRINTING HOUSE
1913

FOR SALE BY
LYON & HEALY, CHICAGO
M. H. GILL & SON, DUBLIN

DEDICATED

TO THE

VENERATED MEMORY

OF

MY PARENTS

WHOSE TUNEFUL TASTES

AND

MEMORIZED MELODIES

ARE CHERISHED

AS A

MOST PRECIOUS HERITAGE

PREFACE

No class of Irish worthies has been treated with less consideration in biographical literature than Minstrels and Musicians. The Bards, as far as Poets, Lawgivers and Genealogists are concerned, have had their meed of recognition from the annalists and historians, but the fourth order, or Musicians, have been much less glorified.

Mirth is God's medicine, and never was there an agency better qualified to administer it than the favorites of the Muses in all lands.

Pitiably few are the harpers, unrivaled in their art, whose names even have been preserved. ◄To casual mention, rather than deliberate purpose, we owe not a little of our meagre store of knowledge concerning some of the very greatest performers of their day, and had it not been for the thoughtfulness of Bunting in having the personal recollections of Arthur O'Neill, the celebrated harper, committed to writing in the first decade of the nineteenth century, scarcely a tradition of their existence would now remain. As the harp declined the vogue of the Irish, or Union bagpipe increased. Accomplished performers on this improved and highly developed instrument became as famous as their predecessors, the harpers. They filled theatrical engagements in the principal cities of the Kingdom, and even entertained royalty on numerous occasions. Now their status is less enviable than that of the harper a century ago, and similarly their utter extinction—sad to say—is among the probabilities of the not distant future.

Histories of music are so wanting in certain features, as to be little better than dry catalogues of names and dates; and while other nations have perpetuated the memories of their worthy musicians, no Plutarch has arisen to immortalize the forgotten though deserving Minstrels and Musicians of Ireland.

The desire to contribute something helpful towards that end, stimulated by the brief notices in Grattan Flood's works was the underlying motive which led to this undertaking. The flattering reviews of *Irish Folk Music: A Fascinating Hobby,* and the eager interest evinced by people of similar tastes from near and far indicated unmistakably that to many the subject was still of vital consequence.

In preparing chapters descriptive of Irish Folk Music, and the lives of eminent Irish pipers, intended for an enlarged edition of the work named, data and material accumulated in such quantities, that the original design developed into a more comprehensive purpose.

Although no available source of information has been overlooked in the compilation of the biographical sketches, errors and omissions are inevitable. Even so, something has been accomplished in a neglected field which invites further endeavor.

Unrestrained by the dictates of commercial wisdom, fervid zeal may have silenced the voice of discretion. Should the student of Irish music lore however appreciate the diversified contents of this labor of love, the author can endure with complacence the personal sacrifice which the publication of such a large volume entails.

Words can but faintly express the writer's sense of obligation to the score

7

and more of kindred spirit, who unselfishly volunteered such information as they possessed to aid in the promotion of a cherished cause. Not only that, but an unexpected number on their own initiative, engaged actively in tracing and bringing to light elusive details, and stories of famous but well-nigh forgotten musicians of bygone days.

For their faithful and tireless cooperation special credit is due to Mr. John S. Wayland, founder of the Cork Pipers' Club; Prof. P. J. Griffith of the Leinster School of Music; Mr. M. Flanagan, Dublin; Mr. Patrick Whelan, of Scarawalsh, Ballycarney, Wexford; Prof. Patrick D. Reidy, London; Mr. Nicholas Burke, Brooklyn, New York; Mr. Morgan P. Jageurs, Parkville, Melbourne, Victoria; and Mr. Patrick O'Leary, Parkside Adelaide, South Australia.

To Dr. Grattan Flood, K. S. G., we owe a double debt of gratitude. Not only were his published works an inspiration and an aid, but his unfailing kindness and liberality in communicating any desired information deserve much more than this simple tribute of acknowledgment.

Not less willing to be helpful in any way in which their counsel or research might be of service were many others to whom thanks are due and whose names the writer records with pleasure: Mr. Patrick Dunne Kilbraugh, Ballingarry near Thurles, Tipperary; Seamus ua Casaide of the Dublin Pipers' Club; Mr. William Halpin, Newmarket-on-Fergus, and Mr. Patrick Powell of Tulla, County Clare; Hon. John O'Neill, J. P. Sarsfield Court, Glanmire, County Cork; Mr. George A. M. Leech, San Francisco, California; Mr. Patrick E. McCormick, Seattle, Washington; Capt. Michael Dunn, Milwaukee, Wisconsin; Mr. William F. Hanafin, and Mr. John Finley, Boston, Mass.; Mr. Patrick J. Touhey, Mr. Patrick Fitzpatrick, and Mr. Frank O'Coffey, of New York City. In the City of Chicago as might be expected much valuable information was obtained. Chief among the contributors in this respect were Mr. John Gillan, Mr. Denis Maloney, and Mr. Richard Sullivan; Police Officers Timothy M. Dillon, and William Walsh; Sergt. James Early, and Mrs. Jane Early; and Prof. W. H. Cahill.

Words fail to express our sense of obligation to Lieut. John McLennan, former head of the Department of Police, Edinburgh, Scotland, for his courtesy in furnishing necessary information relating to Duncan McDougall; and to Inspector James R. Motion of the Glasgow police, who kindly rendered a like service concerning Peter Kelly, the last performer of note on the Irish pipes in Scotland.

Few can realize the difficulties encountered in the quest for reliable information on which to base the brief biographies of the class dealt with in this work. As a consequence sketches had to be amended from time to time, patched out with each new crumb of intelligence that came to hand, and rewritten as often as the circumstances required.

Now that a forward step has been taken in this line of inquiry and effort, others who may follow will obviously be relieved of many perplexities and find fewer obstacles in their path.

Chicago, July 4, 1913.

Francis O'Neill

AUTHORITIES QUOTED

Anthologia Hibernica, 1793-1794.
Alday: *A Pocket Volume of Airs, Duets, Songs and Marches; Circa* 1800.
A German Prince; *Tour in England, Ireland, and France*, 1832.
Armstrong; *The Irish and the Highland Harps*, 1904.
Barnaby Rich; *A New Description of Ireland*, 1610.
Browne's *Pastorals*, 1625.
Bacon; *Sylva Sylvorum*, 1627.
Bunting; *A General Collection of the Ancient Irish Music*, 1796.
Bunting; *A General Collection of the Ancient Music of Ireland*, 1809.
Bunting; *The Ancient Music of Ireland*, 1840.
Brand; *Observations on Popular Antiquities*, 1813.
Brewer; *The Beauties of Ireland*, 1825.
Bartlett, Willis, and Coyne; *The Scenery and Antiquities of Ireland. Circa* 1841.
Bennett; *The History of Bandon*, 1869.
Burke, Rev. Thomas N. *Lectures and Sermons*, 1872.
Bernard; *Life of Samuel Lover*, 1874.
Brown and Stratton; *British Musical Biography*, 1897.
Chaucer; *Canterbury Tales*. Author died, 1400.
Camden's *Britannia—Ireland*, 1586.
Campbell, Dr.; *Philosophical Survey of the South of Ireland*, 1778.
Carr; *The Stranger in Ireland*, 1806.
Crofton Croker; *Researches in the South of Ireland*, 1824.
Carleton; *Traits and Stories of the Irish Peasantry*, 1830.
Conran, Prof.; *National Music of Ireland*, 1850.
Durer, Albrecht—Works. First published, 1603.
Dublin Penny Journal, 1832-1836.
Dublin Monthly Magazine, 1842.
Dublin Illustrated Journal, 1862.
De Burgh; *Landowners of Ireland*, 1878.
Davis, Thomas; *Prose Writings*, 1889.
Evelyn's *Diary*, 1668.
Fuller; *History of the Holy Warre*, 1639.
Frair Clyn; *Annals of Ireland*. Published, 1849.
Forbes, Dr.; *Memorandums Made in Ireland*, 1853.
Fraser, Duncan; *Some Reminiscences and the Bagpipe*, 1906.
Fitz Gerald; *Stories of Famous Songs*, 1906.
Gallilei; *Dialogue on Ancient and Modern Music*. 1581.
Gentleman's Magazine, 1751. (Commenced 1731.)
Giraldus Cambrensis; *Topographia Hibernia* (Translated), 1867.
Gaskin; *Varieties of Irish History*, 1869.
Grove's *Dictionary of Music and Musicians*, 1879-1889.
Grattan Flood; *A History of Irish Music*, 1905.
Grattan Flood; *The Story of the Harp*, 1905.

Grattan Flood; *The Story of the Bagpipe,* 1911.
Galpin; *Old English Instruments of Music,* 1911.
Hogarth's Works—First published, 1768.
Hardiman; *Irish Minstrelsy,* 1831.
Hall, Mr. and Mrs.; *Ireland; Its Scenery and Character,* 1840.
Hall, Mr. and Mrs.; *A Week in Killarney,* 1843.
Haverty; *Three Hundred Irish Airs,* 1858.
Haweis; *Music and Morals,* 1871.
Irish Penny Journal, 1841.
Joyce, P. W.; *Ancient Irish Music,* 1872.
Kohl, J. G.; *Ireland,* 1844.
Knight; *Old England,* 1845.
Keating; *History of Ireland*—English edition, 1866.
Lynch; *Cambrensis Eversus,* 1662.
Ledwich; *Antiquities of Ireland,* 1792.
Logan; *The Scottish Gael,* 1833.
Lewis; *Topographical Dictionary of Ireland,* 1837.
Lady Chatterton; *Rambles in the South of Ireland,* 1839.
Lover; *Legends and Stories of Ireland,* 1848.
Leslie's Popular Monthly, 1877.   (Commenced Jan. 1, 1876.)
Lady Wilde; *Ancient Cures, Charms and Usages of Ireland,* 1890.
Le Fanu; *Seventy Years of Irish Life,* 1893.
Lilly Grove; *Dancing,* 1901.
Major; *Greater Britian,* 1521.
Madden; *Infirmities of Genius,* 1833.
Mooney; *History of Ireland,* 1857.
Manson; *The Highland Bagpipe,* 1901.
Milligan Fox; *Annals of the Irish Harpers,* 1911.
McGoun; *The Repository of Scots and Irish Airs, circa,* 1803.
O'Conor; *Dissertations on the History of Ireland,* 1766.
O'Halloran; *A General History of Ireland,* 1788.
O'Farrell's *National Irish Music,* 1797-1800.
O'Farrell's *Pocket Companion for the Irish or Union Pipes,* Books 1 & 2, 1806.
O'Farrell's *Pocket Companion for the Irish, or Union Pipes,* Books 3 & 4, 1810.
Owenson, Miss; *Patriotic Sketches,* 1807.
O'Donovan; *Annals of the Kingdom of Ireland by the Four Masters,* 1851.
O'Curry; *Manners and Customs of the Ancient Irish,* 1873.
O'Reilly, Boyle; *The Poetry and Song of Ireland,* 1889.
Powell; *The History of Cambria,* 1584.
Plumptre; *Narrative of a Residence in Ireland,* 1817.
Ryan; *Worthies of Ireland,* 1821.
Stanyhurst; *De Rebus in Hibernia Gestis,* 1584.
Smith; *History of Cork,* 1750.
Séward; *Topographia Hibernica,* 1795.
Surenne's *Songs of Ireland,* 1854.
Shelton Mackenzie; *Bits of Blarney,* 1884.
Thompson; *The Hibernian Muse,* 1787.
Trotter; *Walks Through Ireland,* 1819.
Thackeray; *The Irish Sketch Book,* 1842.
Walker; *Historical Memoirs of the Irish Bards,* 1786.
Walker; *History of Music in England,* 1907.

CONTENTS

LIST OF ILLUSTRATIONS

MUSICAL EXAMPLES

IRISH MINSTRELS AND MUSICIANS

CHAPTER I

BARDS AND THE BARDIC ORDERS

"You too ye bards whom sacred raptures fire
To chaunt your heroes to your country's lyre;
Who consecrate in your immortal strain
Brave patriot souls in righteous battle slain;
Securely now the tuneful task renew,
How nobler themes in deathless songs pursue."

No subject relating to Ireland in ancient times whether it be law or literature, militarism or music, can be discussed intelligently without reference to the bards. Consequently so much has been written concerning the bardic order, that it may be said to constitute a literature in itself, for in no other country did they exist in such numbers, or exert such dominant influence on the national life.

With the grey dawn of legendary history the bards make their first appearance, and they continued to exercise their peculiar sway in uninterrupted succession down to the days of Turlogh O'Carolan in the eighteenth century. In all those early ages when war was the chief business of society and commerce was but little known, the romantic scenery of Ireland echoed to the strains of her bards. Their songs in the language of Brewer, an English writer, stimulated the warrior to enterprise and raised enthusiasm in the hall of triumph.

The professors of the divine arts of poetry and music were rewarded with honors and emoluments proportionate to the value of their efforts to elevate the national feeling, and exploit the deeds of distinguished warriors. The harp of Ireland which constituted its pride in prosperity proved its solace in adversity, and stimulated a spirit of romance in real life.

Under ancient laws by which social grades were distinguished according to the number of colors in their garments, the peasantry and lower orders were to have but one. The principal nobility or knights were allowed to wear five colors; the *Ollamhs* or dignified bards six, while royalty itself wore but seven. High as the profession of arms was held among the Irish it is clear that letters were more highly respected.

It is undeniable that poetry and music were held in high esteem by all nations in all ages, but it does not appear that those arts were more respected than the profession of arms in any nation but Ireland, warlike though its people always have þeen.

Seven centuries before the Christian era the renowned Ollamh Fodhla monarch of Ireland, made a law that the dignity of an antiquary, a physician, a poet, and a harp-player, should not be conferred but upon persons descended from the most illustrious families in the whole country.

17

In this aristocracy of intellect ranking next to royalty there were four principal orders, the first or highest being that of the poets—*Ollamhain Re Dan* or *Filidhe* (Filea). They versified the maxims of religion, recited the martial odes to inspire a sentiment of military ardor, celebrated the valor of their chief or prince, and sang his personal praises. As entertainers at the festive board they modulated their voices to the sweet sounds of the harp, an instrument which Conran says every member of the bardic order could touch with a master hand.

The *Filidhe* who were also heralds accompanied their chiefs in war, and marched at the head of their armies in the field of battle arrayed in their distinctive robes, surrounded by the *Oirfidigh* or instrumental musicians.

As D'Arcy McGee says:

> "Our race was mighty once when at the head
> Wise men like steadfast torches burned and led;
> When Ollamh's lore and royal Cormac's spell
> Guided the Gael all things with them went well."

They watched the progress of the combat for the purpose of describing the feats of arms in future epics. Theirs was also the duty of composing birthday odes as well as lamentations for the dead—the caoines which continued to be heard in the wilder and more primitive parts of Ireland until comparatively recent times.

The second order were designated *Breitheamhain* (Brehons) or legislative bards who promulgated and recited the laws in a kind of monotonous chant seated on an eminence in the open air. The Brehons acted also in the double capacity of judges and legislators; dispensing justice as well as assisting in framing the laws.

The *Seanachaidhe* or third order were antiquaries, historians, and genealogists. They recorded remarkable events, and preserved the genealogies of their patrons in a kind of unpoetical stanza like the French and English heralds of the middle ages. Having in mind the duties and accomplishments of the genealogists, Dean Swift said: "Barbarous and ignorant as we were in former centuries, there was more effectual care taken by our ancestors to preserve the memory of times and persons, than we find in this age of learning and politeness as we are pleased to call it."

Entirely distinct was the fourth order—the *Oirfidigh*, or performers on the different kinds of musical instruments, each class being appropriately named from the instruments they professedly played. The head or director of this order was named *Ollamh Re Ceol,* or Musical Doctor.

In a poem describing the duties of his order Dubthach, a bard who lived in the days of St. Patrick, says: "The learned poets and antiquaries shall be ready to direct the kings and nobles according to the laws, preserve the records of the nation, and the genealogy of the families, and instruct youth in the arts and sciences."

It is from such of their chronicles as escaped the destructive fury of the invading Danes and Normans, that historians derive most of what passes for ancient Irish history. However much we may be inclined to rely on such noted authorities as Walker, Bunting, and others, we must allow that modern critical study of ancient records and manuscripts appear to justify a growing belief that the significance attached to the term Bard was much too general in its application. From the *Ancient Laws of Ireland* we learn that the profession of poet was of the highest rank and comprised seven grades or orders the highest that of Professor or Bard being attainable only after seven to twelve years' study at a native Irish college.

Of one of the latter named Brae, who usurped the Sovereignty, but who lacked a proper conception of kingly hospitality, the chronicler says: "The knives of his people were not greased at his table, nor did their breath smell of ale at his banquet. Neither poets, nor their bards, nor their satirists, nor their harpers, nor their pipers, nor their trumpeters, etc., were ever seen engaged in amusing them at court."

Many extracts from ancient writings could be submitted in support of the opinion that the term Bard should be understood in a much more restricted sense. Entirely at variance with our accepted estimate of their exalted rank is the statement in the fourth volume of the *Ancient Laws of Ireland* "A Bard now is one without lawful learning, but his own intellect." This definition is by no means inappropriate to a class of ambitious persons who may be considered their lineal successors. Men of limited education but possessing much native ability, keen of wit, and fluent in flowers of fancy, Ireland bred at all times in abundance. Sometimes in honor but more often in derision, they have been hailed as Bards and treated with varying consideration.

Robert Bruce Armstrong, author of *The Irish and the Highland Harps,* says as a result of his research, that the profession of poet and musician were quite distinct. The term Bard is of infrequent mention in Irish MSS, and when it is used by English and Anglo-Irish writers of the sixteenth century, it is solely with regard to "poets, rimers, or reciters." The term Bard does not appear ever to have been used to indicate a harper or musician, unless the person so designated was also a minor poet or "rimer."

The same may be said of Scotland, for Martin, the historian says, each chieftain retained a physician, orator, poet, bard, musician, etc., so that neither in Ireland nor Scotland were the designations poets, bards and harpers, interchangeable terms. In Hardiman's *Irish Minstrelsy* the author's mention of Bards has reference to poets. Neither are Bards noteworthy in the *Annals of the Four Masters,* while events concerning poets, harpers, minstrels, and musicians, were recorded with prominence and frequency.

The heads of the professions comprised under the general term of Bard were called *Ollamhs.* They as well as their wives enjoyed special privileges. Bards and musicians had portions of land assigned them for their maintenance. The high honors and emoluments attendant on their art, must naturally have produced eminence in many of its numerous professors.

Giraldus Cambrensis (Gerald the Welshman), who scarcely allows the Irish any other good quality, confesses their ascendancy in music. "I can only praise their excellence in music," he says, "in which they are skilled incomparably beyond any other nation I have seen."

The *Ollamhs* of music, or those raised to the highest order of musicians of ancient Erin, were obliged by the rules of the order to be perfectly accomplished in the performance of three peculiar classes of music, namely: the *Suantraighe*— soothing, or sleep-producing music; the *Goltraighe*—dolorous, grief producing, or lamentation music; and the *Geantraighe*—joy, merriment and laughter-producing music.

This development, and specialization of music it must be understood, was of very ancient origin.

From Prof. O'Curry's *Manners and Customs of the Ancient Irish,* we learn that it existed long before the arrival of the Milesians. Daghda, the great chief and druid of the Tuatha De Danaan, on the recovery of his harper Uaithne and his harp, carried off by the Fomorians on their retreat, played "the three musical feats which gave distinction to a harper, namely: the *Suantraighe,* (which from its deep murmuring caused sleep) ; the *Geantraighe,* (which from its merriment caused laughter) ; and the *Goltraighe* (which from its melting plaintiveness caused crying)."

In the opinion of Prof. Conran, author of *The National Music of Ireland,* (London, 1850), Irish airs admit of five classifications as follows: Amorous; Festive; Rural; Martial; and Dirge Music.

In the vicissitudes of time and the untoward conditions resulting from invasion and spoliation the bardic order declined in number an importance until finally the poets, brehons, seanachies, and other attendants of royalty and nobility entirely disappeared, leaving no survivals of their privileged class but the bards of the late centuries, who doubly dowered by nature combined the twin arts of poetry and music.

As Walker says: The character of the bard once so reverenced in Ireland began to sink into contempt in the reign of Queen Elizabeth.

No wonder that under the accumulated woes of her reign, Irish prestige almost faded away and the muse winged her flight from the fated land, or wept and wailed over sorrows that no bravery could dispel, or no courage avert. Gradually, slowly, yet surely, the race of bards became extinct. The years have long passed by when every clan had its lord, and every chief his minstrel.

From a powerful caste the bards in course of time participating in the misfortunes of their chieftains and people, became personal attendants of individual chiefs and finally became wandering minstrels partaking of the hospitality of the reduced gentry of the ancient race, and even of the upstart squireens in their last degenerate days.

From the following petition by one of the once powerful McCarthys appealing to the "Lords Justices" for the restoration of his patrimony about the middle of the eighteenth century, we may form some conception of the impoverished condition to which a scion of that princely race had been reduced by the confiscation of his inheritance. His case was no doubt typical of the times in which it was written, and we can well realize that neither bards, harpers, nor other musicians, could long survive the fallen fortunes and decay of their historic patrons.

> Most Worthy Gentlemen:
> I, Dennis McCarthy, a poor indigent, miserable, deplorable, lamentable, needy, distressed, friendless, unfortunate, misfortunate, student, and scholar, learner and disciple, and follower, and lover, and admirer, and friend, to the tuneful Nine, and Heliconian Choir, do exposulate, invoke, obsecrate, beg, pray, and beseech your worships, and lordships, and majestical powers, grandeurs, highnesses, and mightinesses, and excellencies, to commisserate, pity, and take compassion, and bemoan, and touched with the state and condition of me, Mr. McCarthy, extracted, descended, and derived, and sprung, and come from the most powerful, most mighty, most wise, most witty, most learned, most exquisite, most refined, most polished, most finished, most accomplished, most polite, most established, most consummate, most deserving, most meritorious, most eminent, most honorable, most liberal, most free, most glorious, most noble, most

splendid, most bright, most heroic, most illustrious, most magnani-
mous, most warlike, most brave, most renowned, and most courageous race, stock, lineage, pedigree, genealogy, and generation, of the
princely regal, royal, martial and grand McCarthys, of the County of
Kerry, whose noble actions, and exploits, achievements, performances, transactions, labours, and works, will never be forgotten,
defamed, disannulled, annihilated, antiquated, obliterated by tradition, time, antiquity, or even eternity; but raised historied, and ennobled, aggrandized, eternized, advanced, promoted, extolled, elevated by following and ensuing, and coming-after posterity, and children, and succeeding and future time, and recorded, commemorated, and related, and reached, and accepted, and dictated, and
rehearsed, and established in histories, records, registries, annals,
memories compendiums, and libels of glory, and fame, and character,
and reputation; who am son and heir, and proprietor, and poor dear
child, of the strong, fierce, bold, daring, terrible, and formidable, and
stout and brave, Timothy, Thady, McTiege, McOwen, McDerby,
McFlorence, McCharles, McDaniel, McCarthy (Lord Muskerry),
formerly, and antiently living, and inhabiting, dwelling and resorting
in the county of Kerry, who then and at that time, there, and at that
place had and held, kept and possessed, and enjoyed a plentiful and
bountiful, copious, hospitable, and open house, dwelling and habitation and abode for all sorts and sizes of people, young and old, men
and women, boys and girls, gentle and simple, proper and common,
generous and rustical, poor and rich, that came east and west, north
and south, this way and that way, and every way, for many and several years and months, and was ruler and rector, and governor and
protector, and chief head magistrate, and Justice of the Peace, and
used to wear broadcloth, and fine linen, and ruffles, and a silver-
hilted sword, and boots and spurs, and a three-legged wig and was
provost of a town, city and corporation in said county, out of which
he was with the strongest violence, compulsion and expulsion, forced
out and turned out, and obliged to go out, and now said place, is far
alienated, transferred and removed, and made over from me and my
benefit, emoluments, in the hands, and lands, tenor, and possession,
of Mr. W——— F———, Esq., and magistrate, and Justice of the
Peace, and quorum; and one of his majesty's subjects.

May it therefore please your honours, qualities, qualifications,
and ordinances, worships, and dignities, to help, relieve, assist and
succour, your poor, necessitous, and calamitous petitioner, me, Mr.
McCarthy, who was and is, and has been, and will be banished,
finished, perished, deprived of his vital spirit by cold, fugitated by
famine, unless you consider his state and condition, and want, and
necessity, and calamity, past, present, and to come, by giving, aiding,
assisting, enforcing, and making over upon him, something, or anything or nothing, or some where, or any where, or no where, or every
where, to buy beer, bread, brandy, coat, waistcoat, or breeches, to
circumdate, circumferate, surround or cover, or protect, or defend
my disordered, and distempered, and disfigured abused and soiled
felt, health, skin, hide, that have, and was, and is, and will be ex-
toxicated, scorched, perished, tortured, burnt, and destroyed, by the

fervent, and ardent burning and scorching, sultry heat, and pinching, penetrating piercing of the cold past, present, and future weather. The premises and foregoing of the few mentioned of the aforesaid imprecations, orations, and supplications, and petitions, tenderly and compassionately considered; these ruminated and properly weighed, your petitioner will forever with protection, and satisfaction, to the well-disposed donor, giver, or bestower in contribution, now, and then, and there and forevermore.

Asserted, assured, verified and truly demonstrated to be true,

By me myself,

DENNIS McCARTHY, ESQ.

This literary curiosity in all its pedantic verbosity no doubt pictures the typical misery which beset the native gentry whose holdings and estates had been confiscated.

Though Turlogh O'Carolan is commonly regarded as the last of the bards, he was by no means the last of the poets or harpers. Renowned as a poet and musical composer he was undistinguished as a harper. Admittedly he had no successors who possessed in such an eminent degree the arts and attributes associated in the public mind with the bardic profession. Gifted poets of the people always abounded. They were most of them hedge schoolmasters who were forced to conceal in Gaelic their Jacobite sentiments, and their indigence, genius and learning presented strange incongruities.

The description of Bridget Brady by her lover Thaddeus Ruddy, a bard, who lived about the middle of the seventeenth century is perhaps unique as a specimen of local simile.

"She's as straight as a pine on the mountains of Kilmannan;
    She's as fair as the lilies on the banks of the Shannon;
    Her breath is as sweet as the blossoms of Drumcallan,
    And her breasts gently swell like the waves of Lough Allan;
    Her eyes are as mild as the dews of Dunsany,
    Her veins are as pure as the blue-bells of Slaney;
    Her words are as smooth as the pebbles of Terwinny,
    And her hair flows adown like the streamlets of Finny."

A bare century since O'Carolan's death, saw the last of the great harpers; but lineal descendants of the Filea or poetic bards—the hedge poets and song writers—continued in existence down to the early years of the nineteenth century. Still downward, those minor poets degenerated into the itinerant ballad singers of recent times; the inglorious and vanishing survivals of an order or profession which for untold centuries had ranked next to royalty.

CHAPTER II

OUR readers know what immense influence the ancient Irish harpers or bards wielded. They were the counselors of their princes, and no expedition or feat of war was undertaken without consulting them. They sat in the chair of honor at the festive board, and as the mead or wine-cup went round their plaintive love ditties or martial chants were listened to with delight. They were ever welcome in the ladies' bower according to an able writer in *The Emerald* of forty odd years ago. They headed the troops on their march to battle with harp in hand, and sword on thigh, singing the chant of war; and many a swinging blow they struck too. Their skill was a subject of universal wonder; and even the bitterly anti-Irish Giraldus Cambrensis praised the unequaled beauty of their music and playing in the most enthusiastic terms.

The English early discovered the influence of the bards so hostile to them, and made the most desperate efforts to suppress the bardic institutions. They even offered rewards for the slaying of the Irish harpers, but all in vain. The Norman invaders themselves adopted the system of having a bard in their household; and in this and other respects, acquired the reputation which was intended by England as a reproach; that they were more Irish than the Irish themselves. More remarkable still; it was complained in England, that no sooner had the Cromwellian invaders settled down on the confiscated estates than they began to adopt Irish customs, and keep harpers in their houses. Indeed the same was said of the followers of William of Orange.

In the olden times the bard had the privilege of paying *Cuairt,* or a visit to any prince or chief he pleased, and he was always sure to be treated with the greatest respect and hospitality; for one good reason if for no other; the bards were dangerous persons to offend for their powers of satire were terrific and much dreaded.

The history of Ireland is studded all over with the deeds of he bards and musicians. But in the course of time the harpers began to fade away and the harp of Erin may now be said to be silent forever.

Before introducing to our readers the harpers immortalized in the Irish Annals, it might be well to quote the opening paragraph of Prof. Eugene O'Curry's Lecture on "Music and Musical Instruments in Ancient Erinn."

"The early cultivation of music and melody, and a special respect for the professors of the art bespeak a peculiar civilization, which implies no small degree of refinement of habit and of taste in a people. If there ever was a people gifted with a musical soul and sensibility in a higher degree than another, I would venture to assert that the Gaedhil of Ancient Erinn were that people.

"In no country in Europe, at least I believe so, is the antiquity and influence of the harp thrown so far back into the dark regions of history as in Erinn. Our traditions are more distinct than those of the Greeks, for they give time and place, name and occasion. Ours is not the shadowy myth of Orpheus going to the realms of Pluto, and by his lyre softening the obdurate heart of the grim monarch of the infernal abodes. It possesses something much more of real life, and belongs more to definite history. From the very remotest period to which our oldest traditions with any degree of circumstantiality refer, we find music, musical instruments, musical performers, and the power and influence of music spoken of."

It is not within the scope of our purpose to include the names of bards and musicians in the very ancient poems translated by O'Curry. The figurative language in which poets and genealogists of olden times clothed their thoughts, has given rise to the belief in the minds of modern writers that some of their characters were mythical or fictitious.

Coming down to the borderland between legendary and authentic history, Prof. O'Curry mentions Craftine a celebrated harper, who flourished about four and a half centuries before the Incarnation. One of the several legends concerning him, is to the effect that his instrument having sustained some injury he went to a wood to find a tree suitable for his purpose and selected a willow.

In a manuscript quoted by the above named antiquarian it is recorded that among the retinue of Conaire Mor, who was killed in the year 33 B. C., were three poets, nine pipe-players, and nine harpers.

Roderic, King of Wales in the sixth century, was so celebrated both at home and abroad for power, munificence and princely virtues, that a King of Ireland sent a Joculator or Jongleur to the Welsh court to examine the truth of what fame reported. Being admitted, a writer in *Anthologia Hibernica* of 1793 continues, he sang and played on the harp and tambour and delighted the King and his nobles on the Christmas holidays, after which the King ordered rich presents to be brought to the bard.

No one will question our being on reliable ground, when relating that a harper named Ilbrechtach accompanied Mac Liag, chief poet of Ireland on his visit to Brian Boru at the beginning of the eleventh century.

From the Annals of Ireland we learn that in 1168 Amhlaeibh Mac Mnaighneorach, chief Ollamh of Ireland in harp-playing died.

In the year 1269 Hugh O'Finnachty, a learned minstrel died.

It is recorded in the Annals of Clonmacnoise that Mulronie Mac Kerval, (Caruili), the blind chief Musician of the Kingdom, with his brother and many others, were slain in an uprising of the English in 1328. No man in any age ever heard, or shall hereafter hear, a better timpanist. In other accounts Mac Kerval, or Mac Caruill, is proclaimed "as great a minstrel as the world ever heard." By timpanist is to be understood a minstrel or harper.

In the Annals compiled by Friar John Clyn, of Kilkenny, under date of 1329, vigil, of Penticost, he mentions Cam O'Kayrwill, a famous timpanist and performer on the cythar; a "fenix" in execution, and so pre-eminently distinguished with his school of about twenty musicians, that though he could not be called the inventor of stringed musical instruments, he was the master and director of all his own contemporaries, and superior to all his predecessors.

O'Carroll, like O'Carolan, was allowed to be the foremost bard of his age. With his pupils and his patron, Lord Bellingham, he met a tragic fate, for they were all cruelly massacred by an armed multitude which rose to oppose the oppressive measures of the nobles.

Donslevy Mac Carroll, a noble master of music and melody, died in 1357. He was the best of his time.

Gilla-na-naev O'Connmhaigh, (now Conway), chief professor of music in Thomond, died in 1360.

Magrath O'Finnachty, chief musician and timpanist to the Sil-Murray, died in 1361.

John MacEgan and Gilbert O'Bardan, two accomplished young harpers of Conmaicne in the barony of Dunmore, County Galway, died in 1369.

William, son of Gilla Ceach Mac Carroll, the most eminent of the Irish in music, died in 1379.

The keenness of a harper saved the life of Art Mac Murrogh, an uncompromising opponent of the English in the year 1395. The latter accepted an invitation to a banquet from the Lords of the Pale. Not suspecting treachery, he was only accompanied by one attendant and his harper. Seated near a window the minstrel delighted the company with his music after the feast. The sudden change from festive melodies to the *"Rosg Catha,"* or war song invited his master's reprimand, and the resumption of it drew down upon his loyal head the nobleman's anger. Upon arising from the table to remonstrate, Mac Murrogh saw that the house was surrounded with armed men. Quickly brandishing his sword he cut his way through the surrounding forces and mounting his horse escaped in safety.

Mathew O'Luinin Erenagh, of Arda, County Fermanagh, died in 1396. He was a man of various professions and skilled in history, poetry and music.

Boethius Mac Egan, a man extensively skilled in Fenechus law and in music, died in 1399.

Gilla Duivin Mac Curtin Ollamh of Thomand in Music, died in 1404.

Finn O'Haughluinn, chief timpanist of Ireland, died in 1490.

James the Fourth of Scotland, himself a famous performer, was quite partial to Irish harpers. In the Accounts of the Lord High Treasurer, many entries are found showing payments to them in the late years of the fifteenth century and the early years of the sixteenth. "It is interesting to find," Bruce Armstrong says, "that Irish music was appreciated by King James, who was, we know, accustomed to hear Italian minstrels, luterers, fiddlers, English Lowland, and Highland harpers, and other skilled musicians."

It must not be forgotten that the development of their instruments kept pace with their proficiency, for Gallilei, in his *Ancient and Modern Music,* published at Florence in 1581, states that the Irish harp of his time had 54 to 60 strings, the majority being of brass—a few being of steel for the higher notes as in the Clavichord.

Richard Stanyhurst, whose work, *De Rebus in Hibernia Gestis,* was published at Antwerp in 1584, is the only Irish writer who is not appreciative of Irish harpers and their music. He was fortunate, however, in meeting with one whose performance pleased him.

"Cruise, a contemporary of our own, is by far the best harper within the memory of man. He is entirely opposed to that barbarous din which others elicit from their discordant and badly strung harps. Such is the order of his measures, the elegant combination of his notes, and his observance of musical harmony that his airs strike like a spell on the ears of his audience, and force you to exclaim not that he is the most perfect merely, but in truth almost the only harper." From his views of exclusiveness Dr. Lynch, author of *Cambrensis Eversus* and Rev. Dr. Geoffrey Keating, the historian, emphatically dissent. Assuredly there was never a time prior to the nineteenth century when Ireland could boast of only one distinguished harper.

The above named historian in a poem translated by Prof. O'Curry, pays a glowing tribute to his harper Tadhg O'Cobthaigh, or O'Coffey. The author asks:

Who is the artist by whom the cruit is played? by whom the anguish of the envenomed spear's recent wound is healed, through the sweet-voiced sound of the sounding-board, like the sweet-streamed peal of the organ?

Who is it that plays the enchanting music that dispels all the ills that man is heir to? To which he gives answer in the following translated lines:

> Tadhg O'Cobthaigh of beauteous form,—
> The chief-beguiler of women,
> The intelligent concordance of all difficult tunes,
> The thrills of music and of harmony.

Keating was born in 1560 and died in 1635.

Through the painstaking researches of Grattan Flood, the names of many harpers and pipers hitherto unknown or forgotten, have been brought to light. Of the great number imprisoned under proclamations designed for their extermination, not a trace is left save what an examination of the State Papers may reveal.

The heroic harpers and pipers suffered for their loyalty to their leaders in times of national strife. Some were fortunate enough to obtain freedom through the mediation of persons of prominence while the names and fate of all others are lost in oblivion.

Ignored in history and literature, the sole record of their adult existence in most instances was that preserved in the official files of pardons among the State Papers.

The first pardon to an Irish minstrel of which we are aware is that recorded in a Patent Roll of 1540 in King Henry the Eighth's reign in favor of

Owen Keynan of Cappervarget, in the County of Kildare, harper; otherwise called Owen Keynan, servant of Gerald, late Earl of Kildare; otherwise Owen Keynan, the Rymour, otherwise Owen Keynan, the poet, otherwise Owen Keynan, Keyeghe Berde (blind bard), and for

Cornelius Keynan, of Cappervarget, son of Owen Keynan, Keyeghe, otherwise Cornelius (the) Berde.

Richard O'Malone of Donore, County Westmeath, enjoyed the distinction of being the first musician pardoned by Queen Elizabeth, the date being 1565.

From that time until 1586, the following named harpers were pardoned:

Donogh Mac Crydon, of St. John, Nenagh, Tipperary.

Thady Credan, of Drangan, Tipperary.

Mac Loughlin roe O'Brennan, County Galway.

Walter Brenagh, (Walsh in English).

Maelconry Mac Shane, of Castletown-roche, County Cork, indicted.

Russell Mac Russell, of Ballinacarrig, County Cork.

William MacCruddan, or Creedan.

Melaghlin roe O'Brennan, County Galway, (probably the MacLoughlin roe O'Brennan, before mentioned, first pardoned in 1581, now pardoned in 1585).

Gillaglass O'Shallow.

Dermot McGrath, of Hospital, County Limerick.

No pardons to harpers appear on record during the years intervening between 1586 and 1601. During the latter year Her Majesty and her Lord Deputies in Ireland must have been in a particularly gracious mood for besides clemency extended to a correspondingly large number of pipers, no less than eleven harpers were pardoned, namely:

John O'Lynch.

Art Mac Gillegrone MacDonnell.

Geoffrey McGlade.

Tadhg O'Dermody, harpmaker, County Kilkenny.

Nicholas dall (blind), Rattoo, County Kerry. (The famous Nicholas dall hereinafter mentioned.)

Dermot O'Sgingin, of Donore, County Westmeath.

Donal Mac Conmee, County Westmeath.

Richard Forstall, of Cloghnageragh, County Wexford.

James O'Nolan, of Donore, County Westmeath.

Melaghlin O'Duane, of Cloghkelly.

Tadhg Mac Donal Mac Rory, of Townagh, County Clare, composer of "Teague's Rambles," which appeared in *Playford's Dancing Master,* 1651, as "The Irish Lady or Anniseed-water Robin."

The year 1602 was almost as fruitful of pardons as the preceding one. Following are the names of the beneficiaries:

Gillaglass O'Shalvey, of Annaghmore.

Owen O'Shalvey, of Annaghmore.

John O'Maloney, Pallas, County Longford.

Rory Albanagh (Scott) Castleroe, County Westmeath.

Owen Mac Kiernan, of Kildare.

Tadhg O'Laffan, of Scablerstown.

Edmund O'Gibney, of Mulrankin, County Wexford.

Shane ballagh McGeough, County Monaghan.

Cormack Mac Gillecosgellie, Clogher.

A proclamation issued January 28, 1603, by the Lord President of Muntser, in which the marshal of the province was charged to exterminate by martial law all manner of bards, harpers, etc., was followed by Queen Elizabeth's orders to Lord Barrymore, "to hang the harpers, wherever found, and destroy their instruments."

> "When England would a land enthrall,
> She doomed the Muses' Sons to fall,
> Lest Virtue's hand should string the lyre,
> And feed with song the patriot's fire."

This was bad news for imprisoned harpers as well as those at liberty, yet a short time before her death which occurred less than two months after the date of Lord Barrymore's orders, the queen yielding to some powerful entreaty —it could not have been mercy or remorse—pardoned one piper, and the two following named harpers:

Owen Mac Dermot reagh Mallow, County Cork.

Dermot O'Dugan, Garryduff.

This renowned harper was also bard for the Earl of Thomond, and it was doubtless the intercession of that powerful nobleman, which secured O'Dugan's release.

Around the beginning of the seventeenth century there flourished at Clonmaurice, County Kerry, a renowned harper named:

Nicholas Pierce, commonly referred to as Nicholas dall, he being blind. Celebrated for his capacity for composing laments, and other ancient strains, he enjoyed the distinction, O'Curry tells us of having three odes written in his praise. It appears that he fell into disfavor with the government for it is recorded in the State Papers that Nicholas Dall, Rattoo, County Kerry, was pardoned with nine others in 1601 by Queen Elizabeth and her Lord Deputies in Ireland.

In concluding this chapter it may be pertinent to remark, that while her deputies were carrying out her orders in regard to the hanging of Irish Minstrels in Ireland, Queen Elizabeth's fondness for Irish music, dancing and festivities, was notorious in England, and it was in her reign that we find the greatest number and variety of dances; and taking part in a jig or other lively dance was a common practice with Elizabeth and her pleasure-loving knights and dames. For her personal entertainment she kept an Irish harper, Cormac Mac Dermot, who no doubt did much to popularize Irish songs and melodies at the English Court from the time of his engagement in 1590 to the date of her death in 1603. He continued in favor with King James I., and his name appears in the list of Court musicians, "receiving annuities and fees from the Crown," in March, 1607. Another Irish Minstrel, Donal *duibh* O'Cahill, at the same date was harper to Queen Anne, the consort of King James.

CHAPTER III

In the minds of the English-speaking races of the present day, the bagpipe is invariably associated with scenes of Irish and Scottish life, yet the instrument in some shape or other turns up in every quarter of the globe. Omitting the various names by which it is referred to in scriptural times, we find that it was known in Persia as the *nei aubana;* in Egypt as the *Zouhara;* in Greece as the *askaulos;* and by the Romans as the *tibia utricularis.* In Germany they had the *sacpfeiffe* and *dudel-sac;* in Italy the *Zampogna,* and the *cornamusa;* in France the *musette* and *chalumeau.* In Russia the bagpipe is termed *volynska;* in Spain, *gheeyita;* in Norway *jockpipe;* in Lapland *walpipe;* in Finland *pilai;* and in Wales *pyban;* differing but little from *pipai* the generic name for all kinds of bagpipes in Ireland and Scotland.

Anyone desiring to learn all about the origin and pedigree of the bagpipe in all its guises and developments among all races and in all ages from savage to civilized, should lose no time in consulting Grattan Flood's latest work, *The Story of the Bagpipe.*

THE BAGPIPE IN IRELAND

No better proof of the antiquity of the bagpipe in Ireland need be adduced according to the author, than the reference to it in the Brehon laws of the fifth century. On this point, in his lecture on the "Music and Musical Instruments in Ancient Erinn," O'Curry says: "Like the pipers themselves, I have not met in any ancient composition more than one reference to the *Pipaireadha* or pipers. This reference is preserved in a fragment of ancient laws in the library of Trinity College, Dublin. The article contains a list of the fines or recompense, paid to professors of the mechnical arts for insults or bodily injury, and concludes in these words: 'These are base, that is inferior professions, and entitled to the same amount of fines as the *Pipairedha* or pipers; and the *Clesamhnaigh,* or Jugglers; and the *Cornaireadha* or trumpeters; and the *Cuislennaigh* or pipe blowers.'" This paragraph is valuable, O'Curry adds so far as to show that the *Cuislennaigh* or pipe blower, was a different person from the *Pipaire* or piper.

The *Cuisleannach* or pipes were among the favorite musical instruments at the great triennial *Feis* at Tara which continued from pre-Christian days to the year 560 A. D., when the glories of "Tara's Hall" came to an end.

Mention is also made in Irish writings late in the tenth century of pipers and *mna-caointe* attending a king's funeral. Even at religious service in early Christian times the bagpipe was utilized occasionally according to Grattan Flood, "either as a solo instrument or to sustain the sacred chant."

Although Giraldus Cambrensis does not mention the bagpipe specifically as an instrument in use in Ireland in his time, there can be no doubt that it was known, as it is enumerated among the musical instruments at the fair of Carman, held triennially, commencing with the eighth century. The sixty-third stanza of the poem describing the fair begins thus:

> "Pipes, fiddles, chainmen,
> Bone-men, and tube-players."

29

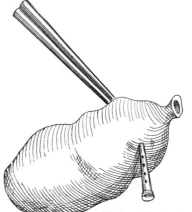

Tibia Utricularis
Bagpipe of the Ancients
From a Bas relief in Roman Palace

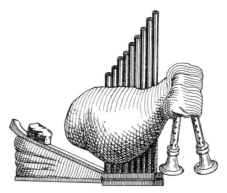

From a Medal of Nero
Suggestion of the Organ

From Harleian Ms
of the XIV Century

From an Initial Letter
Dinnseanchus Mss A.D.1300

Roman Bagpiper
From a Bronze Figure

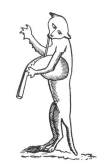

From Harleian Ms
of the XIV Century

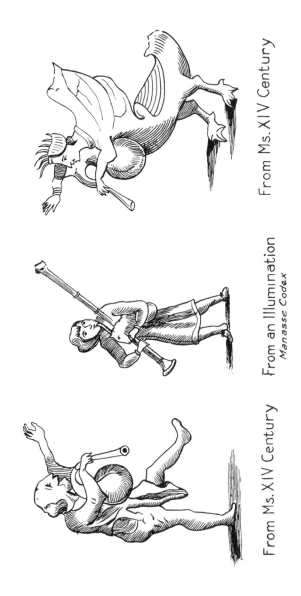

From Ms. XIV Century

From an Illumination
Manasse Codex

From Ms. XIV Century

From *Stultifera Navis*, XV Century

A Russian Piper

French Musette Player (XVII Century)

When Cambrensis wrote, the harp or *clarseach,* always the glorified instrument, had attained such popularity as to relegate the bagpipe to comparative obscurity, its use being confined to the peasantry exclusively even long after the Norman invasion. There is no evidence to show that it was used in war or as a military instrument prior to the fourteenth century. The mention of "Goeffrey the Piper" and "William the Piper" in the years 1206 and 1256 respectively, among the deeds of the Priory of the Holy Trinity, Dublin; (Christ Church Cathedral,) sets at rest all doubts of the existence of the bagpipe in Ireland when Giraldus Cambrensis wrote.

It is also a matter of record that Irish pipers were among the Irish troops led by the Prior of Kilmamham, who in 1475 accompanied King Edward the Fourth to Calais.

From the picture of a warpiper in Derrick's *Image of Ireland,* published in 1581, even if not strictly accurate, we may obtain a fair idea of the costume and instrument of those times. A much finer type of the Irish warpiper is that credited to Albrecht Durer early in the sixteenth century. The original painting adorns a gallery in Vienna. Unlike the German piper painted in 1514 by the same artist, the Irish piper is not listed in any copy of his works which we have seen. At any rate the picture is unmistakably that of an Irish warpiper, for a glance will convince the most incredulous of the general resemblance it bears to that in Derrick's work above named.

We may wonder how the great Bavarian painter came to meet such a subject for his brush, but when we come to consider that he traveled extensively in Europe, visiting Alsace and the Netherlands twice, and that Irish Kerns, accompanied of course by their pipers were engaged in the campaign at Tournay, Belgium, in 1513, and that Irish pipers accompanied the Irish troops at the siege of Boulogne in 1544, the question ceases to be a matter of speculation.

All throughout the centuries when warpipes were used by the Irish as a part of their military equipment, little Irish history was made in their absence, though their participation in the activities of warfare was not specifically mentioned. In forays and battles the pipers took literally a foremost part, being always in the lead, and heroically remaining to encourage their troops with spirited war tunes, until death or defeat silenced their strains.

The Irish advanced to the charge at the famous battle of *Bel-an-atha-buidhe,* or the Yellow Ford, in 1598 to the stirring strains of the warpipes, and many instances are cited by Grattan Flood where the warpipes were used effectively. In the language of Standish O'Grady: "They were brave men those pipers. The modern military band retires as its regiment goes into action. But the piper went on before his men and piped them into the thick of the battle. He advanced sounding his battle-pibroch, and stood in the ranks of war, while men fell all around him."

It was the patriotism and loyalty of the pipers, more than anything else that led to the enactment of the Statutes of Kilkenny in 1367. In the reign of Edward the Third, pipers or minstrels, storytellers, bablers, rimers, etc., were attainted and imprisoned as well as those of the English in Ireland "who receive or give them anything." One piper, Dowenald (probably Dhonal) O'Moghane, was exempted from the operations of this law by special enactment because "he had constantly remained in the fealty, peace and obedience of the king; and that he had inflicted divers injuries on the Irish enemies for which he durst not approach near them."

This harsh law was the first severe blow struck at the popularity of the

IRISH WARPIPER

(From Derrick's *Image of Ireland,* 1581.)

AN IRISH WARPIPER

(From a painting at Vienna.)

A German Piper.
by Albrecht Durer, 1514.

BRETON PIPER
Playing at a Wedding

bagpipe, although in course of time the rigors of its enforcement subsided, and those against whom the law was directed, went among the English and exercised their arts and minstrelsies, and returned to the "Irish enemies" with whatever information they secured.

While we may not be particularly concerned in the identity of the warpipers who accompanied the Irish Kerns in their campaigns in Scotland, and on the continent, in the fifth decade of the sixteenth century to bolster up the interests of English royalty, we cannot help voicing our regret that history has not preserved the names of the pipers who rendered such valiant service at the battle of *Bel-an-atha-buidhe* (Yellow Ford) in 1598, and at the battle of Curlew Mountain one year later, and above all at the battle of Fontenoy in 1745.

For the description of the bagpipe, or warpipe as it existed in the sixteenth century, we are indebted to Richard Stanyhurst, who, writing about the year 1584, says: "The Irish likewise, instead of the trumpet, make use of a wooden pipe of the most ingenious structure to which is joined a leather bag, very closely bound with bands. A pipe is inserted in the side of this skin, through which the piper, with his swollen neck and puffed-up cheeks, blows in the same manner as we do through a tube. The skin, being thus filled with air, begins to swell, and the player presses against it with his arm; thus a loud and shrill sound is produced through two wooden pipes of different lengths. In addition to these, there is yet a fourth pipe, perforated in different places, which the player so regulates, by the dexterity of his fingers in the shutting and opening the holes, that he can cause the upper pipes to send forth either a loud or a low sound, at pleasure. The principal thing to be taken care of is, that the air be not allowed to escape through any other part of the bag than that in which the pipes are inserted. For if anyone were to make a puncture in the bag, even with the point of a needle, the instrument would be spoiled, and the bag would immediately collapse, and this is frequently done by humorous people when they wish to irritate the pipers.

"It is evident that this instrument must be a very good incentive to their courage at the time of battle, for by its tones the Irish are stirred up to fight in the same manner as the soldiers of other nations by the trumpet."

Illustrations of the *Piob Mor* or warpipes of this period described by Stanyhurst, from the brush of different artists, prove conclusively that the instrument was both ornate and imposing, and it would appear superior in workmanship to the warpipes of today.

Some writers assume that the terms *"Cuisle* pipes" and *"Uilleann* pipes" are synonymous or interchangeable. On this point there appears to be a hook on which to hang an argument. That there were two methods of holding the bag admits of no question. In the more ancient pictures of pipers, it will be noticed that the instrument is suspended by a strap or band passed over the shoulders, while the bag rests on the performer's breast and stomach as in Albrecht Durer's paintings of a German piper, and an Irish piper at the beginning of the sixteenth century. The picture of the Irish warpiper in Derrick's *Image of Ireland,* published in 1581, displays a similar arrangement. This style would naturally be called the *"Cuisle* pipes," as the pressure on the bag to expel the air is exerted by the forearms or wrists—hence, *cuisle,* or pulse.

A later development of the warpipe was in placing the bag, much diminished in size, under the arm, in which position the necessary pressure is administered by the elbow or *Uilleann.*

The war pipe may be of either design when blown from the mouth, but it will be noticed that *Uilleann* as a descriptive term for the bagpipe did not come into use before the last quarter of the sixteenth century—1584, Grattan Flood says, and that was about the time when the change just menioned took place. However, the *Uilleann* pipes of those days were still the warpipes or *Piob Mor;* and they must not be confounded with the *Uilleann* or Union pipes which were practically a new instrument, developed in the early years of the eighteenth century.

Shakespeare's "woollen bagpipe," so frequently alluded to, and of late plausibly explained as meaning *Uilleann* bagpipe, affords no cause for speculation in the edition of his works in the writer's library, published in 1803, for the expression is plainly printed "swollen bagpipe"; a designation singularly appropriate.

After the *Uilleann* pipes had been modified in tone, and blown with a bellows, and had the drones arranged compactly and horizontally in a stock, the instrument was more in demand at social gatherings, and such festivities as weddings and christenings; but this type, on which the piper played while seated, did not by any means supplant the *Piob Mor* at funerals, football and hurling matches. Only a generation or so ago, Mr. Wm. Halpin of Newmarket-on-Fergus headed the Clare hurlers on their way to compete with their Limerick rivals, playing on a set of Highland pipes, which was in fact the *Piob Mor* of both Scotland and Ireland for many a day, though a third drone had been added.

As Grattan Flood says, "from grave to gay, the bagpipe was requisitioned, and no important Irish funeral took place unless headed by a band of war pipers." At the burial of a remarkable dwarf piper named Mathew Hardy, in 1737, the funeral cortege was led by "eight couple of pipers, playing a funeral dirge composed by O'Carolan. Gradually the warpipes were superseded by the Union pipes for domestic use, and by trumpets and drums for military purposes. The last occasion of which there is any historical mention of Irish pipers in war was at the battle of Fontenoy, May 11, 1745, when the Irish Brigade in the service of France turned the tide of battle against the English troops. Very appropriately. two of the tunes those intrepid expatriated pipers pealed out were "The White Cockade" and "Saint Patrick's Day in the Morning."

In *Dissertations on the History of Ireland,* published in 1766, the learned Charles O'Conor of Belanagar says: "The instrumental music in the chase, as in the field of battle, was sounded by wind instruments, what they called *Adharcaidh Cuiul.*" This term is literally musical horns, and not a musical bag, as translated by Walker and others. What words could more aptly describe a set of bagpipes of the old type than musical horns?

In his correspondence with Dr. Walker at a much later date, O'Conor mentions the *Cuisle Cuiul* as "a simple kind of bagpipe, loud-toned and confined to a bare octave." This number of notes agrees exactly with the primitive bagpipe pictured in Dr. Ledwich's *Antiquities of Ireland,* which has but six vents for the fingers and one for the thumb. An additional vent for the little finger of the right hand, of later introduction, increased the capacity or compass of the so-called warpipe chanter.

When the *Piob Mor* or warpipe was transformed into the Irish or Union pipes, is largely a matter of conjecture, as the old form continued in use long after the transformation was made. The first performer on the improved instrument of whom we have any historical record was Lawrence Grogan of Johnstown Castle, Wexford. Grattan Flood credits him with the authorship of both words and music of "Ally Croker," in the year 1725. We must, therefore, place the origin of the Irish pipes some few years before that date.

As the harp declined, the new type of bagpipe, improved from time to time, gained immensely in popularity. The extent to which it had been developed from a loud-toned instrument of but one note more than an octave in compass, to two full octaves, may be realized from Dr. Burney's description in 1775: "The instrument at present in use in Ireland," he says, "is an improved bagpipe, on which I have heard some of the natives play very well in two parts without the drone, which I believe is never attempted in Scotland. The tone of the lower notes resembles that of a hautbois and clarionet, and the high notes that of a German flute, and the whole scale of one I heard lately was very well in tune, which has never been the case of any Scots bagpipe that I ever heard." The Irish bagpipe in its improved form had not been deemed unworthy of the ear of royalty, at least a score of years before the date of Dr. Burney's description, for a footnote in Walker's *Historical Memoirs of the Irish Bards* informs us "that George the Second was so much delighted with the performance of an Irish gentleman on the bagpipes that he ordered a medal to be struck for him."

Modern writers assure us with confidence that the qualifying word Union, as applied to the improved Irish bagpipe, is simply a corruption of the Irish term *Uilleann,* in use for over two hundred years. Quite as plausibly might we advance the claim that the word Union is aptly descriptive of the modern Irish instrument, which is in fact a union of two instruments—namely, the simple bagpipe and the organ. Since the adoption of the regulators which produce the organ tones, the Irish or Union pipes have been frequently alluded to as the Irish organ.

It will be noticed that Dr. Burney, above quoted, makes no mention of keys or regulators on the "improved bagpipe" of his day, nor are there any on the fine old specimens of an Irish bagpipe pictured on page 40 of Duncan Fraser's work on *The Bagpipe,* although it has four drones closely set in the stock. Elaborate instruments or "sets," equipped with keyed chanter and regulators, were turned out between 1770 and 1790, by the elder Kenna, a renowned pipemaker of Dublin, and it was about that time, or perhaps later, that the Irish bagpipe became known as the "Union Pipes." As a specimen of a still earlier development of the Union bagpipe, the picture of the Carlow instrument presents an interesting study.

This name, as far as the present writer is aware, was first seen in print in *O'Farrell's Collection of National Irish Music for the Union Pipes,* published about the end of the eighteenth century. The following extract from the author's introduction would seem to justify the name:

"The Union Pipes—Being an instrument now so much improved as renders it able to play any kind of Music, and with the additional accompanyments which belong to it, produce a variety of pleasing Harmony which forms as it were a little Band in itself."

Not a few combining both musical and mechanical genius contributed to the further development of the Union pipes, down to late in the nineteenth century. The number of regulators were increased to three in standard instruments; then a fourth, and even a fifth, was ultimately added, until, as Manson the Scotch authority says, the Irish pipes have been elaborated to such a degree that they have almost ceased to be bagpipes.

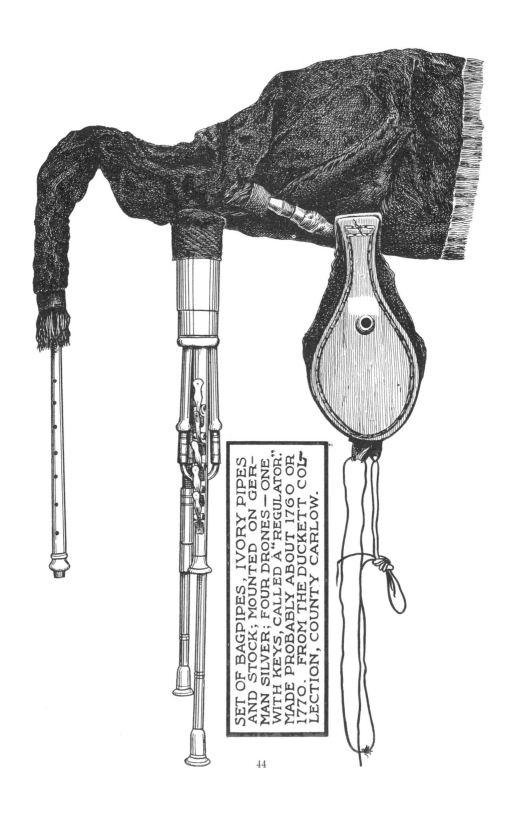

SET OF BAGPIPES, IVORY PIPES AND STOCK; MOUNTED ON GERMAN SILVER; FOUR DRONES—ONE WITH KEYS, CALLED A "REGULATOR." MADE PROBABLY ABOUT 1760 OR 1770. FROM THE DUCKETT COLLECTION, COUNTY CARLOW.

44

The soft, plaintive tones of the pipes manufactured by Kenna, Coyne, and Egan, so delightful in the parlor, proved too weak to produce the desired effect in concert halls and theatres of modern times, so William Taylor, a Drogheda pipemaker, who came to New York City in 1872, and settled in Philadelphia about 1874, developed an instrument of powerful tone and concert pitch, which met all requirements in that respect.

As the limit of development had been reached, the vogue of the bagpipe had declined, and notwithstanding the agitation for its revival in recent years, the outlook to an enthusiast presents but little ground for optimism.

It is unfortunate that the teaching of Irish pipe music has not been standardized, as that on the Highland pipe has been. The system of execution on the latter instrument is uniform; and as all Highland pipers learn from written music, under competent instructors, whether in Scotland, England, Canada, or the United States, they are enabled by the uniformity of their system to play together, in perfect accord, upon all occasions.

That a school of *Piob Mor* or warpipe music existed in Ireland as late as the middle of the seventeenth century, is beyond question, for we find that *Domhnall Mor,* or Big Donald MacCrimmon, son of John, the founder of the famous College of Pipers, in the Isle of Skye, was sent by his chieftain, MacLeod, to a school or college of pipers in Ireland, to perfect himself on the instrument.

From this it would appear that before government persecution chilled their ardor, the Irish pipers were as renowned in their line as were the harpers.

What might be written on this subject would not alone fill a volume, but several of them, for in recent years three separate volumes have been written on the bagpipe—two by Scotch authors, Duncan Fraser and W. L. Manson, and one by our own Grattan Flood, Mus. Doc. Even so, they did not by any means exhaust the subject. In Manson's work, a whole chapter is devoted to the shafts of ridicule and uncomplimentary criticism aimed at the Highland bagpipe and its music, all of which might have been said as deservedly of the Irish warpipes, especially if out of tune, and in the hands of an incapable performer. Yet, strange to say, although the English pipers were also favorite targets for the scoffers in their day, nothing except that which is commendable has come down to us concerning the Irish pipers or their performance.

THE BAGPIPE IN SCOTLAND.

It is now generally admitted that the Scotch got their musical instruments, as they got their music and language, from Ireland. Since the colonization of Scotland from Dalaradia in Ulster, about the year 504, regular intercourse between the two countries has ever since been kept up.

However long the bagpipe may have been in use in Scotland, historical mention of it had been wanting until early in the fourteenth century. The precise date of the bagpipe's introduction to Scotland is unknown a writer in an Edinburgh publication of 1911 says: "Certainly it was in evidence during the twelfth century, and authentic records show that pipers formed a part of the king's retinue during the fourteenth." From all we can learn there was no essential difference between the Scotch and Irish warpipe until early in the eighteenth century, when the third or bass drone was added to the Scotch instrument. About the same time the Irish warpipe was transformed into the Union pipes already described.

To discuss the origin of the bagpipe in Scotland, or Ireland, would lead

A Piper of a Highland Regiment.
From Grose's Military Antiquities. 1786.

to nothing definite, as the diversity of views expressed by writers on that subject is simply bewildering. The opinion that it was derived from the Romans has been discarded by such modern authorities as Manson, Duncan Fraser, and Grattan Flood.

The bagpipe belonged to the Celts, and its existence can be traced to their colonies all the way from ancient Scythia via the Black Sea, and the Mediterranean to the shores of Britain. In the absence of evidence, much is left to conjecture, yet the claim is now confidently made that the bagpipe arrived with the Celts long before the Roman invasion. "Tell me where the old Celt settled," says Duncan Fraser, "and I will tell you where to look for the bagpipe."

After disclaiming any obligation to the Scandinavians, Romans, English, or continental nations for the introduction of the bagpipe into Scotland, W. L. Manson says: "Ireland indeed can put forward a good claim,—Christianity came from there, the peoples are the same, and the relations between the two countries in early days were very close—but there is less to uphold the claim than there is to show that the pipes are native to the Highlands."

In their migration from the borders of the Black Sea, along the Mediterranean shores, and thence northward by way of the Iberian peninsula, the Celts would be certain to colonize Ireland long in advance of their advent in Caledonia. Besides, we must not forget that Ireland was better known to the ancients than Britain. There can be no question, however, that the bagpipe in form, development, and use, was essentially the same in both countries down to the beginning of the eighteenth century when radical changes took place.

As an instrument of war and peace with tones clear, powerful and penetrating, it voiced the national melodies. It had been associated with all the activities of Gaelic life from the cradle to the grave. No single musical instrument ever devised by man united in itself so wide a range of utility as the *Piob Mor* of the Gael. In the language of Lieut. MacLennan of Edinburgh, it pealed forth merry melodies in the halls of the chieftains at the birth, and baptism of the heir. At marriages convivial parties, festive gatherings, dances, and other amusements, it was indispensible. It accompanied the workman to lighten his labor. Its steady measured notes assisted and solaced the soldiers in their long and painful marches, through rocks, rivers, and deserts. It summoned the clansmen when danger was near, and it stimulated and inspired the Highlander with courage and determination on the field of battle. It had from remote times its share in solemn acts of devotion in the sanctuary, and at funerals the melancholy wailing of the lament played on the bagpipes, could give expression to the grief of the relatives better than any other instrument.

Coming from the pen of W. L. Manson, a Scotch writer, the subjoined quotation from *The Highland Bagpipe* cannot fail to be of interest to the general reader particularly as his views cannot have been the result of either partiality or prejudice.

"Passing from debatable ground, the result of our assortment of quotations, seems to be that the first thoroughly authentic reference to the bagpipe in Scotland, dates from 1406, that it was well known in Reformation times, that the second drone was added about 1500, that it was first mentioned in connection with the Gaelic in 1506 or a few years later, that it was classed in a list of Scottish musical instruments in 1548, that in 1549 and often afterwards it was used in war, that in 1650 every town had a piper, that in 1700 the big

THE BAGPIPER
From Painting by Sir D. Wilkie, R. A.

THE BLIND PIPER.

drone was added, and that in 1824 the Scots were enthusiastic about the pipes. There is not the slightest doubt of course, that the instrument was used in Scotland for many years, probably for centuries before we can trace it, but previous to the dates given we have only tradition and conjecture to go by."

The Highlander in his time of greatest adversity, the same author says, stuck to the pipes so the pipes seem determined to stick to the Highlander in spite of the tendencies of latter day civilization.

The transition from the harp to the bagpipe was spread over two centuries. In the middle of the sixteenth century both instruments were in use, but in the seventeenth century, there were few harpers while the civil wars gave bagpipe music an impetus, on account of its superiority in the noise and tumult of battle as a military instrument. Besides supplanting the harp—Manson continues—the pipes also supplanted the bards themselves. The clan piper was second in importance to the chief.

The Scottish bards hated the growing popularity of the pipes, as ardently as the Irish pipers despised the introduction of brass bands, but the world moves, and the keenest satire of the former and the bitterest invective of the latter, were alike powerless to retard or stay the progress of either rival.

The last clan bard, Neil Mac Mhuirich, died in 1726, and the last clan harper in 1739, when the hereditary pipers were in all their glory, living from generation to generation in the family of the chieftain at the head of their respective clans. Not only were the clan pipers of superior rank to other retainers of their chief but they were provided a servant or *gille* to carry their pipes. And though the pipers of our day have fallen from their high estate so have many of their historic patrons. Today the McLeod of Dunvegan, is a poor man. In a year of famine to keep the crofters from starving he emptied his own purse.

The use of the *Piob Mor,* or Highland pipe in connection with Highland regiments, has well served to maintain its popularity as the national instrument, there being at the beginning of the twentieth century twenty-two pipe bands in the British army. It is said that from the year 1750 to 1800, the Isle of Skye in the Hebrides alone furnished 500 pipers for military service.

A curious circumstance is the favor shown this class of music by ancient races. "The only foreign music the Chinese masses have shown any interest in is the skirling of the bagpipes of the Cameron Highlanders," the American Consul General at Tientsin tells us, and although wealthy Chinese occasionally purchase pianos they use them simply as pieces of furniture.

Differing in the arrangement of the drones from all other representations of the Scottish bagpipe with which we are familiar, is that drawn by Sir David Wilkie R. A. in "The Bagpiper," one of his earliest paintings; and "The Blind Piper," from the brush of J. Naysmith, another famous Scotch artist, of about a century ago.

It is worthy of note that the so-called Brian Boru Warpipes lately manufactured in London are modeled after those peculiar instruments.

THE BAGPIPES IN ENGLAND

It has been generally conceded that the Romans introduced the bagpipe into Britain about the middle of the first century. It was the military instrument of the Roman infantry, while the trumpet was assigned to the cavalry. Yet if the Celtic inhabitants of Hibernia and Caledonia were in possession of the bagpipe before the Roman invasion as now claimed by such authorities as Manson, Duncan Fraser, and Grattan Flood, there can be no reason to doubt that it was known to the ancient Britons also.

That it was the pastoral instrument of Britain in the ninth century is evident, for we find the shepherd in *Evans' Old Ballads* whom King Alfred visits in disguise declares that his

> "Bagpipes shall
> Sound sweetly once a year,
> In praise of his renowned king."

Although the earliest mention of the bagpipe in English literature is to be found in the prologue to Chaucer's *Canterbury Tales,* evidence is not wanting to show that it was by no means rare at least a century before his time. Illustrations, cathedral windows, and payments to pipers, attest the bagpipe's popularity in the fourteenth century. Its crowning glory, however, was the inclusion of pipes in the royal bands. Queen Elizabeth's "Band of Musick" in 1588 consisted of 16 trumpets, 9 minstrels, 8 viols, 6 sackbuts, lutes, harps, 3 players on the virginals, 2 rebecs, and 1 bagpipe.

The bagpipe also enjoyed the favor of Kings Edward the Second, and Edward the Third, who retained performers on the instrument in their musical establishments. King Henry the Eighth of unsavory memory, who had musical as well as more reprehensible tastes, left in his collection four such instruments "with pipes of ivorie."

The English bagpipe until the year 1300, or so, consisted of but the bag, blowpipe and chanter. The first instrument pictured with a drone is to be found in the Gorleston Psalter, written about 1306, the second drone being added a century later. Thus improved it is frequently referred to as the "Drone" or "Dronepipe."

In the pages of Knights' *Old England* describing the customs and habits of the outlaws of Sherwood forest in the days of Robin Hood, we read "of enjoyment in their shooting and wrestling matches, in their sword fights, and sword dances, in their visits to all the rustic wakes and feasts of the neighborhood. How the outlaws would be visited by the wandering minstrels coming thither to amuse them with old ballads, and to gather a rich harvest of materials for new ones. The legitimate poet-minstrel would be followed by the humbler gleeman forming one of a band of revelers, in which would be comprised a taborer, a bagpiper and dancers and tumblers."

The above refers to times a generation or so before Chaucer introduces his miller who led the procession from Southwark to Canterbury and the shrine of Thomas a Becket.

> "A bagge-pype wel coude he blow and soune
> And therwithal he broughte us out of toune."

The author tells us that a bagpiper marched or rode in front of the bands of pilgrims on their way to some favorite shrine—a frequent sight in those days—cheering on the weary-footed with his gay music.

It will be observed that the bagpipe which immortalized Chaucer's miller as well as others of the fourteenth century, had no drone; neither had the instrument played by the piper accompanied by the drummer which illustrates the

CHAUCER'S MILLER (XIV Century)

"A bagge-pipe wel coude he blowe and soune
And therwithal he broughte us out of toune"

scenes of the early part of the seventeenth century in Chapter 3, Vol. 2 of
Knights' *Old England*.

In mediaeval England the bagpipe was used in connection with church
services, as it was used in Ireland and Scotland, especially in processions and
outdoor religious ceremonies, but it was at games and May Day dances that
the bagpipe was given preference over other instruments.

> "I have seen the Lady of the May,
> Set in an arbour on a holy day,
> Built by the May-pole where the jocund swains
> Dance with the maidens to the bagpipe's strains."

Illustrating this quatrain from *Browne's Pastorals,* written in 1625, the
piper is seated on a tall barrel or puncheon near the Maypole, while the dance

English Piper, 1733.
From Hogarth's Southwark Fair.   English Piper, 1637.

goes gaily on all around him. In this picture the bagpipe is equipped with two
drones, and so is the instrument played on by the piper in Hogarth's "Southwark Fair."

Though enjoying the favor of royalty during several reigns, it does not
appear that the bagpipe was ever used in war in England. Pipers flourished
in goodly numbers early in the seventeenth century, and were as conspicuous at
Fairs and outdoor entertainments as their brethren in more recent times in
Ireland.

At no stage of its development was the English instrument at all comparable
in style or finish with the *Piob Mor* or Warpipe of Ireland or Scotland.

Reign of Queen Elizabeth, 1558–1603.
"With a good old fashion when Christmas was come,
To call in all his old neighbors with bagpipe and drum."

The English bagpipe survived with varying degrees of popularity until early in the eighteenth century, although the Northumbrian pipes—a distinct and much improved variety—remained in favor for a generation or two afterwards; and from recent accounts it is not yet altogether extinct.

THE BAGPIPE IN WALES

We can safely assume that the bagpipe was known to the Cambrians long anterior to its mention in authentic history, for we are assured by no less an authority than Prof. Kuno Meyer, the renowned philologist, that the Gaels of Ireland made various settlements in Wales in the third and fourth centuries, and the intercourse between the two countries was always of a friendly character and long continued.

Being in great favor with Gruffydth ap Conan King of North Wales, it was given much prominence at an Eisteddfod or Feis held in the year 1100, on which occasion Grattan Flood tells us an Irishman was the prize-winner.

Much earlier reference to the bagpipe, perhaps in a simpler form, is that found in the institutions of the Welsh King, *Howel Dha,* (Howel the Good), about the year 942: "Every chief bard to whom the prince shall grant an office, the prince shall provide him an instrument; a *harp* to one, a *crwth* to another, and *pipes* to a third; and when they die, the instrument ought to revert to the prince."

Brompton, an English historian enumerates the bagpipes among the Welsh musical instruments in 1170, and Giraldus Cambrensis corroborates him in 1185. The popularity of the harp overshadowed it to such an extent in the next century that the bagpipe may be said to have disappeared in Wales at the opening years of the fourteenth century.

CHAPTER IV.

IN the design to give publicity to the gleanings of years in this field of inquiry as far as it relates to the lives of famous or forgotten performers on the *Uillcann* or Union pipes, the aim of including the names of all Irish pipers of note or historical interest has been kept well in view.

Now that Grattan Flood has made known to us the names of so many performers on the *Piob Mor,* or Warpipes of earlier times, can we be censured for availing ourselves of the opportunity to add them to the list, in this belated endeavor to enhance their fame.

Far more dangerous to England's interests than the harpers were the pipers considered, as they invariably headed all hostile incursions into the Pale. Con sequently they were outlawed as a class, and indiscriminately imprisoned in times of public unrest or rebellion.

Whether from the expense of their maintenance in times of peace or through the intercession of powerful friends, pipers were pardoned occasionally, and it is from the official records of such instances of clemency that we have been made aware of their existence.

State pardons were granted from the year 1550, to 1585, to the following named pipers:

Hugh *buidhe* (yellow).

Cormac the piper.

William the piper.

John O'Doran, of Brittas, County Wicklow, at the request of the Protestant Archbishop of Dublin.

Morighane piberre (*Morogh an piobaire*), or Morgan the piper. There were gentlemen pipers even in those days it seems, for this man whose address was the Park, near Gorey, Wexford, was one of the parties to a treaty with the then Lord Deputy of Ireland in relation to their estates.

Conley McFannin *fionn.*

Manus the piper.

Thomas McShane.

Brian Fitzpatrick.

Conor MacLoughlin.

Owen the piper.

Thomas reagh, (brown) Kings County.

Morgan the piper. The date of this pardon was 1584, although he had been previously pardoned in 1574.

Alexander the piper of the Park, Gorey County, Wexford.

Donogh Casey.

Donogh Mac Cormac, County Limerick.

John Piers, "chief musician and piper to Sir Gerald Fitzgerald of Dromana."

One of the most distinguished pipers in the latter part of the sixteenth century according to Grattan Flood, was Dermot Mac Grath. He fell under the ban of the law nevertheless, for a pardon was granted to him in 1597 by the intercession of Fineen Fitzpatrick, "Lord of Upper Ossory."

Fineen Fitz John, was pardoned two years later through the influence of Edmund Viscount Montgarret.

Another batch of pardons to pipers is recorded in the State Papers for the years 1601 to 1603, both inclusive; and from the large number so liberated we can readily conceive how active in the national cause were the Irish pipers at this period, although it appears they were more in their glory half a century later. The *Piob Mor* or Irish warpipe continued in favor whenever the Irish engaged in battle, and the brave pipers always led on the army in times of warfare. Following is the list:

Murtagh Mac Coyne, Kilmallock, County Cork.
Owen Mac Hugh *na bralie.*
John *intlea,* a wandering piper from County Cork.
Cosney Mac Clancy, of Cloonanna, County Limerick.
Bryan Mac Gillechrist, County Wexford.
Fergus O'Farrell, County Wexford.
Donal Mac Fergus O'Farrell, County Wexford.
Patrick oge O'Farrell, County Wexford.
Daniel O'Cullinane Burren, County Cork.
Conor O'Cullinane Burren, County Cork.
Richard *buidhe* Mac James, County Wexford.
Turlogh the piper, of Tubberdower.
Owen O'Delaney, of the Park, Queen's County.
Dermot O'Delaney, of the Park, Queen's County.
John O'Tracy Liscarroll, County Cork.
Donogh O'Cullinane, of Mara, County Cork.
Cathal O'Kelly, County Wicklow.
Donogh *buidhe* O'Byrne, County Wicklow, and Donal the piper, pardoned at the special instance of Mountjoy Lord Deputy.
Donal O'Killeen, of Cloghan, County Westmeath.
Owen O'Killeen, of Ratra, County Roscommon.
Donal Mac Donogh, gankagh (pugnosed) County Cork.
Bryan *buidhe* O'Clabby, County Sligo.

After the death of Queen Elizabeth the rigors of government persecution of the Irish Minstrels, were gradually abated. Still instances are not wanting to prove that pipers were not infrequently treated with harshness and even barbarity.

CORNELIUS O'BRIEN.

From official records of Cromwell's time, Grattan Flood notes an entry relative to one Cornelius O'Brien, an Irish piper, who in 1656, was "Sentenced to receive twenty lashes on the bare back," in addition to a sentence of transportation to the Barbadoes, a penal colony in the West Indies, where numbers of his profession had preceded him.

JOHN CULLINAN.

Even as late as 1676, John Cullinan was prosecuted for being a bagpiper. The specific complaint was that when the company (soldiers) went to the parish church at Ringrone, County of Cork, he went piping ahead of them to church.

COSNEY AND DONOGH, *gankagh;* (pugnosed).

The official records to the effect that the above named pipers were brought to account in the year 1661 for "piping before a corpse to the church," remind us that the bagpipe whether in its primitive or improved form was until comparatively recent times, associated with every Irish custom and ceremony from the cradle to the grave.

CHAPTER V

FAMOUS HARPERS IN THE SEVENTEENTH AND LATER CENTURIES

> The rolls of fame I will not now explore,
>   Nor need I here describe in learned lay
> How forth the minstrel fared in days of yore,
>   Right glad of heart, though homely in array,
>   His waving beard and locks all hoary grey;
> While from his decent shoulder decent hung
>   His *Harp*, the sole companion of his way;
> Which to the whistling wind responsive rung,
> And ever, as he went, some merry lay he sung.   —Beattie.

The old Irish harp has now perhaps no existence unless in the repositories of the curious. It has passed away among many other interesting relics of earlier times, which had yet a lingering existence at the close of the eighteenth century. How much more true to day than when penned by a writer in *The Dublin Penny Journal* eighty years ago.

Prior to the beginning of the nineteenth century, when a much simpler state of society prevailed, the harper was an honored guest whose appearance never failed to produce much animated excitement wherever he came, laden with the music, the provincial intelligence, and the family gossip, amassed during half a year or more tuneful peregrination. Well may we exclaim in the words of Samuel Lover:

> "Oh give me one strain
> Of that wild harp again,
>   In melody proudly its own,
>   Sweet harp of the days that are gone!
> Time's wide-wasting wing
> Its cold shadow may fling
>   Where the light of the soul hath no part;
> The sceptre and sword
> Both decay with their lord,
>   But the throne of the bard is the heart!"

Manson in his great work, *The Highland Bagpipe,* says: In Scotland the use of the harp ceased with the pomp of the feudal system, while in Ireland the people retained for many generations an acknowledged superiority as harpers.

As this feature of the subject is dealt with in a separate chapter there is no necessity for digressing from our purpose, which is the consideration of the famous harpers who flourished subsequent to the reign of Queen Elizabeth.

MR. CLARK

Through an entry in his diary of 1653-4, John Jocelyn, an Englishman, has immortalized Mr. Clark, a gentleman of quality and parts who was brought up to the practice of the harp since his fifth year.

"Come to see my old acquaintance, and the most incomparable player on the Irish harp, Mr. Clark after his travels. He was an excellent musician and a discreet gentleman. Such music before or since, did I never hear, that instrument being neglected for its extraordinary difficulty, but in my judgment far superior to the lute itself, or whatever speaks with strings."

Though born in England, Clark following the customs of his professional brethren in Ireland, visited his patrons periodically all over the country. The date of his birth may be ascribed to the first decade of the seventeenth century.

WILLIAM FITZ ROBERT FITZ EDMOND BARRY

Strange as it may appear the above named, a blind harper, according to the records, was in the service of Lord Barrymore, who had been commissioned by Queen Elizabeth to exterminate the harpers. But this was a dozen years after her death.

MYLES O'REILLY

This eminent harper, as Bunting terms him, was born about 1636, and hailed from Killincarra, County Cavan. He was universally referred to by the harpers assembled at Belfast in 1792 as the composer of the original "Lochaber," an air so called from the circumstance that Allan Ramsay wrote a song to it entitled, "Farewell to Lochaber, Farewell to My Jean." The original air referred to as "The Irish Tune," was printed in Thomas Duffet's *New Poems, Songs, Prologues, and Epilogues, etc;* published in 1676, a copy of which may be seen in the British Museum. Allan Ramsay's song appeared in the *Tea Table Miscellany.* Fuller information concerning this air may be found in *Irish Folk Music: A Fascinating Hobby.*

SIR EDWARD SUTTON

Having such a wealth of famous harpers of our own, it is not with any sinister design the above named gentleman-harper is introduced in those pages. Evelyn the English diarist, writing of him in 1668, says: "I heard Sir Edward Sutton play excellently on the Irish harp, but not approaching my worthy friend, Mr Clark, who makes it execute lute, viol, and all the harmony an instrument is capable of."

THADY KEENAN

This harper, who flourished early in the seventeenth century, won immortality by his composition of that delightful air, *"An Tighearna Mhaigheo,"* (Lord Mayo).

The circumstances which led to its inspiration were as follows: David Murphy undoubtedly a man of genius, who had been taken under the protection of Lord Mayo through benevolent motives, incurred his patron's displeasure by some misconduct. Anxious to propitiate his Lordship, Murphy consulted a friend, Capt. Finn, of Boyle, Roscommon. The latter suggested that an ode expressive of his patron's praise, and his own penitence, would be the most likely to bring about the desired reconciliation. The result was in the words of the learned Charles O'Conor, "the birth of one of the finest productions for sentiment and harmony, that ever did honor to any country."

Apprehensive that the most humble advances would not soften his Lordship's resentment, Murphy concealed himself after nightfall in Lord Mayo's hall on Christmas Eve, and at an auspicious moment poured forth his very soul in words and music, conjuring him by the birth of the Prince of Peace, to grant him forgiveness in a strain of the finest and most natural pathos that ever distilled from the pen of man.   Two stanzas will show the character of his alternating sentiments.

> "Mayo whose valor sweeps the field
>   And swells the trump of Fame;
> May Heaven's high power thy champion shield,
>   And deathless be his name.

> "O! bid the exiled Bard return,
>   Too long from safety fled;
> No more in absence let him mourn
>   Till earth shall hide his head."

LORD MAYO

Rory Dall O'Cahan.

It is doubtful if any harper of any age was so renowned as Rory Dall O'Cahan if we except the glorified Turlogh O'Carolan.   The *O'Cahans* were a powerful clan in the portions of Antrim and Derry called the O'Cahan country, and were loyal lieges of Hugh O'Neill, whose harper, Rory Dall, was said to be.

Ruaidri, or Rory, born in 1646, was nicknamed *Dall* or blind, after losing his eyesight, it being a term commonly applied to those similarly afflicted.   He early devoted himself to the harp not as may be surmised, with a view to following music as a profession for the tradition invariably preserved of him in the North is that he traveled into Scotland attended by the retinue of a gentleman of large property, and when in Scotland, according to the accounts preserved there also, he seemed to have traveled in the company of noble persons.

GIVE ME YOUR HAND

Proud and spirited, he resented anything in the nature of trespass on his dignity.   Among his visits to the houses of the Scottish nobility, he is said to have called at Eglinton Castle, Ayrshire. Knowing he was a harper, but being unaware of his rank, Lady Eglinton commanded him to play a tune. Taking offence at her peremptory manner, O'Cahan refused and left the castle. When she found out who her guest was her ladyship sought and effected a speedy reconciliation. This incident furnished a theme for one of the harper's best compositions, *"Tabair Dam Do Lamh,"* or "Give Me Your Hand!" The name has been latinized into "Da Mihi Manum."

The fame of the composition and the occasion which gave birth to it reaching the ear of King James the Sixth, induced him to send for the composer. O'Cahan accordingly attended at the Scottish court, and created a sensation.

His performance so delighted the royal circle that King James familiarly laid his royal hand on the harper's shoulder. When asked by one of the courtiers if he realized the honor thus conferred on him, to their consternation Rory replied: "A greater than King James has laid his hand on my shoulder." Who was that man? cried the King. "O'Neill, Sire," proudly answered Rory standing up.

Four of the nine tunes to be found at the end of Bruce Armstrong's fine work on *The Highland Harp,* are attributed to "Rorie Dall," namely "Lude's Supper;" "The Terror of Death;" "The Fiddler's Content;" and "Rorie Dall's Sister's Lament." Others of his compositions not previously named are "Port Athol;" "Port Gordon;" and "Port Lennox."

It is a curious coincidence that after spending many years with McLeod, of Dunvegan, in the Isle of Skye, O'Cahan should die at Eglinton Castle about the year 1653. In some unaccountable way during his long sojourn in Scotland he became known as Rory Dall Morrison, and this has so clouded his origin and identity as to involve his very nationality in question.

John and Harry Scott.

Contemporary with Rory Dall O'Cahan were the above named brothers, natives of the County Westmeath. Bunting says they were particularly distinguished for their *caoinans* or dirge pieces. They composed pathetic lamentations for Baron Purcell of Loughmoe, County Tipperary, and for Baron O'Hussey of Galtrim, County Meath.

Gerald O'Daly.

The reputed authorship of *"Eibhlin a Ruin,"* is all that has preserved O'Daly's name from oblivion. Even his name is in dispute. In Bunting's *Ancient Music of Ireland; Grove's Dictionary of Music and Musicians;* and *British Musical Biography;* the name is given as above; while in *The Gentleman's Magazine,* 1827; Hardiman's *Irish Minstrelsy,* 1831; and in Fitz Gerald's *Stories of Famous Songs,* 1906; it is Carrol O'Daly.

All, however, agree in associating the name with the famous melody.

Bunting, who refers to him as a contemporary of O'Cahan, who died in 1653, is of the opinion that from the marks of high antiquity apparent throughout the air, it is probable that he only adapted the Irish words to it. On the other hand Fitz Gerald tells us that at a venture he would suggest about 1450 when *living* money was still in use, as the probable date of the song, for the hero says; he would spend a cow to entertain his ladylove.

The date of his death is given as 1405 by Mrs. Milligan Fox in her *Annals of the Irish Harpers.*

The earliest printed version of the song appeared in Coffey's *Beggar's Wedding,* 1728 or 29. The song with music followed in 1731.

THOMAS O'CONNELLAN

This bard and musical genius whom Arthur O'Neill called "Tom Conlan, the great harper," was born at Cloonmahon, (anciently known as Clonymeaghan), County Sligo. The date of his birth is variously given as about 1625 and 1640. His celebrity in Ireland was very great although it would seem he was no less popular in Scotland where according to Arthur O'Neill he attained to city honors as "baillie" in Edinburgh. After a sojourn of a score of years in Caledonia, he returned to his native land in 1689 and died while a guest at Bouchier Castle, near Lough Gur in County Limerick in 1698. "His remains were reverently interred in the adjoining churchyard of Temple *Nuadh,*" Grattan Flood says, "and over his grave a few pipers appropriately played by way of a funeral dirge the introductory and concluding phrases which O'Connellan had added to Myles O'Reilly's "Irish Tune;" the version being known as "The Breach of Aughrim."

A banshee we are told wailed from the top of *Carrig na g-Colur* while his funeral procession was passing to the burial ground. The mournful cooing of the wild pigeons from which the rock takes it name, may account for this quaint fancy.

The "Great Harper" was the composer of "The Dawning of the Day;" also known as "The Golden Star;" "Love in Secret;" "Bonny Jean;" "The Jointure;" "Molly St. George;" "If to a Foreign Clime I Go;" "Planxty Davis;" and seven or eight hundred others now forgotten. The last named: Planxty Davis, is known in Scotland as "The Battle of Killicrankie."

"By Lough Gur's waters, lone and low the minstrel's laid—
Where mouldering cloisters dimly throw sepulchral shade.
Where clustering ivy darkly weeps upon his bed,
To blot the legend where he sleeps—the tuneful dead!
And fallen are the towers of time, in dust in lone,
Where the ringing of his fairy chime, so well was known!
Where song was sweet and mirth was high, and beauty smiled
Thro' roofless halls the night winds sigh, the owl shrieks wild."

LAURENCE O'CONNELLAN

who is referred to by some writers as William, was a younger brother of the renowned harper and composer, Thomas O'Connellan. Born in the same home the difference in their ages is said to have been five years.

Laurence, who affected a different style from his more famous brother, produced many pieces of high merit. Among them are mentioned "Lady Iveagh;" "Saedbh Kelly;" and "Molly MacAlpine," otherwise known as "Molly Halfpenny" and "Poll Ha'penny," as a dance tune. It will be remembered that "Molly MacAlpine" was the air to which Tom Moore sung, "Remember the Glories of Brian the Brave."

After the death of his elder brother, Laurence went to Scotland, bringing with him and popularizing several of the deceased minstrel's compositions, among them being, according to James Hardiman, author of *Irish Minstrelsy* " 'Planxty Davis,' since well known as the 'Battle of Killicrankie,' and also a prelude to the 'Breach of Aughrim' universally admired under the name of 'Farewell to Lachaber.' "

John Murphy

Arthur O'Neill, who may be regarded as the historian of the harpers, told Bunting of a famous harper named Murphy, a Leinster man, the son of a very indifferent performer, who had borne a higher reputation as a performer, than any other harper who had been O'Neill's contemporary.

On his return from the continent in 1719, after a stay of eleven years, his conceit was insufferable. He had played with approbation before Louis XIV.— Louis le Grand—of France, and proud of this distinction he assumed airs and ostentatious finery, which naturally aroused the jealousy and ill-will of his professional brethren. The father on learning of his son's arrival in Dublin in great grandeur promptly called on him, only to be kicked down stairs, for his shabby appearance. On another occasion O'Carolan, notwithstanding his blindness, nearly beat him to death in a tavern at Castle Blayney, County Monaghan. Murphy in his lofty impudence sarcastically alluded to the Bard's compositions as being but "bones without beef." O'Carolan attacked him, and as he was screaming with pain and terror his irate assailant kept shouting into his ear, "Put beef to that air you puppy!" with every kick. The interference of onlookers saved the egotist's life.

In his *Story of the Harp* Grattan Flood says, that Murphy as harp solist, was one of the attractions at a special performance on February 14th, 1738—the year in which O'Carolan died—at Smock Alley Theatre, Dublin. His death took place in 1753 after several seasons' playing at Mallow, County Cork, then a popular health resort.

Cornelius Lyons

This renowned musician, who in his day was household harper to the Earl of Antrim, was a native of County Kerry, and flourished in the latter part of the seventeenth, and the early part of the eighteenth centuries.

Agreeable in personality, his reputation both as a man and a musician was admirable. Though a rival in art and even in composition, Lyons was O'Carolan's loyal friend and companion. Famous as an arranger of variations in more modern style to such airs as "Eileen a Roon;" "The Coolin;" etc., only one of his original compositions—"Miss Hamilton"—has been preserved.

The Earl of Antrim was a wit and a poet, and notwithstanding his rank, was quite democratic in his manners. Once while in London accompanied by Lyons, they went to the house of a famous Irish harper named Heffernan, who kept a tavern there, but agreed on a plan before entering.

"I will call you cousin Burke," said his lordship. "You may call me cousin Randall or My Lord as you please." It was not long before Heffernan was made aware of the dignity of his guest, from the conversation and livery of his lordship's servants. Heffernan being requested to bring his harp complied willingly and played a good many tunes in grand style. The Earl then called upon his "Cousin Burke" to play a tune. After many apologies and with apparent reluctance the supposed cousin at length took the harp and played some of his best airs. Heffernan after listening a while started up and exclaimed, "My lord you may call him 'Cousin Burke' or what cousin you please, but *Dar Dia* he plays upon Lyons' fingers."

Mr. Heffernan.

The above described episode was the first meeting of Lyons and Heffernan. Lord Antrim then retired, leaving the minstrels to enjoy themselves to their heart's content which Arthur O'Neill assures us they did like "bards of old."

The story of the trick which had been played on Heffernan soon gained circulation and it was not long before the Duke of Argyle came to the tavern with a large company to hear him play. Unheeding his lordship's call for a Scotch tune Heffernan played "The Golden Star," a plaintive Irish melody. When the nobleman complained that it was too melancholy for a Scotch tune the harper replied, "You must know my Lord it was composed *since* the Union."

The remark touched a sensitive spot, for the Duke, who was an advocate of the Union of Scotland with England, hastily left the tavern with his company in no pleasant frame of mind.

Mr. Maguire.

A celebrated harper named Maguire, from the County of Fermanagh, settled in London about the year 1720, and opened a wine shop or tavern near Charing Cross. His house attracted the patronage of some of the very best people in the city, including the Duke of Newcastle and several of the ministry. On one occasion he was asked why the Irish airs were so plaintive and solemn. He replied that the native composers were "too deeply distressed at the situation of their country, and her gallant sons to compose otherwise; but remove the restraints which they labor under, and you will not have reason to complain of the plaintiveness of their notes."

He had committed the impardonable sin! The expression of such warm sentiments of patriotism gave offence, his house became gradually neglected,— in modern idiom, boycotted—and he died broken-hearted a year or so afterwards.

Owen Keenan.

Born in 1725 and therefore contemporary with Echlin O'Cahan, a harper named Owen Keenan, of Augher, was no less reckless, turbulent, and adventurous. Becoming enamored of a French governess at the residence of Mr. Stuart at Killmoon near Cookstown, County Tyrone, which he often visited, he proved that love laughs at other obstacles no less than at locksmiths. Blind as he was the impetuous Romeo made his way to the room of his Juliet by means of a ladder from the outside. This breach of the proprieties resulted in his commitment to Omagh jail.

Another blind harper named Higgins hailing from Tyrawley, County Mayo, who traveled in better style than most others of the fraternity, hearing of Keenan's predicament, hastened down to Omagh, where his respectable appearance and retinue readily procured his admission to *see* his friend. The jailer was not at home but his wife was. She loved music and cordials and being once a beauty was by no means insensible to flattery even from men who could not see. She fell an easy victim to their wiles, and the blind harpers contrived to steal the keys out of her pocket, oppressed as she was with love and music,

They did not forget to make the turnkey drunk also, and while Higgins remained behind *soothering* his infatuated dupe, Keenan escaped with Higgins' boy on his back to guide him over a ford in the river Strule, by which he took his route back to Killymoon, and repeated the offence for which he had been previously imprisoned.

After narrowly escaping conviction at the County assizes, Keenan finally carried off the governess and married her. Seldom does an affair of this kind end otherwise than happily in the story books, yet rumor compels us to add that after their emigration to America, the fickle French woman proved unfaithful to her romantic Romeo.

HUGH O'NEILL

An honorable exception to the generality of the harpers of his day Hugh O'Neill was a man of conspicuous respectability both in character and descent. He was born at Foxford, County Mayo, late in the seventeenth century, and his mother being of the MacDonnell family, was a cousin to the famous Count Taaffe.

Having lost his sight by smallpox when but seven years old, he devoted himself to the study of music as an accomplishment. In later years this acquirement was turned to good account when he was beset with reverses of fortune.

From the respectability of his family and the propriety of his deportment, he was received more as a friend and associate than a professional performer by the gentry of Connacht.

To the generosity of Mr. Tennison of Castle Tennison, County Roscommon, he owed the possession of a large farm at a nominal rent. Though sightless he enjoyed a hunt with the hounds which in an open country like Roscommon subjected him to comparatively little physical danger.

JEROME DUIGENAN

We are indebted to Arthur O'Neill, the Plutarch of the harpers, for all that is known of this remarkable performer on the harp, who was born in County Leitrim in the year 1710.

"There was a harper before my time," he says, "named Jerome Duigenan, not blind, an excellent Greek and Latin scholar, and a charming performer." Of the numerous anecdotes heard by O'Neill concerning him, that which pleased him most was the following:

Duigenan lived with a Colonel Jones of Drumshambo, who was one of the representatives in parliament for the County of Leitrim. The Colonel being in Dublin at the meeting of parliament, met with an English nobleman, who had brought over a Welsh harper. When the Welshman had played some tunes before Colonel Jones which he did very well, the nobleman asked him had he ever heard so sweet a finger. "Yes," replied the Colonel, "and that by a man who never wears either linen or woolen." "I'll bet you a hundred guineas," says the nobleman, "you can't produce anyone to excel my Welshman." The bet was accordingly made, and Duigenan was written to and ordered to come on immediately to Dublin and bring his harp and dress of *Cauthach* with him; that is a dress made of beaten rushes, with something like a caddy or plaid of the same stuff. On Duigenan's arrival in Dublin the Colonel acquainted the members with the nature of his bet, and they requested that it might be decided *in the House of Commons* before business commenced. The two harpers performed before all the members accordingly, and it was unanimously decided in favor of Duigenan, who wore his full *Cauthach* dress, and a cap of the same stuff shaped like a sugar loaf with many tassels. He was a tall handsome man and looked well in it. Mr. Bunting says this conical cap was unquestionably the *barradh.* of the old bards, and corresponds with the costume of the head carved on the extremity of certain ancient Irish harps.

DOMINIC MUNGAN

A harper of great renown in the first half of the eighteenth century was Dominic Mungan, whose story Edward Bunting learned from Henry Joy, Esq., of Belfast, who often heard him play.

Born blind about the year 1715 in the pastoral and poetical county of Tyrone, his profession was determined by his affliction, and in it he acquired such fame as to embalm his name in the annals of Irish musical literature. He was long famous for his excellent performance throughout the north of Ireland "where he regularly went the Northwest circuit with the bar." An admirable performer, those janglings of the strings so general among ordinary practitioners were never heard from the harp in his hands. His "whispering notes" were indescribably charming. They commenced in a degree of *Piano* that required the closest approach to the instrument to render them audible, but increased by degrees to the richest chords.

Mungan was conversant with the best music of his day such as that of Corelli, Handel, and Geminiani, select adagios from which he often played.

Being a man of prudence and economy he was enabled to give his three sons a liberal education. Mark, the eldest, destined for the priesthood finished his studies in France where he obtained more than two score premiums for classical learning. In consequence of his intense application his health failed on his return home, and he died at Strabane in his father's house.

John, the second son, became a physician and won distinction in his chosen profession, abandoned the creed of his parents, and lost his life in an accident returning from the Middleton races.

The youngest son, Terence, also apostatized, and was appointed dean of Ardagh, from which he was promoted to the bishopric of Limerick in the Established Church.

John the doctor had fallen in love it is said with a protestant young lady, who refused his suit on account of his creed. Having recanted he again sought her hand, and was scornfully rejected. She "would not demean herself by marrying a turncoat." To add still further to his humiliation his father refused to speak to him thereafter.

ECHLIN O'CAHAN [ACKLAND KANE]

Strong as the wandering proclivities of the Irish harpers have been for centuries prior to their extinction, it is doubtful if any of them indulged this propensity to such an extent as did the subject of this sketch, who was born at Drogheda, County Louth in 1720.

Such was his love of adventure, that notwithstanding his blindness, he visited Rome early in life where he played before "the Pretender," then resident there. In his subsequent travels through France and Spain in which a large number of exiled Irish had settled, he was treated with great liberality and introduced to the notice of His Catholic Majesty. The design of favoring him with a pension which the king had in contemplation, was frustrated by his own indiscretions, and after exhausting the patience and patronage of his countrymen at Madrid, O'Cahan set out on foot for Bilboa on his way home, carrying his harp on his back. As he was a very strong, tall and athletic man he reached his destination safely.

It does not appear that he spent much time in Ireland after his return, for all mention of his name and fame thereafter down to the time of his death in 1790 is in relation to Scottish events.

While on a tour of the Isles in 1775, he was at Lord Macdonald's of Skye, where he recommended himself so much by his performance, that his host presented him with a silver harp key that had long been in the family, "being unquestionably," Bunting says, "the key left by his great predecessor and name-sake, Rory Dall O'Cahan." But the dissipated rascal sold it in Edinburgh and drank the money.

His behavior was not at all times so exemplary, for Mr. Gunn relates that the Highland gentry occasionally found it necessary to repress his turbulence by clipping his nails; thereby "putting him out of business" for a time.

His execution and proficiency were a credit to his teacher, Cornelius Lyons, harper to the Earl of Antrim. Manini often spoke of him at Cambridge with rapture, as being able though blind, to play with accuracy and great effect the fine treble and bass parts of many of Corelli's concerts, in concert with other music. Had he been but moderately correct in his conduct he might with certainty have raised the character of the wandering minstrel higher than it had stood for a century before.

THADY ELLIOTT

In describing harpers of note we would hardly be justified in ignoring Thady Elliott of County Meath, the blind minstrel, who taught Rose Mooney. His general character, though spoken of disparagingly by Edward Bunting, was viewed with more liberality and toleration by Arthur O'Neill, who experienced nothing but kindness at his hands.

Elliott's chief claim to fame or rather notoriety, rests on an act bordering on sacrilege which but few outside of Bedlam would have the hardihood to attempt.

A practical joker of a type not yet extinct, knowing that he was to play at the celebration of Mass on Christmas morning at the town of Navan, took him to a public house or tavern the evening before, and bribed him with the promise of a gallon of whiskey to strike up "Planxty Connor," one of O'Carolan's lively tunes, at the time of the Elevation.

With all due decorum Thady played sacred music until the appointed time, when true to his word, he swung into "Planxty Conner" to the horror of the officiating priest who well knew the apocryphal nature of the melody.

Other means of showing his displeasure being unavailable, the priest repeatedly stamped his foot. Some who thought his emphatic movement was but an irresistible response to Thady's spirited strains, whispered *"Dhar Dhia tha an Sagart ag Rinnce."* The daring and irreverent harper after a few rounds of the Planxty resumed the sacred airs, but that didn't save him from denunciation and dismissal after the service.

A harper named Harry Fitzsimmons, who was engaged to play at the later Masses, had no easy time of it, escaping Elliott's vengeance. The latter though blind, secured a club and laid in wait outside the chapel door for his intended victim. After a while some one seeing the priest coming out said *"Ta se ag teact"* (He is coming). When the footsteps indicated striking distance Thady made a sweeping blow which, had it hit his reverence instead of the chapel door, would have seriously injured him.

Humiliated like the lion who loses his prey by miscalculating the length of his spring, Thady Elliott re-entered the sanctuary and publicly apologized for his misbehavior.

He was born in 1725, and notwithstanding his vices and his follies, Bunting says he was a capital performer, and generous and hospitable in the highest degree.

"Old" Freney

Mingled with mother earth in some ancient church yard in his native province, for more than a century, lie the mortal remains of "Old Freney the Harper," described in *The Dublin Penny Journal* of October 20, 1832.

Freney or Frene, as he was sometimes called, was not less than ninety years old at the end of the eighteenth century. Of medium size and bent with age, his head of Homeric cast was crowned with hair of the whitest, and he was a welcome visitor in every respectable family in many of the western counties. His harp, as the writer could recollect its appearance was a dark framed antique looking instrument, closely strung with thin brass wires, which produced that wild, low ringing music poetically compared to the "ringing of fairy chimes." The effect of this was heightened by the old man's peculiar expression of intense and sometimes pleased attention to his own music as he stooped forward, holding his head close to the wires, as he swept them over with a feeble, uncertain and trembling hand—the too obvious effect of extreme age. His appearance thus bowed beside the instrument, which towered far above his white head, was of the most picturesque character. But the old minstrel had no rallying of tuneful power—his harp strings seemed to have caught the wandering, querulous and feeble dotage of his infirm age and echoed mournfully of departed power and life.

It now adds much to the interest of his memory, that he could not have been the welcome guest, which at that time he was for the sake of his music alone. He was a venerable ruin of those good old times which were felt to be passing away with the harper. "Old" Freney had lived among their grandfathers, and had been prominent in the gay doings of those less refined, but more joyous and hospitable times. He was full of old stories about persons whose names and deeds had still an interest in the memory of their descendants; and those stories were listened to with a delight which can now be little understood.

CHAPTER VI

TURLOGH O'CAROLAN AND HIS TIMES

To do anything like reasonable justice to such a celebrity as the great Irish Bard in a few pages is a hopeless task. And what adds to the difficulty is, not the lack but rather the amplitude of material available. Nothing less than a good-sized volume would meet the requirements.

Turlogh O'Carolan was born about the year 1670 at a place called *Baile Nuadh* or Newtown, near Nobber in the County of Westmeath, but in his youth his father migrated to County Leitrim, where he settled on a farm near Carrick-on-Shannon. Though gifted with a natural genius for music and poetry he displayed no precocious disposition for either. Had he not lost his sight when 16 or 18 years of age from an attack of smallpox, it is doubtful if he would ever have won undying fame through his minstrelsy. Accident or rather chance determined his vocation, and he continued it more by choice than necessity. Respectably descended, possessing no small share of Milesian pride, and entertaining a due sense of his additional claims as a man of genius, he neither played for hire nor refused a reward if offered with delicacy, and he always expected and invariably received that attention which he deserved. His visits were regarded as favors, and his departure never failed to occasion regret. He seldom extended his travels beyond the province of Connacht, where he was such a universal favorite, that messengers were continually after him to one or other houses of the principal inhabitants; his presence being regarded as an honor and a compliment.

Instinctively understanding that hospitality has its limitations, he made a good natured reply of which the following is a translation, to a gentleman who was pressing him to prolong his stay.

> "If to a friend's house thou should'st repair;
> Pause and take heed of lingering idly there;
> Thou mayest be welcome but it's past a doubt;
> Long visits soon will wear the welcome out."

In his *Historical Memoirs of the Irish Bards;* Walker says O'Carolan must have been deprived of sight at a very early period of his life; for he remembered no impression of colors. His merry saying: "My eyes have been transplanted into my ears," does not necessarily imply early blindness. Other authorities mention sixteen, and eighteen years respectively, as his age when afflicted, while Grattan Flood extends the date to his twenty-second year.

"He was unquestionably a great genius both as a composer, and a poet; but it is equally certain that he never excelled as a performer," according to Edward Bunting: "This may be attributed to the fact that he did not begin to learn the harp till he was upwards of sixteen, at which age the fingers have lost the suppleness that must be taken advantage of in early years, to produce a really master hand."

Turlogh O'Carolan

Love does not always enter at the eyes for O'Carolan became enamored of Miss Bridget Cruise of Cruisetown in County Longford several years after he had lost his sight, and though this lady did not reciprocate his affection; yet the song in which her name is immortalized is regarded as his masterpiece coming as it did, warm from his heart while his genius was in its full vigor.

Near his father's house was a rath, in the interior of which one of the Fairy Queens or "good people" was believed by the country people to hold her court. This rath or fort was the scene of many a boyish pastime with his youthful companions; and after he became blind, he used to prevail on some of his family or neighbors to lead him to it, where he would remain for hours together, stretched listlessly before the sun. He was often observed to start up suddenly, as if in a fit of ecstasy, occasioned as it was firmly believed by the preternatural sights which he witnessed. In one of these raptures he called hastily on his companions, to lead him home, and when he reached it, he sat down immediately to his harp and in a little time played and sung the air and words of a sweet song addressed to Bridget Cruise, the object of his earliest and tenderest attachment.

So sudden and so captivating was it, that it was confidently attributed to fairy inspiration. From that hour he became a poet and composer. "Bridget Cruise" is the only one of O'Carolan's airs composed in the traditional style.

BRIDGET CRUISE

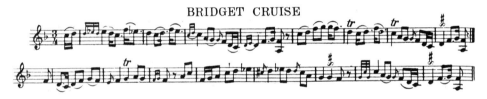

One of his earliest patrons, George Reynolds of Letterfian Leitrim, who was something of a poet himself, remarked to O'Carolan in the Irish idiom: "Perhaps you might make a better hand of your tongue than of your fingers." He suggested a text by telling him that a great battle had been recently fought between the fairies or "good people" of two hills in the neighborhood. The influence of the folklore of his boyhood and the day dreams in which he indulged at the rath, contributed not a little to the inspiration which produced "The Fairy Queens" in 1693, a much more ambitious composition than "Bridget Cruise."

No more successful in his courtship of Margaret Browne—the "Peggy Browne" of his muse—than of Miss Cruise, he consoled himself with the charms of Mary Maguire, a young lady of good family in the County of Fermanagh, whom he married in his fiftieth year. Though she was proud and extravagant they lived in connubial harmony through life. After his marriage he occupied a small farm near Mohill in County Leitrim, but hospitality more suited to his mind than his means, soon caused embarrassment, and he was soon left to lament the want of prudence without which the rich cannot taste of pleasure long, nor the poor of happiness.

Equipped with a good horse and an attendant harper furnished by his generous patroness and lifelong friend, Mrs. MacDermott Roe of Alderford House, County of Roscommon, O'Carolan commenced the profession of an itinerant harper or bard in 1693. Wherever he went the gates of the nobility and others were thrown open to him; he was received with respect and a distinguished place assigned him at the table. In all respects he was a genuine representative of the bards of old.

It was during his peregrinations that he composed all of the two hundred airs which have immortalized his fame. He thought the tribute of a song (with music of course) due to every home in which he was entertained, and he seldom failed to pay it; choosing for his subject either the head of the family or the loveliest of its branches.

THE FAIRY QUEENS

One of O'Carolan's earliest friends was Hugh MacGauran, a County Leitrim gentleman, who had a happy poetic talent, and excelled particularly in ludicrous species of poetry. He was the author of the justly celebrated song of *"Plearaca na Ruarcach"* freely translated as "O'Rourke's Feast," which he prevailed on the bard to set to music. The fame of the song having reached the ears of Dean Swift, he requested of MacGauran a literal translation of it in English. The Dean was so charmed with its beauties that he honored it with an excellent version of his own. MacGauran's original composition in Irish appears to have been lost, but O'Carolan's "Planxty O'Rourke" composed about 1721, has been preserved.

PLANXTY O'ROURKE
(O'Rourke's Noble Feast)

Although O'Carolan delivered himself but indifferently in English, he did not like to be corrected for his solecisms, Hardiman tells us in his *Irish*

Minstrelsy. A humorous instance of this weakness has been handed down. A self sufficient gentleman surnamed O'Dowd or Dudy, as it was sometimes pronounced, once criticising his English, asked him why he attempted a language of which he knew nothing. "Oh I know a little of it" was the reply. "If so," said the egotist, "can you tell me the English for *Bundhoon?*" "Yes," said the bard with an arch smile, "I think the *properest* English for that word is Billy Dudy." This grotesque repartee turned the laugh against the critic who was ever after nicknamed "Billy Bundhoon."

O'Carolan seldom exercised the keen satirical powers he possessed, although occasionally they were aroused by inhospitality—to him the only unpardonable sin. At the house of a parsimonious lady who was sparing in her supply of O'Carolan's favorite beverage, a butler named O'Flynn, who objected to his freedom of the wine cellar—a customary privilege—had his name preserved from oblivion in the couplet—

> "What a pity hell's gates are not kept by O'Flynn!
> So surly a dog would let nobody in."

The incident which led to the birth of "O'Carolan's Devotion" was a chance meeting with a Miss Featherstone of County Longford, who was on her way to church at Granard one Sunday in the year 1719.

"Your servant, Mr. O'Carolan," she saluted.

"I thank you. Who speaks to me?" he replied.

"It is I, sir, one Miss Featherstone."

"I've heard of you, Madam: a young lady of great beauty and much wit. The loss of one sense prevents my beholding your beauty; and I believe it is a happy circumstance for me, for I am assured it has made many captives. But your wit, Madam! I dread it."

"Had I wit, Mr. O'Carolan, this is not a day for its display. It should give place to the duty of prayer. I apprehend that in complying with this duty, you go *one way*, and I go *another*—I wish I could prevail with you to quit *your* way for *mine*."

"Should I go your way, Madam, I dread you yourself would be the chief object of my devotion."

After some bantering of this nature, Miss Featherstone invited the bard to visit her house, assuring him of a hearty welcome, and admonishing him to pray for her at his church. Very gallantly O'Carolan responded: "Could I withdraw my *Devotion from* yourself, I would obey; but I will make the best effort I can. Adieu, adieu."

"Adieu to you, O'Carolan—but remember——"

The event justified his fears. Instead of praying for Miss Featherstone, he neglected his religious duties to compose a song on her, which has been described as "humorously sentimental, but in bad English. The music, however, was of a high order.

Irish hospitality and his mode of life led to his fondness for the "flowing bowl," as it does almost invariably with his humble brethren of the present day. Inordinate gratifications bring their own punishment, and from the consequence O'Carolan was not exempt. Physicians assured him that unless he corrected his habits, his mortal career would soon come to an end. He determined to abstain thereafter from the forbidden yet delicious cup. He wandered about the town of Boyle, County Roscommon, at that time his principal residence, dejected in spirit and brooding in melancholy. His gayety had forsaken him, and his harp lay in some obscure corner of his habitation, neglected and unstrung.

Passing one day by a grocer's shop, our Irish Orpheus, after a six weeks' quarantine, was tempted to step in, undecided what course to pursue. "Well, my dear friend," cried he to the young man who stood behind the counter, "you

O'CAROLAN'S DEVOTION

see I am a man of constancy; for six long weeks I have refrained from whiskey. Was there ever so great a case of self-denial? But a thought strikes me, and surely you will not be cruel enough to refuse one gratification which I shall earnestly request. Bring hither a measure of my favorite liquor, which I shall smell to, but indeed shall not taste." The lad indulged him on that condition; and no sooner did the fumes ascend to his brain than every latent spark within him was rekindled. His countenance glowed with an unusual brightness, and the soliloquy which he repeated over the cup was the effusion of a heart newly reanimated. Contrary to the advice of his medical friends, he once more quaffed the forbidden draught until his spirits were sufficiently exhilarated and his mind had resumed its former tone. Inspiration returned, and he immediately set about composing that much admired song known as "O'Carolan's Receipt," or "Planxty Stafford." That same evening, at Boyle, he commenced the words and began to formulate the air, and before the following morning he sang and played this noble offspring of his imagination in Mr. Stafford's parlor at Elphin.

O'CAROLAN'S RECEIPT FOR DRINKING
(Planxty Stafford)

When O'Carolan was enjoying the hospitality of Thomas Morris Jones, Esq., of Moneyglass, County Leitrim, in the year 1730, he signalized the occasion by composing a song, according to his custom. While so engaged he was overheard by one Moore, who had a ready ear for music and played tolerably well on the violin. After completing his inimitable piece, O'Carolan proudly announced that he had now struck out a melody which he was sure would please the Squire. Moore, in a spirit of mischief, insisted the air was an old and common one, and to prove his contention he actually played it note for note on the violin. This, of course, threw the bard into a rage. However, when his passion calmed down, an explanation took place, and all misunderstandings were duly drowned in the good old-fashioned way.

Another version of this story is to the effect that O'Carolan and Baron Dawson happened to be enjoying, with others, the hospitalities of Squire Jones, and slept in adjoining rooms. The bard being called upon by the company to compose a song or tune in honor of their host, retired to his apartment, taking his harp with him, and under the inspiration of copious libations of his favorite beverage, not only produced the melody now known as "Bumper Squire Jones," but also very indifferent words to it. While the bard was thus employed, however, Baron Dawson was not idle. Being possessed of a fine musical ear as well as considerable poetical talents, he not only fixed the melody in his memory, but actually wrote the noble song now incorporated with it before he retired to rest.

At breakfast the following morning, when O'Carolan sang and played his composition, the Baron, to the astonishment of all present, and the bard in particular, stoutly denied O'Carolan's claims to the melody, and to prove his contention, sang it to his own words amid shouts of laughter and approbation. The bard, whose anger knew no bounds, was eventually mollified by explanations. Not few were the practical jokes of a similar character that had been perpetrated on the blind bard in his time.

All accounts of O'Carolan's life make mention of a romantic incident which occurred about 1713, during his pilgrimage to "St. Patrick's Purgatory," in an island in Lough Derg, County Donegal. On his return to shore he found several pilgrims awaiting the arrival of the boat which had conveyed him to the penitential cave. In assisting some of those devout pilgrims to step on board, he chanced to take a lady's hand, and instantly exclaimed: *"Dar lamha mo chardais Criost"* (by the hand of my gossip), "this is the hand of Bridget Cruise." His sense of feeling did not deceive him; it was the hand of her whom he had adored —his first love.

His musical capacity had been severely tested more than once when the craze for Italian music had crossed the Channel from England, but he never failed to acquit himself with credit.

The story goes that an Italian voilinist named Geminiani, then residing in Dublin, hearing of O'Carolan's fame, took steps to put it to the proof. Selecting an elegant piece of music in the Italian style, he altered it here and there in such a manner that none but a keen musician could detect the mutilation, and sent it to the bard at Elphin, County Roscommon. The latter, on hearing it played, declared it to be a fine piece of music, but humorously remarked in Irish: *"Ta se air cois air bacaige!"*

He rectified the errors as requested, and when the music score was returned to the Italian maestro in Dublin, he pronounced O'Carolan to be a true musical genius.

On another occasion, at the beginning of the eighteenth century, according to the historian Sylvester O'Halloran, the then Lord Mayo brought from Dublin the celebrated Geminiani to spend some time with him at his seat in the county. O'Carolan, who happened to be visiting his lordship at the same time, found himself greatly neglected, and complained of it one day in the presence of the foreigner. "When you play in as masterly a manner as he does," replied his lordship, "you shall not be overlooked." O'Carolan, whose pride was aroused, wagered with his rival that though he was almost a total stranger to Italian music, yet he would follow him in any piece he played, and he himself would afterwards play a voluntary in which the Italian could not follow him. The test piece happened to be Vivaldi's fifth concerto, which the foreigner played on the violin. The blind bard was victorious, and "O'Carolan's Concerto" was the result.

The death of his wife in 1733, which was his first bereavement, threw a gloom over his mind, that was never after entirely dissipated. Realizing that the sands of his life were fast running out, he commemorated his final departure from the hospitable home of his great friend, Robert Maguire of Tempo, County Fermanagh, with the production of that plaintive melody, "O'Carolan's Farewell."

O'CAROLAN'S FAREWELL

Hastening on his way and making a few hurried visits to cherished friends in County Leitrim, he reached his destination—Alderford House—the residence of his lifelong friend, Mrs. McDermott Roe, where he died on the 25th of March, 1738, in the sixty-eighth year of his age. Shortly before his death, he called for his harp, and with feeble fingers wandering among the strings, he evolved his last composition, the weirdly plaintive wail, "O'Carolan's Farewell to Music."

O'CAROLAN'S FAREWELL TO MUSIC

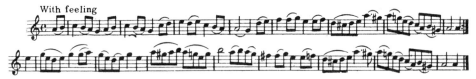

O'Carolan's funeral was a memorable event. The wake lasted four days, and he was buried on the fifth, in the McDermott Roe vault at Kilronan Ardagh, County Westmeath. Upwards of sixty clergymen of different denominations, a number of gentlemen from surrounding counties, and a vast concourse of country people assembled to pay the last mark of respect to the great bard. Hospitality was lavish, a keg of whiskey on either side of the hall was replenished as often as emptied, and the music of the harp was heard in every direction.

During his forty-five years of itinerant minstrelsy, he is said to have composed upwards of two hundred pieces of music, many of which have been irretrievably lost, including all but one of the fifteen addressed to Bridget Cruise, the object of his youthful yet hopeless attachment.

A harper who attended the Belfast Harp Festival in 1792, and who had never met the bard, had acquired more than one hundred of his tunes, it is said. Although half a dozen or so of his productions had been included in J. and W. Neale's *Collection of Irish Tunes,* in 1726, and at least as many more were printed in Wright's *Aria di Camera,* two years later, nothing purporting to be a collection of his compositions appeared until nine years after his death.

Under the patronage of Rev. Dr. Delaney of Dublin, O'Carolan's son, who had little musical genius, published by subscription a small edition of his father's works in 1747, but selfishly and unfilially omitted several of the best of them.

O'Carolan was the first of the Irish harpers who departed from the purely Irish style in composition. Bunting says he delighted in the polished compositions of the Italian and German schools, yet he felt the full excellence of the ancient music of his own country.

Uniting in his person the fourfold avocations of his race—poet, composer, harper, and singer—he may well be regarded as the last true bard of Ireland; but he possessed none of their ruling spirit, for he was more festive than patriotic. Welcome alike to hall and cottage, he spent his days in cheering their inmates, as Bayle Bernard says, with his love songs and his planxties, and doubtless did so all the more in being himself the happiest harper who has ever repaid the loss of sight by the felicities of sound.

Though nearly two centuries have passed on the wings of time since Turlogh O'Carolan was "gathered to his fathers," he still lives in his own deathless strains; and while the charms of melody hold their sway over the human heart, the name of the great Blind Bard will be remembered and revered. As a fitting conclusion to this brief biography, we quote the expressive words of Charles O'Conor of Belanagar, his loyal friend: *"Turlogh O'Carolan, the talented and principal Musician of Ireland, died. May the Lord have mercy on his Soul, for he was a moral and religious man."*

CHAPTER VII

HARPERS OF NOTE

MISCELLANEOUS MENTION

DURING his comprehensive tours throughout the four provinces, Arthur O'Neill not only picked up all the information and current gossip relating to his predecessors, but met all the prominent harpers of his own time. Not included in the list of those already mentioned were a few whose attainments he deemed worthy of special note.

Foremost among them were three brothers named McAleer, encountered in Tyrone. Edward, the oldest and most accomplished, spent five years in the Irish Brigade in France, and of course learned the language of the country as well as some other acquirements less praiseworthy. Assuming the name "Leeriano" for professional purposes, after his return to Ireland, he started out as a traveling minstrel. Down in County Cavan, at a gentleman's home, he was set to perform in a hall where some tailors were at work, and gave a fine exhibition of jig and reel playing. After some time, the lady of the house said she was much disappointed in his performance, as some of her own countrymen could excel him. "Leeriano" sarcastically responded that as he had been ordered to play in the hall, he appropriately played tailors' and servants' music. This outspoken reflection on the "knights of the goose" aroused them to fury, and had it not been for some peacemakers coming between them, the "French" harper may not have escaped with his life.

Of fourteen harpers encountered at Cavan, O'Neill says, "Ned" McCormack was by far the best of them all. The first and best which claimed his attention in County Tyrone was "Paddy" Ryan, a cherished friend next to Hugh O'Neill. Ryan's father was a Munsterman, and his kindly biographer adds: "Indeed, 'Paddy' was not inferior to any man I ever heard on the harp." Besides, it appears Ryan was honorable, and devoid of the "low ideas of jealousy common to itinerant musicians."

Hugh Quinn, one of "Con" Lyons' pupils, comes in for special mention. "He was a gentleman's son, and as such conducted himself." He reflected nothing but credit on his teacher.

Also in Tyrone he came across his namesake, "Peggy" O'Neill, "who played very decently on the harp." Her special claim to fame, however, was founded on her ability to play "all O'Carolan's planxties extremely well."

While at Bantry, County Cork, he met a blind harper named John O'Gara, from the County of Sligo, who was a good performer. He was also evidently a man of spirit, for when offered part of his confiscated estates, he declined to compromise, and so forfeited the whole.

Others of some note mentioned in Arthur O'Neill's Memoirs, recently published in the *Annals of the Irish Harpers,* by Mrs. Milligan Fox, are: "Ned" Maguire, a blind harper of County Mayo, who was drowned in the River Shannon at Limerick; Mathew Ormsby of County Sligo, a good performer, but so peevish as to be unendurable; Owen O'Donnell of Roscommon, a very genteel young man, but blind; and Andrew Victory, a blind harper from County Long-ford, whose name gave rise to much banter and pleasantry.

Renowned Minstrel—Cormac Common

While Turlogh O'Carolan may be regarded as the last of the Bards, Cormac Common was undoubtedly the last of the Order of Minstrels, called Tale-tellers, or *Fin-Sgealaighthe.*

He was born in May, 1703, at Woodstock, near Ballindangan, in the County of Mayo, although he spent many years of his adult life in the adjoining County of Galway. His parents possessed little but a reputation for honesty and simplicity of manners. Smallpox deprived him of sight before he had completed the first year of his life, so that blindness and poverty conspired to deprive him of the advantages of education. While he could not read, he could listen to those that did, and though lacking in learning, he was by no means deficient in knowledge, for a receptive mind and tenacious memory made amends for his misfortune.

Unkind fate seemed relentless, for a generous gentleman who procured him a teacher on the harp died suddenly when his protege Cormac had received but a few lessons, and so the poor blind boy's musical prospects came to an end. His taste for poetry was still unquenched, and though too poor to buy strings for the harp, it cost nothing to listen to the songs and metrical tales which he heard sung and recited around the fireplaces at his father's and neighbors' houses. Having stored his memory with all he heard, and being without other means of obtaining a livelihood, he became a professional tale-teller.

At rural wakes, and in the hospitable halls of the native gentry, he found a ready welcome for his legendary tales, and being blessed with a sweet voice and a good ear, his recitations were not infrequently graced with the charms of melody. He did not recite his tales in an uninterrupted monotone, like those of his profession in Oriental countries, but rather in a manner resembling the cadences of cathedral chanting.

But it was in singing the native airs that he displayed the powers of his voice to the best advantage, and before advanced age set the seal of decadence on his vocal cords, he never failed to delight his audience. He composed several airs and songs in his native Irish language. One—a lament for John Burke, Esq., of Carrentryle—is preserved in Walker's *Historical Memoirs of the Irish Bards.*

We find that the highly romantic story of *"Eibhlin a Ruin"* and her elopement with Carroll O'Daly was derived from Cormac Common's repertory.

Twice a widower, his offspring were not few, and when immortalized by Walker in 1786, he was living with a daughter near Dunmore, County Galway. In his old age he continued to be led around by a grandson to the homes of the neighboring gentry, but it would appear that with his faculties much impaired by the tooth of time, he was endured rather than admired. The date of his death is not a matter of record.

Patrick Byrne, "The Blind Harper"

Of all the minstrels trained by Arthur O'Neill in the school founded by the Belfast Harp Society in 1807, none achieved such fame as a performer as Byrne, "The Blind Harper," as he was called. Of his early life nothing is known, except that he was born at a place called Farney, in the latter part of the eighteenth century. He was said to be about sixty years of age in 1843 or 1844,

PATRICK BYRNE.

when his picture was taken at Edinburgh, in the flowing garments of the harpers of earlier centuries, according to Bruce Armstrong, in his great work, *The Irish and the Highland Harps,* published in 1904, but that was an over-estimate, we are satisfied. Byrne, however, had played in Edinburgh and throughout Fifeshire for a considerable period before the date on which his picture in ancient costume had been taken.

Although from his estimated age, Armstrong thought that the Irish minstrel had commenced the study of the harp before the end of the eighteenth century, we must regard a Dublin gentleman in whose house Byrne played in 1860 as the better authority on that point. In an article in *The Emerald* of New York City, in 1870, he gives an account of the old minstrel's manner of playing "Brian Boru's March," which reminds us of Owen Lloyd's performance of the same tune at the Munster Feis, in 1906.

Byrne's command of the harp was complete, the writer tells us. His touch was singularly delicate, yet equally firm. He could make the strings whisper like the sigh of the rising wind on a summer eve, or clang with a martial fierceness that made your pulses beat quicker. After quaffing a generous tumbler of punch, he would say, "Now, ladies and gentlemen, I am going to play you the celebrated march of the great King Brian to the field of Clontarf, when he gave the Danes such a drubbing. The Irish army is far off, but if you listen attentively you will hear the faint sound of their music." Then his fingers would wander over the upper range of strings with so delicate a touch that you might fancy it was fairy music heard from a distance. Anything more fine, more soft and delicate than this performance, it is impossible to conceive. "They are coming nearer!" And the sound increased in volume. "Now here they are!" And the music rolled loud and full. Thus the march went on; the fingers of the minstrel's right hand wandering farther down the bass range. You find it hard to keep your feet quiet, and feel inclined to take part in the march yourself. You fancy you see the troops dashing fearlessly onward with the great old King and the fierce and stalwart Morogh at their head. "Hist! we are nearing the field of battle." Then the music became stronger and louder, and there is a deeper rumbling of the bass, with an occasional harmonic third with the right hand, producing a remarkable effect. "Now they're at it—Irish and Danes!" The music suddenly changes to the middle range; it is hard and harsh—clang! clang! like the fall of sword or axe on armor, the blows showering thickly; and that harmonic third aforesand comes frequently, but on a higher string, which gives it a sterner and more fitting effect. The right hand produces an artistic confusion with starts and rugged chords, while the left continues playing the melody, but more quickly. Presently the right rushes down pell-mell among the bass strings. "The Danes are broken! They are falling back!" Then the fingers of the left hand suddenly sweep up along the treble strings, producing a shriek-like sound. "That's the Irish cry of victory." Immediately the music assumes a merry, lightsome character, as if it were played for dancers. "Rejoicing for the victory." But this abruptly ceases; there is another shriek and discord, jangling and confusion in the upper bass strings. The harper explains as usual, "They have found the old King murdered in his tent." Then the air becomes much slower and singularly plaintive. "Mourning for Brian's death." There is a firmer and louder touch now, with occasional plaintive effects with the left hand. "They are marching now with the brave old King's body to Drogheda." The music now assumes a slow and steady tone, the tune being played on the middle range. Gradually the tone is lowered, and grows momentarily louder and louder, till finally it dies away, as Sheridan Knowles would say: "A sound so faint, there's naught 'twixt it and silence." And all these marvelous effects are produced upon what is used as a simple dance tune in the south of Ireland.

Hearing such a player at this late day, one can understand the enthusiasm of Giraldus Cambrensis when he listened to the playing of the great Irish harpers seven hundred years ago. Alas! that those glories of the past should so easily fade away.

When Byrne, "The Blind Harper" played "Brian Boru's March" in Dublin, as above described, he must have been past the allotted Scriptural age. He died at Dundalk in 1863, and although he was the last of the great Irish harpers, he passed away, for all we know to the contrary, "unwept, unhonored, and unsung," within a few miles of the capital of his native land!

CHAPTER VIII

HARPERS AT THE GRANARD AND BELFAST MEETINGS

THE GRANARD MEETING

THE harpers who assembled at Granard, County Longford, in 1781, to play at the Grand Ball instituted for the encouragement of harp music by Mr. James Dungan of Copenhagen, were:

Charles Fanning,
Arthur O'Neill,
Patrick Kerr,
Patrick Maguire,
Hugh Higgins,
Charles Byrne, or Berreen,
Rose Mooney.

First, second, and third prizes were awarded to Fanning, O'Neill, and Rose Mooney, respectively. The decision, it appears, was not unanimous, for a Mr. Burrowes, one of the stewards, found vent for his anger by thrusting his cane through a window.

The second ball, held early in the next year, was more numerously attended than the first; yet notwithstanding the publicity, and the fame of Mr. Dungan, who was a native of Granard, only two new competitors came forward—namely, Edward McDermott Roe and Catherine Martin. Owing to some fancied slight, Hugh Higgins, though present, did not play at all. The prize-winners were the same as at the first ball.

In point of numbers, the third ball, held in 1783, was a magnificent success. It was attended by its founder, Mr. Dungan, in person, and by Lord and Lady Longford. Two additional candidates—Lawrence Keane and James Duncan—presented themselves on this occasion.

For the third time the prizes were awarded to Fanning, O'Neill, and Rose Mooney. Jealousies and animosities began to do their deadly work, and even the originator and financier of the harp revival movement was not exempt from their shafts.

A suggestion from Arthur O'Neill that a subscription be taken up for the benefit of the harpers who had not won premiums was favorably received. The result was quite satisfactory, for the amount distributed to each exceeded the value of the prizes.

The experience of the patriotic Mr. Dungan was so disheartening that he did not afterwards interest himself in the renewal of those interesting assemblies.

THE BELFAST HARP MEETING

Every age—and every generation, it may be said, for that matter—produces its enthusiasts who, undeterred by the failure of their precursors, undertake to break through the barriers of stagnation and indifference, and accomplish the ambition of their lives.

Of such were Doctor MacDonnell, Robert Bradshaw, Henry Joy, and other estimable citizens of Belfast, who founded the "Belfast Harp Society" in 1791. Originated for the purpose of reviving and perpetuating the ancient music and poetry of Ireland, it fulfilled its mission to a degree not equaled by any prior or subsequent endeavor in that line. The concluding paragraph of their prospectus, which follows, was well calculated to appeal to the sympathies of all music-loving Irishmen:

"An undertaking of this nature will undoubtedly meet the approbation of men of refinement and erudition in every country. And when it is considered how intimately the spirit and character of a people are connected with their national poetry and music, it is presumed that the Irish patriot and politician will not deem it an object unworthy his patronage and protection."

The ten harpers who responded to the invitation to attend the Harp Festival at Belfast in July, 1792, were:

Denis Hempson, blind..... Native of Derry ....age 97 years
Arthur O'Neill, blind..... Native of Tyrone ....age 58 years
Charles Fanning .... Native of Cavan ....age 56 years
Daniel Black, blind....... Native of Derry ....age 75 years
Charles Byrne .... Native of Leitrim ....age 80 years
Hugh Higgins, blind...... Native of Mayo ....age 75 years
Patrick Quin, blind....... Native of Armagh ....age 47 years
William Carr .... Native of Armagh ....age 15 years
James Duncan .... Native of Down ....age 45 years
Rose Mooney, blind...... Native of Meath ....age 52 years

A Welsh harper named Williams also played. His execution, which was very great, was in marked contrast to the sweet, expressive tones of the Irish instrument. He died on shipboard soon afterward.

The first premium of ten guineas was adjudged to Charles Fanning, and the second of eight guineas was awarded to Arthur O'Neill. All of the others received six guineas each. After the meeting, which lasted four days, all of them were liberally entertained at his residence by Doctor MacDonnell.

Edward Bunting, who had been selected to take down the airs played by the harpers, says Fanning was not the best performer, but that he succeeded in getting the first prize by playing "The Coolin" with modern variations, a piece of music at that time much in vogue with young practitioners on the pianoforte.

A prejudice in favor of "The Coolin" still exists, for not a few who proclaim a love for Irish melody have no ear for any other strain. Most of the harpers convened at that historic meeting were men advanced in life, yet little was known to them of the origin of the tunes they played. To them, all of their tunes, even then, were ancient and handed down traditionally from their predecessors.

Patrick Lyndon

While making his way to Belfast to attend the Harp Festival, Arthur O'Neill met Patrick Lyndon, a most interesting harper and poet, who was anxious to accompany him if his wardrobe had not been so scant and shabby. Knowing Lyndon to be an excellent bilingual scholar and a desirable representative of the profession, he furnished him with a presentable suit of clothes. Lyndon was so delighted with his improved appearance in the newly acquired raiment that he went rambling around in such elation of spirits as to forget to keep his appointment with his benefactor, who was reluctantly obliged to continue his journey without him.

Lyndon, who was a native of County Armagh, boasted of his boyhood acquaintance with Turlogh O'Carolan. Patrick Quin, who played at the Belfast Harp Festival, was one of his pupils.

O'SHEA

Another harper of acknowledged ability, named O'Shea, was prevented by extreme debility from attending the Belfast Meeting. Though an octogenarian, he was still an enthusiast in everything connected with Irish feeling, a characteristic common to practically all natives of Kerry, the county from which he hailed.

ARTHUR O'NEILL

The most celebrated of all the harpers in many respects was Arthur O'Neill, who was born in 1734, at Drumnaslad, in the County of Tyrone. Intelligent, liberal, and companionable, this exemplary minstrel honored the traditions of his illustrious ancestry. His manners and acquirements, Bunting tells us, were such as would not have been inconsistent with the pretentions of many country gentlemen.

Stored in his tenacious memory, he preserved an array of facts, anecdotes and reminiscences concerning his predecessors and contemporaries, but for which the very names of many of them would have passed into oblivion. From his manuscript memoirs, written out by one Thomas Hughes at Belfast, about the year 1809, Edward Bunting and other writers derived most of such information as is now available relating to the Irish harpers of the late centuries.

Both parents, as well as his paternal and maternal ancestors for generations indefinitely back, were O'Neills. In fact, he had no relatives, to his knowledge, of any other surname. An injury to his right eye, when but two years old, led to his total blindness, and he commenced the study of the harp at the early age of ten, under the tuition of Owen Keenan, who continued to be his instructor for three years. Although he set out as a traveling harper at the immature age of fifteen, there is no doubt but that he subsequently received some training at the hands of Hugh O'Neill, a blind harper from County Mayo, for whom he always entertained the greatest friendship and veneration.

Accompanied by a boy as guide, young Arthur O'Neill directed his footsteps southward, wandering through the provinces of Leinster, Munster, and Connacht successively, and arriving at the home of his parents about the year 1760.

While visiting Murtagh Oge O'Sullivan, at Dunboy Castle, Berehaven, at Christmas time, his guide came to his bedside one morning in great alarm, telling him to bless himself. Being asked why, he replied: "Och, sir! there's a pipe of wine and two hogsheads of some other liquor standing up in the hall, with the heads out of them, and a wooden cup swimming in each, for any one that likes to drink their skin full." Similar instances of reckless and wholesale hospitality came to his notice elsewhere in Munster.

At an entertainment given by Lord Kenmare (annually) to the Mac's and O's or principal Milesian families in the district, all were represented but the O'Neills. Murtagh Oge O'Sullivan told his lordship he could supply a young man who could fittingly represent the name.

Arthur O'Neill was sent for accordingly, and when dinner was announced he groped his way to a seat among the Munster chieftains. Lord Kenmare, addressing the young minstrel, said: "O'Neill, you should be at the head of the table, as your ancestors were the original Milesians of this kingdom." "My lord," promptly responded Arthur O'Neill, "it's no matter where an O'Neill sits; let it be at any part of the table. Wherever I am should be considered the head of it."

This impromptu reply was greeted with a universal burst of applause, and his arm was almost shaken from his body, in appreciation of his ready wit.

It was in the year 1760, shortly before completing his first tour of the provinces, that Arthur O'Neill performed the memorable act of playing on the harp of Brian Boru through the streets of Limerick.

While enjoying the hospitality of Councillor McNamara of that city, he was shown the framework of the historic instrument at the councillor's town house, and, as he says in his Memoirs, in consequence of the national esteem he held for the memory of its owner, he strung and tuned it, after its silence of over two hundred years. It was at the suggestion of his host, that O'Neill hung the harp from his neck, being then young and strong, and paraded through the streets of the patriotic city, followed by an enthusiastic audience of five or six hundred people—gentle and simple—as he played the melodious strains of "Savourneen Dheelish, Eileen Oge," and other tunes not named.

Tiring of the monotony of his life with his parents and friends around Dungannon, he resumed the life of a wandering minstrel again, but confined his circuit to the Ulster counties, especially Cavan, where he enlarged his list of acquaintances among the harpers, and of whom he tells many an amusing story in his Memoirs.

He attended the three celebrated balls held at Granard, County Longford, in 1781, '82, and '83, respectively, and won second prize at each, the first prize in all three going to Charles Fanning, more on account of his shabbiness and evident want of money, it was said, than the superiority of his performance.

Even in his dress, Arthur O'Neill never failed to uphold the respectability of his ancestry. The buttons of his coat, which were of silver and of half crown size, had the Red Hand of the O'Neills engraved thereon.

These balls, it will be remembered, were instituted by Mr. James Dungan, a native of Granard, and a wealthy merchant of Copenhagen, for the purpose of encouraging the promotion of harp music.

During his peregrinations some time about the end of the eighteenth century, the renowned minstrel called at the home of Mr. James Irvine of Streamstown, County Sligo, who was an enthusiastic lover of music, and possessed an ample fortune. His four sons and three daughters were all proficient performers on various instruments. At a meeting in his house there were forty-six musicians, enumerated at follows:

Three Misses Irvine at the piano	3
Arthur O'Neill at the harp	1
Gentlemen flutes	6
Gentlemen violoncellos	2
Common pipers	10
Gentlemen fiddlers	20
Gentlemen clarionets	4

ARTHUR O'NEILL

When O'Neill received from Dr. James MacDonnell the invitation to attend the Belfast Harp Meeting, in 1792, he was visiting Philip O'Reilly of Mullagh, County Cavan, at whose hospitable home he had spent the Christmas holidays for eighteen successive years. Suffering as he was with rheumatism in the two principal fingers of his left hand, he would have declined had not his friend and host insisted upon his attendance. Handicapped as he was in consequence of this affliction, he won second prize, the first being accorded to the incomparable Denis Hempson, who plucked the strings with crooked finger-nails, in the ancient style.

During the succeeding ten years of his life he made his headquarters at Castle Hamilton in County Cavan, the residence of Colonel Southwell, who treated him as a friend and companion.

On the formation of the Belfast Harp Society, in 1807, Arthur O'Neill was unanimously chosen to conduct the Harp School, which he did so creditably that on its decline in 1813, for lack of funds, he was provided with a pension of thirty pounds a year for life, by a few generous and musical enthusiasts of Belfast. He returned to his native district in County Tyrone, to pass the few remaining years of his life. An ideal minstrel, he never married, and passed away in peace in 1818, in the eighty-fifth year of his age, at Maydown, County Armagh, being the last of the old line of harpers.

Denis Hempson

Of the ten harpers who competed at the Belfast Harp Meeting in 1792, Denis O'Hempsey, or Hempson, then ninety-seven years old, was the only one who literally played the harp with long, crooked nails, as described by the old writers. In playing he caught the strings between the flesh and the finger-nail, while the other harpers pulled the strings by the fleshy part of the finger alone. Bunting tells us he had an admirable method of playing Staccato and Legato, in which he could run through rapid divisions in an astonishing style. The intricacy and peculiarity of his playing often amazed Bunting, who could not avoid perceiving in it a vestige of a noble system of practice, that had existed for many centuries; strengthening the opinion that the Irish were at a very early period superior to the other nations of Europe both in composition and performance of music. "In fact," Bunting adds, "Hempson's Staccato and Legato passages, double slurs, shakes, turns, graces, etc., comprised as great a range of execution as has ever been devised by the most modern improvers."

Hempson was born in 1695, at Craigmore, near Garvagh, Londonderry. At the early age of three years he was deprived of sight by an attack of smallpox, and when twelve he began to learn the harp under the tuition of Bridget O'Cahan. In those days, women as well as men were taught the harp in the best families. He studied under John C. Garragher, a blind traveling harper, Loughlin Fanning, and Patrick Conner, successively, all hailing from the Province of Connacht —the prolific mother of musicians.

At the age of eighteen he began his professional career, being provided with a harp by the generosity of Councillor Canning, Squire Gage, and Dr. Bacon, of his native place. A tour of Ireland and Scotland, lasting ten years, furnished him with a fund of anecdotes and experiences, which rendered his conversation as entertaining as his music was entrancing.

He was fifty years old when a second trip to Scotland was undertaken, in 1745. Prince "Charlie," the Pretender, being in Edinburgh when Hempson

DENIS HEMPSON OR O'HEMPSEY

arrived, the renowned harper was called into the great halls to play. After a time, four fiddlers joined in, and the tune they played was "The King Shall Enjoy His Own Again." Hempson was brought into the Pretender's presence, it is said, by Colonel Kelly of Roscommon and Sir Thomas Sheridan.

On his return to Ireland, the celebrated harper played in the houses of the nobility and gentry and in the principal cities throughout the country. Like all traveling musicians, his memory was stored with an inexhaustible assortment of interesting, gossipy narratives.

He had been in O'Carolan's company when a youth, but never took pleasure in playing his compositions, preferring such ancient strains as "The Coolin," "Eileen a Roon," "The Dawning of the Day," etc.

He was not entirely free from egotism, the proverbial professional failing. In conversation with Bunting in 1793, the year after the Belfast Meeting, he said, with conscious pride, "When I played the old tunes, not another of the harpers would play after me."

A gay bachelor at the age of eighty-six, he married a woman at Magilligan, in his native county, who bore him a daughter, with whom he spent the last years of his life. Commenting on his belated matrimonial venture, he remarked: "I can't tell if it was the devil buckled us together, she being lame and I being blind."

The day before his death, on hearing that Rev. Sir H. Harvey Bruce had come to see him, he desired to be raised up in bed, and his harp placed in his hands. Having struck some notes of a favorite strain, he sank back, unable to continue, taking a last farewell of an instrument which had been a companion even in his sleeping hours and a solace through a life protracted to the astounding span of one hundred and twelve years.

CHARLES FANNING

As a winner of prizes against all competitors, Charles Fanning, a native of Foxford, County Mayo, and a contemporary and rival of Arthur O'Neill, stands pre-eminent. For the excellence of his performance at the meetings of harpers at Granard, County Longford, in the years 1781, '82, and '83, respectively, he was awarded the first prize. This success he repeated at the Belfast Harp Festival in 1792.

Born in 1736, he was the son of Loughlin Fanning, a comfortable farmer who played well on the harp, although the instruction of the son was entrusted to a County Roscommon harper named Thady Smith.

Charles Fanning preferred Ulster to his native province, and although certain important episodes in his life happened at Tyrone, his chief haunts were in the County of Cavan. The mistake of his life was marrying the kitchen maid of one of his early patrons, a Mrs. Baillie, who was a good performer on the harp herself, and who had entertained him at her table, and introduced him to genteel company. The result is well expressed in the concise language of Bunting: "He was also patronized by the celebrated Earl of Bristol, the great Bishop of Derry; but in consequence of having married a person in low life and corresponding habits, he never attained to respectability or independence."

JAMES DUNCAN

The gentlemanly conduct of this distinguished competitor at the Belfast Harp Festival in 1792 attracted much attention. Musically inclined in his youth, he was taught to play the harp as an accomplishment and not as a means of obtaining a livelihood, his tutor being Harry Fitzsimmons.

Litigation connected with the settlement of his paternal estate in County Down drained his financial resources, and he had recourse to his harp as a means of securing funds to defray the expenses thus incurred. Fortunately, the lawsuit was decided in his favor, although he did not live long to enjoy his success. He died about the year 1800, in the fifty-third year of his age.

In his Memoirs, Arthur O'Neill describes him as an excellent performer, who knew very little of ancient Irish airs, but played a great variety of modern airs very well.

HUGH HIGGINS

This distinguished harper, mentioned at some length in connection with Owen Keenan's escape from prison, was a good performer, and outranked in social standing most of the professional harpers of his time. He was born at Tyrawley, County Mayo, in 1837, his parents being in comfortable circumstances. Blindness in early life led him to the study of the harp, and being gifted in a musical sense, he made rapid progress.

Well dressed and genteel in appearance, Higgins aimed at supporting the character of a gentleman harper, and traveled in a manner befitting the best traditions of Irish minstrelsy. He attended the Granard Balls and the Belfast Meeting in later years, but won no premiums. In fact, he did not play at all at the second ball at Granard, having taken offense at something connected with the arrangements. Arthur O'Neill's avowed friendship for Higgins was a guarantee of his respectability.

PATRICK QUIN

One of the youngest of the harpers who played at the Belfast Harp Festival in 1792 was Patrick Quin of Portadown, County Armagh, a pupil of Patrick Lyndon of the Fews, in the same county.

Early in the nineteenth century, he was taken under the patronage of the eccentric but enthusiastic John Bernard Trotter, whose extravagance led to his bankruptcy in 1817, and death a year later.

Modesty, it would seem, was not Quin's most conspicuous virtue. He was so elated at his being selected to play at the O'Carolan Commemoration Meeting held at Dublin in 1809 that, on his return to his own country, he scorned to play the fiddle, as before, at public gatherings, although it had been his chief source of income in former years, ere he had fallen a victim to megalomania.

ROSE MOONEY

The most noted of the women harpers was Rose Mooney, winner of third prize three years in succession at the Granard Balls. She also attended the Belfast Harp Festival in 1792, where no third prize was on the programme.

She hailed from County Meath, where she was born about the year 1740. Her teacher, Thady Elliott, as well as herself, was blind, and being an incorrigible wit and joker, he was much disliked and seldom out of trouble.

Accompanied by her maid as a guide, Rose Mooney adopted the life of an itinerant harper, but in the course of time sacrificed her popularity and in a sense her life to a fondness for conviviality, a weakness which was decidedly more pronounced in the maid than the mistress. Some accounts intimate that she died when the French fleet were at Killala in 1798, but Bunting's notation of having taken down "Planxty Charles Coote" from her in 1800 conflicts with that view.

CHARLES BYRNE

Charles Byrne, or Berreen, namesake and guide of his blind uncle, to whom O'Carolan had such an aversion, was born about 1712, in the County of Leitrim. He attended the three Granard Balls and the Belfast Harp Festival, but won no prizes at any of them. Though not excelling as a performer, as an entertainer with anecdotes and Irish songs he had no superior.

He was not far from being a centenarian at the time of his death, which was subsequent to the year 1810, and for many of the later years of his life he was in the habit of spending the Christmas holidays at the hospitable home of John Lushington Reilly of Scarva, County Down.

DANIEL BLACK

Little can be said of Daniel Black, one of the competitors at the Belfast Harp Festival, except that he was one of the five harpers upon whom Edward Bunting relied for authentic information concerning the traditions of their art.

He hailed from County Derry, and was born about the year 1717. Bunting, who visited him in 1796, and noted down four of his airs, informs us that Black's chief resort when in Antrim was Mr. Heyland's seat near Glendaragh. He was blind, and sang to his music very sweetly.

WILLIAM CARR AND OTHERS

Nothing like an extended account can be given of the six other harpers who attended the Granard and Belfast Meetings, as little information relating to their lives has escaped the obliterating hand of time.

William Carr was a mere lad of fifteen, hailing from the County of Armagh, when he played at the Belfast Meeting. Of Patrick Kerr, Patrick Maguire, and Edward McDermott Roe, who played at the Granard Balls, nothing is available but their names.

Catherine Martin, the last of the list, was, like Rose Mooney, a native of County Meath. Her favorite airs were those composed by "Parson" Sterling, the reverend piper and composer of Lurgan, in County Cavan. It is much to be regretted that Mr. Bunting neglected to take advantage of the opportunity to preserve some of the compositions of this renowned musician.

CHAPTER IX

HISTORIC ESTIMATE OF IRISH MUSIC

THAT the ancient Irish cultivated the music of the voice and of instruments, is proved in every page of their history. To quote the language of Mooney, the historian: "Music mixed in every ceremonial. In their sun worship, the song of praise and thanksgiving was raised to the giver, in their opinion, of fruits, and regulator of the seasons. At funerals, the voice of lamentation was vented under the control of musical notation. In the battle, the harper bards led on the warrior hosts. At the festive board, and in the banquet hall, there also the voice of music stimulated the joyous passions. On all these occasions, the harper bards caught the most touching sounds of human sensations as they rose, and copied them on their harpstrings. These were, upon succeeding occasions, repeated musically to kindle in other hearts emotions similar to those which gave them birth. In this manner, a series of the most touching sounds was formed by the Irish bards into a code of melody which has lasted through innumerable ages."

The National Melodies of Europe sprang from her bards and troubadours, and are highly expressive of the races they belong to, says Bayle Bernard, biographer of Samuel Lover. In Irish airs, even the most wildly inspiring and jubilant, as well as the most intensely pathetic, a vein of peculiar plaintiveness pervades the structure—the result, no doubt, of the tragedies of history.

Ruskin has demonstrated that the art of a country is the direct expression of the mind of its people, and if this be true of the arts in general, it is pre-eminently true of music in particular; for of all the arts, the most direct, the most subtle, and by far the most expressive, is music.

The Music of Ireland was classed by Edward Bunting under three heads,— the very ancient; the ancient; and the modern. The first comprises all that is believed to have existed before the Christian era, such as "The Lamentation of Deirdre Over the Sons of Usnach"; "The Children of Lir"; and the Chants to which Fenian poems ascribed to Oisin and Fergus were sung, like the "Battle of Erragan Mor," and the "Death Song of Oscar."

The second class includes compositions dating from that period until the days of O'Carolan; while the third class contains nothing of a date much older than the generation in which the great Blind Bard flourished. Little folk music can be traced to his muse; in fact, his compositions furnish no standard; for Irish music of that inimitable vein of tender expression which winds through the very old strain in every mood, major and minor, is too often sought for in vain.

Little music, if any, that can be identified as originating in the early centuries has come down to us, although allusions to the pre-eminence of Ireland in its cultivation and practice are by no means rare. In the life of St. Keiven, quoted by Mooney, it is stated that "the King of Munster, so early as A. D. 489, had the best band of harpers of any in his time, who accompanied their music with singing." When Nivelles Abbey was established, at the close of the sixth century, under the auspices of King Pepin, Gertrude, his daughter, sent to Ireland for musicians and choristers to serve in it. "A band of these Irish harpers and choristers came from thence, who imparted their music and rules to all the Franks, which were adopted by the court and the nation." In like manner, Charlemagne, in the eighth century, appointed two Irishmen—Clement Albanius and Dungin—preceptors for the two great Universities of Pavia and Paris, which he established. Testimony such as the above cannot be regarded lightly in upholding the claim of Ireland's renown among the nations over a thousand years ago.

Such was the celebrity of the music of Ireland in the eleventh century that the Welsh, according to their own historians, received their improved musical system from the "Land of Song."

About the year 1100, Gruffydth ap Conan, King of North Wales, "who being on the one side an Irishman, by his mother and grandmother, and also born in Ireland, brought over with him out of that countrie *divers cunning musicians* into Wales, who," the Welsh historian Powell asserts, in his *History of Cambria,* translated by Lloyd, edit. 1584, "devised in a manner all the instrumental musicke that now is there used, as appeareth as well by the books written of the same, as also by the names of the tunes and measures used amongst them to this daie."

In this assertion Powell is corroborated by the learned Selden, an English jurist, who, in speaking of the Welsh, says: "Their musique for the most part came out of Ireland with Gruffydth ap Conan, prince of North Wales about King Stephen's time." Another Welsh writer, Caradoc of Llancarvan, and Wynne, the historian, take the same view.

The result of the introduction of the "cunning musicians" from Ireland was soon apparent. At a great feast given by Rhys ap Gruffydth, at Cardigan Castle, in 1176, and to which all the bards and poets of Wales were invited, the bards of North Wales, among whom it is natural to suppose were some of their Irish instructors, proved their superiority and were awarded the prizes.

Johannes Brompton Abbot of Jereval, in Yorkshire, who wrote early in the last half of the twelfth century, and before the Norman invasion, states that the Irish had two kinds of harps,—the one bold and rapid, the other soft and soothing; and although "the music was headlong and rapid, it was nevertheless sweet and pleasant, the modulations crisp, and the small notes intricate." He further stated that the Irish taught in secret, and committed their lessons to memory.

No commentator on early Irish music is so universally quoted as Gerald Barry—Giraldus Cambrensis—Bishop of St. David's, in Wales. He had traveled, as the companion of Henry the Second, all over Europe, and had heard the best music of every country in the most refined society. With Prince John, he visited Ireland in 1186, and subsequently wrote an account of his observations, entitled *Topographia Hibernica.*

Concerning the development of music among the Irish, he says: "The attention of this people to musical instruments I find worthy of commendation; in which their skill is beyond all comparison superior to that of any nation I have seen; for in these the modulation is not slow and solemn, as in the instruments of Britain to which we are accustomed; but the sounds are rapid and precipitate, yet at the same time sweet and pleasing. It is wonderful how in such precipitate rapidity of the fingers, the musical proportions are preserved, and by their art faultless throughout, in the midst of their complicated modulations, and most intricate arrangement of notes, by a rapidity so sweet, a regularity so irregular, a concord so discordant, the melody is rendered harmonious and perfect.

Whether the chords of the diatessaron or diapente are struck together, yet they always begin in a soft mood, and end in the same: that all may be perfected in the sweetness of delicious sounds, they enter on, and again leave their modulations with so much subtilty, and the tingling of the small string sport with so much freedom under the deep notes of the bass, delight with so much delicacy, and soothe so softly that the excellence of their art seems to lie in concealing it.

"It is to be observed, however, that Scotland and Wales—the latter in order to disseminate the art; the former in consequence of intercourse and affinity—strive with rival skill to emulate Ireland in music. In the opinion of many at this day, Scotland has not only equalled, but even far excels her mistress Ireland in musical skill; wherefore they seek there also the fountain as it were of the art."

The peculiarities of Irish music in rhythm and execution must have deeply impressed the distinguished Welsh prelate, for he admits it was superior to that of Wales, the latter "being of a grave and solemn nature, whereas that of the Irish was soft, lively and melodious, their fingers passing rapidly over the strings of the harp, preserving a true musical proportion, nor in any part injuring the art among the shakes of the notes, and a multiplicity of intricate musical sounds, such as soft and pleasant notes divided by just proportion into concords and discords, making a complete melody, all of which depended upon the power and variety of the sounds, and the lengths of the Irish vowels, and to which the Welsh language is a stranger."

Perhaps the circumstance that the Irish harps were strung with brass wire instead of thongs and even horse hair, as the custom was in Wales, may account in a measure for the "soft and pleasant notes" of the Irish instrument.

As Borde, the Welsh poet said in 1542:

> "For my harp is made of good mare's skin
> The strynges be of horse-heare it maketh a good dyn."

Speaking of the effects of music, Cambrensis has in the following passage recorded the extreme love of the Irish for the music of the harp. "The sweetness of music not only delights with its harmony, it has its advantages also. It not a little exhilarates dejected minds, it clears the clouded countenance and removes superciliousness and austerity. Harmony is a kind of food to the mind. Whatever be our pursuit, music assists application and quickens genius; it gives courage to the brave and assists the devotion of the pious. Hence it is that the bishops, abbots, and holy men in Ireland, are used to have their harp about them, and piously amuse themselves with playing it. Music has a power to alter our very nature," he continues, "hence the Irish, the Spanish, and some other nations, amidst their funeral wailings bring forth musical lamentations, either to increase or diminish their grief."

Keenly appreciating the music and performance of the Irish harpers, Cambrensis says that "those very strains which afford deep and unspeakable mental delight to those who have skillfully penetrated into the mysteries of the art; fatigue rather than gratify the ears of others who seeing, do not perceive, and hearing, do not understand; and by whom the finest music is esteemed no better than a confused and disorderly noise, and will be heard with unwillingness and disgust."

The widely divergent emotional attitude of men in modern times no less than in the days of Giraldus Cambrensis reminds us that Voltaire hated music with intensity, while Calvin and Knox denounced it as a bait held out by the evil one to lure the souls of the unwary. Even Goethe, German in heart and soul knew nothing of, and cared nothing for music. Again some there be like the young violin student described by a writer in the *Musical Leader* who never heard anything at a concert, but fiddle technic, and who used to figure out sympathetically on his coat sleeve every single passage and writhe in envy during every difficult one. Beauties of tone and melody did not exist for him. Every emotional appeal flew over his head. Music held nothing for him but finger twiddling.

But to return to the current of our subject from a digression pardonable perhaps under the circumstances: John DeFordun " a canon of Aberdeen, the earliest Scotch historian," who was sent over to Ireland at the end of the thirteenth century to collect materials for his *Scotichronicon* expressly states that "Ireland was the fountain of music, (in his time), whence it began to flow into Scotland and Wales."

From the pages of Dean Lynch's *Cambrensis Eversus* we learn that Polydore Virgil, who lived in England in the first half of the sixteenth century paid a glowing tribute to the musical faculties of the Irish at that time. "The Irish practice music and are remarkably skilled in it," he says. "Their performance both vocal and instrumental is exquisite, but so bold and impassioned that it is amazing how they can observe the rules of their art amidst such rapid evolutions of the fingers and vibrations of the voice, and yet they do observe them to perfection."

About the same time we are told by John Major in his *Greater Britain,* published in 1521, that the Irish and the wild Scots were pre-eminent as performers on the harp. In his panegyric of James the First of Scotland, he styles that prince "another Orpheus who touches the harp more exquisitely than either the Highlanders or even the Irish, who were the most eminent harpers then known."

At a later date Count de Hoghenski, a musical authority testifies that "of all the people the Irish are esteemed the best performers." Still more explicitly he continues, "They use the harp whose strings were of brass and not of animal gut; on this they make the most pleasing melody."

Were further testimony needed on this score it has been furnished by Vincentio Gallilei, a noble Florentine in his *Dialogue on Ancient and Modern Music* published in 1581. In this work he eulogises Irish harps and harpers, remarking that "the strings are generally of brass with a few steel for the highest notes."

In all historical comment on the Irish harp and its music which has come to our attention, there is but one dissenting voice and strangely enough the critic is a native born Irishman. In 1584 Richard Stanyhurst, whose ancestors for many generations resided in the vicinity of Dublin, records in a work entitled *De Rebus in Hibernia Gestis,* that "the harper uses no plectrum but scratches the chords with his crooked nails and never marks the flow of his pieces to musical rhythm, nor the accent and quantity of the notes, so that to the refined ears of an adept it comes almost as offensively as the grating of a saw."

It is gratifying to learn, however, that he encountered one harper named Crusius, or Cruise, who measured up to his ideal, and on whom he lavishes unlimited praise; but even so his strictures on the harpers of his day in general were not permitted to pass unquestioned by such able writers as Dean Lynch and Geoffrey Keating.

Barnaby Rich, an English gentleman, who visited Ireland in the reign of James the First and embodied his impressions of the country in *A New Des-*

cription of Ireland, says: "They have harpers and those are so reverenced among the Irish that in the time of rebellion they will forbear to hurt either their persons or their goods."

From an essay on "The Ancient and Modern Manners of the Irish," to be found in *Camden's Britannia,* published in 1586; written by J. Good, an English priest, who conducted a school at Limerick about the year 1566, we extract the following—his only reference to music: "They are particularly fond of music especially of the harp with brass strings which they strike harmoniously with their crooked nails."

Pretorius, author of a work on Musical Instruments, published in 1619, says "The Irish Harp has rough thick brass strings, forty-three in number, and is beyond measure sweet in tone."

Referring to the Irish harp in *Sylva Sylvorum,* published in 1627; years after the author's death, Bacon declares "it maketh a more resounding sound than a Bandora, Opharion, or Cittern, which have likewise wire strings, and no instrument hath the sound so melting and prolonged as the Irish harp."

To the same general effect is the testimony of Thomas Fuller, author of the *History of the Holy Warre,* published in 1639. In his account of the crusade conducted by Godfrey de Boulogne in the last years of the eleventh century, he says: "Yea we might well think that all the concert of Christendom in this warre would have made no musick if the Irish harp had been wanting."

In Hardiman's *Irish Minstrelsy,* the author mentions an unpublished History of Ireland written about the year 1636, reposing in the Royal Irish Academy, Dublin, from which he quotes the following: "The Irish are much addicted to musick generally, and you shall find but very few of their gentry either man or woman, but can play on the harp; also you shall not find a house of any account without one or two of those instruments and they always keep a harper to play for them at their meals, and all other times as often as they have a desire to recreate themselves or others which come to their houses therewith."

M. de la Boullaye Le Gouz, who journeyed from Dublin to the principal cities and towns in Ireland in 1644 and whose description of the country has been translated by Crofton Croker, says of the people: "They are fond of the harp on which nearly all play as the English do on the fiddle, the French on the lute, the Italians on the guitar, the Spanish on the castanets, the Scotch on the bagpipe, the Swiss on the fife, the Germans on the trumpet, the Dutch on the tambourine, and the Turks on the flageolet." After describing their weapons and their dexterity the French traveler adds, "they march to battle with the bagpipes, instead of fifes; but they have few drums."

As to the ancient Irish music it is confessed to be original, and in what remains of it to this day there is found a wonderful softness and pleasing harmony, according to the learned Sylvester O'Halloran whose *History of Ireland* appeared in 1778. The Abbey of Benchoir got its name from the melody of its psalmists, and when in the next century the Abbey of Nivelles was founded, Gertrude, daughter of Pepin, sent to Ireland for doctors to instruct in church discipline, and for musicians and choristers for the church music.

Writing in 1779 on *The Power of Music* John Wesley said: "Generally, if not always, when a fine solo was sung; when the sound has been an echo to the sense; when the music has been extremely simple and inartificial........the natural power of music to move the passions has appeared. This music was calculated for that end, and effectually answered it. Upon this ground it is that so many persons are affected by the Scotch or Irish airs. They are composed not according to art, but nature; they are simple in the highest degree. There is no harmony according to the present sense of the word therein; but there is much melody."

In Walker's *Historical Memoirs of the Irish Bards,* which came from the press in 1786, we read that "The Irish music is in some degree distinguished from the music of every other nation, by an insinuating sweetness which forces its way irresistibly to the heart, and there diffuses an ecstatic delight that thrills through every fiber of the frame, awakens sensibility and agitates or tranquilizes the soul. Whatever passion it may be intended to excite it never fails to effect its purpose. It is the voice of nature and will be heard. We speak of the music of the ancient Irish for music like language, the nearer we remount to its rise amongst men, the more it will be found to partake of a natural expression."

The same author adds: "The great Irish families even to the last century, entertained in their houses harpers who were the depositories of their best pieces of music. These remains which we consider as classics have obtained for Ireland the honorable title of *A School for Music."*

That Ireland was the "School for Music" as well as for learning in its broadest sense, from which Scotland derived not a little of its earliest training is well attested by their own writers and historians, a few of whom have been already quoted.

In the pages of *A Philosophical Survey of the South of Ireland* comprising a series of letters to Dr. John Watkinson, in 1775, the author, Rev. Dr. Campbell, speaks with the confidence of an authority who is master of his subject.

It may be of interest to add that Dr. Campbell, who was rector of Galloon, in County Fermanagh, and chancellor of Clogher in County Tyrone, reckoned among his friends such notables as Burke, Johnson, Boswell and Goldsmith.

"From what has been now observed relative to the distinguished excellence of the Irish musicians, particularly in ancient times, compared with what has been proved in former letters, that Ireland was the old *Scotia,* it will not, I flatter myself, be difficult to trace the origin of what is now called Scots music.

"We have seen that there is proof positive from their own chronicles that the Welsh received their instruments from Ireland, let us now see whether there be not proof presumptive, the strongest which the nature of the thing is capable of, that the British Scots borrowed their music also from the same quarter.

"It is vain to say, as is generally said, that David Rizzio was author of the Scots music. There is an internal evidence against such a supposition; the wild and pastoral singularity of the Scots melodies is incompatible with the grave and learned compositions of Italy. And there is evidence still more strong. Rizzio was secretary and not musician to the Queen of Scotland. His father had been a musician by profession, but we do not find that he was one himself. That he might, however, have played, improved, and collected the Scots airs is very probable, but that a young dissipated Italian—busied in the intrigues of a court and attendance on a Queen so fair, and so condescending as Mary—could in a few years have disseminated such multifarious compositions through a nation which despised his manners, and hated his person is utterly incredible.

"Nor is it to be believed what is still more credible that James the First of Scotland was the author of the Scots tunes, though Buchanan does say that he excelled in music more than became a king.

"The honor then of inventing the Scots music must be given to this country the ancient *Scotia* so renowned for music in old times; from whence as we have incontrovertibly proved, the present *Scotia* derived her name, her extraction, her language, and her poetry."

There can scarcely be a question that the melodies preserved in the Scottish Highlands such as those performed on the bagpipe, and rustic dance tunes, clan tunes and other Celtic melodies which continue to be sung to Gaelic poetry or words, in the affecting traditional way flow entirely in the Irish manner and had a common origin.

Contrasting conditions as he found them to exist in his *Tour of Ireland and England* in the year 1828 and 1829, "A German Prince" records that "the love of music in England is a mere matter of fashion. There is no nation in Europe which plays music better or understands it worse." To which may be added a quotation from Gaskin's *Varieties of Irish History* of a later date: "Many old authors from the tenth to the sixteenth centuries, speak in the highest terms of the music of Ireland. Ireland and Scotland far excel England in those compositions, for which she has been denied the gift of melodious uterance. Ireland and Scotland though less favored in other respects, teemed with the harmonious productions of bards who have left no other monument behind them—not even in most cases their names."

Coming down to still more recent times, we have the opinion of the distinguished German traveler, Kohl, who published a work on *Ireland* in 1844. Speaking of his visit to the residence of a gentleman at Drogheda, he says: "The harp was brought in and a blind young harper advanced who was, I was told, one of the most accomplished harpers in the neighborhood; and in fact his music enraptured us all. The first piece he played was 'Brian Boru's March.' The music of this march is wildly powerful, and at the same time melancholy. It is at once the music of victory and of mourning. The rapid modulations and wild beauty of the airs was such that I think this march deserves fully to obtain a celebrity equal to that of the 'Marseillaise' and the 'Ragotsky.'

"The march of 'Brian Boru' was followed by an air called the 'Fairy Queen,' which I was told was a very old melody. Old or not I can testify that it is a charming piece of music, so tender, so fairy like and at the same time so wild and sweetly playful that it can represent nothing, but the dancing and singing of the elves and fairies by moonlight. I afterwards heard the piece on the pianoforte, but it did not sound half so soft and sweet as from the instrument of the blind young harper. Of all the fine arts music is the one of whose beauties it is most impossible to convey any adequate idea by criticism or description."

In the foregoing pages ample historical evidence has been submitted, although much more might be produced to sustain Ireland's claim to eminence among the most advanced nations in the knowledge and practice of music, from the earliest ages down to comparatively recent times, when the tragedies of her history paralyzed the progress of the arts for which she had been so long distinguished.

CHAPTER X

IRISH FOLK MUSIC—A PRECIOUS HERITAGE

A voice beside the dim, enchanted river,
    Out of the twilight where the brooking trees
Hear the Shannon's druid water chant forever
    Tales of dead kings and bards and shanachies;
A girl's young voice out of the twilight singing
    Old songs beside the legendary stream—
A girl's clear voice, o'er the wan waters ringing,
    Beats with its wild wings at the Gates of Dream.

The flagger leaves, whereon shy dewdrops glisten,
    Are swaying, swaying gently to the sound;
The meadow-sweet and spearmint, as they listen,
    Breathe wistfully their wizard balm around;
And there, alone with her lone heart and heaven,
    Thrush-like she sings, and lets her voice go free;
Her soul, of all its hidden longing shriven,
    Soars on wild wings with her wild melody.

Sweet in its plaintive Irish modulations,
    Her fresh young voice tuned to old sorrows seems,
The passionate cry of countless generations
    Keenes in her breast as there she sings and dreams.
No more, sad voice; for now the dawn is breaking
    Through the long night, through Ireland's night of tears.
New songs wake in the morning of her awaking
    From the enchantment of eight hundred years.
                                            —*Dr. Todhunter.*

WHAT charm there is in the name? What memories does it not awaken? What feelings does it not arouse in the breasts of the sons and daughters of Erin, whose hearts beat true to the cherished institutions of their race, since human emotions found expression in musical tones? Folk Music is the music of the song that lives in the hearts and voices of the people—to use the words of the great Dominican, Father Tom Burke—the national songs you will hear from the husbandman in the field following the plow; from the old woman singing to the infant on her knee; from the milkmaid coming from the milking; from the shoemaker at his work, or the blacksmith at the forge while he is shoeing the horse; or as Dr. Joyce expresses it: the people's pastimes, occupations, and daily life were mixed up with tunes and songs. The women sang at the spinning wheel; plowmen whistled tunes to soothe their horses; girls sang their gentler milking songs which the cows enjoyed. Parents and nurses put their children to sleep with their charming melodies, laborers beguiled their work with songs of various kinds to which their fellow workmen listened with quiet enjoyment, and at the last scene of all, the friends of the dead gave vent to their sorrow in a heartrending *caoine* or lament.

The Folk Music and songs of a nation are treasured, because they were conceived as a melodious poetic expression of the sentiments and feelings of the people. Genuine expression of a nation's soul in tuneful melody cannot be produced to order, for the strains which live are the offspring of inspiration or the spontaneous flow of thought in timely accord with the general social conditions of the people.

Folk Music then is the true national melody handed down traditionally for centuries with surprising fidelity, until in the more ciivlized and cultured time it has been interpreted into musical notation. Irish music has been admired wherever its melting strains have been heard, and it has been said that the Irishman's whole life is set to song. He is crooned to sleep in his cradle by immemorial lullabies, and the weird wail of the *caoine* follows him to the grave, for as Ida Haggerty Snell says: "Music seems to be a part of man's nature by which he expresses thoughts that otherwise could not be revealed."

Music was held in much repute in the ancient world as a curative agent, Lady Wilde says in her quaint work. *Ancient Cures, Charms, and Usages of Ireland* besides being the inspiration that gave force to life, stimulating or soothing as the moment required, for music above all the arts has a subtle power over the nervous system, and is able to interpret and direct, all the sudden, swift and varied phases of human emotion, it can stir the soul to its inmost depths till the tears fall in silent sorrow or fill the brain with a passionate enthusiasm which is a prophecy of victory.

The Irish from the earliest times have shown their belief in the mystic influence of music upon life, and their legends record how the musician could sooth the wounded and calm the dying.

Practically all Irish music may be classed as Folk Music, for original composition distinctively Irish in character, we are told ceased on the death of "Piper" Jackson, and "Parson" Sterling late in the eighteenth century.

In the world of modern music Irish composers—many of them—have won distinction since that time, but the songs and ballads of the people continued to be sung to the old traditional strains, and few indeed were the musicians who would care to play any tunes but the haunting melodies of the olden days.

O'Carolan alone of all the bards was the exception who, influenced largely by the music of Geminiani departed from the purely Irish style in composition. In conceding that he has produced some airs of surpassing tenderness and of purely Irish structure, we may ask; who sings or plays them, and why are they neglected while a thousand folk airs and tunes, of unknown paternity are in promiscuous circulation?

The Italian peasant while working in the vineyard, Father Burke tells us, has no music except two or three high notes of a most melancholy character. The peasants of Tuscany and of Campagna, when after their day's work they meet in the summer evenings to have a dance, have no music but the beating of a tambourine. But go to Ireland; listen to the old woman as she rocks in her chair, and pulls down the hank of flax for the spinning; listen to the girl coming from the field with the pail of milk on her head, and what do you hear? The most magnificent melody of music. Go to the country merry-makings, and you will be sure to find the old fiddler or old white haired piper, an infinite source of the brightest and most sparkling music.

Never was there a nation which had such a wealth of Folk Music—an infinite variety—tender love songs, witty ballads, deeply emotional poems set to haunting melodies as Ireland and the Irish.

"Few musicians have been found to question the assertion that Irish Folk Music is on the whole the finest that exists; it ranges with wonderful ease over the whole gamut of human emotions from the cradle to the battlefield, and is unsurpassed in poetical and artistic charm," writes Dr. Ernest Walker in his *History of Music in England.* "If musical composition meant nothing more than tunes sixteen bars long, Ireland could claim some of the very greatest composers that have ever lived, for in their miniature form the best Irish folk tunes are gems of absolutely flawless lustre, and though of course some of them are relatively undistinctive, it is very rare to meet with one entirely lacking in character."

To those who retain the pure simplicity of man's nature such music born of emotion, and untrammeled by rules, possesses charms of a more lasting and touching kind than the finest works produced from the fancy and brain of the most skillful musician of a cold and artificial age. The simple folk tunes are endeared to us by association, and like the nectar of the flowers, they can be stored in the hive of our faculties to sustain us through all the bleak days of sorrow, or cheer us in the bright days of prosperity.

Irish music has all the sweetness, tenderness, humor, pathos, fervor, grandeur, and tragedy of real life, because it sprang from the heart of a race which underwent every phase of human experience and existence. Haydn, on hearing a National Irish melody for the first time, without knowing its origin, exclaimed that such music could only belong to an oppressed and unfortunate race.

The Folk Music of Ireland, intimately associated with the joys and sorrows and pastimes of the people, has been preserved from generation to generation among the peasantry and perpetuated largely through the agency of the minstrels whose wandering mode of life was well calculated to effect that purpose. In the language of the illustrious Dr. Petrie, "Irish Music is characteristic of their ardent and impassioned temperament and expressive of the tone of feeling that has been for ages predominant. The upper class are a different race—a race who possesses no national music, or if any, one essentially different from that of Ireland. They were insensible to its beauty for it breathed not their feelings, and they resigned it to those from whom they took everything else, because it was a jewel of whose worth they were ignorant. He therefore who would add to the stock of Irish melody must seek it not in the halls of the great, but in the cabins of the poor; at the peasant's humble hearth or follow him as he toils at his daily labors." In the same vein John Boyle O'Reilly says: The Irish in the late centuries "carried the ancient wordless music in their hearts; the wandering piper and harper played the dear melodies and planxties to them; the plowboy whistled and the milkmaid sung the archaic airs; and so they were preserved, like the disconnected jewels of a queen's necklace."

Apropos of Dr. Petrie's remarks: When J. Bernard Trotter was traveling through Ireland in 1817 he frequently heard the loud songs of the laborers returning from work. They sang airs in the Irish language with surprising beauty and effect. Their airs were not always plaintive for some were finely martial. "You cannot imagine how we enjoyed them," he writes. "Often as the evening had in her sober livery all things clad, have we listened with redoubled pleasure to this really fine music. Loud and sprightly, it wantoned through the distant air, seemed the call to war, and heroic deeds of a great and valorous people; or assuming softer tones, invited to gay reveling the merry dance and the sportive joys of love! Who could fail to think he heard the venerable harp accompanying these evening hymns? Who could forbear to rush into the mists of antiquity to find the people who formed, who cultivated, who listened to such music? How pleased too, one is to leave modern history for these fascinating versions of peace and joy, which will rise up in deeply considering of the remote times, of Erin's early sons! The kind delusion soothes the soul. How I long to see the merry dance and the rural groups of the redressed and happy! — the light feet beating gaily responsive to their lively planxties."

In the pages of *The Stranger in Ireland,* published in 1806, John Carr, Esq., the author, describes the peasantry as being "uncommonly attached to their ancient melodies some of which are exquisitely beautiful. In some parts of Ireland the harp it yet in use, but the Irish bagpipe is the favorite instrument. The stock of national music has not been much increased in late years. The Irish of all classes are fond of music. Amongst the higher orders of Irish capable of appreciating the unrivaled extent of his genius in music I heard the name of Viotti mentioned with the admiration which is due to his talents." Quite so: Instead of encouraging or cultivating the national music the "higher orders" of the alien race followed the fashionable fad of the times and patronized the musicians of the continent.

Irish music was never the offspring of fashion or caprice. It was literally the voice of the people. Whether excited by joy or sorrow, or love or injustice, their feelings found vent in music, Mrs. Hall says. Their grief for the dead was relieved by a dirge; they roused their troops by song and offered their prayers in chorus and chant; their music was poetry and their poetry was music. In the words of Lady Wilde all the various strings of the Irish harp have been touched, and made to give up the strange fitful and wayward music, that can move at will to tears or laughter, and which never fails to vibrate in the Irish heart, for music and song are part of the life of the people. Through music and song the Irish race have always uttered the strongest emotions of the vivid Celtic nature.

"It has often been remarked and still oftener felt," says Tom Moore, "that in our music is found the truest of all comments upon our history. The tone of defiance succeeded by the languor of despondency—a burst of turbulence dying away into softness—the sorrows of one moment lost in the levity of the next, and all that romantic mixture of mirth and sadness, which is naturally produced by the efforts of a lively temperament to shake off or forget the wrongs which lie upon it."

The musical compositions of the older minstrels were admirably in keeping with the national sentiment. The wild melodies and inspiring lilts that we find among the old melodies, are the productions of the bards to a considerable extent, but the author of each particular piece is unknown.

Witness the effect of those airs on the son or daughter of Erin who has any inclination for music—and who has not? Few indeed are they who can escape response to some form of music, any more than they can fail to respond to any and all forms of the beautiful. People whose emotions remain unaffected by a symphony, will smile in response to some homespun melody. They may even denounce an opera, yet enjoy a simple hymn or sway in sympathy with an old man's jig.

To the exile of Irish birth, the melodies of the old land will bring back memories of the fireside, the lakes, the moors, and clear flowing rivers, the towns and villages and above all the flower-spangled green fields of their native land, for nothing is so certain to survive of a people as their songs and music.

Many a homesick exile weary of the meaningless music which his American daughter had acquired at the academy, has been assailed by conflicting emotions such as the author describes in the following verses:

THOSE OLD IRISH AIRS

Come Katie avourneen touch up your piano,
　　And play off the tunes that your father likes best;
You've been taxing your brains with those German composers—
　　Let's hear from Tom Moore, just by way of a rest.
Your teacher has told you no doubt that they're trashy,
　　And nothing but simple and common affairs;
To some they may be, but to me they're entrancing,
　　So just play a few of Those Old Irish Airs.

Ah, Moore was the man to put *grah* in his verses;
　　To reach the right spot sure, 'twas he knew his art;
A magician in troth with a wonderful latchkey,
　　That opened the door of each Irishman's heart;
He never would stop and apply for admittance,
　　But softly creep in and make off with your cares,
And well may his countrymen cherish his mem'ry
　　For putting such words to Those Old Irish Airs.

Was there ever such music—so soft and so soothing,
　　So mournful and wild, so exciting and gay?
Such melody clear as the stream from the mountain,
　　Which splashes along in its own artless way;
The blast of defiance, the sigh of oppression;
　　From the lilt to the lullaby nothing compares—
All the moods mixed in an Irishman's nature
　　Are clearly expressed in Those Old Irish Airs.

If it's mournful you feel or in vein sentimental,
　　Just choose any book that you find will include
"The Last Rose of Summer;" "The Exile of Erin;"
　　"Believe Me;" "The Coolin;"—they'll answer your mood.
If stirred be your soul by the wrongs of your sireland,
　　You know courage will win while the coward despairs.
And the spirit that breathes in "Let Erin Remember,"
　　Is enshrined for all time in Those Old Irish Airs.

If it's mirthful you feel, and in need of diversion,
　　Look over the feast, there's enough and to spare
See "The Maid on the Green" with her chum "Nora Chreena"
　　At "The Top of Cork Road" with "The Rakes of Kildare."
Don't tell me there's naught to admire in such music;
　　'Twas made for all time, you can see how it wears,
Why the blood rushes up to my cheeks at the sound,
　　And my heart beats the time to Those Old Irish Airs.

In the war for the Union with my Irish companions
　　I've heard those airs played when the battle was nigh,
And I've marked the wild look in their eyes as they listened,
　　As if it were glory to fight then, and die,

And when I lay wounded and death hovered o'er me,
  The music would haunt me and mix in my prayers;
And I wondered at times if the angels in heaven,
  Have songs that would equal Those Old Irish Airs.

Don't tell me the music is trashy or common
  That fills men with motives so unselfish and high.
There is not a bar in your famous composers
  That would stir us to fight for a cause till we die.
If lost be that cause for a time—well, no matter;
  The spirit to conquer will survive in our heirs,
And the hope smold'ring deep in an Irishman's bosom
  Will be fanned into flame by Those Old Irish Airs.

Then, Katie, avourneen, play off the dear music,
  And please your old father—if but for tonight;
Though it may not show art, nor display execution,
  It's all in the taste, and we both may be right.
Play off the dear music that breathes of the shamrock,
  The moor and the mountains, the fields and the fairs.
Though tyrants may strangle a cause and a people,
  They never could smother Those Old Irish Airs.

Music which in the words of Agnes Gordon Hogan, "is a language without an alphabet, a speech without a tongue, a power without a limit," still retains its subtle influence over the Irish heart, although over one hundred years ago Lady Morgan—then Miss Owenson—in her *Patriotic Sketches,* bewailed the "regrettable and undeniable fact, that the warm, ardent sprit of national enthusiasm which hung delighted on the song of national melody to which many an associated idea, many an endeared feeling lent their charm, has now faded into apathy, and neither the native strain nor sentiment which gave it soul touches on the spring of national sensibility or awakens the dormant energy of national taste."

Music was to the Irish a living delight, a mysterious key to a host of undiscovered emotions, hoarded in the secrecies of the soul. Irish music haunts the memory unlike certain modern compositions of which a critic in the Chicago *Musical Leader* says: "It comes and it goes but when it is gone there's not even an echo of it left in the mind of the listener." Wherever the Irish go—and where have they not gone?—their music or the memory of it clings to them through life. A selection conveying a sorrowful cadence in its burden will awaken thoughts of home, kindred and early associations, filling the mind of the auditor with emotion and sorrow, writes Cornelius O'Donovan, an exile in Canada, but a change in the metre substituting animation for sentiment, will produce a corresponding change in the feelings, and the heart that but a short time ago was "bowed down," has again resumed its gayety. How aptly the poet voices the spirit of vain regrets which torture our very souls, when we contemplate the havoc which the tragic trinity of persecution, pestilence and proscription has wrought in the historic Green Isle—the once renowned "Land of Music and Song."

OLD TIMES

"Where is that spirit of our prime,
      The good old day!
Have the life and mirth of that honored time
      All passed away!
When old friendship breathed,
And old kindness wreathed
      The cot and castle in kindred claim,
And the tie was holy,
Of high and lowly,
      And neighbor was a brother's name.
Then kindly welcome held the portal free,
      To none denied.
His song the wandering minstrel brought
      From far and wide;
The strains rose lightly,
And young eyes shone brightly;
      And in sunshine ever life's stream rolled on,
And no thought came hither
How fate could wither;
      Yet time stole by, and they are gone!"

CHAPTER XI

IRISH FOLK MUSIC WANING

In olden times music was the only avocation or profession available to the blind; hence we find that so many harpers, pipers, and fiddlers were bereft of sight. The renowned harpers, Rory Dall O'Cahan, Turlogh O'Carolan, Denis Hempson, and Arthur O'Neill were blind, and so were most of the celebrated Union pipers. Some, like O'Neill, lost their sight through accident, but the great majority were victims of the ravages of smallpox. Pitiable indeed was the plight of the young, to be thus deprived of the blessings of vision at an age when the blossoms of intelligence had but just awakened an interest in the delights of life. Sadder still was the misfortune of those stricken in infancy, at the very threshold of existence, who had no conception of light or colors, and to whom even the memory of departed pleasures was denied. Their eyes may have been transplanted into their ears, as some say; but who can read unmoved of their yearnings and despair as pictured in Hannah F. Gould's pathetic poem?—

A Blind Boy's Song

Oh! tell me the form of the soft summer air,
That tosses so gently the curls of my hair!
It breathes on my lip, and it fans my warm cheek,
Yet gives me no answer, tho' often I speak.
I feel it play o'er me, refreshing and kind,
Yet I cannot touch it—I'm blind! oh! I'm blind!

And music, what is it? and where does it dwell?
I sink and I mount with its cadence and swell;
While touched to my heart with its deep, thrilling strain,
Till pleasure, sweet pleasure, is turning to pain.
What brightness of hue is with meekness combined?
Will anyone tell me? I'm blind! oh! I'm blind!

The perfumes of flowers that are hovering nigh,
What are they? on what kind of wings do thy fly?
Are not they sweet angels who came to delight
A poor little boy that knows not of sight?
The sun, moon, and stars are to me undefined;
Oh! tell me what light is: I'm blind! oh! I'm blind!

The harpers from time immemorial were the great composers. Honored, fostered, and glorified, they produced the best that was in them, undisturbed by the present and unmindful of the future; and though their melodies were unwritten, many of the thousands which have survived are listened to with delight the world over in this late day of musical culture and advancement. Despite a concatenation of untoward circumstances, Irish Folk Music exists in greater volume than that of any other nation, there being, according to Dr. P. W. Joyce, over three thousand distinct melodies, exclusive of variants; and this is all the more remarkable in view of the assertion of Bayle Bernard, in his biography of Samuel Lover, that out of some five thousand operas written since the beginning of the past century, not more than a hundred have survived, and that in the main they owe their preservation to their melodies and their dramatic interest.

Those who minister to amusement are everywhere popular characters, and amongst the Irish—a jovial, fun-loving people—none were more welcome than the wandering pipers and fiddlers, upon whom devolved to a large extent the burden of supplying entertainment and promoting good humor in the community. The harpers, it is true, were of more ancient lineage, but their art and talents had been devoted to the service of the rulers rather than the people. Always treated with respect and consideration, there was yet something about them not in perfect accord with the habits and feelings of the majority, on account of their association with persons of rank and wealth.

Not so with the pipers and fiddlers; they were the minstrels of the multitude. They mingled in every feature of Irish life, from the cabin to the castle, especially where the ancient race predominated. Never at a loss for a bed or for board; every door was open to them and every purse untied. With seldom a worry except the rivalry of professional brethren, Irish minstrels and musicians were peculiarly free from care.

Living and circulating in an atmosphere of happiness, hearing little but mirth, and experiencing nothing but kindness at festivities and merry-makings, the pipers and fiddlers in the heyday of their popularity were the "source and centre of all good and friendly feelings." Who will say that life was less worth living then than now?

James Lynam Molloy, of Cornolare, Kings County, hardly thought so when he penned the following lines:

I think of the Irish Piper
As o'er the hills at close of day
He came with a breath of music
That made you dance in spite of yourself
As soon as you heard him play,
The moment you heard him play.
And, "Save you kindly," he would cry,
With merry voice and twinkling eye;
"There's no divarsion can compare
With an Irish dance and an Irish air!"
And we danc'd away to the Piper's tune,
Laughing under the rising moon;
And, ah! it seems but yesterday,
Tho' years of life have pass'd away.

And who but the Irish Piper,
When times were dark and wild with care,
Came up to the mountain shieling,
And made us laugh thro' all our tears,
When the hunger was hard to bear,
And the hunger was hard to bear.

He sang the glorious songs of old,
Of Irish Kings and chieftains bold,
And fairy tales of the little men
That lived below in the haunted glen.
And 'twas oh! the touch of a loving hand
That made the music wild and grand,
And charm us to forget our woe
In the wistful dreams of long ago.

Tho' the great Atlantic rolls its waves between
And we're only dreaming of days that once have been,
Our hearts are over the water,
And throb with many a tear,
For the friends we've left in the old land,
And that land is oh! so dear.
And we dream again of the mountain home,
The dance and song and the Piper's tune;
And tho' the years are old and grey,
It's fresh in our hearts as yesterday,
It's fresh in our hearts as yesterday.

Ah, yes; many are they from every province, county, and parish in Ireland who think of the Irish piper now, when he is following the footsteps of the harper into Dodoland; but we never miss the water till the well runs dry.

The conditions under which minstrels and musicians prospered no longer exist. Gone are the days when their merry music, heard on every hand, memory gathered like nursery jingles and retained without effort. The mind was led captive by the iteration of musical phrases in dance tunes, like

"An echo from a measured strain
In some old corner of the brain,
With haunting sameness in the rhymes,
That came and went a thousand times."

And much as we may cherish the memory of the "Days of Auld Lang Syne" when the Green Isle was a "Land of Music and Song," we are being brought face to face with the inevitable, for

"It is written in the sunshine
As it gilds the shining dome;
It is written in the joyous smile
That lights the hearth of home;
It is written on all fairest things
Beneath the sun's bright ray,
That all were made for one brief hour,
That all must pass away."

Too true! The old must give way to the new; but what blessings has the change brought to Ireland? Mainly monotony, and melodeons made in Germany.

England is the only country where laws were enacted against music, and while the results of their barbarous enforcement are incalculable, it must be conceded that influences originating in Ireland cannot be held blameless of contributing to the musical decadence of the late centuries.

Nothing clings to the expatriated sons of the Gael so tenaciously as the memory of the pleasures and pastimes in which music and song played a part. How aptly the tuneful J. I. C. Clarke voices the reminiscent longing in his "Pictures of Ireland":

"Do you ever think of night-time round the fire?
The rosy little children, their mother and their sire;
    The crossroads and the fiddle,
    With the dancers in the middle,
While the lovers woo by moonlight in the lane?
For Irish love has e'er your heart been fain?
    A many a time, a many a time.

"Did your mother by your cradle ever croon,
For lullaby, some sweet old Irish tune?
    Did an Irish love song's art
    Ever steal into your heart,
Or Irish war chant make your pulses thrill?
Do haunting harps yet sound from Tara's hill?
    A many a time, a many a time."

The Irish peasantry cannot resist the witching tones of the violin or Union pipes or other popular instruments. "If you would keep them in their seats," says an English traveler, "you must fasten them down." How expressive is the sad, sweet wail of Louis Davoren, whose verses betray a wistful desire to relieve his attack of nostalgia by a return to the scenes of his youth,

"Where innocent pastime our pleasures did crown
Upon a green meadow miles out from the town."

THE IRISH PIPES

I heard them once in the long ago,
    But the memory lives today,
Though the sound is hushed and the player dead,
    And I am far away.

I think of them now when twilight throws
    Over earth its chastening spell;
And the feelings that surge through my yearning heart,
    None but myself can tell.

I think of the happy moments spent
    'Neath the yellow harvest moon,
When, the day's work o'er, my feet kept time
    To the piper's merry tune.

And many a tale they call to mind,
    Of the dark, dark days of old,
When for Freedom's cause, in the battle fierce,
    Fell many a hero bold.

Their music hath power no tongue can tell,
    Nor Irish heart resist,
They bring the past to memory back
    From out of the ages' mist.

I long to be back in Ireland again—
    To wander at will and free,
And to hear again the skirl of the pipes
    As once they played for me.

When Congreve conceived the idea that "Music hath charms to soothe a savage breast," though an Irishman, it is hardly probable that he had in mind the strident skirl of the Irish warpipes or the Highland instrument. Yet who knows, in view of the following, for tastes will differ:

A few years ago, dressed in full regalia, with the October zephyrs fanning his unclad knees, a Highland piper sailed into the Morrisania police court in New York City, awakening the echoes with the exultant strains of "Garryowen." It took the combined efforts of three bailiffs to stop him, so enthusiastic was he in his performance.

"He came out of the subway at two o'clock this morning with a stranglehold on his instrument," testified the policeman who had him in charge, "and I placed him under arrest. We danced all the way to the station, and he hadn't stopped playing until this minute."

"Can you play 'Comin' Thro' the Rye'?" asked the magistrate with some display of interest. McGregor could and did, but divining the nationality of the questioner, he diplomatically switched to a rollicking reel. The effect was soon apparent, and the court officers had to use more than persuasion to keep Judge Finn in his seat.

"Here, take this," exclaimed His Honor, handing the piper a five-dollar bill. "You've done me more good than a dozen doctors. Call the next case."

A lilt will put life in the limbs of the weary and quicken the pulsations of the most sluggish heart. The aged, reminiscent ever, live their lives over again under the stimulus of a haunting strain, and the young are stirred to ecstasy, while nothing "shortens the road" for the plodding traveler like the turn of a tune or a verse of a song.

Who can tell by what secret means all our faculties, mental and physical, are enthralled by the charms of simple melodies? How does its subtle influence steal along our thrilling nerves, through every recess of our frame, even changing the expression of our features at will?

"When whispering strains do softly steal
    With creeping passion through the heart;
And when at every touch we feel
    Our pulses beat and bear a part;
When thrills can make a heartstring break,
    Philosophy can scarce deny
    The soul can melt in harmony."

A striking instance of the rejuvenating effect of Folk Music on the aged is that of Peg Fryer, a retired Irish actress, mentioned in Walker's *Historical Memoirs of the Irish Bards*, 1786. Having admirably played the part as grandmother in the *Half-pay Officers,* in 1720, after fifty years' retirement, "she was brought again upon the stage to dance a jig at the age of eighty-five. She came tottering in, seemingly much fatigued, but all on a sudden, the music striking the 'Irish Trot,' she danced and footed it almost as nimbly as any wench of five and twenty."

From the anonymous account of a traveler's excursion through Ireland in 1751, published in the twenty-first volume of the *Gentleman's Magazine,* we get a glimpse of the social customs of that period. "Every village has a bagpiper who every fine evening after working hours collects all the young men and maids in the village about him, where they dance most cheerfully, and it is really a very pleasing entertainment to see the expressive though awkward attempts of nature to recommend themselves to the opposite sex."

> "Twilight's soft dews steal o'er the village green
> With magic tints to harmonize the scene;
> Hushed is the hum that thro' the hamlet broke,
> When round the rim of some venerable oak
> The peasants flocked to hear the minstrel play,
> And games and dances closed the busy day."

The appearance of a piper, fiddler or fluter, or even a man with a jews-harp, was sufficient to draw a crowd of the youth of both sexes to enjoy a dance or listen to the music; and night after night the same youthful hearts would gather around some blazing turf fire, and if there happened to be no musician to stir the dancing spirit, some sweet peasant voice would make up for the loss by singing of love or war, or perhaps some incident which had caught the popular fancy and been versified for the ballad-singers—those degenerate descendants of the bards—whose powerful and melodious voices enlivened the scene at every fair and market in the land in days gone by. With them has vanished much that was interesting in Irish life, as well as the airs which their songs kept alive and in circulation among the people.

CHAPTER XII

IRISH FOLK MUSIC EXEMPLIFIED

As CROFTON CROKER says, the Irishman, like the Frenchman, sings his conquests, his prosperity, his defeats, even his miseries and misfortunes. Conquering or conquered, in plenty or want, happy or distressed, sorrowful or gay, he always sings. To this disposition we may attribute our treasures of melody and our bewildering plenitude of song.

> "The old, old songs, and the dear dead songs,
>   And the songs that we hear no more,
> Like a phantom race, they haunt the place
>   And the scenes that were loved of yore.
> Oh, the dear old songs, I can hear them yet,
>   When the weary world's asleep
> 'Neath its comfort gray, with the stars alway
>   Their ward o'er its dreams do keep."

In Irish Folk Songs, no less than in Folk Music, there is an individuality of feeling and character which distinguish them from English songs—a certain humor and quaintness of expression with an exquisite simplicity and other peculiarities easily recognizable.

A numerous and characteristic class of Irish airs which the ballad-singers kept in promiscuous circulation have come to be facetiously termed "Come, all ye," on account of the comparatively large number of songs which commenced with these words, such as, "Come, all ye sporting gentlemen"; Come, all ye blooming country lads"; "Come, all ye tender Christians; I hope you will draw near," etc. Another hackneyed introduction was, "As I roved out" on a summer's morning, or evening, or any other time or date pertinent to the theme. Much less common was, "Ye Muses nine, with me combine," since the days of the hedge school-master, who reveled in mythology and soared in classical allusions far above the heads of his unlettered audience. The minstrel or balladist of the olden time seized upon every battle, murder, execution, wonderful or laughable event, as a theme for his muse, and, being the purveyor of the latest news and gossip available in his circuit as well, his coming was everywhere welcomed.

Any traditional air suitable to the metre of a new song was liable to be pressed into service; so that in course of time many songs were sung to the same air, thereby confusing its origin and history.

No better description of this class of airs can be presented than that given by a writer in the *Dublin Examiner* of August, 1816: "They are for the most part formed of four strains of equal length—the first soft, pathetic and subdued; the second ascends in the scale and becomes bold and energetic and impassioned; the third, a repetition of the second, is sometimes a little varied and more florid, and leads often by a graceful or melancholy cadence to the fourth, which is always a repetition of the first."

Of this class are the airs known as "The Foggy Dew," "The Enniskillen Dragoons," "The Maid of Sweet Gurteen," "Billy Byrne of Ballymanus," "Irish Molly O," "Good Morning, Fair Maid"; or, "The Roving Pedlar," "The Tossing of the Hay," "Father Tom O'Neill," "Sweet Beaulieu Grove," "The Colleen I'm Courting Just Now," "I'll Build a Tower in My Love's Breast," *"Seamus Mo Mile Stor,"* and many others.

THE TOSSING OF THE HAY

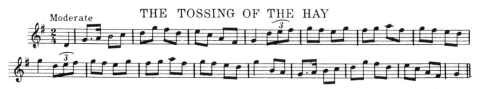

A typically Irish air of this variety is that wedded to John Parry's English lyric, "Vilikins and Dinah," a love tragedy in seven verses, the first of which follows:

> 'Tis of a rich merchant who in London did dwell;
> He had but one daughter, an unkimmon nice young gall;
> Her name it was Dinah, scarce sixteen years old,
> With a very large fortune in silver and gold.
> Singing to la lol la ral lall to ral lal la.
> (Chorus repeats three times to same melody.)

VILIKINS AND DINAH

An American song of love betrayed, named "Joe Bowers," was set to an air unmistakably Irish, in the days of the California gold excitement in 1849. In accepting Joe's proposal of marriage, the prudent Sally Black suggested that "before they hitch for life" he "ought to get a little home to keep a wife." California was the place to "raise a stake" in those days. So, encouraged with "a kiss to bind the bargain," and a dozen thrown in for good measure by the liberal Sally, Joe set out and "worked both late and early in rain, in sun, in snow"; he was working for his Sally, " 'twas all the same to Joe."

The first letter from his brother Ike, in the old Missouri home, put an end to his dream of bliss and faith in woman's constancy. Not only was Sally married to a butcher whose hair was red, but, to crown his agony, the letter conveyed the information that the baby's hair was of the same radiant hue!

JOE BOWERS

Among the airs of this class in which the third strain varies from the second are, "The Lowlands of Holland," or "Holland Is a Fine Place," "The Boys of Wexford," "Willy Reilly," "The Lovely Sweet Banks of the Suir," and "The Banks of Claudy."

WILLY REILLY

An air memorized from my father's singing, the refrain of which was "My Darling, I am Fond of You," possesses peculiarities somewhat exceptional. The second strain is repeated after the fourth, evidently to correspond with an extra line in the verse. Perhaps no Irish melody better illustrates "the placid succession of lengthened tones which swell on the sense and insinuate themselves into our most inmost feelings" described by Webb in his work on *Poetry and Music*.

MY DARLING I AM FOND OF YOU

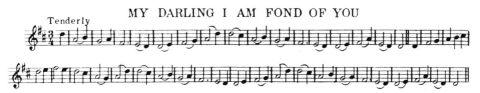

Another air named, "Margaret Sheehan," is peculiar in the sense that while regular in composition there is no repetition of strains.

MARGARET SHEEHAN

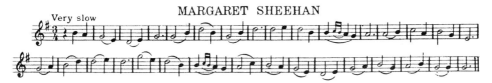

"If we are to form our opinion of the original genius of Irish music from the accounts handed down by Cambrensis," says Lady Morgan, in her *Patriotic Sketches,* over a century ago, "the pathos which it now betrays was certainly not its primeval character. 'But music feedeth the disposition which it findeth.' The popular feelings of a nation may be frequently discovered to a certain degree in the character and idiom of its native melodies, and the very key in which these melodies are composed may give a refined intimation of the political circumstances under which they were first breathed. Thus the Irish, during the long series of their sufferings, effused not their tuneful sorrows in the cheery, open fullness of the major mood. Their voices, broken and suppressed faintly, rose by minor thirds, and the sentiment of anguish communicated to the song of the persecuted bard by 'his soul's sadness' still breathes in Irish music, even though the efficient cause from whence it stole its plaintive character may no longer exist." Hence we find that "even the most rapid Irish air will be found to contain some lurking shade of pathos, even to possess something of that melancholy luxury of sound which characterizes the Arabian music."

Passing a very small rustic cot near Cong, in 1817, John Bernard Trotter, in his *Walks Through Ireland,* heard an old Irish air sung with Irish words by an aged woman turning her spinning wheel. "It was mournfully and remarkably melodious," he says, "sung very low, and with astonishing and true pathos. The sweet and affecting memories of the past days of Ireland, surviving all her sorrows in an humble cottage in Connacht, appealed powerfully to the heart."

> "Old songs! old strains! I should not sigh;
> Joys of the earth on earth must die;
> But spectral forms will sometimes start
> Within the caverns of the heart,
> Haunting the lone and darkened cell
> Where warm in life they used to dwell.
> Hope, youth, love, home, each haunting tie
> That binds, we know not how or why—
> All! all that to the soul belongs,
> Is closely mingled with old songs."

One objection to Irish airs in this generation is the mournful or plaintive key in which so many of them are pitched. Exceptions are by no means rare, and of these some are enlivened with a rollicking chorus.

The three great bardic classes of music previously described in Chapter I might be judiciously increased to twice that number, such as Slumber or Lullaby; Dirge or Lamentation; Rural; Amorous; Festive and Martial.

LULLABIES

No form of music can have greater claims to antiquity than lulling or sleep-inducing music, for even the birds croon to their nestlings. In some form it was common to all nations and in all ages, but among no people were lullabies as numerous and varied as in Ireland and the Scottish Highlands. The "Shuheen Sho" of the Gaels—anglicised into "lullaby"—has been modernized into "cradle song." One cannot fail to notice that almost all lullabies or cradle songs are made up, with little variety, on the same plan, regardless of the age or nation in which they may have originated.

Following is the first verse of a lullaby of great beauty, translated from the Irish. It purports to be the song of the fairy nurse in the rath of Lisroe for a child stolen by the "good people."

> Sweet babe! a golden cradle holds thee,
> Shuheen sho, lulo lo!
> And soft the snow-white fleece enfolds thee,
> Shuheen sho, lulo lo!
> In airy bower I'll watch thy sleeping,
> Shuheen sho, lulo lo!
> Where branchy trees to the breeze are sweeping,
> Shuheen sho, lulo lo!

A LULLABY OR SHUHEEN SHO

DIRGES OR LAMENTS

Irish music is rich in laments for the dead—a form of composition probably among the very oldest. Rev. Dr. Campbell, in his *Philosophical Survey of the South of Ireland,* in 1775, says: "Their finest airs are of the plaintive turn, and are supposed to have been set to elegies for renowned warriors, or to the sighs of complaining lovers."

The form of the lament varied in different parts of Ireland, but the cadences are often inconceivably plaintive and affecting. Did ever a wail make a man's marrow quiver, and fill his nostrils with the breath of the grave, queries Thomas Davis, like the *Ullulu* of the north or the *Ullagone* or *Wirrasthrue* of Munster?

Besides the *caoine,* or dirge for the dead, there were also lamentations for the living, expressive of every form of regret, such as for eviction, emigration, loss of valued property, or other calamities. Unlike lullabies, lamentations display much diversity of composition. The most ancient, such as "The Lamentation of Deirdre for the Sons of Usnach," "Ossian's Lament," and even lamentations composed around the year 1600, make no appeal to modern ears.

"Ormonde's Lament," which can be assigned to the early years of the eighteenth century, is now quite generally known as "Billy Byrne of Ballymanus." Songs entitled "A Lament for Thomas Flavell" and "The County of Mayo" have been also set to the same air.

So quaint and plaintive is "Crotty's Lament," which dates from about the year 1742, that a setting of it is herewith presented:

CROTTY'S LAMENT
Composed about 1742

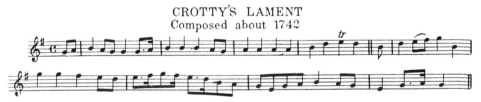

An air named "Sarsfield's Lament," entirely distinct from the melody of that name in modern publications, may not be devoid of interest. It is among the contents of *The Hibernian Muse,* published in London in 1787.

SARSFIELD'S LAMENTATION
From the Hibernian Muse. pub. 1787.

"Owen Roe O'Neill's Lamentation," if not the product of O'Carolan's genius, as claimed by several authorities, is by no means unworthy of the renowned bard.

"*Caoine Cill Cais,*" or "The Lament for Kilcash," an ancient seat of the Ormondes, a few miles northeast of Clonmel, originated early in the eighteenth century. Some dozen songs of varied character were sung to this popular melody, one of the most recent being "The Fair at Dungarvan."

THE LAMENTATION OF OWEN ROE O'NEILL

Every ballad having capital punishment or other harrowing death as a theme was sung to a peculiarly mournful air, in southwest Munster at least, in the last half of the nineteenth century. This lament, which escaped the vigilance of Dr. Petrie and was alluded to as the "hanging song," was published in O'Neill's *Music of Ireland,* in 1902, as "The Martyr's Lament." It has been pronounced by a distinguished vocalist and lecturer to be unsurpassed among traditional Irish dirges.

THE MARTYR'S LAMENT
(The Hanging Song)

Not less expressive of woe, if more modern in musical phraseology, is a lamentation composed in 1904 on the death of a young collegian of brilliant promise in Chicago.

LAMENT FOR ROGERS O'NEILL

Among the lamentations not of a tragic nature we may mention *"Ullulu mo Mhailin"*—the old woman's lament for the loss of her little bag and its contents. "Rocking the Cradle," or "Rocking a Baby That's None of My Own," and "The Old Woman Lamenting Her Purse." In the song to the first of these airs, the old woman, in response to questions, recounts in details the contents of the bag. A good description of "Rocking the Cradle" may be found in the biography of John Coughlan, the Australian piper.

THE OLD WOMAN LAMENTING HER PURSE

RURAL MUSIC

Under this head may be classed Plough tunes, Spinning-wheel tunes, Milk-maid songs, and Loobeen or Luinig airs. Comparatively few of any of these varieties have been preserved, and all of them may be regarded as obsolete by this time.

PLOUGH TUNES

"Amongst the numerous classes of melodies which a people so music-loving as the Irish, invented to lighten the labor and beguile the hours devoted to their various occupations," says Dr. Petrie, "there is perhaps no one of higher interest, and certainly no one that I have listened to with deeper emotion, than that class of simple, wild and solemn strains which the ploughman whistles in the field to soothe or excite the spirits of the toiling animals he guides, as well as to fill his own ears with sounds expressive of peaceful and solemn thoughts."

SPINNING-WHEEL TUNES

From the number of melodies of this class yet remaining in Dr. Petrie's time, it would appear, he says, that there was no sort of occupation or labor, indoors or out, that the use of song was not resorted to with a view to sustain the spirits and lighten the toil.

Differing from the plaintive and solemn plough tunes, spinning-wheel airs were of a lighter and more mirthful kind, and from Bunting's description they were generally songs in which several singers took part. Following are his words: "The Loobeen is a peculiar species of chaunt, having a well-marked time and a frequently recurring chorus or catchword. It is sung at merry-makings and assemblages of the young women when they meet at spinnings and quiltings, and is accompanied by extemporaneous verses, of which each singer successively furnishes a line. The intervention of the chorus after certain phrases gives time for the preparation of an appropriate line or reply by the next singer. The airs themselves bear all the appearance of antiquity."

As might be expected, tunes of this class were also very common in the Scottish Isles and Highlands. The name *Luinigs,* or *Luinnochs,* by which they are known, signifies cheerful chorus music.

An air and song of this class picked up in our boyhood days near Bantry will convey some idea of the possibilities of a song of that nature for unlimited extension.

IF ALL THE YOUNG LADIES
A "Luibin" Air

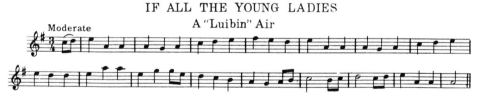

Dr. Petrie, in his *Ancient Music of Ireland,* published in 1855, gives as examples of this rare class of occupational tunes, the music and responses of a ploughman and his two assistants, working and worrying, at the lateness of their dinner, and "The Smith's Song," or "Ding, dong, didilium." The latter name represents the ring of the hammer on the anvil as the smith and his helper strike and respond.

MILKMAID SONGS

Familiar as we are with the name, it does not appear that milkmaid songs enjoyed any special characterization. However, it is well understood that milch cows are not indifferent to familiar tones and persons, for the Bossy that would stand contentedly for one would not tolerate another. This brings to mind Tim O'Neill's story of a neighbor's cow which "would kick the daylights out of any person attempting to milk her" unless the affecting strains of "Nell Flaherty's Drake" greeted her ears, so accustomed was she to the tones of that soothing refrain on such occasions.

Without assuming that all cattle are influenced by music, we are certain that some are keenly alive to its attractions, and will even follow it, with evident delight, until restrained by the limits of their enclosure.

In the exuberance of youth, milkmaids are prone to give their emotions vocal expression, and the nature of their singing or lilting when milking is more than likely to be an indication of their frame of mind for the fleeting moment.

Amorous, or Music of the Affections

Many of the finest traditional Irish melodies are of this character, among them being *"Eibhlin a Ruin,"* the oldest of all Irish folk airs, according to Prof. Carl Hardebeck, of Belfast, and other distinguished authorities. The weight of evidence seems to establish its origin in the latter part of the fourteenth century, though others place the date a century and a half earlier. In a general way such melodies may be described as of a narrative, or excited discoursing character— animated and energetic in their movement, yet marked with earnest tenderness and impassioned sentiment—more or less tinged with sadness, though rarely sinking into tones of extreme or despairing melancholy.

In the same classification might be enumerated such popular airs as *"Ceann Dubh Dilis"* or "The Black-headed Deary," "Molly Asthore," "The Coolin," "The *Paistin Fionn,"* *"Caithilin Thriall,"* "Nora of the Amber Locks," "Have You Been at Carrick?" "The Dark Maiden of the Valley," "The Foggy Dew," "The Lowlands of Holland," and *"Mo Mhuirnin na Gruaige Baine"* or "My Fairhaired Darling." The last named, being the least known, is presented as a specimen of this class of melodies.

MY FAIRHAIRED DARLING
(*mo muirnin na gruaige baine*)

The Irish language is rich in terms of endearment, and as one would naturally be led to expect, love and affection are the themes of a large number of folk songs. The Irish, as everyone knows, are not lacking in chivalry, still there is a limit to the ardor of the most enthusiastic occasionally in their devotion to the fair sex when it comes to the supreme sacrifice. Few, however, will be inclined to condemn a man who was willing to do as much as James Doherty for the young lady of his choice, whom he evidently idolizes:

> I'd swear for her,
> I'd tear for her,
> The Lord knows what I'd bear for her;
> I'd lie for her,
> I'd sigh for her,
> I'd drink Lough Erne dry for her;
> I'd "cuss" for her,
> Do "muss" for her,
> I'd kick up a thundering fuss for her;
> I'd weep for her,
> I'd leap for her,
> I'd go without any sleep for her;
> I'd fight for her,
> I'd bite for her,
> I'd walk the streets all night for her;
> I'd plead for her,
> I'd bleed for her,
> I'd go without my "feed" for her;
> I'd shoot for her,
> I'd boot for her
> A rival who'd come to "suit" for her;
> I'd kneel for her,
> I'd steal for her,
> Such is the love I feel for her;
> I'd slide for her,
> I'd ride for her,
> .I'd swim against wind and tide for her;
> I'd try for her,
> I'd cry for her,
> But—hang me if I'd die for her
> Or any other woman!

FESTIVE OF MIRTHFUL MUSIC

What other strains but those of *Geanntraighe* or merry music could have inspired the author of the following lines on "The Power of Music"?

> "Can I be thus in vision blest,
>   Or can such bliss arise from sound?
> By some sweet madness I'm possessed,
>   Or is the air enchanted round?

> "Wild raptures in my bosom swell,
>   And my soul floats in fond delight;
> For every note conceals a spell
>   That pictures scenes long lost to sight."

Though the tragedies of her history have indelibly stamped the music of Ireland with characteristic plaintiveness, a race so noted for humor and joviality could not fail to have the spirit of cheerfulness and vivacity also reflected abundantly in their music and song. Take, for instance, such animated airs as "The Parson Boasts of Mild Ale," "Teig Moira's Daughter," "The Lough Carra Fisherman," "The Peeler and the Goat," and the drinking song, *"Beidmaoid ag Ol'sa Poga na m-Bean."*

What music could be more gay and spirited than the hop or slip jig in nine-eight time, a metre peculiar to the Gaelic race, not to mention other varieties of jigs and reels to which songs without number had been sung before their conversion into dance tunes by the pipers and fiddlers?

And then we must remember there were planxties by the score, all breathing a spirit of untrammeled gladness and conviviality, such as "Planxty O'Rourke" or "O'Rourke's Noble Feast," and "Bumpers Squire Jones"—compositions of the great bard O'Carolan. Even so, not a strain conceived in the prolific brain of O'Carolan, or his contemporaries, which has come down to us is at all comparable with the simple melody, "Tow row row" in giving musical expression to the mirthfulness and buoyancy of the Irish mind.

TOW ROW ROW, JOHNNY WILL YOU NOW?

MARTIAL MUSIC

No enemy speaks slightingly of Irish music, and no friend need fear to boast of it, says Thomas Davis. Its antique war-tunes such as those of O'Byrne, O'Donnell, Alastrum, and Brian Boru stream and crash upon the ear like the warriors of a hundred glens meeting; and you are borne with them to battle, and they and you charge and struggle amid cries and battle axes and stinging arrows.

The War Song of the Irish Kerns was called *Pharrah.* Walker tells us in his *Historical Memoirs of the Irish Bards;* that while an army was preparing for the onset, the song was sung at the head by a *Filea* to the harsh but spirit-stirring accompaniment of the different martial instruments. He further adds that each chieftain had a war cry peculiar to his tribe. The Scottish clans had their *Piobaireachd* and *Cruinneachd* compositions which may be regarded as a species of martial music.

A setting of "The Pharrah or War March," obtained from Dr. Petrie in 1835 is to be found in Bunting's *Ancient Music of Ireland,* published in 1840. It consists of nine parts or strains, and it is worthy of note that this ancient march has been converted by the pipers into a spirited jig called "The Gold Ring."

Little need be said of a martial tune so well known as "Brian Boru's March," unless we might point out that its structure and rhythm would seem to indicate an origin much later than the eleventh century. An appreciation from the pen of Kohl, the German traveler who heard it played on the harp at Drogheda in 1843, cannot fail to be of interest. "The music of this march is wildly powerful and at the same time melancholy. It is at once the music of victory and of mourning. The rapid modulations and wild beauty of the air was such that I think this march deserves full to obtain a celebrity equal to that of the 'Marseillaise' and the 'Ragotsky.' "

The wild and inspiring martial air entitled, "The Return from Fingal," which Dr. Petrie learned from the Munster pipers is evidently of much earlier origin. It was supposed to have been the march played or sung by Brian Boru's Munster troops on their return home from the glorious but dearly bought triumph at Clontarf in 1014 and was expressive of the mixed feelings of sorrow and triumphs which had been excited by the result of that memorable conflict.

Such splendid martial airs as "Rory of the Hills," "Paddies Evermore," "The Boyne Water," "O'Donnell Abu," and the "Green Flag Flying Before Us," need no special comment, so we will discuss a tune with a history, the antique "Alastrum's March," or "MacDonnell's March" as Bunting calls it.

Few indeed are the warpipe tunes that have come down to us from the seventeenth century. Passed on from one generation to another traditionally we must expect such as have been preserved to vary in some degree from the original composition, which to find proper expression on the *Piob Mor* must not exceed a compass of nine or at most ten notes.

Of this class "Alastrum's March" is historically the best known. Dr. Smith in his *History of Cork* published in 1750, refers to it as "a very odd kind of Irish music well known in Munster by the name of 'Mac Allisdrum's March' being a wild rhapsody made in honor of this commander, to this day much esteemed by the Irish."

This revered hero was Sir Alexander (in Irish Alastair) MacDonnell, an Irish general of great bravery who was basely assassinated by an English soldier, after the Irish had been defeated at the battle of Knockinoss, fought November 13, 1647, between the English or Parliamentary forces under the command of Lord Inchiquin and the Irish under Lord Taaffe. Four thousand or one half the entire strength of the latter were left dead on the field.

A party of Scotch Highlanders in the Irish army headed by MacDonnell, nicknamed Colkitto [left-handed], contested their ground in a most determined and gallant manner, and were inhumanly butchered by the victors.

All possible honors were shown the remains of the brave Colkitto, and his funeral procession was headed by a band of pipers playing what Grattan Flood terms "a specially composed funeral march, ever since known as 'Mac Alistrum's March.' "

Differing from Dr. Flood as to its origin, Crofton Croker says in *Researches in the South of Ireland*, which came from the press in 1824, "That wild and monstrous piece of music known by the name of 'Ollistrum's March' so popular in the south of Ireland, and said to have been played at Knockinoss should not, it appears to me be considered an Irish air." After quoting Walker in support of his contention, Croker continues: "The estimation in which it is held in Ireland is wonderful. I have heard this march, as it is called, sung by hundreds of the Irish peasantry who imitate the drone of the bagpipe in their manner of singing it. On that instrument I have also heard it played and occasionally with much pleasure from the peculiar and powerful expression given by the performer."

"Not one of our native musicians understand a note of music, as the pipers in general are blind," says the lady who noted it down, "and yet the air has been handed or rather (if I may use the expression) *eared* down, I imagine with very little alteration, having heard numbers perform it in the same irregular way."

ALLISTRUM'S MARCH

This ancient war march presents a typical instance of how Irish tunes have been both preserved and varied, in their transmission traditionally from one generation to another throughout the nation. Bunting's setting of "Mac Donnell's March," printed in his third volume was obtained in 1802, from a piper at Westport, county of Mayo. It consists of but three parts.

A variant of this march with but two strains and named "Sarsfield's quickstep" is included in Haverty's *Three Hundred Irish Airs,* published in 1858-1859.

MISCELLANEOUS MELODIES

Before terminating this chapter—already extended far beyond anticipation, it may not be unwise to take advantage of this opportunity for presenting a few specimens of unclassified tunes.

From Mr. Quinn, a famous Irish piper of Chicago, his friend Sergt. James Early many years ago learned an odd jig called "The Goat's Song" in which the bleating of that sportive animal is an ever-recurring tone. Its antiquity is undeniable for an almost identical version of the tune under its Irish name "*Cronan Gabhair*" is to be found in Logan's *Scottish Gael.*

THE GOAT'S SONG
(*An Cronan Gabhair*)

By a strange coincidence a roll of manuscript music, after passing through many hands in two hemispheres came into the possession of the present writer. It proved to have been originally owned by an O'Mahony—a maternal relative— of Dunmanway county of Cork. Among its contents was a tune so peculiar and staccata in its movements that it naturally suggests the jockeying of a child on the nurse's knees. The rapid alteration of long and short notes, as in a strathspey renders it rather difficult of execution except on the violin.

DANCING THE BABY

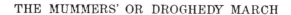

In an age when the knowledge of the customs and social life of our immediate ancestors is little more than legendary, few could be expected to have any conception of the Mummers of the olden time or their annual festivities.

More ancient than the Wren Boys of St. Stephen's Day who also had their characteristic song and tune the Mummers were according to Walker strolling companies of young men and maidens who like the English Wassailers went about carousing from house to house during the Christmas holidays attended by rude musicians. Each mummer personates an eminent saint, and before the dance begins, these different characters form themselves into a circle, and each in his turn steps forward declaring at the same time his assumed name, country, qualification and other circumstances, in a kind of rhyme.

After scanning the contents of the Bunting, Petrie and Joyce collections of Irish music in vain, kind fortune finally favored us. Unexpectedly a setting of "The Mummers' March" with other valued contributions reached us from the hand of the helpful and versatile Patrick Whelan of Scarawalsh Ballycarney near Ferns county of Wexford. Were Ireland blessed with more men of his type Gaelic Revivals would be unnecessary.

THE MUMMERS' OR DROGHEDY MARCH

CHAPTER XIII

THE DEVELOPMENT OF TRADITIONAL IRISH MUSIC.

THE saying that the invention of writing injured the power of memory, finds much support from the fact that musicians ignorant of written music, possess the faculty of memorizing tunes to a far greater degree than those who acquire their repertory from that source.

We have all heard of Irish seanachies and professional story tellers of Oriental countries, who could recite hundreds of tales and genealogies in identical phraseology from day to day and year after year. Neither historians nor those who read their works could hope to rival them in that respect.

Music it must be granted surpasses every other aid to memory in that it brings its influence most directly and most movingly to the heart. The old song or strain possesses a power which will turn back the years even to the cradle no less than the odor of forgotten flowers.

We must not forget however that memory is capricious, and preserves a baffling independence of the will. We cannot always summon up forthwith the images or combination of tones which we desire. Neither can the untrained ear be always relied on when we wish to reproduce the words or musical forms casually impressed on it.

The bards, like their predecessors the druids, concealed with jealous care all knowledge from the vulgar eye. The harpers in their turn, Brompton, the English abbot, tells us, taught in secret and committed their lessons to memory before the Norman invasion—a practice they continued down through the centuries.

Neither harpers nor pipers made use of printed music even when available in the eighteenth and nineteenth centuries, as in fact the majority of them were blind and of necessity obliged to learn and teach by the oral method only.

Musicians of talent, harpers principally, have exercised their skill in elaborating simple melodies, and adding variations to the original strains. All of the four dozen airs in Burk Thumoth's collections published in 1742-1743, whether Irish, Scotch, or English, are embellished with variations, and the same can be said of popular Irish and Scotch airs in O'Farrell's, Alday's, and other collections, down to the early years of the nineteenth century.

Fired by the same ambition, the pipers and fiddlers invoked their muse to emulate the example of the harpers and set about composing additional "parts" and florid finishes to their simple dance tunes, especially jigs, and before long it was nothing unusual to find a jig with from three to half a dozen "parts" or strains. Not a few had been enlarged to seven, eight, and nine parts. In *O'Farrell's Pocket Companion for the Union Pipes* (third collection about 1810), "The Little House Under the Hill" jig has no less than eleven "parts," while a nameless long dance in the Petrie collections is extended to twenty-four parts!

Though Bunting tells us that the harpers invariably played and transmitted their tunes precisely as they had been taught them, it is but reasonable to make some allowance for lapses of memory and individual taste; for even Bunting himself included in his later collections variants of airs he had previously printed under different titles.

Quite obviously memorized music disseminated from one generation to another by vocal or instrumental means would inevitably lead to the formation of many variants from original versions.

Traditional music unlike any form of modern composition is not the work of one man but of many. Indeed it can hardly be said to have been composed at all. It is simply a growth to a certain extent subject to the influence of heredity, environment, natural selection, and the survival of the fittest.

It may be regarded as axiomatic that the older the melody the simpler the strain. Melodies consisting of but one strain are to be found in the Petrie and Joyce collections.

The purpose of this chapter is not so much the discussion of the subject, as the practical demonstration of the changes which time and taste have brought about in some pieces of Irish music, and how dance tunes particularly have been evolved from vocal airs and other forms of the same melody.

The Irish Fox Hunt, or The Fox Chase

No piece of Irish music is so widely known by name in the land of its origin at least as "The Fox Chase." As an instrumental composition it is attributed to Edward Keating Hyland, a celebrated blind piper who received some lessons in theory and harmony from Sir John Stevenson in Dublin. The melody or theme on which it was founded was an ancient lamentation to which was sung some verses in both Irish and English reciting a dialogue between a farmer and a fox which he had detected with the "goods" on him in the shape of "a fine fat goose."

From this air then called *"An Maidrin Ruadh"* (Modhereen Rua), Hyland developed the famous descriptive piece, introducing the sounds of the chase such as the tallyho, baying of the hounds, death of the fox, etc., and winds up the performance with "The Foxhunters' Jig" as an expression of the general delight at the result.

Fortunately we can present a copy of "The Irish Fox Hunt," as printed in *O'Farrell's Pocket Companion for the Irish or Union Pipes,* published about 1806. This being but seven years subsequent to the date of its composition according to Grattan Flood, it can be safely assumed that O'Farrell's setting is authentic.

The next version, entitled "The Fox Hunt," is that found in the manuscript collection of Henry Hudson, 24 Stephens Green, Dublin, completed in 1842. A notation indicates that Mr. Hudson copied this and other tunes from an older collection owned by F. M. Bell.

Through the kindness of the princely Prof. P. J. Griffith of the Leinster School of Music we are enabled to submit the genial professor's own version of "The Fox Chase," the version by the way which, enhanced by his skillful execution, won the seal of supremacy at various contests.

The fourth and final example of "The Fox Chase" is that which appears in O'Neill's *Music of Ireland* published in 1903. Although we had been led to believe that the setting was that played by the great Munster piper, Stephenson, it turns out that "Patsy" Touhey obtained it from John L. Wayland of the Cork Pipers' Club, and that it primarily came from Mrs. Kenny of Dublin.

We trust the settings or versions of the once popular piece of music herein presented will serve to relieve the anxiety of several correspondents who feared that it would be utterly lost, although were it necessary several other versions could have been submitted.

THE IRISH FOX HUNT
from O'Farrell's Pocket Companion for the Irish or Union Pipes
Vol 1 Book 2 circa 1806

THE FOX HUNT
from H. Hudson's Manuscript Collection, 1841 A.D

THE FOX CHASE—*Tipperary Version*
by Prof. P. J. Griffith Dublin

THE FOX CHASE
from O'Neill's Music of Ireland

THE BLACKBIRD

Deservedly popular whether as an air or dance tune in the late generations, "The Blackbird" was one of those allegorical songs much in vogue in the days of the "Old Pretender" in the beginning of the eighteenth century.

The earliest printed setting of this melody which we have been able to discover is that found in *A Pocket Volume of Airs, Duets, Songs, Marches, etc.,* vol. 1, published by Paul Alday at Dublin about 1800-1803. Included among "Six Favorite Original Airs never printed till now" we find:

THE BLACK BIRD
from Paul Alday's- A Pocket Volume etc

The following version was taken from *O'Farrell's Pocket Companion for the Irish or Union Pipes, etc.,* published about 1806 and entitled:

THE BLACK BIRD_ Very old
from O'Farrell's Pocket Companion for the Irish or Union Pipes
Vol 1 Book 2 circa 1806

It is indeed surprising to find that no setting or version of this noted tune can be found in the Petrie Collections of Irish music.

The setting of this melody which Bunting credits to "D. O'Donnell, harper, county Mayo," although obtained in 1803—the same year in which Alday's version was printed—was withheld until the publication in 1840 of *The Ancient Music of Ireland,* his third volume. This florid setting serves to illustrate what skillful instrumentalists can accomplish in the elaboration of the most simple compositions.

As Bunting's version of "The Blackbird" with a traditional and long dance setting are included in Appendix C, of *Irish Folk Music: A Fascinating Hobby,* their reproduction in this work is unnecessary.

Had we then possessed the ancient versions above presented they also would have been included in that work.

Fagamaoid sud mar ata se, and THE FIRST OF MAY

A prominent advocate of traditional Irish music who was enthusiastic in his praise of a hornpipe known as "The First of May" was asked if he considered it a very old tune. Unhesitatingly he replied that it was one of the very oldest. A brief discussion which followed gave the learned gentleman much food for thought for the evidence of its derivation from a much older melody was most convincing.

We can assume that no one will question the antiquity of the air called

"Fagamaoid sud mar ata se." By no means a rare melody, two settings of it being in the *Complete Petrie Collection,* Dr. Joyce, who includes a version of it in his *Ancient Irish Music,* says: "Several songs, both English and Irish, are sung to this air which is well known all over the Munster counties." Many will remember that "Darby O'Leary," or "The Galbally Farmer," was one of them.

A comparison of the air which is in six-eight time, with the hornpipe in common time, will show that they are identical in strain and differ only in arrangement. Plainly enough, the hornpipe was evolved from the old air, as in many similar instances.

Fagamaoid sud mar ata se
LET US LEAVE THAT AS IT IS

THE FIRST OF MAY (HORNPIPE)

Rodney's Glory

Not the least popular of the Long dance tunes of a generation or so ago, was "Rodney's Glory." In this form it is simply an adaptation from the song of that name composed in honor of Lord Rodney, the English admiral who won some signal victories over the Spanish and French fleets in 1780 and 1782 respectively. The melody, no doubt much older, was also called "My Name is Moll Mackey" and "The Praises of Limerick." Following is the air of "Rodney's Glory" as sung by my father:

RODNEY'S GLORY (SONG)

RODNEY'S GLORY (LONG-DANCE)

'THE GARDEN OF DAISIES

Similarly this once popular Long dance tune, of which there are several versions, was evolved from a slow song air, which the present writer often heard in boyhood days. From the drift of one line remembered—"My hook began to glitter, and my flail it was in order"—it would appear that the song was of the narrative class, describing the adventures of one of those who migrate annually to engage in harvest work in more fertile fields.

YOUNG ROGER WAS A PLOUGHBOY

This old air taken from Dr. Joyce's *Ancient Irish Music* will serve to illustrate how readily a strain so simple may be converted into a typical Irish hornpipe.

YOUNG ROGER WAS A PLOWBOY (AIR)

ROGER WAS A PLOWBOY (HORNPIPE)

THE CAMPBELLS ARE COMING, and MISS MCLEOD'S REEL

No tunes have enjoyed greater popularity for many generations than the above named. "The Campbells are Coming," or *"An Seanduine,"* as it is called in Ireland, was printed as early as 1750, and it is historically certain that "Miss McLeod's Reel" was one of six tunes played by the Galway pipers in 1779, for the entertainment of Beranger, the French traveler. The antiquity of both tunes is therefore beyond question, and ordinarily one would not suspect their close relationship.

Any discriminating musician who will examine their structure and compare their similarity of strain cannot escape the conviction that both tunes had a common origin or that "Miss McLeod's Reel" was derived from "The Campbells are Coming," or its Irish equivalent *"An Seanduine."*

JIGS DERIVED FROM MARCHES

In stating that most if not all traditional Irish jig tunes were originally marches or song airs, we have the authority of the illustrious Dr. Petrie. Obviously Jackson's compositions, published in his lifetime, are not of this class. Some have come down to us but little altered from their most ancient settings; while not a few others have been so disguised in the process of evolution as to almost lose their identity.

For instance, who would question the antiquity of a jig so generally known as "The Rakes of Kildare?" Yet when compared with "Get Up Early," an ancient march melody which Bunting obtained in 1802 from R. Stanton at Westport, county of Mayo, it is plainly evident that the march is the parent tune. "Very ancient author and date unknown," is Bunting's notation on the latter.

GET UP EARLY

THE RAKES OF KILDARE

JIG AND REEL FROM SAME STRAINS

Instances of jigs and reels being evolved from the same strain, or of one being derived from the other, are more numerous than is generally supposed. Some pipers and fiddlers are surprisingly expert in that line of composition, or adaptation. A change of arrangement especially if in a different key, will often-times constitute an apparently new tune.

The most ordinary ear can discern the relationship existing between "The Templehouse Jig" and its offspring, "The Templehouse Reel." Each in its class is a tune of distinct merit, though identical in tonality.

THE TEMPLEHOUSE JIG

THE TEMPLEHOUSE REEL

JACKSON'S MORNING BRUSH

A good example of a jig which grew from two to four strains in much less than one generation is "Jackson's Morning Brush," the best known of "Piper" Jackson's compositions. Following is the version of it as played by Bernard Delaney and others of our best traditional musicians in Chicago.

The earliest setting of this favorite jig is probably that taken from a MSS. collection of 1776 by Grattan Flood and published in his recent work, *The Story of the Bagpipe.* It consists of only the first and third strains of Delaney's version. The setting which we find in volume one of *Aird's Selection of Scotch, English, Irish, and Foreign Airs*, published in 1782, comprises the first, second and third strains of our example without the second finish to the third.

Bunting's setting of this tune obtained from a piper in 1797 was extended to four strains in the same order of sequence as ours, but besides lacking the second finish before mentioned there are a few minor differences not at all to its advantage.

JACKSONS MORNING BRUSH

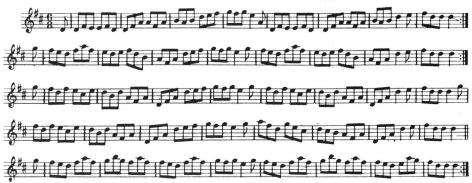

While engaged in this line of demonstration we may as well submit for consideration two settings of a popular reel which presents unmistakable evidence of having been the subject of somewhat similar development. The first setting as printed in Haverty's *Three Hundred Irish Airs* is named "The Unfortunate Cup of Tea."

THE UNFORTUNATE CUP OF TEA

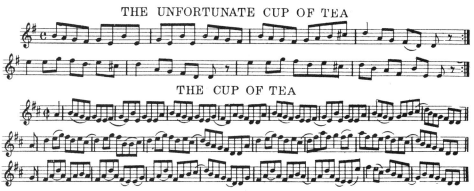

THE CUP OF TEA

The setting of this fine reel as printed in O'Neill's *Dance Music of Ireland,* was the version noted down from the playing of James Kennedy, one of the famous fiddlers of the Irish Music Club of Chicago. Among the "craft" it was called "The Cup of Tea."

TRADITIONAL MUSIC

Although convincing evidence has been presented, much more is available to support the claim that traditional Irish music has quite generally wandered from its originals, in all of its different varieties. Even that "Queen of Irish airs," "The Coulin" has its "Old Coolin" and a still more primitive version in the Petrie collections, and such a slashing marching tune as "The Boyne Water" is represented by two apparently older versions—Nos. 1529 and 1530—in the same repository of ancient Irish music, disguised under Irish names of different import.

A volume, much less a chapter, would scarcely do justice to this subject, but we trust examples enough have been submitted to furnish food for thought especially to those who in their self-complacent attitude of musical infallibility, will tolerate no standard of excellence or perfection but their own.

CHAPTER XIV

FAMOUS COLLECTORS OF IRISH MUSIC

LOVE of music for its own sake is invariably the inspiring motive which prompts and sustains the musical antiquarian, or collector of Folk Music in every age, and in every country. Like the benefactors of their race who have devoted their lives and even their fortunes to the acquirement of rare manuscripts, historical documents, and other interesting things, collectors of folk lore, and Folk Music, are all enthusiasts in their chosen subjects.

Affected no doubt by the tragic vicissitudes of their country, the Irish did not begin the work of collecting the melodies of Erin until long after the English and Scotch had invaded the field, and incorporated many stray Irish tunes in their publications.

As early as 1594 a manuscript collection of music, including several Irish airs, was compiled by William Ballet, a Dublin actor. In musical bibliography it is known as *William Ballet's Lute Book,* and is preserved in Trinity College Library.

Although many musical works were printed in England in the first half of the seventeenth century it was not until 1650 that any great collection of music without words was undertaken. From that date and for seventy-five years thereafter various editions more or less enlarged of *The English Dancing Master,* commonly called *Playford's Dancing Master,* continued to come from the press, among the contents being not a few Irish tunes.

The same English publisher, John Playford, compiled and published in 1700 the first collection of Scotch music consisting of but sixteen pages and of which there is known to exist but one copy.

Though the subject of Music Collections has been dealt with at some length in Chapters XII and XIII of *Irish Folk Music: A Fascinating Hobby,* the occasion seems opportune to present brief biographies of certain collectors whose conspicuous labors in the line of original research can never be too highly appreciated. In fact theirs were the storehouses from which many minor collectors and publishers freely helped themselves.

JOHN AND WILLIAM NEALE

The first music publishers of any note in Dublin were John and William Neale, father and son, and it is recorded, they played an important part in matters musical in their day, even to the extent of managing most of the entertainments in the city. The elder Neale or O'Neill—as the surname was sometimes referred to, was in 1723 connected with a musical club which afterwards developed into a very important musical association.

Their meeting place was at a tavern at Christ's Church Yard, and it is worthy of note that it was at this location the Neales published in 1726, (or 1720 according to Bunting) a little volume with the modest title: *A Book of Irish Tunes.* About the same time they brought out *A Collection of Irish and Scotch Tunes;* three books of English Airs, and a volume of Country Dances. Two thin folio volumes of songs and airs from the *Beggars' Opera* which abounded with Irish airs followed in 1729, but their special claim to distinction in this connection lies in the fact that they were the pioneer collectors and publishers of Irish music.

The Neales were also the builders of the Musick Hall in Fishamble street opened in 1741, and in which Handel conducted his first public performance in Dublin.

John Neale died before this event, but the son, William, survived to an advanced age, the date of his death occurring in the year 1769. Musical taste and talent persisted in the family for William's son, Dr. John Neale, became the best amateur violinist of Dublin.

Burk Thumoth

After the Neales, Neills, or O'Neills, as they were variously called, the next collector of prominence was Burk Thumoth, whose fame rests on his two celebrated collections, *Twelve Scotch, and Twelve Irish Airs,* with variations, etc., and *Twelve English, and Twelve Irish Airs,* with variations, etc., published about the years 1742 and 1745 respectively. Both volumes are "Set for the German Flute, Violin or Harpsichord."

No details of Thumoth's life are available except that he was an Irishman and a famous performer on the flute.

In his third volume Bunting refers to Burk Thumoth's *Collection of Irish Tunes* as having been published about 1725. That this date is much too early is clearly set forth in *Grove's Dictionary of Music and Musicians.* On the title page of the first edition it is stated that they were printed for John Simpson, but it appears that Simpson did not engage in the publishing business until long after that date. Again James Oswald's two collections of *Curious Scots Tunes* are advertised on the title page of Thumoth's first "Book." Yet Oswald's volumes were not printed before 1742.

Omitting the date of publication, formerly a common practice, still prevails, but less frequently, hence the discrepancies which naturally arise.

O'Farrell

A celebrated Irish piper, first name unknown, who flourished in the latter part of the eighteenth and first part of the nineteenth centuries, must be reckoned as one of the most famous collectors of Irish music, but being listed among the notables of his profession in Chapter XIX further reference to him in this connection is unnecessary.

Edward Bunting

The selection of Edward Bunting to reduce to musical notation the tunes played at the Belfast Harp Festival in 1792 immortalized his name and gave his talents that trend which eventually led to such important results. To this circumstance, probably, he owes the preservation of his name from the oblivion which was the fate of most of his professional contemporaries.

Edward Bunting was born in the town of Armagh in 1773, his mother being the daughter of an Irish piper named Quinn, whose ancestor, Patrick Grauna O'Quinn, lost his life in the rising of 1641. His father was an English mining engineer from Derbyshire, who came to Ireland to open a coal mine in county Tyrone. The three Bunting brothers, Anthony, John and Edward, studied music at Armagh and became professional organists. Contrary to the general belief that the subject of this sketch had no previous acquaintance with traditional Irish music, it appears that young Edward mingled freely with his mother's kindred in his boyhood days, and confessed to a liking for the native music, which increased on more intimate acquaintance in later years.

So rapidly did he progress in his musical studies that he outclassed his teachers and the organists who employed him in a subordinate capacity. Teaching pupils much older than himself was not without its embarrassments, especially when they happened to resent his exercise of authority. Not only did he excel in music but in the mechanical skill to tune and repair the instruments.

Recognized as a prodigy, hero-worship came near spoiling him. Petted and pampered, he grew peevish and indolent, and like many another genius of brilliant prospects, Bunting may have disappointed the expectations of his early years, had not the event which laid the foundation of his fame occurred, when he was but a rosy-cheeked blue-eyed boy of nineteen.

For four years after the Belfast Harp Festival of 1792, Bunting tells us, he devoted himself to the work of collecting airs. Encouraged and financed by the patriotic Dr. MacDonnell and other liberal citizens of Belfast he travelled into Tyrone and Derry, visiting the centenarian Hempson at Magilligan after his return from Belfast, and spending a good part of the summer in the mountainous districts around Ballinascreen, where he obtained quite a number of admirable airs from the country people.

His principal acquisitions he claims to have collected in the province of Connacht where he was the guest of the celebrated Richard Kirwan, founder of the Royal Irish Academy. Having succeeded beyond his expectations he returned to Belfast, and in the year 1796 produced his first volume containing sixty-six native Irish airs never before published.

No sooner had this tangible result of Bunting's painstaking labor come from the press than a Dublin pirate-publisher brought out a cheap edition, undersold Bunting's half guinea volume, and robbed him of the fruits of his enterprise. And that was not all. When Tom Moore at the suggestion of W. Power, his publisher, commenced his renowned *Irish Melodies* he found Bunting's volume of garnered airs ready at hand for his purpose.

From Moore's own memoirs we learn that Robert Emmet was an eager listener, as he played over the airs from Bunting's collection at Trinity College. Wedded to Moore's inimitable verses the airs gained in popularity, but the profits from this source went to the poet and his publisher and not to Bunting.

Writing of the latter's work in 1847 Petrie says: It has now been long out of print and too generally forgotten, but the majority of its airs have been made familiar to the world by the genius of Moore, to whom it served as a treasury of melody, as may be gathered from the fact that of the sixteen beautiful airs in the first number of the *Irish Melodies,* no less than eleven were derived from that source. Even Lover did not disdain to seek inspiration in its pages for "The Angels' Whisper."

Regardless of the fact that his efforts were unrewarded by due financial return, and that others had reaped both fame and fortune as a result of his labors, Bunting continued persistently in his work of research and accumulation as opportunity offered. To him it was a labor of love to be indulged in, during the intervals of his occupation as organist and teacher.

In 1809 he published his second volume: *A General Collection of the Ancient Music of Ireland, Arranged for the Pianoforte and Voice,* and containing "An Historical and Critical Dissertation on the Harp." The author had intended to

Edward Bunting.

have Irish songs set to the 77 airs in the work, but as Patrick Lynch, a capable Irish scholar whom he had engaged to assist him in this feature of the project became involved in the political complications of the times, the plan was abandoned and English verses by Thomas Campbell, Miss Balfour and others were utilized instead.

This splendid work placed Bunting in the foremost rank of British musicians and at the head of those of his own country. Yet fame and worry was all he got out of it. Had it not been for the liberality of his Belfast subscribers its sale at one pound six shillings a volume would not have defrayed the expenses of publication. Failing to dispose of his elaborate work otherwise he ceded his interests to the publishers for a trifling sum.

A musical prodigy in childhood, though an orphan in early youth, his talents procured him adulation and an easy living. As his years advanced, his fame increased, his company was sought in the best society, and he formed the acquaintance of distinguished men of letters, as well as the most eminent in his own profession.

A confirmed diner-out, and enjoying life thus pleasantly and even luxuriously, Bunting remained unmarried until his forty-sixth year.

Many of his collected airs were as yet unpublished and it was hardly probable that he would venture to repeat his bitter experience, with a family now dependent on him for support had not the persuasion of friends and the goading of Dr. Petrie stirred his indolent spirit into renewed activity.

Although Moore, eager for additional airs suitable for his lyrics, pronounced the great collector's third volume, *The Ancient Music of Ireland,* published in 1840 "a mere mess of trash," the genial Tom made amends soon after by acknowledging his indebtedness to Bunting for his acquaintance with the beauties of native Irish music, graciously admitting that it was from his early collections his "humble labors as a poet have since then derived their sole lustre and value."

This last and in many respects his greatest work contained in addition to its hundred and a half airs and musical examples, much valuable information relating to the characteristics of Irish melody, ancient musical terms, notices of remarkable airs and sketches of famous harpers. It also included "An Essay on the Harp and Bagpipe in Ireland, by Samuel Ferguson, Esq., M. R. I. A.," and other interesting articles.

Highly appreciative notices of the work were printed in *The Atheneum* and other influential periodicals. "We close with regret Mr. Bunting's volume because we believe that with it we take leave of the genuine Music of Ireland," wrote Robert Chambers in *Chambers Edinburgh Journal.* "It must not be regarded as a musical publication alone, but as a National Work of the deepest antiquarian and historical interests." Dr. Petrie proclaimed it, "A great and truly national work of which Ireland may feel truly proud. To its venerable editor Ireland owes a deep feeling of gratitude, as the zealous and enthusiastic collector and preserver of her music in all its characteristic beauty, for though our national poet Moore, has contributed by the peculiar charm of his verses, to extend the fame of our music over the civilized world, it should never be forgotten that it is to Bunting the merit is due of having originally rescued our national music from obscurity."

Bunting did not long survive his final triumph, but his last years were soothed by the consolation that his life-work was duly appreciated. He died suddenly while preparing to retire on the evening of December 21, 1843, at the scriptural age of three score and ten.

Farquhar Graham states in the Introduction to *Surenne's Songs of Ireland* that Bunting "died at Belfast and was interred in the cemetery of Mount Jerome." Hence our error in *Irish Folk Music: A Fascinating Hobby*.

The great collector died in Dublin, to which he removed in 1819 at the time of his marriage. Our esteemed friend, Prof. P. J. Griffith of the Leinster School of Music who reminded us of our error, obligingly sent us a drawing of the granite monument in the Dublin General Cemetery, Mount Jerome, on which the following is inscribed:

Sacred
to the memory of
Edward Bunting,
who died 21st December, 1843,
aged 70;
Mary Anne Bunting,
his wife,
who died 27th May, 1863,
and their only son,
Anthony Bunting,
who died 10th July, 1849,
aged 29.

R. M. LEVEY

Of the host of Irish musicians whose talents have immortalized their names during the last century, the subject of this brief biography is one of the few who paid more than casual attention to the native dance music.

R. M. Levey, whose true name was Richard Michael O'Shaughnessy, was born at Dublin in 1811 and died there in 1899. Displaying a decided predilection for music in boyhood days, he served an apprenticeship to James Barton from 1821 to 1826, after which he entered the Theater Royal Orchestra, being then but fifteen years old. A few years later he became musical director.

As a violinist of unusual gifts he was well known at the Crystal Palace Handel Festivals, and other musical events in London, and the incident which led to his change of name occurred on the occasion of his first visit to the metropolis. When asked, his name by the official in charge of enrollment, he promptly replied "Richard Michael O'Shaughnessy." "O'whatnessy?" echoed the astonished official. "O'Shaughnessy," repeated the bewildered violinist. "My friend," volunteered his questioner, "you can never hope to make a success in professional life with an unpronounceable name like that. By the way what was your mother's maiden name?" When told it was Leavy, the official wrote down Levey, and announced to the abashed musician, "Hereafter you will be known as R. M. Levey in this establishment." And true enough it is by that Hebraic cognomen he is known in musical history.

Wallace and Balfe were among his most intimate friends and he toured Ireland in 1839 with the latter's opera company. In all, Levey composed fifty overtures and arranged the music for forty-four pantomimes, and he often alluded with pardonable pride to Sir Robert Stewart, and Sir Charles Villiers Stanford, as his pupils. He was also professor of the violin at the Royal Irish Academy of Music, of which he was one of the founders.

His oldest son and namesake, born in 1833, became a violinist of renown and won distinction at concerts in Paris and later in London where he was known

as "Paganini Redivivus." Another son, William Charles Levey, no less talented, also won recognition in Paris, and was subsequently conductor at Drury Lane and Covent Garden theaters.

With all his accummulated honors this famous Irish musician did not disdain the simple folk music of his ancestors. On the contrary all through life he cherished a love for the unpretentious melodies of the Green Isle, which he noted down from the playing of traditional fiddlers and fluters in Dublin and London. In the latter city he published in 1858, and 1873, two unclassified collections of *The Dance Music of Ireland,* each containing one hundred tunes. Only in one instance, he tells us in a footnote, did he alter in the slightest degree the tunes which he obtained as above stated. Levey's was the first work ever printed devoted to Irish dance music exclusively.

George Petrie, L. L. D

One of the most learned and versatile of the distinguished sons of Erin was the amiable George Petrie—artist, archaeologist, journalist and musician. Born at Dublin in 1789, he was the son of James Petrie, also a native of the Irish capital but of Scotch ancestry. When ten years old George entered the school of Mr. White at which Sheridan, Moore, and several others of his famous countrymen were educated. In due time he studied art under his father who was a talented portrait painter, among the subjects of his brush being Lord Edward Fitzgerald, Philpot Curran and Robert Emmet. The son soon became noted for his skill in water colors, and was in much demand in illustrating works on travel and topography, because his drawings were peculiarly imbued with truthfulness and possessed that indescribable charm which has been styled feeling. It was while engaged in this congenial pursuit that he acquired the vast fund of antiquarian information which enabled him to accomplish more in the interest of Irish archaeology than had been done by a single individual before or since.

He became librarian of the Royal Irish Academy in 1830, was associate editor of the *Dublin Penny Journal* in 1832, founded the *Irish Penny Journal* in 1840, and was the projector of the museum of said academy for which he collected over 400 ancient Mss., among them being the original manuscript Annals of the Four Masters.

From 1833 to 1846 Petrie was actively engaged in the Ordnance Survey of Ireland, had charge of its historical and antiquarian department, and numbered among his staff Prof. Eugene O'Curry and Dr. John O'Donovan, the translator of the Annals before mentioned.

The most notable of Petrie's numerous antiquarian writings was *The Ecclesiastical Architecture of Ireland, Anterior to the Anglo-Norman Invasion, Comprising an Essay on the Origin and Uses of the Round Towers of Ireland.* The Essay on the Round Towers, originally written in 1833, won the gold medal and prize of fifty pounds offered by the Royal Irish Academy for the best essay on the subject.

Not less noteworthy were Dr. Petrie's patriotic services in another field of endeavor. From his seventeenth to his seventieth year he was an assiduous collector of Irish Folk Music. During his sketching raids his mind was not altogether absorbed by the beauties and romance of the scenes through which he passed. He possessed a perfect ear and was proficient on more than one instrument. Wherever he went through the country and heard an ancient Irish tune that was new to him he carefully noted it down, even sometimes on a sketch book page. In this manner was formed his singularly interesting and invaluable collection of ancient Irish airs, the great majority of which but for his instinctive care would have been buried in oblivion; the old inhabitants of the districts where he found them in use, being long since dead, and the younger generations having emigrated or dispersed. The first step in each locality visited was to make inquiry concerning people who could sing or play music, or even whistle tunes. So gentle and unassuming was Dr. Petrie and so charming his personality that he found no difficulty in gaining the confidence of the people who met him by appointment in some commodious kitchen generally, when he noted down such tunes as caught his fancy.

Not a few of his melodic treasures were obtained from ballad singers. Invariably gifted with fine voices they attracted crowds at every fair and market in those days, and contributed more than any other influence to keep alive and in circulation the simple melodies of the peasantry.

Manuscript collections of music that otherwise might have never gained the light of publicity proved a prolific source of pleasure and profit to Petrie, such as those compiled by Mr. Patrick O'Neill of Kilkenny in 1785, and the amiable *sagart,* Father M. Walsh, P. P. at Iveragh, County Kerry, who, is is said, was the original of A. P. Graves' "Father O'Flynn."

How or when the subject of this sketch learned to play the fiddle and the flageolet, or by whom taught does not appear to be a matter of record, but we know that he was proficient on both, and that he rendered the native music enchantingly on the former instrument, but played only to a sympathetic audience. Furthermore he had little patience with the affectation of the would-be "quality" of the provinces who favored quadrilles and gallopes instead of the native dances. "But what a monstrosity—to dance quadrilles in Galway!" he exclaims. "Dance indeed, no but a drowsy walk and a look as if they were going to their grandmothers' funerals. Fair Galwegians—for assuredly you are fair—put aside the sickly affectation of refinement which is equally inconsistent with your natural excitability and with the healthy atmospheric influences by which you are surrounded. Be yourselves, and let your limbs play freely and your spirits rise into joyousness to the animating strains of the Irish jig, the reel, and the country dance; so it was with your fathers and so it should be with you."

From his own pen of later years we learn that he was a passionate lover of music from childhood and of melody especially, "that divine essence without which music is but as a soulless body," and that the indulgence of this passion had been indeed one of the great if not the greatest source of happiness in his life. Though he had been at all times a devoted lover of music and more particularly of the melodies of his country, which he considered to be the most beautiful national melodies in the world, neither the study nor practice of music, had been anything more than the occasional indulgence of a pleasure during hours of relaxation from the fatigues of other studies, or the general business of life. Neither had he contemplated giving even a portion of his collection publicity in his own name.

With characteristic liberality and unselfishness, Petrie contributed a number of airs to the poet Moore which for the first time appeared in his *Irish Melodies,* and shortly afterwards he enriched Francis Holden, Mus. Doc., with a much larger number which were first printed in his father's, Smollett Holden's *Collection of Old Established Irish slow and quick Tunes* published in 1806.

Petrie's acquaintance with Bunting began shortly after the publication of the latter's second volume in 1809. Interested only in the preservation of the melodies which he had accumulated, Petrie generously offered him the use of the whole

George Petrie

collection or such portions of it as Bunting may select, provided that due acknowledgement be made of the source from which they had been obtained.

After the acceptance of over two dozen airs, of which he printed only seventeen, Bunting could not be persuaded to accept even one more lest the public might say that the greater and better portion of his third volume published in 1840 was derived from Petrie.

Enthusiast as he was, the latter kept on adding to his store year by year, cherishing the hope that some fortunate circumstances might intervene and lead to the publication of his melodic treasures eventually. And he had not hoped in vain, either, for the formation of the Society for the Preservation and Publication of the Melodies of Ireland, in December, 1851, presented the desired opportunity.

George Petrie, then sixty-two years old, was elected president. Nine of the ten vice-presidents were noblemen, and all members of the council—twenty-three in number—were men of learning and distinction.

Encouraged and sustained by this notable galaxy, Petrie set to work, and published in 1855 a handsome folio volume (containing 147 assorted numbers) entitled *The Petrie Collection of the Ancient Music of Ireland, Arranged for the Pianoforte, edited by George Petrie, LL. D., R. H. A., V. P. R. I. A., Vol. I.* Several other impressive honors and announcements on the title page are omitted, but enough has been stated to show that the movement did not fail for lack of patrons of prominence, and although the airs and dance tunes were "illustrated by a great quantity of criticism and observation" which was of absorbing interest, yet fail it did, owing to the same cause that paralyzed so many similar attempts at popularizing Irish music—public apathy and indifference.   ,

The editor's misgiving as to the success of his work on account of the decline of the "racy feeling of nationality and cultivation of mind so honorable to the Scottish character" was justified by the result. Though his treasury of melodies would fill many volumes, only one, containing less than one-tenth of them, was published, and the undertaking so full of promise at its inception was abandoned.

Although checked in his cherished aims, his ardor in adding to his collection suffered no diminution. During a visit to the Arran Islands in 1857, with a party of friends, they made their headquarters at a cottage near Kilronan. The same course was pursued as on other like occasions, and when the persons "who had music" were assembled, night after night, the work of taking down the names and words in Irish was assigned to Prof. Eugene O'Curry, while Dr. Petrie, equipped with fiddle and writing material, scored the music bar by bar as it was sung to him by each vocalist, who in rotation "took the chair," or rather the stool, in the chimney corner. When the "proofs" had been corrected Dr. Petrie would play the airs or tunes over and over again, to the astonishment and delight of his audience. Respected and lamented universally, the amiable enthusiast died in 1866, leaving four daughters but no son.

A small supplement to *The Petrie Collection of the Ancient Music of Ireland,* containing thirty-six airs, saw the light of day in 1882—sixteen years after his death—but it was not until the Irish Literary Society of London engaged Sir Charles Villiers Stanford to hunt up his almost forgotten manuscripts and take charge of their publication, in 1902 and 1905, that Dr. Petrie's dream was ultimately realized.

Patrick Weston Joyce, LL. D., M. R. I. A

Few men have been so favored with fame and fortune in their lifetime as the genius whose name heads this sketch. Gifted with literary as well as musical talent, Dr. P. W. Joyce is the author of several works of antiquarian value, notably *Irish Names of Places,* published in 1869.

Born in 1827 at Ballyorgan, among the Ballyhoura Hills, which divide south-eastern Limerick from the County of Cork, he was nurtured in an atmosphere of tradition, and, loving music, instinctively, like his prototype, Petrie, he learned to play the fiddle, and mingled with the peasantry in their pastimes and entertainments.

In the Preface to his *Ancient Irish Music* he says: "I spent all my early life in a part of the country where music and dancing were favorite amusements; and as I loved the graceful music of the people from my childhood, their songs, dance tunes, *keens* and lullabies remained on my memory almost without any effort of my own. I had, indeed, excellent opportunities, for my father's memory was richly stored with popular airs and songs, and I believe he never sang or played a tune that I did not learn. Afterwards, when I came to reside in Dublin and became acquainted with the various published collections of Irish music, I was surprised to find that a great number of my tunes were unpublished, and quite unknown outside the district or province in which they had been learned. This discovery stimulated me to write down all the airs I could recollect, and when my own memory was exhausted, I went among the peasantry during vacations for several successive years, noting down whatever I thought worthy of preserving, both music and words."

Shortly after Mr. Joyce went to reside in Dublin, in the early bloom of manhood, a copy of the prospectus of the Society for the Preservation and Publication of the Melodies of Ireland fell into his hands. Becoming interested in the project, he ventured to call on Dr. Petrie, the president of the organization. The timidity, which at first almost unnerved the young man, soon vanished on finding that the learned antiquary was a charming, kindly and unpretentious old gentleman whose gentle voice and manners soon made him feel quite at ease. Dr. Petrie was evidently surprised at the extent of his caller's repertory of strange tunes, and, finding that the young musical enthusiast could write music, he requested him to jot down a few dozen of his best.

"With a little book filled with airs, all from memory, I returned at the end of a week." Dr. Joyce writes: "The good doctor looked at the MS. and fell upon it much as a gold miner might fall upon a great and unexpected nugget. And so commenced my collection of Irish airs, at first entirely from memory, all of which I handed over to Dr. Petrie, book after book, according as each was filled. And this continued for several years."

Dr. Petrie acknowledges his indebtedness to "Mr. Joyce" all through his collections, but as the death of the venerable collector in 1866 put an end to any lingering hope that he would bring out a second volume of *The Petrie Collection of the Ancient Music of Ireland,* Dr. Joyce wisely undertook to publish his collection himself.

Accordingly, in 1873 there came from the press *Ancient Irish Music: Comprising One Hundred Irish Airs Hitherto Unpublished, Many of the Old Popular Songs, and Several New Songs:* Collected and Edited by P. W. Joyce, LL. D., M. R. I. A. The descriptive text accompanying each number is by no means the least interesting part of the volume. This was followed in 1888 by *Irish Music and Song: A Collection of Songs in the Irish Language, Set to Music.*

A far more pretentious work than either is *Old Irish Folk Music and Songs: A Collection of 842 Irish Airs and Songs Hitherto Unpublished*—Edited with

Annotations for The Royal Society of Antiquaries of Ireland, by P. W. Joyce, LL. D., M. R. I. A., President of this Society.

This very interesting work is made up of three separate collections, the largest and best, consisting of 429 numbers, being from Dr. Joyce himself. The Forde MSS., compiled in the second quarter of the nineteenth century by William Forde, a distinguished Cork musician who edited the *Encyclopedia of Melody,* published before 1850 in London, yielded 256 more; while the Pigot MS. collection, assembled by John Edward Pigot, of Dublin, M. R. I. A. and honorary secretary to the "Society for the Preservation and Publication of the Melodies of Ireland," contained 157 selections.

Still hale and hearty in his eighty-sixth year, and devoted to the enjoyment of his cherished hobby, Dr. Joyce is likely to be heard from again in the world of music before be becomes a nonogenarian or joins the "heavenly choir."

CHAPTER XV

THE IRISH PIPER IN IRISH LIFE

I will take my pipes and go now, for the bees upon the hill
  Are singing of the summer that is coming from the stars.
I will take my pipes and go now, for the little mountain rill
  Is pleading with the bagpipes in tender, crooning bars.

I will go o'er the hills and valleys, and through fields of ripening rye,
  And the linnet and the throstle and the bittern in the sedge
Will hush their throats and listen while the piper passes by,
  On the great long road of silver that ends at the world's edge.

I will take my pipes and go now, for the sand-flower on the dunes
  Is a-weary of the sobbing of the big white sea,
And is asking for the piper, with his basket full of tunes,
  To play the merry lilting that sets all hearts free.

I will take my pipes and go now, and God go with you all,
  And keep all sorrow from you, and the dark heart's load.
I will take my pipes and go now, for I hear the summer call,
  And you'll hear the pipes a-singing as I pass along the road.
                     —*Donn Byrne.*

In the language of Mrs. S. C. Hall, who wrote of Irish life and character in the second quarter of the nineteenth century, the pipers were at one period the great originals of Ireland. The race of minstrels was even then gradually departing, or at least sobering down into the ranks of ordinary mortals; but there was a time, as described in previous chapters, when the piper stood out prominently upon any canvas that pictured Irish life.

Closely as the harp and the music of its strings are associated with the history of Hibernia in happier days, no class of minstrels was in such perfect accord with popular sentiment, or was so intertwined with tradition, story, legend and poetic fancy as the pipers.

Not only were they an essential element in every phase of life's activities, but they were, according to common belief, not infrequently kidnapped by the fairies, so fascinating was their music, and forced to entertain their captors at their subterranean festivities.

Whether in the land of the living or the realm of shades, a halo seems to encircle the head of the piper in the mysticism of the Irish mind. To those who still find pleasure in relaxation from the materialism of the present to indulge in the contemplation of the past, the stories comprising Chapter XXXI, and the experiences of Turlogh McSweeney, "The Donegal Piper," in Chapter XXII, will no doubt prove of more than ordinary interest.

THE IRISH PIPER

A quotation from Robertson's "Fairy Pipers" may serve to illustrate one feature of those quaint fancies.

"Weary is the way, and I'm a weary man tonight—
    Ah, the fairy pipers that awoke me long ago,
When the mists began to shiver at the coming of the light,
    And the wind was in the heather, soft and low!

"The grey hills flushed to purple, and the east was like a rose;
    They called me to the long road with piping shrill and clear;
Rest and rust and dull content, the mortal never knows
    Who may once the fairy pipers chance to hear.

"Over hill and valley, he must follow till he fall;
    Jeweled gossamers at dawn that shine about his feet,
Love, and wealth, and honor—he must break and leave them all
    When the fairy music calls him, shrill and sweet.

"Weary is the way, and I'm a weary man tonight—
    Ah, the fairy pipers that awoke me long ago,
Still they're calling as they called me when my heart and foot
        were light,
    And the wind was in the heather, soft and low."

After the siege of Limerick, the *Piob Mor,* or Warpipe, as it is now termed, shared in Ireland's fallen fortunes, and its use practically terminated about the middle of the eighteenth century. Historically, it is unheard of after the battle of Fontenoy, in 1745—a fitting finish for an instrument so renowned in association with deeds of Irish bravery.

The Union pipes, of milder tone and enlarged compass, invented and developed at least a score of years earlier, won immediate recognition, and before the end of the century, performers on the improved Irish instrument vied with the harpers in fame and popularity. But it must be borne in mind that the addition of regulators, on which concords could be produced, contributed not a little to its charm. From its earliest development, men of wealth and title took to playing the pipes, and it was not considered beneath the dignity of the clergy even to become performers on the fascinating, soft-toned instrument, the music of which,

"Like the whistling of birds,
    Like the humming of bees,
Like the sigh of the south wind
    Through the crest of the trees,"

soothed the soul while it entranced the mind. Household pipers became the vogue as the harp declined, and a capable performer was never at a loss for an engagement at castle, or hall, in the homes of the gentry, with a stipend of fifty pounds a year, and a "horse and saddle" at his pleasure. And when we come to contemplate the patronage and perquisites which pipers enjoyed generations ago, as compared with their oppression and neglect in more recent times, their former number and celebrity ceases to excite our astonishment.

In one of his stories Shelton Mackenzie says: "One set of pipes is worth a dozen fiddles, for it can 'take the shine out of them all.'" But then these same pipes can do more than make a noise. The warrior boldest in the field is gentlest at the feet of his lady love; and so the Irish pipes, which can sound a strain

almost as loud as a trumpet-call, can also breathe forth a tide of gushing melody—
sweet, soft, and low as the first whisper of mutual love. You have never felt
the eloquent expression of Irish music if you have not heard it from the Irish
pipes."

In this connection it may not be out of place to mention that after trying
every other instrument with a view to imitate the human voice, Kempelen, the
Austrian professor, found that the tones of the Irish chanter were the most in
accord with it. Yet, though soft, pleasing and haunting as the music of the
instrument may be, the truth is that the pipes are delicious or abominable just
according to the skill of the hand that rules them; but when skilfully manipulated they are what John Augustus O'Shea termed them, "a hive of honeyed
sounds." Even the English writer, Mrs. Lilly Grove, in her great work on
Dancing, concedes that "the modern Irish bagpipe has the sweetest sound of all
instruments of this description."

Although less renowned as minstrels than the harpers, the Union pipers
came closer to the hearts of the bulk of the people. The professional or traveling
pipers were the news carriers of their times, and their advent was an event of
no small importance in any community. They were everywhere hospitably
received and treated with the utmost cordiality wherever they went, and besides
the cheering notes of their "merry pipes so gaily O," there were many other
considerations which added fervor to their welcome. A paraphrase on Theo.
Garrison's "Welcome Guest" aptly expresses our conception of the Irish hospitality
to which the piper was ever welcome:

> Oh! here's the open door for you,
> *Ceud mile failthe go deo* for you,
> A cheering cup and more for you
>   As long as you want to stay;
> For love of that gay voice of yours—
> That calling to rejoice of yours—
> The very sun comes in with you
>   And dances when you play.

In a sense, the wandering piper or minstrel was a combination of mail service,
news agency and general entertainer; for whoever heard of a piper who was
not a repository of song and story, while his wit, sharpened by contact with the
world, was a never failing source of delight to his audience, old or young.
Neither were pipers illiterate, as a class, when blest with sight, for among them,
then as now, were men of uncommon attainments. A letter from one about a
century ago, requesting payment for his professional services, is a quaint specimen
of this acquired polish:

> MADAM: The Bearer hereof is the piper that played for your
> Lordable family at the Terrace on the twelfth instant, and I am
> referred to your Honor for my hire. Your Ladyship's pardon for
> my boldness would be almost a sufficient compensation for my labor.
>   PATRICK WALSH.

At a wedding in those times, Crofton Croker tells us, the best apartment
was reserved for the bride and bridegroom, the priest, the piper, and the more
opulent and respectable guests, such as the landlord and his family and the

neighboring gentry. The second apartment was appropriated for the neighbors in general, and the third, or an outhouse, for less welcome guests. After the ceremony two collections were taken, one for the priest and the second for the piper; but the succeeding festivities seldom ended before daylight in the morning.

The following, from Mrs. Hall's description of an Irish wedding nearly a generation later, further illumines the pages of Ireland's social history: "The piper and fiddler, who during dinner had been playing some of the more slow and plaintive of the national airs, now strike up, and the dance immediately commences. First single parties dance reels, jigs and doubles; country dances then succeeded, in which, as in the single dances, priest and laic, old and young, rich and poor, the master and his maid, the landlord and his tenant's daughter, as well as the landlord's daughter and his tenant's son, all join together without distinction."

Just as the custom is generally preserved among the Scottish nobility of today, the Irish gentlemen of consequence in bygone days had their pipers to entertain them at mealtimes. In a letter dated September 20, 1775, describing his visit to "Mr. Macarty of Springhill," Tipperary, Rev. Dr. Campbell in his *Philosophical Survey of the South of Ireland,* says: "Here we were at meals, even on Sunday, regaled with the bagpipe, which to my uncultivated ear is not an instrument so unpleasant as the lovers of Italian music represent it." The reverend author wrote, in the days of the renowned "Piper" Jackson, when Union pipers were supplanting the harpers in the homes of the Irish aristocracy. The zenith of their fame was reached a generation later, after which the vogue of the piper began to decline.

Patron days, or festivals in commemoration of the days on which the early churches or sanctified places, such as fountains or wells, were dedicated to their respective saints, were observed quite generally down to the early years of the nineteenth century. Their original religious character, it appears, gradually degenerated into frivolities and abuses, which led to their suppression. Almost every tent or booth in which food and refreshments were for sale had its piper, for dancing and diversion succeeded the performance of rounds or other observances. So busily engaged were the musicians on those occasions, that in a painting by Grogan, a native artist, the piper is represented as drinking from a jug of porter, held to his lips by a friend, while he continued the music uninterruptedly for the dancers in front of him.

It is needless to expatiate on the demoralizing influence of the famine years— from 1846 to 1849—on Irish music and minstrelsy. That is self-evident. The decline of pipe music, however, had already set in. Brass bands, nearly as numerous as the branches of the temperance societies instituted as a result of Father Mathews' crusade, drove the Union piper and fiddler out of fashion, and dancing, of course, shared the same fate, although not long before every public house had its piper or fiddler, who kept traditional music in promiscuous circulation.

Changed conditions, lack of patronage, and other well-understood causes, forced this class of minstrels, many of them blind, to take to the highways for support—a form of mendicancy which brought their once honored calling into disrepute. The more robust and adventurous made their way beyond their native shores, to find life more enjoyable in Scotland, England and America, and even in distant New Zealand and Australia. The extent to which they had migrated may be judged from the fact that while on a tour of Scotland in early manhood, the famous Turlogh McSweeney, "The Donegal Piper," found not less than sixteen of his profession in one Edinburgh lodging-house. We must not lose sight of the fact, however, that Irish pipers as well as harpers had been passing into Scotland from time immemorial and leaving their impress on the music of our kinsmen beyond the North Channel.

The capricious exercise of authority which forced the discontinuance of the time-honored crossroads and farmstead dances gave the death blow to Irish minstrelsy and music, and made Ireland the anomaly among nations—a land without pleasures or pastimes.

"There is no mirth or laughter to be heard any more in the country," pathetically remarked a peasant to Lady Wilde in 1880; "the spirit is gone from the people, and all the old fun is frozen."

Even though the same influences which led to such deplorable results are now, with belated wisdom, actively aiding in the Irish Revival, who that cherishes a love for the traditions and institutions of his race can contemplate with equanimity the spectacle of a world-wide struggle to foster and preserve the historic features and social customs associated with their motherland as a distinct nationality?

In speaking for himself the brilliant John Augustus O'Shea but voices the sentiments of the multitude: "I am afraid that the old Irish piper, like the old Irish wolf dog, is dying out; but I had the luck to hear one in Cork, nevertheless. It was in a by-street he humored the bellows of Æolian winds, fingered the keys, and worked lullabying drones wrapped in the charm he evoked, as if he veritably loved it. I listened to him until I was wet through with rain, but Apollo is god of medicine as of music, and he did not permit a devotee of the latter to stand in need of the former. Alas! that the Irish piper such as he who erst roused the blood of warriors at Donnybrook, coaxed the birds off the bushes at courting season in the glen of Aherlow, and soothed the seagulls from an eyrie in the cliffs of Moher—alas! that he should be let die out. I would rather hearken to one Irish piper playing 'The Fox Chase' than fifteen politicians bellowing on ancient themes political. To his instrument—hive of honeyed sounds—the biniou of Brittany, the pipe of Pan, or of Calabrian pifferari, the shrill bag of reedy quavers of the Scottish Highlander, or Algerian Turco, are as naught. By the soul of Conor McNessa, I conjure Irishmen to respect and preserve the piper, the walking treasury of the spirit of our bardic prime, the descendant of those who wore the robe of honor of six colors, and the gold circlet on their brows, and sat at the boards of princes."

Though many and earnest have been the appeals to Irishmen to respect and cherish the piper and his music, by such distinguished worthies as O'Curry and O'Shea and the leaders of the Irish Revival movement, in all candor we must confess that the situation painfully reminds us of Father Mullen's wail for "The Celtic Tongue":

> " 'Tis fading, O, 'tis fading! like the leaves upon the trees!
> In murmuring tone 'tis dying like the wail upon the breeze;
> 'Tis swiftly disappearing, as footprints on the shore
> Where the Barrow, and the Erne, and Lough Swilly's waters roar."

Passing over many of the various phases of Irish life in which the pipers were by no means inconspicuous figures, we cannot refrain from adverting to the sad and all too common failings incidental to their mode of life. The wandering Irish piper should be more than mortal to resist the temptations which bestrew his path. At christenings, weddings, and other festivities, conviviality is the order of the day. Where so likely for music to attract an audience as in the vicinity of a tavern or public house? Then the admirers of minstrelsy, in an outburst of feeling which they mistake for generosity or friendship, ply the musician with liquor, to his ruin, instead of contributing to his prosperity in the coin of the realm. This pitiable and perverted conception of liberality and hospitality has long prevailed in Ireland, and still continues to blight the prospects of brilliant promise in the lives of others besides pipers and fiddlers.

Much as we may deplore the minstrel's cardinal failing, as we do the conditions which give rise to it, we feel assured that all who cherish a sincere regard for the traditions of Irish minstrelsy and music will view this frailty more in the light of pity than prejudice. For, after all, the plaintive, haunting, dulcet tones of the real Irish national instrument—the Union pipes—like the poetry of Robert Burns, James Clarence Mangan, and Edgar Allan Poe, is not the less appreciated because of their predilection to worship at the shrine of Bacchus.

In compiling the following sketches of famous pipers, no source of possible information has been overlooked, and all available data have been interwoven, regardless of the source. As a matter of expediency, distinctive classification has been attempted chiefly for the purpose of bringing out in stronger relief the fact that the bagpipe had its votaries in all walks of Irish life. To be a performer on the Union pipes involved no loss of social prestige until the degenerate days succeeding the famine.

The piper was a character whom his countrymen loved and respected, and in every instance treated with the kindness and cordiality due to a relative, Carleton says. Indeed, the musicians of Ireland are as harmless and inoffensive a class of persons as ever existed, and there can be no greater proof of this than the very striking fact that in the criminal statistics of the country the name of an Irish piper or fiddler has scarcely if ever been known to appear.

CHAPTER XVI

FAMOUS BAGPIPE MAKERS

THE inordinate passion which the Irish have in all ages displayed for music must have eventually produced an eager pursuit of such means as would tend to its gratification. Musical instrument makers were to be found in many of the smallest towns of Ireland, and generally among men of the lowest professions, Lady Morgan tells us in her *Patriotic Sketches,* published in 1807.

In this work she mentions the case of a poor hedge carpenter in the town of Strabane, County Tyrone, who obtained some degree of excellence in making violins and flutes, built a small organ, and was frequently called in by the most respectable families in the neighborhood to tune or mend pianofortes, harpsichords, and other instruments.

Another instance was that of a young Connachtman then residing in Dublin, who, though but a common carpenter, made a small piano on which he performed, self-taught in theory of music as in the construction of a musical instrument.

"A remarkably fine-toned organ with six stops," she continues, "has been lately placed in the Roman Catholic chapel at Mullingar, built by a poor wheelwright, a native of the town. He had commenced as a bagpipe maker a few years before, without any previous instruction, and shortly after completed a good pianoforte."

The genius to whom Lady Morgan, then Miss Sydney Owenson, refers, was

TIMOTHY KENNA

Originally a maker of household spinning-wheels, and a mechanic of conspicuous excellence, he turned his attention to the making of Union pipes, and became the most famous in that line in Ireland, not alone in his day, but of all time, until Michael Egan, of Liverpool, won recognition and renown in the early forties of the nineteenth century.

Kenna flourished between 1768 and 1794, but the date on which he transferred his business to Dublin cannot be stated.

Judging by the splendid instrument pictured in Grattan Flood's *Story of the Bagpipe* which Kenna made in 1770 for John MacDonnell, the development of the Union pipes was far advanced. This instrument, now the property of Lord MacDonnell, late Under-Secretary for Ireland, may be seen at the Dublin Museum, where another set of Kenna's make is also on exhibition. And, by the way, it may interest the reader to know that John S. Wayland, founder and secretary of the Cork Pipers' Club, rejoices in the possession of a set of Union pipes made by Kenna in 1783, which had passed through the hands of five previous owners.

There having been two makers of bagpipes in Dublin with this surname (probably father and son), the subject of this sketch is generally referred to as "the elder Kenna."

THOMAS KENNA

"The younger Kenna" flourished in the first quarter of the nineteenth century, and by all accounts he ably sustained the family reputation. He kept shop at

No. 1 Essex Quay, Dublin. Mysterious and secretive, "the younger Kenna" was a "close corporation," and would not allow anyone, idler or stroller, about his place to see him take off a single shaving. A young farmer named Boylan, possessing remarkable mechanical skill, came one day into Kenna's shop with a chanter and asked him to fit a reed to it, hoping to gain a little knowledge by seeing him work. Kenna, who always maintained a respectable appearance— he wore top boots, if you please—put on his hat and coat, left the shop at once, locked the door, and, turning to Boylan, said: "Come at this hour tomorrow, sir, and your chanter will be ready." And so it was, but Boylan was no wiser.

MAURICE COYNE

This well-known maker of Union pipes was one of four brothers, respectable young farmers, who lived in the parish of Carbury, County Kildare, a few miles from the town of Edenderry. Maurice took to "playing the pipes" as a youth, migrated to Dublin, and acquired the tools and business of the "younger Kenna" on the latter's death. Coyne's shop was at No. 41 James Street, Dublin.

Instruments of Coyne's make, of which many are yet in existence, display neat workmanship and, though lacking in volume, are pure and sweet in tone.

THE MOLONEY BROTHERS

The discovery that the magnificent set of Union pipes of peculiar design picked up by Prof. Denis O'Leary in Clare in 1906 was manufactured by the Moloney brothers—Thomas and Andrew—at Kilrush, in that county, presumably solves a puzzling problem.

The trombone slide, which is a conspicuous feature of the instrument, was also a prominent characteristic of the splendid Irish pipes seen in the pictures of Captain Kelly and William Murphy in this volume. As neither of the noted pipemakers—Kenna, Coyne, Harrington, or Egan—turned out instruments of that type, there is nothing inconsistent in attributing their manufacture to the Moloneys.

It was while acting as Gaelic League organizer in 1906 that Professor O'Leary became acquainted with a Mr. Nolan, of Knockerra, near Kilrush, a good amateur piper and an enthusiast on the instrument, though then well advanced in years. In early life he knew intimately Thomas and Andrew Moloney of the same town-land, who made on the order of Mr. Vandaleur, a local landlord, what is claimed to be the most elaborate set of bagpipes in existence. Thomas was a blacksmith and Andrew was a carpenter, but both were great performers on the Union pipes. According to Mr. Nolan's story, they did not manufacture many sets of pipes, but they were always most obliging towards the piping fraternity in repairing their instruments.

It may be objected that mechanics of their class would be incapable of turning out such fine technical work, but in view of the fact that Egan, the famous harp-maker of Dublin, was originally a blacksmith, and that the elder Kenna was by trade a wheelwright, there appear to be no just grounds to question the authenticity of the Moloney claims.

When seen by the present writer at Mr. Rowsome's shop, 18 Armstrong Street, Harold's Cross, Dublin, in 1906, Professor O'Leary's treasure was disjointed and apparently long out of use, but it seems Mr. Rowsome experienced no difficulty in putting it in order. It was a massive ebony instrument, the chanter being eighteen inches in length, and, according to its present owner, "of exquisite sweetness and fullness, much superior to an Egan or Harrington chanter." It has five regulators, with twenty-four keys, and the tones of both basses resemble those of an organ. There are two splendid drones. The tubing and keys are of pure silver and artistically turned out, and the various pipes are tipped with ivory. Experts estimate the original cost at one hundred pounds, or five hundred dollars. The date of their manufacture is not known, except that it was early in the nineteenth century, when the makers were in good circumstances. As the young man for whom the instrument was intended met with an injury, it remained on their hands, unsalable because of its expensiveness.

The disastrous famine years ruined the Moloneys and they were obliged to part with their masterpiece for a trifling sum. The purchaser, Mr. O'Carroll, of Freagh, near Miltown-Malbay, was a farmer of independent means, and an excellent performer on the Union pipes. People used to come from far and near to hear him play and to examine the wonderful instrument. He died about the year 1890, and as none of his family could manipulate this "hive of honeyed sounds," it remained silent as a mummy until Mr. Rowsome restored its voice as before stated.

JOHN EGAN, OF DUBLIN

Many besides the writer were under the impression that John Egan, the famous Dublin harpmaker, who flourished in the early part of the nineteenth century, was also a bagpipe maker.

Speaking of his prominence in his profession, Miss Owenson, afterwards Lady Morgan, says in her *Patriotic Sketches:* "By an invention of which he has all the merit, he has so simplified the machinery that the springs hitherto found necessary to return the pedals he has laid aside, which renders the harp less liable to get out of order, much easier to repair, and enables the ingenious inventor to sell a pedal harp nearly one-half cheaper than it could be imported."

What more reasonable to suppose than that John Egan was the maker also of the many fine sets of Union pipes on the stocks of which the name "Egan" is found engraved? Few except old-time pipers were aware that the expert piper and mechanic who made those splendid instruments was Michael Egan, of Liverpool, and not John Egan, of Dublin.

This explanation, however, offers no solution of another Egan problem. On the silver ferrule of the stock of Lord Edward Fitzgerald's pipes in the Dublin Museum there is engraved the owner's name, a coat of arms, and the date, "1768. Made by Egan, Dublin."

Now the question arises, who was this Egan? The writer acknowledges his indebtedness to Grattan Flood for the information that John Egan's father made bagpipes, although Irish literature is silent on that score.

MR. HARRINGTON

That an able pipemaker of that name once turned out fine instruments in the city of Cork is beyond question, for the name is alluded to by various authorities in that connection. The indefatigable John S. Wayland was unsuccessful in adding to our meagre knowledge. Some light has dawned on us through the medium of John O'Neill, Esq., J. P., of Sarsfield Court, Glanmire, who knew him in his boyhood days.

Harrington, whose first name Mr. O'Neill failed to remember, was the son of a small farmer, but he couldn't be kept away from music. He went to the city and lived on Hanover Street, where our informant often saw him making pipes. "Over fifty years ago," says Mr. O'Neill, "the first exhibition in Cork was held. Harrington made a set of Irish pipes for the occasion. The keys and ferrules were of silver, and he sold them at the exhibition for fifty pounds. At the Munster Feis at Cork, about eight years ago, I complimented one of the pipers, named Cash, from the county of Wicklow, on the beauty of his pipes. He drew my attention to the words, 'Harrington, Cork,' branded on every stick of them. I have an old set of Harrington's make left me by a piper named John O'Neill."

Discouraged by the direful condition of affairs resulting from the famine, Harrington emigrated to America and all trace of him was lost.

THOMAS FLANAGAN

A bagpipe maker of the above name, we are informed by Grattan Flood, occupied the premises at No. 35 Broad Lane, in the city of Cork, about the year 1820, but no further information concerning him is available.

MICHAEL EGAN

Among bagpipe makers none holds higher rank than the subject of this sketch. His name engraved on the stock of an instrument was a synonym for purity of tone and a guarantee of first-class workmanship since early in the nineteenth century.

Exact dates are unascertainable at this late day, but some leading facts in the life of this fine musician and excellent mechanic can be stated with certainty. He belonged to the town of Glenamaddy, barony of Ballymoe, County Galway, according to Mr. Burke, who associated with him in New York City. John Cummings, of San Francisco, who enjoyed his acquaintance at Liverpool away back in the fifties, says Egan hailed from the village of Cultymaugh, in the County Mayo. How he came to be a piper and pipemaker, or why he chose Liverpool instead of Dublin for his place of business, we have never learned. It goes to show, however, that Irish pipers existed in considerable numbers in England around the middle of the nineteenth century.

The famous Flannery came to America in the year 1844, or perhaps a year later. The great set of pipes which added to his fame no less than to that of Egan, who made them, he brought across the Atlantic with him. From this date we are justified in assuming that Egan had been established in business at Liverpool probably as far back as 1830, and perhaps earlier.

As stated in the sketch of John Coughlan, the so-called Australian piper, he came to America on the recommendation of the elder Coughlan, with whom he lived for some time. He kept a workshop on Forty-second Street, between Ninth and Tenth Avenues, New York, until his death, which occurred in 1860 or 1861.

The splendid set of pipes which Charles Ferguson pretended was presented to him on the orders of Queen Victoria was made by Mr. Egan in his shop in New York City during Ferguson's visit to America.

Then no more than now was bagpipe-making and repairing a lucrative business, it seems, for notwithstanding his skill and popularity, Egan died on the threshold of poverty, like that other celebrated piper and pipemaker, "Billy" Taylor, of Philadelphia. A benefit party was gotten up for him by his friends in his last illness, and Mr. Burke tells us he remained with him to the last minute.

MICHAEL MANNION

In discussing the merits of the instrument which he made for Patrick Flannery, Mr. Egan lets us into the knowledge that there was another pipemaker in Liverpool besides himself, namely, Michael Mannion.

The following is his language: "Until I made Flannery's pipes there was no more thought of my pipemaking than there was of Michael Mannion's, of Liverpool, or of Maurice Coyne's, of Dublin."

EDWARD WHITE

When Michael Egan died just before the Civil War, he left no successor to carry on the pipemaking business in New York, so to meet the want, "Ned" White, popularly known as the "Dandy Piper," started a pipemaking shop at Roxbury, Mass., a suburb of Boston.

Of course, reedmaking and repairs were most in demand, but White turned out quite a number of new sets during his time, of which it can be said that the tones of his drones, if equaled, were never surpassed by those of any pipemaker known to Americans.

Born at Loughrea, County Galway, he came to the United States about the middle of the nineteenth century and settled in Boston. During the years of the Civil War, 1861 to 1865, he was in the zenith of his fame, and conducted a dance hall at Roxbury. Prosperity was loudly proclaimed by his fashionable wardrobe, and such was his pride in his apparel that he never appeared in public uncrowned with a tall silk hat. Hence his nickname, "The Dandy Piper."

"Patsy" Touhey, who knew him well in his old age, says he was "a nice player," and the fact that John Coughlan, the best piper in Australia in after years, was sent by his father from New York to finish his studies under White, speaks well for his reputation when in his prime.

MICHAEL CAROLAN

For many years there lived at No. 842 Greenwich Street, New York City, a good performer on the Union pipes, named Michael Carolan. A native of the County Louth, he was born about the year 1810, and learned the art of pipemaking in his youth. His execution was of the old close-fingering or staccato style, and his training must have been very thorough, for he could play off the printed page with the greatest facility. Long past his eightieth milestone, he died in 1894, in comparative obscurity.

WILLIAM TAYLOR

Equally celebrated as a piper and pipemaker in America, "Billy" Taylor, of Philadelphia, came by his talents naturally. Born about 1830 in the historic city of Drogheda, County Louth, where his father was a piper, pipemaker, and organ builder, the son grew up in the trade and continued it until the day of his death, in 1891.

When the elder Taylor came to realize that as a performer he was excelled by his son, he kept right on with the business, but he had lost all taste for playing himself thereafter.

The rapid decline of pipe music in Ireland in the third quarter of the nineteenth century determined William Taylor and his stepbrother, Charles, to emigrate to America and try their fortunes on the other side of the Atlantic. Their first stand was at New York City, in 1872, and they lived with a friend named Gaffney.

Tom Kerrigan's pipes were the first made by Taylor in America, and he turned them out in a little workshop fitted up in Kerrigan's basement, corner of Eighth Street and Avenue D. After a stay of a year or so in that locality they went to Philadelphia, opened a shop, and gradually built up a business, most of which for a time consisted in repairing old sets of pipes.

A short experience of the changed conditions prevailing in the United States convinced them that the mild tones of the ordinary Irish pipes were too puny to meet the requirements of the American stage or dance hall, being a note or more below concert pitch. Genius that he was, "Billy" Taylor experimented, remodeled and developed a compact, substantial instrument of powerful tone, which blends agreeably with violin and piano. So successful was it in meeting the popular demand that the Taylor type of Irish bagpipe has superseded the old mellow-toned parlor instrument almost altogether.

"Charley" Taylor was a fine mechanic but not a musician. When experimenting, "Billy" would play, while his brother, stationed some distance away, would pass judgment on the music. Both were kept busy, and, though money came in liberally, their Irish weakness was taken advantage of by people one would naturally expect to have better principles.

A saloonkeeper who contrived to keep track of their mail instinctively knew when a check had arrived. A gang of leeches were promptly on hand to trespass on their hospitality, and, even though the Taylor brothers did not indulge in liquors which intoxicate, the money was dissipated just the same. Oh! when will the Irish misconception of hospitality—the national curse—give way to saner customs?

Pouring over manuscript music, of which he had a large store, with a view to improving it, was "Billy's" chief diversion. Occasionally he gave instructions to aspirants, one of his pupils being "Eddie" Joyce, of Boston, who bade fair to rival his teacher when death intervened.

We are credibly informed that Highland pipes, as well as Irish pipes, were manufactured by the Taylors in Drogheda, and it is quite probable such was the case, because Highland pipes were turned out in the Philadelphia shop. Some medals were awarded the Taylors at the Centennial Exposition held in that city in 1875.

The renowned musician and mechanic died in 1901, and his brother "Charley" followed him in about a year, but as neither had ventured to embark on the stormy sea of matrimony there were neither widows nor orphans to mourn their loss. They were sincerely lamented, however, by all the Irish pipers in the land, for to them the death of the Taylors was a veritable calamity.

WILLIAM ROWSOME

Another notable instance of heredity of musical talent is to be observed in the Rowsome family. Mr. Samuel Rowsome, a "strong" farmer of Ballintore Ferns, County Wexford, was a fine performer on the Irish pipes, by all accounts. His sons, William and Thomas, of Dublin, need no introduction to the lovers of pipe music in this generation. Perpetuating the name and fame of the family, young Samuel Rowsome, son of William, has already achieved distinction as a piper.

During a brief visit to Dublin in the summer of 1906, the present writer made the acquaintance of the subject of this sketch at his residence, No. 18 Armstrong Street, Harold's Cross. Being favorably impressed by his manner and music, the visit was repeated in the company of Rev. James K. Fielding, of Chicago, next day. Of course, Mr. Rowsome "put on the pipes" and played his favorite tunes at a lively clip—a trifle too lively for a dancer, we thought. That, however, is a mere matter of opinion. But the spirit of the music was in the performer, unmistakably, for while he touched the keys of the regulators airily and in good rhythm, his eyes sparkled with animation and his whole anatomy seemed to vibrate with a buoyancy which found suitable expression in the clear tones of his chanter. The instrument on which he played and that used by Prof. Denis O'Leary, winner of the first prize at the Munster Feis a few days before, were Mr. Rowsome's own make. In finish and tone there was no cause for criticism, unless possibly a greater volume of tone might be more desirable in a large hall.

Old-time instruments in all stages of dilapidation were strewn about the shop awaiting repairs, the most remarkable being an immense set made on an original design, and which had lain unused in a Clare cabin for many years. Always an impulsive enthusiast, my reverend countryman, Father Fielding, was bound to take a shot at it with his ever-ready kodak. Yours truly was persuaded—very reluctantly, though—to hold up the framework of the wonderful pipes to the proper level, it being understood that I was to constitute no part of the target. Standing sideways and leaning backward as far as equilibrium would permit, my outstretched arms presented the derelict instrument in front of the camera. Three months later the morning mail brought me a souvenir from the reverend photographer in which my distorted likeness was more prominent in the picture than the pipes I had been holding!

Commendably circumspect in his language and reference to others in his profession and trade, during our few hours' stay, Mr. Rowsome has been almost as fortunate as "Billy" Taylor, of Philadelphia, in winning and retaining the good will of his patrons and associates. The artistic temperament, however, may be accountable for many little misunderstandings which sensitive natures magnify into grievances.

Never was there a greater surprise sprung on "the old folks at home" and the promiscuous array of pipers, fiddlers and fluters at Ballintore and vicinity than the discovery that "Willie" Rowsome had become an accomplished performer on the Union pipes. Having moved to Dublin and married there in early manhood, he was remembered by the people at home in Wexford only as a fine freehand fiddler who could also do a little at the pipes.

Blood will tell, and so heredity asserted itself in his case. When he paid a visit to the old homestead in the summer of 1911, his general execution and command of the regulators was a revelation to his family and friends. Replying to a question as to the relative merits of William and Thomas Rowsome, John, the senior brother, said: "That is largely a matter of opinion; some would rather 'Willie's' playing, others would prefer 'Tom's.' I believe 'Willie' is just as good as 'Tom,' and his style is more staccato."

In the language of an admirer who is himself a versatile musician, "his staccato style is a marvel of dexterity, as it entails an expenditure of muscular energy beyond ordinary manual effort. His tipping and tripling are admirable, and his manipulation of the regulators may well, in these degenerate days of piping, be regarded as an innovation in the art. In playing dance music, which he prefers,

WILLIAM ROWSOME

his chords, save at the end of the strain, are never sustained beyond the duration of a crochet, so that the bars of his accompaniment in reels and hornpipes are regularly filled with four crochets each, and not infrequently varying to the same number of quavers with equivalent rest intervals alternating."

Much more from the pen of a friendly biographer might be added, but believing it would be injudicious to cater unduly to personalities, especially in the case of a musician still in the land of the living, we must forego the pleasure it would afford us to be more generous with space under different circumstances.

R. L. O'MEALY

It is with anything but confidence or complacency we approach the task of writing a brief sketch of Mr. O'Mealy, who as piper and pipemaker has earned an enviable reputation in both capacities since the formation of the Gaelic League. Much that would be interesting to the general reader from our point of view, and rather complimentary than otherwise, is omitted in deference to our subject's wishes. Biography of the living is as much out of place, anyway, as *ante-mortum* epitaphs, for be it known we are all prone to view ourselves in the delusive mirror of self-esteem.

A man of education and ability, Mr. O'Mealy, now of No. 17 Edinburgh Street, Belfast, was born generations too late for his merits to be appreciated as they deserve.

A native of County Westmeath, near the birthplace of O'Carolan, where his father, also a fine piper and pipemaker, was a comfortable farmer, O'Mealy traces his ancestry to the historic O'Malleys of County Mayo, where his great grand-father, Thomas, was born. The latter, though a builder by occupation, is said to have been a noted piper and pipemaker. The trade and talent passed down from father to son through four generations; and as the flattering testimonials of the press in Belfast, Londonderry, Coleraine, Newry, Dublin, and Glasgow, proclaim the excellence of his performance on the Irish or Union pipes, we are furnished with a conspicuous instance in which talent is hereditary.

In his young days Mr. O'Mealy had the pleasure of playing at a concert with the renowned Canon Goodman, who in his opininn was the best piper in the province of Munster.

The young man's talents, though acknowledged, were unappreciated, and, failing to secure a position in any line of remunerative employment in Cork, he directed his course to Belfast, where he was more successful. Realizing that an instrument fuller in tone than the Kenna, Coyne, or Egan type of bagpipe, would be more suitable for modern conditions, he has followed Taylor's example in raising the tone to concert pitch, and increasing its volume. The old-style bagpipe, be it understood, was much below concert pitch, though very pleasing as a parlor instrument.

Never has a question been raised as to O'Mealy's excellence as a performer on the Union pipes or the quality of his workmanship. In the manipulation of the regulators, his accompaniment of the chords evokes much flattering comment. "He is a most interesting psychological subject," writes one correspondent, "artistic and sensitive; but a decenter fellow than O'Mealy you could not meet. As a performer of airs, he is most expressive, but as to dance tunes—jigs, reels, and hornpipes—he can turn them off with the greatest rhythmic point and humor. Only to know him socially would not lead one to think him gifted in this way. His playing of the reels is full of that ineffable, buoyant flow that only the best

R.L. O'Mealy
Piper and Pipemaker

pipers know the secret of. His finger technique is as complete as any I've known, and his use of the regulators, the expressive ringing tones of his tremolo (or, more correctly, his vibrato) are wonderful.

"As a pipemaker he is no less remarkable. All the work—wood work, brazing, turning ivories, curing skins for bellows and bags—is done by his own hands. What he doesn't know about the making and repairing of pipes isn't much. It was in the blood of the family."

It is claimed that at the Oireachtas in 1901, and also in 1902, prizes were awarded Mr. O'Mealy for his workmanship, and he is also said to have received an award at the Dublin Feis Ceoil in 1897 for unpublished tunes.

Liberally endowed with the artistic temperament, O'Mealy seems well equipped for his profession. He claims to have worked certain improvements in various parts of the instrument which do away with many of the difficulties with which the learner had formerly to contend. If Irish piping becomes a lost art it will not be for want of skillful pipemakers in this generation.

Since the death of William and Charles Taylor of Philadelphia in 1901 no capable successor in the art has appeared on the American continent. We emphasize the word capable because an amateur in Massachusetts turns out a set once in awhile which though pleasing to the eye is disappointing to the ear. In fact, the drones of a nice looking set owned in Chicago cannot be fitted with guills at all, by the most expert in that line in the city.

Robert Hutton

of Wilmington, Delaware, an excellent turner and general mechanic, got possession of all "Billy" Taylor's tools and equipment after his death. Mr. Hutton is an enthusiast on bagpipes, both Scotch and Irish, and we are informed enjoys turning out an instrument occasionally, such is his love of everything connected with them. But it takes more than a mechanic to put the true tones in a set of Union pipes, and besides it is an art that all can't learn, try as they may.

Sergt. James Cahill

Had there been any scarcity of Union pipes in Chicago in recent years, several of our citizens could have risen to the occasion and supplied the want. Sergt. James Cahill, a native of Kildare, one of the group of pipers in the Irish Music Club, was an expert wood turner. In a workshop attached to his residence he has turned out at least a dozen chanters—flat and sharp—equal to the best, and fully equipped with keys.

James Carbray

Another musician-mechanic to whom nothing comes amiss has devised reamers which bore out chanters as true in tone as any that ever came from the hands of Taylor. In evidence thereof it can be stated that Sergt. James Early and Bernard Delaney, our celebrated policeman piper, use Mr. Carbray's chanters in preference to those which belong to their sets of Taylor pipes.

Mr. Carbray, who is a florist in the employ of the West Park Commissioners, Chicago, loves to dally with the Irish pipes, but his execution thereon is not at all comparable to his mastery of the violin, though he never saw Ireland or the sky over it, being a native of Quebec, Canada, to which his parents had emigrated from the county of Tyrone in the fifties of the last century.

JAMES WILLIAMSON

Among the exhibits at the Irish Harp Festival in Belfast in 1903 were "several sets of pipes made by James Williamson, Belfast." From the press we learn that he "played magnificently on the Irish pipes" on that occasion.

Another exhibit was a "set of Irish Union pipes" attributed to a maker named Kennedy.

In the vicissitudes of human life with its changing moods and fashions, the pipemakers—not so long ago a flourishing fraternity—have dwindled almost to the vanishing point.

CHAPTER XVII

REVEREND MUSICIANS

IN A country like Ireland, where the people were proverbially vivacious and light-hearted and where every pastime, function and celebration was associated with music, the clergy could hardly be expected to remain uninfluenced by their musical environment. Nor did they in many instances. Not a few musically inclined had already acquired passable proficiency on various instruments, before their vocation had been determined. If college life may have tended to check their progress in music, the question of resuming its practice after ordination presented no insuperable difficulties.

With such cases as those of Bishop Campbell of Kilmore and Bishop Touhy of Limerick before us, who can claim that playing on the bagpipe was any bar to clerical advancement?

That the clergymen of England utilized the bagpipe in connection with the exercise of their sacred calling, though not in such a commendable way as Bishop Campbell, is evidenced by the following quotations from a rare work published in London in 1561: "I knewe a priest (this is a true tale that I tell you and no lye) which when any of his parishioners should be maryed, woulde take his Backe-pype and go fetche theym to the Churche, playnge sweetelye afore them, and then would he laye his instrument handsomely upon the Aultare, tyll he had maryed them and sayd Masse. Which thyng being done, he would gentillye bring them home agayne with Backe-pype. Was not this Priest a true ministrell, thynke ye? for he did not counterfayt the Ministrell, but was one indede."

Peasants and princes, parsons, priests and prelates were alike addicted to "playing the pipes"; nearly all but the first named being for obvious reasons restricted to the privacy of their own homes while indulging in their musical hobbies. This restraint tacitly imposed by convention on rank and calling, has doomed many a fine musician to the obscurity of the flowers in the wilderness which were "born to blush unseen." Hence the brevity of their annals.

There is ample evidence in early Irish writings to show that the bagpipe was used in religious processions, and the custom of having pipers lead funeral processions to the cemetery, and play a lament over the grave, survived down to the middle of the seventeenth century at least. We must bear in mind, however, that only the Warpipe or *"Piob Mor"* could be used for marching purposes. Even in this generation performers on the Union pipes have played sacred music at the celebration of Mass, as instanced elsewhere in this work.

RIGHT REV. ANDREW CAMPBELL, D. D.

Perhaps the most remarkable case in which the bagpipe has been utilized in the interests of religion is that mentioned by Cardinal Moran of Melbourne, Australia. In 1885 an English gentleman who happened to pay a passing visit to His Grace, Dr. James Brown, Bishop of Kilmore, in County Cavan, was astonished to see in the sitting room the picture of a Highland piper in full costume, occupying the place of honor between the pictures of two of Bishop Brown's predecessors. His surprise was by no means lessened when informed that the "Highland Piper" was none other than Right Rev. Dr. Campbell, a former bishop of the diocese, who ruled the see from 1753 to 1769. In the penal days when his episcopate was outlawed he availed himself of his skill as a piper, and the costume which effectually disguised him while ministering to the spiritual wants of his scattered flock.

RIGHT REV. TIMOTHY J. O'MAHONY

For the following dramatic story describing the means by which another resourceful prelate utilized his musical talent in the interests of religion, we are indebted to our versatile friend, Prof. W. H. Cahill, editor of *The Chicago Citizen*.

Towards the spring of the year 1875 the Right Rev. Timothy J. O'Mahony, a native of Cork, was Bishop of Armidale, Australia. He had been a student at Rome and was a scholar of considerable distinction. His early days as a priest had been spent in Cork, his native diocese, where he succeeded beyond all expectations in elevating the youth of the large parish wherein he labored for many years. His success having attracted the notice of the authorities in Rome, led to his signal advancement.

In the early days of his episcopate in Australia he labored strenuously to gather from his scattered flock, almost all of whom were his own countrymen, sufficient funds to erect the most modest buildings for his church. The hardworking prelate tried every means his prolific mind could devise to induce the men of a certain mining district to contribute, but the great trouble was that when he called to that particular district not one of them could he find, although the mines were filled with Irish workmen. Leading in their own way a miner's reckless life, they always hid whenever their spiritual superior called to see them— always baffling him in his search.

The faithful bishop was in despair, not only for the funds he so much needed, but much more for the spiritual condition of the poor fellows who seemed so anxious to avoid him. At last a happy thought struck him, and the next time he called at the camp he brought with him a fiddle upon which he was an accomplished performer. Upon entering the camp he divested himself of his Episcopal insignia, and at once wended his way slowly yet none the less surely among the hills, playing every Irish air that long practice and skill had made him so brilliant a master of. The answer quickly came. First one head appeared, then another over the knolls and hills. Still the bishop advanced until he reached the opening of the mine by which time quite a large number of the boys had gathered around. Some were crying at the sound of the once familiar airs; others were dancing with joy at the fact that at last a real Irish musician had appeared among them. Within another half hour every man and boy with a drop of Irish blood in his veins had appeared and was taking part in this unexpected and most welcome treat.

However, all good things must come to an end, and at the opportune moment the bishop in a most impassioned appeal to the love they bore their native Erin revealed his identity. His victory was complete, and as the boys said to him afterwards: "Bishop, as the Yankees say, 'You put one over on us that time.'" Ever afterwards he was the most welcome visitor to the mining camp. He built his churches and when Prof. Cahill last saw him before his death, he was shown by the venerable prelate some very large nuggets of gold, the gifts of some one or other of the men who in his early days did all they could to avoid meeting him.

Great indeed is the power of music over the Irish mind, and never was it better illustrated than at the first meeting of the Irish miners of Armidale, Australia, with the Right Rev. Timothy J. O'Mahony, their revered bishop.

Rev. Edward Sterling ("Parson" Sterling)

This renowned musician, who flourished in the second quarter of the eighteenth century was appointed rector of Lurgan, County Cavan, in 1737. As a piper and composer, "Parson" Sterling, as he was called, was almost as famous as "Piper" Jackson, who, though his junior by about a score of years, may be called his contemporary.

Bunting tells us that he "composed many capital airs which he performed on the bagpipes." Jackson's compositions on the other hand were jigs, reels, and hornpipes. Both are said to be the last who composed Irish melodies in the ancient traditional style.

The only one of the "Parson's" airs now known by name is "The Priest of Lurgan," but it is doubtful if its music or identity is known in this generation.

Catherine Martin of County Meath is mentioned by Arthur O'Neill as a good harpist who confined herself to "modern compositions" by "Parson" Sterling. Bunting, however, did not see fit to take down any of her tunes; consequently they are all forgotten.

Rev. John Dempsey

would probably have lived and died unknown to fame outside the confines of his own parish but for his skill as a performer on the Union pipes.

He flourished between the years 1770 and 1790, according to Grattan Flood, was a native of County Wexford, but was affiliated with the diocese of Kildare, and served as assistant priest for twenty years in the parish of Killeigh in Kings County.

As a piper his ability must have been exceptional, otherwise the memory of his reputation would hardly have survived the obliterating vicissitudes of time, since his death in 1793 at the round Scriptural age of seventy-six years.

Rev. Charles Macklin

of the Episcopal Church, it appears, was a more enthusiastic but less discreet votary of the fascinating Union pipes than Father Dempsey. According to Lady Morgan, this reverend piper "was a marvelous performer on the Irish bagpipes, that most ancient and perfect of instruments."

He was a nephew of Charles Macklin, the celebrated actor and dramatist, who was born in 1690 and lived to be one hundred and seven years of age. The family name was McLaughlin, but owing to the difficulties his English friends had in pronouncing it the uncle abbreviated it to Macklin in 1743. Naturally enough his immediate relatives, including the subject of this sketch, followed his example.

Wit, originality, and eccentricity were in the Macklin or McLaughlin blood, and this in a measure accounts for his whimsical prank of playing out his congregation with a solo on the bagpipes after the service. For this breach of religious decorum he was dismissed frim his curacy in the diocese of Clonfert, County Galway.

Rev. Charles Bunworth

This liberal and patriotic Protestant clergyman of Baltdaniel, County Cork, who was rector of Buttevant for many years, was greatly distinguished for his patronage and knowledge of Irish music. At the trienniel "sessions" or competitions of the Munter bards held at either Charleville, County Cork, or Bruree, County Limerick, between the years 1730 and 1750, he was five times chosen president or umpire. Those meetings, at which the prize winners in the various department of poetic competition were publicly crowned, were eventually suppressed by the operation of the penal laws.

The reverend gentleman was himself a very capable performer on the Irish harp, and at the time of his death, about the year 1770, had in his possession no less than fifteen harps, bequeathed to him at various times by the minstrels as the last mark of respect and gratitude for his kindness and hospitality. During a temporary absence of the Bunworth family from home, a servant, finding them stored in the granary and not having any conception of their value or interesting associations, broke all of them up for firewood! His own harp, made in 1734 by John Kelly of Ballynascreen, County Derry, on the borders of Tyrone, came into possession of the noted writer, Thomas Crofton Croker, his maternal great-grandson. On the latter's death in 1854 the harp was disposed of to an enthusiastic harp collector of London. In his youth, John Philpot Curran was under financial and other obligations to the generous clergyman, whose musical genius has immortalized his name.

REV. ALEXANDER NICOLLS

When "Aleck" Nicolls was ordained a minister of the Established Church late in the first quarter of the nineteenth century, he was given a lucrative living in the barony of Carrigallen, County Leitrim, not far from Crossan, his birthplace. But the lady by whose influence the desirable gift had been obtained, it turned out, expected to secure the handsome clergyman for a brother-in-law.

Unaware of the "Big Parson's" aversion to womankind notwithstanding his manly attractions, she felt mortified on his declining to marry her sister. Embittered by the miscarriage of her cherished scheme, she caused the cold and unresponsive parson to be deprived of the living which in her selfishness she had obtained for him. So he had to be satisfied with an uncoveted assignment at Kilgariff thereafter.

An incorrigible woman hater, he consoled himself in the isolation of his rectory with the music of his beloved bagpipes, on which he had been taught to perform quite cleverly by his cousin, Augustus Nicolls, a local landlord. Often would he play for hours at a time in the solitude of his library, undisturbed by comment or applause. No less austere than Saint Kevin; no woman was ever permitted to invade the parsonage, his only servant or factotum being "Mickey" Byrne, who, like Dean Swift's man, was something of a humorist in his way.

Between them, master and man did their own cooking. One morning while "Mickey" was presiding over the pots, he informed the parson that what meal he had was insufficient for the measure of water in the stirabout pot. After the parson had added another handful from the bag, "Mickey" slyly poured in more water and still complained of the thinness of their prospective breakfast. More meal was reluctantly supplied and more water followed it surreptitiously as before, until "Mickey" declared to the puzzled parson that the more meal he put in the thinner it got!

RIGHT REV. BISHOP TUOHY

Of this distinguished performer on the Union pipes who was Bishop of Limerick from 1814 to 1828, little can be said except that it was under his tuition

Charles Ferguson laid the foundation of his fame as an Irish piper on both sides of the Atlantic.

If the acquirements of the pupil are to be regarded as but the reflection of the talents of the teacher, we must accord the endowed prelate high rank as a performer on the most distinctive of Irish musical instruments.

Tradition has it also that the generous prelate, recognizing young Ferguson's talents, procured him suitable musical training. From the circumstance that the celebrated piper's repertory was mostly confined to airs and sacred music, it would appear that his instruction was such as he would naturally receive under Bishop Tuohy's tuition.

REV. JOHN A. HEMLOCK

"Success, the mark no mortal wit,
Or surest hand, can always hit;
For whatsoe'er we perpetrate
We do but row; we're steered by fate."

In contemplating Father Hemlock's musical proclivities, and his versatility as a performer on a variety of instruments, one naturally speculates as to the factors which determined his calling.

This gifted priest was born in an Irish settlement about a dozen miles or so from Milwaukee, Wisconsin, in 1855, his parents being natives of Kinsale, County Cork. As a result of his early environment among foreign-born pioneers he not only acquired a good knowledge of idiomatic Irish, but speaks the German language so correctly that his Irish ancestry is not suspected.

The writer remembers that when Father Hemlock was a curate at St. Bridget's Church, Chicago, in the early eighties, he could play on any instrument in the orchestra at the church fair. Charmed by John Hicks' splendid performance on the Irish pipes, the reverend enthusiast took up the study of that difficult instrument. His youthful ardor, however, did not long survive the blighting influence of clerical isolation and exclusiveness, as far as the practice of Folk Music is concerned.

Nothing is so stimulating to the musical instinct as congenial companionship, and on the contrary nothing is so disheartening as the absence of it. Without appreciation and encouragement the most ardent musicians grow indifferent.

On the occasion of a recent visit to St. Patrick's Church, Lemont, some twenty-eight miles from Chicago, a glance into the rectory from the veranda proved we were at the right place, for there on the open desk lay a practicing chanter for the Highland pipes. During our brief stay, convincing proof of Father Hemlock's linguistic and musical abilities were by no means few or inconspicuous. Two ordinary cases in which reposed valuable violins graced two corners of the dining room; the piano in another corner was crowned with a cornet; a fife, piccolo, and keyed flageolet kept company less obtrusively in a bookcase, while a set of the *Piob Mor* or Highland bagpipes, and a neat ebony set of the Irish or Union pipes (made by Coyne) were carefully stored away on top.

An ideal Soggarth though he be—cheerful, kindly, and sympathetic—it seems little sort of sinful and calamitous to maroon in an obscure American town a man of Father Hemlock's exceptional artistic endowments.

REV. J. T. WALSH

Aroused from the lethargy of more than a score of years by the publication of O'Neill's *Music of Ireland,* Father J. T. Walsh, pastor of St. Patrick's parish,

East Hampton, Connecticut, opened up a correspondence with the writer. It turned out that the good priest, a native of County Waterford, was a great lover of Irish music and a fine fiddle player in his younger days. Marooned for a quarter of a century among the New England Yankees, he had lost interest in almost everything but the spiritual welfare of his congregation.

Desirous of helping along the good work of preserving Ireland's musical remains, the patriotic *Sagart* forwarded pages of manuscript tunes which he had personally written out from the pent-up stores of his memory. One gem in particular has been embalmed in our later publications as "Father Walsh's Hornpipe."

REV. FATHER M. WALSH

An examination of Dr. Petrie's Collections of Irish Music discloses the fact that no less than twenty-five fugitive melodies were obtained from Father Walsh, parish priest at Sneem, bordering on Kenmare Bay. It appears that his reverence, an enthusiastic musician, had compiled a manuscript collection of Irish music, from which Dr. Petrie was welcome to select tunes at pleasure. It is generally believed that he was the original of A. P. Graves' "Father O'Flynn."

REV. CANON GOODMAN, M. A.

"He was remarkable for his great charity to the poor, and repaired sets of pipes for all comers free of cost. If blessings do any good, he certainly obtained an abundant supply."

Such were the words of one who knew intimately the amiable Rev. James Goodman, Canon of Ross, and Professor of Irish in Trinity College, Dublin What better credentials could be presented at the gates of Paradise?

Universally respected wherever known for his sterling qualities of head and heart, Canon Goodman came prominently into the limelight when the Gaelic League launched the Irish Revival. Irish music, games, and pastimes had declined almost to the vanishing point. The oldtime traditional musicians were seldom seen at fair or feast; their instruments were put away and not a few of them, blind or helpless, found a humiliating refuge in the poorhouse.

All through those long years of national decay Canon Goodman continued to indulge his taste and love for music, and his favorite instrument was the Irish or Union pipes, upon which he had become an excellent performer.

The circumstance of a man of his cloth—a canon of the Established Church—being an accomplished Irish piper, naturally attracted public attention, and the esteem in which he had always been held grew into admiration; undiminished to the day of his death, January 18, 1896.

He was born at Dingle, County Kerry, in the year 1828, and he grew up in that most western town in Ireland, where he acquired his mastery of the Irish language. His father and grandfather had been rectors of Dingle, although the latter Rev. John Goodman also held the family living of Kemerton, in Gloucestershire, England.

All members of the Goodman family spoke Irish fluently and conversed in it even when visiting other countries, so that the future professor, always modest and democratic, had no trouble while associating intimately with his schoolmates and their people in picking up the airs and tunes which formed the nucleus of his manuscript collections, now deposited in Trinity College Library. In this respect he enjoyed exceptional opportunities in the acquaintance of Eugene Whelan, a piper of renown, brother of Michael Whelan, no less distinguished as a fiddler.

His first assignment after ordination was the curacy of Ardgroom, Castletown, Berehaven, and it was while there he commenced the study of the Union pipes, according to Mr. Wayland of the Cork Pipers' Club.

Few indeed are those who acquire command of any musical instrument, particularly the Irish pipes, who did not commence the study in early life. Curate Goodman was an exception, for although he was a fine fluter since boyhood, he did not begin to practice on the set of pipes which he obtained from his fellow curate, Rev. John Holahan, now dean of Ross, until he was past thirty years of age.

Self-taught in music and in the delicate art of making reeds and guills, he overcame difficulties which are the despair of most pipers. His skill and generosity soon made his house the Mecca to which many a poor, perplexed piper bent his weary steps to have his instrument put in order, and none was ever disappointed.

From "Tom" Kennedy, an old Kerry piper who followed him to Ardgroom, his son—Dr. Goodman—tells us his father took down several hundred tunes not previously reduced to musical notation, and he never neglected an opportunity of collecting unrecorded strains from wandering minstrels.

After a few years at Abbeystrewry, to which parish he had been transferred from Ardgroom in 1867, he was promoted Canon of Ross, and appointed Professor of Irish in Trinity College, Dublin.

In this historic institution, "Anglicising denationalizing Trinity," as some are pleased to term it, he kept up his practice on the pipes, usually in concert with John Hingston, the steward, one of his old-time parishioners near Skibbereen, who was also addicted to this form of enjoyment. Members of the faculty were by no means the least enthusiastic of the privileged audience which met on those occasions in the room of Joseph Marshall, a most genial and intelligent man of musical and antiquarian tastes, who succeeded to the stewardship on Hingston's death in 1893.

"Generous, genial, hospitable Goodman—how well I remember his appearance in his rooms in the college," writes Mr. M. Flanagan; "his fine set of pipes with crimson cover set off by his white necktie, while with his foot—often with his two feet clad in plain shoes—he kept time to his splendid music."

On his visits to the old rectory at Skibbereen it was no uncommon sight to see the reverend piper seated comfortably under the shade of the trees in the lawn, where his friends and neighbors were always welcome to enjoy his company and his music. Besides it was his custom to accompany his playing with songs in Irish, of which he had an abundance, for he could sing in the old traditional way which still survives among the glens of West Munster.

His rendering of "The Fox Chase" was a remarkable performance and the expression he gave to some of the plaintive old Irish airs could only be accomplished by one who had a thorough knowledge of the Irish language, character, and feeling, and also musical perceptions of a high order.

Quite noticeable was the way his face lighted up with an almost ecstatic vision, as touching the notes of his instrument he passed on from melody to melody, and from tune to tune, as though he could not stop, he was in such rapture.

His last public performance was in connection with a lecture delivered by Sir Robert Stewart, on the Irish and Scotch bagpipes.

His funeral, which took place January 21, 1896, was of "enormous dimensions," according to the local press. The procession composed of all classes and creeds in the community was singularly sad and imposing. Signs of universal

Rev. James Canon Goodman

grief were everywhere observable and all business was suspended as a mark of respect to the memory of the venerated canon, who endeared himself to all by his charity, humility and kindly disposition.

His generosity to the poor left him without wealth at the end. Yet he died rich, for money could not buy the esteem and respect of his countrymen which were his without limit or reserve.

The Goodman Family

From the statement that Canon Goodman's grandfather, rector of Dingle, also held the living of Kemerton, Gloucestershire, we would naturally infer that he was a native of England. Be that as it may, it is certain that the Goodmans have been settled in Ireland since early in the seventeenth century. The name appears in the list of English Puritan colonists who landed at Kinsale on the invitation of Lord Cork after the departure of the Spanish fleet. Based on information which proved to be incorrect it was stated in *Irish Folk Music: A Fascinating Hobby,* that P. Goodman, Professor of Music in Central Training College, Dublin, was Canon Goodman's son. The latter's only surviving son is Dr. Frank Goodman, in practice at Brigg, Lincolnshire, England.

It appears that Rev. Thomas Goodman, born in 1657, was percentor of Ross, and that his son Richard was vicar of Ballymodan in 1692, and for years thereafter figured extensively in church affairs in that part of the country. Another son, Thomas, was vice-choral of Ross, "where he was licensed to keep school at his residence in the churchyard."

Premature Burial

When Richard's wife Hannah died, the coffin was laid in the family vault at Ross Cathedral. Before daylight next morning, the sexton, who thought the diamond ring he noticed on her finger would be of more service to him than to the dead, entered the vault, with a view to gaining possession of it. Finding its removal no easy matter, he gave the finger a twist to break it off from the hand, but was startled by a groan, which paralyzed him for the time. Reassured by the stillness, he renewed the attempt, but when he bent the finger backwards the "corpse" sat bolt upright and with a yawn inquired, "Where am I?" The ghoulish sexton didn't wait to answer the lady's polite question but fled in terror.

Realizing her predicament, the poor woman, weak as she was, and aided by the lantern which the sexton had dropped in his fright, made her way to the house of her brother-in-law, Rev. James Goodman, just outside the churchyard. Imagination only can picture what followed, but it is certain she lived happily with her husband for many years thereafter and gave birth to a son whose life-long boast it was that "he was born after his mother was buried."

The story in all its gruesome details can be found in Bennett's *History of Bandon,* pages 568-72.

Very Rev. John Canon Scallan

Far from regarding the practice of music and dancing inimical to the welfare of his flock, like so many of his cloth, Father John Scallan, P. P. of Bree, County Wexford, not only encouraged both but indulged in the pleasures of melody himself. Born in 1812, he was ordained in 1839, and died in 1895 at the patriarchal age of eighty-three, beloved and lamented by all, for he was the typical "Sogarth Aroon" of whom the poets loved to sing. He was a votary of the violin during the greater part of his lifetime, and swung the bow with grace and skill to a ripe old age. Although a man of Herculian physique, he was during the later years of his life subject to recurring attacks of nervous prostration. When confined to his room in such cases, he found some solace in playing the fine old airs of his country, the "Coolin" and the "Blackbird" being his special favorites.

Father Scallan organized and supplied the funds to finance a fife and drum band at Bree in 1879, which has been doing service in every popular movement since then. Not only did he tolerate farm house and barn dances on winter evenings, but encouraged such recreations. When the mummers dressed out for the winter season's practice, they always honored the kindly canon by giving their first public performances in front of his halldoor, and right hospitably did he entertain them.

Thomas Whitney of Merton Lodge, near Bree, a Protestant gentleman who prided himself on his accomplishments as a violinist, once met Father Scallan in friendly conference over a business transaction. Although Whitney lived the life of a recluse and was otherwise eccentric, the priest's affability and charm of manner—and indeed one could not name a good quality of mind or heart he did not possess—won his esteem to such an extent that he took his fiddle from the case and played some choice selections for the entertainment of his reverend guest, and then proffered the fiddle to Father Scallan for a return of the compliment. "Old Whitney," as he was commonly styled, listened with rapt attention to his guest's rendering of "The Coolin" and "The Last Rose of Summer." Evidently much impressed with the performance, and feeling that he should do something out of the ordinary to surprise his rival and assert his own fancied superiority, he took the fiddle in his right hand, and the bow in the left, and played a tune with as good grace and as much expression as if he had been handling the instrument in the ordinary way. To most persons this story may seem improbable, but the feat has been practically duplicated by Patrick Cummins, one of Whitney's neighbors. Cummins lost his left hand by a mishap while engaged in blasting a rock, but the genius of music was so strong that by reversing the strings and making some small structural alterations in his fiddle, he nullified the effects of his misfortune. An appliance of his own invention by which the bow could be attached to his left wrist enabled him to acquire a wonderful degree of proficiency and maintain his enviable reputation as a musician, although by no means a young man when the accident occurred.

Canon Scallan was the lifelong friend of the renowned "Jemmy" Sinnott, a sketch of whose life will be found in another chapter. Together they would visit the band room "to see how the boys were getting on." "O'Donnell Abu" played on the highest pitch attainable on the fife was the priest's favorite, while to "Jemmy's" more sensitive ear it was excruciating.

The good pastor liked to be present at the annual ball inaugurated by the Total Abstinence Association, and our correspondent, Mr. Whelan, assures us that his exuberant sallies of wit and humor were by no means the least enjoyable features of the entertainment. He always contended that the tone of his fiddle was much improved coming from the hands of Sinnott after the famous "Jemmy" had manipulated it for an hour or two.

Canon Scallan was a native of Ballyvalloo, barony of Ballaghkeen, County Wexford, and as a priest, entering into the home life of his people in a spirit of accord and helpfulness, it is little wonder that he was universally respected and revered, and exercised a gentle yet effective influence for the best interests of the community.

Rev. Robert Leech,

Protestant rector of Drumlane, Belturbet, County Cavan, was an expert and enthusiastic performer on the German flute. A native of Ballynascreen, Londonderry, he was a graduate of Trinity and was, according to his son, George A. M. Leech of San Francisco, a teacher in that institution. Possessed of fine literary ability, he contributed articles on various subjects to the press for many years.

Rev. James Mease

Another clergyman to whom Dr. Petrie was indebted for six melodies was the subject of this sketch. As the tunes were obtained in the counties of Donegal, Tyrone and Kilkenny by the Rev. Mease, the limits of his circuit must be left to conjecture.

Rev. Richard Henebry, Ph. D.

Coming down to our own times, who is more prominent in the realms of traditional Irish music than Dr. Henebry, former professor of Gaelic in Georgetown University at Washington, D. C., present professor of Gaelic at University College, Cork, and author of a treatise on Irish music, embracing a dissertation on ancient scales, modes and keys. Born in Portlaw, County Waterford, where Irish language, music and tradition still survive, and possessing the musical instinct, he became a fine freehand fiddler in his youth.

Among the happiest days of our life were those in which the genial doctor favored us with his music at our residence in Chicago in 1901, playing solo or in concert with the Irish-American pipers, fiddlers and fluters whom he subsequently immortalized in current literature.

Rev. William Dollard

Not less distinguished as a fiddle player than his friend Dr. Henebry was the amiable and unassuming Father Dollard, brother of the brilliant poet-priest, Rev. James B. Dollard.

A native of the parish of Mooncoin and born in the early sixties, he learned to play the fiddle and flute equally well, and being endowed with a fine voice he was a welcome acquisition to the parish choir.

When the writer was favored with his acquaintance, Father Dollard was rector of a parish at Saint Johns, New Brunswick, British America, and while the "Mac" and "O" proclaimed the Irish ancestry of the majority of his congregation, the traditions and sentiments of their forebears were conspicuous by their absence. What wonder then that an Irish priest, yearning for more congenial associations, felt like a schoolboy on vacation when mingling with members of the Irish Music Club during his visit to Chicago in 1901.

A born musician, he was equally at ease performing on either fiddle or flute. Faultless in time and tone and with a repertory of tunes as select as it was extensive, Father Dollard endeared himself to the Irish music devotees who met for mutual enjoyment at the hospitable home of Sergt. James Kerwin on Wabash Avenue. The kindly and talented clergyman died in the prime of life a few years later.

Father Gleason

Along in the seventies of the last century, his reverence, then curate in the parish of Rosenallis, in the barony of Tinnahinch, Queens county, was a violinist of recognized ability, while

FATHER BRENNAN

of the adjoining parish of Clonaslee was equally famous as a performer on the flute.

FATHER KENNY,

parish priest of said parish, was also an accomplished fluter. He had organized a band to play in the choir, and when mass was over, they struck up lively music as the congregation filed out of the chapel in deference to the pastor's inclination.

As he died intestate his property, by no means inconsiderable, it is said, was claimed by the government under Maynooth regulations.

FATHER JAMES DERMODY

A native of Kilkenny, now pastor at Goldfield, Nevada, not only can play the fiddle, but can when in the humor dance a double and reel with the best of them. Of course these cherished accomplishments were acquired before his college days, but whatever may be said of "the light, fantastic toe," it is not likely that his skill with the bow will be ever in abeyance.

REV. BERNARD J. MAGUIRE

A native of County Fermanagh, now assigned at St. Patrick's Church, Lewiston, Maine, is as devoted to the music of his native land as he is loyal to his creed. Practically self-taught, he is an excellent violinist, but unlike the majority of our best traditional performers he is an adept at playing from the printed score.

Were Irish musicians in general as liberal and practical in their patronage as Father Maguire, who buys—not borrows—such publications as suit his fancy, the interests of Irish music would be much enhanced.

REV. JAMES K. FIELDING

In bringing this chapter to a close, it may appear ungenerous to ignore Father Fielding, the Chicago priest so widely known as a proponent and promoter of traditional Irish pastimes.

Of course we all know what he can do to the "Modhereen Rua" when he gets his trusty flute adjusted to the proper angle athwart his beaming countenance—the version of it he learned at Mooncoin, County Kilkenny, where he was born nearly forty years ago.

No shrinking shyness deters the display of James K.'s musical talents; nor is there anyone endowed with the divine afflatus more keenly alive to the applause which greets his musical performance.

However we may view in conspectus the Saint Patrick's night entertainments which his reverence has provided for years; there can be no question of their success. As an advertiser he has nothing to learn, for like the thrifty Irish jobber, if he had only a *banabh*, he'd be in the middle of the fair with it. Halls, including the Auditorium, which yawn with vacant seats when grand opera, and concerts, and symphonies conducted by the most noted leaders constitute the attractions, have been filled to overflowing repeatedly by audiences eager to enjoy Father Fielding's "Night in Ireland."

So long as achievement is the goal and glory of human endeavor, it is "hats off" to the man who succeeds.

CHAPTER XVIII

GENTLEMEN PIPERS

When music finds a lodgment in the soul of man, neither rank nor station, creed nor calling, is exempt from a yearning desire to give it vocal or instrumental expression in all ages of the world's history.

Who has not heard that the Emperor Nero fiddled while Rome burned? Be that as it may, it can be stated on better authority, that he was famed as a performer on the primitive bagpipes of his day. James the Sixth of Scotland bore an enviable reputation as a Highland piper, and so did "Bonnie Prince Charlie." Frederick the Great of Prussia, who delighted in playing the flute, affected his audience to tears. But, however, much English, French and Spanish royalty may have appreciated and enjoyed the music of the Irish or Union pipes in the late centuries, it is not a matter of record that there were any royal performers on that fascinating instrument, unless we except the many descendants of Irish kings of untainted blood and unquestioned pedigree who won fame if not fortune as Irish pipers. Not a few were the men of rank and wealth who have been immortalized, on account of their prominence as performers on the Irish pipes. For obvious reasons they never courted publicity in the indulgence of their hobby, but enjoyed the distinction of being designated "Gentleman Pipers."

In the hands of a good performer, Walker, in his *Historical Memoirs of the Irish Bards,* remarks the bagpipe is not unworthy of the ear of royalty, and adds that George II, about the middle of the eighteenth century, was so much delighted with the performance of an Irish gentleman on the bagpipe that he ordered a medal to be struck for him.

Lord Edward Fitzgerald

Without a rival among the nobility in the hearts of his countrymen, this distinguished patriot was the fifth son of the Duke of Leinster and was born at the family residence, Dublin, October 15, 1763.

The story of his life, self-sacrifice and tragic death is a glorious episode in the history of Ireland and need not be dwelt on in connection with the purpose of this work.

Loving the music of his native land as dearly as its freedom, he learned to give it proper expression on the Union pipes, a sweet-toned instrument as characteristically Irish as the native language.

A set of Union pipes made of ivory and silver and said to be the instrument on which he played was deposited in the Dublin Museum. For some reason a plain wooden chanter has been substituted for the original ivory one. On the silver collar of the stock is engraved the name "Lord Edward Fitzgerald," the family arms, and the date "1768. Made by Egan, Dublin."

Our interest in the exhibit is naturally much lessened, and the authenticity of the relic itself brought into question, when we come to consider that the noble embryo piper was but five years old in 1768, when the instrument is alleged to have been made.

PIERCE POWER

The earliest of the "Gentleman Pipers" of whom we have any available record is Pierce Power of Glynn, whose fame is perpetuated in the song called *"Plearaca an Gleanna;"* or, "The Humors of Glynn," which he composed in the first quarter of the eighteenth century.

Robert Burns, who was always on the lookout for attractive airs, adopted it for his song known as "Their Groves o' Sweet Myrtle." Words and music to the air "Humours of Glen" are included in *The Irish Minstrel* published by R. A. Smith in 1825 at Edinburgh. A florid setting of the melody under the same name with eight variations is to be found in McGoun's *Repository of Scots and Irish Airs,* printed at Glasgow about 1803.

The Glynn from which the air takes its name is a small romantic country village situated at either side of the Suir, not far from Clonmel, being partly in the the counties of Waterford and Tipperary. Glynn was anciently the residence of a branch of the Powers, to which family it probably still belongs. One of them, Pierse Power, called *Mac au Bharuin* (the Baron's son, for his father was the Baron of an annual fair held there), was celebrated as a poet and musician, and there is a tradition among his descendants that he was the author of the popular air of "The Humors of Glynn." We may as well add that Grattan Flood ascribes its composition to O'Carolan.

LAWRENCE GROGAN

A contemporary of Pierce Power of Glynn, Lawrence Grogan of Johnstown Castle, County Wexford, was still more celebrated as a piper and composer, though, like Power, his fame rests chiefly on one air—"Ally Croker"—which caught the popular fancy. It was taken up immediately by the ballad-singers, circulated far and wide, and within a few years had been incorporated in three operas.

The authenticity of the air has been questioned in recent times, by Chappell, an English publisher, and Sir Villiers Stanford, because it first appeared in print in an English publication.

We are informed by Crofton Croker, an excellent authority, that the song and music of "Ally Croker" were composed about the year 1725, by Lawrence Grogan, a gentleman piper. It is not easy to see how its appearance in the opera of *Love in a Riddle* five years later renders its Irish origin improbable. Its popularity became more widespread on being introduced by Foote in 1753 into his comedy, *The Englishman in Paris,* and by Kane O'Hara in *Midas,* seven years afterwards. In 1803 the air was wedded by George Colman to a song entitled "The Unfortunate Miss Bailey."

Tom Moore's song, "The Shamrock," set to the air of "Ally Croker," has been excluded from the Stanford edition of *Moore's Irish Melodies—Restored.*

Like the gentlemen of his day, "Larry" Grogan, as he was called, was devoted to hunting and horse-racing. Widely known, he was immortalized in verse in his prime, but no account of him since the middle of the eighteenth century can be traced.

Following is a jig bearing his name, to be found in the first volume of *Aird's Selection of English, Scotch, Irish and Foreign Airs,* published in 1782 at London.

LARRY GROGAN

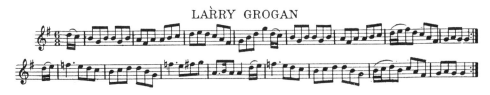

WALTER JACKSON ("PIPER" JACKSON)

The most celebrated Irish piper of the eighteenth century, or perhaps of any age, taking all things into consideration, was Walter Jackson, better known as "Piper" Jackson. He flourished in the prime of his glory about the middle of the eighteenth century. A gentleman of wealth and landed estates, he won undying fame not alone for his skill as a performer on the Union pipes but for his versatility as a composer of music suitable for that instrument. His residence near Ballingarry, County Limerick, called "Jackson's Turret," commanded an extensive view of the surrounding country. From the fact of his leaving sixty pounds a year to the poor of Ballingarry parish, half to be distributed by the Catholic pastor and half to the Protestant rector, according to Grattan Flood, there can be no doubt as to his having lived in that part of the country.

The present writer remembers having read somewhere that Jackson belonged in the County Monaghan, where he owned an estate. A correspondent from South Australia, Mr. Patrick O'Leary, of Drumlona, Eastwood, Adelaide, who is a man of prominence in that country, tells a story which unexpectedly strengthens the presumption that County Monaghan had as much claim to him as County Limerick.

Referring to what is said of Jackson in *Irish Folk Music: A Fascinating Hobby,* Mr. O'Leary says: "You struck a sympathetic chord in my memory in your altogether too meagre reminiscences of the famous and never-to-be-forgotten 'Piper' Jackson, of Creeve, near Ballibay, County Monaghan, for well do I recollect the expression of delight that would light up my mother's face—God rest her!—when talking about the famous Jackson, his tunes, and his playing. Her father, being a good fiddler himself and a neighbor of the renowned musician, was also something of a crony of his, and enjoyed the latter's friendship for years.

Jackson belonged to a well-known family. They were linen lords in Ulster for over a century, and were also mill owners, and possessed a stable of race horses. Differing materially from the Anglo-Scottish squirearchy of Ulster of their time, or any other time, they were liberal, broad-minded and hospitable. During my boyhood I have heard fifty or sixty tunes, reels and jigs, that were credited to the famous piper, such as 'Jackson's Soho,' 'Jackson's Flowery Garden' ('The Rose in the Garden' in your great work), 'Jackson's Maria,' 'Jackson's Drowsy Maggie,' etc."

Commenting on "Jacky Latin," a tune printed in O'Neill's *Dance Music of Ireland,* Mr. O'Leary continues: "This fine old reel is said to have been composed in honor of a young man, John Duffy—better known as 'Jack' Duffy—who lived in the townland of Lattan, near Jackson's home in the parish of Aughnamullen. Duffy being a fine, strapping young man, a local Adonis, and an incomparable dancer in those days when dancing was a fine art in Ireland, he won Jackson's friendship and esteem to such a degree that the great composer immortalized him in the beautiful tune, 'Jack o' Lattan.'" A very romantic story indeed. Truth compels us to add, however, that among the contents of Waylet's *Collection of Country Dances,* published in 1749, is "Jack Lattin." Whether this fact militates against its probability is a question which is open to speculation.

Practically all Jackson's tunes bore his name; such, for instance, as "Jackson's Morning Brush," his best known composition. After its introduction by John O'Keefe in *The Agreeable Surprise,* in 1781, this popular jig has been included in almost every collection of Irish music since that time, although by no means superior to the majority of Jackson's tunes.

A small volume of his melodies published by Sam Lee of Dublin in 1774, and reprinted in 1790, is now so rare that the principal book agency of London has been unable to procure a copy of it for the present writer.

Most of Jackson's tunes, kept alive traditionally for more than a century, have lost their original titles as well as their original settings, but from an examination of various collections of Irish music at hand, commencing with *Aird's Selection,* etc., in 1782, the following have been found retaining the composer's name, exclusive of those mentioned by Mr. O'Leary: "Jackson's Morning Brush," "Jackson's Nightcap," "Jackson's Over the Water," "Jackson's Welcome Home," "Jackson's Frolic" (now known as "Kitty of Oulart"), "Jackson's Bouner Bougher" (original of "Morgan Rattler" before being embellished with variations), "Jackson's Bottle of Brandy," "Jackson's Cravat," "Jackson's Frieze Coat," "Jackson's Jug of Punch," "Jackson's Rambles," "Jackson's Rolling Jig," "Jackson's Maggott," "Jackson's Bottle of Punch," "Jackson's Jig," "Jackson's Punch Bowl," "Jackson's Coge in the Morning," "Jackson's Dream," "Jackson's Maid at the Fair," "Jackson's Cup," "Jackson's Rowly Powly," "Jackson's Favorite," "Jackson's Bottle of Claret," "Jackson's Maid," and "Jackson's Delight," which, by the way, is identical with "The Irish Washerwoman." Besides the above named, we find "Copey's Jigg" ("Jimmy O'Brien's Jig" in the O'Neill Collections) and "Pither in enugh," attributed to Jackson in Clinton's *Gems of Ireland.* Many other well-known tunes, such as "Cherish the Ladies" and "The Little House Under the Hill," are ascribed to Jackson. The original simple two-strain melodies were doubtless the products of his prolific fancy, but the variations—four in the first case, and nine in the second—were the work of later composers. It may not be out of place to add that an "Irish Air" in *The Poor Soldier,* to be found in *The Hibernian Muse,* published in 1787, is unmistakably a simple version of "The Little House Under the Hill."

A violinist of ability, as well as a performer on the Union pipes, Walter Jackson has been immortalized as "Piper" Jackson because of his enthusiasm and love of the instrument and its music, while all his forebears and descendants have been forgotten.

EDWARD BLAKE

Casual but provokingly meagre mention has been made of a "Gentleman Piper" named Edward Blake, of Castlegrove, near Tuam, County Galway. He is said to have been "a beautiful performer." Having been referred to as an ancestor of the late Edward Blake, M. P. for Longford, he probably flourished in the early part of the nineteenth century.

Capt. William Kelly

No book on pipers and pipering would be complete without an account of Capt. William Kelly, the great County Kildare piper, who was born in New Abbey House, County Kildare, early in the last quarter of the eighteenth century. He played before King George IV when that monarch visited Ireland, and was presented with a set of pipes—ebony, silver-mounted—which is shown to visitors at Kilkea Castle, Maganey, County Kildare. After his death, his widow gave this set of bagpipes to a Mrs. Bailey, of Newtown Bert, near Athy, whose son, Samuel Bailey, was also a famous piper. The latter, after playing on them for years, died in August, 1895, and two years later the historical instrument was obtained from his daughter, Mary, and is now at Kilkea Castle, as before stated. Round the stock is engraved "William Kelly, Esq., 1809."

"Sporting" Captain Kelly, as our hero was affectionately called, typifies the best qualities of his race, with few or none of its failings; and as a man of his prominence and parts deserved much more than the recognition which current history accords him, we have deviated from our main subject in order to make partial amends in that respect. Not the least of Captain Kelly's claims to the veneration of Kildare people is the circumstance that he trained Dan Donnelly, the boxer, for his contest with Cooper, the Englishman, champion pugilist of his time. Donnelly was born in Townsend Street, Dublin, and on one occasion Captain Kelly saw the yet untrained man dispose with a single box each of three bullies who had set upon him. The sporting gentleman at once recognized Donnelly's powers and undertook to develop them, with the result we have all heard of, both in poetry and prose. Captain Kelly was well known on the turf; for many years he kept a racing establishment at Maddenstown Mansions, Curragh, and named several of his horses after parts of the pipes, as "Chanter," "Drone," etc. Drone was a particularly fine gray horse, and his successes are recorded in the Racing Calendars of the period. Captain Kelly had several protegés among the pipers of his time, one of the most distinguished being John Hicks, who left his native country for Liverpool and eventually made his way to New York, Chicago and other American cities.

The fighting as well as the sporting instinct was well developed in the Kelly family. Two brothers of "the Captain" served in the British army—Col. Ponsonby Kelly, who commanded the Twenty-fourth Regiment, and Capt. Waldron Kelly, who served in the Forty-first. The Captain's first cousin, Col. Edward Kelly, performed brilliant service on the field of Waterloo.

Capt. William married his first cousin, Miss Orford, of Rathbride Manor, and had issue, seven sons and one daughter. After a long and brilliant career on the turf, the Captain retired to his town house, Clontarf Crescent, and after a few years' residence died there about the year 1858.

The custodian of the family traditions, records, heirlooms, etc., is Mrs. Jane Ellis-Bailie, granddaughter of Captain Kelly, who lives at "The Porch," Castleblaney, County Monaghan, and whose picture graces the opposite page. Besides being imbued with an intensely national patriotic spirit, the Kellys would seem to have been endowed with the faculty of choosing suitable mates. At the time of his death, December, 1911, there was no more popular man in Monaghan County than the late Mr. Robert Ellis Bailie, crown solicitor; his funeral was three miles long.

It was through Mrs. Ellis Bailie that the picture of the Captain was obtained, having been copied from an oil painting in the lady's possession. She has also

"SPORTING"CAPT. WM. KELLY
of the Curragh of Kildare.
COPIED FROM PAINTING IN POSSESSION OF HIS GRANDDAUGHTER, MRS BAILIE

an oil painting of the celebrated racer, Drone. In addition, there may be seen also at "The Porch" a unique collection of plates, glass, china, etc., as Mrs. Bailie has been a collector for many years. She has specimens of even the spurs which used to be fitted on game cocks. As showing Mrs. Bailie's benevolence, it may be mentioned that she is a life governor of four Dublin hospitals and an active member of the guild founded by Lady Dudley for affording aid to young women in choosing a profession.

It often happens that family traits, after lying partially dormant for one or two generations, manifest themselves with added force in a third or fourth. This truth is strikingly exemplified in the person of Mr. Robert John Ellis Bailie, son of Mrs. Ellis Bailie, consequently great-grandson of the celebrated piper. He hunts the country from his seat, Shortstone, Dundalk; he is a perfect horseman, a keen judge of blood stock and breeder of race horses; he is twenty-two years old and six feet in height. He is very musical, but he will scarcely ever play on his great ancestor's pipes, the instrument, as already stated, being kept at Kilkea Castle, where it is greatly prized by the family of Lona Walter Fitzgerald.

A grand-aunt of Mrs. Bailie's was the lady who staked her coach and four and a heavy sum in cash on Dan Donnelly. This notice may appropriately end with a quotation from the well known song:

> Long life unto Miss Kelly, she's recorded on the plain;
> She boldly stepped into the ring, saying, "Dan, what do you mean?"
> Saying, "Dan, my boy, what do you mean, Hibernia's son?" said she;
> "My coach and horse I have bet on you, Dan Donnelly."

Augustus Nicolls

A renowned performer on the Union pipes in his day was "Gusty" Nicolls, a landlord who lived on his estate near Carrigallen, in the southern part of County Leitrim. He had probably reached early manhood at the beginning of the nineteenth century, for it was from him James Quinn, of Cloone, who was born about that time, learned to play the pipes.

Mr. Quinn, an excellent piper himself in later years, spoke in the highest terms of the ability of his generous teacher, both as a performer and composer, his most popular piece being "Gusty's Frolics," a hop or slip jig of seven strains. The versatile "Gentleman Piper" was the instructor of his cousin, "Parson" Nicolls, whose sketch will be found in the chapter devoted to "Reverend Musicians."

Blessed with manly beauty, musical talents, and worldly wealth, Augustus earned the reputation of being an irresistible heartbreaker also.

Robert Brownrigg

Unaffected by wealth or station, and enjoying the respect and confidence of rich and poor alike, Robert Brownrigg, of Norrismount, barony of Scarawalsh, County Wexford, was the type of Irish gentleman—none too numerous—whom all men honor. A really fine performer on the Union pipes, 'twas his delight to entertain with his music those who partook of his hospitality.

In every sense of the word a "Gentleman Piper," he was a magistrate in those days when none but the landed proprietor and city magnate were entrusted with the commission of the peace, and all his sons entered the learned professions.

Mrs. Jane E. Bailie.

Mr. Brownrigg not alone practiced but patronized Irish music in true traditional style. To such a degree did its influence enter into the activities of his life that it was his custom to attend the weddings and merry-makings of the peasantry, and go wheresoever good pipers might appear, in order to participate in the festivities and indulge what might justly be termed his ruling passion.

On one such occasion he secured an engagement to assist where the great Hugh Kelly—long dead and almost forgotten—had been already installed as official piper. After tuning their instruments to an even pitch, they started in to entertain the company, but it was not long before Kelly, though blind, discovered the identity of his partner and told him so in a confidential whisper. The only response was a gentle pressure on the blind piper's toe, which conveyed all the assurance necessary. So they played away together until morning for a company which had no suspicion that the pipers had ever met before.

The unknown piper, who of course was Mr. Brownrigg in disguise, received his stipulated fee from the host and liberal donations from the assembled guests, all of which, with the addition of a small gold coin of his own, he stealthily slipped into the pocket of his comrade of the night's diversion.

The adventurous "Bobbie," however, was not always so successful in preserving his incognito. At another time he made his appearance at a popular benefit ball where he encountered a great army of pipers. Competitions in both music and dancing were the order of the night, the winners to be decided by popular acclaim. When it came to our hero's turn to display his musical abilities and compete for the honors at stake, much speculation was rife in the audience as to the capabilities of the unknown piper. Not the least disconcerted by the evident anxiety of the crowd to learn what county or province he hailed from, he commenced his performance, quite carelessly, but it was plainly seen that his indifference was only affected. Warming up to his work, a murmur of approbation greeted his ears, and so he began to let himself out in great shape, finally winding up with one of his peculiar flourishes. This characteristic wind-up betrayed his identity and he was greeted with a tumult of applause from all over the house, interspersed with remarks such as "Well done, Brownrigg!" "More power to your elbow!" "That your bag and bellows may never fail you!" and other phrases indicating the esteem in which he was held as a man and a musician.

He did not tarry long to receive the congratulations of his ardent admirers, or the prize which he had inadvertently won, but hastened away to temporary obscurity, from which he was sure to emerge when suitable opportunity was presented.

A remarkable character in many ways, Robert Brownrigg died about the middle of the nineteenth century at a ripe old age.

HENRY BROWNRIGG

The oldest son of Robert Brownrigg, he not only inherited his father's patrimony at Norrismount, County Wexford, but his musical taste and talent, for, though a barrister by profession, the melody of the bagpipes had more attractions for him than the intricacies of the law.

Henry Brownrigg as a musician was best known to fame in association with the great Highland instrument, of which he had many. One of the costliest of them, in a tolerable state of preservation, still remains a souvenir at the Rowsome home at Ballintore.

Little less eccentric than his father, nothing seemed to afford him greater pleasure than to take out a set of Highland pipes on a fine evening and play them on the slopes above Norrismount and Whitewell. Often in the night-time the clear, ringing tones of his instrument could be heard for miles along the valley through which the River Banna winds its serpentine course. Played under such conditions—and we agree with him—music produces its most charming effects.

There is a tradition in connection with his memory which still holds good, that his music haunted the valley and was heard even after his death, which occurred about the year 1860.

Surviving his father only ten or twelve years, he probably lacked a decade of reaching the scriptural allotment of three score years and ten.

DUDLEY COLCLOUGH

Of this "Gentleman Piper" little can be told except that he lived in the nineteenth century and that he was one of the landlord class, whose estates of over thirteen thousand acres included Tintern Abbey, in the southwestern part of the county of Wexford.

For more than three centuries the Colcloughs lived in great style on their property and were the leading magnates in that part of the county bordering on Bannow Bay. Living among their tenantry and spending their income for useful purposes at home, unlike most landlords, they enjoyed uncommon popularity.

One of them, Anthony Colclough, who became a Catholic and joined the "rebels" in '98, was duly hanged for his patriotism.

DR. O'DONNELL

Many were the accomplished performers on the Irish bagpipes who played only for their own pleasure and yet could hardly be classed as "Gentlemen Pipers," for this distinction seems to have been always associated with rank or title. Men endowed with the musical instinct had little choice as to the means of giving it musical expression in Ireland, since the decline of the harp, except as between the flute, fiddle, and pipes. Being inexpensive and always in order, the flute was the great favorite. From the humble tin whistle to the keyed concert flute, dozens were to be found in every parish, and the gamut being somewhat similar to that of the chanter of the bagpipe, ambitious fluters naturally graduated into practicing on the more difficult and elaborate instrument.

That many of them by natural talent and assiduous practice became famous performers on the Irish pipes, is a fact beyond question, for be it known it was by that method all, or nearly all, pipers, peasant or noble, lay or cleric, amateur or professional, acquired their skill on that instrument which for some has such peculiar fascination.

Following a paragraph in praise of the music of the Irish pipes, Shelton Mackenzie tells us of an apothecary, named O'Donnell, who was the last performer of any note on the instrument in the town of Fermoy, County Cork. He died about the year 1869, but when living he certainly could discourse "most eloquent music." "It was almost impossible," he says, "to listen with dry eyes and unmoved heart to the exquisite manner in which he played the Irish melodies—the *real* ones, I mean, not those which Tom Moore and Sir John Stevenson had 'adopted' (and emasculated) for polite and fashionable pianoforte players and singers."

DUDLEY COLCLOUGH

Mackenzie speaks of Charles Ferguson, "whose performance on the Irish pipes may be said to equal—it could not surpass—that of O'Donnell." This is high praise, indeed, for Ferguson's fame as an air player was world-wide in his day.

LORD ROSSMORE

This aristocratic performer on the Irish or Union pipes was a wealthy landlord, owner of the town of Monaghan and no doubt other estates in the county. He was born in 1765, ennobled in 1796, and died in 1843. His son, the third baron, was also an accomplished Irish piper.

In a work compiled by Hussey De Burgh, entitled *The Landowners of Ireland,* we learn the family name from the following entry: "Lord Rossmore—Derrick Warner William Westenra, 4th Baron—14,839 acres County Monaghan. Residence Rossmore Park, Monaghan."

An examination of the *Complete Petrie Collection* shows that six tunes were obtained from Lord Rossmore, who personally noted down some of them from the playing of "Paddy" Coneely, the famous Galway piper. Three others were credited to Colonel Westenra, of the same family, possibly the Captain Westenra of Bumper Hall, County Meath, mentioned in Arthur O'Neill's *Memoirs.*

HON. WILLIAM PHAIR

A great lover of Irish music and an ardent performer on the Union pipes, the late Alderman William Phair, chairman of the water works committee of the city of Cork, was none other than a genuine "Gentleman Piper."

Inheriting neither wealth nor title, he acquired both by the exercise of those admirable qualities with which nature so liberally endowed him. A familiar figure in the life of the city for over a quarter of a century, both as Alderman and Councillor, Mr. William Phair departed this life March 9, 1912, in the sixty-sixth year of his age. His death occasioned the deepest regret among all classes of the community, for a more respected and popular gentleman did not live in the province.

A native of the parish of Dunisky, southeast of Macroom, he migrated in early life to the city on the Lee, and was elected to the reformed corporation at its inception in 1883. From that date until shortly before his death he was elected and re-elected to offices of responsibility, and often unopposed, so completely had he won the respect and confidence of the citizens.

In everything that conduced to the uplifting of his native land, Alderman Phair's support was ever at the call of his country. A native Irish speaker, the Gaelic Revival found in him a warm advocate, and the revival of Irish music a splendid champion. A great admirer of the Irish bagpipes, he was the chief patron of Robert Thompson, the forgotten minstrel, who through the aid supplied by his enthusiastic friend traveled to Dublin to attend the first *Oireachtas* and outclassed all competitors in the manipulation of the melodious Irish instrument. And by the same token 'twas on the alderman's pipes he played, for he had none of his own for many a year.

The Cork Pipers' Club, founded in 1898, elected Alderman Phair its first president, and though the flippancy and levity of some of its members on his appearance at a meeting in a fur-trimmed coat and tall silk hat, after attending a council session, offended his dignity, he never lost interest in its welfare. Poor "Bob" Thompson, whose health had subsequently failed, found in him a steadfast and generous friend.

Ald. William Phair
City of Cork

When attending the Munster Feis in 1906, it was the writer's good fortune to form the acquaintance of the able but unassuming official, who called to tender us the hospitality of Gilabbey House, which is poised on a precipice overlooking the "Pleasant Waters of the River Lee."

The proverbial hospitality of an Irish gentleman needs no description, but it certainly was worth "a day in the garden" to be entertained by a man of such distinction with a tune on the pipes—aye, and dozens of them at that. John S. Wayland, so prominent in the Music Revival, was no silent partner in contributing to the pleasures of the evening, and what with the kindly solicitude of Mrs. Phair the remembrance of our enjoyable evening at Gilabbey House will always remain a milestone in our memory.

CHAPTER XIX

FAMOUS PERFORMERS ON THE IRISH OR UNION PIPES IN THE EIGHTEENTH AND EARLY PART OF THE NINETEENTH CENTURIES

THE classification of Irish pipers not included in the two preceding chapters, with a view to draw lines of distinction for the convenience of readers, is by no means as simple as it seems.

The idea of listing them as "amateurs" and "professionals" was abandoned for the reason that an amateur in modern days has come to be regarded as a beginner rather than a non-professional.

Drawing the line at the century was no less objectionable. Some pipers had flourished in one generation and died young. Others, again, blest with longevity, lived and flourished in two centuries, and in one case at least even in three. The divisions adopted, though somewhat indefinite, will, we trust, be found not objectionable.

JOHN MACDONNELL

In the state of society which prevailed in Ireland in the eighteenth century we can well imagine how exclusive were the "Gentlemen Pipers" as far as the public was concerned. It appears, however, from an incident mentioned by John O'Keefe, the celebrated dramatist and comedian, in his *Recollections,* published in 1826, that there was another class of "Gentlemen Pipers" intermediate between the titled and the plebeian, as the following stories of the times about 1770 will show:

SPIRIT OF AN IRISH PIPER

"MacDonnell, the famous Irish piper, lived in great style—servants, grooms, hunters, etc. His pipes were small and of ivory, tipped with silver and gold. You scarcely saw his fingers move, and all his attitudes while playing were steady and quiet, and his face composed. One day that I and a very large party dined with Mr. Thomas Grant at Cork, MacDonnell was sent for to play for the company during dinner. A table and chair were placed for him on the landing outside the room, a bottle of claret and glass on the table, and a servant waiting behind the chair designed for him: the door left wide open. He made his appearance, took a rapid survey of the preparation for him, filled his glass, stepped to the dining-room door, looked full into the room, and said: 'Mr. Grant, your health and company!' drank it off, threw half a crown on his table, saying to the servant, 'There, my lad, is two shillings for my bottle of wine, and keep the sixpence for yourself.'

"He ran out of the house, mounted his hunter, and galloped off, followed by his groom.

"I prevailed on MacDonnell to play one night on the stage at Cork, and had it announced in the bills that Mr. MacDonnell would play some of O'Carolan's fine airs upon the *Irish Organ.* The curtain went up and discovered him sitting alone in his own dress; he played and charmed everybody."

MacDonnell possessed several exquisite sets of pipes. One of them, made

194

by the elder Kenna and dated 1770, Grattan Flood tells us, passed into the Mac-Donnell family of County Mayo and is now in the Dublin Museum on loan from Lord Macdonnell, late Under-Secretary for Ireland.

It is a most elaborate instrument, and if the date is correct it proves conclusively that the *Uilleann* or Union pipes had been developed into a keyed instrument with regulators much earlier than generally supposed, and certainly long before Talbot was born.

James Spence

None but those of moral fibre and strong power of resistance may hope to withstand the demoralizing influence of conviviality in at atmosphere of adulation which conspicuous talent invites. James Spence, who was famous as a piper in his teens, was not one of those, for the sands of his life ran out at the early age of twenty-eight.

This brilliant performer on the Union pipes was born near Mallow, in the County of Cork, about the middle of the eighteenth century. Little or nothing is known of his early years except that his fame was widespread throughout Munster.

Emulating the example of so many others of his profession, he visited Dublin and at once won favor with the students and faculty of Trinity College, but lost discretion, health and life in short order, as before stated.

Patrick Courtney,

who flourished in the latter part of the eighteenth and the early years of the nineteenth century, was a piper of renown in his day. Like most of his class, he traveled extensively in Scotland and England. At the performance of the pantomime of *Oscar and Malvina* at Covent Garden Theatre in 1791 it is recorded that Courtney played the Union pipes with much effect, and in 1798, according to Manson, author of *The Highland Bagpipe,* he "played a solo on the Union pipes in the quick movement of the overture, with good effect, in a performance founded on Ossian's poems."

A writer in the *Freeman's Journal,* March 21, 1811, commenting on the capabilities of the Irish bagpipe, says "the celebrated Courtney has fully established the captivating sweetness of the notes in alt."

We learn from Grattan Flood that he spent many years in England and was not only a good performer but a good teacher. More than that, he was a composer of many popular dance tunes not easily identified at this late day. He died in London, but the date, 1794, conflicts with the account in Manson's work, above quoted.

John Crampton

Meagre indeed was the information available concerning the life of this noted piper, until we came across an article on the evolution of the Irish bagpipe, published in an issue of the *Freeman's Journal* of 1811, the year of his death.

Speaking of Crampton, the writer says: "Possessing musical taste and judgment far above any other performer on the Irish bagpipe, he managed the bass or drone tubes with such skill as to form a very pleasing accompaniment, and plainly showed what might be effected were that attention paid which is devoted to other instruments. Besides, he gave a softness to the general tone that was peculiarly pleasing, and his style was so chaste, so completely divested of anything piperly, that no doubt can now remain of the bagpipe being capable of as much feeling and expression as the organ or harpsichord."

In the *Story of the Bagpipe* the author names Crampton as one of the three most famous Irish pipers at the birth of the nineteenth century. Though a brilliant instrumentalist, he was not endowed with the gift of composition.

In a notice printed in the *Freeman's Journal* of April 13, 1812, describing the attractions of Dignam's tavern, at No. 14 Trinity Street, Dublin, we are informed that the proprietor has engaged the "celebrated Munster piper, Mr. Talbot, a pupil of the late Cramp, to play every evening after eight o'clock, Sundays excepted." But who was Cramp? None other than Crampton, whose name had been abbreviated colloquially into Cramp, and even corrupted into Crump. By the latter name he was immortalized by Dr. Petrie.

It was in writing a sketch of "Paddy" Coneely, the Galway piper, in 1840, that the amiable and gifted Petrie refers to Crump, whose instrument Coneely then possessed.

"As to the bagpipes," in Petrie's words, "they are of the most approved Irish kind, beautifully finished, and the very instrument made for Crump, the greatest of all the Munster pipers, or we might say Irish pipers of modern times, and from which he drew singularly delicious music. Musical reader! do not laugh at the epithet we have applied to the sounds of the bagpipe. The music of Crump, whom we have often heard from himself on these very pipes, was truly delicious, even to the most refined musical ear. He was a Paganini in his way—a man never to be rivaled, and who produced effects on his instrument previously unthought of and which could not be expected."

Those pipes after Crump's (or Crampton's) death were saved as a national relic by the worthy and patriotic historian of Galway, James Hardiman, who in his characteristic spirit of generosity and kindness presented them to "Paddy" Coneely, as a person likely to take good care of them and not incompetent to do them justice.

Mr. O'Farrell

Should an adequate work on Irish musical biography ever be undertaken, it is sincerely to be hoped the Union pipers—true national minstrels—no less than the harpers will receive due consideration.

In vain we scan the pages of *Grove's Dictionary of Music and Musicians* and *British Musical Biography* for the names of such renowned Irish musicians and composers as "Piper" Jackson, "Parson" Sterling, or even O'Farrell, an Irish piper and publisher of no inconsiderable fame in London for at least a score of years at the end of the eighteenth and beginning of the nineteenth century.

Quite likely English writers and publishers had no conception of Irish music as performed on the improved Irish bagpipe, regarding both instrument and music as being no better than the rude performances of the pipers and street fakers of England as pictured by Hogarth and other English artists. Irish pipers were no rarity on the London stage since the last decade of the eighteenth century, and it is a matter of history that some of them, brilliant performers, were commanded to present themselves for the entertainment of royalty. With such recognition and patronage, it "passeth understanding" how the most prominent of them, and particularly one who published three notable collections of music between the years 1797 and 1810, could be utterly ignored in such standard works as those named.

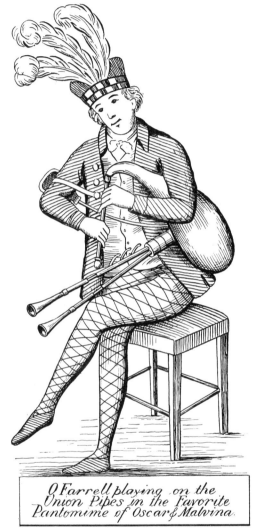

O Farrell playing on the
Union Pipes in the Favorite
Pantomime of Oscar & Malvina.

Copied from Title Page of O'Farrell's National Irish
Music for the Union Pipes

To the researches of the indefatigable Grattan Flood we are indebted for much of what little information we possess concerning this talented and enterprising piper. Of his early life we know nothing. His introduction to fame dates from the year 1791, when he played the Union pipes in the pantomime of *Oscar and Malvina* at London. A man of affairs, evidently, he was practical and farseeing, for after years of preparation, no doubt, he published a work entitled *O'Farrell's Collection of National Irish Music for the Union Pipes; Comprising a variety of the Most Favorite Slow and Sprightly Tunes Set in Proper Stile and Taste, etc., etc.; also a Treatise with the most perfect Instructions ever yet published for the Pipes.*

Although music and a tutor for the Highland pipes had been published by Rev. Patrick MacDonald in 1784, O'Farrell's *Treatise* was the first ever printed for the improved Irish instrument; and, by the way, the present writer procured through the courtesy of Grattan Flood a transcript of said *Treatise* from the copy of O'Farrell's work in the National Library at Dublin—the only one in Ireland, it is said—and inserted it as "Appendix A" in *Irish Folk Music: A Fascinating Hobby.* Since the publication of the latter work, in 1910, we have ascertained that O'Farrell's collections repose in the National Library and not in the Trinity College Library, as therein stated.

Again in 1804 there came from the press *O'Farrell's Pocket Companion for the Irish or Union Pipes, etc., etc.,* two small volumes of music, chiefly Irish, suitable for the instrument. These were followed in 1810 by two others similarly named.

This remarkable man, who must have been an excellent performer on the Union pipes, preserved, through his thoughtfulness and energy, many fine airs and dance tunes that but for his efforts would have been lost. His volumes are frequently quoted by Alfred Moffatt in tracing the history of many of the airs in his *Minstrelsy of Ireland.*

One of his own composition, called "O'Farrell's Welcome to Limerick," would seem to indicate that he had traveled in Ireland and that probably Limerick had been the place of his nativity.

That the unexpected sometimes happens was curiously illustrated in the experience of the writer recently. One of a dozen rare musical works sought through the medium of a London book agency whose specialty is filling such orders, turned up with some rubbish. To my delight, it proved to be a perfect though discolored copy of O'Farrell's first volume, of which there was but one copy in all Ireland! At last here was O'Farrell's likeness in a vignette on the centre of the title page, garbed as he appeared on the London stage, and from it the etching on the opposite page has been reproduced. The set of Union pipes on which he played are quite distinct and unlike any other instrument we have ever seen. But possibly the artist was to blame and neglected to include the small drone and tenor with which such instruments are equipped.

JEREMIAH MURPHY

Another noted performer on the Union pipes of the same period was Jeremiah Murphy, a Galway man from Loughrea. In an issue of the *Freeman's Journal* of Dublin, in September, 1811, Murphy's arrival in the city is announced as follows:

THE IRISH PIPES

Jeremiah Murphy, late of Loughrea, begs leave to acquaint the lovers of national music that he at present plays at Darcy's Tavern, Cook Street, where he humbly hopes his exertions to please will obtain for him that encouragement with which he has for so many years been honored by the gentlemen of Munster and Connacht.

Early in 1813, Murphy transferred his services to the Griffin Tavern, on Dame Street—a sort of "Free-and-Easy" establishment. After 1815 he gave up entertaining the public in taverns, and his subsequent career is not a matter of record.

James Sheedy

Available information concerning the subject of this sketch is decidedly meagre. Among the contents of Petrie's *Complete Collection of Irish Music* are two unnamed jigs contributed by Dr. P. W. Joyce, "as played by James Sheedy." One of them is an old Munster single jig set by Dr. Joyce in 1852 from the whistling of Michael Dineen, a farmer at Coolfree, parish of Ardpatrick, in County Limerick. The latter had learned it in his youth "from the playing of James Sheedy, a celebrated Munster piper, who died a very old man, more than thirty years ago."

As the above quotation was penned by Dr. Petrie in 1855, Sheedy must have been in his prime in the last quarter of the eighteenth century.

William Talbot

In a country so renowned as Ireland for the beauty of its melodies and the excellence of its musicians for so many long centuries, it was by no means surprising that famous performers on the harp and Union pipes abounded throughout the Green Isle until comparatively recent times.

One cannot help remarking that wherever mentioned in literature, almost all Irish pipers were alluded to in their respective circuits as "the greatest piper in Ireland."

A few, in the more modest estimate of their friends, were declared to be "the best piper in the county and the next one to it as well." Who does not crave fame, the goal of universal aspiration? If exceptions exist, seek not for them among musicians. Following closely upon the heels of fame came rivalry and unhappiness, for no sooner was a piper's reputation established than peace fled and anxiety commenced. Challenges from rivals eager to strip him of his title are anything but conducive to tranquility of mind, and, being blind—most of them—they never could tell when a disguised competitor was among their audience, picking up their best tunes and gaining information which might be an advantage and guide for future contingencies.

On a fact so generally known, it is scarcely necessary to quote Carleton, the celebrated Irish novelist, as an authority in saying that Union pipers were most numerous in the provinces of Connacht and Munster and fewest in Ulster, his native province.

It is much to be regretted that but comparatively few have escaped the oblivion to which the many have been thoughtlessly consigned. No one was more capable of the task of immortalizing the great pipers who we have no doubt came within the scope of his observation than Carleton. Yet only two have been so favored, namely, Talbot and Gaynor, though two others are briefly mentioned.

Born near Roscrea, in northeast Tipperary, in 1780, this celebrated musician and mechanic lost his eyesight when but fifteen years of age, as a result of an attack of smallpox. It is indeed a melancholy alternative that destines the poor sightless lad to an employment that is ultimately productive of so much happiness to himself and others. So the blind boy devoted his attention to music, and soon acquired such efficiency on the Union pipes that in a few years he was locally famous and in request for all festive gatherings at the seaside near the city of Waterford, where his family had settled after his misfortune. Having traveled about by land and sea for some years, he became a professional piper in 1802, when twenty-two years of age.

Though totally blind, Talbot possessed constructive genius of a high order, and was surprisingly delicate and exact in manipulation, not merely as a musician, but as a mechanic as well. His performance, singularly powerful and beautiful, charmed his audience wherever he went.

It is said that he opened a tavern in Little Mary Street, Dublin, yet it is certain he played in others. His playing of the Union pipes at a performance of *Oscar and Malvina* at Crow Street Theatre in 1816, Grattan Flood says, upheld his reputation as a master of the instrument. He used to play in Ladly's Tavern, in Capel Street, where he arrived every night about eight o'clock and remained until midnight, or even later, occasionally. He was very sociable and, when drawn out, displayed much genuine Irish humor and rich conversational powers. Sometimes at a late period of the night he was prevailed upon to attach himself to a particular party of pleasant fellows who remained after the house was closed, to enjoy themselves at full swing. Then it was that Talbot shone, not merely as a companion, but as a performer. The change in his style and manner of playing was extraordinary; the spirit, the power, the humor and the pathos which he infused into his execution were observed by everyone; and when asked to account for so remarkable a change, his reply was, "My Irish heart is warmed; I'm not now playing for money, but to please myself."

"But could you not play as well during the evening, Talbot, if you wished, as you do now?"

"No, if you were to hang me. My heart must get warmed, and Irish—I must be as I am this minute."

This indeed was very significant, and strongly indicative of the same genius which distinguished Neil Gow, O'Carolan, and other eminent musicians.

An appeal for continued patronage in behalf of Mr. Dignam, proprietor of the O. P. Tavern, printed in the *Freeman's Journal* of April 13, 1812, announced as an attraction that "Mr. Talbot, the celebrated Munster piper, a pupil of the late Cramp, has been engaged to play every evening after eight o'clock (Sunday excepted) at his house, No. 14 Trinity Street." The notice is addressed "To the Lovers of Harmony."

Though blind, Talbot used to employ his leisure hours in tuning and stringing pianos, organs, and mending almost every description of musical instruments that came within his reach. His own pipes, which he called the "grand pipes," were at least eight feet long, and for beauty of appearance, richness and delicacy of workmanship, surpassed anything of the kind that could be witnessed, and, when considered as the product of his own hands, were indeed entitled to be ranked as an extraordinary musical curiosity.

This talented blind musician played before George IV and appeared at most of the London theatres, where his performances were received with the most enthusiastic applause. In person Talbot was a large, portly-looking man, red-faced and good-looking, though strongly marked by traces of the smallpox. He always wore a blue coat, full made, with gilt buttons, and had altogether the look of what is called in Ireland a well-dressed *bodagh,* or "half-sir," which means a kind of gentleman farmer.

His pipes indeed were a very wonderful instrument, or rather combination of instruments, being so complicated that no one but himself could play upon them. The tones which he brought out of them might be imagined to proceed from almost every instrument in the orchestra—now resembling the sweetest and most attenuated notes of the finest Cremona violin, and again the deep and solemn diapason of the organ. Like very Irish performer of talent that we have met, he always preferred the rich old songs and airs of Ireland to every other description of music, and, when lit up into the enthusiasm of his profession and his love of the country, has often deplored, with tears in his sightless eyes, the inroads which modern fashion had made and was making upon the good old spirit of the bygone times. Nearly the last words Carleton ever heard from his lips were highly touching, and characteristic of the man as well as the musician: "If we forget our own old music," said he, "what is there to remember in its place?"—words, alas! which are equally fraught with melancholy and truth.

The man, however, who ought to sit as the true type and representative of the Irish piper is he whose whole life is passed among the peasantry, with the exception of an occasional elevation to the lord's hall or the squire's parlor—who is equally conversant with the Irish and English languages, and who has neither wife nor child, house nor home, but circulates from one village or farm-house to another, carrying mirth, amusement, and a warm welcome with him wherever he goes, and filling the hearts of the young with happiness and delight.

The true Irish piper, Carleton continues, must wear a frieze coat, corduroy breeches, grey woolen stockings, smoke tobacco, drink a tumbler of punch, and take snuff; for it is absolutely necessary from his peculiar position among the people that he should be a walking encyclopedia of Irish social usages; and so he generally is, for to the practice and cultivation of these the simple tenor of his inoffensive life is devoted.

"Piper" Gaynor

The most perfect specimen of this class Carleton ever was acquainted with was a blind man known by the name of "Piper" Gaynor. His beat extended through the county of Louth, and occasionally through the counties of Meath and Monaghan. Gaynor was precisely such a man as has been described, both as to dress, a knowledge of English and Irish, and a thorough feeling of all those mellow old tints which an incipient change in the spirit of Irish society threatened even then to obliterate.

As before stated, he was blind, but, unlike Talbot's, his face was smooth, and his pale, placid features while playing on his pipes were absolutely radiant with enthusiasm and genius. He was a widower who in his earlier years had won one of the fairest girls in the rich argicultural county of Louth, in spite of the competition and rivalry of many wealthy and independent suitors. But no wonder, for who could hear his magic performance without at once surrendering the whole heart and feelings to the almost preternatural influence of this miraculous enchanter? Talbot? No, no! After hearing Gaynor, the very remembrance of the music which proceeded from the "grand pipes" was absolutely indifferent. And yet the pipes on which he played were the meanest in appearance you could imagine, and the smallest in size of their kind, at that. It is singular, however, but no less true, Carleton says, that he could scarcely name a celebrated Irish piper whose pipes were not known to be small, old-looking, and marked by the strains and dinges which indicate an indulgence in the habits of convivial life.

Many a distinguished piper had the novelist heard, but never at all any whom he could think for a moment of comparing with Gaynor. Unlike Talbot, it mattered not when or where he played; his ravishing notes were still the same, for he possessed the power of utterly abstracting his whole spirit into his music, and anybody who looked into his pale and intellectual countenance could perceive the lights and shadows of the Irish heart flit over it with a change and rapidity which nothing but the soul of genius could command.

Gaynor, though comparatively unknown to any kind of fame but a local one, was yet not unknown to himself. In truth, though modest, humble and unassuming in his manners, he possessed the true pride of genius. For instance, though willing to play in a respectable farmer's house for the entertainment of the family, he never could be prevailed on to play at a common dance, and his reasons, often expressed, were such as exhibit the spirit and intellect of the man.

"My music," he would say, "isn't for *the feet* or *the floor,* but for *the ear* and *the heart;* you'll get plenty of foot pipers, but I'm none o' them."

When asked what he thought of the Scotch music in general, he replied, "Would you have me to speak ill of my own? Sure they had it from us."

"Well, even so; they haven't made a bad use of it."

"God knows, they haven't," he replied; "the Scotch airs, many of them, are the very breath of the heart itself."

The experience of a night spent by Carleton in his youth at a farmer's house in Gaynor's company is too long to be reproduced in full, so we will bid adieu to this paragon of pipers and quote his biographer's closing paragraph:

"Such is a very feeble and imperfect sketch of the Irish piper, a character whom his countrymen love and respect and in every instance treat with the kindness and cordiality due to a relation. Indeed, the musicians of Ireland are as harmless and inoffensive a class of persons as ever existed, and there can be no greater proof of this than the very striking fact that in the criminal statistics of the country the name of an Irish piper or fiddler, etc., has scarcely if ever been known to appear."

EDMUND KEATING HYLAND

The authorship of a great poem or musical composition is the key which opens the portals to the hall of fame. Mr. Hyland's claims to distinction as an Irish piper, however, do not rest alone on his reputation as the composer of that delightfully descriptive piece of music, "The Fox Chase," with its imitation of the horns, the tallyho, the hounds in full cry, and the death of the fox, etc. He was an excellent musician, but his performance of "The Fox Chase" is said to have been unrivaled.

Born at Cahir, County Tipperary, in 1780, the same year in which Talbot was born, like the latter also, Hyland lost his sight in early youth, and was apprenticed to a local piper. His talent for music must have been conspicuous to have attracted the notice of Sir John Stevenson, under whom he studied musical theory in Dublin when twenty years of age.

This circumstance brought him into prominence, which, coupled with his wonderfully clever performance, led to his being "commanded" to play before King George IV, on his visit to Dublin in 1821. As a mark of recognition, his majesty ordered him a new set of pipes costing fifty guineas. The popularity of the Irish or Union pipes by this time was much enhanced as a result of the improvements effected by Talbot.

If Hyland composed "The Fox Chase" in 1799, as stated by an authority, his precocity was remarkable, he being then but nineteen years old and as yet uninstructed by Sir John Stevenson. In according him all due credit, we must bear in mind that the original lamentation, or *"Maidrin Ruadh,"* consisting of but eight bars, on which the piece was founded, was much older than Hyland's generation. The renowned performer and composer died at Dublin in 1845.

Elsewhere in this volume will be found several versions of this celebrated piece, obtained from widely different sources.

John Murphy

Accomplished Irish pipers, with few exceptions, like their predecessors, the harpers, traveled extensively throughout Ireland, Scotland and England, until comparatively recent times. Some followed a regular circuit periodically and returned to their native homes to end their days. Others, again, finding life quite agreeable among the English or Scotch, settled down permanently in the sister island. Of this latter class was John Murphy, whose talents secured him the enviable position of family piper to the Earl of Eglinton, at Eglinton Castle, Ayrshire, Scotland.

Murphy was evidently no ordinary performer, but a piper and musician of distinction, for in 1820 he published, *A Collection of Irish Airs and Jiggs with Variations by John Murphy, performer on the Union Pipes at Eglinton Castle.*

Thomas O'Hannigan

Neither history nor tradition shed their illuminating rays on the career of O'Hannigan as far as the present writer was aware until a sketch of his life appeared in *The Story of the Bagpipe,* by Grattan Flood, recently published. Some allusions to him have come to hand since then, however.

Born in 1806 at Cahir, County Tipperary, whence Hyland, the famous piper, also hailed, O'Hannigan was a full-fledged popular Union piper in the second quarter of the nineteenth century. Having become blind at the age of eleven, he took the usual course in such affliction, and served an apprenticeship of four years to various Munster pipers.

Following the example of others in his profession who had attained local celebrity he went to Dublin. In 1837 we are informed he filled an engagement of five nights at the Adelphi Theatre. Seven years later his performance at the Abbey Street Theatre evoked merited applause. He is next heard of at London in 1846, where he remained six years, adding to his fame, and earning the coveted distinction of playing before Queen Victoria and the Prince Consort, and also at an Oxford University commemoration.

Like other exiles he yielded to the desire to return to his native land but died within a year at Bray, County Wicklow, from a stroke of apoplexy.

PATRICK O'SULLIVAN

This surname was as numerous in West Cork and Kerry, as the Smiths were in the old German settlements in Pennsylvania, and equally as insufficient for the purposes of identification without a subtitle or nickname. The writer in his boyhood days at the Bantry National School could enumerate seventeen branches of the Sullivans, as they were commonly called, and the list was by no means complete.

"Paddy O'Sullivan" is referred to by Grattan Flood as "O'Connell's famous piper," although "Mickey" Sullivan, *Cumbaw* of Castlecove, elsewhere sketched, claimed to be hereditary piper to Daniel O'Connell's family. At any rate he was taught the art of piping by another Sullivan, his uncle and a band master. Piper Mr. Sullivan, *"Coshier,"* is mentioned by Lady Chatterton in her *Rambles in the South of Ireland,* in 1839.

More interested in his personal appearance than in his music, she is silent as to the latter, but describes the former in considerable detail, adding that the nickname *"Coshier"* was given to a particular branch of the O'Sullivans from which he claimed descent, for a peculiarity in using a sword in battle. "A most singular figure he was; originally tall and thin, his height is now diminished," she says, "in consequence of a fall, the result of which was to incline his head greatly to one shoulder, and his jocose countenance has acquired an air of knowing familiarity characteristic of his profession."

"This excellent performer," according to Grattan Flood, flourished from 1825 to 1840, but as he could not be induced to wander far from Derrynane, he could not have been the celebrated piper of that name mentioned by Carleton who pursued a rival named Reillaghan for eighteen months through the whole province of Munster in order to challenge him to a contest for supremacy.

Not everyone is aware that Thomas Sullivan, a famous military band master, and father of Sir Arthur Sullivan, was also a native of Kerry.

PATRICK FLANNERY

Chronologically this famous blind minstrel is entitled to first place among Irish-American pipers, as far as our information goes.

He was a native of Ballinasloe, County Galway, but neither the date of his birth nor any account of his early life has come to our knowledge, except that his fame was widespread even in his youth.

He was well along in years when he came to America, about 1845 and as he had no family, he lived for years with Mr. James Quinn in New York City. Money was showered on him as he played in the streets, so keen was the appreciation of his wonderful music, which we can well believe was voluminous as well as melodious.

This grand old minstrel, towering in talent as well as in physique, played his way into paradise, where no doubt he was eagerly welcomed, if we are to place any faith in Irish folk lore, for he had his pipes buckled on, with the lively strains of "The Bucks of Oranmore" rolling in rhythmic tones from the chanter, when the summons to eternity came, as he was entertaining a fascinated audience on the streets of Brooklyn in the year 1855.

In the estimation of Mr. Quinn, a great piper himself, Flannery, of all the pipers he had ever heard, was "the best jig-player that ever laid a finger on a chanter."

"I've heard of Flannery from my boyhood," says Mr. Burke. "He was before my time, but from all accounts he was a great player."

Concerning his splendid instrument the statement of Michael Egan to Mr. Burke is of unique interest: "I made his pipes in Liverpool. I made him a good instrument, and the right man got it. It made a great name for him and also for me. Until I made Flannery's pipes, there was no more thought of my pipemaking than there was of Michael Mannion's of Liverpool, or Maurice Coyne's of Dublin."

The renowned piper had lived at least ten years in America, and taking into consideration his advanced age on arrival, we can safely assume that his birth may be dated a score or so years back into the eighteenth century.

Flannery's grand set of pipes, in which Mr. Egan, their maker, took so much pride, became the property of Mr. Quinn, his friend, who honored the old minstrel with a decent burial. Ald McNurney, into whose hands they passed subsequently, found them too large for convenience, so he traded them for a more suitable instrument to Bernard Delaney, who can wake the echoes with them again, although they are far below modern concert pitch.

James Gandsey (King of Kerry Pipers)

As a performer on the Irish or Union pipes, the subject of this sketch appears to have been unrivaled in his day, at least as far as musicians of his class had come within the scope of Mr. and Mrs. S. C. Hall's observation in their comprehensive travels throughout Ireland in the thirties of the nineteenth century.

Much prominence has been given the celebrated piper and his talents on pages 39 and 40 of *Irish Folk Music: A Fascinating Hobby,* in connection with the history of the "Fox Chase," and which therefore need not be repeated here. Much supplementary information, however, concerning this charming character, having since come to hand; it is submitted with great pleasure for the edification of those interested in Irish musical biography.

Gandsey was long distinguished as "Lord Headley's piper" and it was his privilege for many years to receive instruction beneath his lordship's roof, where his fine original talents were applied to what was worthy of care and cultivation, and where his attention was riveted to the most exquisite melodies of the mountains and glens.

The venerable bard (who died in 1857 at the patriarchal age of ninety) had much Saxon blood in his veins; for his father was an English soldier, who, being quartered at Ross Castle, fell in love—most naturally—with a pretty Kerry girl. Having espoused him and his fortune, she followed them to Gibraltar, bequeathing her child James to her mother's care. An attack of smallpox left him nearly blind, but he could just tell how many candles were lighting on the table. Possibly the skillful surgery of the modern oculist could have effected a cure, as the sight had not been totally destroyed.

The child evinced early genius for music, turning when absolutely an infant the reeds of the lake into musical instruments. When old enough, his grandfather sent him to one of the rustic schools where Latin was taught; and not only the master, but the pupils, loved to instruct and aid the precocious blind boy. Gandsey possessed original talent in many ways. His wit was ready and keen, and he threw the genuine character of the strain into his performance.

But, gentle reader, from the words of Mrs. Hall you are invited to judge for yourself. "The door opens and the blind old man is led in by his son; his head is covered by the snows of age, and his face, though it retains traces of the fearful disease which deprived him of sight, is full of expression. His manner is elevated and unrestrained—the manner of one who feels his superiority in his art, and knows that if he do not give you pleasure, the fault is not his. Considering that perhaps you do not understand sufficiently the beauty of Irish minstrelsy, he will test your taste by playing some popular air or quadrille; and you already ask yourself if you are really listening to the droning bagpipes. His son accompanies him with so much taste and judgment on the violin as to cause regret that he is not practiced on his father's instrument, for you would have the mantle hereafter—and long hence may it be—descend upon the son. You ask for an Irish air, and Gandsey, still uncertain as to your real taste, feels his way again, and plays, perhaps, 'Will You Come to the Bower?' so softly and so eloquently that you forget your determination in favor of 'original Irish music' and pronounce an 'encore.' Do not, however, waste any more of your evening thus; but call forth the piper's pathos by naming 'Druimin dhu dheelish,' as an air you desire to hear; then observe how his face betrays the interest he feels in the wailing melody he pours not only in your ear but into your heart.

"What think you of that whispering cadence—like the wind sighing through the willows? What of that fine-drawn tone, melting into air? The atmosphere becomes oppressed with grief, and strong-headed, brave-hearted men feel their cheeks wet with tears.

"Said we not that Gandsey was a man of might? The piper feels the effect of that air himself; and as he is not a disciple of Father Mathew, a flagon of ale or a mixture of mountain dew will 'raise his heart' and put him in tune for a planxty. There it comes; ringing, merry music— joy giving, light-hearted strain, the overboiling of Irish glee.

"Some of the martial gatherings are enough to rouse O'Donoghue from his palace beneath the lake—one in particular, 'O'Donoghue's whistle,' is full of wild energy and fire. In but too many instances these splendid airs have not been noted down. The piper learned them in his youth from old people, whose perishing voices had preserved the musical traditions so deeply interesting—even in an historical point of view—to all who would gather from the wrecks of the past, thoughts for the future. There are few of those memories of by-gone days that Gandsey does not make interesting by an anecdote or a legend; and in proportion as he excites your interest, he continues to deserve it."

The instrument on which he performed to the great delight of Mrs. Hall, and in fact all who ever heard him, was a bequest from his friend and instructor, Thady Connor, who asserted Gandsey was the only musician in that part of the country worthy to inherit so precious a gift. When questioned as to the accuracy of the authority for a certain story, the kindly old man smiled and bowed but made no verbal reply. As he did not express any doubt concerning its truthfulness, we may as well repeat the story as told to the amiable authoress by no less a person that Sir Richard Courtenay himself, in a chapter devoted to "Irish Pipers in Literature."

PATRICK WALSH

Little is known of this migratory Irish piper except that he was a native of Mayo, large in stature, and flourished about the middle of the nineteenth century.

Like so many others of his profession he encouraged the belief that he was indebted to the fairies for his musical excellence.

Finding the life of a traveling piper in Ireland not to his liking, he made his way to England, where money was more plentiful than in Connacht. Settling down in some town in Lancashire, he secured an engagement to play nightly in a barroom at regular weekly wages, and being a fine piper, even-tempered and accommodating, his employer's increased patronage proved his popularity.

To Walsh it began to look like a life job. Yet in the midst of our joy there may lurk the germ of trouble, and so it was in this case.

One evening a gang of navvies who came in, seeing a fiddler of their acquaintance at the bar, rudely ordered the piper to put up his pipes and let the fiddler play.

Under ordinary circumstances he would be well pleased to get a rest while some other musician continued the entertainment, but the insulting tone in which he had been addressed so stirred his hot Milesian blood that he could not overlook the insult.

The herculean piper, six feet three inches in height, deliberately unbuckled his instrument and put it away carefully after detaching the bellows. With the latter as a weapon in his muscular grip he sailed into the crowd and put them to rout, fleeing in all directions for their lives.

After this incident, either from a dislike to the country or the desire to escape the penalties of the law for his onslaught, he returned to his native province, content with whatever the future had in store for him to the day of his death. He settled at Swineford, County Mayo, and taught his art to many pupils who came from near and far for instruction on the pipes.

His method of dismissing his pupils was as unceremonious as his own departure from England. When one had mastered a tune Walsh took the pupil's hat and flung it outdoors as a signal for the owner to follow it. Without any unnecessary words another aspirant for musical learning was taken in hand and treated similarly.

DANIEL O'LEARY

Down to within comparatively recent times, capable performers on the Union pipes, like their predecessors the harpers, were attached to the households of families of distinction, not alone in Ireland but also in Scotland and England occasionally. No little honor and prestige accrued to the position or connection, but to regard the office as hereditary is, we think, claiming too much. Musical talent is more often sporadic than inherited, and the mediocrity of famous men's sons has become proverbial; the dullness of the bard O'Carolan's only son being a notable instance.

The subject of this sketch presumably is spoken of in *The Story of the Bagpipe,* as one of the last household pipers to the "O'Donoghue of the Glens" in the forties and fifties of the last century, and regarded as little inferior to Gandsey. Earlier mention is made of Daniel O'Leary, the "Duhallow Piper," by a traveler who made his acquaintance in the early thirties at the cabin of a herdsman whom the piper visited periodically in his wanderings.

He is described as a dwarfish hunchback, with a knowing cast of countenance and a keen observant eye. After the customary *cead mile failthe* and the ordinary exchange of compliments O'Leary yoked on his pipes to play as a courtesy to the stranger and rendered "Eileen a Roon" and "O'Carolan's Farewell to Music" with exquisite taste and feeling.

"I have listened to much music," to quote the traveler's words, "but Jack Pigott's 'Cois na Breedha' and O'Leary's 'Humors of Glin' are in my estimation the *ne plus ultra* of bagpipe melody."

A very entertaining but lengthy story of O'Leary's adventures and experience with the fairies at the fort or rath of Doon will be found in another chapter.

John McDonough

Far more truly can it be said that Galway was the "Mother of Pipers" than that Virginia was the "Mother of Presidents." Although obviously inadvisable to institute comparisons, yet in introducing the subject of this sketch as second to none in his profession from Galway, or any other county in Ireland for that matter, we are but voicing the opinion which prevails among old-time musicians.

"John McDonough was the best player of Irish music on the pipes known in his day," Mr. Burke tells us. "He always claimed the parish of Annaghdown, on the banks of Lough Corrib, as his native home (the same in which I was born), but he traveled about from place to place during the greater part of his life."

Even fifty years after his death, which occured in 1857, old people speak of this remarkable piper's facility in giving to the music an appeal and expression peculiarly his own. An all-around player, capable of meeting all demands, he had a preference for piece or descriptive music.

Much of his time was spent in Dublin, and we are informed by his daughter, Mrs. Kenny, "Queen of Irish Fiddlers," that while in that city he had for a brief period been engaged by the late Canon Goodman at Trinity College, either for the purpose of teaching his art, or furnishing entertainment.

In this Mrs. Kenny is simply mistaken, for her father died ten years before the Canon's appointment to a professorship in Trinity. McDonough may have entertained the faculty or students in earlier years, in Goodman's sophomore days, or what is more probable he may in his wanderings through Ireland have met the reverend piper when a curate at Berehaven, or Skibbereen, and there given him instruction.

Whatever the occasion may have been, McDonough's name was placarded conspicuously in Dublin as the celebrated Irish piper from Annaghdown, County Galway, especially on the bridges crossing the Liffey.

While playing on the streets one evening, to the keen delight of an appreciative audience, some well-to-do gentry who came along were so captivated by his inimitable execution that they took him into a clubhouse or hotel in the vicinity. No doubt he was treated with much liberality, but when he reappeared on the street some time afterwards, it was noticed that he was under the influence of intoxicants. This so angered the waiting audience that they stoned the building, and didn't leave a whole pane of glass in the windows within reach of their missiles.

In his native province and even beyond it John McDonough was commonly referred to as "*Mac an Asal*" from the following circumstance: His father, who was a dealer in donkeys or asses, made a practice of getting "Johnny" to play the pipes along the highway to fair or market while mounted on the back of one of them. Whether the father's motive was parental pride in his son's musical precocity, or a shrewd appreciation of the value of commercial advertising, we are unable to say, but it certainly attracted attention. Later in life, from one of his favorite expressions, he was called "Home with the rent."

To no class in the community did the terrible famine years prove more disastrous than to the pipers. Those who lived through plague and privation found but scanty patronage thereafter. "The pipers were gone out of fashion," as one of them ruefully expressed it, so poor John McDonough, the peerless piper, finding himself crushed between poverty and decrepitude, took sick on his way back to his native Galway and died neglected and ignored in the Gort poorhouse.

His splendid instrument, made specially for him by Michael Egan, the most famous of all Irish pipemakers, while both were in Liverpool, was treasured by his widow for seven years after his death. Necessity however forced her to sacrifice her sentiments, and though costing originally twenty pounds she disposed of it for a trifle to a pipe-repairer named Dugan, of Merchant's Quay, Dublin.

KEARNS FITZPATRICK

It appears that Edmund Keating Hyland and William Talbot were not the only Irish pipers who had the honor of playing for the entertainment of King George IV during his visit to Dublin in 1821.

Kearns Fitzpatrick enjoyed that distinction also, but probably on account of the tones of his instrument being deficient in volume for such a large auditorium, he was not equally successful in appealing to the royal generosity, although his playing of "St. Patrick's Day" and "God Save the King" was greeted with applause.

How the prestige of having "played before the king" affects a musician's reputation, is well illustrated by a quotation from the letters of a German prince who toured Ireland in 1828, addressed to his sister:

"In the evening they produced the most celebrated piper of Ireland, Keans Fitzpatrick, called the 'King of the Pipers,' having been honored with the approbation of 'His most gracious majesty, King George the Fourth.' Indeed the melodies which the blind minstrel draws from his strange instrument are often as surprising as they are beautiful, and his skill is equal to his highly polished and noble air. These pipers, who are almost all blind, derive their origin from remote antiquity. They are gradually fading away, for all that is old must vanish from the earth."

The prince, evidently much impressed with the piper and his instrument, took occasion to cultivate a closer acquaintance. Four days later he writes: "As Fitzpatrick the piper, whom I had sent for to my party yesterday, was still in town, I had him come to play *privatim,* in my room while I breakfasted, and observed his instrument more accurately. It is as you know peculiar to Ireland, and contains a strange mixture of ancient and modern tones. The primitive simple bagpipe is blended with the flute, the oboe, and some tones of the organ, and of the bassoon; altogether it forms a strange but pretty complete concert. The small and elegant bellows which are connected with it are fastened to the right arm by means of a ribbon, and the leathern tube communicating between them and the bag lies across the body, while the hands play on an upright pipe with holes like a flageolet which forms the end of the instrument, and is connected with four or five others joined together like a colossal Pan's pipe. During the performance the right arm moves incessantly backwards and forwards on the body, in order to fill the bellows. The opening of a valve brings out a deep humming sound which forms an *unisona* accompaniment to the air. By this agitation of his whole body, while his fingers were busied on the pipes I have described, Fitzpatrick produced tones which no other instrument could give out.

"The sight in which you must picture to yourself the handsome old man with his fine head of snow-white hair, is most original and striking; it is, if I may say so, tragi-comic. His bagpipe was very splendidly adorned, the pipes were of ebony ornamented with silver, the ribbon embroidered, and the bag covered with flame-colored silk fringed with silver.

"I begged him to play me the oldest Irish airs; wild compositions, which generally begin with a plaintive and melancholy strain like the songs of the Slavonic nations, but end with a jig, the national dance, or with a martial air. One of these melodies gave the lively representation of a fox hunt; another seemed to be borrowed from the Hunters' Chorus in the Freischutz; it was five hundred years older.

"After playing some time the venerable piper suddenly stopped and said, smiling, with singular grace, 'It must be already well known to you, noble sir, that the Irish bagpipe yields no good tone when sober; it requires the evening, or the stillness of night, joyous company, and the delicious fragrance of steaming whiskey-punch. Permit me, therefore, to take my leave.'

"I offered such a present as I thought worthy of this fine old man, whose image will always float before me as a true representative of Irish nationality."

How strange that Irish writers should regard such types of Irish life as Fitzpatrick and his class unworthy of their pens.

The prince had been enjoying the hospitality of a Mr. O'R—— at or near Bansha, Tipperary, when he encountered the grand old minstrel Keans or Kearns Fitzpatrick.

Peter Cunningham

In the early years of the nineteenth century there came from Westmeath into the barony of Carbury, County Kildare, a young piper named Peter Cunningham. He soon disappeared however, but some years later, after having rambled all over Munster, came back a finished performer. He settled in the parish of Dunfort at least to the extent that any roving piper can settle. A victim to a peculiar feature of Irish hospitality, he had acquired an unfortunate taste for drink.

On one occasion he visited at Powers' distillery in Dublin some country friends employed in the establishment, and sampled their wares to the number of seventeen glasses of whiskey at that bout. His only regret on leaving was that he had not drank enough while the liquor was going cheap. To finish the slaking of his thirst he went into a convenient pawn office and pledged a five-pound set of pipes for three tenpennies or half a crown.

In his last years he had of course nothing, and was provided with a lodging in a barn by "Pat" Boylan, of Killinagh, about four miles from Edenderry, Kings County.

Peter was visited by the priest who administered the last sacrament. Being prepared for the long journey he called for his pipes, and after dashing off a few rounds of the "Humors of Glin" announced, "That is the last tune I will ever play," and soon fell into the sleep which knows no waking.

John Rotchford

In the early years of the nineteenth century a piper of some renown named "Jack" Rotchford flourished in the barony of Slieveardagh, County Tipperary. He must have been favored with attributes not especially conspicuous among traditional musicians to have earned the nickname *"Seaghan a Beannuighthe"* (Shaun a Vanee) or "John the Blessed."

All too meagre are the details of his life which have come down to us, but from the text of the following legendary story communicated to us by Mr. Patrick Dunne of Kilbraugh, it can be inferred that he was one of those known as family pipers.

Tradition has it that Shaun was "enchanted, so wonderful was his music, and although he never knew a note, he was able to charm the birds to come and sing near him."

"Old Butler," of Williamstown, while entertaining some neighboring gentleman at his residence on one occasion made a bet that he had a better piper than his guest. So Shaun and the other piper met according to the arrangements and played alternately all night and until the break of day, because the judge was unable to decide as to their respective merits. The question of supremacy may never have been determined had not a skylark—proverbial for melody and early rising—lit on the window sill and tapped his approval on a pane of glass when Shaun struck up "The Little House Under the Hill," and endeavored to accompany him with bird music while the tune lasted. Of course Shaun was proclaimed the winner and "Old Butler" won the bet.

In their complacent yet pitiable egotism pipers of prominence affected an air of mystery now and then, and encouraged a rather prevalent notion in days gone by that the friendship and influence of the fairies had not a little to do with the current of their lives. Shaun, who was one of this class, is himself responsible for the following:

One fine morning while watching a cow which needed some care and attention, he thought he may as well entertain himself with a tune or two on the pipes when not otherwise engaged. Choosing the shady side of a rath or fort he sat down and played and sang some favorite airs, for be it understood cows are by no means insensible to the charms of melody. Loud shouting and clapping of hands greeted the finish of his performance. Startled by such unexpected appreciation he was about to hasten away, when requested to continue the music. After obliging the fairies with another tune—for as no one was in sight who else could it be?—they cheered again, and as an evidence of their regards, announced, "Go over to your cow now and you'll find she has a heifer calf."

James Coady

At a later period, say about the middle of the last century, a piper of at least local celebrity named James Coady, hailing from the same part of Tipperary as "Jack" Rotchford, traveled about the country. Whatever virtues he possessed, he was not without a few of the cardinal failings of his fellows. Referring to him by the name which he preferred—*Seamus an Choadhe*—his wife complained that he gave her no money on his periodical visits home, and alleging that whatever *Choadhe* would earn during the day *Seamus* would spend in the night. Drunk or sober he had a great reputation for putting a demoralized set of pipes in good order, a faculty which not all of even the most noted performers possessed.

Timothy Shelly

While making inquiries concerning the history of "Pat" Spillane, a musical genius who first saw the light at Templetouhy, County Tipperary, it developed that an accomplished piper named Timothy Shelly had kept a public house or tavern in that town for many years.

As his musical performance was restricted to that locality his fame was necessarily circumscribed. Intemperance led to his ruin eventually, and he died in the poorhouse about the year 1870, according to Mr. Patrick Dunne, our obliging correspondent.

Hugh Kelly

This great piper's name, like that of so many others of his profession, would have passed into oblivion but for the linking of his performance with the pranks of Robert Brownrigg, the eccentric "Gentleman Piper" of Norrismount, County Wexford.

Kelly, although blind, was one of the circulating pipers of a century ago, and a good one he must have been to have enjoyed the patronage of Mr. Brownrigg.

If further testimony were needed in support of his reputation it was furnished by a lately deceased centenarian of poaching proclivities, who in praising a favorite hound said it had "a tongue as sweet as Hugh Kelly's pipes," and that was no small compliment we can well believe.

"Soldier" Farrell

Not the least distinguished of the many Irish pipers who rejoiced in the patronymic of Farrell or O'Farrell, was one whose story as related by Mr. Flanagan of Dublin cannot fail to arouse our sympathy regardless of other diversified emotions. Considered from any point of view the outcome reflects anything but credit on those responsible for the poor musician's predicament.

When our versatile Dublin friend was a young man "learning the pipes" he was occasionally visited by Farrell, whose home was at Shannon Harbor in Kings County. The latter was a fine performer on the double chanter. In person he was tall and erect with hair as white as snow, and having served twenty-one years in the army was in receipt of a pension of some six or eight pence a day. "As you are aware," says our informant, "O'Connell came along addressing the people and levying the Repeal rent to maintain his campaign, though he betrayed no aversion to the fat salaries his relatives were drawing from the government. The Liberator being expected somewhere in Farrell's locality, the parish priest proposed to the piper that he should take his place in a cart and head the procession with his music. To this prominence Farrell objected, pointing out that he was dependent to some extent on the government, and that it would be injudicious for him to take part in a demonstration hostile to it.

"Naturally the priest prevailed, and the piper-pensioner, much against his judgment, played as requested on the assurance of his reverence that he would see to his safety from unpleasant consequences. When the old soldier was about to be deprived of his pension, the priest on whom he relied told him all he could do for him was to write to O'Connell.

"To the appeal made to him by the patriotic priest in Farrell's behalf, the illustrious Dan, indifferent to the sacrifice, replied curtly that he 'hoped to get Repeal without the assistance of any military men.'"

The pension was forfeited, and though the clergyman pursued the course on which he had relied for its retention, poor Farrell in his old age was left to suffer the pangs of poverty as well as the anguish of misplaced confidence.

There was also a piper named Martin Farrell, who circulated in that part of the country. Though a very fair performer "he wasn't a patch" on the soldier piper of Shannon Harbor.

Patrick Coneely

Immortalized by the eminent George Petrie in the *Irish Penny Journal* of 1840, "Paddy" Coneely, the Galway piper who flourished in the second quarter of the nineteenth century, alone of the many accomplished pipers hailing from that county lives in history.

PATRICK CONEELY

Few indeed are they who do not know that Petrie, artist, antiquary and musician that he was, delighted in nothing more than the indulgence of his hobby of collecting folk music, and it was his desire to increase his store of melodies that brought him to seek the piper's acquaintance in 1839.

Famous though he was in that part of Connacht, "Paddy" Coneely was not the equal of John Crump, or Crampton, the Munster piper whose instrument had been secured after his death by the generous Hardiman and presented to his countryman, the Galway piper.

According to Petrie, " 'Paddy' was simply an excellent Irish piper—inimitable as a performer of Irish jigs and reels, with all their characteristic fire and buoyant gaiety of spirit—admirable indeed as a player of the music composed for and adapted to the instrument, but in his performance of the plaintive or sentimental melodies of his country, he was not able, as Crump was, to conquer its imperfections; he plays them not as they are sung, but—like a piper.

"Yet we do not think this want of power attributable to any deficiency of feeling or genius in 'Paddy'—far indeed from it—for he is a creature of genuine musical soul; but he has had no opportunities of hearing any great performer like that one to whom we have alluded, or of otherwise improving, to any considerable extent, his musical education generally. The best of his predecessors whom he has heard he can imitate, and rival successfully; but still 'Paddy' is merely an Irish piper—*the* piper of Galway par excellence; for in every great town in the west and south of Ireland there is always one musician of this kind more eminent than the rest, with whose name is justly joined as a cognomen the name of his locality."

"Paddy" was away from home on a tour of the county when Petrie and his party visited the City of Galway; consequently they did not meet until a fortunate coincidence brought them together on the Connemara highway. The piper was on his way home for a change of clothing with the intention of spending an evening with a party of gentlemen who had engaged him to play at a regatta coming on in a few days. Though quite blind, yet at any hour of the day or night, he could find his way from his house at Newcastle to any given place in the county. It is said he might often be seen leading another poor blind man by the hand to the latter's destination.

Despite his protestations "Paddy" was actually kidnapped and this was effected only by the seizure of his pipes. His captors explained to him that the Galway gentlemen could often hear him, while they may never have the opportunity again of doing so. So he had to come.

Like the American bobolink which sings almost as soon as it is caged, they had "Paddy" crooning old Irish songs for them and pointing out and even describing all the objects of any interest as they passed along as accurately as if he were blessed with eyesight; though in fact he was stone blind from infancy. More reliable than a barometer, he was an infallible authority on the weather, foretelling a storm in sunshine, and a clearing up on a dismal day, with equal certainty though no indications of impending changes were apparent to others.

After keeping the kidnapped piper with them for two weeks, he was brought home safe and sound and financially better off than if he had kept his engagement with the gentlemen of the regatta.

During the trip, Petrie noted down seventeen of Coneely's tunes, all of which, with six others scored by Lord Rossmore a few years later, are included in Petrie's Complete Collection, published in 1902-1905.

The amiable "Paddy" was in tolerably comfortable circumstances Petrie tells us, having a neat cottage and a few acres of land which he cultivated. He had a great love of approbation—who hasn't?—a high opinion of his musical talents, and a strong feeling of decent pride. He played only for the gentry or comfortable farmer, and would not lower the dignity of his professional character by playing in a tap room or for the commonality, except on rare occasions, when he would play gratuitously and for the sole pleasure of making them happy.

Although he had a wonderful repertory of Irish music; instead of firing away with some lively reel or still more animated Irish jig, he pestered Petrie, in spite of his intensely Irish nationality, with a set of quadrilles or a gallope such as he was called on to play by the ladies and gentlemen at the balls in Galway.

Popular and patronized as he was in his prime, poor "Paddy," like many other celebrities, outlived his fame. He so far resembled many of his fellow votaries of the muses, who moved in a more exalted sphere, that he rarely "thought of tomorrow." The famine years proved disastrous to him in many ways. Sadness instead of gaiety universally prevailed, and music had lost its appeal even were our hero—then in broken health—capable of furnishing it. Paralysis gradually sapped his strength and he passed away in 1850, relieved of anxiety for the welfare of his two boys, who were cared for by the Christian Brothers.

As a specimen of his composition "O'Connell's Welcome to Clare," in 1828, is herewith submitted:

O'CONNELL'S WELCOME TO CLARE

OWEN BRENNAN

of the barony of Mohill, County Leitrim, who flourished in the second quarter of the nineteenth century, was a piper of no ordinary ability. The following story on the authority of Mr. John Gillan of Chicago, who was personally familiar with the circumstances, illustrates his superiority over his contemporaries in that territory.

A few years before the middle of the nineteenth century the estate of Col. Francis Nesbit at Derrycarn, in southeastern Roscommon not far from Drumod, came into the possession of an Englishman at an auction sale. The purchaser, who was passionately fond of pipe music, gave a barbecue to his new tenants, at which no less than thirty pipers attended. From this number the new landlord selected nine of the best performers to compete for prizes. "Owney" Brennan was proclaimed the champion after the contest, his rendering of "Lady Kelly's Reel" being viewed with special favor. One of the Galway Joyces received second prize, while the third went to a piper who hailed from Drogheda.

Riding in a donkey cart and playing the pipes as if for a wager, it was Brennan's invariable custom to accompany any of his friends or acquaintances leaving for America, from their home to the town of Longford, where they embarked on a boat to continue their journey. He was neither lame nor blind, but took to minstrelsy for a livelihood from natural inclination.

Edward Fraher

In the parish of Emly—the Imlagh of Ptolemy—and barony of Clanwilliam, County Tipperary, a piper of good repute and fine ability named "Ned" Fraher flourished before the middle of the nineteenth century. Not from necessity but rather from musical instinct did he become a piper, for in early life he was in full possession of all his faculties.

After leading the ordinary life of a professional piper for some time, he went to England, where he is said to have won fame and fortune. At any rate he had money and medals when he returned, and there was no one to dispute his claim that he had played before royalty and received the splendid instrument he brought back as an evidence of royal appreciation.

Stricken with sudden blindness, his affliction, idiomatically termed a "blast," was attributed to the malevolence of the fairies. His misfortune exempted him from the clerical proscription then in force, and he was allowed to play on Sunday afternoons. He was about fifty-three years of age in 1857 when our informant, Mr. Denis Maloney, an excellent musician himself, came to America.

Edward Lee and Son Denis

of Ballylanders, County Limerick, are said to have been excellent performers on the Union pipes. The father, who flourished in the second quarter of the nineteenth century, was blind, and often instead of playing in concert with him Denis danced to his music.

In his young manhood the latter emigrated to England, and being of splendid physique he obtained a position on the police force. An Irish Adonis, a dancer, and musician, he became a prime favorite in short order, and his admirers presented him with a most expensive set of Union pipes, as he had neglected to bring his own with him from Ireland.

As our informant, who had been one of his neighbors at Ballylanders, emigrated to the United States in 1857, the subsequent career of the Lees—father and son—must remain unrecorded.

CHAPTER XX

OLD TIMES IN WEXFORD AND HER FAMOUS MUSICIANS

At the eleventh hour, so to speak, there came to hand more than half a hundred pages of manuscript, from the facile pen of our tireless contributor, Mr. Patrick Whelan of Scarawalsh, County Wexford. The subject would make an interesting booklet in itself, for not only does it portray certain features of social life in that and contiguous counties in days gone by, but it has rescued from oblivion the names of many whose talents and idiosyncrasies left an impress on local history not yet wholly obliterated. From its contents we gladly glean much that is suitable to our purpose.

The fair of Scarawalsh comes down from the past as a time-honored institution, and tradition holds that it had its origin in a "patron," because the indications—such as a spring well, monastic ruins, and a graveyard found in the vicinity—all point that way.

As the festivities lasted two days—"Lady Day," the fifteenth of August, and the day following, which was the fair day—an event so notable attracted a large attendance, including of course a goodly number of those peculiar types who look to such gatherings for their chief source of income. Although this once celebrated fair went out of existence over fifty years ago, there be those yet among the living who have not forgotten it, even though the mental picture is becoming blurred as it recedes into the mists of time.

First in the list of famous musicians who thronged to this once popular resort stands the name of

"Old Jemmy Byrne the Piper,"

who for many years of his life was saddled with the offensive nickname of "Scut" Byrne as distinguished from another piper of the same patronymic from Glencree, County Wicklow. Gossip is not agreed as to the origin of the sobriquet. One story is to the effect that he demeaned himself and insulted the sentiment of his people by playing party tunes, such as "Croppy Lie Down," at the orgies of the yeomen subsequent to the Rebellion of '98. In extenuation of his alleged offense, it is claimed that mutilation or death would have been the penalty of his refusal. In another account, tradition has it that a parish priest of Ballon, County Carlow, whilst engaged in a militant warfare against the cross-roads dances and other peasant amusements, took occasion to remark in the course of an address to his congregation on the iniquity of dancing and kindred practices: "How dare this 'Scut' come into my parish with his bagpipes to corrupt and demoralize my flock in defiance of my expressed wish?"

Although little of this piper's early life history has been transmitted to posterity, and few incidents of his career recorded, we may safely assume that he was in his day a performer of good repute, from the fact that his fame has survived his death so far, by at least three quarters of a century, while the name of whoever was responsible for his opprobrious nickname is utterly forgotten.

"Old Jemmy Byrne" had three sons—pipers of varying degrees of merit—who also played at the fair of Scarawalsh as long as they lived or remained in the country. In the order of seniority they were Thomas, James, and John, but the sequence was reversed as far as musical efficiency was concerned.

John Byrne

Few men in the community were as presentable as John Byrne. Handsome and erect, his splendid physical proportions were set off to advantage by a broadcloth suit, beaver hat, and a pair of top boots then much in vogue with people of wealth and fashion. A man of intelligence, his address and conversational powers were quite in keeping with his appearance. As if to preserve a due sense of proportion, his set of Union pipes was of the largest size manufactured by Maurice Coyne of Dublin. The wood was ebony with massive ivory mountings, and the brass keys of the regulators, always highly burnished, flashed the reflected rays of the sun like a mirror, under his rapid manipulation, while the green velvet covering of the bag, with tinseled fringe, enhanced the general effect of the whole picture.

Though but a piper dependant on public patronage, John Byrne's exalted ideals and polished manners would honor a prince, and if he could not be classed as a "gentleman piper" in the accepted sense of the phrase, he was endowed liberally with the qualities of head and heart which ranked him as one of "nature's noblemen."

He traveled into Munster periodically and enjoyed an exceptional patronage for obvious reasons. Concerning his musical attainments, Michael Doyle, the most celebrated dancing master in the province, said: "There is something in his playing to commend him to the dancer, which I cannot find in any other man. His brother James is also gifted in this way but John is decidedly the better."

As might be expected from a piper of his reputation, his circuit was less confined than that of the late lamented "Jem" Cash, who was best known in his native county, so that his attendance at the fair of Scarawalsh was not habitual. Like all traveling minstrels he had his favorite haunts; the choice in that neighborhood being the home of Mr. William Murphy, an extensive farmer of Craanrue, who was a flute player of good local repute. Byrne's visits were always hailed with delight, and the news of his arrival which spread quickly brought the youth of the countryside for miles around to the scene. Some of the more joyous spirits came provided with cordials, and perchance something more exhilarating, and we can well believe that the outbuilding in which they congregated to hold the dance never had a dull moment while the festivities lasted.

Such visits, usually of about a week's duration, were regarded by this exemplary piper as a time of relaxation or holiday making, and we get a clearer insight to a character so unique by his refusal to accept any monetary consideration for his music on those occasions. Competitive dancing was one of the principal features of the merrymaking incidental to Byrne's sojourn at Craanrue. Need it be said that his fame and popularity were no less pronounced in his day than what "Jem" Cash enjoyed at a later period?

Good pipers found the Curragh of Kildare a profitable field for their profession, and no point in his peregrinations was so favored by John Byrne as that celebrated centre of sport and gayety, and if tradition can be relied on, he received a weekly stipend of thirty shillings from the military stationed there, to play for their entertainment.

This paragon of pipers emigrated to America about the year 1860—just before the beginning of the Civil war—but no authentic information concerning his history thereafter reached his friends and admirers in his native country.

JAMES BYRNE

Next in order of musical merit comes James, an elder brother of John, and whose name tradition links inseparably with the long extinct fair of Scarawalsh.

All the crack dancers of the three parishes—and they were by no means few—and many more from far beyond thronged to that fair. The two Coopers, "Dick" and "Will," "Lawrence Piper," "Matty" Tobin, and several other disciples of Terpsichore of less renown, would be holding high heads for days in happy anticipation of "Jemmy" Byrne's arrival, for simultaneous with that event might be expected another of scarcely less moment—the appearance of Michael Doyle, the dancing master.

All the celebrities met at the widow Piper's farmstead, and thrifty and accommodating individual that she was, she secured a limited license for the occasion, and we may be certain that the attractions of piping and dancing to be enjoyed on the premises assured her a liberal patronage. Besides, her oldest son Lawrence was Doyle's best pupil, at least in Wexford, for as Mr. Whelan says: "You would have to cross the granite ridge of Mount Leinster, and go out into the County of Carlow, where there lived another of Doyle's pupils named James O'Neill, before you would meet any who could compete with a tolerable chance of coming out even."

Be it understood that the fair of Scarawalsh, held annually on the sixteenth day of August, came in the middle of the harvest season, which may be early or late according to climatic conditions. Now it so happened at one time that the piper and dancing master were on hand a few days before that date, and the widow had a field of oats "rotten ripe" which must be reaped before the fair, or it would not be cut until "God knows when," or perhaps altogether lost. Now here was a predicament in earnest. The day before the fair being "Lady Day" there remained but one working day in which to get it done. True, there was but little more than a day's work in it under normal conditions for the three men available—her son and the two Coopers—but unfortunately they were undergoing a course of training for the dancing contests.

A "plan of campaign" formulated by the widow's resourceful son Lawrence which met with favor was promptly put into execution. "Jemmy" Byrne with his pipes and a chair; Michael Doyle, the dancing master, with a door, and Lawrence Piper and the two Coopers, armed with reaping hooks, hastened to the field early in the morning. Two of the reapers slashed away at the oats; the third mounted the prostrate door and took his dancing lesson under the supervision of Doyle, while Byrne seated in his chair close by supplied the enlivening music. Each dancer's term of practice lasted while one swath was being reaped across the field; and thus the trio danced and reaped alternately throughout the livelong day except when food or refreshments were partaken. The result was most gratifying, for not only was the work of three men done by two, but each dancer had also his full meed of practice into the bargain.

During the holiday afternoon and the entire day of the fair, dancing would be at a premium. "Jemmy" Byrne was usually to be found "discoursing sweet music" on the widow Piper's premises, while his father and brothers were located among the tents.

Occasionally the music, dancing, and associated convivialities would be inter-rupted abruptly by the breaking out of a fight in which the tents would be dis-mantled and the wattled framework broken up into convenient lengths to supply the gladiators with munitions of war.

In those days the tunes now termed "single jigs" were known as "jigs" with-out any qualifying word. The other varieties were called "doubles" and "hop jigs." With jigs and reels alternating, there was no "let up" to the dancing in the tents favored with music.

Sometimes a young man or woman of exceptional repute appeared, and such was the desire to witness their exhibition of skill, that all other forms of entertain-ment would be suspended for the time being. Should the "star" happen to be one of the fair sex, a suitable partner was pressed into service; if a young man, and no partner was forthcoming, instead of dancing a "double" according to custom, he not infrequently "took the door" provided for such contingencies all by himself and danced a "naked step"—usually some favorite hornpipe.

The tent which harbored the best piper was certain to have the largest patron-age, and naturally the most skillful dancers. Of all the trim colleens who ever graced the green when the fair of Scarawalsh was the event of the year in that territory, the name of Katie Morgan—the late Mrs. Ward—stands pre-eminent A match any day for "Larry" Piper, her preferred partner, in exhibition dances; her blandishments were irresistible in coaxing the coin from the pockets of the most penurious, in exchange for her stock of fruits, candies and confections.

"Jemmy" Byrne was her favorite piper—and who so keen to appreciate a good piper as a good dancer—but she married John Ward, an excellent performer on the flute and dulcimer. Wealthy at one time, the enforced change in social life and customs ruined her business and brought her to the verge of want in later years. Yet such was her spirit even in old age, that she would lay down her basket and dance with surprising agility on hearing any of her favorite tunes played by some wandering minstrel.

Thomas Byrne

Compared with his father and younger brothers, Thomas Byrne was incon-spicuous. Even so, he was a fairly good piper of wandering habits, and followed the fairs and festivals while capable of traveling. He survived his brother James, but when or where he died remains an unsolved problem. The fact that he had some professional intercourse with John Rowsome and George Carroll, within the period of their activity as pipers, affords plausible grounds for believing that he was among the living up to 1880 and perhaps a few years later.

The Byrne Family

Collectively the Byrnes belonged to Shangarry, in County Carlow, from whence they radiated to the "patrons," fairs, and races in that and neighboring counties, returning again at stated intervals to enjoy a season of domestic reunion on their replenished purses.

After the death of "Old Jemmy" Byrne sixty years or so ago, and the subse-quent emigration of John to America, the home at Shangarry was broken up. "Young Jemmy" emigrated to the vicinity of Ballycarney, where he lived with a man named "Matty" Rigley, whose brother Ben was a good amateur piper. While at Mr. Rigley's he was frequently visited by John Cash and Samuel Rowsome, who became noted pipers themselves.

Here we have a musical chain the most complete of any which has come to our attention. "Old Jemmy" Byrne, the Carlow piper, and his three sons all professionals, of whom young "Jemmy" communicated his art to Samuel Rowsome of Ballintore, County Wexford, who in turn transmitted it to his three sons. The art is still further perpetuated in his grandson, Samuel Rowsome, Jr., of Dublin, who recently gained distinction as a prize winner at the age of sixteen, being the fifth generation of pipers of note. 'Twas in the blood of the Byrnes and the Rowsomes, though in the latter family music was a pleasure rather than a profession.

When Mr. Rigley removed from Ballycarney to Knockmarshal near Enniscorthy, seven miles from the former home, "Jemmy" Byrne accompanied the family with whom he lived to the end of his days. His death, which was rather sudden, occurred about the year 1867 and before he had rounded out three score years.

For many a year at Shrove-tide, he made a trip to his native Carlow to play at the weddings, for it appears that the music of the Union pipes retained its hold on popular sentiment more tenaciously in that county than in Wexford.

Michael Brandy of Ballycarney, a veteran of seventy-four, to whom Mr. Whelan, our correspondent, is indebted for not a little of his information, relates that once when Byrne was about to start on one of his annual expeditions, finding that his funds were exhausted, asked for a loan of five shillings until his return. Brandy being then young and unmarried was glad of the opportunity to oblige such a friend with twice that amount. A month or so later the piper returned, repaid the ten shillings, "treated" his generous friend to all he cared to drink, and still had left a balance of six pounds in his pocket.

Henry Roberts

Another Irish piper of local fame who frequented the fair of Scarawalsh was Henry Roberts of Bunclody. He was best remembered by his rendering of the "Fox Chase," in which the cry of the hounds, the sound of the horns, the tallyho of the huntsmen, the galloping of the horses, and the shouts and cheers of the enthusiastic votaries of the chase, and even the agonizing wail of the gamey fox, as he yielded up his life in the last struggle against overwhelming odds, were all reproduced with startling vividness.

In those days of unrestrained merriment, when custom gave license to the many to "let their bursting spirits out," often at the expense of the unwary pleasure seeker, some practical jokes bordering on criminality were liable to be perpetrated. Even the piper it seems was not exempt from being victimized. One fine day Roberts was playing away contentedly while seated in a car unyoked for the purpose on the sloping sward of the fair green, in close proximity to the brink of the river Slaney. Taking in the situation at a glance, a villianous wight noted for misconduct, and who years afterwards perished by violence, seized the shafts and swinging the car free of its fastenings let it roll into the river. Before the astonished piper could realize his danger he was plunged headlong into a deep pool while his instrument with drones still humming from the air in the inflated bag floated away on the current. Eager hands promptly came to his rescue, and saved both himself and his pipes, but his earning capacity for the rest of that day at least was ruined beyond repair.

And so ends our chronicle of the days of "Old Lang Syne," as condensed and abbreviated from the correspondence of our indefatigable friend, Mr. Patrick Whelan. Many and interesting accounts of the pipers, fiddlers and fluters of more recent times will be found elsewhere under their proper headings.

CHAPTER XXI

FAMOUS PIPERS WHO FLOURISHED PRINCIPALLY IN THE SECOND HALF OF THE NINETEENTH CENTURY

CHARLES FERGUSON

This celebrated piper, who is said to have been a native of Limerick, was more fortunate than most members of his profession in being immortalized by Shelton Mackenzie in *Bits of Blarney* and by Duncan Fraser in *Some Reminiscences and the Bagpipe,* even though the references to him are disappointingly meagre.

A footnote in the first named work reads, "There is now in New York a gentleman named Charles Ferguson, whose performance on the Irish pipes may be said to equal—it could not surpass—that of O'Donnell."

Ferguson's pipes are pictured in Duncan Fraser's work with the following notation:

"THE GREAT IRISH PIPE

WITH DOUBLE BASS REGULATOR AND 27 KEYS

This pipe is made of ebony and ivory with brass mountings, and was said to have been a gift from the late Queen Victoria to one Ferguson, a blind piper in Dublin." The author adds that Ferguson played in and out of the large hotels in Dublin in the early part of the last century.

To have played before royalty was an honor only exceeded by that of having been presented with an instrument as a mark of special distinction, and though tradition delights in perpetuating stories of such royal favors, few will stand the test of authenticity. Queen Victoria no doubt was endowed with many admirable qualities, but neither generosity nor liberality, especially to an Irishman, can be reckoned among them. In the case of Ferguson, we can clearly acquit her of making any exception in his favor.

Attracted by his splendid execution when playing around the prominent Dublin hotels, Catherine Hayes, the great Irish singer, engaged Ferguson to accompany her on a concert tour of the United States and Canada in 1851. His financial circumstances having materially improved in America, he sought out Michael Egan, the famous pipemaker, who had moved his business from Liverpool to New York, and ordered made the set of pipes supposed to have been presented to him as before stated. Read what Mr. Nicholas Burke has to say on this subject:

"Charles Ferguson, after he came back from San Francisco, lived in Brooklyn, New York. Those pipes you mention in *Irish Folk Music—A Fascinating Hobby,* that he claims he got presented to him by Queen Victoria, were made for him by Michael Egan in his shop in Forty-second Street, between Ninth and Tenth Avenues, New York City.

"We had a benefit party for Egan when he was sick a short time before he died, and this was how the tickets were worded: 'Benefit party for Michael

Egan, the maker of the celebrated Harmonic Irish Union Pipes; also the maker of Professor Ferguson's pipes, which are supposed to have been presented to him by the Queen of England.'

"Egan was well satisfied with the wording of the ticket. He said he never denied Ferguson's qualities as a player, and he had no right to deny that he made the set of pipes for him."

After settling down permanently in Brooklyn, Ferguson and William Connolly played together at picnics and church fairs, Ferguson's forte being airs and slow music. Connolly was in demand to play jigs, reels, and hornpipes for the dances, and, in the language of Mr. Burke, " 'Tis he could do it to the queen's taste."

Ferguson is said to have learned most of his music from Rt. Rev. Dr. Tuohy, who was Bishop of Limerick from 1814 to 1828, a notable performer on the Irish pipes. From this we can account for the pupil's ability to play the sacred music at the celebration of mass in a Brooklyn Catholic church in later times, and his preference for airs, to the exclusion of dance music.

Eventually, when well advanced in years, he married a wealthy old lady in Brooklyn, who professed a great desire to take care of him, and no doubt she did, for he dropped out of view completely thereafter.

James Quinn

An early settler on the shores of Lake Michigan, James Quinn enjoyed the distinction of being the first Irish piper who became a resident of Chicago. Famous as a musician and popular as a citizen, he was regarded as an old-timer when the writer made his acquaintance in 1873.

Mr. Quinn was born in the parish of Cloone, barony of Mohill, County Leitrim, about the year 1805, and he died in Chicago in 1890, at a patriarchal age. Being uncommonly bright and precocious, he attracted the notice of his landlord, Augustus Nicolls, commonly called "Gusty" Nicolls, a noted piper and composer of pipe music, who took him in hand and gave him a thorough schooling on his favorite instrument.

Following some years' experience as a professional piper, Mr. Quinn was engaged as a house-piper by a gentleman in the adjoining county of Cavan. Every man of prominence prided himself on his piper in those days, for whoever had the best piper was sure to have the most company. Whimsical as prima donnas, pipers were always noted for their eccentricities. No inducement which his employer could offer would restrain one remarkable performer of Mr. Quinn's acquaintance from taking to the road with the first troop of tinkers that came the way in the spring. The gypsy life which that class of nomadic artisans led in the summer time appealed to him irresistibly, and not until the inclemency of winter weather drove them from the highways did this unconventional piper seek a re-engagement.

Fifty pounds a year and the use of a saddle horse was the ordinary annual allowance for a family piper, and this James Quinn received during his ten years' stay in Cavan. Letters addressed to him in New York in 1840 indicate his emigration to America before that date. Little is known of his life in New York except that for four years preceding his death the great piper Patrick Flannery lived with him. Mr. Quinn was interested in the livery business after his coming to Chicago, but later he became a coal and wood dealer, in which gainful calling he continued up to the time of his death.

He was commendably liberal with his music in public and in private, and he never failed to entertain his callers to their heart's content. His style of execution was close staccato of the classic Connacht school of piping, and, like most old-time players, he was inordinately addicted to embellishing his tunes with a surprising number of variations. Many a rare tune has been preserved through him. Besides John K. Beatty, Michael McNurney, afterwards alderman, and Sergt. James Early, who were his pupils, "Pat" Coughlan and John McFadden, famous fiddlers, played in concert with him for many years in Chicago, and consequently acquired and perpetuated his music.

As a wit and a story teller he was in a class by himself. Keen, observant and gifted with a phenomenal memory, we can well believe that his fund of anecdotes was endless. Revered in death as he was loved when living, this typical piper and minstrel, although summoned to eternity over a score of years ago, is still affectionately referred to as "Old Man Quinn" by a large circle of surviving friends, as well as by his numerous descendants.

John Hicks

Most Irish musicians have their specialties, and this characteristic is particularly true of the pipers. Some who can play the most difficult dance music with ease and unconcern seldom attempt to entertain an audience with airs, marches or other slow measures except when called for; while others, on the contrary, who enjoy playing airs and even modern compositions, are incapable of rendering the sprightly dance tunes with that peculiar rhythm and swing which instinctively sets our feet in motion.

The subject of this sketch was a notable exception. He had neither fads nor favorites, for he was equally proficient and charming in all kinds of music, ancient and modern, which came within the compass of his instrument.

From his own lips in Chicago I learned that he was a protegé of "Sporting" Captain Kelly of the Curragh of Kildare. His musical precocity when a boy attracted the Captain's attention, and many a time, perched on his patron's knees, did the youthful prodigy play on his flute for the entertainment of company.

To Mr. M. Flanagan of Dublin, a fine musician himself, we are indebted for some interesting information concerning Hicks' early life. He was born on the edge of the Curragh, about the year 1825, and was left without a father when quite young, the only son of his widowed mother. His musical proclivities endeared him to his generous patron, who, by the way, was an enthusiastic piper himself, and loved the music of his country as dearly as he loved the turf. What could better exemplify this intensity of feeling than his custom of naming his stud of racers after parts of the instrument, such as Chanter, Bellows, Drone, etc.? The inheritance of musical talent survives in his grand-nephew, Mr. John Kelly Toomey, a Dublin attorney, but it finds expression on the fiddle instead of the Union pipes.

And, by the way, Captain Kelly did not monopolize the sporting blood of the family, for it was his sister, Mr. Flanagan says, who staked an immense sum and her "coach and four" on Dan Donnelly when he fought and defeated Cooper, the English champion pugilist, on the Curragh of Kildare.

But to return to our subject, "Johnny" Hicks became a piper under the patronage and instruction of Captain Kelly. He turned out to be an apt pupil, and if we are to judge of the teacher by the style and execution of those who graduated under his tuition, the renowned turfman must be ranked among the best pipers of his day.

How Hicks got started as an independent piper is best told in Mr. Flanagan's own words, which follow:

"I am sure you will be interested to learn that I was born and brought up within a stone's throw of a little wayside public house where Hicks played many a day and many a night. This was before my advent in the family, but the piper lived in the memory of my elders. He was introduced into the neighborhood by a fiddler named 'Patsy' Kilroy, and the piper soon 'cut the roots' of the fiddler to such a degree that Kilroy bitterly rued his unselfish act. One night the piper and fiddler were playing in concert a reel called 'Fisher's Fancy,' at the public house referred to, when in comes 'Bill' Thompson, the local blacksmith and farrier. 'Bill,' who was as fine a specimen of the Irish peasant as I ever laid eyes on, listened patiently while the musicians played a few rounds of the tune. Placing his brawny hand on Kilroy's shoulder, he softly said, 'Put up that wash-staff *avic* and let the man play the pipes.'

"The public house which John Hicks had made his headquarters was situated on the Dublin and Galway mail-coach road, about midway between Edenderry and Innfield. It was kept by the widow Cleary and was a place of great resort, because in those days there was something of a population in rural Ireland. Hicks must have left the neighborhood in or about 1850. He was then quite a young man and was a promising rather than a finished player. In fact, there was in the parish at the time a much superior piper, 'Tim' Ennis, who afterwards taught me all I know on the instrument. Although denationalized in many aspects, the people of my parish had the old *gra* for the Union pipes, and a fiddler got but little countenance. Yet when I took up the study as a young fellow there was not another young piper within a radius of ten miles."

"The Kildare piper" must have come direct to America in 1850, for he was well known in all the cities along the Atlantic coast almost a generation before his visit to Chicago in 1880, an account of which can be found in *Irish Folk Music—A Fascinating Hobby.*

His playing was wonderfully even and rhythmical, and the tones were clear, full and melodious. Other performers heard in Chicago at later dates excelled him in brilliant execution and variations, but no piper of our acquaintance was so popular with a mixed, or American audience as John Hicks, because of his versatility in playing all kinds of modern music, including polkas, waltzes, and schottisches. One great favorite which never failed to please was "General Grant's Grand March," a composition which served equally well as a schottische. He was also a fiddler, and could transpose written music into keys suitable for the pipes when necessary.

He ventured on the stormy sea of matrimony more than once, his second wife being a lady of fortune. Her death before the birth of an heir, under the provisions of the ante-nuptial contract, deprived him of the inheritance.

Clerical in attire and appearance though he was, it did not protect him from being the victim of a fatal assault late one night in the year 1882. He was on his way home to New York after playing at an entertainment on the Jersey side of the Hudson River. Just as he reached the Hoboken ferry-dock someone whose identity was never ascertained struck him on the head with a sandbag. No attempt was made to rob him, but he died in a short time without regaining consciousness.

In the account of his tragic death, the press honored his music and himself with many flattering paragraphs, due no doubt in some measure to his amiable personality and freedom from those failings which so often mar cordiality in the musical profession.

WILLIAM CONNOLLY AND JOHN CONNOLLY

Among the pipers of whom we have any record, few if any were so successful financially and none possessed the nomadic instinct to such a degree as William Connolly, who was born at Milltown, County Galway, about the year 1839. His father, known as *"Liam Dall,"* or "Blind William," born at the beginning of the century, was a piper of great repute.

In his young days he went to Liverpool, accompanied by his brother, John, but their experience not being up to their expectations, they decided to cross the Atlantic. While John remained in the United States, William's restless temperament impelled him to try his luck in Canada. Fortune favored him in this venture, and, finding things to his liking, he tarried in that country for an unusually long time, playing on the steam packets plying up and down the St. Lawrence River.

Having made considerable money, he longed for a change of scene, returned to the United States, and settled in Brooklyn, New York, where he bought a house. This property he disposed of in 1863, fearing he would be drafted into the Federal army, the Civil War being then at its height. Besides, he realized that it was much easier for him to handle a chanter than a rifle, so he lost no time in getting back to Liverpool, in which cosmopolitan city he remained four years.

Before his return to America, when all danger had passed, this inveterate bird of passage took occasion to pay a visit to the old home in Galway. Modesty evidently was not his most conspicuous virtue, for we are told that he engaged a boy to carry his set of bagpipes through Milltown, with a view to impress the people with a due sense of his importance.

Brooklyn, New York, his next destination, soon lost the distinguished piper, for he went to Waltham, Massachusetts, and built a dance hall in which he was to be the great attraction. Golden visions eventually lured him to California, so San Francisco enjoyed a musical treat for some time; but as happiness is always at the end of the rainbow, which recedes as we approach, Connolly retraced his steps to the Atlantic coast. After a brief stay in the East he again headed for the Golden Gate.

Still restless and dissatisfied, he bade a final adieu to California, intent on purchasing Hibernian Hall, Brooklyn; but as his wife would not consent to the sale of her home in Waltham, the project had to be abandoned. Another move was the result, this time to the city of Pittsburgh, Pennsylvania, where he died a few weeks later, after acquiring possession of a prosperous saloon.

Mr. Burke, to whom we are indebted for the above information, says "William Connolly was the best general player on the Irish pipes on either side of the Atlantic." Michael Egan, the famous maker of the Irish or Union pipes, who knew all the best pipers of his day, was of the same opinion.

His brother John, it seems, was something of a rambler also, for in an article in *The Advocate* of Melbourne, Australia, issued August 17, 1912, we find that an Irish piper named J. Connolly returned to San Francisco, after a few months' residence in Melbourne many years ago." "Patsy" Touhey, who regarded him as a fair performer, reports that he died about the year 1895 at Milford, Massachusetts.

WILLIAM MADDEN

On the authority of Mr. Burke we are told that this piper was a great performer, excelled only by William Connolly. Little is known of him except that he was a native of Ballinasloe, county of Galway, and that the renowned piper Patrick Flannery was his uncle. After the latter's death, in 1855, Madden, accompanied by John Coughlan, visited Ireland, where he remained two years before returning to New York.

In Madden's case, necessity was not the motive for his choice of a profession, for all his faculties were unimpaired. The predilection for music not infrequently proves irresistible, and where social position or some lucrative calling presents no hindrance or restraint, the profession of wandering musician is taken up as an agreeable means of obtaining a livelihood.

OWEN CUNNINGHAM

This great performer on the Irish pipes, who was known among his own people as Cunnigam, belonged to the city of Galway, although Mr. Cummings of San Francisco claims he lived at Athenry, his own native place. Both may be right at different periods. The date of his birth is unknown, but he flourished around the middle of the nineteenth century. According to Mr. Nicholas Burke, he was much given to rambling and was seldom to be found at home. Going from one gentleman's place to another's, all over the country, he remained at each for an indefinite period, as did the harpers in their day.

Captain Clancy of the Chicago police, who was born some eight miles northeast of Galway City, remembers Cunnigam's visits to his father's house in the fifties. The piper drove his own jaunting car when traveling on his annual summer tours, and he put up for a week or so among his selected patrons.

During his stay at the Clancy homestead the people flocked from miles around to hear him, and so did the pipers within reach—to listen, learn, and *keep still,* for they admitted his superiority.

The Captain, who has a clear recollection of the piper and his instrument, describes him as rather tall and thin, with high cheek bones and sallow complexion. His pipes were longer, slimmer, and softer in tone than the modern concert instrument made by Taylor of Philadelphia.

'Twas Cunnigam's proud boast, and one often repeated, that he received one hundred pounds a year from the Duke of Northumberland for staying at the castle and playing when required for six or eight weeks around the Christmas holidays.

He also claimed to have played before royalty and to have filled engagements at one of the most fashionable of London hotels. His return to his native home in Galway, in prosperous circumstances only in the summer season, gave color of probability to his story, especially as the duke was known to be a great lover of Irish music and a liberal patron of accomplished Irish pipers.

Cunnigam was an incorrigible rambler, and his peregrinations in the year 1861 extended to America, but his travels in the "land of the free" were confined to the cities of Boston, New York, Brooklyn, and vicinity. Restless in spirit as the "Flying Dutchman," his stay in America was short, for the demon of discontent seemed to possess him and keep him forever on the move. So he returned to Ireland, but from an article on "The Irish Music Revival" which appeared in the issue of *The Advocate,* August 17, 1912, we learn that "Owen Cunningham, formerly of Boston, U. S. A.. formerly played in the streets of Melbourne and Sydney in 1868."

Like Ferguson, Cunnigam was an exception among pipers. A splendid performer, he played airs, marches. and descriptive pieces to perfection, yet, to quote the language of Mr. Burke. "he wasn't much on jigs, reels, or hornpipes."

Eugene Whelan

No piper of his day or generation enjoyed such fame as an accomplished musician as Eugene Whelan, who confined his circuit to his native Kerry.

At Oakpark, a few miles north of Tralee, there lived early in the nineteenth century a rich farmer named Whelan, who was keenly disappointed on the birth of his first-born because it was not a boy. You may be sure that when a second and a third daughter arrived they were anything but welcome. The exasperated Mr. Whelan took no pains to conceal his displeasure at not having an heir to perpetuate his name and inherit his wealth. More than once he told his neighbors that he would rather have three blind sons than three daughters possessed of all their faculties.

His people looked upon his attitude as a defiance of God's will, which invited merited punishment, and it was no more than they expected when three blind sons were born to him following the three daughters. This story, for which our genial friend, Officer "Tim" Dillon, is responsible, can claim more originality than that of Prof. P. D. Reidy, which follows: A beggar woman, accompanied by half a dozen children, sought alms at the Whelan farm-house one day. Being in an ungracious mood at the time, "the woman of the house," who was not long married, ignored the plea for charity, comparing the beggar woman and her offspring to a sow and her brood. To the proverbial widow's curse is attributed the subsequent misfortunes of the Whelan family. According to Professor Reidy, three brothers—Maurice, Eugene, and Michael—were born blind, and a sister, Kitty, nearly so. Maurice, who was a first-class fiddle player, was living as late as 1840 at least. Michael, who was also a violinist, was the last survivor of the family. Eugene was the most accomplished performer on the Irish or Union pipes Professor Reidy, the renowned dancing master, ever heard. His command of tune was faultless, and his versatility even extended to the flute and fiddle also. Speaking of his playing of the *Ceoil Sidhe* (Keolshee), the professor says: "The lights were extinguished, and as I entered the room in the farmer's house I had to study to know where Eugene was sitting, the music was so soft and melodious."

Exhibitions of dancing on the kitchen table by professional or noted dancers were very popular forms of entertainment in Cork and Kerry in former times. When playing for such experts it was Whelan's custom to shut off the drones and use the chanter only. Order and quietness were preserved by the old men, so that every tap of the dancers' performance could be distinctly heard.

When Professor Reidy and Edmund Denis O'Loughlin, another celebrated dancer, gave an exhibition at Mr. Craig's residence, near Ferranfore, in 1866. Eugene Whelan, who played for them, was in failing health. and he soon had to take refuge in the Union Infirmary in Tralee, where he did not long survive.

So great was his reputation as a performer when in his prime, that professional pipers from far and near came to hear him, not only out of curiosity, but also with a view to profit by his example. Conviviality, that bane of professional musicians, led to excesses, and though his end was unhappy he was by no means friendless.

William Boyle

According to Mr. Burke, William Boyle, hailing from the city of Galway, was a fine general player on the Irish pipes and was equally proficient on the fiddle. Caring little for travel, he never went far from home until he came to America, about 1885 or 1886, being then well advanced in years.

After a short stay in New York City, he settled in Newark, New Jersey, where he died. He kept a dance house in that town, and when Owen Cunnigam would be around they would play together at balls and parties and other entertainments.

Boyle was taught pipe music by Michael Touhey, a famous piper from Loughrea, Galway, grandfather of Patrick J. Touhey, the renowned American performer. His father, who was a piper also, kept a dance house in the city of Galway.

John Williams

The maxim that temperance or sobriety tends to prolong life, finds no endorsement in the case of John Williams, a blind piper from the town of Athlone, on the banks of the Shannon. Being a fine performer on the Irish pipes, he was a great favorite with the soldiers at the barracks.

After coming to America he told Mr. Burke that he played for fourteen years in the "canteen," and during that time he never went to bed a night sober. Many and many a night he had been picked up, bag and baggage, pipes and all, and taken home, helplessly intoxicated. He was past middle age when he emigrated to this country with his wife and daughter, but he had two sons in America years ahead of him. He died at the beginning of this century, a very old man.

John Morris

This truly great piper, better known as Morris Sarsfield, belonged to Clida, a short distance from the town of Headford, County Galway. How he came by the name Sarsfield is not clear, but it quite likely originated from hero-worship of the famous general. Under the name *"Muiruich"* (as near the writer can get it) he was known also in that part of the country, natives of which now residing in Chicago remember him by name and reputation.

In the language of Mr. Nicholas Burke, "he was a powerful man and a great player on the pipes," and we find he had a decided aversion to remaining long in one place. Much of his time was spent in England, but if he happened to be at home at the time, he was sure to be off with the crowd that went harvesting to that country every year.

On one occasion he went to Wales and got along swimmingly with the miners until asked to play the "Collier's Reel." Unfortunately, this was a "new one on him." "Tim" Callaghan's excuse or proposition to "give them one as good" was not satisfactory. To be unable to play the tune so named after their trade or calling was to be unworthy of their patronage, and the story goes that Morris was chased out of town for this deficiency in his repertoire.

Neither the date of his birth nor death can be stated, but it is certain that he flourished in the third quarter of the nineteenth century.

Peter Hagerty

More than half a century ago—in 1860, to be exact—the present writer, not yet in his teens, listened for hours with awe and delight to the music of Peter

Hagerty's pipes. Peter "Bawn," as he was called on account of his fair hair, was a tall, dignified man of about fifty years of age. The ravages of smallpox, which destroyed his sight and pitted his face, had not entirely obliterated the comeliness of his classic features.

The "patron" at Colomane Cross, at which he played every Sunday afternoon in summer time, was the event of the week to the peasantry for miles around. Besides the actual enjoyment of attending it, free rein was given to the pleasures of anticipation and memory. The *"Piobaire Ban"* was a busy man, for there was no let up to the dancing while daylight lasted, and every dance meant an increase of income to the piper.

Close by, in Crowley's *mointan,* those who preferred athletics to music and dancing, indulged in hurling, jumping, and stone-throwing to their hearts' content, and although Harrington's shebeen was taking in an odd shilling, there was never a complaint of crime or disorder in connection with those popular peasant gatherings.

Of course the piper was not dependent on the weekly "patrons" for patronage. His music was much in demand, especially in the winter months, to play at weddings, christenings and other festivities, and it was the writer's good fortune to hear him again, even though his delicious strains were subdued by the stone wall which intervened.

There were great dancers in those days, and they were lavish of their praise of Peter "Bawn" as being the ablest performer on the Irish pipes in the southwestern baronies of the County of Cork.

The parish priest, Father David Dore, was a gentleman of the old school. He habitually wore velvet knee breeches, preached in both Irish and English, lived in peace and harmony with his flock, and died wealthy; but he encouraged rather than interfered with the time-honored customs of the people. His successor, Father Wall, was of a different type altogether. Austere and puritanical, his coming was like the blight of a heavy frost on a blooming garden. All forms of popular pastimes were ordered discontinued. No more dances or diversions relieved the monotony of peasant life, and the poor, afflicted piper, with his avocation gone, had no alternative but the shelter and starvation of the poorhouse.

Rumor has it that in after years there was some dispute or rivalry as to who should give him his passports to "kingdom come."

PATRICK O'NEILL

In the days before brass bands put them "out of business" Irish pipers not infrequently enlivened the dull hours with their music and consequent dancing on passenger boats, both in Ireland and America.

Mr. John Connors, the Nestor of our Chicago pipers, lately deceased, played for years on one of the famous Mississippi packets, sailing out of Memphis, Tennessee, before the Civil War.

In his delightful volume, *Seventy Years of Irish Life,* Mr. Le Fanu introduces to his readers the amiable musician on the "Garry Owen," a boat plying between Limerick and Kilrush in his college days.

On the voyage, which generally took about four hours—sometimes five or more, if the weather was bad—the passengers were cheered by the music and songs of a famous character, one "Paddy" O'Neill, whose playing on the fiddle was only surpassed by his performance on the bagpipes. He was, moreover, a poet and sang his own songs, with vigor and expression, to the accompaniment of his own music.

Rare indeed are men of such versatility, and however willing we may be to concede all that is claimed for him as a piper, fiddler, and vocalist, we must in all fairness acquit him of the accusation of being a poet, on the evidence submitted by Mr. Le Fanu himself.

At what date "Paddy" O'Neill gave up steamboating we are not informed, but we know he had a successor on that line in the person of

JOHN QUINLAN,

commonly known as "Jack the Piper." Born in the County Limerick, he began his career as a piper, playing on the River Shannon excursion boats between Limerick and Kilrush. It is said he accumulated a lot of money in this way, but, growing tired of the monotony of his daily life, or perhaps the decline of interest in his music, he abandoned his accustomed post on the boat and took to the road as a roving piper, choosing the County of Clare as his field of operations, and seldom going beyond its boundaries for any purpose.

He attended all fairs of any importance, and wherever there was a bit of fun going on "Jack" was sure to be in the midst of the crowd, "standing on one leg," while the other leg hung on a short crutch which held it in the same relative position as if he were seated, so that the end of the chanter could rest thereon.

Quinlan was a good piper, but the decrepitude of his instrument was a sad handicap to his proficiency. To those who spend their holidays at Lahinch and Lisdoonvarna he was no stranger, and he could often be seen sitting on the wall, squeezing out some lively strains for the boys and girls, to whom nothing is more enjoyable than "to tip the light fantastic toe" to the "merry pipes so gaily O."

"MICKEY" DUNNE

of Mountrath, Queens County, had quite a reputation as a professional piper for at least a score of years in the middle of the nineteenth century, and

MICHAEL DUNN,

a well-to-do farmer of Affaly, near Clonaslee, in the same county, was no less proficient as a performer on the Union pipes. His instrument, a small but neat set made by Maurice Coyne of Dublin, is now in the possession of his son, Capt. Michael Dunn, of the Milwaukee Fire Department, who has inherited his father's musical taste and talent. In addition, Captain Dunn is an expert and ingenious mechanic in all that pertains to the fittings of the most modern Irish chanter.

MICHAEL SCANLAN,

whose home was at the Ivy Bridge, a mile or so from Castleisland, County Kerry, is said to have been a very good piper, according to Richard Sullivan of Chicago, who knew him well in the seventies of the last century. In 1869 he played for Prof. P. D. Reidy's dancing class, the same year in which the renowned professor gave an exhibition of artistic dancing at Ballybunnian to the music of "Tom" Carthy's pipes. Good dancers are keen to appreciate good players, so we feel we are on safe ground when relying on such authority.

"Mick" Scanlan, as he was called, was blind, but he traveled all over with his son "Andy" as his guide and dancer to his music. The professionals who dance on a "slab" on the American stage evidently did not originate that circumscribed footing for their act, for "Andy" Scanlan carried about with him a miniature wooden platform, barely eighteen inches square, on which to display his Terpsichorean abilities. When we come to consider the condition of the highways and fields in Ireland when it rains—and that is often—we cannot but admire "Andy's" thoughtfulness.

John Moore

"Jack" Moore, as he was known to his neighbors, did not claim to be a gentleman in the sense that he was an aristocrat or above being engaged in some useful occupation. He was simply a wealthy farmer who lived about one mile from Newcastle-West, County Limerick. He was also an excellent performer on the Irish bagpipes—the best in Ireland, according to his friends—who played in his own home for his own pleasure and the entertainment of his company. He was above playing for money, and that, we believe, is where the line can be drawn between the gentleman piper and the professional. It is related of him that he communicated through the means of his music outside the prison walls with a prisoner closely confined for some political or government offense. At any rate, the intent of Moore's piping was understood and had the desired effect.

Moore, who owned two fine farms, was in the habit of taking a cart-load of butter at a time to the Cork market. His neighbors, among whom he was very popular, always timed their trips so as to accompany him, for, besides entertaining them at his house the night before their departure, he was liberal on the road, and took care that they were justly dealt with by the butter merchants at the city.

Mr. Dillon, a respected member of the Chicago police, now retired, had the honor of dancing "The Blackbird" and "The Humors of Bandon" to Moore's music in his boyhood days. Being childless, the farmer-piper willed his fine instrument to his nephew.

Maurice Moore

The latter, who was not musically inclined, for more than four years did not trouble himself to unwrap the package in which his uncle's gift had been given him. One night he had a very vivid dream in which the late lamented "Jack" Moore appeared to be much displeased because his pipes had been left so long neglected and unused.

Maurice of course excused himself, as he had never learned to play, but the uncle insisted he could if he tried, giving his diffident nephew to understand that there could be no peace for either while the pipes remained silent and smothered in the green bag.

Maurice awoke, worried and perplexed. Try as he would, he couldn't fall asleep again. There was nothing else to do but get up, for the impulse was irresistible. 'Twas long after midnight but yet some time before cock-crow— the weird hours in which the spirits and fairies haunt their former homes—when Maurice put the disjointed pipes together and yoked them on as he had seen his uncle do many a time. To say he felt uneasy and nervous is putting it mildly; but after catching a long breath he pumped the bellows under his arm and commenced fingering the unaccustomed chanter — *Moladh's buidheachas le Dia!* (Praise and thanks be to God). Out came the music in a flood of melody, the same as if old "Jack" Moore himself had them on! To his astonishment, Maurice found he could play like an expert on his dead uncle's pipes without having been taught at all.

Not satisfied with this instance of musical skill supernaturally acquired, our veracious informant, Mr. Dillon, went on to say that in a week or ten days—he couldn't say for sure—a circus happened along and, being a little short on talent, the manager prevailed on Maurice Moore to entertain the audience with some music on the wonderful pipes as a special attraction.   Maurice had some misgivings about playing so conspicuously, but the story goes that his performance met all expectations, for the gift with which he had been so suddenly and mysteriously endowed betrayed no evidence of decline or deterioration up to the day of his death, which occurred some forty-odd years ago.

The Bohan Brothers

Owen and Patrick R. Bohan, who flourished about the middle of the nineteenth century, were natives of a place called Clonbare, County Galway.   Mr. Nicholas Burke, of Brooklyn, New York, who heard them play in his boyhood, says "they had a great name as Irish pipers."

Being neither lame nor blind, they enjoyed traveling, not alone in Ireland, but in England.   Many trips were made to Liverpool, for that great commercial city was almost as Irish as Dublin, in which they eventually settled down, although "Paddy" spent much of his time in England.   Owen seems to have been soon lost sight of, but his younger brother's name,

Patrick R. Bohan,

has been embalmed in modern literature.   An Irish-American writer named Barry, speaking of the modern Irish bagpipes, says: "In its original form it had nothing like the range of capabilities which now enables Mr. Bohun to perform on it not only the 'Humors of Ballinahinch,' 'Shaun O'Dheir an Gleanna,' 'Paddy O'Carroll,' 'The Fox Chase,' and 'The Blackbird,' but serious productions such as Corentina's song from *Dinorah* and Bach's *Pastorale* in F major."

Corroborating Mr. Barry's appreciative comment, a Dublin correspondent adds, "In the use of the regulators, Bohan was far ahead of all other players of his day."

If he ever heard of Father Mathew it is certain he ignored his teachings, consequently he was always a frequent if not welcome guest at the various city police barracks.   Early in the year 1867, on a winter evening, Bohan was returning to town after playing in the viceregal kitchen, feeling *maith go leor*.   A young constable, noticing the foreign-looking individual in a slouched hat and wearing chin whiskers, accosted him, and while speaking felt of the green bag, which contained a whopping set of pipes that he took for a new-fashioned pike, in joints, or some other dangerous weapon.   A character so suspicious-looking could not be allowed to escape the official vigilance.   The new recruit escorted his prize to the barrack, reporting to his station sergeant that he had just captured a dangerous Fenian.   His visions of immediate promotion were rudely dispelled, however, when the sergeant, after a glimpse of the captive, exclaimed, "Musha, bad cess to you and your Fenian; sure that's 'Paddy' Bohan, the piper!"

In his old age the minstrel was evidently far from prosperous, and he was indebted for many favors to the generous John Hingston, steward of Trinity College.   The latter, who was Canon Goodman's particular friend, appreciating Bohan's great superiority as a performer on the Irish pipes, fitted him out with a presentable suit of clothing and played in concert with him at the Viceregal Lodge before the Prince of Wales, afterwards King Edward VII.

Although a man of herculean build and a piper of no mean ability himself, John Hingston many a time danced to the piping of "Paddy" before the inroads of age stiffened the joints of both.

In his prime "Paddy" Bohan was a perfect piper, and his art was perpetuated in his no less distinguished pupil, "Dick" Stephenson, "The Prince of Pipers."

Not a little whimsical speculation as to the origin and orthography of the surname has been indulged in, but as neither Bowen nor Bohun conforms to the genius of the Irish language, the characteristic final as in Bohan is used. The name O'Beoain as written in the *Annals of the Four Masters* is probably its most ancient form.

JAMES O'BRIEN

From personal knowledge the present writer can testify that "Jimmy" O'Brien was a fascinating performer on the old-style soft-toned Union pipes. We have listened to others who excelled him in execution and versatility, but no one had the faculty which he possessed of producing combinations and turns by a dextrous movement of the bottom of the chanter on his knee.

The amiable and modest "Jimmy" was born at Swineford, County Mayo, about 1823. Neither halt nor blind, he took to music through pure love of it, and, being well acquainted with Cribben, a celebrated piper, he became his pupil in early manhood. O'Brien later struck up an acquaintance with "Paddy" Walsh, another famous Mayo piper, but found him far less liberal with his tunes than the good-natured Cribben.

"Paddy" Walsh, although a good teacher of pipe music, would never allow his pupils to beat time with the foot when learning. The test of proficiency was in playing the lesson tune three times over without a slip. When this was accomplished successfully, Walsh, without a word, would pick up the pupil's hat or cap and fling it out, as a hint for the owner to follow it and get the rest of the air outdoors.

After graduating, O'Brien emigrated to England, where he obtained employment in a stone-quarry in Yorkshire. An injury to his spine which he sustained at this work unfitted him for manual labor the balance of his life, so he was obliged to depend on playing the pipes for a livelihood thereafter. He played in taverns and at picnics all over the north of England, particularly in Yorkshire and Lancashire, and even wandered as far south as Devonshire on one occasion.

While sauntering along a highway one day he came to a fine-looking mansion, and, being thirsty, he went up to the hall door and rang the bell. An old lady, whose head was crowned with a wealth of snow-white hair, responded. When O'Brien announced the object of his call she asked him where he came from. On learning that he was an Irishman she further inquired if he knew a place called Ballinamuck. Of course he did, for it was close to his birthplace. Then the mystery of her interest in Irish topography was revealed.

Her son, an officer in the English army, was killed in that vicinity a little while before the battle of Ballinamuck, in September, 1798. When the Irish and French troops were marching towards the town, followed closely by the English, a French soldier dropped out of the ranks, too ill to proceed farther, and crawled behind a stone wall to die. Seeing the English force marching by a short time later, he took deliberate aim at an officer and shot him dead. The victim was the white-haired lady's son.

Notwithstanding a bereaved mother's cherished grief, O'Brien's thirst was assuaged with a beverage stronger than water.

In the early sixties he came to the United States, landing at Portland, Maine, and he played all through the Irish settlements in that state. Boston, Massachusetts, was his next destination. Having friends and relatives in Chicago, he settled eventually in the western metropolis in 1875 and made the home of Roger Walsh, whom he had known in Portland, his headquarters for a long time. Many a pleasant hour the present writer spent listening to "Jimmy's" delightful music and memorizing his tunes, many of which were not in circulation until given publicity through our efforts.

At that time Officer William Walsh was but a strippling of fifteen, and 'twas as good as a play to hear old Roger, his countenance aglow with parental pride, address the boy in alternate terms of encouragement, admonition and endearment as he "trebled and ground" to O'Brien's piping.

The amiable and accommodating piper had the peculiar and oft-times embarrassing habit of suddenly stopping the music to voice a passing sentiment or indulge in conversation when elated. After his death, in 1885, his pipes were treasured by John Doyle while alive, and then passed into the possession of Sergt. James Early.

MICHAEL WALLACE

Born somewhere between Ballina and Westport, in County Mayo, this most celebrated of two brothers, in the opinion of some critics, rivaled the renowned William Connolly as a performer on the Union pipes. Mr. Burke says, "I have heard arguments between players about the Wallace brothers; some claimed that Michael Wallace was a better player than Connolly."

In the latter's biography we have quoted Michael Egan as awarding him the palm of superiority as an Irish piper "on either side of the Atlantic." As Egan, the piper and pipemaker, was a competent judge, we must regard the question of supremacy as settled.

FRANK WALLACE

All that can be said of Frank is that he was inferior to his brother Michael as an Irish piper, but at that he was an excellent performer. As far as known, they traveled together, but never extended their circuit beyond the British Isles. The Wallace brothers flourished about the middle of the nineteenth century and some years later.

The Wallace brothers and the Bohan brothers, elsewhere mentioned, had associated for years in England with a well-known if not distinguished piper-fiddler of dance hall fame in Brooklyn, New York. An appeal to that thrifty minstrel evoked promises and evasions in plenty, but no enlightenment. But perhaps we were expecting too much, with no reward in sight, from natures grown callous and avaricious by long practice in "passing the hat" on both sides of the Atlantic.

JOHN CRONAN

An Irish piper of that name who flourished in comparatively recent times is said by Burke to have been "a good player on the pipes." Nothing concerning his antecedents is known except that he hailed from the county of Waterford and was born about the year 1838.

Some years after the Civil War, a man named Reagan, who kept a "Free and Easy," or concert hall, in Pittsburgh, Pennsylvania, decided that an Irish piper would add much to the attractions of his place. Accordingly, he went to New York City and called on Thomas F. Kerrigan, a famous piper who conducted a similar institution at No. 316 West Forty-second Street. Mr. Kerrigan referred him to John Egan, the "Albino piper," but the latter, not caring for adventures so far from home, sent him to John Cronan, who without hesitation accompanied Reagan back to the "Smoky City," where he remained for about eight years.

On his return to New York, Cronan formed a sort of partnership with his old-time friend, Egan, and they continued to play together at picnics, parties, and various entertainments for a long time thereafter. He made his home at his daughter's house in New Jersey for some years, but he died in 1905 in the City of New York.

Bernard Delaney of Chicago, who met him at Pittsburgh, says he was an amiable, quiet spoken man and a fine, even player on the Union pipes.

John Foraghan

Around the early sixties of the nineteenth century there flourished in Tullamore, Kings County, a good performer on the Union pipes named "Jack" Foraghan. Though a wagonmaker by trade, he was what might be termed a semi-professional, for he played at weddings and christenings and other occasions when favored with an engagement.

He was the proud possessor of an ass and dray of his own, the latter being an object of much interest to his neighbors on account of the facility with which it could be used on sidehill ground. It was provided with an extra wheel of larger diameter than the other two. By substituting the large wheel for a small one on either side, as the circumstances required, the body of the cart was kept pretty much on a level.

Foraghan, who died when but thirty years of age, had a liberal repertory of dance tunes, and his music was to an appreciable degree the source from which Bernard Delaney derived his inspiration.

John Egan

"The Albino piper" was a native of Dunmore, County Galway, and like his whilom partner, "Patsy" Touhey, was *ciotogach,* or left-handed. Born about the year 1840, he studied pipe music under the instruction of William Connolly the elder, familiarly known as *"Liam Dall,"* or "Blind William," and also from the latter's grandson, John Burke, a capable performer.

Since coming to America most of his time was spent in New York City, the only exception being the years in which he toured the eastern states with "Patsy" Touhey and John Cronan.

Supplementing the latter's praise of Egan's proficiency on the Irish pipes, Mr. Burke adds, "He was a grand player and very powerful in his music." Egan died in New York City about 1897, a comparatively young man.

Touhey is no less eulogistic of his former partner, from whom no doubt he learned some of the artistry of his phenomenal execution on the regulators, and "Patsy's" estimate can always be relied on as impartial and judicial, although he is charitably silent concerning Egan's temperamental peculiarities.

Martin Kenneavy

In connection with "Paddy" Bohan's superlative manipulation of the regulators, Mr. Flanagan remarks: "The best piper I ever heard used neither drone nor regulator—merely the chanter. He must have commenced as a child, so inimitable was his execution. His name was Martin Kenneavy. He enlisted and served six years either in the Ninth or Twelfth Lancers, and on the completion of his military service married one of Bohan's daughters.

"In 1887, after a long absence from my native land, I heard him play in Gibney's tavern, at the top of Knockmaroon hill, Phœnix Park, and from him I picked up some fine tunes."

Kenneavy died at Newcastle-on-Tyne about the year 1890.

The Hogans of Cashel

Who has not heard of the Hogans of Cashel, Tipperary, the famous family of pipers and fiddlers? Great as was their reputation a generation or two ago, most of what little information concerning them has trickled down to us was vague and legendary rather than reliable.

Out of the gloom of uncertainty we have recently been led by Mr. Wayland of the Cork Pipers' Club, who in his boyhood days enjoyed the acquaintance of one member of the tuneful family. Supplementing his personal knowledge, he has favored us with certain authentic facts derived from his old-time friend, "Con" Dwyer of Cashel.

According to popular report there were four brothers—two pipers and two fiddlers—but we find that the numerical strength of the family was underestimated (a very un-Irish error). In reality the father and three sons were noted Union pipers, while two other sons were distinguished fiddlers. All of the brothers but Michael were afflicted with defective eyesight.

Michael Hogan

The father of this interesting family was a native of Cashel, Tipperary, where his sons also were born. He was a professional piper and flourished in the second and third quarters of the nineteenth century. Thurles, it seems, had been his place of residence for some time, for he died there about the year 1890, at an advanced age, outliving his oldest son by several years, but was buried with his ancestors in his native town.

Thomas Hogan

The eldest of the quintette was not alone a noted piper but a fine fluter and an expert violinist as well. Bernard Delaney, the polished policeman-piper of Chicago, who met "Tom" Hogan at Tullamore, Kings County, in the early sixties, describes him as a tall, dark-complexioned man, always very neat and dressy and wearing a stylish hat. His appearance indicated prosperity, and well he deserved it, for he was equally at home on all kinds of music, ancient and modern, and could play to suit any variety of musical taste. Left to his own choice, "Tom" Hogan ordinarily first played an air, or descriptive piece of music, and followed it up with some spirited dance tune.

John S. Wayland got his first inspiration from "Tom" Hogan's piping when the latter, accompanied by his son-in-law, "Mickey" Walsh, the dancing-master,

Ned Hogan of Cashel

used "Johnny" Hickey's commodious kitchen on the Wayland farm for a dancing-school. The piper died at Cashel, his native place, in 1884. The dancing-master, his son-in-law, who is yet living and long past ninety, it would appear, was at least as old as "Tom" Hogan, his father-in-law. He claimed to be over ninety years of age when serving as one of the judges of the Feis at Thurles in 1906, and could dance a few steps even then. He was the recipient of a handsome present in money from Cardinal Vanutelli, Papal Legate, when at Cashel a few years ago, when he learned that "Mickey" Walsh was a member of the Papal Brigade that fought against Garibaldi in 1870. A son of "Tom" Hogan's who is a splendid fiddler lives in Cashel.

EDWARD HOGAN

Next in order of primogeniture came "Ned" Hogan, who it is alleged was the best piper in Ireland in his day, according to "Billy" Taylor, of Drogheda and Philadelphia. Be that as it may, there can be no doubt that he enjoyed an enviable reputation as a performer on the Union pipes, although a competent authority still living in Dublin is of the opinion that he had no advantage over "Dick" Stephenson.

Whether the story, like several similar ones, is apocryphal or not, it is claimed that "Ned" Hogan was presented with a silver-mounted set of pipes by the Prince Consort, grandfather of the reigning King George V. Dublin had been his headquarters for some years, but in 1888 the generous John Hingston, elsewhere mentioned, fitted him up with a suit of olive green Irish broadcloth cut in the Irish style, put a set of good pipes under his arm, and paid his passage over to the London Exhibition. It is quite possible that the medal which he wore when his picture was taken was won at that time. He settled in Shoreditch, East London, and died there.

From London he came back in a coffin in 1897, his remains being forwarded to Dublin by his pastor, who took up a subscription to defray the expenses. Two daughters, both musicians, were supposed to be living in the capital on that date.

JOHN HOGAN

The youngest of the five Hogan brothers was John. Less distinguished, possibly, as a piper than "Tom" and "Ned," he is also less known to fame. Full forty years ago Mr. John K. Beatty of Chicago heard him play in County Westmeath. His performance was very creditable. Though still living, his present whereabouts is unknown, and being a traveling piper, like so many of his profession, he probably finds life in England or Scotland more to his liking than in his native country.

MARTIN O'REILLY

A typical blind piper belonged in the city of Galway, where he kept a dance house for some years. Emigration, decline of public interest, and other causes ruined a once profitable patronage. Sightless and old and unable to make a living by other means than music, he was obliged, like many another unfortunate Irish minstrel, to take refuge in the poorhouse as his only escape from starvation.

However, his reputation as a fine piper survived his inhumation in this grave of hope and ambition. So when the Gaelic League undertook to revive an interest in native music and language, O'Reilly was taken out by some enthusiasts and conveyed to Dublin, where, out of practice and all as he was for years, he gained distinction by winning first prize in the pipers' competition at the annual Feis in 1901.

A Dublin newspaper, describing the Pipers' Festival in the "Large Concert Hall of the Rotunda," has the following: "A notable incident was the playing of Mr. Martin O'Reilly, who played a selection entitled "The Battle of Aughrim," descriptive of the advance, the trumpets of the British, the battle onslaught of the Irish soldiers, and the wail of the women. Aughrim was of course a lost field, but, nothing daunted, the gallant old piper, throbbing with a spirit that might long to play his countrymen into battle, fired them with a stirring and strident version of the victorious march of Brian Boru." He played in perfect tune and produced marvelous tones on his instrument.

The famous Galway piper was the central figure at several entertainments at various cities for some time thereafter. At the Belfast Harp Festival in 1903 he was the hero of the occasion, his favorite pieces being "The Fox Chase" and "The Battle of Aughrim." "The wonderful old man," says one press report, "played the ancient airs with such a feeling expression and profound understanding of their suggestions and meanings that he simply took the house by storm. Later he played for the dancers."

A half-tone picture of this now celebrated piper from a photograph by Father Fielding in Dublin was inserted as a frontispiece in O'Neill's *Dance Music of Ireland* in 1907.

It is humiliating to relate that when the excitement subsided, instead of providing suitably for this grand old traditional musician, or establishing him in a way to teach his precious art, we find him back again in the Gort poorhouse, in which·ignoble institution he has since died.

And when we come to consider the heartless indifference of the people towards Martin O'Reilly and his talents, can we be blamed if we sometimes question the sincerity of the agitators who have talked themselves hoarse in their advocacy of a regenerated Ireland?

As an object lesson, the case of Martin O'Reilly serves well to remind us that a vast gulf still separates theories from practical methods in Ireland.

THOMAS MAHON

From far-away Australia came all the information we possess of Thomas Mahon, an Irish piper, of peculiar celebrity in his day. The interest awakened by Mr. M. P. Jageurs' article on the Irish Revival in *The Advocate* of Melbourne last August brought Mahon to the surface from the pool of oblivion.

In a communication to the same weekly a few months later, James Clarke of Albert Park writes: "From childhood to the present date, I have been an enthusiastic admirer of Irish pipe music, a taste stimulated through having lived in boyhood days close to the home of the late Thomas Mahon, 'Professor of the Irish Union Bagpipes to Her Most Gracious Majesty, Queen Victoria.'"

When the late Queen first visited Ireland in 1849 a number of Mahon's friends used their influence to obtain for him an introduction, and an opportunity of performing before royalty a selection of national music on a national instrument, and they succeeded. However, when the ambitious minstrel arrived in Dublin he found to his keen disappointment that the royal party had left earlier in the day for Balmoral. With a persistence worthy of a better cause, Mahon followed with fevered haste, and delayed only by inevitable formalities, was ushered into the royal presence in dire trepidation, with "his knees bending under him."

MARTIN O'REILLY
The Blind Piper of Galway

A few kindly words of encouragement from the Queen's Highland piper, who was present, soon reassured him, so that when her majesty through a page conveyed her request for the "Royal Irish Quadrilles," "St. Patrick's Day," "Garryowen," etc., he acquitted himself very creditably, but was surprised when he learned that not only the Queen, but the Prince Consort was familiar with the best gems of Irish music.

The Prince Consort, then in his prime, seemed to be enthusiastic over Mahon's performance, and the Queen, to signalize her appreciation, directed that thenceforth Mahon may bear the proud title as above quoted.

After spending a few weeks at Balmoral Castle, playing for a few hours daily for the royal household, he gave a series of recitals in the principal towns of Scotland before returning to his humble home in the historic little town of Finea, in the county of Westmeath. Mr. Clarke heard him play at a party in 1882, and again in 1889, at which period he must have been over eighty years of age, and though the flight of time had left its stamp on his furrowed face, he was still the brilliant performer on his favorite instrument. When in the zenith of his career he accepted engagements from the wealthier class only, but with increasing years and less prosperous times, his services were available for less favored classes. Two of his sons, after learning to play fairly well, Mr. Clarke tells us, went to America.

Commenting on the respective merits of Mahon, and Coughlan, "the Australian piper," he says: "The latter was quite the equal of the former, as a player of dance music, but as an exponent of the higher branches of the art, Mahon, who had through the kindness of a wealthy patron the advantage of a sound musical education, was as might reasonably be expected the more accomplished musician."

A year or so subsequent to the last date of which Mr. Clarke writes, Mr. Jageurs, author of the article which inspired the discussion, met Mahon and danced a "moneen" jig to his music while on a visit to his native land. The minstrel was then very old and feeble, and though the unexpected coming of an Irish-Australian to that secluded part of Westmeath caused him some little excitement, still his infirmities prevented him from playing very much on the beautiful set of pipes he possessed. His jig music, Mr. Jageurs continues, was well rendered, but in a reel his memory failed him, with the result that parts of other tunes became intermixed with the original. His forte was still manifest in his execution of descriptive pieces, for the rapid fingering and other quick movements incidental to dance music were too much for his enfeebled condition. In the slower musical expression of the melodies, and other almost forgotten ancient airs, he played well enough to convince his visitor that the great reputation he bore in his day, particularly around the "bonnie, bonnie banks" of Lough Sheelin, was well deserved.

The grand old minstrel, whose circuit seldom extended beyond the counties of Westmeath, Longford, and Cavan, died early in the nineties, aged about eighty-five years. In personal appearance his resemblance to Tom Moore was quite remarkable, and the similarity in other respects was no less noticeable, for both had a taste for stealing a few hours from the night as the best of all ways to lengthen their days.

The Union pipes upon which Mahon was heard to the greatest advantage, according to Mr. Clarke, were formerly the property of Sir Godfrey Kneller, one of whose descendants married a nobleman residing near Finea. This is interesting if true. Sir Godfrey was born at Lubeck, Germany, in 1648, and died in

England in 1723. Taking into consideration that the Union pipes in their most primitive form were but just then developed from the Warpipes, we may be pardoned for regarding the story of the famous painter's original ownership of Mahon's instrument as highly improbable.

PATRICK McDONAGH

Shortly after the Cork Pipers Club had been organized in 1898, Jeremiah O'Donovan, its first secretary, mentioned to John S. Wayland, its founder, that a very accomplished old piper named Pat McDonagh lived in the city of Galway. O'Donovan, who was an authority on the subject, said he never heard his equal.

Mr. Wayland, whose interest had been aroused, had long wished to meet a piper so highly spoken of. His curiosity was gratified at last on seeing the "man from Galway" facing the judges among at least a score of competitors. On hearing them play Mr. Wayland and Father Quinlan, an amateur piper who sat beside him, agreed that McDonagh was far and away the best of them all.

"When the steward conducting the contest announced that all was over, and the audience began to disperse," writes Mr. Wayland, "I walked over to McDonagh, a most respectable little man with white hair, and wearing blue smoked glasses; and addressed him in Gaelic, saying how glad I was to meet him, having heard of his ability. I had hardly said that in my opinion he had won first prize, if he got fair play, when the steward having got the verdict from the judges, clapped for silence and to my delight proclaimed the highest award—five pounds—to Pat McDonagh.

"He was certainly a beautiful player, with the sweetest chords I ever heard, and grand 'passes' up the scale, and no jarring notes.

"I met him in the street the next day near the Rotunda and was inquisitive enough to ask him where he was going. 'Back to Galway,' he replied. 'Why, Mr. McDonagh,' I said, 'aren't you a very foolish man not to wait for the *Feis Ceoil* competition which comes off in three days?' He had intended going home and possibly coming back, but I prevailed on him to remain." So he did, and won first prize again, a matter of three pounds more. This was in 1903, and before another year had passed Pat McDonagh was numbered with the dead. Another account has it that he died in 1908.

Whatever may have been McDonagh's career in early life, in later times he kept a small shop or store in the city of Galway, and bore an excellent reputation. For a man of his rare musical ability his modesty was truly refreshing. and though conscious of his gifts, he was much disinclined to display them away from his own home.

No relationship other than that of surname and nativity existed between him and John McDonough, the renowned piper of an earlier generation.

JOHN MOORE

Unique, even tragic, was the career of "Johnny" Moore, a piper of good repute residing for many years in Brooklyn, New York. He was born in or near the City of Galway about the year 1834, and was but a boy when his father died. The widow Moore soon found consolation in a second marriage, her choice being Martin O'Reilly, the celebrated blind piper; and it was from him the subject of this sketch acquired his musical training. Shortly after his coming to America, Moore enlisted in the United States navy and remained in the service for quite a few years.

Subsequently he became a professional piper around New York. He accepted an engagement with Powers' Ivy Leaf company, the same with which "Eddie" Joyce and "Barney" Delaney had previously traveled, but took sick at Springfield, Ohio, in 1887, and was sent to a hospital. On Mr. Powers' urgent request, Moore's place was temporarily filled by Delaney, who was loaned from the Chicago Department of Police to tide over the emergency.

While on the circuit after his recovery "Johnny" Moore called on the Delaneys at Chicago later in the season. He was explaining how he had tripped and fallen on the sidewalk, while bringing home a pail of coal from the fuel yard, when Mrs. Delaney exclaimed in surprise: "A pail of coal! Why, I should think it would be cheaper to buy a ton at a time." His brow clouded as he glanced at her suspiciously, as if questioning her seriousness, and replied in an injured tone: "A ton at a time! What do you think we are? Millionaires?"

As far as known Moore's life was otherwise uneventful, until in 1894 he decided to return to his native home for the purpose of bringing Martin O'Reilly, his stepfather, back to America with him. The night before his departure from New York he visited "Patsy" Touhey and Patrick Fitzpatrick, brother pipers to whom we are indebted for much of our information. It was remarked that his condition was none of the best, but at that it was by no means alarming.

A week later the newspapers announced that a passenger named John Moore died on the voyage to Ireland, when the boat was within sixty miles of land, and was buried at sea on his own request.

Mr. Fitzpatrick says that Moore was not particularly distinguished for brilliancy of execution on the chanter, but in the manipulation of the regulators he had few if any superiors. Often when the reed in his chanter proved refractory or did not "go" to suit him, he would play the whole tune through on the keys of the regulators.

JOHN MURPHY

Though but little known to fame the subject of this sketch was a prodigy on the pipes. Like his contemporaries, "Patsy" Touhey, "Eddie" Joyce, and many others of the fraternity, "Johnny" Murphy come of piping stock. Bartley Murphy, his father, under whose training "Patsy" Touhey's musical talents were developed, was himself taught by James Touhey, "Patsy's" father.

Young Murphy was a Boston boy, born in 1865. Under his father's instruction he progressed rapidly, and soon was ranked with "Eddie" Joyce, than which no greater compliment could be paid him.

From a former companion, John Finley, the noted dancer and now promising piper, we learn that in 1885 when Murphy was but twenty years old he was matched to play against Joyce for a stake of five hundred dollars, their respective backers being Richard K. Fox of sporting fame and the renowned pugilist, John L. Sullivan. For some reason the contest never came to an issue. Quite likely Murphy's declining health may have tended to discourage the proposition, for we are told by Mr. Finley, to whom we are indebted for the information, that he died in 1887 lamented by all who knew him.

WILLIAM MURPHY

A splendid performer on the Union pipes named William Murphy, commonly known as *Liam Mor* (Big William) on account of his great height, flourished

William Murphy

some twenty-odd years ago on Dublin Hill in the city of Cork. Little else is now remembered concerning him, as Irish piping was then at its lowest ebb in Ireland.

Murphy's picture, secured through the efforts of our obliging friend Mr. Wayland, reminds us of President Abraham Lincoln, who was also a man of extraordinary stature. His instrument, which was both large and elaborate, is of the same type as those displayed in the pictures of Captain Kelly and Prof. Denis O'Leary, the bass tubes being adjusted with a trombone slide. We have not learned the maker's name. The easy and confident pose of *Liam Mor* is seemingly that of a performer who knew his business.

Patrick Spillane

A native of Templetouhy, barony of Kerrin, County Tipperary, had a great reputation as an Irish piper a generation or so ago. According to "Tom" Higgins, a famous fiddler of Hennessy Road, city of Waterford, "Pat" Spillane was the best performer on the Irish pipes he had ever heard. We were apprised that Mr. O'Mealy, piper and pipemaker of Belfast, entertained a very high opinion of Spillane's abilities, but our letter of inquiry brought no appreciable information from that quarter.

To the tireless and accommodating John S. Wayland of the Cork Pipers' Club we owe the intelligence that the subject of our sketch was a fine performer, a thorough musician, and at one time the leader of a band, and spent some time in France.

Though born a "Tip," he lived much of his life and died in Cork, some fifteen or twenty years ago.

Thomas McCarthy

This celebrated centenarian, who lived in three centuries, was born in the year 1799 and died in 1904 at the remarkable age of one hundred and five years. A native of north Kerry, within a mile of Ballybunnian, he lived all his life in that part of the county. Unlike the majority of his class he was neither lame nor blind, yet he learned to play the Irish or Union pipes and maintained himself as a professional piper up to the time of his death.

On account of his great age and picturesque appearance he was a favorite subject for the photographers for many years, and post cards adorned with his likeness were in general circulation.

"Tom Carthy," as he was familiarly called, made Ballybunnian his headquarters, since it became famous as a summer resort. The rocky spur of land called Castle Green, always regarded as a common, was his favorite haunt until it was claimed as belonging to one of the local estates. The parish priest took issue with the claimant, and finally won the suit after spirited litigation. The old piper was restored to his accustomed stand by the victorious pastor, and assured of undisturbed possession thereafter, a tenure which lasted for full sixty-five years.

The instrument on which he had played for generations, we are told by Mr. Richard Sullivan of Chicago, who often danced to his music, passed on his death into the possession of a man named Sullivan, of Ballyheige in the same county.

As a citizen, and as a piper, this remarkable man bore an enviable reputation. His longevity no doubt was attributable in some measure to his outdoor life, and the salubrity of the climate on the Atlantic coast.

Tom Carthy.
Who lived to the wonderful age of 105.
Irish Piper. Ballybunion, Co. Kerry.

John Coughlan (the Australian Piper)

The supremacy of John Coughlan among the few performers on the Irish or Union pipes who emigrated to Australia was undisputed from the time of his arrival in 1862 until the day of his death, April 23, 1908. He was the eldest son of Thomas Coughlan and Margaret O'Connor of Portumna, County Galway, but was born at Butler's Bridge, County Cavan, in 1837, where his parents resided temporarily. In childhood he met with an accident, which lamed him for life. This mishap practically determined his future career, and being frequently in the company of Patrick Flannery, the renowned blind piper, he acquired from the latter the first rudiments of piping. The Coughlan family accompanied by Flannery emigrated to America in 1845 and settled in New York City, where the subject of our sketch received instructions for a time from "Jacky" Quinn, a County Longford piper. Young Coughlan had also the advantage of precept and example from William Madden. a performer on the Union pipes almost as celebrated at Patrick Flannery, his uncle.

The elder Coughlan's ambition, stimulated probably by John's predilection and progress, led to the latter's transfer to Roxbury, Massachusetts, where he attended school and lived with "Ned" White, "The Dandy Piper," who took charge of his musical education in the evenings and made a finished piper of him. In 1835, when but eighteen years old, young Coughlan accompanied William Madden to Ireland and toured the country with him for two years before returning to New York.

Prompted no doubt by parental pride, the father induced Michael Egan, the famous piper and pipe maker of Liverpool, England, to come to New York and live with him. After practicing with Egan for some time and becoming possessed of two splendid sets of Union pipes specially made for him by the latter, young Coughlan in his twenty-third year started out as an independent piper. His first public appearance was at Tremont Temple, Boston, in 1859, at which he was assisted by his friend William Madden. From that forth for some years he filled engagements all over the United States, traveling as far south as Charlestown, South Carolina, and even crossing the continent to San Francisco on the Pacific coast.

Conceiving that the disturbed condition of public sentiment arising from the Civil War was unfavorable to his prospects in America, he took passage with some members of the family for Melbourne, Australia, in June, 1862.

It may be said, however, that the abundance of money in circulation during the continuance of the war contributed not a little to the prosperity of the pipers who remained.

Coughlan was warmly received by his countrymen at Melbourne, and he played for a time at the rooms connected with Pat Hannan's Galway Club Hotel, now the site of the General Postoffice, and later at Dan Moloney's Exford Hotel in Russell Street, both places being popular resorts of young Irishmen who had preserved an enduring love for the music and dances of their native land. The migration of his sons was no part of their father's ambition, and so keen was his disappointment at the miscarriage of his cherished plans, according to his friend Nicholas Burke, that he returned to his native land and bought a farm a few miles distant from the City of Galway.

Ever in pursuit of the pot of gold at the end of the rainbow, the report of rich gold discoveries on the west coast of New Zealand lured the versatile but unstable Coughlan to the land of the Maoriès. After wandering from camp to

JOHN COUGHLAN
(*The Australian Piper*)

camp with his wonderful music he engaged in the hotel business at Canary, conducted dancing rooms of his own at Charleston and Dunedin successively, but returned to Melbourne in 1883, where he was made the beneficiary of several complimentary concerts.

Never content, seldom satisfied, this really excellent piper transferred his talents to Sydney in 1884, in which city and its surroundings he played for a number of years. He appeared in Her Majesty's Theatre in "Arrah-na-Pogue," in 1901, and later in the opera, "The Emerald Isle."

"The frail old man," writes Morgan P. Jageurs in *The Advocate*, "looked quite a pathetic little figure in his velveteen knickers and long stockings, as he limped to his seat on the stage. Once seated, the attention of his audience became riveted on his pipes. Plaintive, haunting melodies followed one another with indescribable sweetness until the theatre became as silent as a mortuary, when hey! a turn of the wrist broke the stillness with the merry nine-eight hop jig of 'The Rocky Road to Dublin.' Double jigs, hornpipes and reels followed in quick succession and added to the gaiety. It was impossible to keep one's feet still. Like the Pied Piper of Hamelin, he controlled his audience at will, but never satisfied them. Their demand was for more, more—and still more." Much of the following is in Mr. Jageurs' language:

His *goltraighe,* or war tunes, such as "Brian Boru's March," "O'Donnell Abu," "Lord Hardwick's," "Napoleon's," "Captain Taylor's," and other military marches, were played with great spirit. The more uncommon marches of "Alastrum McDonnell" and "Feach Mac Hugh O'Byrne" were, however, not in his repertoire.

His merry reels were his best effort. Few pipers, fiddle or flute players could equal him in that class of dance music. His playing of "Miss Gunning's Reel," in particular, was something to remember, and worthy of that beautiful lady herself. Other good reels he rendered well were "The Bright Star of Munster," "Lord Gordon's Reel," "Bonny Kate," "The Bucks of Oranmore," and "Erin's Hope."

Who, too, could resist his inspiriting jigs, notably "The Yellow Wattle," "The Black Rogue," and "Paudheen O'Rafferty"? His daughter Lizzie was famed for her "American Sand Jig," which she danced to her father's piping. The air and dance were acquired from the late Tom Peel (or Radley), a clever Irish-American dancer, resident in Melbourne, who was also an excellent Irish reel exponent.

Amongst the many other frolicsome tunes played by Coughlan were a few of those irregular ones associated with figure or long set dances. He played the "Blackbird," "The Job of Journey Work," "The Suisheen Bawn," "Rodney's Glory," and "The Garden of Daisies." These were danced to Coughlan's music by noted old-time Melbourne dancers, particularly the late Denis Lyhane (who was accidentally drowned in New Zealand), Edward Tobin, J. Fitzgerald, Tom Hartnett and John Daly. The last-named is the sole survivor of this group of really fine Irish long set dancers.

Most of the famous Munster pipers elsewhere mentioned played all the long set dance music known to Coughlan, and many other pieces in addition, such as "Sean ua Duibhir an gleanna," "Bonaparte's Retreat," "The Jockey Through the Fair," "The Three Sea Captains," "The Humours of Bandon," "The Battle of Killiecrankie," "The Downfall of Paris," "The Blackthorn Stick," "An Stucaire," "Rub the Bag," "The Funny Tailor," etc. Of exponents of Irish dancing in Melbourne, there are now only two or three left who have any knowledge of these fast disappearing Irish dances, and, unfortunately, the other States of the Commonwealth, as far as can be ascertained, are in no better condition. Sydney, however, has two magnificent dancers in Messrs. Purtell and Hennessy.

Turning to other branches of Irish music, Coughlan played a very fine setting of "St. Patrick's Day," with variations, but whether original or not it is difficult to say. It was certainly uncommon. Of ancient Irish melodies he possessed a good knowledge. His rendering of them was traditional, but marred at times by the undue prolongation of certain notes—a fault common to many Irish musicians, who, like himself, played by ear. He was a piper by nature, and loved his music as his most precious possession. At times he betrayed much emotion and introduced a singular pathos into the melodies that was most affecting to his hearers. He was also variable in his temperament. On some occasions he could not be induced to play, whilst at other times he would go on for hours almost oblivious of those present. His best melody of the *Geantraighe* or love song class was "The Coolun," which he played admirably. Other favorites of his were *"Mo cailin deas cruidte na m-bo,"* "The Dear Irish Boy," "The Colleen Bawn," "O'Carolan's Farewell to Music," and "Young Mat Hyland." He was particularly fond of the "Star Spangled Banner," which he played most sympathetically.

Of the too little known descriptive music of Ireland—that allied with occupations, such as trades, hunting, cradle, spinning, and milking, Coughlan was a fine exponent. In his *suantraighe* (sleep music), "The Old Man Rocking the Cradle," the audience was usually as much amused by the portrayal of the old fellow's dilemma as they were pained by the sobs or fretful screams of the thirsty infant. They certainly heard the crooning of the lullaby, but could conjure up the anxious, nay, despairing, look on the old man's face, as he, ever and anon, glanced towards the door, expecting the return of the absent "ma-ma." Then again, Coughlan would, as it were, fill the concert room with red-coated huntsmen, horses and dogs, as they met for "The Fox Chase." Every stage of the hunt was then vividly illustrated on his pipes—the meet, the cover, the scent, the view-halloa, the long drawn out chase, with its galloping of horses, and the baying and yelping of the hounds, and finally, the kill. Then followed his rendering of "The Fox Hunter's Jig"—a fitting finale to one of the finest descriptive pieces of Irish music in existence.

Turning from the gay to a plaintive theme, Coughlan's rendition of the lament, "The Battle of Aughrim," which he learned from his old tutor Flannery, a native of the district, illustrated another item of his large repertoire. So descriptive was it of battle sounds, and particularly of the subsequent wailing, that the latter might be regarded as the concentrated expression of all the misfortunes which befell the Irish troops from the battle of the Boyne to the fall of Limerick. Another fine plaintive air, viz., "Limerick's Lamentation," to which Moore has wedded his "When cold in the earth," was also played by him. This air was composed for the war pipers who accompanied the Irish regiments to France after the fall of Limerick in 1690. It was afterwards played for many years in various military camps of the Irish soldiers on the continent, and in 1746 was taught by Colonel Fitzgerald to musicians in the Scottish camp before the battle of Culloden. It has ever since been preserved by the Scottish people, but is now known by the title of "Lochaber No More." "Limerick's Lamentation" is only one gem of hundreds of similar Irish airs thus annexed by British and foreign musicians and used to this day for social, church and operatic purposes.

John Coughlan left a widow and seven surviving children, who now reside in a Melbourne suburb. His pipes were bequeathed to his brother Thomas, professionally known as "Tom Buckley, the Irish Comedian," throughout the theatres and music halls of Australasia. Tom played, as far back as 1859, with Wolfenden's Star Minstrels, in Abington, Massachusetts, U. S. A., and made his first appearance in Melbourne, Australia, in 1869, with Weston and Hussey's American Minstrels. Since then he has toured in India and Australasia. Though he has now been some fifty-three years on the boards, he is still hale and hearty, and since his brother's death has added selections on the Irish Union pipes to his other stage items. He is also a very creditable performer on the drums, guitar and banjo.

Mr. Jageurs of Parkville with many prominent Irishmen of Melbourne endeavored time and again to induce this fine performer to establish a school for the instruction of a class of Irish-pipe students to perpetuate his art, but all to no purpose.

Yielding to the persuasion of his best friends he promised more than once to comply with their wishes, but just as often disregarded his word and honor and failed to put in appearance. Disappointed, disgusted, and indignant, his stanchest supporters, the Irishmen of Melbourne, washed their hands of him eventually.

It is sad and regrettable to see such a spirit manifest itself in a man gifted as he undoubtedly was.

"In rendering airs or slow music," writes Mr. Patrick O'Leary of Parkside, South Australia, "Coughlan's performance was not always all that could be desired, but when playing jigs or reels he was a revelation—something like your inimitable townsman, Bernard Delaney. The picture card which I enclose is said to be an exact counterpart of the great piper, and was reproduced from a photograph taken at Boston, U. S. A., in 1862."

On the reverse of said card is printed the following:

MASONIC HALL, BALMAIN

A CONCERT AND SOCIAL WILL BE GIVEN TO

MR. JOHN COUGHLAN,

THE WORLD'S RENOWNED IRISH PIPER,

By his friends and admirers Balmain in the above Hall Saturday night on 17th December, 1898. Champion Irish and Scotch Dancers, together with Professional Vocalists, also a Marvelous Mouthorgan Performer, will assist. Doors open at 7:30. Concert at 8 p. m. Quadrille party from 10 to 12. Single ticket, 1 shilling.

In the matter of getting out attractive advertising circulars, the "Kangaroos" certainly have little to learn, judging by the handiwork of the "live wire" who schemed out the handbill of which the following is a copy:

THE BARDS OF ERIN

Will appear in this town on the above date and respectfully solicit the patronage of the ever-generous public. The company comprises a party of lady and gentlemen Irish national entertainers, who acknowledge no rivals in the business, foremost amongst whom is

JOHN COUGHLAN,

THE WORLD'S GREAT IRISH PIPER AND BARD OF ERIN,

The most phenomenal artist living who plays the Irish pipes. It has been acknowledged by every nation in Europe that music was cultivated in Ireland when melody was scarcely known in other countries. Pope, the great poet, calls *Ireland the mother of sweet singers,* the truth of which is verified in a most natural gift to the manor born in the above great player, who will discourse the sweetest music ever heard, on Ireland's sweetest of national instruments, the Irish Pipes, carrying his audience with him at will with the plaintive strains of his dear native land.

> Cold must the heart be,
> And void of emotion,
> That loves not the music
> Acushla Machree.

During the evening Mr. Coughlan will perform several imitations on the Irish Pipes, both ancient and modern music, notably:

THE CELEBRATED FOX HUNT

A perfect imitation of the hounds in full cry—Breaking Cover —Losing the Scent—In the Cornfield—On the Trail—The Death.

CATH EACHROMA, OR THE BATTLE OF AUGHRIM

The Irish cries of the females for the dead friends and husbands found in the battlefield—Sounds of Trumpets—Sarsfield's March to Limerick. (The Irish cry is of remote antiquity, a period beyond the reach of memory.)

THE OLD MAN ROCKING THE CRADLE

Mr. Coughlan will imitate the human voice on the Irish Pipes, making the instrument speak plain English in this old Irish piece.

Some three or four years later, after the Irish Music Club of Chicago had been organized, overtures were made by Mr. Coughlan to the officers with a view to his coming to that city provided his expenses were advanced. As the proposition did not meet with favor he was obliged to remain at the Antipodes.

"To make enough money to carry me home again," he says in his letter to Sergt. Early, "is the everyday thought of my life. You see there is no scope for me out here. Were I at home (in America) I could make my fortune with the dear old pipes." The unreliability of men of his class is proverbial, and though we may condone such common failings as jealousy and selfishness, we are unprepared for such an exhibition of exasperating conceit as his letter discloses. Hear him:

"I stand pre-eminent over all Irish pipers of the present day, without a doubt the most celebrated piper living this day. Yet I am out here wasting valuable time, instead of making a fortune for myself and keeping revived to the hearts of all the sweetest strains of music of our forefathers. It nearly breaks my heart when I think that when I am gone there is not one left to keep such music of the old ancient bards such as Carolan, Madden, Flannery, and the celebrated James Kelly and others long since deceased. I have all their music, reels, jigs, long dances, marches, pieces, etc., of which my enclosed programme will explain. Were sufficient funds raised among the brother pipers and countrymen, that would enable me to return home (if it was only to hear the dear old Irish pipes played as they should be played) I could teach my music to either lady or gentleman desirous of learning them, and thus leave behind me such famous and delightful music."

And yet this musical egotist, with all his blarney and breaking heart lest the art of music die with him, is the same aggravating Orpheus who could not be persuaded or induced to teach anyone in his adopted country.

Coughlan, who was undoubtedly a fine performer, died soon after in the land of his adoption, but the music still lives and so do others who are his superiors on the "dear old pipes," at least in dance music, according to competent authority quoted elsewhere.

JOHN CASH

A description of the circumstances attending this patriarchal minstrel's presence at the Mansion House Reception at Dublin in 1906, where the writer made his acquaintance, may be found on page 228, *Irish Folk Music: A Fascinating Hobby,* and therefore need not be repeated here.

Through the courtesy of Mr. William Rowsome of Dublin we have been favored with an excellent sketch of his life and that of his talented son from the able pen of Mr. Patrick Whelan of Scarawalsh, Ballycarney, County Wexford, a versatile musician himself.

"Cash the Piper" has been for over fifty years to all lovers of traditional melody as well as those who affected the display of the "light fantastic toe" in Wexford and adjoining counties, a popular and familiar phrase, and although as an honored title, it is now derelict, there is no indication that it will pass into oblivion for many a day to come.

The name was borne in common by two contemporary pipers, with the distinctive qualifying terms "Old" or "Young," for they were father and son—John and James respectively.

John Cash, who was a native of County Wexford, was born in the year 1832, the historic landmark of his birth being March, after the tithe massacre of Bunclody, commonly called the battle of Newtownbarry, which occurred in 1831. He learned the art of playing the Union pipes from his uncle, James Hanrahan, an Irish piper of repute, a Tipperary man whose wife was an excellent violinist also.

Bred in an atmosphere of music, and as his various callings tended to bring him generally within a musical environment, and being endowed with much talent, it is little wonder he attained the distinction of being one of the most famous pipers of the latter half of the nineteenth century.

He married early in life, his wife, "Polly" Connors, being a tidy and industrious woman who could foot a dance against any who ever "took the floor." To his trade of tinsmith he combined that of horse dealer, and his enterprise soon made him comparatively wealthy.

John Cash

Fortified with capital, Cash could import as many as six or seven score of Connemara ponies and young horses in one season into the southern counties of Leinster.

To all interested in the dance and music of the motherland he was known as "Cash the Piper," but from Waterford City to the Curragh of Kildare and from Enniscorthy to far-off Ballinasloe, among those more interested in horse-flesh than in music, he was simply "Johnny Cash." Although always having an established home occupied by some members of his family, he kept abroad himself pretty much at certain seasons of the year in the pursuit of his avocations, and we may well believe that he was a welcome guest at the wealthiest farmers' houses, and enjoyed to the fullest the best accommodations wherever he went, for he was never without his melodious pipes on his horse-trading expeditions.

John Cash was a man of fine personal appearance, well above medium height, with proportionate muscular development, amiable of disposition and with good conversational powers. Unlike the typical piper and fiddler, he was not loquacious; neither was he an egotist. Although conversant with all the dance music common to the south of Ireland, he never set himself up as an infallible authority in such matters, but would play anything called for without comment or delay; yet, like the majority of his class, he was quick of wit and keen of repartee.

His advent to the barony of Scarawalsh on the occasion of his periodical visits to the fair of Enniscorthy was always regarded by young and old with pleasurable anticipation. He invariably stayed overnight at the snug home of Mr. Lawrence Piper, who was Doyle the dancing master's best pupil, and was also one of the best nonprofessional dancers of his day or any other day. As the saying goes, "Larry was as fine a dancer as ever stepped in shoe leather," and, as an admirer once said of him, "kicked dance around the house and in all directions away from him," and could beat one, two, three, consecutively against a wall as easily as kiss his hand, and besides he was as imposingly handsome a figure as imagination could conceive. Talk about the poetry of motion, of which he was a superb exponent. There is a poetry of just proportion in the symmetry of muscular development in the human form which you realized the moment he stood on the floor. This Adonis scorned vest and cravat as accessories of his holiday attire, and as for braces, why, he never indulged in such superfluities. For fancy, flashy shirts he had a strong weakness, while a broadcloth coat and a shining silk beaver hat completed his wardrobe and his happiness. With the two latter articles of apparel laid aside, he was ready "to take the floor."

The young people always expected a rare treat when "Cash the Piper" was around, and it is but the simple truth to say they were never disappointed, although their patience was sorely tried occasionally by the piper's protracted delay in getting started. Oftentimes Mr. Cash, with the pipes thrown carelessly across his knees, would suspend operations to talk to "Larry" of "the days of old lang syne" when they met at the fairs and the races at which they were by no means inconspicuous figures.

Invariably they had to be recalled from their reminiscent reverie by the importunities of an expectant audience, but after the music and dancing had commenced in earnest the scene can be better imagined than described.

"Larry" Piper had all the distinguishing qualities of the great Irish dancer. As an athlete he had no rival worthy of the name, except John Nolan, "The Fairy Man," whose almost superhuman feats of strength and muscular dexterity became proverbial during his life time. Without any of the swaying body-movement or ridiculous and grotesque arm motion that characterizes the mediocre, his perform-ance proved a psychic treat.

With arms drawn closely to his sides, and rather backward to the elbow, from which joint they were relaxed with a forward inclination, his body otherwise motionless, he carried in a vertical line wherever he changed his position. The precision and rapidity of his footwork and evolutions, while appreciated by the eye, defy the pen to describe.

On such occasions Cash invariably played the "Londonderry Clog" in five parts almost identical with the setting in O'Neill's *Music of Ireland,* in his inimi-table style, it being one of his favorites, and locally known as "Cash's Hornpipe" on that account. Even those who were wont to advocate the claim of James Byrne of Bagnalstown, County Carlow, to the premiership of Leinster, were forced to admit that the acme of good pipering was here to be enjoyed.

In common with all musicians of his class, Cash disliked playing for "sets" or quadrilles, yet he never failed to meet the expectations of his host or audience, though jigs, reels, and hornpipes, were his cherished favorites.

"Alec." Leary and "Kitty" Carton were always in evidence as the sturdy representatives of oldtime customs and manners, and would take the floor and "welt it for further orders," and could calculate on the hearty support of Mrs. Piper and "Polly" Cash.

The superb "Larry" Piper's health had been declining for a long time, but a month prior to his death, when John Cash called around, he mounted the kitchen table and grasping a pole that crossed the house within above his head, made the board "tell" in response to every note emitted by the chanter. We can scarcely conceive the mutual feeling of admiration or rather veneration which existed between these two worthies—piper and dancer.

Although Cash's visits were only of periodical recurrence, and of brief dura-tion, yet they did much to influence the popular musical taste along traditional lines, and to still direct it in the channel through which it flowed for centuries. The same may be said of him wherever he went. He had a long and honorable career as an Irish piper. Otherwise he was an industrious man who led a useful and, it must in truth be stated, a blameless life. He died in 1909 at his residence in Wicklow town, where he lived for many years, surviving his beloved "Polly" only a brief twelve months.

The old minstrel's picture was obtained from John Rowsome, who on handing it to Patrick Whelan remarked: "There it is, and it is more like the poor old fellow than he was himself!" Sir Boyle Roche couldn't do better.

A song popular in the counties of Wicklow and Wexford, in which our hero is the leading character, may not be out of place in concluding the biography of this exemplary man:

> My name is "Cash the Piper,"
>   And I'm seen at race and fair;
> I'm known to all the jolly souls
>   From Wicklow to Kildare;
> I've played at dance and wedding
>   From Bray to Clonegal,
> But the cream of entertainment
>   Was at "Mick the Dalty's" ball.

I received a special order
    To attend at eight o'clock;
I took the train to Rathdrum,
    Then walked to Glendalough.
The boys around the neighborhood
    Assembled one and all,
Saying, "You're welcome, 'Cash the Piper,'
    To 'Mick the Dalty's' "ball."

And when I entered I beheld
    A table brimming o'er
With beef and bread and bacon,
    And stout and punch galore;
We all sat down and ate our fill,
    Like cattle in a stall,
For "eat and drink"—it was the word
    At "Mick the Dalty's" ball.

The feast being o'er, the cloth removed,
    I played a dashing reel,
When one young lady on the floor
    Displayed a toe and heel,
With "Will the Dalty," "Will the *gaum*,"
    For such I must him call;
He slapped his flat foot on the floor
    At "Mick the Dalty's" ball.

The family names were "Jim" and "Will,"
    With "Andy" and old "Mick";
The guests were "Tom" and "Paddy," too,
    And Martin, Hugh, and "Dick";
There was Mary, Kate, and Nancy,
    With one they did not call—
All danced before me on the floor,
    At "Mick the Dalty's" ball.

And when the dance was over,
    The dancers all sat down;
In tumblers, tins and teacups,
    The punch went steaming round,
While rough and ready Hugh struck up,
    And sang the "Ould Plaid Shawl,"
Which brought three cheers with laughter loud
    At "Mick the Dalty's" ball.

The longest night must have its dawn,
    The sweetest pleasures end,
The jolliest crowd must part at last,
    And home their footsteps bend,
So when loud upon our revels rang
    The cock's loud morning call,
We all shook hands and took our leave
    Of "Mick the Dalty's" ball.

JAMES CASH

James, commonly known as "Young Cash," in contradistinction to the elder —his father—is believed to have been one of the most brilliant lights of the profession which his native province of Leinster has produced, as far as we have any definite knowledge. Inheriting the musical faculty and nurtured under condition which gave every facility to the unfolding of latent talent, he graduated as a sterling Irish piper whilst yet but a boy. Possessing marvelous execution on the chanter in the rendering of reels, doubles, and hornpipes, and dance music generally, he was no less an adept in playing waltzes, marches, airs, and miscellaneous compositions.

His acumen and dexterity in the manipulation of the regulators in producing harmonic accompaniments was such as to win the approbation of the wealthy and refined, and commend him to the patronage of the nobility of the land.

Unlike his father, James Cash never learned or followed any other trade or calling, his sole ambition being directed towards becoming a piper of fame in his day, and his efforts were singularly successful in that respect, so far as giving practical manifestation of phenomenal ability. But, alas, "fell death's untimely frost" nipped him in the flower of his manhood and effervescent genius.

To be duly appreciated he should have been born three generations earlier, when great musicians attracted distinguished patrons and the blight of famine and proscription had not done their deadly work. He came unfortunately at a time when the greatest apathy prevailed in all that pertains to the noblest Celtic tradition in music, and when the country, with a greater degree of justice than ever, might be described as a "corpse upon the dissecting table."

An incident of his early life, as told by his mother, shows the bias of his early inclinations.

At the early age of nine years, while the family lived in the town of Wexford, he occasioned great distress by his protracted absence from home one day. As evening waned and night came on, anxiety became intensified to alarm, when his father and mother went forth in search of the truant. Attracted by a noisy crowd of juveniles which they saw assembled in the main street, to their great relief they found in the centre of the throng the youthful James, who, with a miniature set of bagpipes, had been making a circuit of the town, with more small silver and copper coins upon his person than he could comfortably carry.

For the purpose of improving and giving a polish to his education, this prodigy early decided on making a prolonged tour of Munster and Connacht. Some of his earlier experiences in this enterprise were by no means reassuring or encouraging, according to his own statement.

It had been the zest of his ambition to invade the County and City of rebel Cork, and when he was well across the frontier, while traveling one day, he entered a house by the wayside. The only occupant at the time was a precocious boy of rather diminutive stature who, regarding him with evident interest, soliloquized, "Oh! is this another new piper we've got?" Young Cash admitted the implied accusation. "Will you let us hear you play?" asked the self-possessed one.

James played one of his best and most catchy tunes in confident style, expecting to astonish the listener, but it seems he didn't, for the latter only remarked: "Not a bad player at all if you had a good instrument."

The invading piper, who had not only prided himself on having a good set of pipes but in being a competent judge as well, was taken somewhat aback, laid them down on the seat beside him to await the outcome of what had become to him a very interesting turn of affairs. The boy advanced, took hold of the chanter and looked it over critically with the eye of an expert.

"This ought to be a good chanter if there were a good reed in it," he announced.

Cash, perceiving he was about to draw the chanter from its stock, interposed with the observation: "Be careful of what you do, my boy; those reeds are delicate and are very easily injured."

The boy, without taking apparent notice of the remonstrance, took out the chanter, withdrew the reed, put the stem to his lips, drew the air in through it so as to produce the "crow," and said reassuringly to the perturbed owner, "I make reeds for the pipers who circulate around here and they consider me not a bad hand at the business."

Reaching up to a hole in the "scraw," he drew from under the thatch a small box full of miscellaneous articles, saying as he did so, "I may have a reed to suit this chanter." After searching through the contents of the box he selected one, tried its "crow" in the manner described, adjusted it in proper position, put on the pipes and played a tune, to Cash's astonishment, in such a manner as left little doubt in his mind that his own best efforts were but poor in comparison. [This is a very nice story, but what has become of the phenomenal young piper and reedmaker?]

James Cash rapidly rose to distinction in his chosen profession and filled appointments in the Metropolitan Theatre and music halls, and, being a young man of handsome appearance, he enjoyed, or perhaps suffered from, that peculiar popularity or adulation accorded only those displaying conspicuous artistic talents. To some the fascination proves irresistible.

Like many another of brilliant genius, he was beset by adversity, lost his emoluments, and yielding to the pressure of circumstances traveled about as a wandering piper.

All of the family—boys and girls—were born at Kilmore, County Wexford, the date of his birth being October, 1853. After a short but eventful life, this gifted musician died at Rathdrum in 1890, ere he had attained his thirty-eighth year. Too much conviviality, an evil almost inseparable from his profession, led to certain infirmities from which neither age nor youth may hope to escape.

"My estimate of the younger Cash, based on acquaintance and general experience, is," writes Mr. Wm. Rowsome, the versatile piper and pipemaker of Dublin, "that he was the star piper of the whole globe. I had the opportunity of hearing the best pipers of Ireland. Among them were many marvelous performers who could play an Irish tune to suit the most critical, but James Cash could play a tune in ten different styles before he would finish, and, what was still more astonishing, he could converse on any subject while doing so. Many a conversation I had with him in my old home at Ballintore when he was playing a difficult hornpipe for a noted dancer named Lawrence Murray, now living at Avoca Mills, County Wicklow."

During the whole period of his meteoric career he was a frequent visitor at the picturesque and commodious farmstead of Mr. Samuel Rowsome of Ballintore, Ferns, County Wexford, himself a fine performer on the Irish pipes. By this hospitable family his memory and that of his father as well are religiously cherished, and his technique of pipe-playing adopted by the younger generation of that famous family of pipers.

Imitation being the sincerest form of flattery, no tribute could excel that of the Rowsomes who are carving niches in the Temple of Fame; but let it not be forgotten that whosoever aspires to the musical mantle of the lamented James Cash must aim high indeed.

THOMAS F. KERRIGAN

Many who read these lines can testify from personal knowledge, as well as the writer, that "Tom" Kerrigan was a splendid Irish piper in every respect.

He came to Chicago in 1873, from New York, on the invitation of Mr. McNurney, a wealthy horseshoer and alderman, who was himself an enthusiastic dilettante on the pipes, and created something of a sensation by his skill on the new style instrument.

Homesick or perhaps tired of the saloon business in which he had been set up by the generous McNurney, the lionized Kerrigan, after a brief stay, started for the east without even the formality of leavetaking, and we next hear of him as the proprietor of a "Free and Easy" called "Kerrigan's Pleasant Hour," at No. 316 West 42nd Street, New York City.

All callers were welcome to free seats in the hall back of the barroom while listening to the music or singing, but the activity of the aproned waiters parading up and down the passage-ways to take orders for drinks and cigars, left us in no doubt as to where the profits were to come in. On the stage Kerrigan played the pipes to the accompaniment of a piano from four to six o'clock every afternoon, and again after supper until closing time. He varied this, however, with an occasional tune on the "coffeepot." This clown instrument consists of a tall, rather slim coffeepot, with a teapot-like spout on the side. Holes are punched in the tin opposite the spout, to correspond with the holes of a tin flageolet soldered within. The player blows through the spout, and fingers the tune on the holes in the coffeepot.

Although the manipulation of the gamut differs to some extent from that of the Irish pipes, Kerrigan was equally at home on either instrument.

It must not be imagined that the manager, as he called himself, played continuously all those long hours, for that would be beyond the endurance of mortal man. We were much surprised to find that every waiter was a specialist in some line of entertainment, such as singing, dancing, or playing on some odd musical instrument, and it was amusing to see the man who served you with refreshments throw off his apron, step up on the stage and do an artistic hornpipe or clog dance, and then resume his keen quest for orders among the audience.

As for Kerrigan himself, his music was all that could be desired. Time, tune, taste, and rhythm were all there, but from the monotony of his perennial practice he played automatically, hardly an effort of the will being required in his wonderful command of such a complicated instrument.

Often with eyes closed, and head resting against the wall back of his chair, and seemingly half asleep from pure weariness, his fingers never forgot their mission. With unerring certainty they reached for the proper keys on the regulators even in the most lively dance music, and never a discord or false note marred "Tom" Kerrigan's playing during the two hours the writer enjoyed in his "Pleasant Hour" a quarter of a century ago.

When little more than a child he came with his parents from Granard, County Longford, Ireland, and grew to be a strikingly handsome man. He died in the year 1901 at the comparatively early age of sixty years, from a severe attack of rheumatism.

His splendid set of pipes, the first made by the famous William Taylor after arriving in America, are treasured as a precious heirloom by his children.

Thomas F. Kerrigan

Edward Joyce

It is generally conceded that "Eddie" Joyce, familiarly called "The Kid," was the most precocious and in many respects the most remarkable performer on the Union pipes which America has produced. Pipering was in his blood, for not only was James Joyce, his father, a good piper, but several relatives of his name from County Galway were also good performers on that instrument.

It can safely be assumed that much of the facility with which he mastered the intricacies of the Irish chanter were in no small degree attributable to the influence of heredity.

Born at Boston in 1861, and originally taught by his father, "Eddie" completed his musical education and training under the renowned William Taylor of Philadelphia, a thorough master of his business in every sense of the word. It was the pupil's boast that the suppleness of his fingers enabled him to excel even his teacher in difficult technical execution. In fact, the latter took such a liking to him that he generously assigned many of his engagements to the talented pupil.

Undersized and boyish-looking for his age, he soon fell a victim to the blandishments of impressionable females, and was caught in the meshes of matrimony while yet in his teens.

Unfortified by discretion or determination, the train of evils which follow the footsteps of fame soon undermined a constitution never robust, and at the early age of nineteen, while playing for the "Ivy Leaf" company in Chicago, he was obliged to give up his engagement and go to a hospital for treatment.

As an honored guest in the homes of his admirers, many months were spent pleasantly after his recovery, and many an hour did he devote to practice on the pipes. Like the professional pedestrians who when they first start out, wear heavy-soled shoes, young Joyce wore gloves with holes cut in the fingers of them adapted to the holes in the chanter. Relieved of the impedimenta of gloves he would play like "a house on fire," and arouse the enthusiasm of his audience. Entertainments were given for his benefit, but the phenomenal fingering for which he was so justly renowned gradually degenerated into a kind of choppy execution subversive of both rhythm and melody.

For an Irish piper his repertory was not comprehensive, being limited to a dozen or so of each variety of Irish airs or tunes, but all of those he could play exceptionally well on the chanter unaccompanied by the concords of the regulators, which he seldom used.

Much as mankind is inclined to condone the failings of those conspicuously endowed with artistic talent, nothing short of reasonable rectitude in our idols will ensure permanent popularity. Having fallen from his pedestal, "Eddie" Joyce, the erstwhile paragon of pipering, returned to his home town in shattered health and waning fame. He died in 1897 at Bridgeport, Connecticut.

Admired for his genius, pitied for his foibles, and lamented for his loss, young Joyce—"The Kid Piper," disappointing the promise of earlier years—passed away in obscurity like a meteor in its fall. His fine instrument, made for him specially by Taylor his teacher, was sold to "Billy" McCormick of Chicago in 1897 to defray the funeral expenses.

Michael O'Sullivan (Cumbaw)

To such an extent had pipers dropped out of Irish life, that the discovery of an odd one still in the flesh, in out of the way places, was quite often the result of chance or coincidence.

Edward Joyce

"Meeting at a *Scoruideacht* of the Cork branch of the Gaelic League, a professor of the Basque language, who had come to this part of the country to study Irish," writes Mr. Wayland, "I remarked to the philologist what a splendid performer on the Union pipes Mr. Thompson was. 'Yes, he is,' said he, 'but I have heard as good, if not better, at Castlecove in Kenmare Bay.'

"I was surprised to think a good player should be living in Munster, at least of whose existence I was not cognizant. I commenced operations at once by writing to Mr. O'Shea, the local school teacher. True enough, the piper referred to by the professor was there; by name, Michael Sullivan (Cumbaw), the latter being the nickname of one of the numerous branches of that historic family.

"I soon had the new-found out, familiarly called 'Mickey,' imported to Cork, where he was received with due honors; and as he was a sweet, expressive player, I had several of his masterpieces recorded, such as the *'Maidrin Ruadh'* (Modhreen Rua) and *'Gol na m-Ban.'*

"My experiences with 'Mickey' would fill a volume; he was such a funny little man with a head full of 'quare' notions, 'pishogues and the like.' He was induced to try his luck playing on the streets of the city, but, being stone-blind, he was provided with a suitable guide, glad of the opportunity of earning a few coppers."

From the start, the blind musician was liberally patronized, but, unfortunately, one of his many whims seized him and put an end to his dreams of prosperity. A hallucination that it was fairy butter the landlady put before him changed the whole current of his thoughts and caused him to quit the house on short notice.

A very pious man in his way, he had a habit of crossing himself repeatedly when he thought he was in the company of uncongenial spirits. Often would he caution Mr. Wayland, "Look out for yourself now, Mr. Whalen, you have enemies here."

Early to bed and early to rise was a maxim religiously observed, his custom being to do most of his praying while standing, at the same time making sweeping motions with his hands.

One lightsome evening, while performing his usual devotions, "Mickey's" strange motions attracted the attention of a storekeeper on the opposite side of the street. Thinking a tragedy was being enacted, the latter, in great alarm, rushed over coatless and hatless to tell Mrs. Moore that one of her lodgers was committing suicide upstairs. "Mickey" Sullivan's misunderstood movements were simply intended as a safeguard against the approach of evil spirits, during the night, any closer than the reach of the outstretched arm in making the Sign of the Cross. This form of demonstrative devotion among a people to whom nothing was more real than disembodied spirits had some vogue in former days in the southwestern counties.

The first night of his stay, Mrs. Moore's servant made rather an amusing blunder. When he had reached the head of the stairway she called after him: "Oh, excuse me, Mr. Sullivan, I forgot to give you your candle." 'Twas all the same to the poor man, doomed to darkness for life—there was no light for him this side of the grave.

Michael Sullivan was born at Castlecove, near Waterville, in Kerry, in the thirties, and came of a family of pipers. His claim to having been hereditary piper to Daniel O'Connell's family appears to be chronologically out of joint. Yet it may be true, although his father or uncle may have had better claims to that distinction. He emigrated to America in early life and located at Worcester,

Massachusetts, where his wife and daughter still live. "Patsy" Touhey, the great American piper, who met him in that city, speaks very kindly of him.

Not less characteristic of his freakish ways in Ireland, was an incident in his career in America. Accompanied by a little boy as a guide, one day he started out to play at a wedding. Before reaching his destination, the guide, seeing some carriages and a crowd in front of a building, concluded he had arrived at the right place and entered with his charge. They were conducted through a long dark hallway and given seats in the back parlor. Being blind, of course, Sullivan could not see what was going on in the front room, but not a word uttered by the clergyman, who had already commenced the service, escaped his sharp ear.

"It is true that this is a most solemn occasion," the clergyman was saying, "but let us try to look upon the more hopeful side. It may all be for the best. Who among us can tell? Let us remember that behind the darkest cloud the sun still shines. It is our duty to try to believe that our friend has entered into a happier state. It is true that he will mingle with us no more; we shall not again be cheered by his bright smile. All that once seemed so dear to him he has had to resign; he has met the common fate of Adam's sons, but it is not for us to decide that this is to be the end of all for him."

Unable to restrain himself longer, and not suspecting that it was a funeral and not a wedding that was being conducted, "Mickey" leaned over to the man in front of him and said in a tone loud enough to be heard all over the room: "Do you know what? If I was the father of the bride, I'd give that fellow a taste of my stick!"

Sullivan's provoking oddities may have had much to do with originating the hoax which induced him to return to Ireland to inherit an alleged fortune in money and lands.

Under the guardianship of the indefatigable Wayland, "Mickey" journeyed to Dublin and tied with Denis Delaney for second prize at the Feis Ceoil competition in 1899, but not being awarded the first prize, he attributed his ill success to the fairy butter served him at Mrs. Moore's establishment, and also to the malign influence of a dead man's breeches he wore.

It appears that certain members of the Cork Pipers' Club had fitted him out for the occasion with a suit from a "ready made" shop, but nothing could convince "Mickey" that he had not been draped in a dead man's garments. Rather than run any future risks of being "overlooked," he decided to hasten back to his friends in Kerry; but before setting out on the journey he carefully parceled up the bewitched breeches and flung it violently into the little shop where it had been purchased, remarking that it was hard for him to take first prize with the fairy butter stuck to him and a dead man's spirit haunting him, or, in other words, "with God in his heart and the devil in his breeches."

His guide who accompanied him to Castlecove served in that capacity with him in Kerry, but, having been "fed up" as they say and pretty well dressed, he pined for the sound of Shandon Bells and the home allurements beside the "pleasant waters of the river Lee." Lest his youthful guide, blest with perfect eyesight, might go astray, the simple, superstitious, but conscientious, blind piper actually returned with him to Cork.

Obligingly he played his best tunes into an Edison phonograph, but a scowl instead of a smile overspread his handsome features when he heard the machine reproduce the tunes. Evidently regarding this as another instance of the devil's

Michael O'Sullivan

handiwork, he aimed several whacks of his cane at the enchanted box before he could be restrained.

His splendid instrument was purchased by Major-General Foster, a native of Kilkenny, and an enthusiastic piper himself; but as the general had been transferred to England from Queenstown, and subsequently to Quetta, British Beluchistan, Sullivan's famous pipes, like many of her talented sons, are lost to Ireland forever.

Old, feeble, and friendless, and far from those upon whom he had legal and sentimental claims, Michael Sullivan, talented, eccentric, and a scion of illustrious ancestry, found a final refuge in the Cahirciveen poorhouse, where he died soon after; but, whether numbered among the living or the dead, his memory will remain ever fresh and green with Mr. Wayland and the other members of the Cork Pipers' Club of Saint Fionn Barr's famous city on the Lee.

"Jimmy" Barry

The strangest old piper who attended an inaugural meeting of said club, in 1898, was "Jimmy" Barry, a "lefthander." He was *NOT* a teetotaler. In some of his jolly moods, Mr. Wayland tells us, he would burst forth into song so loud and voluble as to render the music of his pipes inaudible, anon raising the chanter almost over his shoulder and in other ways displaying the exuberance of his spirits.

"Nance the Piper"

From him was learned the story of a woman known as "Nance the Piper," who flourished at Castlelyons and who had become a performer from dire necessity, on the death of her husband. She was an especial favorite with the dancers, and it is quite likely that she must have had some previous training to have acquired such proficiency. None but the best can play for those who are called stage or platform dancers. Without a blink of light in her eyes, she was able to discern each step-dancer by the sound of his feet.

Not the least entertaining part of the performance was the fusillade of comments she kept up all the time, such as: "Wisha, darlin' to ye, Patsy Magner. Yerra, I wouldn't doubt your father's son." "Wire into 'em, Mickey Joe Sullivan, there is not the batins of ye anywhere for a gorsoon. Faith, 'tis little boastin' the Mulcahey's of Grange will have whin ye are a year or two oldher." "Now, Darby Tom, don't ye let it go with 'em. Ah, 'twas kind father for you to be handy with your fut, me bouchal."

Her originality was phenomenal and she never was at a loss for a word of encouragement to stimulate the dancers as well as to keep the crowd in good humor.

A character so quaint and unique as this blind woman piper, if "Jimmy" Barry's story be true, should have been immortalized in Irish literature.

John O'Neill

For many years prior to the Gaelic League agitation in behalf of an Irish Ireland, and the restoration or rehabilitation of her games, music, language, and literature, the wandering minstrels and musicians were few and far between. As elsewhere stated, the oldtime festivities and celebrations had been discontinued and those of the pipers not doomed to the poorhouse by reason of old age or blindness sought some other means of obtaining a living.

Shane O'Neill

Their instruments were put away, and in course of time even themselves, as well as their tunes, were forgotten.

The nucleus or "foundation stone" of the Cork Pipers' Club, Mr. Wayland, its founder, tells us, was "Shane" O'Neill.

When resurrected, as it were, the old piper explained to his discoverers that he had not "touched a chanter in more than twenty years. Oh, sure, the old people died out and the young people, most of them, left the country," he pathetically added; "who was there to listen to me?" Poor "Shane's" case was typical of scores of others who had been "silenced" and whose lives had been blighted by the ban on "patrons" and dancing.

The subject of our sketch was born near Macroom in the western part of the County of Cork, where it converges with Kerry and Limerick. Traditional music, the Gaelic language, and Irish folk lore, found a refuge in that secluded part of the province of Munster; and it is a noteworthy fact that natives of that locality carried off the majority of prizes awarded for original composition and story-telling in the Irish language, at the annual Feis contests, in recent years.

"Shane," or John O'Neill's brief biography may be condensed to the simple statement: "He lived and he died." His death took place a few years ago at the patriarchal age of ninety-three years.

From him Mr. Wayland obtained certain lamentation parts of the "Fox Chase" not known to pipers of greater repute, which he had learned from his teacher, "Mickey" Connell, who also hailed from Macroom.

Though not a great performer, "Shane" played in excellent time, but this art he paid for dearly and never forgot to the day of his death. While "serving his time," young O'Neill was playing for some step-dancers. One of them, increasing his speed, the apprentice piper, fancying he was doing a clever thing, "followed him up." In a twinkling he was sent sprawling on the floor, pipes and all, by a thundering box on the ear from the veteran teacher. 'Twas explained to him *NEXT DAY*, when he had recovered from the shock, that he must on all occasions preserve correct time and never "slow down" or "hunt up" a step-dancer for love or money. We can well believe that an admonition of such a striking character left an indelible impression on the pupil's mind.

MICHAEL CONNELL

Better known as "Caunheen," following the example of so many of his countrymen, "to better his fortune had crossed the deep say," according to my informant, Mr. Wayland. His "tour of America" about the middle of the nineteenth century, to use his own words, was very likely confined to the Atlantic towns and cities, in one of which he accepted a challenge to play against a local celebrity.

A tremendous crowd filled the hall on the night appointed for the contest. They cheered lustily when his American competitor repeated every tune that the greenhorn piper from Ireland rattled off. The latter was thinking about giving up, when some faithful "towny" from Ballyvourney yelled from the gallery: *"Wisha 'Caunheen' a gradh geal, cadh mar geall an Ceoil Sidhe?"* The voice from home, giving fresh courage and inspiration to the man from Macroom, he put his whole soul into the execution of the enchanted air, and as the Yankee champion could not follow him into the realms of fairy music, our hero won the wager.

The decision, however, was received with anything but satisfaction by the supporters of the American piper, for in almost all such cases popular sentiment is with the local favorite. "Caunheen's" exultation soon gave way to alarm at the hostile attitude of so many in the audience. So he discreetly decided on making himself scarce, and seeing a side door hospitably open and convenient, he lost no time in closing it from the outside.

What became of him after that is left to conjecture, but a few of the old-timers from whom Mr. Wayland got the story of "Mickey" Connell's exploits were not a little proud of the fact that they had entertained him after his triumphant return from America.

RICHARD STEPHENSON

The "Prince of Pipers," as "Dick" Stephenson preferred being called, was born at Clonakilty, County Cork, in the forties, but when quite young went to reside at the village of Shanagolden, County Limerick, near Foynes, on the banks of the Shannon, a circumstance which led to the belief that he was a native of the latter county. It is known that he studied music under Owen and "Paddy" Bohan, natives of Clonbare, County Galway, and he certainly was a credit to them as far as proficiency on the Union pipes was concerned.

He served for a short time in the Cork Artillery Militia, afterwards going to England as piper with the "Leaves of Shamrock Company."

None but an exceptionally fine performer would have been selected by the great baritone, Professor Ludwig, to accompany him on his American tour in 1886. Stephenson had few equals and possibly no superior in playing hornpipes, but in jig and reel playing, according to competent judges in Chicago, he had no advantage over pipers familiar to the people of that city. His execution was decidedly rapid.

The effects of too much conviviality, arising largely from the ill-advised conception of Irish hospitality, were beginning to tell on the piper. Such was his desire for a "bracer" that he had been observed anxiously parading the streets of Chicago awaiting the earliest hour in the morning that his longing for a drink could be legally gratified.

Having heard Stephenson's performance at the Ludwig entertainment, Sergeant Early went around to the stage entrance, where he was cheerfully greeted by the piper.

"Are you acquainted around here, sir?" eagerly inquired Stephenson, producing a slip of paper; "here's a name—maybe you'd know him."

"I'm the man," said the sergeant, glancing at it.

"Oh, Mr. Touhey told me you were a grand gentleman, sir," exclaimed the stranger, delightedly.

"Then you've met Mr. Touhey?"

"Oh, yes; he's a grand gentleman and a grand player, and I'm very glad to meet you, sir; I heard so much about you," replied the "Prince of Pipers." "I'm very dry, sir, can't we have a drink?"

The generous sergeant, although a Father Mathew man himself, could not ignore the obligations of hospitality, but no sooner had poor Stephenson swallowed a bumper of bourbon than he pleadingly asked: "Will you let me have another one, sir?"

On Stephenson's return to Ireland he entered on an extensive tour of the country, particularly the province of Munster, accompanied by an excellent fiddle player, one of Bob Thompson's sons, and Johnny Dunne, a capable vocalist and banjo player. Well attuned, all three played together, and their performance

Dick Stephenson   John Dunne

was well received wherever they went. A very trifling incident at Ballyhaunis, County Mayo, wrecked the harmony of their partnership for good.

Stephenson got an extra coin for his playing of the "Fox Chase" (his great favorite), while his partners had to stand inactive, not being able to follow the "variations." Dunne remarked he wouldn't hunt a fox that cold night for any consideration. A rejoinder from Stephenson to the effect that "maybe he couldn't" was the spark that fired the flames of jealousy, and a round of fisticuffs put an end to years of friendship and companionship, although the Dunnes and Stephensons and Thompsons were all intermarried.

Broken in health and spirit at last, and unable to continue his wandering minstrelsy, the "Prince of Pipers" found a resting place in the infirmary and workhouse at Rathkeale, County Limerick, where he died in 1897.

When Robert Thompson was being persuaded to enter the lists of competitors on the pipes at the first Feis Ceoil in that year, he remarked to Mr. Wayland, "I would not be a feared of any piper in Ireland barring Stephenson." Not a few claim that, as an all-round player of airs and dance music, Thompson was not his inferior. The fact that the latter having won first prize at the annual Feis two years in succession and was barred from competing thereafter adds much to uphold that view of the case.

Both pipers have since joined the silent majority, but their families have been linked by marriage—one of Thompson's sons having married Stephenson's daughter. Were talent hereditary, great results might be expected from this union.

As a performer on the Union pipes, in the opinion of competent judges in Dublin, Stephenson outranked his contemporaries, but his integrity was of the "good old piperly stamp." Canon Goodman, who sold him a set of pipes for a few pounds, never succeeded in getting either the pipes or money.

After the Canon's death, his claim was corroborated in an unexpected way. The two sets of pipes which Stephenson possessed at the time of his death were bought in for three half crowns (less than two dollars) and one of them proved to be an excellent instrument.

It appears that "Dick" Stephenson had a brother "Jack," who was a piper also, but a much less capable performer. When but fifteen years old Mr. Timothy M. Dillon, now a retired police officer of Chicago, won a dancing contest from young "Dick" Stephenson of Shanagolden, the great piper's nephew.

Morgan Galwey

Around Christmas time in the year 1890 two globetrotting brothers, just returned from Australia, named George and Morgan Galwey, paid a passing visit to Mr. M. Flanagan, a versatile musician and writer of Dublin. Morgan, the younger brother, was a good performer on the Union pipes, hardly inferior to Canon Goodman, but the pitch of his instrument was so low that Mr. Flanagan found it no easy matter to accompany him on the violin.

Nothing could be more touching than the veneration with which Morgan was regarded by his elder brother. Prodding his host on the shoulder with the shank of his pipe, George asked: "What instrument leads the band?" "Well, I've always heard that the clarinet is the first fiddle of a military band," replied Mr. Flanagan. "Right you are," agreed George. "There's your clarinet," pointing to Morgan. "Follow him and you'll do."

Morgan was certainly a skilled musician, and wrote correctly in every detail, from memory, a tune his host had long sought in vain. He was the only musician Mr. Flanagan ever met that played "The Foxhunter's Jig" in the key of G major, and certainly he played it well.

In 1896 Morgan was heard of as an inmate of Honan's Home, Tivoli, in his native County of Cork.

Well educated, courteous, and evidently of good family, the Galwey brothers for many years led a nomadic life, but their most conspicuous characteristic was an unconquerable aversion to water externally applied.

JOHN HINGSTON

Not less enthusiastic as an Irish piper than Canon Goodman, with whom he had been associated for many years, both in Southwest Cork and in Dublin, was the magnificent John Hingston. Music was in the family, for his brother was also a performer on the Union pipes.

Born on a farm not far from Skibbereen, County Cork, Mr. Hingston was a splendid specimen of the Munster peasantry, considerably over six feet in height, and it is little wonder that his prowess as a life-saver in Phœnix Park attracted the attention of Prince George, Duke of Cambridge, who, in recognition of his heroism, secured him the position of head steward in Trinity College Dublin. His experience on the St. Lawrence river, Canada, in early manhood, schooled him in the knowledge which in after years he turned to such good account.

The Feis Ceoil Association has been taken to task by "An Old Piper," in an interesting communication to a Dublin paper, for making no mention of Canon Goodman and Mr. Hingston, who above all others should be credited with having kept pipe music alive in its darkest days. He claims that it was owing to their exertions and liberality that any sets of Union pipes remained in the country at the time of the musical revival, such was the demand for them in America.

Mr. Hingston was a much less masterful player than Canon Goodman, but many an evening during a period extending over some years did the two old pipers take off their coats and play in concert in the apartment of the genial Joseph Marshall (now steward), while the heads of the University, instead of frowning on that variety of Irish entertainment, dropped in from time to time to enjoy and show their appreciation of the performance.

Hingston played before King Edward VII, then Prince of Wales, at the Vice Regal Lodge, accompanied by "Paddy" Bohan, a perfect piper whom he had equipped for the occasion.

Well, they have both joined the heavenly choir; the life saver in 1892 and the gentle Canon in 1896, but while in the land of the living they nobly upheld the best traditions of the Irish race in music, language and liberality. In addition they furnish a striking instance of the descendants of an alien race becoming more Irish than the Irish themselves.

ROBERT THOMPSON

When the Gaelic League agitation in the last decade of the nineteenth century set the life blood pulsating through the moribund arteries of a decadent nation, it brought to light many a forgotten genius whose artistic flame had been quenched by public apathy and national indifference.

Who could have imagined that the modest "Bob" Thompson, who was proclaimed the best piper in Ireland two years in succession at the annual Feiseanna, had not played a tune nor even owned an instrument in the ten preceding years?

John Hingston

More; his next door neighbors were unaware that a man of such musical abilities lived in their midst.

It does not speak well for the spirit of the citizens of Cork, to be so callous to the beauties of their national music, as to allow a piper of such distinction to dwell among them unappreciated and unknown, for so many years, dragging out a cheerless existence at the gloomy business of making hearse-plumes.

To Alderman Phair of Cork, an enthusiastic amateur piper himself, belongs the credit of discovering Thompson, after John S. Wayland had exhumed Shane O'Neill. It didn't take the Alderman long, kind-hearted man that he was, to have his prize ensconced in his parlor with the Alderman's own pipes on his lap. At reed and quill making the newly discovered piper proved to be an expert, and before an hour had elapsed Gillabbey House resounded with the merry music of the Union pipes such as its astonished proprietor had not heard in a lifetime. Thompson's performance was a revelation.

Installed as teacher of his art at the newly organized Cork Pipers' Club, of which Alderman Phair was president, his name and fame spread like fire on a mountain. At concerts, entertainments and festivities of all kinds he was the great attraction, but the conviviality common to such occasions proved disastrous to his health, which had been far from robust for years.

Thompson, who had a cool finger and splendid execution, took first prize among thirteen competitors at the first *Feis Ceoil* at Dublin, 1897, and repeated his triumph at Belfast the following year. Lest his continuous success should discourage less gifted pipers from competing, the Committee formulated a rule under which he was ineligible to enter future contests.

Equally at home playing strathspeys, waltzes and quadrilles, his repertoire was by no means confined to Irish music. Yet he had his peculiarities in a musical way; an aversion to the "Fox Chase," and to the humming of the drones, being the most pronounced. The latter can hardly be viewed as an evidence of fine musical taste, for few sounds produced by nature or art are more soft and soothing than the mellow hum of well-tuned drones of the Union pipes. Unsupported by them the tones of the chanter lose much of their charm, and it has been noticed that a piper's dislike of the sustained tones of the drones is always associated with his inability to tune them properly.

"Bob" Thompson, with some members of the family, was born at Lisburn, County Antrim, although his father hailed from Ballyclough, a small village near Mallow, County Cork. The latter was an Irish scholar and at one time was a teacher of the Irish language at Belfast. He was also a skilful performer on the Union pipes and taught the rudiments of the art to his son, who had inherited his musical tastes, and later took lessons from Daniel Crilly, a noted Dublin piper. Involved in financial difficulties by the introduction of machinery, and domestic infelicities, "Bob" was reduced to the necessity of pawning his pipes. When "Paddy" Meade's pawnshop was wrecked by fire soon after, both pipes and prospects perished with it, and the forlorn piper considered the curtain had finally fallen on his piping.

Mr. Wayland, founder and secretary of the Cork Pipers' Club, to whom we are indebted for a vast fund of information in this and other cases, says: "Thompson was a nice man to talk to, most conversational, and above all modest as to his own abilities as a piper and reed maker."

With "Tim" Murphy, a champion step-dancer, Thompson once went to play at a concert at Mitchelstown. When Mr. Wayland called the manager's attention to the curious coincidence that the piper was a maker of hearse-plumes, and the

Robert Thompson

dancer a builder of coffins, the witty Milesian carelessly answered: "Oh well, if they are both in the funeral business I don't think there's any necessity for a rehearsal!"

On another occasion, while returning by train from Schull, a remote town in West Carberry where he had been repeatedly engaged to play at concerts, he was entertaining Edward Cronin, brother of Rev. Dr. Cronin, editor of the *Buffalo Catholic Times,* and Mr. M. Donovan of Skibbereen, with a round or two of "The Dear Irish Boy"; a telegram was received announcing the death of Thompson's mother. His reverence and the journalist humbly apologized for asking him to play, not knowing of his mother's illness. Nothing disconcerted by the sad news, the bereaved *orphan* continued playing the plaintive melody, casually remarking, "Wisha then, 'twas time for her, after her ninety-three years." All three are now in the land of shades, and all three—nature's noblemen—have left their impress on their times.

The insistent friendship and misdirected hospitality of his admirers—too often a source of inconvenience and embarrassment—eventually ruined Thompson's health utterly, and he died early in 1903. Two of his three living sons are skilled violinists; "Mattie" being engaged in teaching a violin class at Schull. Another married the daughter of "Dick" Stephenson, the celebrated piper.

Poor Robert Thompson, though not blessed with much of this world's wealth, enjoyed the fullness of deserved popularity during the later years of a checkered life, and in death he has the honor of taking his final rest beside another famous Corkman—Collins the explorer—in the elevated and picturesque old churchyard of Currakippane, a few miles above the city on the banks of the river Lee.

CHAPTER XXII

IRISH PIPERS OF DISTINCTION LIVING IN THE EARLY YEARS OF THE TWENTIETH CENTURY

NICHOLAS BURKE

ALTHOUGH our kinsmen of Caledonia have at all times cherished the traditions and customs of their race and clans, and possess reliable records of all their famous musicians—harpers, pipers, and fiddlers—the Irish, no less patriotic and tenacious of their national ideals, have been woefully negligent in that respect.

Since Giraldus Cambrensis, late in the twelfth century, wrote his panegyric on the harpers of Ireland, proclaiming them to be "beyond all comparison superior" to those of any nation he had seen, much of what little we know of that class of minstrels was derived from Arthur O'Neill, the celebrated blind harper of Tyrone, whose reminiscences were first given publicity by Edward Bunting in the year 1840.

The Union pipers were, however, closer to the hearts of the people and quite as famous in their line as the glorified harpers, passed away on the current of time, as unnoticed by the journalists and biographers as floating chips on the Shannon's waters on the way to the sea. An awakened interest in the subject brings us to a realization of what we have irretrievably lost, and the meagre mention of the few notables immortalized by Grattan Flood in *The Story of the Bagpipe,* instead of satisfying our longing, serves but to emphasize the national delinquency.

To do partial though tardy justice to a worthy and for a time numerous class of typically Irish minstrels, would indeed be a labor of love, but at this late day, where is information to be obtained concerning the great Irish musicians and composers who flourished since the middle of the eighteenth century? Stories more legendary than reliable were to be picked up here and there, while an occasional nugget of authentic biography would prove invaluable in piecing out an otherwise disjointed story.

Years of unremitting inquiry resulted in but a tithe of the material one would reasonably expect to accumulate on this subject. In fact the gleanings were so disappointingly incomplete that this work may never have been undertaken but for the fortuitous discovery in Brooklyn, New York, of Mr. Nicholas Burke, who knew and remembered the Irish pipers of his generation as well as Arthur O'Neill knew the harpers of his day.

A glance at his picture will show that he had attained the patriarchal age, and being a music lover and musician, hospitable and helpful to those of similar tastes, every piper and fiddler of prominence who crossed the Atlantic since the middle of the nineteenth century made his acquaintance.

On learning the nature of the purpose in view, Mr. Burke obligingly "took his pen in hand" and wrote out pages upon pages of interesting memoirs dealing with nearly a score of pipers about whom we knew practically nothing, besides giving supplementary information concerning many others already on our list. In fact Mr. Burke may aptly be termed the Plutarch of the pipers.

Mr. Nicholas Burke

Born in the parish of Annaghdown, on the banks of Lough Corrib, County Galway, in 1837, he emigrated to America in early manhood. From his trade as carpenter he developed into a skilful draughtsman, and eventually became a successful and prosperous builder. Like many others of his countrymen, from being an excellent performer on the flute, he took to playing the Union pipes, on which he also became proficient, but be it remembered that Nicholas Burke played only for his own pleasure or the entertainment of his friends, and invariably in his own home. In Ireland he would be called a "gentleman piper."

His instrument, it will be observed, is of the most elaborate pattern, with a chanter of fine-grained ivory instead of wood. As Taylor, the maker of this type of Irish bagpipes, has joined the "silent majority" some years ago, and left no successor, the picture may be regarded as one possessing no little historical importance. Though in his seventy-fifth year, Mr. Burke's memory is singularly retentive and clear and he possesses in an eminent degree the rare faculty of imparting desired information in a manner both concise and complete.

JOHN K. BEATTY

Crowned with a snow-white fringe of once luxuriant hair, through which his well-developed bump of self-esteem invites attention, and with a patriarchal beard of the same hue adorning his florid and expressive countenance, no one could more fittingly typify the dignified bard of ancient Erin in this generation than John K. Beatty, the nonogenarian dean of the Chicago pipers.

Though enfeebled by age and no longer able to play in the manner described in *Irish Folk Music: A Fascinating Hobby,* no tastier, livelier, jollier young man ever left the parish of Drumrany, Ballymore, in the county of Westmeath, than "Johnny" Beatty.

As jig and reel dancer he was equal to the best, and though not a musician in his youth his lilting was simply incomparable; his inconceivable combination of syllabic staccato accurately expressing every tone and shading of the most complex tune.

About eighteen years old when he landed at Brooklyn, New York, in 1839, he took to the trade of bricklaying for some years. In 1860 we find he was a member of the Illinois militia, and on the breaking out of the Civil War was actively engaged in the commissary department.

About this time Mr. Beatty commenced his musical studies under the instruction of the veteran piper James Quinn, a sketch of whose life will be found in the preceding chapter. A good set of Egan pipes which he owned were laid aside after "Billy" Taylor of Philadelphia had developed a more powerful instrument. To Mr. Beatty Dame Fortune proved fickle, yet the failure of his enterprises never chilled the warm glow of his optimism and good nature. As the sun shines behind the darkest cloud, so was ultimate prosperity in store for the genial minstrel. With the first returns from a lucrative position, a *carte blanche* order for a new set of pipes was given Mr. Taylor, and it was on this triumph of the great pipemaker's art that John K. Beatty so distinguished himself.

So supreme was he at lilting that on hearing him vocalize a tune in that way, the renowned Taylor said: "Ah, Mr. Beatty, if you could only play it that way you'd be a wonder." But he couldn't. Neither could anyone else, for such rhythmic staccato was beyond their powers of execution.

Mr. Beatty's headlong execution on his superb set of pipes was as much of a surprise to Turlogh McSweeney, the "Donegal Piper," as was his lilting. After watching his acrobatic performance on the huge instrument for a time, Mc-

Sweeney remarked quizzically: "Begor, Mr. Beatty, you have a great shower of fingers." And so he had.

In the exuberance of his spirits and anxiety to impress his audience with a due sense of his superlative execution, he not infrequently left much to be desired in the way of rhythmic precision, it must be confessed; and if the drones and regulators after a round or two of such strenuosity insisted on disagreeing with the chanter, it must not be regarded as a reflection on the maker, or the conduct of the instrument under milder treatment.

Like a true bard he composed and sang his own songs, mainly on topical subjects, and had his practice on the pipes been commenced in his youth instead of his manhood, the true spirit of the minstrel so dominant in his character would doubtless have gained him more enduring fame.

JOHN CUMMINGS

The ablest and most distinguished looking of the capable Irish pipers brought to light since the inception of the Gaelic Revival is the octogenarian Prof. John Cummings of San Francisco, California, whose likeness with that of his friend, Mr. George A. M. Leech, graces the opposite page.

In execution and versatility he is classed by competent authorities with "Patsy" Touhey and "Barney" Delaney. In this generation no greater compliment could be paid him. As one of them put it: "If not as light-fingered as Touhey now, it is safe to say that Touhey won't play as well as Mr. Cummings at the age of eighty-four years."

This "grand old man" was born at Athenry, County Galway, in 1828, and was taught by his father, Patrick Cummings, to whom quite a few pipers owe their early musical training. It appears that Prof. Cummings' ancestors kept a college for pipers at or near Athenry for generations, the name in those days being Cummins.

Before coming to America in 1892 John Cummings had lived in England for forty years. Though an accomplished piper he was not a professional one. While in Liverpool he worked for builders, and later in the city of London he had much to do with the handling and care of horses. Only when thrown into the company of people whose tastes were similar to his own, did he indulge in his passion for music, but his most enjoyable experience was the acquaintance and companionship of Michael Egan, the famous piper and pipemaker of Liverpool, about 1850.

Amiable as he is venerable, this patriarchal minstrel fittingly typifies the bards of old in the heyday of Ireland's glory, but fate decreed his birth a thousand years too late. In these degenerate days pipe music falls on callous ears. The German accordeon or melodeon has supplanted the Union pipes and fiddle in the land of the Gael, for the "sets" which may be extracted from the foreign instrument are more "polite" than the jig, reel and hornpipe of our ancestors. And besides it never gets out of tune, and anyone can bring music out of it.

Had John Cummings been a contemporary of Crampton and Courtney, his name like theirs would have found a place in literature.

It is only within a year or so that his existence and phenomenal musical ability were incidentally disclosed at the Golden Gate, and now that he has reached the eighty-fourth milestone on the way to eternity the incubus of age has begun to dim the eyes, unsteady the nerves, and blight the faculties of one of Erin's most talented yet neglected sons.

Mr. Leech, to whose zeal and devotion in the cause of Irish music we are under many obligations, induced Prof. Cummings to pose for the picture which,

Geo. A. H. Leech   Prof. John Cummings

let us hope, will contribute something to the perpetuation of a worthy man's name and fame.

Even at his advanced age, when he hears an old tune, or a new one for that matter which captivates his fancy, his spirit revives like an old warhorse at the sound of the bugle, and buckling on his beloved instrument, he strikes up the tune in such a masterly way, with graces and curls, as to put those who inspired him entirely in the shade. When in the humor at the social gatherings of Irish musicians at the home of his daughter, Mrs. Hogan, with whom he lives, Mr. Cummings would roll off a score of reels, that none of his audience "ever heard before or since," as Mr. Leech expresses it.

"One night I played 'The Raveled Hank of Yarn,'" the latter writes, "and the old man shook his head reminiscently, remarking, 'I had forgotten that tune and didn't play it for forty years.' Gradually the smile came over his face, and he commenced to pump the bag, and out came the tune, but with such grace notes, embellishments, and variations, that I stood aghast, enraptured by the soul of music which brought me back to the time when Erin was melodious with our own dear strains."

Among his father's pupils were Michael Kenny, a good Irish piper who made some pretention to original composition, and "Patsy" Mullin, who also won distinction as a performer on the Union pipes. Another was Michael Twohill or Touhey, who Prof. Cummings believes was the grandfather of "Patsy" Touhey, the celebrated Irish-American piper and comedian—the best known of living performers on the Union pipes in this generation.

Daniel O'Mahony

Of the two noted performers on the Union pipes still surviving in London and representing a once numerous fraternity, Daniel O'Mahony, whose stage name is "Michael O'Hara," is regarded by Prof. P. D. Reidy as being in the same class as Thomas O'Hannigan, of an earlier generation, who played before royalty.

O'Mahony was born at Bermondsey, London, England, in 1837, and was taught music by his father, a native of Cork. In rendering dance music his rhythm and execution were faultless, and it was a rare treat for admirers of such spirited melodies to hear O'Mahony and William O'Kelly, another expert on the pipes, play in concert. The latter fell from grace many years ago but managed to reach Sydney, New South Wales, Australia, by working his passage.

So moribund is Irish sentiment as far as the old music is concerned, coupled with the lack of suitable equipments for his instrument, that the famous old minstrel confines his execution to the chanter alone in late years.

Thomas Garoghan

One of the pleasant surprises which conduced to render the Oireachtas of 1912 particularly interesting and enjoyable, was the introduction of Thomas Garoghan, the London piper, to a Dublin audience. He played on a full set of boxwood pipes, and according to one account, the performance was "splendid and refined, but the tone of his instrument was too weak to be effective in a large concert hall." He did not have his pipes with him at the little assembly at Groome's hotel, but on the stage of the Rotunda each evening his music was much admired, and by uttering intelligibly on the chanter, "Polly put the kettle on," the unique trick aroused the audience to enthusiasm.

Thomas Garoghan

"Prof. Garoghan," as he prefers to be called, was born in Coventry, Warwickshire, England, in 1845, his parents being natives of County Mayo, Ireland. He learned to play the Union pipes from James O'Rourke of Birmingham and Michael McGlynn of Aughamore, who were well known in the midland counties of England half a century ago.

Piper Garoghan is a fluent Irish speaker, having acquired the language from his parents, and the Irishmen who come in large numbers every year to reap the English harvest; but the event which was the crowning glory of his life was his eight months' engagement with the "Shemus O'Brien" opera company at His Majesty's Theatre, London, some years ago. Always spry and active, he has kept the Irish pipes to the front for forty-five years, and in a country in which there was said to be an Irish piper for every day in the year less than two generations ago, he is now one of the very few remaining. He is back again in London, for after indulging a very natural desire to visit the land of his forefathers, he finds that, after all, "There's no place like home."

Peter Kelly

At the annual picnic of the Highland Pipers' Band of Chicago in 1912, the present writer complimented a member of it for his proficiency. "The Irish bagpipe is what I would like to play," he answered, pointing to Adam Tobin, who, seated under the shade of a convenient tree, was manipulating such an instrument. We inquired where he had heard an Irish piper before, and learned that he had often listened with pleasure to an Irish piper of fine ability at Jamaica bridge, Glasgow. His name he did not know, but the location mentioned furnished a clew which, through the courtesy of Inspector James R. Motion of the Glasgow department of police, led to the information desired.

In London there are still surviving two capable performers on the Irish or Union pipes—Daniel O'Mahony and Thomas Garoghan—but the death of Peter Kelly, the man alluded to by McPhail on the first day of April, 1910, at the age of seventy-three, ends the race of Irish pipers in Scotland.

Peter Kelly was born in the historic City of Galway, and was stricken with blindness when but a few months old. Arriving at a suitable age, his parents arranged to have him taught by the celebrated Martin O'Reilly, with whom they were well acquainted. He proved to be an apt pupil, and a set of pipes then about forty years old were with the aid of friends procured for him at Liverpool, and it was this set he played on to within a few days of his death.

He was about thirty years of age when he went to Glasgow on a visit with a fiddler named John Crockwell, and finding that thriving city to his liking he made it his permanent home. His widow and three of his nine children survive him.

In the early years of his married life, the Irish bagpipes being comparatively new to Glasgow, Kelly was quite prosperous, and it was no unusual thing for him to take in one pound ten shillings or even two pounds on a Saturday night alone, but of late years and up to the time of his death, his receipts diminished to not over one-fourth of those amounts.

Occasionally he would take a trip to Edinburgh, and during the summer season to Portobello, and reap a better reward than when at home. About thirty years ago he played at one of the theatres in Edinburgh at a benefit given to a then well-known Irish comedian named "Pat" Feeney.

At the invitation of Dr. Boyd of Belfast, Kelly went to that city in 1898 to play at a competition, and notwithstanding his being awarded but third prize by the local judges, he was honored by being selected by the Lord Mayor to play at a reception given at the city hall that same evening, a circumstance which goes to show that his performance was appreciated by the authorities.

Shortly after this event a similar competition was arranged to take place in the National Halls, Glasgow. Only three players came forward, these being Kelly and two farmers—-father and son, natives of Ireland—from a remote part of Scotland. Kelly was adjudged the winner without hesitation.

In Glasgow his services were in great demand at gatherings of the Ancient Order of Hibernians; United Irish League, etc.; and his proficiency and popularity on such occasions always insured him a warm welcome and a good fee.

This ideal old minstrel was a well-known figure for many years in the vicinity of the Jamaica and Albert bridges, and opposite the Queen Street Station, but instead of sitting down while playing he stood upright, resting his right leg above the knee on a short crotched stick so as to manipulate his instrument successfully. He had the reputation of being a particularly skilful and sweet player, and Mr. Henderson, the famous bagpipe maker who made his reeds, speaks in very high terms of his capabilities as a musician. Kelly played all his music by ear, and so quick was he in picking up a tune, that if he heard it played, sung, or whistled once, he could repeat it on the pipes without making a mistake. His favorite melodies were "The Coolin" and "The Blackbird."

Very often he was accompanied by another blind man named Smith, who played the flute, and the two were looked upon as inseparable cronies, and both were equally fond of their pint of porter, though by no means drunkards. Kelly was at his usual stand on the Albert bridge on the Saturday evening preceding his death from pneumonia four days later.

Dire want drove his widow to a pawnshop with the pipes shortly after, and the generous (?) pawnbroker said, had not the chanter been worn nearly through by the finger marks he could afford to have given much more than the ten shillings he allowed her.

THOMAS RUDD

of Clone, near Ferns, County Wexford—a gentleman farmer whose name comes down to us as a piper of no inferior merit—was an early contemporary and friend of Mr. Rowsome's. He used to enliven the harvest-work of his employes by bringing his pipes to the field and playing to them the popular melodies which they loved and were accustomed to hear, and which in those days when the peasantry had few comforts and no luxuries, constituted one of the greatest joys of their existence.

Mr. Rudd was one of the leading farmers of Wexford in his time. As none of his family inherited his musical proclivities his instruments, of which he possessed more than one valuable set, passed after his death, which occured fifty years ago, into the hands of the late John Cash.

A defective chanter which Mr. Rudd owned, after undergoing an overhauling at the hands of his friend Mr. Rowsome, was declared to be the "truest he ever handled."

PATRICK GALVIN (THE NEW ZEALAND PIPER)

As widely dispersed all over the English-speaking world as the most adventurous of their countrymen, were the tuneful Irish pipers, although it is by the merest chance that we learn of their existence on the other side of the globe.

PATRICK GALVIN
(*The New Zealand Piper*)

Had not Mr. Galvin returned from Shingle Creek Hotel, Otago, New Zealand, to visit the scenes of his childhood at Corofin, County Clare, at the end of the century, after forty years' exile, his picture would not have been included in our gallery of famous Irish pipers.

He looks the part in every sense of the word though out of practice for many years. He visited the Cork Pipers' Club during his stay, and "Bob" Thompson supplied reeds and guills for a new set of pipes which Mr. Galvin had purchased from C. Butler & Sons. Returning to New Zealand, he took with him a step dancer to revive the Irish pastimes at the Antipodes.

Toirdhealach Mac Suibhne (Turlogh McSweeney)

No Irish piper of ancient or modern times, unless it be "the piper who played before Moses," has been the subject of so much publicity as McSweeney, "the Donegal Piper," since brought to light by Mrs. Hart and installed at "Donegal Castle" on the Midway of the World's Columbian Exposition at Chicago in 1893.

In the evolution of time and the decay of ancient Irish institutions during the nineteenth century, the professional piper sometimes was obliged to abandon his calling and seek a livelihood by more profitable means, and so it was with McSweeney.

On his arrival in Chicago, McSweeney found that his instrument from age and disuse was entirely unfit for the service required; and had it not been for the kind helpfulness of Sergt. James Early, it would have been scarcely possible for him to fulfil his mission.

While the "Donegal Piper" played outside the main entrance to "Donegal Castle," "Patsy" Touhey, the great Irish-American piper, was the center of attraction within; and no two musicians on the Midway, representing their respective countries, won more attention or elicited more praise than they.

As McSweeney enjoyed the hospitality of Sergt. Early from Saturday evening until Monday morning, during his six months' stay in Chicago, we were afforded ample opportunity to hear him at his best.

For an Irish piper, his coldness and reticence were in marked contrast with the manners of most persons of his class. This taciturnity may have been constitutional; yet who knows but it was the visible effect of maintaining the dignity befitting a distinguished piper, conscious of his descent from the chieftains of the once powerful *Clan MacSuibhne* of *Tir-Conaill*. Be that as it may, he rarely relaxed his reserve. With his host and benefactor, Sergt. Early, and with Mr. Gillan, a great admirer of his music, he was more communicative and almost cordial.

INSPIRED BY THE FAIRIES

It was while in one of his gracious moods that he confided to them how he came to be such a great piper. In his young days McSweeney was no musical prodigy, as one may surmise from his subsequent reputation. In fact, he was not much of a player at all, according to his own account, though having the advantage of heredity and example; for his father and grandfather, particularly the latter, were fine pipers in their day. "There was no music in me," is the way he tells of his lack of talent, but he was anxious to learn and be a credit to his name and ancestry.

Despairing of other means of attaining success, it occurred to him to make an appeal to the fairies on the rath of *Gaeth-Doir* on the hilltop, half a mile away. One moonlight night, he plucked up courage, and with his pipes buckled on all ready for playing, he made his way up along the "boreen" and across the fields and timidly entered the fort. But perhaps the reader would prefer to read the story in his own words:

"Well, as I was saying, when I got to the center of the *Plasog,* as near as I could tell, you may be sure I wasn't any too comfortable. Anyhow, I addressed myself to the king of the fairies, saying: 'I'm Turlogh McSweeney, the piper of Gwedore, and I hope you will pardon my boldness for coming to ask your majesty to play a 'chune' on the pipes for me, and I'll return the compliment and play for you.' Yerra, man, like a shot out of a gun, the words were hardly out of my mouth when the grandest music of many pipers, let alone one, playing all together, filled my ears; and that wasn't all, for lo and behold you, what should I see but scores of little fairies or *luricauns,* wearing red caps, neatly footing it, as if for a wager. Believe me, I was so overcome with fright at such a strange and unexpected sight that I ran for the bare life, my pipes hanging to me and dropping off piece and joint along the way; and by the time I reached home, the dickens a bit of my whole set of pipes was left to me but the bellows and bag, and they couldn't let go, as they were strapped round my waist.

"Picture to yourselves the kind of a night I spent after what happened. Anyway, by sun-up in the morning I ventured out and started to try and pick up the disjointed sections of my pipes, as I knew well enough the route I ran. My luck relieved my misgivings when I found the last missing part, which had dropped off at the very entrance to the rath or fort when I ran away.

"I lost no time in putting the now complete instrument in order, and to keep my word and fulfil my promise made to the king of the fairies the night before, I struck up 'The Wild Irishman,' my favorite reel. Words can't express my astonishment and delight when I found I could play as well as the best of them. And that, gentlemen, is how I came to be the best Union piper of my day in that part of the country."

ENTERTAINS A FAIRY UNAWARES

"Many years after that, when I was living alone in the little cabin after my mother died—God rest her soul—there came to the door in the dusk of the evening a stranger and nothing less than a piper, by the way, who with a 'God save all here,' introduced himself as was customary. I invited him in, of coorse, and after making himself at aise he says, 'Would you like to hear a 'chune' on the pipes?' 'I would that,' said I, for you know a piper and his music are always welcome in an Irish home. Taking his pipes out of the bag, he laid them on the bed beside him, and what do you think but without anyone laying a finger on them, they struck up 'Toss the Feathers' in a way that would make a cripple get up and dance. After a while, when they stopped, he says, 'Will you play a 'chune' for me now?' I said I would and welcome, pulling the blanket off my pipes that were hid under the bedclothes, to keep the reeds from drying out. 'Give us *Seaghan ua Duibhir an Gleanna*' (Shaun O'Dheir an Glanna), says I to the pipes, and when they commenced to play, the mysterious stranger, who no doubt was a fairy, remarked, 'Ah! Mac, I see you are one of us.' With that, both sets of pipes played half a dozen 'chunes' together. When they had enough of it, the fairy picked up his pipes and put them in the green bag again. If I had any doubts about him before, I had none at all when he said familiarly, 'Mac, I'm delighted with my visit here this evening, and as I have several other calls to make I'll have to be after bidding you good night, but if I should happen to be passing this way again, I'll be sure to drop in.'

Turlogh McSweeney
"The Donegal Piper"

"We must be always careful to not offend the 'good people,' but as I traveled around through the Northern Counties a great deal after that, and even into Scotland, of course he couldn't blame me if I wasn't at home to entertain him if he happened to call during my absence."

AMERICAN EXPERIENCES

On another occasion McSweeney was the centre of attraction at a house party gotten up in his honor by Mr. John Gillan. Naturally all present were musicians or music-lovers, and taking into consideration the lavish hospitality of an Irish host, it occasioned no surprise when, under the mollifying influence of a few tumblers of screeching hot punch, "the Donegal Piper" relaxed his customary reserve and became almost sociable.

When he realized that "Billy" McCormick, a local piper present, was an admirer instead of a rival, and that he could converse with him in his native Irish, he "took" to him at once and invited him out during a lull in the festivities. Instead of speaking to McCormick, however, his mysterious mutterings seemed to be addressed to someone else not visible in the darkness. McCormick began to feel uneasy, and his dismay was not lessened when McSweeney abruptly asked him, "Would you like to have the scum lifted from your eyes? If you do, I'll show you something," at the same time slipping him an old country jobber's penny. Keenly alive to the insidious liberality of the dreaded recruiting sergeant, and the fatal consequences of accepting gifts from the fairies, McCormick did not wait to answer, but headed for home as fast as his legs could carry him, and without observing the merest formalities of leave-taking. Convinced that "the Donegal Piper" was either a fairy himself, or their agent, McCormick carefully avoided meeting him thereafter.

'Twas nearly midnight when that ardent music-lover Mr. Gillan, the genial host, called for "Cherish the Ladies," his favorite jig. When the star of the evening, McSweeney, had played it to the satisfaction of all present, he deliber- ately lit his pipe and announced: "Now, Mr. Gillan, I've been playing for you all night, and I think it is about time I should play something for *ourselves.*" With that he took the whiskey jug, yet far from being empty, opened the backdoor, and peering into the backyard, said in a familiar tone, as if inviting intimate friends: "Boys, everybody come here and help yourselves." Suiting the action to the words, he deposited the precious jug on the platform, just outside the door, where it is presumed the fairy host regaled themselves to their hearts' content. From that time, and until near daylight, McSweeney, who had changed from the parlor to a seat near the kitchen door, played for the fairies without stopping or uttering a word, and you may say 'twas he had the bag full of tunes. Mr. Gillan, who was listening in rapt attention all the time, and ought to know, being an excellent judge of music, assures us that the music Mac played for the fairies' entertainment was much superior to his performance in the parlor in the early part of the night.

At what hour the invisible audience departed, we are unable to say, but when the good lady of the house came down stairs in the morning, the piper lay on the kitchen floor, pipes and all, with his head projecting half way under the stove, while Mr. Gillan himself was sound asleep in an easy chair. The jug was empty and as the host "wasn't taking anything," who could have drained it if the fairies hadn't?

PROFESSIONAL JEALOUSY

Professional jealousy, especially among musicians, that bane of fellowship and concerted effort, is sure to find a vent, and although Turlogh McSweeney betrayed no evidence of membership in the "knockers' club," that didn't save him from being the subject of a poem (God save the mark), calculated to disparage his musical pretentions. It emanated from the fertile brain of the versatile John K. Beatty, who, to insure its preservation, sang it haltingly into an Edison phonograph to the tune of *"Fagamaoid sud mar ata se."* As a sample of what a poetical piper can perpetrate when he gets his muse in motion, a few verses are here reproduced, with apologies to the reader:

THE DONEGAL PIPER

Ye sons of Apollo come listen to me,
And a comical story I'll tell unto ye;
Of a musical janius that came 'cross the sea,
    To represent all Irish pipers.

When he came from New York to the great World's Fair,
He met champion Murphy of the auburn hair,
And big blowhard Ennis from the County Kildare,
    Who call themselves all Irish pipers.

When he got his engagement, late in the spring,
He took his seat with an air that would rival a king.
Some friends went to see him and presents did bring,
    And called him "The Donegal Piper."

He had but one reel called "Up the Broomstick,"
And all other reels he would pitch to "Ould Nick";
The way that he played it was but an old trick,
    For that man called "The Donegal Piper."

He played every day from the time he got there,
And the Touheys and Flahertys came in for their share,
Such trios as they, sure would make a man swear,
    That e'er heard a genuine piper.

When his flat-throated chanter and pipes gave a squall
They were like a screech owl or a whipperwill's call!
Why, Mozart or Beethoven wasn't in it at all
    With this man called "The Donegal Piper."

I've heard all the pipers from 'round Skibbereen,
And from Ballinafad up to Sweet College Green;
Arrah! such a mimic on Irish was never yet seen
    As this man called "The Donegal Piper."

But now he is gone and our spirits are low,
And I say God be with him, *Go deo's go deo*,*
Since Ireland was scourged by that villain Strongbow,
    You never have heard such a piper.

---

* For ever and ever.

Search Ireland all o'er from seashore to seashore,
From the cliffs of Cape Clear to the rath of Gwedore,
And you'll ne'er meet man such a musical bore
    As the one called "The Donegal Piper."

And so ends the story of the "Donegal Piper," partly as told by himself in all seriousness to men not much his junior in years. For obvious reasons such tales are never debatable, yet those who came in contact with the taciturn minstrel felt that there was something strange, inscrutable, and even uncanny, in his whole demeanor.

Wonderfully even and correct was his rendition of Irish airs, and his systematic manipulation of the regulators or concords in difficult and varied pieces plainly demonstrated that his instructor had an apt pupil. And still, withal, the coldness of his character was reflected in his music. Faultless in time as the tones of a hand organ, the spirit of the Irish tune seemed lacking—that spirit which, even at the hands of a less capable performer, invigorates our system and impels us to dance or beat time to the rhythm.

To an issue of *The Christian Age* in 1909, kindly sent by Mr. J. S. Wayland, we are indebted for the following:

A DESCENDANT OF KINGS IN RECEIPT OF OLD AGE PENSION

"In the varying fortunes of its people, the history of few countries presents more striking examples than that of Ireland. The many and fierce internecine wars with which Ireland was distracted in her early days, followed by the Anglo-Norman conquest of the country in the twelfth century, has tended to bring about a state of affairs, by which at the present time, some families who formerly ranked among the highest in the land, are now in poverty, while others have been raised from obscurity and are at present in possession of wealthy estates.

"A notable example of the reverses of fortune is afforded by the subject of this picture, in the person of Turlogh McSweeney. A reference to O'Hart's *Irish Pedigrees* will show that the ancestors of this remarkable old man, born in 1829, and who has followed the occupation of professional Irish piper, were formerly princes closely connected with the royal line of Ireland. The records of his race have been so carefully preserved that his pedigree can be traced to Eremon, first king of Ireland, in the year 1690 B. C."

Then follows a list of the names of comparatively modern ancestors, ending with *Donnchad Mor* (last of the McSweeney chieftains), son of Sir Miles McSweeney of Doe castle.

No wonder his dignity and reserve were well nigh impenetrable.

In a letter to Mr. Wayland from Strabane, County Tyrone, in 1909, the writer, who chanced to meet our hero, has this to say of him: "McSweeney is a very queer old man, and will give no information about pipes or piping whatever. He still claims to have a book of instruction for the pipes, and has it for over sixty years, but would not part with it, as 'tis the only one in existence at the present time. He has had offers for it several times, but *money could not induce him to part with it.* He would give no information in regard to the book, or how he got it. He would give lessons on the pipes, but would not make known the terms. He has no pupils. Neither of his two sons plays the pipes, but it is rumored that one of his five daughters could. (As she as well as the others of his children have scattered far and wide, I could not trace her.)"

PROFESSIONAL RATING

In the pipers' competition at the first Dublin Feis Ceoil in 1897, where Mr. Wayland met him, McSweeney was awarded the second prize. Robert Thompson, winner of the first prize, was similarly honored at the Belfast Feis the following year.

Being in line with the tales of fairy enchantment, his mysterious allusions to a book of "instructions" all through his career have served to make him an object of peculiar interest to people of his class everywhere. No human eye, except his own, has ever been permitted to profane this treasure by even a glance. As a concession to his benefactors before named, he presented them with a scale of the natural notes on the Irish chanter, which, upon comparison, we find is identical with that to be found in *O'Farrell's National Irish Music* and reprinted in Appendix A of *Irish Folk Music: A Fascinating Hobby*.

It is claimed that the only copy of O'Farrell's work in Ireland is in the library of the Dublin Museum. By way of information, it may be added that another copy, recently procured through a London book agency, occupies an honored place in the writer's library. Even so, the "Donegal Piper" may well regard his treasure as priceless, cherishing, as he undoubtedly does, the hallucination that he possesses the only copy in existence of one of the rarest and most unique works ever printed on a British press.

To add to his fame, he has been immortalized by the poetess, Anna Johnston (now Mrs. Seumas McManus) in a poem bearing his name.

A health to you, Piper,
    and your pipes silver-tongued, clear and sweet in their crooning.

> Full of the music they gathered at morn
>   On your high heather hills from the lark on the wing,
> From the blackbird at eve on the blossoming thorn,
>   From the little green linnet whose plaining they sing,
>   And the joy and the hope in the heart of the spring—
>   O Turlogh MacSweeney!

Although five more verses and a peroration follow from the same gifted pen, we must bid adieu to the "Donegal Piper," and wish him long life in his eighty-fourth year.

GEORGE McCARTHY

No name has appeared so frequently in the list of prize-winners at Dublin Feiseanna as that of George McCarthy. In the years 1900, 1902, 1904, and 1905 he was awarded second prize. In 1903, he was not so fortunate, getting but third prize. To crown his successes he gained first prize in 1907, and from the records it appears that in 1900 he also was awarded third prize for his collection of "Unpublished Irish Airs."

Although the name would indicate a Munster origin, McCarthy was a native of Cavan, where generations of his forebears had lived. The McCarthy family evidently had a strong predilection for the pipes. Four brothers, including George's father, were performers on that instrument. George being lame, became a professional piper, after some time spent under the instruction of "Billy" Taylor at Drogheda. He invariably played on a double chanter, and was in no wise niggardly in the purchase of a suitable instrument.

After his triumph in 1907 he played in the neighborhood of Blackrock, County Dublin, for some months, but eventually took refuge in the Ardee Union Workhouse, where he died in 1908, being then about sixty-five years of age.

McCarthy's fine silver-mounted set of pipes, made by the famous Taylor, was sold for twenty pounds to pipemaker R. L. O'Mealy of Belfast, who can appreciate their value.

John O'Gorman

"The blind piper of Roscommon," born in the early sixties, and brought up on the DeFreyne estates, first saw the light at Ballaghaderreen, County Mayo, a few miles from the boundary line. Being blind from childhood, he began the study of the Union pipes at an early age under the tuition of Patrick Vizard, a relative, and, like many others of his class, he was unable to procure a good instrument. So superior was his skill, however, that it made amends for that drawback, and in a short time his splendid performance attracted wide attention in that part of the country.

One day, while playing at a crossroads dance, his performance so charmed Lady DeFreyne, who happened along in her carriage, that she stopped to listen to the fine music played by the blind minstrel. Drawing closer, she asked him to play a favorite Irish air. He willingly complied, and impressed her so deeply by his manner no less than by his delightful rendering of the touching melody, that she presented him with a splendid set of pipes and started him on the road to fame.

With the new instrument his popularity increased and people came from far and near to hear him. He was in great demand throughout County Roscommon to play at weddings and other festivities.

One young man now living in Chicago, named Edward Creaghton, a prize-winner in the flute contest in the Chicago Feis of 1912, who attended a wedding where O'Gorman played, thus describes the event: "I was delighted to get an invitation, for I was anxious to hear him play. When I got near the house, I could hear the strains of his fascinating music, and when I entered I beheld the famous blind piper mounted on a little stage in a corner of the room. His music was such as to set every foot in motion, for it seems no one could keep still. He had a fine set of pipes, which took up a lot of room, but there was melody issuing from every one of them, and the fine reels which he rolled out on that evening, although years ago, are still ringing in my ears."

O'Gorman was universally respected. Whenever any event of importance was coming off, the first thing to be done was to send after him in a side car, a conveyance in which he was taken home again when his engagement was ended. Generous and liberal with his music, he played for all who asked him; in fact, his whole soul was in the beloved instrument, which responded in seeming sympathy with his touch. In close fingering and "peppering" he was an expert. The first prize awarded him at the Oireachtas in 1902 was no more than his due—George McCarthy and Denis Delaney getting second and third prizes, respectively. In 1908 O'Gorman did not fare so well, being defeated for first prize by Delaney.

In the long line of immortal minstrels which Hibernia has produced, "The blind piper of Roscommon" deserves a worthy place, and the province of Connacht, in which so many of them were born, shall long cherish the name of John O'Gorman.

Nicholas Markey

An advertisement in the Dublin press of 1910 announces that "Nicholas Markey, 45 St. Joseph's Place, Nelson Street, Dublin, pupil of the celebrated 'Willie' Taylor of Drogheda and Philadelphia, gives tuition on the Irish Union Bagpipes."

For several years Mr. Markey has been instructor in the Dublin Pipers' Club, and it is said that his pupils have won distinction at the annual competitions. For obvious reasons, teachers are not inclined to take part in contests of skill, and this reluctance no doubt accounts for the absence of his name from the lists of prize winners at the annual Feiseanna, which have come to hand.

The publication of the likeness of this fine type of the Irish minstrel is a source of no small pleasure to the writer, and even though we cannot subscribe to the opinion of his friend, Mr. Deegan, the honorable secretary of said club, that Mr. Markey "is the best living piper," we can readily concede that for an Irish piper his modesty is truly refreshing. But after all what else could be expected from such a prepossessing representative of his race and profession, but the manners of a gentleman?

Stephen Ruane

Another of the few surviving pipers, famous but forgotten, which the Gaelic League has resurrected, is Stephen Ruane, of Shantalla, Galway. That ardent revivalist, John S. Wayland, of the Cork Pipers' Club, traced him up and paid him a visit at his home just outside the "City of the Tribes." Ruane displayed wonderful execution on the chanter, but did not manipulate the regulators, possibly on account of their being not properly equipped with reeds.

Persuaded by Mr. Wayland, he attended the Dublin Feis in 1906, and was awarded the first prize, notwithstanding his long seclusion and want of practice. His fine execution on the chanter at the Feis in 1912, in which there were seventeen competitors, was remarked, but as his instrument was in wretched tune it militated against his success accordingly. Ruane, who was originally a farmer, is a very tall man of quite respectable appearance.

Samuel Rowsome

In early and middle life this typical amateur piper enjoyed a great local reputation in the barony of Scarawalsh, County Wexford. Far-famed as a jig player—the jig which has become unfashionable in his old days—it was no vain boast that he had a hundred of its several varieties at his finger tips. A man of untiring energy in all respects, Samuel Rowsome was an indefatigable piper. On one occasion, Mr. Whelan his friend tells us, he supplied the music unaided at a ball held at "The Harrow," where eighty-four couples assembled, and in the words of one who was present "gave them all dancing enough." In fact, Mr. Rowsome could "fill the house with music." Contemporary with the late John Cash, his inborn love of the native music and talent for playing it on the Union pipes was developed under the tuition of the famous but almost forgotten minstrel, "Jemmy" Byrne, the piper of Shangarry, County Carlow.

Mr. Rowsome, who was an extensive and prosperous farmer and whose commodious dwelling typified Irish hospitality, adopted pipe playing not as a vocation but as an accessory to pleasure and recreation, for he was ever an advocate of pastimes and social intercourse.

Nicholas Markey

He attended the "'patron,' race, and fair," and went everywhere a good piper was to be heard. Not many indeed were the wandering musicians worthy of note in that part of the country he had not come across, and few were the tunes they played that he did not memorize, if new to him, and reproduce at will.

A piper of acknowledged ability, he was no less skilful in equipping and repairing the instrument from bellows to reeds, so that we can well conceive how much in demand a man must be who combined the various endowments of Samuel Rowsome of Ballintore, whose hospitable home sheltered many a wandering minstrel in times of stress and stringency.

How could the later generations of Rowsomes escape their musical tendencies if heredity is to be considered as a factor in influencing our lives.

Mrs. Rowsome, born Mary Parslow, was not only one of the finest dancers of her day, but also an excellent violinist by all accounts, being taught by her father, William Parslow, of Ballyhaddock, a townland adjoining Ballintore. Not only that, but her brother Thomas was a piper of good local reputation. Example, heredity, and environment could hardly fail to produce conspicuous results under such circumstances.

At the patriarchal age of eighty-four, Mr. Rowsome is still living at the old homestead.

John Rowsome

"For power of extracting a strong, voluble tone from the chanter, and imparting a beautiful expression to the music, he has few peers and certainly no superior." Such is the language of an enthusiastic admirer in describing the accomplishments of John Rowsome, the eldest son of Samuel Rowsome of Ballintore Ferns, County Wexford, who resides on the old homestead and is consequently unknown to fame. As Mr. Whelan is a very interesting though somewhat partial writer we will let him continue: "There are surely none more conversant with the law of modulation in music. To hear him play a great Irish reel is like listening to the warring elements of nature. The music from his chanter comes with the impetuosity of the wind, which gathers force in its gambols down the mountain side to accelerate its wild career over the plain. And anon it lingers or seems to linger, and goes on again with increased velocity. It comes in undulating waves of sound, and breaks upon the ear as the swells of the ocean break upon the beach and disperse around the feet of the spectator.

"Who that has listened to the roar of the distant cataract in the stillness of the night would fail to be impressed with a sense that a greater volume of water overleaps the rock, and plunges into the chasm below with correspondingly increasing fury at certain intervals than at others?

"Any or all of the above similes might be taken as illustrations of his music, yet they are but poorly or indifferently put, for still the music swells, breaks, leaps, curvets, sighs, murmurs, ripples, laughs, rolls, thunders, on the ear of the enraptured listener.

"The noise emitted through the chanter and from the strings of many of the swelled heads, is mere musical chatter in comparison to his playing, nor is it to be wondered at, since the musical faculty with him was inborn, and James Cash, that 'prince of pipers,' was through all his early years his most intimate associate, friend, and tutor."

But coming back to earth from Patrick Whelan's aerial flights, we hasten to inform the reader that John Rowsome, as well as his brothers Thomas and William, studied music under Herr Jacob Blowitz, a German professor, who

John Rowsome

resided in Ferns from 1878 to 1885, and became efficient performers on various orchestral instruments. John was famous on the cornet, on which he could play jigs as fluently as William could on the violin. Strange to say, heredity overcame their training under Professor Blowitz, and all three owe their present fame to their skill as performers on the Union bagpipes.

Since succeeding his father in the management of the farm, John has not played in public, nor has he continued his practice of music except in a desultory way in private. Just as he would be warming up to his work and when his audience would be anticipating a musical treat, he would strike a few chords on the regulators and put away the instrument heedless of protest or entreaty.

Nearing the half century milestone in age, he is unostentatious in the extreme, though active in all that pertains to the revival of interest in Irish music, and the art of giving it traditional expression on Ireland's national instrument. He has furbished, repaired, renovated, and reeded more foundered sets of bagpipes, for the unskilful, than any other man in the south of Ireland.

Neither is this splendid type of the whole-souled Irishman inclined to "hide his light under a bushel," like so many excellent pipers whom we could name.

John Rowsome sees no glory in taking his art or his tunes to the grave with him, like so many small-bore musicians afflicted with atrophied consciences. On the contrary, to his great credit, he is teaching his art, as his generous-hearted father did before him, to all who cared to learn. Among his present pupils are his young neighbors, David and Bernard Bolger, of the manufacturing firm of "David Bolger and Sons," and their maternal uncle, Joseph Sinnott, draper at Enniscorthy, who is active and enthusiastic in Gaelic circles.

Wealthy, popular, and patriotic, three members of the Bolger family represented constituencies in the first election assembly which supplanted the Grand Jury system in Wexford, and it is quite within the bounds of probability that in the near future two "gentlemen pipers" of the name will succeed their honored relatives in the same capacity.

THOMAS ROWSOME

Of this member of the Rowsome family of pipers we can say nothing from personal knowledge, but we are reliably informed that Thomas Rowsome is not inferior to his brother William as a performer on the Union pipes. In fact, some are inclined to believe that, in rendering Irish airs with the manipulation of the regulators, Thomas has the advantage. At any rate it speaks well for the latter's ability that he was awarded first prize at the Dublin Feis Ceoil competition among pipers in 1899. Winning third prize even, in 1897, when "Bob" Thompson of Cork and Turlogh McSweeney, "the Donegal piper," were awarded first and second prizes respectively, was no small honor indeed.

From a discriminating pen we learn that "Tom" Rowsome is a fine, steady player, and at times even a brilliant one. At single jigs it would be hard to beat him, though in general execution his style may be considered too open and flute-like. However, that is a matter of individual taste. As regards time, he stands pre-eminent; his last bar of a jig or reel, in fact of any tune, is played in precisely the same time as the first, and no dancer can influence him to accelerate his pace or tempo.

Mr. O'Mealy, the well-known piper and pipemaker of Belfast, who played in concert with him on various occasions, speaks very highly of his social qualities. Nothing else could have been expected from his father and mother's son, anyway.

Thomas Rowsome

Differing from his brother, John and William, at least in one respect, he stuck to his first love—the Union pipes—and, notwithstanding his musical education acquired under Herr Blowitz of Ferns, his taste for traditional Irish music remained uncorrupted and undiminished. All three became skilful pipers under the instruction of their father, Samuel Rowsome, the famous farmer-piper of Ballintore, Ferns, County Wexford, and all three have won distinction in that line of musical art.

The "Harvest Home" was an established institution at Ballyrankin, Clobernin, Farmley, Morrison's, St. Aidan's Palace, and many other residential seats of the wealthy in north Wexford. The attendance of the three brothers was ever in requisition at those annual celebrations, "Willie's" reputation as a violinist being less than that of his elder brothers as pipers, only in the degree that the fiddle is deemed an instrument inferior to the Union pipes in giving to traditional Irish music its characteristic tonality. The "Harvest Home," be it understood, was essentially the same as the "Flax Mehil" in other parts of Ireland—all private festivals—the assembly consisting of the family, friends, employes, and invited guests.

During this period Thomas Rowsome became closely associated with the late James Cash in his periodical visits to the Rowsome homestead. Together "Young Cash" and the youthful enthusiast would proceed to a secluded nook in the garden, or, the weather being unfavorable, to a private room in the house, and indulge in long-sustained spells of practice, for everything new in music which the wanderer had picked up on his rambles through Munster and Connacht he would impart to his beloved protege. More than once old Mr. Rowsome would come upon them in the act of playing one instrument together, each with one hand fingering the chanter.

"Tom, you will become a great piper yet," Cash would say, as a presentiment of his own impending death would cloud his brow. "The music of your chanter will thrill audiences when the name of James Cash will be but a reminiscence or merely the subject of unsympathetic gossip." The forecast was prophetic, for he died in his thirty-eighth year, while his friend Thomas Rowsome, now a municipal employe of the city of Dublin, has made a name for himself in the world of music. His engagements are many, not alone in his native land, but on the stage and in the halls of London, Glasgow, and other cities and towns across the Channel, where the mellifluent tones of the "Irish organ" in the hands of a capable performer never fail to arouse the most enthusiastic applause.

About forty-six years of age, over six feet in height, handsome and of impressive appearance, "Tom" Rowsome may not owe all his popularity to his musical gifts. He is also accused of being both genial and kindly, yet apparently insensible to female charms. Whoever the "King of the Pipers" may be, an ardent admirer insists "he is one of the Princes and Heir Presumptive." Still there are others.

SAMUEL ROWSOME, JR.

Murder will out, and so will music, and, though the days of fostering patronage and encouraging recognition are past, the divine art, whether begotten of nature's whim, or vitalized as a manifestation of the laws of heredity, may be relied on to find some outlet for expression, but it will be noticed that environment and opportunity have much to do with determining the favored instrument.

To maintain the traditions of his family, what else could this promising scion be but an Irish piper, his father, and grandfather, before him having been worthy

Samuel Rowsome

representatives of the class? Had they been fiddlers, no doubt he would have followed in their footsteps. Still we must rejoice in his choice, for, while we are likely to have with us always raspers, fiddlers, and even violinists, we cannot but regret that performers on the Union or Irish pipes—the real national instrument of the people—are declining in numbers year by year and may eventually become extinct, like the harpers, their predecessors.

This young musical aspirant, on whom will depend to a considerable degree the preservation of his art, is the eldest son of William Rowsome, piper and pipe-maker of Harolds Cross, Dublin, and grandson of Samuel Rowsome of Ballintore, Wexford, elsewhere mentioned.

Born September 25, 1895, he commenced his musical practice under his father's tuition when but twelve years of age. Such was his proficiency on both chanter and regulators that he won many prizes, and had been highly commended for taste and style by the best judges of pipe music, though but a boy of only sixteen birthdays.

If appearance counts for anything, we are justified in assuming that the future has no small distinction in store for him.

The instrument on which he is represented as playing in the picture was manufactured by his father, and is of full tone and concert pitch, blending harmoniously with violin and piano.

DENIS DELANEY

One of the few surviving, good, old-time players of the rollicking style lives in his native town of Ballinasloe, County Galway. Robust in build and ruddy of complexion, he is one of the central figures in its life, and in its celebrated fair.

Though totally blind, he is, strange to say, unsurpassed as a judge of cattle and other kinds of farm stock, and so well recognized is his skill in this respect that at fair and market his opinion is eagerly sought when trading is in progress. Stranger still is the fact that furniture moving is his principal occupation. With a table on his head, or a cupboard on his back, he can make his way safely all over town. To see him thus engaged and without a trace of timidity in his footsteps, a stranger would never suspect that he was blind.

Gifted with great conversational powers, an endless fund of humor, and a tenacious memory, he is naturally the life of every gathering which he attends. With such attractions, not to mention his qualifications as a prize-winning piper, we can understand how he won the heart and hand of a buxom young colleen half his age, it being his second matrimonial venture.

The jolly Denis, having "seen" to the burial of an old friend and brother piper, naturally "came in" for his beautiful set of pipes. He disposed of his own superannuated set, made by the elder Kenna in 1781, to Mr. Wayland, the irrepressible enthusiast and untiring promoter, of Cork, he being the fifth proud possessor of this specimen of Kenna's handiwork.

The first owner after coming from the hands of the maker was a Mr. Burke of Tyrquinn, near Athenry, County Galway, and their cost ten pounds. By bequest they became the property of Mr. Burke's nephew, Mr. C. Natton, of Kingstown, Dublin, from whom Denis Delaney purchased them in 1873.

In friendly rivalry at a big concert in Dublin, Mr. Delaney and Prof. P. J. Griffith played their respective versions of the "Fox Chase," and, while both delighted the audience with their performance, it was freely conceded that Prof. Griffith's version of that famous but much varied composition was the better.

The humor of the situation so appealed to the versatile "member from Cork"—John Smithwick Wayland—that he unlimbered his muse, so to speak, took his pen in hand and dashed off the following racy dialogue which led to striking effects:

WARPIPES VERSUS FIDDLE

Said the fiddle to the warpipes, "What is all this noise I hear?
You have challenged me to combat, so 'tis whispered in my ear;
Your form is most ungainly, and your arms and legs too long,
Puffed up with cheek and pride, you can't accompany a song."
Said the warpipes to the fiddle, "'Tis just what I'd expect—
You're like a barque forlorn, on the point of being wrecked;
And don't you talk to me, sir, of puffing or of blowing,
For I'd much prefer that kind o' work to scraping and a bowing,
And it shows that I've the wind in me, to help me through the battle,
While you have to rely on but an empty, worthless rattle;
And if you stood before me, you would soon be on the ground,
For we know that empty vessels always make the greatest sound."
The fiddle then got "crusty" and his bow he did let fly:
There was varnish, hair, and resin, flying everywhere sky high;
The fiddle turned yellow, and the warpipes turned blue,
Each returned to the onslaught, angry words they did renew.
Said the fiddle to the warpipes, "You're all made up of drones,
You can boast of but one octave, and you have no semitones."
Said the warpipes to the fiddle, as his eyes now flashed with fire,
"For untruthfulness and impudence you come second to the LYRE—
You mentioned just awhile ago about my arms and legs,
But you can boast of none at all, for you have only pegs;
And what is more, I say, sir, that your head is only glued,
And anyone can see, sir, that you're very often screwed."
Said the fiddle, "I've a belly and a back and sides, moreover,
And a shift or two at intervals, my nakedness to cover;
I've a head-piece and a tail-piece, and though I'm often tight,
I've a bridge to rest my bones upon when I retire at night;
My audience I can move to tears, with feelings of emotion,
Without using golden syrup or any other lotion."
Said the warpipes to the fiddle, "You are talking all *rameis,*
For I am far more welcome at a concert or a Feis;
I can be heard two miles off in spite of wind and weather,
While your puny, squeaky music cannot scrape a crowd together.
You can amuse the children, so can a penny rattle,
But you will ne'er be fit, like me, to lead men into battle."
Here the "seconds" gave a signal, simply by a beck:
And with that the warpipes rushed and caught the fiddle by the neck,
But this grip did not undo him, and only caused some fun,
For 'twas very soon discovered that a windpipe he had none.
"I defy you to come out here," said the pipes, in accents bold;
"Of course you won't, you coward, you're afraid of catching cold,
For your bridge would fall, your strings would snap, your voice would turn hoarse,
While the fresh air only strengthens me and gives me greater force.
This tap-room is no place for me, a coward I'll be never,

DENIS DELANEY

So, Mr. Fiddle, you and I will have to part for ever.
Another word I would not parry with you for a guinea—
Your "case" is lost and badly lost in spite of Paganini,
And though you boast your parentage to Stradivari of Cremona,
My lineage goes further back to ancient Babylonia."
The warpipes then marched up the hill with erect and manly stride,
While Mr. Fiddle, whose pride was hurt, committed suicide.
"Hung by the neck," the verdict ran, as the neighbors all predicted;
'Twas agreed by every juryman that the act was self-inflicted.

Why the author should ignore the perfected Union pipes, in favor of the primitive instrument, in his dramatis personæ, is not quite clear, yet the outcome in a manner betrays the direction in which his sympathies lay. The fiddle's finish is pitiably sad, and one cannot help regretting that the talented author did not relent in the last act, and with a magnanimity befitting the occasion, let the contest end in a "draw" at least.

As long as might continues to rule the world, and nations honor and ennoble the inventors of weapons for the wholesale destruction of human life, what chance has a flimsy, finical fiddle against a shrieking, windy warpipe?

As a prize-winner at pipers' competitions all over Ireland, we know of nothing to equal Denis Delaney's record. Since 1897—the date of their origin —he has to his credit 29 first, 12 second, 6 third, and 1 special prizes up to the year 1912, according to his own account

Accustomed as he had been to winning distinction for over a dozen years, his bump of self-esteem suffered no diminution in the flight of time, and however much we may approve the decisions of the adjudicator in awarding the prizes to others at the Dublin Feis in 1912, we cannot help sympathizing with Delaney, whose pride had sustained a shock so severe that he hastened away without waiting to enjoy the subsequent festivities, or sit in the group of competitors for a picture.

Sergt. James Early

A piper and a lover of piper music, kindly, unassuming, patient, tolerant, helpful, and hospitable—such is James Early as a man among musicians.

Free from professional jealousy, a proverbial affliction, he has been to the Union pipers of America what the lamented Canon Goodman was to the pipers of Ireland a generation ago—their unfailing friend in distress. An expert at putting a demoralized set of pipes in order, he had no superior as a reed maker, and although he had no monopoly in this line of delicate workmanship, the difference between his dealings and that of some others was the difference between liberality and covetousness, or between candor and duplicity.

From Boston to San Francisco, and from New Orleans to Manitoba came appeals for reeds, from pipers, amateur and professional, who were unable to fit their own chanters. They knew their man and they never appealed in vain. Many a time have we seen pipers come to Chicago from cities and towns a hundred miles away, for the special purpose of having their instruments put in order, and they were always hospitably entertained at the Early residence during their stay.

From Saturday evening until Monday morning Turlogh McSweeney made Sergt. Early's house his home all throughout his engagement, which lasted six months, at the World's Fair held in Chicago in 1893. Neither does "Patsy"

JOHN McFADDEN   SERGT. JAMES EARLY

Touhey concern himself about hotel accommodations when filling his theatrical engagements in the young giant city on the shore of Lake Michigan in more recent times. And that is not all, for many are the callers during the genial "Patsy's" welcome visits, and no one need be told what happens in an Irishman's house on such occasions.

Born at Cloone, near Carrigallen, County Leitrim, in the late forties, James Early learned to play the flute and fiddle when quite young; but, coming to America when but a boy, his practice was interrupted for many years while struggling with the vicissitudes of life in the mining territories of the Northwest. Coming to Chicago, he became a member of the police force in 1874 and fortunately met his friend and relative James Quinn, who enjoyed an enviable reputation as an Irish piper.

To acquire proficiency in music, everyone knows that early training is indispensable. Even so, our friend, infatuated with Mr. Quinn's playing, though in the prime of manhood became the latter's pupil. Rapid progress was the reward of taste and assiduous practice, and it was not long before he could play for dances with the best of them.

For a generation past Sergt. Early, in concert with John McFadden, a traditional fiddler of phenomenal execution, has played at public entertainments all over Chicago, and even in other cities in this and adjoining states on important occasions, their last being at the Chicago Feis, August 3, 1913, for the dancing contests.

With rare forethought the Sergeant kept a memorandum book in which he noted down the first few bars of "Old Man" Quinn's tunes, from which he could always refresh his memory. As McFadden had also played with Mr. Quinn for years, many melodies derived from the latter were preserved and published for the first time in O'Neill's *Music of Ireland*.

Although now retired from active service, like the writer, and living on the "sunny side of Easy street," Sergt. Early has many pleasant years of life yet in prospect. Consequently we may hope to enjoy the music of our sires which he and his light-fingered partner "Mac" can render so delightfully in perfect time, tune, and execution, for many a year to come.

BERNARD DELANEY

Quiet and unassuming, and silent as to music, unless the subject was under discussion, "Barney" Delaney betrayed no outward indication of being the marvelous jig, reel, and hornpipe player that he was. In fluency and rhythm on the chanter his execution left nothing to be desired—his style was truly the dancers' delight, for he put the music right under their feet.

Like Gandsey, the Killarney piper, who in his childhood made music with the reeds which grew on the banks of Lough Lene, young Delaney fashioned a set of pipes from the *feleastroms* growing in the meadows near Tullamore, his birthplace, in Kings County. Music was in him and it early found expression on a penny whistle. In fact, to this day his self-taught system of fingering and tongueing on a whistle or flageolet is scarcely equaled by his execution on the chanter.

With the exception of a little primary instruction he received from "Jack" Foraghan, a Tullamore piper, Delaney was self-taught, and though capable of "cranning" or playing in the Connacht staccato system of execution, the free and rolling style with a liberal sprinkling of graces and trills was his favorite.

Bernard Delaney.

By dint of economy, while working as a laborer at the Baldwin Locomotive Works in Philadelphia after coming to America in 1880, he saved the price of a small set of pipes made for him specially by "Billy" Taylor, the great pipemaker of that city. Equipped with these he started for the west and finding appreciative people in Chicago, among them the present writer, he settled in the western metropolis permanently.

For a time after his arrival in Chicago, Delaney played in a concert hall, but was induced to accept an engagement with Powers' Ivy Leaf theatrical company in place of "Eddie" Joyce, who took sick in that city. So satisfactory did he prove in every respect that his temporary engagement was made permanent with an increase of salary.

His friends and admirers in Chicago were bound to get him back, however, so the writer contrived to intercept the play in New York, and escort the piper home to Chicago, where a position in the Department of Police awaited him. But this was not his only theatrical experience. Some years later he was given leave of absence to help Mr. Powers out of a similar difficulty during the sickness of John Moore, the company's piper.

During his residence of over a quarter of a century in Chicago, he has played at one time or another on every important stage in the city, including Central Music Hall and the Auditorium; at picnics and excursions without number, and he has been practically kidnapped more than once by delegations going to New Orleans in cars specially chartered for some important occasion. From an incident in his younger days in Philadelphia we get a sidelight on his popularity with dancers. Once while playing at a dance, Taylor, said to be the greatest Irish piper of his day, was called away temporarily. To oblige him, Delaney put on the pipes and played for the dancers during his absence. The rhythm and swing of his performance were so pleasing that the dancers insisted on his continuing after Taylor's return.

Unconcerned and self-possessed under all circumstances in public or private, he plays on undisturbed by an excited partner, who forgets when to change or repeat; and, to crown all, his instrument is sure to be in perfect tune, for in the mechanical art of putting or keeping an instrument in repair he has nothing to learn. Writing to a friend, of his experience while visiting Chicago in 1905, Father Jones of Ballyferriter says: "While at the musical entertainment that out-and-out wonderful piper, 'Barney' Delaney, held me spellbound during those hours of gladness."

The simplest tune at his hands took on a new expression and became a marvel of melody, so instinctive was his fancy and finished his execution.

Following this litany of perfections we must admit that we do not regard Delaney as a fit subject for canonization. In his earlier years he poured out his melodies without restraint, but when he found that they were being memorized and played by others, he became secretive and regaled his hearers, even his best and most intimate friends, with nothing but "chestnuts."

Occasionally, when in the right humor and the listeners had no capacity for memorizing, he would play a string of rusty ones preserved for special use. Yet in the matter of enlarging his own repertoire no one was more acquisitive. Deprecating the decadence of Irish music, and deploring the decline of Irish piping, like John Coughlan the great Australian piper, Bernard Delaney could not be induced to teach his art to old or young.

Were he a "knocker" or afflicted with proverbial jealousy we would be inclined to believe that he cherished the conviction so common among his class, that when he died the last of the pipers was gone. But he is neither. Liberal as an entertainer, he was a miser with his tunes, and it is a certainty that quite a few of them, if not already forgotten, will die with him.

Being a good business man he has grown wealthy for a piper or policeman. After twenty-four years' continuous service with a clear record, he retired on a liberal pension on the first day of March, 1912, to enjoy life at his latest home at Ocean Springs, Mississippi, and be fanned by the breezes of the Gulf of Mexico for the rest of his days.

Patrick J. Touhey

The "Only Patsy Touhey" among his admirers, and they are legion, is the youngest of the many distinguished pipers, who hailed from Galway. He ranks easily at the head of his contemporaries from his native county and province, and it is contended by many that he has no equal anywhere. He was born at Loughrea, February 26, 1865, and came of a family in which musical talent was hereditary, he being the third generation noted for proficiency as an all-round performer on the Union pipes.

His father, James Twohill (that being the older form of the Irish surname *O'Tuathail*), born in 1839, was an excellent piper who played for the local gentry almost exclusively. The elder brothers, John and "Pat," born in the years 1831 and 1836 respectively, rambled through England as professional pipers. John died in early manhood, but "Pat," who was a fine performer, enjoyed a long life. Michael Twohill, grandfather of the subject of our sketch, born in 1800, in the same county, is reputed to have been a celebrated piper in his day.

Our hero "Patsy," when less than four years of age, was brought to America by his parents. He had not commenced to learn music before his father's death, being then only ten years old, but he was subsequently taught by Bartley Murphy, his father's pupil, a Mayo man, and took what may be regarded as a post-graduate course with John Egan, the "albino piper," elsewhere mentioned.

Together they toured the Atlantic cities for a year or so. Both had great command of the regulators. The resounding organ tones which a skilful performer can produce on them as an accompaniment to the treble, is a never-ending source of wonder to an audience.

While Turlogh McSweeney, the "Donegal Piper," may have fittingly represented an antiquated and oppressed Ireland, playing his ancient instrument outside the entrance to Mrs. Hart's "Donegal Castle," at the World's Columbian Exposition at Chicago in 1893, the hopes and aspirations of a regenerated nation were pleasingly typified in "Patsy" Touhey, the spruce young man in corduroy breeches and ribbed stockings, whose expert manipulation of a great set of Taylor pipes made him the centre of attraction within.

When Myles Murphy, manager of the "Irish Village" at the Louisiana Purchase Exposition held at St. Louis, Missouri, in 1903, determined to obtain the best talent for his concession, he engaged "Patsy" Touhey at the latter's own price, and it proved a capital stroke of business for Mr. Murphy at that.

So novel and captivating was his performance of all varieties of music on the Irish pipes on the stage of the Irish Theatre, that the members of the "International Association of Chiefs of Police," about 200 in number, who attended the play in a body, encored his playing repeatedly, and wanted him to continue his wonderful music indefinitely, but four encores were all the stage manager would allow.

Patrick J. Touhey

Neither sentiment nor early associations had much to do with this acclaim, for the majority of those present were of other than Irish ancestry, and of the latter less than half were of Irish birth.

As comedian and piper Touhey has been before the American public all over the United States for years, and, while at this writing many hundreds of theatrical people are out of employment, it speaks well for his standing with the public that he is rarely without an engagement.

His advent in Chicago to fill theatrical engagements is an event of much concern to his many friends and admirers, who anticipate an afternoon and evening of unalloyed pleasure in his company. "The gathering of the Clans" at the hospitable homes of Sergeants James Early or James Kerwin is always attended with a "feast of music and a flow of soul" unrestrained by diffidence or formalities.

Agreeable in personality and obliging in disposition, he is deservedly popular. A stranger to jealousy, his comments are never sarcastic or unkind, neither does he betray any tendency to monopolize attention in company when other musicians are present. In fact, Touhey is a notable exception in many ways, and if he possesses any less admirable qualities they have escaped the notice of the writer, who has enjoyed his acquaintance for over a score of years.

MICHAEL FLANAGAN

In a much appreciated communication to the present writer in 1911, giving an account of the early life of John Hicks, the "Kildare Piper," mentioned in *Irish Folk Music: A Fascinating Hobby,* Mr. Flanagan not only disclosed certain features of his own boyhood days, but betrayed the fact that, besides being a trained musician himself, he was a man of education and uncommon literary ability.

Restrained by a modesty, oh! so rare among favorites of the muses, his communications to the Dublin press on musical affairs, were published anonymously or otherwise disguised.

Hitherto the classification of performers on the Union pipes, as Professional Pipers, Reverend Pipers, Gentlemen Pipers, etc., presented little or no difficulty. But where does Mr. Flanagan belong? To neither of the first two had he a claim. He would be a splendid type of the third, were not wealth and position so intimately associated in the public mind with the term gentleman. We know that the inheritance of wealth is no guarantee of worth, yet who is independent of custom or convention? In the aristocracy of intellect—nature's dower—few gentlemen rank as high as Mr. Flanagan.

Born almost within hailing distance of Carbury Castle, County Kildare, about the middle of the nineteenth century, the early years of the future philologist were passed in an atmosphere of music and tradition. Many were the pipers of renown who were nurtured not far from where Kildare, Kings and Queens Counties converge. As a boy, young Flanagan caught the "bagpipe fever" from "Tim" Ennis, a local piper, who displayed marvelous execution on the chanter, and, although a few years earlier quite a number were learning to play, he was the only aspirant for fame in that line at the time. Like many another young Irishman of brilliant promise, he joined the British military service, in which he spent over twelve years in India. There his linguistic talents enabled him to acquire the native and other languages so successfully by tireless study, that he is said to be the best all-around Oriental scholar in the British Islands.

M. Flanagan

Armed with certificates of high proficiency in Arabic, Sanskrit, Persian, and Hindustani, issued under the authority of the government of India, Mr. Flanagan submitted his application for the position of lecturer in Oriental languages, advertised for by the authorities of the National University a few years ago. Quite likely the source of his credentials, and the circumstances attending his linguistic studies, militated against his success, for the office, with its stipend of two hundred pounds a year, was given to a clergyman whose learning was derived from books exclusively and who had never set foot on the Asiatic continent.

Popular sentiment against government employes, senseless and unjust though it be in many instances, is still too strong in Ireland to look with favor on the selection of an ex-military schoolmaster to fill an office of distinction in the National University.

Well grounded in the theory of music, and equally proficient as a performer on the Union pipes and violin, Mr. Flanagan, when in the mood, indulges his fancy in the pleasures of composition, especially sets of quadrilles. A man of strong convictions and full of his subject, he is ever ready to engage in controversial tilts, but it must be keenly disappointing to one of his aggressive temperament to seldom find an opponent willing to "break a lance with him."

The facility of diction displayed in his essays and epics proclaims Mr. Flanagan the possessor of rare intellectual gifts. Under more favorable circumstances a man so endowed could not fail to attain to positions of prominence and power.

PATRICK WARD

In addition to the ordinary worries to which mankind in general are liable, pipers and fiddlers have to contend with the exasperating perverseness of refractory reeds and unreliable fiddlestrings. Unlike the latter, serviceable reeds are not easily procured, because Spanish cane, the only material out of which they can be made, is scarce, and when available, few indeed are the pipers who have the knack of making their own reeds. Besides, every chanter possesses an individuality to which the reed must be adjusted, so that a defective or ill-fitted reed is truly the pipers' despair.

From the foregoing we can understand why our correspondent, Mr. Flanagan, speaks so eulogistically of his friend, Patrick Ward, the farmer-piper of Blackbull Drogheda, after some unpleasant experiences with less skilful though more pretentious reedmakers nearer home.

Philosophically he remarks: "If human life has its trials and disappointments, it has also its compensations. While smarting under the sting of insolence and ingratitude, I was fortunate enough to make the acquaintance of little 'Pat.' Ward of Drogheda. It's a good man that performs what he promises, but Ward does more and does it well. In short, his principles would better become a prince than a piper. For over forty years he has been following the plow, and yet so delicate is his touch that he can make the best reeds I ever used. If you give him a piece of written music, reel, jig, or hornpipe, he will read it off for you on his voice, and any tune he plays he can write out in proper key and correctly barred."

Ward was born about the year 1847 in the Parish of Drumconrath, in the County of Meath, and had attained considerable command of the fiddle before commencing the practice of the Union pipes. His first lesson in writing music, he tells us, was not unattended with difficulties. Having neither pen nor ink, he was told by his teacher, "a dark man," to burn a furze stick and write with its

Patrick Ward

318

calcined end.   This expedient served fairly well.   From that day to this he says that whenever he takes a pen in his hand to write music his mind reverts to "The Flogging Reel," which was the first tune set down in the manner mentioned.

In his repertory are many tunes seemingly peculiar to the County Louth. He has played at Feis Ceoil and Oireachtas for the last ten years and has been awarded several prizes.   At the Oireachtas in 1907 he won second prize, the first going to George McCarthy, and in 1911 he again captured second honors.   Taking into consideration that Ward is not a professional piper, but a plowman since early manhood, his execution on the double chanter is indeed remarkable.

George Carroll

A machinist and engineer by occupation, George Carroll is said to be a versatile musician also, his favorite instrument, upon which he is a fine performer, being the Union bagpipes.   With his brother Denis, who is an expert on the fiddle, he devotes much of his spare hours to the practice of music.   The most tempting offers to play in public have been steadfastly declined.   To most pipers, the inducement of a five-pound note for one performance would be irresistible. Not so with George Carroll, for a theatrical manager who made the proposition had no better success.

One day in the autumn of 1911, while engaged "threshing out the barley" for Mr. Fernando Murphy, Fincurry House, Ballycarney, he spied a fine set of pipes made by William Rowsome of Dublin.   When he had planted the machinery to his satisfaction, he left the engine in charge of his assistants, and going into the house hitched on the pipes, and, with O'Neill's *Music of Ireland* open in front of him, played for hours uninterruptedly.

This amateur piper's proudest boast is that he rode upon a "boneshaker" solid-tire bicycle from Kilrush—his home—to Ballintore, County Wexford, a journey of six miles, at frequent intervals for a period extending over half a dozen years, to receive instructions on the Union pipes from Mr. Samuel Rowsome.

Born in 1868, George Carroll is a piper of the transition period—that is to say, the period between the decline and revival of piping—and, though good-natured and genial like most men of ponderous build, his placid features betray less pleasant emotions when he thinks of the decline into which Irish music and Irish national instruments had fallen.

Michael J. Anderson

Of the early life of Mr. Anderson, who was born in Sligo about the middle of the nineteenth century, we know but little.   After making New York City his home since his first arrival in America, many long years ago, he decided to return to his native home early in July, 1912.

He had but recently finished an engagement at the New York Hippodrome, and had also played for the dancing competitions at the Gaelic League Feis, instituted by Donal O'Connor, the Irish organizer, shortly before his departure.

From newspaper accounts we learn that he intended to engage in manufacturing bagpipes when he got settled down finally in the land of his forefathers; and, by giving lessons and arranging music for the pipes, he expected to be "a big boon to the preservation of traditional Irish music."   He took with him five sets of pipes, one set being the product of the celebrated master, Taylor, of Philadelphia, and the others being the handiwork of Mr. Anderson himself.   If time should permit, his intention was to publish a tutor for the Union pipe, an ambition shared with several others of his profession.

During a prior visit to Ireland, Mr. Anderson spent a year in the City of Cork in 1904 and 1905, but alas for the realization of our fondest hopes, a few brief months on this occasion changed the current of his thoughts, and he recrossed the briny deep to the "land of the free" with all his plans unfulfilled. Evidently he was not aware that, notwithstanding the strenuous efforts of the Irish Revivalists, an Irish piper would be a curiosity in most of the Irish counties in this year of our Lord 1913.

Patrick Fitzpatrick

A rarity among pipers, Mr. Fitzpatrick is not only abstemious, and economical in his habits, but a thrifty business man as well. Unafflicted with artistic temperament in the slightest degree, he is both liberal and companionable.

Born at Carrigallen, County Leitrim, in 1860, he learned to play the flute in his youth. When but sixteen years old he went to Scotland, and during his five years' stay took up the practice of the Highland pipes. Shortly after his coming to New York, in 1881, he lent his instrument to John O'Neill, an expert performer, and never saw either since. The latter, by the way, played in Chicago in 1870, and was reputed to be comparatively wealthy.

Mr. Fitzpatrick transferred his attention to the Union pipes thereafter, but was always engaged in commercial pursuits. He built Celtic Hall, in New York City, in 1892, and it became the Mecca for the best class of Irish sociables and gatherings for many years.

Early in the year 1913, Fitzpatrick started out to tour the country with "The Top o' the Mornin'" company, in which "Paddy" Long, late of Cork City, leads the Irish dances, and he it was who played for the dancers at the New York Feis, held on the first day of June in the same year.

His splendid instrument, as represented in the illustration, is one of Taylor's masterpieces, on which, under the supervision of Mr. Fitzpatrick himself, no pains were spared.

James Byrne

Liberally endowed with musical talent, James Byrne as a young man earned an enviable reputation as a fluter in his native town of Ballybogan, at the foot of Tara Hill, in the County of Meath. Born in 1868, he received a fair education, but having learned no trade he found life enjoyable as a "Spalpeen Fanach." Fortune directed his footsteps to the farmstead of Samuel Rowsome of Ballintore, County Wexford, about the year 1887, where the father and three sons were all pipers. The transition from flute playing to piping came naturally and easily, for the Rowsome boys were then all at home and, discovering "Jem's" aptitude, furnished him with an outfit and taught him "the technicalities of the trade," as our informant, Mr. Whelan of Scarawalsh, puts it.

A year or so later Byrne took to the road as a wandering minstrel, a mode of life he has consistently followed ever since. He has traveled every county in the four provinces, it is said, and he has a vast and varied store of music that speaks at his finger tips. First prize was awarded him at the Dublin Feis Ceoil in 1905, but his name does not appear in the list of prize winners again until 1912.

In minor competitions, however, like the Feis Loch Carman, held at New Ross in 1908, he secured first honors.

Pat Fitzpatrick

Rev. Dr. Henebry and Father James K. Fielding, unaware of the existence of any passable piper in that part of the country, were astonished when they met him at Mooncoin in 1904. They took charge of their treasure at once—enthusiasts as they were—and we may be sure that the minstrel's temporal welfare, no less than his spiritual, received due consideration at their hands. Here was the opportunity of their lives to restore Irish music in all its traditional glory. With a real live piper and a good one, of a species thought to be extinct, right within their grasp, what may they not hope to accomplish in the cherished ambition of their lives?

After Byrne had regaled them with his ravishing strains to their heart's content, his tunes were recorded on an Edison phonograph—his masterpiece. "Rakish Paddy," being in their opinion not inferior to "Barney" Delaney's, and he was forthwith installed in suitable quarters to teach his precious art to a class of aspiring youngsters. But the "call of the wild" was too much for the professor. The microbe of vagrancy was too active in his blood to allow him to submit to the restraint of settled residence, or the monotony of steady employment. So away he went to enjoy the pleasures of conviviality and change of scene, leaving his kind-hearted benefactors in a fit mood to appreciate the feelings of the man who undertook to domesticate wild ducks.

Byrne was a fine reel player, but he has failed to realize the cherished hopes of his friends of earlier years. Like too many of his class he had fallen a victim to the perverted conception of hospitality which has prevailed in Ireland from remote times. The ineradicable custom of "treating," founded on racial generosity and hospitality, is responsible for many misfortunes besides the downfall of so many professional musicians.

It is never too late to mend, however, and it gives us much pleasure to relate that James Byrne "tied" John O'Reilly of Dunmore, County Galway, for first prize at the Dublin Oireachtas in 1912. The press reports of the meeting indicate that he was "in full possession of all his faculties, and sporting a temperance badge, played very well on a set which contains little more than the bag, bellows and chanter made by the Rev. Dr. Henebry's brother."

The Mooncoin piper is to be congratulated, for besides becoming a disciple of Father Mathew, it was no small honor to equal the best among no less than seventeen competitors, though we must admit that the possibilities of the Union pipes cannot be demonstrated on a set so incomplete and demoralized as that on which Byrne habitually plays. "He is a master of the *Uilleann* pipes," adds Seamus Clandillon, B. A., "and his handling of the chanter recalls such great pipers as Martin Reilly of Galway, Michael O'Sullivan of Sneem, and Thompson of Cork. He did what he liked with us that night. From 'The Flogging Reel' to 'Chief O'Neill's Hornpipe,' he swept us fairly off our feet, and listening to him one understood what Dr. Henebry meant by 'the dynamic power of a hurrying Irish reel.' "

Brought thus suddenly into the limelight, Opportunity, which is said to knock at least once at every man's door, paid a visit to James Byrne with commendable promptitude. He was showered with attentions and profitable patronage, including engagements on the Metropolitan stage. It is sincerely to be hoped that he can stand prosperity—for many there be who cannot. Yet who among his compatriots is insensible to the fawning of the flatterer, or immune from attacks of megalomania, a temperamental affliction to which the musical fraternity is so lamentably susceptible.

We can conceive of no influence so effective in promoting a knowledge and love of Irish Folk Music as a capable traveling Union piper, equipped with a good instrument, but above all temperate and self-respecting in his habits. A minstrel of that character would be in fact a musical missionary whose vocation would be no less appreciated in the community than profitable to himself.

John Flannagan

An Irish piper like John Flannagan, who has been winning prizes at Feis Ceoil competitions in Dublin since 1897, is justly entitled to recognition as a famous piper under existing standards of excellence.

To win half a dozen prizes classed as second, third, and special, among a score or more of competitors, is no small honor indeed in view of the fact that some winners of first prizes have secured no better than third on other occasions. Born at Dublin in 1870, Flannagan is yet a comparatively young man, and as in many similar instances he is by no means inferior to his father, who was also a piper. He created a sensation by his street playing at Enniscorthy at the great Home Rule Demonstration in August, 1912.

As his wife is a daughter of Mrs. Kenny, "Queen of Irish Fiddlers," we are justified in looking forward with keen concern to evidence of musical heredity in their offspring.

William Andrews

Instinctive talent, nurtured by individual preference, when supplemented by opportunity, seldom fails to determine our career. Such was the case with the subject of this sketch. Possessed of all his faculties, he had no motive other than choice to adopt music as a profession.

William Andrews was born in 1873, in the city of Dublin. He was instructed in the elements of music and piano playing by his aunt, Miss Eva Andrews, for many years a teacher at the Alexandra School of Music in that city. Piano music, however, not being in accord with his predilections, he studied the flute under George Ellard at the Municipal School of Music. It was while playing for dances in the mountainous districts of the county that he acquired a taste for traditional Irish music. As his knowledge grew, his love increased until he finally became afflicted with "piperitis" on hearing Tom Rowsome "wake the echoes" at a Ludwig concert at the Rotunda.

After buying a set of Union pipes at O'Reilly's on Wellington Quay, he settled down at Clontarf, playing the flute frequently for dances at the local Gaelic League gatherings. He joined the Dublin Pipers' Club, which then met in a cellar of McGarvey's tobacco shop opposite Findlater's church, and studied for ten years with Mr. Markey, the club's instructor, who by the way was himself a pupil of the famous Taylor of Drogheda. Andrews profited not a little by his acquaintance and practice with Pat Ward of Blackbull, Drogheda, another of Mr. Taylor's pupils.

Besides playing the Union pipes at nearly all the important Gaelic League meetings, William Andrews played at three performances of the opera "The Lily of Killarney," at the Gaiety Theatre, Dublin, for the Amateur Operatic Society, under the conductorship of Barton McGuckin.

In 1911 he won first prize at the Oireachtas for his playing of the Union pipes for the Dublin pipers' band, and tied with Coughlan of London for first prize on the Warpipes. Daniel Gallery, then a member of the Canadian Parliament, and Dean O'Meara of Montreal, enamored of his musical abilities, offered him a position of emolument provided he undertook to teach his art in that city. Being then

John Flanagan

William Andrews

married, the prize winner was disinclined to sever home ties and leave his native country.

Liberality, and a disposition to aid those financially embarrassed, were by no means conducive to prosperity, so Andrews took to the stage with Sydney Kelly, the dancer—one of the famous Kelly trio. They made their first appearance with great success, in February, 1912, at the Empire Theatre, Dublin, and then went to Liverpool. After touring the principal halls of Lancashire and Yorkshire, Kelly got disabled from blood-poisoning of the hand, and their programme was thus brought to a sudden ending. Having by this time acquired both fame and experience, the versatile William Andrews accepted a permanent position on his return to Dublin, which is said to be remunerative as well as agreeable.

WILLIAM F. HANAFIN

No incident connected with a trip to the Atlantic cities in 1905 is remembered with such pleasure by the writer as a chance meeting in Boston with William F. Hanafin. Young, handsome, and unassuming, he created a favorable impression at once, and we do not recollect having ever met a man of more pleasing personality.

Almost reluctantly he took up an unstrung fiddle, put it in shape, and with a slack bow produced some wonderful tones in the airs and dance music, which he played with equal facility.

He was born on a farm in Callinafercy, not far from Kilcoleman, County Kerry, in 1875. In those days it was customary to have a dancing school every winter, and no place was better suited to the purpose than the Hanafin barn. The opening night in "Willie's" sixth year made a lasting impression on his memory, and no wonder, for a coquettish but clumsy young woman while dancing "Sir Roger de Coverley," darted away from her partner and landed on "Willie's" bare toes. Another event remembered in connection with it was the arrival of the Keel fife and drum band after making a detour of seven miles on the trip.

Some of the best Kerry dancers and fiddlers were in the adjoining parish of Keel, and 'tis many the warm competition Mr. Hanafin tells us he witnessed between the rivals on either side of the river Maine. "Mike" Hurley, the best fiddler in the district, played at the dancing school, and his music so fascinated the boy that he always managed to find a safe place behind "Mike's" chair. Hurley's execution in his prime was equaled only by that of "Dan" Sullivan of Boston, who, it turned out, was his boyhood friend. Hurley's voice it is said was as musical as his fiddle, and when he told his young admirer that he would teach him to play, we can imagine what happy dreams ran riot in his plastic brain that night.

Well, the young enthusiast kept on dreaming and hoping for four or five years, but in the meantime, having such a craze for music, he got a tin whistle and got lessons on it from Florence Hartnett, a flute player and dancing master who fortunately chanced to come to his father's house. Young Hanafin, then but nine years old, was an apt pupil and soon was able to play "sets" for the boys and girls, and though he was becoming quite expert on the flute, his ambition was unsatisfied, and nothing could quench his longing for the music of the fiddle.

The Hanafin farmstead was the goal to which all traveling pipers, fiddlers and dancing masters bent their way in those days. The farmer himself was one of the best dancers in the county, and whenever there was a dancing contest, he had to represent his townsland, and 'twas nothing new for him to "trim" even the dancing masters.

Wm. F. Hanafin   Michael Hanafin

Hearing that Hurley was coming to start a dance for the summer, young Hanafin, full of hope for the realization of his cherished desire, stationed himself on the stile which commanded a good view of the road, and sure enough along came "Mike" poking his way slowly and carefully, for he was blind, with his fiddlebox under his arm, and we may be sure he met with a cordial welcome.

The long delayed music lessons commenced that afternoon and continued in a desultory way for some weeks, the result being that the eager pupil had some knowledge of scale, and could play "The Pigeon on the Pier" and "The Star of Munster" reels, and "Apples in Winter," a nice jig, besides being able to study a little from written music.

We next hear of our hero at Boston, Massachusetts, where he arrived in October, 1889, when but fourteen years old. The musical instruction given in the grammar school which he attended for a few years in that city advanced him on the road to success, and he soon became known as a capable performer. One night he was asked to help out an old man to play at an entertainment given for the benefit of some needy person. It turned out that the elderly musician was the famous "Dan" Sullivan, of whom he had heard so much. From a full whiskered face more Hebraic than Hibernian in appearance, two kindly eyes beamed on the boyish Hanafin, and when saluted with the familiar *"Cionnos ta tu?"* in good Kerry Irish, he felt entirely at ease with the old man, and they became fast friends thereafter.

Mr. Sullivan was also a skilled fluter in his young days, and nothing pleased him better than to play duets on either instrument with his young countryman. Under such circumstances the latter learned a few "wrinkles" from his senior.

Dancing was an accomplishment acquired by the majority of young people, not so many decades ago, especially those who made any pretense to music. Although the dancing school was held in the Hanafin barn, the Hanafin boys were taught by their father, and many's the nail they lost from their shoes at the crossroads contest. The game and the "drop" was in them, and, signs by, the subject of our sketch won the gold medal in 1906 from all competitors in Boston.

At a party held at the old home in honor of the son's return visit from America, his father, three neighboring men, his mother and her three sisters danced an eight-hand reel unsurpassed by any others seen since then. The music was by "Dick" Stephenson, "the Prince of Pipers," and the son, William F. Hanafin.

Many a time did Stephenson find comfortable quarters at the Hanafin farmstead, and it was from that celebrated performer "Billy" Hanafin caught the bagpipe fever. Like "Mike" Hurley with the fiddle, "Dick" Stephenson promised to teach him the next time he called around, and it turned out his intentions were good, for he was on his way to the house when met by some of the boys in town. Needless to say the poor piper fell a victim to Irish hospitality and never reached his destination.

Nothing daunted by the loss of the only opportunity presented for learning pipe music while in Ireland, our young enthusiast bought "a bag and chanter" from John Harney, an amateur piper in Boston. One Sunday while practicing the scales, a guest at the St. Leon Hotel, around the corner from where Hanafin was rooming, hearing a fellow man in evident distress, was kind enough to call around and excuse himself for intruding. He said he played a little on the pipes himself, and hearing something like the sound of a chanter, it attracted his attention. He was handed the rudimentary instrument, but finding it defective and unsuited to his arm—he being left-handed—he laid it aside, saying, "Wait a minute till I come back." "I knew there was something coming by the way he fingered the old thing I had," Mr. Hanafin writes. "There were eight or nine of us in the room. When the piper came back and harnessed on his own set of pipes, you may be sure we got the finest surprise of our lives. He started 'The Maid in the Cherry Tree.' I jumped up, and over the table in the centre of the room, and danced all around it, while the others stared in blank astonishment. His identity was a mystery to me, but I sat down beside him, and accompanied him on the fiddle for an hour. I had heard 'Mike' Hobbs, the bandmaster, talking about a great piper by the name of 'Patsy' Touhey, and thinking this fellow might know him, I asked if he had ever met Touhey in his travels. When he modestly replied, 'I'm the man,' our surprise was hardly less than when he turned loose on his instrument."

Such was the beginning of a lasting friendship. Hanafin came into possession of Harney's set of Taylor's Union pipes, practiced on them assiduously and whenever the genial "Patsy" came to Boston it was a new lesson for his friend. "I got O'Neill's famous book of Irish music and found a lot of the real old music in it," continues Hanafin, "and between the book and 'Patsy' I became a piper, and when I play a tune they ask me: 'Is it from "Patsy" you got that?' or 'What page is it in?'"

As William F. Hanafin took to the pipes, his brother Michael from boyhood days a fluter and dancer, took to fiddle playing, and both having learned their tunes from the same source, they played well in concert. Consequently they are in much demand, and fill engagements at all kinds of entertainments and festivals where good music is appreciated. As the Hanafin brothers are in the prime of life and pink of health, there is no danger that Irish music will be forgotten in the city of Boston or its environs in the near future.

John Smithwick Wayland, Founder of the Cork Pipers' Club

Great movements develop from small beginnings as great oaks from little acorns grow. Who could have foreseen the far-reaching influence which the Cork Pipers' Club—the pioneer of its kind—exercised in the revival of music and dancing in Ireland?

Conceived in the brain òf an enthusiast without prestige or prominence, advocated by men lacking in wealth or power, and organized in the face of indifference and discouragement, the Cork Pipers' Club owes its birth, growth, and continuance to the energy and persistence of John Smithwick Wayland. This Club was organized for the purpose of arousing an interest in the Union bagpipes, there being at that time no pronounced sentiment in favor of reviving the long obsolete Warpipes. Every available piper in the city was present at the first meeting held early in March, 1898—Mr. Thomas Croasdale, Robert Thompson, Shane O'Neill, James Barry, Richard L. O'Mealy (now a famous pipemaker in Belfast), and Morgan Galwey, lately returned from Australia. Alderman William Phair, himself an enthusiastic performer on the Union pipes, was elected first president; P. J. Lawless and John S. Wayland vice presidents, and Jeremiah O'Donovan secretary.

Tireless in advancing the interests of the Club, Wayland and his aids traced out pipers whose instruments had lain unused for a score of years, and gave them public recognition. Classes for the study of music and dancing were formed and placed under the tuition of the best talent obtainable, and so successful has been their training that some of the pupils now excel their teachers.

The founder and later secretary of the Club, whose devotion to Irish music was the passion of his life, without an iota of professional jealousy, taught all he knew of pipe music to whoever wanted to learn, his only reward being the con-sciousness of having contributed so much to the regeneration of the music and pastimes of his native land.

Contending with poverty and even boycotting, Mr. Wayland and the Club which he founded swerved not from their purpose. They were obliged to find means to defray the traveling expenses of those pipers and fiddlers who came from a distance to compete at the annual Feiseanna, besides paying their own expenses when traveling to other celebrations in various parts of Ireland. A debt of thirty pounds in which the Club was involved as a result of a senseless boycott was duly liquidated, and the missionary programme of arousing the dormant interest of the community was maintained uninterruptedly to the present time.

The Cork Pipers' Club survived many difficulties since its inception in March, 1898, and blazed the way to success which similar organizations subsequently followed. In precept and example it was an inspiration, and not only that but convention was disregarded, barriers were broken down, and the musical franchise conferred on the fair sex. The latter have since earned distinction in every branch of study whether vocal, instrumental or terpsichorean, and thus proved the wis-dom of the innovation. If we are correctly informed the first band of kilted warpipers in modern days was organized and equipped at the instigation of the Club's founder.

John Smithwick Wayland, born in 1874, was a native of Clonkelly, between Dundrum and the historic Rock of Cashel of the Kings, County Tipperary, where his father, Palliser Wayland, farmed a fertile slice of the Golden Vein. John was the youngest of ten children and the only one gifted with a musical ear. His predilection for melody found much inspiration in the whistling and flute playing of "Pat" Ryan, one of his father's plowmen, and from "Johnny" Dwyer *(Sean Ban),* a neighboring farmer; but the man from whom he caught the "bagpipe fever" was the celebrated "Tom" Hogan of Cashel, who used to come with his son-in-law, "Mickey" Walsh, the dancing master, to the house of "Johnny" Hickey, another of his father's workmen. Old man Walsh, although bearing the weight of ninety-four years on his frame, could do a few steps yet in 1911. He served as one of the judges at the Thurles Feis a few years earlier. We may be pardoned for digressing from our subject to mention that Darby Ryan, author of the famous song "The Bansha Peelers," or "The Peeler and the Goat," lived near Lisheen, a short distance from Mr. Wayland's birthplace. The following in Irish and English is inscribed on his monument: "Pray for the repose of the Soul of Darby Ryan, Scholar, Poet, and Patriot, born at Ashgrove, April, 1779, died March, 1855, aged 76 years."

The zeal and energy displayed by Mr. Wayland in the organization and main-tenance of the Cork Pipers' Club, if exercised in the interests of an American corporation, would have met with prompt recognition and advancement. To his willing aid we are indebted for much valuable information, and not a few of the original pictures from which our illustrations have been copied.

And the wonder of it all is how a salaried man in anything but affluent circumstances, could have vitalized a movement such as the Cork Pipers' Club, the offshoots of which have extended even to the Antipodes. If not a visionary, as claimed by some, John Smithwick Wayland is unquestionably a successful enthusiast. Not a few who have won recognition and fame in later years owe their inspiration and early training to Mr. Wayland. Among them may be men-tioned Miss Mollie Morrissey, Miss May McCarthy and the genial and generous Mr. Edward Cronin. In fact all the "crack" dancers so conspicuous in America

John S. Wayland

in late years, learned to "trip the light fantastic toe" at the Cork Pipers' Club. Equally proficient on the Union pipes and Warpipes, Mr. Wayland organized and directed one of the best Warpipe bands in Ireland, from which he furnished pipers and drummers on demand to various meetings and entertainments throughout the southwest. His patience and composure while playing for hours for the dancing contests at the Munster Feis in 1906 was simply heroic, in face of the fact that he had been unjustly deprived of first prize on the Warpipes by a discreditable maneuver on the part of one of the judges.

Yielding to the persuasions of certain Irish enthusiasts of Perth, West Australia, this irrepressible organizer set sail for the Antipodes in August, 1912. In a few months we hear of him at his destination giving successful concerts, in which Mazie McCarthy, who accompanied him, shared the honors by her clever dancing.

The excitement which his campaign of Irishry created during the voyage is well told in the columns of *The Irish American* of January 11, 1913, as follows:

"A by-product of the movement for the restoration of the Irish language has been the revival of the bagpipes, an instrument that shared with the harp the distinction of being, if not Irish in its origin, associated with Ireland through twenty centuries of its history. Pipers' bands have been formed all over the country and the members clothed in ancient Irish costume, marching with skirling pipes and beating drums, produce a remarkably picturesque and martial effect. Recently Mr. Wayland of Cork, the first of Irish pipers, left Ireland on a visit to Australia and all piping Ireland is in glee today at the account received of the remarkable effect produced by his pipe playing, en route, in France, Italy and Egypt. The vessel in which Mr. Wayland sailed put in for a day or two at Toulon in France, Naples in Italy, and Port Said, and at each place he disembarked, and clad in Irish costume marched through the streets playing his pipes. At Toulon, the people, attracted by the novel spectacle and the martial music, thronged around him cheering and gesticulating through the streets. One man left his carriage to follow the piper, a barber deserting his customer came running to the procession, and the customer, lathered and towelled, followed after. Returning to the Quays the magic piper had an advance guard of some hundreds of children, a rear guard of men and women, sailors, soldiers and gendarmes, singing and cheering the musician. Before boarding the ship the piper struck up the "Marseillaise," and the Toulonese sang it with frantic enthusiasm. The delight of Toulon in the Irish pipes proved embarrassing for the piper at the close, for it was only with the aid of a French officer he succeeded in getting on board his ship, the people were so clamorous for him to stay.

"At Naples the scenes of Toulon were repeated on a greater scale. Through the streets of the city the piper marched followed by thousands of enthusiastic Italians, and when in front of the Royal Palace some Irish fellow-passengers danced jigs and reels to the piper's music, the enthusiasm rose to fever pitch. The women took possession of the piper, garlanded him with flowers, and like a Roman conqueror he returned to his ship cheered from the shore until the anchor was lifted. At Port Said the scenes of Toulon and Naples were repeated. Every Irish piper is swelling with pride today at the triumph of Mr. Wayland."

Miss May McCarthy

Of the many whose musical instruction was obtained in the Cork Pipers' Club, no one is more distinguished than Miss McCarthy, whose performance on the Union pipes, surpassing that of Mr. Wayland, her teacher, won for her many

Miss May McCarthy

engagements at entertainments not only in Ireland but also in England and Wales. Though not out of her teens, her progress in piping and dancing is said to have been little short of marvelous.

Her parents, who were intimate friends of the brilliant John Augustus O'Shea, hailed from Nenagh, Tipperary. Their talented daughter, however, was born within earshot of the far-famed Bells of Shandon, and while neither big nor brawny this versatile Irish colleen can handle with ease a full-size instrument.

She won first prize at the Munster Feis in recent years, and even successfully competed with men on the Warpipes, and her fame as a performer on the Union pipes is now so well established, that she was invited to cross the Channel to Wales to play at a series of concerts in December, 1910, after which followed engagements at Manchester and Birmingham, England. Following is a press notice taken from the *Daily Sketch* of March 18, 1911:

"The Irish pipes are not seen in active service much in these days, but at the concert at Birmingham last night, those who met to celebrate St. Patrick's Day heard a performer who is probably without an equal, as far as the Union bagpipes are concerned. Miss McCarthy is from the Cork Pipers' Club, and has won many medals for piping and step-dancing. Master Cormac O'Keefe, also from Cork, as a dancer was pre-eminent in his own particular line."

MISS MOLLIE MORRISSEY

The subject of this sketch, whose picture graces the opposite page, was one of the aptest learners on the Union pipes that Mr. Wayland ever instructed, and in the matter of memorizing new strains she had no equal, it being nothing unusual for her to add four or five new tunes to her repertoire of an evening. An extract from the *Ladies' Pictorial* of June 10, 1905, enumerates the accomplishments of this talented young girl:

"I give you an interesting portrait of Miss Mollie Morrissey of Cork, fideogist, harpist, pianist, violinist, bagpiper and stepdancer, at the age of fourteen. I venture to say that not many Irish colleens can boast of such a long list of accomplishments, but such are the attainments of this little girl, whose charming and unassuming manner has endeared her to all who know her. She is the youngest and most proficient female piper in Ireland, playing the famous Irish melodies with great expression, and is also a correct exponent of dance music. She appeared at the Cork International and Industrial Exhibitions with very pronounced success. The clever little artiste is decorated with many medals, won at competitions in piping and step-dancing, and at last year's Oireachtas she carried off first prize in female hornpipe dancing from all comers, her graceful carriage and movements combined with precision being much admired. Recently at Thurles Feis she won no less than three first prizes in step-dancing, and marched to the field in company with another young genius playing the now revived primitive Irish Warpipes. Miss Morrissey got a special invitation from the mayor of Carnarvon to attend a reception during Pan-Celtic week, which she could not accept on account of being indisposed at the time." The genial Edward Cronin, elsewhere mentioned in this volume, composed some appreciative verses in her honor, commencing:

> "Upon the height of steep Glenview
> That looks o'er Shandon's sweet-toned bells,
> A maid with eyes of heavenly blue—
> Fair Mollie of the music dwells."

MISS MOLLIE MORRISSEY : A PRETTY LITTLE IRISH PIPER.

Having blossomed into womanhood since the above was penned, Miss Morrissey has been called to Dublin for training as a national teacher, and we are justified in predicting for her a brilliant future.

JOSEPH W. HOGAN

The great historic city of Philadelphia, in which quite a few Irish pipers besides the renowned "Billy" Taylor lived and died, now numbers among its million and a half inhabitants but one of that class deserving any special mention.

John Rountree and John Morgan have passed away, but the latter left a son, professionally known as Joseph W. Hogan, to perpetuate his fame if not his name.

Born in Philadelphia in the late seventies, "Prof." Hogan, a creditable performer on the Union pipes, is equally proficient on the violin, and personally conducts a serviceable orchestra which enjoys a liberal patronage.

ADAM TOBIN

Evidences are constantly cropping out to indicate that inherent talent for music is no less pronounced in the Irish race in this generation, than it was in the days of their ancestors, whose renown in music was world-wide. Simply, conditions have changed, and strangled the expression of the gift with which the race had been so conspicuously endowed.

In spite of their manifold disadvantages in this respect, pent-up talent will always struggle for some adequate means of utterance. An instance of this nature is presented in the case of Adam Tobin, who, though self-taught, is a very capable performer on three instruments.

In his youth in the parish of Mooncoin, County Kilkenny, where he was born in the late fifties, Tobin learned to play both flute and fiddle. After coming to Chicago he became enamored of "Barney" Delaney's rhythmic execution on the Union pipes, and at once commenced the practice of that fascinating instrument. Notwithstanding the disadvantages imposed by his belated beginning, he acquired very creditable proficiency in an unexpectedly short time.

Though employed in commercial pursuits, Tobin has filled many engagements in this and other cities. Year after year he is the centre of an admiring crowd at the annual picnic of the Highland Pipe Band. His playing for the competing dancers at the Gaelic Feis at Chicago in 1912 for several hours, and subsequently winning first prize in the piping contest against a young man of great pretentions, may be regarded as a flattering evidence of his abilities. He also tied with two rivals for first prize in the playing of jig, reel and hornpipe on the flute, and that is a good record for one day.

WILLIAM McCORMICK

It would be invidious to omit the name of "Billy" McCormick from the list of pipers of prominence in the city of Chicago. He hails from the historic city of Waterford, in which he had learned the printing trade and other arts. Originally a fine free-hand fiddler, his fondness for his favorite instrument forced him to follow the footsteps of Tobin. Like the latter also, his practice on the pipes commenced in mature manhood, although his present proficiency would indicate a much earlier acquaintance with the intricacies of the instrument.

With the cooperation of his faithful friend "Jack" Doolin, McCormick managed to get possession of a splendid set of pipes specially made by Taylor for his pupil, "Eddie" Joyce, who died in 1897, and thus equipped he has attained the ambition of his life.

Unlike others whom we might mention, "Billy" McCormick is not afflicted with temperamental infirmities. In fact he is one of the most amiable of men, always companionable and obliging, and as he holds a permanent position in the municipal service, his music on either instrument is always on tap for his friends

As a musical missionary his coming is always an occasion for rejoicing. He accompanies the playing of others on the pipes or piano with his fiddle, or performs on the pipes while others play the accompaniment, but the most delightful results are obtained when Miss Theresa Geary, a charming violinist and pupil of the Chicago Musical College, swings in on the reels, jigs and hornpipes, which she plays so skillfully while the talented Miss Nellie Gillan presides at the piano. Then there *IS* music.

Not the least of McCormick's claims to consideration is the training he is giving his son Hugh, who is already quite expert in the fingering of a chanter.

PROF. DENIS O'LEARY

Nothing could excel the tactfulness of the curly-headed, smiling, spectacled Denis O'Leary, who acted in the capacity of chairman or stage manager of the Munster Feis in the year 1906 at the City of Cork. His direction of the proceedings in the Irish language exclusively had the charm of novelty, at least to one returning to his native shores after an absence of forty-one years.

Feeling quite secure in our incognito we were not prepared to be approached in the audience and saluted by Mr. O'Leary, and notified of our selection as one of the adjudicators in the musical competitions.

Imagine our surprise next day when the gracious chairman himself competed for the honors as a performer on the Union pipes, and won first prize. In his playing there was none of the free and easy abandon of the seasoned piper about him. He realized his limitations and did not attempt any fancy flourishes, but with his instrument in perfect tune he played airs, and dance tunes, with admirable rhythm and precision.

The tones of his fine set of Union pipes were a trifle keener than those of the Kenna, Coyne, or Egan type, but they were much less sonorous than the concert pitch instrument manufactured by the late William Taylor of Philadelphia, and to our notion much more pleasing to the ear.

By a fortunate coincidence we met again a week or so later at William Rowsome's place, No. 18 Armstrong Street, Harold's Cross, Dublin, where the pipes which had excited our admiration were turned out. Mr. O'Leary had brought with him a most remarkable set of pipes which he had purchased for twelve pounds from an old woman in the County Clare, who had treasured them in an old chest for many long years. Had she been at home when an American called the day before for the same purpose, doubtless she would have received a much better price; but such is luck. The instrument, it is said, was specially made for a scion of the Vandaleurs, but the young man having met with an accident, it was left on the maker's hands.

The subject of this sketch was born January 21, 1877, at Dirrinculling, Ballyvourney, barony of West Muskerry, County Cork; a district bordering on Kerry, in which tradition, song and story, language and native customs, yet survive and thrive to a degree unsurpassed in any part of Ireland. Master of English and

Irish and a graduate of the local national school, in which Irish history was ignored, he was doomed to follow the plow until the Gaelic League movement vitalized the national consciousness.

Ardently cooperating in its aims, young O'Leary took advantage of every spare moment in conferring with shanachies, and carefully committing to writing every fragment of song and story recited by these venerable, old men, thus preserving much valuable material for future Irish literature. He was a constant contributor of Irish articles to the *Weekly Examiner* and *Fainne an Lae* during the editorship of the lamented Denis Fleming, and also to the *Gaelic Journal*.

In the early days of the Gaelic League, he competed regularly at Feis and Oireachtas and won many distinctions, including the Bunting gold medal for original poetry at the Oireachtas of 1900. It was at one of those gatherings, by the way, that he met Mr. Wayland, founder of the Cork Pipers' Club, and influenced by the latter's enthusiasm became imbued with a love for the music of the Irish or Union pipes, an instrument which had become extinct even in such a conservative territory as his native barony. However, many of an older generation remembered *Mikil Piobaire* (O'Hallisy). Conor O'Hallisy, Cronin, who was a Kerryman, and *"Cauhneen"* O'Connell and some others of less note.

Yielding to the persuasions of his friend Mr. Wayland, the embryo professor migrated from Ballyvourney to the City of Cork, in 1900, and took up the study of the Union pipes under his friend's tuition. In 1901 we find him in the town of Roscommon, having the honor of being the first extern teacher of Irish appointed by the Gaelic League to give instruction in the national schools. His success led to his selection two years later, from a large number of candidates, as organizer in Cork, where his urbanity and genial manner proved the wisdom of the choice. Equally successful in County Clare, to which he had been transferred in 1905, he won the affections of the Dalcassians and in evidence thereof at the time of his resignation in 1906, the Gaels of *Corca Baiscin* presented him publicly with testimonials and illuminated addresses.

It was while on this mission he became acquainted with Mr. Nolan of Knockerra, near Kilrush, a good amateur piper, and an enthusiast on the instrument. In his younger days he had known intimately the Moloney brothers—Thomas and Andrew—pipemakers who had manufactured the splendid instrument we had seen at Mr. Rowsome's shop at Harold's Cross. Its description and history will be found in Chapter XV in connection with the sketch of its makers.

Being of studious habits and deeply interested in the teaching profession, Mr. O'Leary conceived the idea of going on the Continent to study foreign languages; so early in 1907 he went to Belgium and entered the Catholic university of Louvain, where he remained two years. During his holidays he also studied at the university of Dijon in Burgundy, and he traveled also in Germany, perfecting himself in his linguistic acquirements.

Wherever he went he was always sure to keep up his practice on his beloved pipes, which, in their soft yet powerful tones, contrasted very favorably with the French *cornameuse*, or the German *dudel-sac*.

After his return to Ireland in the autumn of 1908, Mr. O'Leary was appointed professor of Irish and French at Mount Melleray Seminary, Waterford. During his stay he maintained his interest in pipe music, and had no less than five youths under instruction.

When Desmond College, Ring, County Waterford, was opened in 1909, Prof. O'Leary was assigned to teach classics and modern languages, and as this college

PROF. DENIS O'LEARY

is situated in the midst of an Irish population, no institution affords better opportunities for acquiring a knowledge of the national language.

The professor is quite proud of his proficiency on the pipes—the national instrument—and in spite of his manifold duties finds time for a daily practice. A pleasing feature of his performance is to see a curly-headed baby boy sitting beside him pounding away at the regulators, probably the most youthful performer on the pipes in existence.

CHAPTER XXIII

FAMOUS PIPERS

Miscellaneous Mention

Many a fine performer on the Union pipes flourished in the last half of the eighteenth and the first half of the nineteenth centuries, and even later, whose names have vanished on the wings of time. Others again there were of whom little is now remembered but the names, and even that slight concession to fame is due more to chance than design.

If we have failed to meet the expectations of our readers by the omission of deserving names, or by the paucity of our remarks in other cases, we can only plead that every available scrap of information has been utilized in the preparation of this work, which deals largely with a class conspicuous in Irish life, yet slighted in Irish literature.

It is surprising how many pipers of note came from within a radius of half a dozen miles of the town of Edenderry, in Kings county, close to the borders of Kildare. Trinity Sunday was an eventful day in the parish of Carbury generations ago. A holy well in a gentleman's demesne close to Carbury castle was a Mecca to which hundreds hied on that day. A "patron" originally of a religious character was an institution in that locality, with the usual accompaniments of courting, dancing, drinking, and even fighting. Thither came people from ten or twelve neighboring parishes and those gatherings naturally attracted wandering minstrels from near and far. The consequence was that the district became a rich repository of Irish Folk Music.

Edward Dowdall, who early in life went to Dublin, was born in the same parish as Maurice Coyne, the famous pipemaker. "Eddy" Dowdall, as he was called, was taught either by "Thady" Devaney, or Peter Cunningham. Devaney also taught "Tim" Ennis, the expert chanter manipulator mentioned in the biography of John Hicks. Ennis, Dowdall and Devaney were reckoned very good pipers in their day, which was in the second quarter of the nineteenth century. Another good piper of whom Grattan Flood makes mention was Garret Quinn of Enniscorthy, Wexford. Quite likely he was the "Piper Quinn" who kept a drinking bar and dancing saloon at New Street, Enniscorthy, some sixty or seventy years ago. He played the double bass himself in the string band which was part of his establishment. Old-timers are still living who remember seeing "Piper Quinn and his big fiddle" at the fair of Scarawalsh. His son Patrick was a famous traditional fiddler in a later generation.

Through the kindness of Officer William Walsh of the Chicago police force, we present the names of some Connacht pipers unknown to fame, as they had never rambled beyond the confines of their native province. Though a native of Oughterard, County Galway, Officer Walsh is an accomplished "Highland piper," and a writer of pipe music.

Between the fifties and eighties of the nineteenth century there rambled through the said county, "Paddy" Green, a blind piper from Tuam; "Paddy" Kilkenny, who hailed from Clifden; and John Lennan of Kilkerin, who achieved considerable repute throughout Connemara.

Martin Moran was a native of County Mayo, and Charles Daly, though born in Clare, spent most of his time in Galway. There was another piper, known only by the name *"Eunachaun,"* who for nearly thirty years enjoyed enviable popularity in Iarconnacht. No wedding or christening could be properly celebrated without the piper and his music in that district or in Connemara in the "good old times."

A piper named Martin Curley, whose antecedents are unknown, was, according to Mr. Quinn, a famous Chicago piper, the best reel player he ever heard. Not less famous was a piper named Cribben, of whom we know nothing except that he hailed from Swineford, County Mayo, and that "Jimmy" O'Brien was one of his pupils.

In an Irish lyrical song given by Professor O'Curry to Dr. Petrie, mention is made of Shane O'Finnelly playing "Ree Raw" on his pipes, and by the way, it is said that the professor obtained some fine tunes in 1853 from a piper named Michael O'Hannigan.

Quite a number of the tunes in Dr. P. W. Joyce's collections were noted down from the playing of James Buckley, a piper in the barony of Coshlea, in the southeastern part of County Limerick, who flourished in the third quarter of the nineteenth century.

Anthony Kennedy—briefly called "Tony"—of Carrigrannig, County Longford, although a tinsmith by trade, was a fair performer on the Union pipes. His son, "Tony" the younger, who lacked nothing of equaling his father's abilities either way, played the pipes at his father's wake. This, be it understood, was done in no spirit of levity but, on the contrary, out of respect to the old man's fondness for the music of his favorite instrument.

The O'Farrells of County Longford—father and three sons—were not distinguished for brilliancy of execution on the chanter, and they made no pretense of manipulating the regulators. Yet, playing altogether at the fair of Longford, Mr. John Gillan tells us, they attracted a large and appreciative audience around the middle of the last century.

An excellent piper named Fitzpatrick, who flourished about the same time, frequented Miltown, Malbay, and other places of public resort on the Atlantic coast of the County Clare. He was not much over forty years old when Officer John Houlihan met him in 1860 at the fair of Dunbeg, some five miles northwest of Kilrush.

We are indebted to Grattan Flood for the information that a famous piper named O'Mahony flourished in Wexford in 1832, and that David Cleary was no less distinguished in 1840 in Limerick.

Tradition has preserved the name of Kitty Hanley, a Limerick widow, who on the death of her husband—a blind piper—buckled on his pipes and made a living playing on the streets—a prototype of "Nance the piper" of Castlelyons, County Cork, elsewhere mentioned.

A writer in the *Dublin Penny Journal* of October 18, 1834, briefly refers to a Munster piper named "Jack" Pigott, whose playing of "Cush-na-Breeda" (Beside the River Bride) was the *ne plus ultra* of bagpipe melody. This bare allusion is all that has hitherto preserved from oblivion the name of a piper so proficient, as far as Irish literature is concerned.

Mathias Phelan of Cappoquin, County Waterford, must have been a piper of some consequence to have his instrument deposited in the National Museum, Dublin.

As late as the early sixties a piper named Shannahan, who was a native of Kilrush, County Clare, had a great reputation in Kerry and Limerick. He was the father of Michael Buckley Shannahan, the celebrated violinist, according to Prof. P. D. Reidy.

Another famous piper remembered by the professor was Timothy O'Gallagher, commonly called "Theig O'Gollahoo," as the name sounds in Irish. He hailed from Clonfert, and "played most excellently" for an exhibition in the sixties.

The Daniel O'Leary of Mallow, County Cork, to whose splendid performance at Dinis Cottage, Lakes of Killarney, Professor Reidy listened for hours, in the late sixties, could hardly have been the piper of identical name, mentioned by Grattan Flood as having flourished in the forties and fifties, and being the clan piper of "O'Donoghue of the Glens." Much less probable was he the "Duhallow Piper" described by a writer in the *Dublin Penny Journal* of October 18, 1834, who was a diminutive hunchback.

As far back as the second quarter of the nineteenth century, a farmer named Dudley Gallaher of Lisnatulla, near Ballinamore, County Leitrim, had a wide reputation as an Irish piper. The chanter of his pipes was recently brought to Chicago by James Kennedy on his return from a visit to his native home. The wood is lignum vitæ.

Oldtimers remember the names merely of "Rody" Slattery of Cahir Tipperary, and one Moriarty of Kerry, as being fine performers generations ago, but no details of their lives are now available.

Casual mention has been made of Patrick Gallagher, a capable piper of Lewisburgh, barony of Murrisk, County Mayo, who passed away in the last decade; and of one Malloy, who, when his little crop is sown at Doon, Parish of Killannan, County Galway, resumes his rôle of traveling piper in the "north countrie."

"Pat" McCormack of Ardee, County Louth, would have remained unknown to more than local fame had he not been brought to Dublin to play at the Pipers' Concert in 1903, and delighted the audience with his performance on the double chanter.

Merely as a matter of information, we may add that Ashley Powell of the Cork Pipers' Club—one of Mr. Wayland's pupils—is said to be playing the Irish pipes in the land of the Pharaohs.

ACCOUNTS FROM AUSTRALIA

In a very interesting article on "The Irish Musical Revival," by Morgan P. Jageurs of Parkside, published in *The Advocate* of Melbourne, South Australia, we find many of the missing links not otherwise obtainable in our sketch of John Coughlan, the most renowned Irish piper of the Island continent.

Other Irish pipers in Australia, the author says, were Patrick Clarke of Ballarat, Victoria (1865); J. Connelly, who returned to San Francisco after a few months' residence in Melbourne; Owen Cunningham, formerly of Boston, U. S. A., who played on the streets of Melbourne and Sydney in 1868; also one O'Connor of Sydney, in more recent times, and the late John Fraser of Glenmaggie, Gippsland, Victoria, who was noted as a skilful performer, though unfortunately his talents were confined to the quiet country districts in which he lived. J. Critchley of Rockleigh, South Australia, elsewhere mentioned in connection with Mr. Patrick O'Leary, is described by Mr. Jageurs as equally proficient on the

Union pipes and Warpipes. Other great Irish pipers, not generally known but whom he names, are: Daniel Rahilly of Killarney; Lawrence Minahan, also a Kerryman; and Denis Duggan, the "Duhallow piper" (County of Cork), who on account of his excellence was usually engaged for the dancing competitions.

It would appear that, released from home influences, some of the clergy have been moved to make amends for the attitude of their cloth in the motherland. What else can we understand from the following: "The Perth Irish Warpipe Band, West Australia, founded by the Rev. Fr. T. Crowley, P. P., who, with another *Sagart,* played in its ranks, brought out an expert piper, Mr. Richard Evans, from the City of Cork a couple of years ago. He, too, plays both instruments." And now, by the way, they have induced the tireless enthusiast and organizer, John Smithwick Wayland, founder of the Cork Pipers' Club—the pioneer organization—to emigrate to Perth, with his passage and expenses paid in advance.

More extended accounts of Cunningham and Connelly may be found in the preceding pages.

In his correspondence, John Coughlan, the great "Australian piper," alludes to James Kelly as a performer who ranked with the famous Patrick Flannery and his nephew, William Madden.

A very capable performer on the Union pipes of the few tunes comprising his theatrical repertory, was "Charley" McNurney, the musical member of the "Callahan and Mack" vaudeville combination, which toured Australia very early in the twentieth century.

Some four or five days after their first performance at Sydney, Mack was approached on the street by a man whom he recognized as the occupant of a seat in the front row at every performance.

"Excuse me, sir," said the man; "but would you mind telling what might be the tail of your name?"

"The tail of my name! What do you mean?" answered the piper, in surprise.

"Oh, I mane no offense at all, sir; only surely there must be something afther Mack."

"So there is, indeed," replied the man of music, good-naturedly. "My name is McNurney."

"For God's sake, Mr. McNorney," exclaimed the fascinated exile, "is there only three 'chunes' in the pipes? Night afther night I've been going to hear you play, but never a 'chune' comes out of your chanter but the same three."

Of course the disappointed lover of the music of his motherland was not aware that "Charley" McNurney was but following the custom of musicians and vocalists in the theatrical profession, who seldom vary the favorite numbers in their program.

"Mack" has a bag full of "chunes" for that matter, being the son of Alderman McNurney, a wealthy horse-shoer, and a very capable amateur piper, but those he repeated so frequently on the stage were his masterpieces.

THE DUBLIN GROUP

Great credit is due Michael O'Duibhginn, secretary of the Dublin Pipers' Club, who through his capacity and energy brought to the Oireachtas of 1912 no less than seventeen Union pipers—the largest number of the fraternity ever assembled at such a gathering. And then, to crown his efforts, a versatile member of the club—Seamus ua Casaide—took his pen in hand and gave to the press a

The above interesting photo was taken by Roe McMahon at the instance of the Pipers' Club, Dublin, immediately after the Union Pipes Competition in the Rotunda on Tuesday, the 2nd July, 1912.

Back Row—Stephen Ruane(Galway); John Potts(Dublin); Tom Matthews(Greenanstown, Balbriggan); Thomas Walsh(Dungarvan); M. Flanagan (Dublin); Pat Ward (Drogheda); Nicholas Markey (Teacher, Dublin Pipers' Club); Dan Markey (Castleblayney); W. H. Mulvey (Mohill); Michael O'Duibhginn (Hon. Sec. Dublin Pipers' Club); Risteard O. Foghludha (Chairman Oireachtas Committee); J. J. O'Farrelly

Middle Row—Seamus Ua Casaide (Dublin Pipers' Club); John Kenny (Dublin); Hugh Newman (Athboy); Mrs. J. J. Murphy (Limerick); James Byrne (Mooncoin); J. F. Flanagan (Dublin); Edward Mulvey (Mohill); Michael MacGuinness (Mohill).

Front Row—Seamus Mac Aonghusa(Dublin Pipers' Club); John O'Reilly(Dunmore, Co., Galway); Eamonn Ceannt (Adjudicator); Francis J. McPeake (Belfast).

345

gossipy sketch of the proceedings and those who took part in the event. Interesting as the picture of the group—reproduced in our pages—may be at present, we regret to foresee the day that it may be historical.

Among the pipers who contributed to the success of the Oireachtas, eight had been dealt with elsewhere in our sketches; namely, M. Flanagan, John Flannagan, James Byrne, John Kenny, Denis Delaney, Patrick Ward, Stephen Ruane, and Nicholas Markey.

John O'Reilly of Dunmore, County Galway, the dean of the assemblage, won the highest honors jointly with James Byrne of Mooncoin, County Kilkenny. The former is described as "a blind man of smart appearance with a jet black goatee beard and clean shaven upper lip, which gives him the appearance of a returned Yank." Though seventy-three years of age, not a grey hair gives warning of life's decline. His playing, which was far superior to his performance of previous years, may be attributed in some degree to his splendid set of pipes, recently purchased from William Rowsome, the clever pipemaker of Harold's Cross, Dublin.

Seamus MacAonghusa—otherwise James Ennis—of the Dublin Pipers' Club, who was awarded second prize, is a new Richmond in the field of piping. He was leader of the Dublin Warpipers' Band, which won third prize at the Carnival, while Seamus himself achieved distinction by winning first prize in the individual warpipes contest, and also Francis Joseph Bigger's prize for the best all-around warpiper.

Accompanied by Mrs. Kenny—"Queen of Irish Fiddlers"—this talented young man's playing proved how well the Union pipes and fiddle play in unison. As Union piper, Warpiper, and dancer, this native of the Parish of Naul in his round of triumph exemplified the possibilities of intelligent effort sustained by vitalized national sentiment.

Special prizes were awarded William H. Mulvey, "a pleasant-looking giant" of Mohill, County Leitrim, and Hugh Newman, a tall, thin piper hailing from Athboy, County Meath. Mr. Mulvey, it appears, won third prize at the Dublin Feis in 1905, second prize in 1906, and first prize in 1909—a very creditable record indeed.

Francis J. McPeake of Belfast and Mrs. J. J. Murphy of Limerick were awarded first and second prizes, respectively, in the learners' class of Union pipers. The singing of the young man from the north to the accompaniment of his pipe music was a performance highly appreciated. Originally a pupil of R. L. O'Mealy of Belfast, temperamental difficulties came between them, so he placed himself under the tuition of O'Reilly, who spent some months in the Ulster metropolis.

Daniel Markey, a Union piper hailing from Castle Blayney, County Monaghan, is described as an active, low-sized man, resembling a seaman more than a musician, and a witty conversationalist in Ulster Irish. At the Dublin Feis of 1900, he tied with Denis Delaney of Ballinasloe for third prize, and he also won third prize in 1909.

Of Thomas Walsh, one of the group, nothing can be said except that he came from Dungarvan, County Waterford.

THE DeLACY WARPIPE BAND

Probably the most unique band in Ireland is that composed exclusively of nine members of the DeLacy family, boys and girls, hailing from the townland of Tomsallagh, Ferns, County Wexford. As arranged in the picture their names

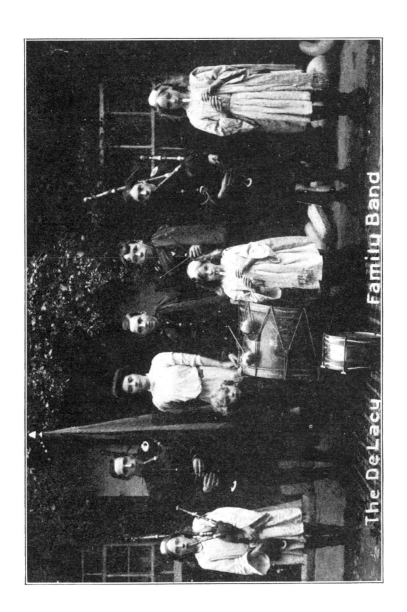

The DeLacy Family Band

347

are, from left to right in rear row: Eva Gertrude (known as Queenie), Patrick Thomas, Catherine Agatha Philomena, James Vincent, Richard Kevin, William Gervase, and Elizabeth Veronica. In front row: Leo Michael and Una Mona.

Just think of it, the DeLacy family of fourteen children brought up in a laborer's cottage with only half an acre of garden! And, by the way, that same cottage and garden won first prize for care and crops for thirteen years. There's a record from any point of view.

To the encouragement, training, and fostering care of Patrick Whelan of Scarawalsh, elsewhere sketched, the DeLacys owe not a little of the renown which their acquirements have won, although their first meeting, and the introduction of warpipes into Wexford, are due to the energy of John S. Wayland, founder of the Cork Pipers' Club.

Judging from the accounts in the papers, it seems like old times again in Wexford. On Sunday evening "Tinnacross was the rendezvous for a genial, warm-hearted gathering from all the district around," says one of them. "The occasion was an entertainment provided by the indefatigable DeLacy Warpipers' Band, and surely never a social gathering was more racy of the best and kindliest Irish characteristics. It is surely an omen of a more healthy social life and an indication of what progress we have already made, along the road to an Irish Ireland. A growing nation—just as, thank God, Ireland is growing—must manifest itself in varying phases, and our concerts and entertainments were as much indicative of racial spirit and racial development as greater events. To the splendid little clan belongs the honor of holding a thoroughly Irish entertainment in Tinnacross, free from every trait of Anglicization and as amusing as concert could well be." Nearly a column is devoted to giving a detailed account of the entertainment and those who took part in it, among them being Miss Una DeLacy and Master James DeLacy, whose dancing elicited repeated applause. "Three Misses DeLacy sang a pianoforte song with beautiful effect, the action being perfect and the singing a marvel." Such a display of versatility in one family is difficult to duplicate.

CHAPTER XXIV

TYPICAL HIGHLAND PIPERS

DANIEL O'KEEFFE

ONE of the most noted characters in Chicago before the great fire of 1871, which practically destroyed the city, was "Dan" O'Keeffe, a dancer and performer on the Highland pipes. He was born at Rathmore, County of Kerry, about ten miles east of Killarney, in 1821, and died in Chicago in 1899, the wealthiest professional piper on record. In his youth he learned to play the flute, but on coming to America in 1847 he took up the practice of the Highland pipes.

Before settling down in the western metropolis he had toured the United States and Canada as a traveling piper. His watchword was "Get the Coin," and he surely got it, for he knew the value of advertising when giving entertainments in many of the small towns in his itinerancy.

Many of his escapades while traveling, when a squint through the peephole in the curtain showed but a slim attendance or "poor house," made him an object of deep interest to the disappointed ticket buyers, who waited in vain for his appearance. Some of "Dan's" practical jokes had no element of humor at all from their standpoint. Should the box office receipts, even with a full house, fall into his hands under any pretext, the transfer of his slim baggage and himself to the first train—passenger or freight—was his only solicitude.

Anyway, the gay and festive "Dan" came to Chicago in the late sixties and opened a saloon on Kinzie Street, near the passenger station of the Chicago and Northwestern Railway, and, being but one square from the Chicago River, it was frequented by sailors, who are proverbially good spenders. But what attracted the most patronage was a large swinging sign over the door, on which was painted a Highland piper in full costume, playing the pipes and dancing to his own music. As a special inducement to the passerby, it was announced on the sign that anyone who beat the proprietor in dancing a jig, reel, hornpipe, or Highland fling, could have his drinks free for a week. Though not specially distinguished as a piper, competent authorities allow that O'Keeffe was an exceptionally fine dancer. As far as we can learn, it is not recorded that any free drinks had been handed out, as a result of the standing challenge.

"Dan" O'Keeffe turned his talents, such as they were, to good account. He made money and invested it wisely in Chicago corner property, now very valuable. Late in life he undertook to play on the Irish pipes, but the attempt did not meet with the success anticipated. Many years after his death, which occurred in 1899, the instrument, dried up and disjointed from long disuse, came into the possession of Sergt. Early, who, after putting it in order, disposed of it to Robert Lawson. The latter, who was an excellent fluter, soon became a capable performer on the O'Keeffe instrument, and secured an engagement to play on the porch of the McKinley cottage in the Irish Village at the Louisiana Purchase Exposition at St. Louis in 1903. Years afterwards this splendid, sweet-toned set of Union pipes of the Egan make was stolen from Lawson at New York City. After playing a few tunes in a Bowery bar-room, the piper was given some "knock-out drops," and when he came to his senses next morning in some out-of-the-way place, he had neither pipes nor knowledge of where he had been "doped." No trace of the instrument has been discovered from that day to this.

WILLIAM McLEAN

Born in Ross Shire in the northern Highlands, in the first decade of the nineteenth century, William McLean was famous as a Highland piper in early manhood, and, if rumor is true, had no superiors when he was twenty-five years old. Among his various avocations was that of cook in seagoing vessels, and his promiscuous intercourse with people of all nations no doubt added something to the natural urbanity of his manners. When the writer made his acquaintance in Chicago in 1875 his pre-eminence as an all-around performer on the Highland instrument was acknowledged. Unlike most Scotch pipers, his repertory was not confined to Scotch music. "Mac" was equally proficient on such Irish dance music as came within the limited compass of his chanter, but it was amusing to witness his bewilderment when he found his system of execution was ineffective on the diatonic scale of an Irish chanter.

He had engaged in the saloon business for a brief period before that date, and his music attracted a large patronage, but so sociable and absent-minded did he become that often he left the day's receipts on the bar while he engaged in conversation with a friend. As a financier he was simply impossible not only in business but in all his transactions, and it was marvelous how he could discover such cheap and cheerless tenements as he invariably occupied with his family.

As we have stated, such was the excellence of his execution that no one but Joseph Cant made any pretense to rivalry. Surprises are always in store, and our hero was the victim of one of them at Milwaukee one Fourth of July. At a competition in which he took part, an obscure, fifth-rate piper was announced as the winner of the first prize, to the astonishment and disgust of the audience. The adjudicator, it appeared, hadn't much of an ear for music, anyway, and as it happened one of the competitors played "The Campbells are Coming," the only tune known to the judge, what could the latter do but award first prize to the one who played it!

Well does the writer remember the winter when McLean filled an engagement to play for hours every evening in the large barroom in the temporary building at the southwest corner of Clark and Jackson Streets, where the Western Union Telegraph "skyscraper" now stands. At home he preferred to play the half-size bellows pipes, but in a barroom, especially of liberal dimensions, they could not compare with the *Piob Mor* in drawing a crowd.

Of all his callers, none was more welcome than "Willy" Walsh—now a dignified officer of the law—for when the latter hove in sight "Mac" knew he was in for a long rest. As the magnet draws the iron, so does the sight of a set of Highland pipes attract the willing Walsh. But to get them away from him, once he starts playing—ah, but that's a problem not so easily solved sometimes.

A birthday party at Bohemian Hall on DeKoven Street, when he was seventy-five years old—about 1880—replenished the old minstrel's depleted exchequer for the time being, but he soon found it advisable to make his home with his daughter at Saint Paul, Minnesota, where he lived to a great age.

Never afflicted with megalomania like so many of the musical fraternity, McLean was always genial, kindly, and helpful, and, though enjoying an occasional glass of kümmel when procurable, he never lost possession of his faculties, and he remained the same good-natured though thriftless genius to the end.

William McLean

Joseph Cant

Another famous Highland piper who may be considered one of Chicago's early settlers was Joseph Cant, a native of Inverness. Born around the middle forties of the nineteenth century, he was an expert carpenter and cabinetmaker also. Coming to Chicago in early manhood he soon became shop foreman, but eventually branched out in the building business for himself, at which he has been quite successful.

Strictly a note player, "Joe" Cant was familiar with all standard Scotch pipe music. Nothing could attest his proficiency more convincingly than the fact of his winning first prize at the St. Andrew's Games at Dexter Park, Chicago, in 1877. A stranger from the west, he journeyed to Buffalo, New York, in 1882, and won the R. B. Adam medal (first prize) for marches, strathspeys, and reels, among nine competitors from Canada and the United States. The genial "Joe" was awarded a gold medal, first prize, played for three times in 1888, at the games of the Highland Society in Chicago and Milwaukee.

A tempting salary induced him to accept an engagement to play for an advertising firm throughout the western states on one occasion, and that was his only lapse into professionalism. An anomaly among musicians, Mr. Cant prefers to listen to others rather than play himself. Always appreciative, never harsh, nor even critical, he is the most companionable of men, and no native of the Green Isle is more keenly alive to the spirit of an Irish jig or reel. In fact, such is the liberality of his nature that he discovers merit in others not even suspected by themselves.

Music must have been in the family, for his brother, Andrew Cant, was for many years household piper to the Earl of Breadalbane.

Occasionally the subject of our sketch turns out a new set of pipes—the half-size reel set with stock and bellows being his favorite. Nothing in a mechanical way comes amiss to his hand, consequently he is the court of last resort to many who find his friendship indispensable.

Patrick Noonan

Contemporary with William McLean and Joseph Cant was Patrick Noonan. Though not so absolute a performer as they, he was better known than either, and for suavity of manner and powers of persuasion, few could hold a candle to him. Born in the County of Limerick about 1825, he had developed considerable proficiency on the Highland pipes before coming to America. After engaging in various occupations, including that of drayman, his blarneyed tongue secured him a life position in the general postoffice, Chicago, in the early seventies.

A born salesman and trafficker, he made a specialty of second-hand sets of bagpipes—Scotch and Irish—and their equipments; and he was forever engaged in negotiations with a view to their purchase or sale. He was quite liberal with his music and without hesitation played all over town as a matter of accommodation, and thus enlarged the circle of his friends and patrons. The writer made a little deal with him once and of course "got stuck." A quiet, almost inaudible, word from his wife, who evidently did not approve of his methods, seemed to have vitalized his conscience much to my advantage.

Always ready-witted and unabashed, he acquitted himself very creditably on the Highland pipes at a great gathering of the Hibernian and Caledonian Gaels in Central Music Hall a generation ago, when the program needed new life. His

Joseph Cant

rendering of Irish tunes on the Scotch instrument left nothing to be desired on that occasion.

As we have stated, trading was his ruling passion, and in supplying pipe fittings he dealt with those at a distance as well as those nearer home. One day Sergt. Early met him carrying a tanned sheepskin under his arm. Being asked what he was going to do with it he answered, "Oh, a Highland piper up in Wisconsin wants it for a new bag."

"But sure a porous thing like that isn't suitable for the purpose," protested the sergeant; "'tis too leaky."

"Arrah, man alive," answered Noonan, complacently, "them Scotch fellows could fill a sieve!"

Keen as Noonan was in effecting a sale, and oblivious as he appears to have been to the restraints imposed by the Decalogue, he was the soul of hospitality once negotiations were concluded, and he would cheerfully spend the profits with the purchaser.

As an agent or promoter under modern commercial conditions, "Pat" Noonan would be simply irresistible, and though his transactions may savor of sharp dealing, his subsequent liberality goes far to show that he was simply yielding to a natural propensity. A "good fellow" as the world goes, he cut no inconsiderable figure in his sphere, but as was to be expected, he enjoyed neither riches nor long life.

Duncan McDougall

When our cherished friend, Joseph Cant, was approached on the subject of introducing his likeness in this work as a representative Highland piper, with characteristic unselfishness he exclaimed, "If you are going to put any Hielander in your book, Frank, tak Duncan McDougall, for he deserves it more nor any one." Then the generous "Joe" went on to tell about McDougall's celebrity, not alone as a piper and pipemaker, but as a typical, proud Hielander, who "wadna tak off his bonnet till no man"—no, not even royalty itself.

Much as his independent spirit appealed to Mr. Cant, we have good reasons for believing that the story of his dismissal on that account is somewhat apocryphal. For the leading facts in his career we are indebted to an esteemed brother Gael, the versatile Lieut. John McLennan of Edinburgh.

Duncan McDougall, a piper and pipemaker of the first rank, was born in the city of Perth, in the shire of that name, in central Scotland, where his forefathers for at least five generations were pipers and pipemakers. He was piper to several gentlemen before his fame gained him the coveted position of piper to the Prince of Wales, afterwards Edward VII. His fall from royal favor was due rather to an excess of conviviality than to a lack of conventional courtesy.

A performer so distinguished could command his choice of engagements. For several years thereafter he served as piper to the Marquis of Breadalbane, but tiring of routine and restraint, both irksome to a man of his temperament, he bade adieu to nobility and took up the ancestral profession of pipemaking at Aberfeldy.

He did not long survive the change, for the path of fame as well as glory leads but to the grave, and he died in 1898, a comparatively young man. In his prime he won many prizes—gold and silver medals, dirks, powder horns, and valuable sets of bagpipes. A glance at his picture will be more enlightening as to his acquisitions in this respect than pages of description. Flattery and frailty are the penalties of fame.

Duncan McDougall

WILLIAM WALSH

An ardent Revivalist who practiced what he preached in the furtherance of Irish regeneration, in all that constitutes distinct nationality, as persistently as did the subject of this sketch, is entitled to a place in our gallery of worthies.

William Walsh was born in 1859, at Oughterard, on the banks of Lough Corrib, County Galway, and, although coming to America with his parents in childhood, he is a fluent speaker and reader of the Irish language, and few are so well versed in the history and lore of his native land.

Self-taught in music, as in most other things, he took up the study of the Highland pipes when but little more than a boy. So zealous was he in his practice that the present writer has seen him lay down his dinner pail on returning home from work and, without waiting to change his begrimed clothing, put on the pipes and play while his mother was preparing supper. We may as well admit, however, that the neighbors were by no means unanimous in their approval of his tireless assiduity.

It would be but natural to suppose that, after listening for months to the mellow music of "Jimmy" O'Brien's Union pipes, young Walsh would favor the Irish instrument, but he didn't. Provided with suitable music, he learned to play by note and eventually to write music according to the Scottish scale, but not a little of his inspiration came from his frequent visits to William McLean, Joseph Cant, and some others, all famous performers on the Highland bagpipes.

Liberal, even lavish, with his music, he was the most obliging of men, and his only lapse into professionalism was a season's engagement with Sells Brothers' circus in 1881. This of course was long before his connection with the Chicago police force, which commenced in 1891. Timidity or bashfulness being entirely foreign to his nature, he makes the acquaintance of every Scotch piper who comes to town, and it is owing to his energy and promptness in this respect that he induced no less than seven of them, on short notice, to enter the contests at the Gaelic Feis held at Chicago in July, 1912, and by the same token the prize winners happened to be only casual visitors in the city.

On that occasion, by the advice of the present writer, Walsh dismantled one of his tenor drones, thereby converting his set of Highland pipes into an Irish warpipe. This metamorphosed instrument served for all, but Walsh easily won the gold medal, the silver trophy being awarded to Walter Kilday. This triumph he repeated in 1913. The second prize was won by James Adamson.

Officer Walsh attends all Scotch picnics as a conservator of the peace, and although he does not compete in the piping contests, often acting as one of the judges, it would indeed be a queer day that he wouldn't take a whirl at them for an hour or two; and whether it be on account of the excellence of his execution, or partiality for the Irish tunes which he plays, he is sure to have a large and appreciative audience.

Possibly with a view to finding an additional vent for his versatility, "Willy" learned to play the flute—by note, of course, for he scorns ear players. Dividing honors with the best of them for the gold medal at the Gaelic Feis before mentioned is no slight testimony to his proficiency. He was equally successful at the great Feis in Comiskey Park in 1913, tying for first honors with Charles Doyle.

The triumphs above set forth, though notable, do not constitute our hero's chief claim to fame. In these days of costly living, William Walsh supports on a policeman's salary a family of fifteen. Thirteen of his fourteen children are living. Oh! what a boon men like Walsh would be to a decadent nation like France, in which the births barely equal the deaths.

WILLIAM WALSH

CHAPTER XXV

THE IRISH FIDDLER

Across the strings his bow he lightly draws,
  And from the vibrant violin
A voice speaks out, a timid, plaintive voice,
  So soft so sweet, so sad, that in
My heart I feel a restless, half-formed joy
  That is to pain akin.

It seems as though the erstwhile silent soul
  Had found a voice in which to tell
Its inmost dreams; it seems as though the heart
  Had found an outlet, in the swell
Of solemn sound that weaves upon the air
  Enchantment's wizard spell.

And like the music of the violin
  Is life; sometimes a jarring strain
Will mar the harmony of joyous chords,
  And yet discordance may be gain;
For pleasure, when we find it doubly sweet,
  Comes in the wake of pain.

Scannell O'Neill.

What a host of light-hearted associations are revived by that living fountain of fun and frolic, an Irish fiddler, says Carleton in one of his character sketches. Everything connected with him is agreeable, pleasant, jolly. All his anecdotes, songs, jokes, stories, and secrets, bring us back from the pressure of cares of life to those happy days and nights when the heart was as light as the heel, and both beat time to the exhilarating sound of his fiddle. His art was a key to the mansions of the rich and great, where his enchanting strains opened the pockets of the men and the hearts of the women.

The only instrument that can be said to rival it is the Union pipes, for which there is in fact a more lasting sentiment. Still the fiddle is, in the minds of many, the instrument of all others most essential to the enjoyment of an Irishman. Dancing and love are by no means antagonistic, and the thrilling tones of the fiddle are never heard without awakening the most agreeable emotions. Its music, soft, sweet, and cheerful, acts like a charm on a susceptible nature. In the language of the great novelist before mentioned, "It opens all the sluices of his heart, puts vigor in his veins, gives honey to a tongue that was, heaven knows, sufficiently sweet without it, and gifts him with a pair of feather heels that Mercury might envy; and, to crown all, endows him, while pleading his cause in a quiet corner, with a fertility of invention and an easy unembarrassed assurance which nothing can surpass."

Victims of the same misfortune, blind fiddlers were far less numerous than sightless pipers, for the quaint, plaintive tones of the old-style Union pipes— much below concert pitch—were more potent and persuasive in their appeal to Irish nature than the crisp yet insinuating voice of the fiddle.

It must be borne in mind, however, that the fiddle was the favorite instrument of those who loved music for its own sake, and indulged their melodic fancies at pleasure, whether among friends in the community or in their own domestic circle, as suggested in the illustration.

FIDDLING AFTER SUPPER

"I love to play the fiddle
    Nearly any time o' day,
When I'm feeling in the notion
    And my fiddle wants to play;
But it's nicer after supper,
    When the day's work's done, you know,
And my thoughts get solemncholy
    And I play right soft and low.

"Then the fiddle seems to join in,
    Like your sweetheart at the gate,
When you're courting in the evening
    And stay out a little late;
And my heart it gets to chording
    With the music in the strings,
And the fiddle gets a-trembling,
    And kind o' sobs and sings.

Michael J. Dunn
"Fiddling after Supper"

"Then my eyes they get to leaking,
  And my voice don't want to speak,
And I feel so awful happy,
  And so kind o' mild and meek,
That I love the whole creation,
  As I play and walk the floor,
And just crave to own a billion,
  So I might help the poor.

"And I most forgot to mention
  That my little daughter, Nell,
Plays the chords upon the organ—
  And you bet she plays them well—
And most always after supper
  We just have a jubilee,
And I get as close to heaven
  As a fellow needs to be!

"For my wife she'll sit a-smiling,
  And the baby'll jump and coo,
And I feel so good and happy
  That I don't know what to do;
And old 'Nancy' and the puppies,
  They think the music's fine,
For they all stand in the entry
  And wag their tails and whine!

"Now you've heard the simple story
  Of the music in me bred,
And I guess 'most everybody
  Will smile at what I've said;
But I tell you there's no happiness
  Like the kind a fiddle brings
When it trembles on your bosom
  And just kind o' sobs and sings!"

The music of the fiddle has a wonderful hold on the affections of the people of West Virginia, Kentucky, and Tennessee, many of whom are the descendants of Irish settlers of the eighteenth century. Even in the state of Indiana the "Old Fiddlers' Contests," held annually and lasting several days, are among the most interesting events of the year.

Who has not heard of "Fiddling Bob" Taylor of Tennessee, who fiddled himself into the House of Representatives at Washington, then into the Governor's chair of his native state, and finally into the United States Senate. In default of money and influential friends in his campaign against a distinguished lawyer and politician in 1878, he tucked his fiddle under his arm and set out to win votes with its melodious strains. And he won. Equally successful was he in the campaign for the Governorship, his opponent in that instance being his own brother, Alfred A. Taylor. Music proved more persuasive than oratory, for it entered the hearts of his audience, while eloquence passed over their heads.

As the sailor to his ship, the sportsman to his gun, so is the fiddler to his instrument, whose tones range from the bass of the resounding drum upward through a chain of a thousand modulations, to the shrill chirrup of the piccolo.

Seemingly simple and uniform in construction, fiddles possess marked individuality, and need we wonder then that, after years of association and manipulation and tuneful accord, the sightless owner affectionately endows his fiddle with personality, and a pet name.

"Old violin, sweet friend and love,
　The world is dark; we're growing old;
The light is vanishing above;
　No more I see your strings of gold.
The love-knots which our Ellen tied
　Around your carved neck long ago
Have faded in the friendless tide
　Of summer heat and winter snow.
　　　Old violin,
　　　Dear violin,
　Companion of my wanderings,
　　　Your golden moans,
　　　Your plaintive tones,
　Plume memory with radiant wings.

"The sunny fields thro' which we've strayed,
　The woods we've sought from sun and rain,
The pebbled brook and chestnut glade,
　Like blessed phantoms fill my brain.
Our welcomes, as with set of sun,
　From purple heaths and hills forlorn,
The villagers with labor done
　Come dancing thro' the yellow corn.
　　　Old violin,
　　　Dear violin,
　Once more like laughter touch my ears,
　　　Once more arise
　　　And fill my eyes
　With floods of unavailing tears.

"How often in those olden times,
　When shadows folded all the east,
And the ivied chapel's pious chimes
　Tolled sweetly for the rural feast,
Have you and I in happy trance,
　O'er green field from the dusty road,
Seen the brown groups of harvest dance
　Till brows were red and ringlets flowed!
　　　Old violin,
　　　Dear violin,
　Even now, with blinded eyes, I see
　　　The roses red
　　　That twined your head,
　The brown ale foaming at my knee.

"Solace of my declining life,
    Heaven blessed us with tranquillity,
In all the moods of peace and strife,
    No pair could more contented be.
We left the monarchs crowned above,
    To act their wise or foolish parts,
And with our strains inspired by love
    Ruled the great universe of hearts.
            Old violin,
            Dear violin,
Tho' fame and fortune could not last.
        We have no fears
        For coming years,
And no repentings for the past."

When Charles II had come to the throne, one of his first acts, we are told, was the bringing over to England of a band of twenty-four fiddlers, each a prodigy in his way, but immeasurably inferior to their leader Baltzar. This man performed such marvels on the four slender strings of the violin that an honest gentleman of the period suggested his identity with Satan and seriously examined his feet in the expectation of finding them cloven.

Miracles of execution even on one string no longer excite our astonishment, for musicians have reached such a state of mechanical perfection that nothing more is to be expected along that line, and while their music may interest the cultivated ear it seldom touches the heart. We all know that the quaint and simple melodies of many tunes will commend them to those for whom an artless air has many charms.

The Irish fiddler, it may be said, is in a class by himself. His music, whether plaintive or spirited, is freely sprinkled with graces, trills, and turns that give to Irish music its peculiar distinctiveness. And though his execution —often original and wayward—may be the despair of the trained violinist, who among the best performers can compare with him in touching the susceptibilities of his audience? How delightfully Hugh F. Blunt expresses these ideas in his poem:

AN IRISH TUNE

Will you listen to the laugh of it,
    Gushing from the fiddle;
More's the fun in half of it
    Than e'en an Irish riddle.
Sure, it's not a fiddler's bow
    That's making sport so merry;
It's just the fairies laughing so—
    I heard them oft in Kerry.

Will you listen to the step of it,
    Faith, that tune's a daisy;
Just the very leap of it
    Would make the feet unaisy.

Hold your tongues, ye noisy rogues,
    And stop your giddy prancing;
It's me can hear the weeshee brogues
    Of Irish fairies dancing.

Will you listen to the tune of it,
    Sweeter than the honey.
I'd rather hear the croon of it
    Than get a miser's money.
Sure, my son, it makes me cry—
    But don't play any other;
May God be with the days gone by
    I danced it with your mother.

Who but an Irish fiddler would think of taking part in an eight-hand reel, and dance to his own music "gushing from the fiddle"? Yet an instance of that kind was witnessed by the writer in his boyhood days in the commodious kitchen of a neighboring farmer. Great as has been the decline of peasant music and pastime since those days, we find that the feat is still in favor, for Mr. Hourigan of Bansha, Tipperary, is reported to have "brought down the house" at a Cork concert in 1912 by a similar performance. Many excellent performers among the traditional musicians had but a very nebulous conception of the value of musical signatures. Their execution, however, was instinctively correct as to tone, and it was only when they undertook to write music that their shortcomings in this respect were betrayed.

The witchery of the violin is not easily explained. In *Music and Morals,* Rev. H. R. Haweis says:

"I have never been able to class violins with other instruments. They seem to possess a quality and character of their own. Indeed, it is difficult to contemplate a fine old violin without something like awe; to think of the scenes it has passed through long before we were born, and the triumphs it will win long after we are dead; to think of the numbers who have played on it and loved it as a kind of second soul of their own; of all who have been thrilled by its sensitive vibrations; the great works of genius which have found it a willing interpreter; the brilliant festivals it has celebrated; the solitary hour it has beguiled; the pure and exalted emotions it has been kindling, for perhaps two hundred years; and then to reflect upon its comparative indestructibility. Organs are broken up, their pipes are redistributed, and their identity destroyed; horns are battered and broken, and get out of date; flutes have undergone all kinds of modifications; clarionets are things of yesterday; harps warp and rot; piano-fortes are essentially short-lived; but the sturdy violin outlasts them all. If it gets cracked, you can glue it up; if it gets bruised, you can patch it almost without injury; you can take it to pieces from time to time, strengthen and put it together again, and even if it gets smashed, it can often be repaired without losing its individuality, and not infrequently comes home from the workshop better than ever, and prepared to take a new lease of life for at least ninety-nine years."

The Old Minstrel

CHAPTER XXVI

SKETCHES OF SOME FAMOUS FIDDLERS

MICHAEL McROREY

IN a character sketch from the facile pen of William Carleton, in 1840, the novelist pays his respects to "Mickey" McRorey, a blind fiddler whom he had known in his boyhood days: "In my native parish (Clogher, County of Tyrone) there were four or five fiddlers, all good in their way," he says, "but the Paganini of the district was the far-famed 'Mickey' McRorey. He had no settled residence, for he was not at home once in twelve months, being 'a kind of a here-and-therian —a stranger nowhere.'"

Blind from infancy, a victim of smallpox, he possessed an intelligent countenance on which beamed that singular expression of inward serenity so peculiar to the blind. His temper was sweet and even, but capable of rising through the buoyancy of his own humor to a high pitch of exhilaration and enjoyment.

To be his guide or carry his fiddle case was an honor much coveted by the youngsters, and Carleton tells of his delirious joy in being the favored one entrusted with that responsibility for seven years when "Mickey" came around. His reception was cordial and vociferous, and, as the saying goes, "they near killed him with kindness." "Blood alive, 'Mickey,' you're welcome!" "How is every bone of you, 'Mickey'?" "Bedad, we gave you up." "Ah, 'Mickey,' won't you sing that song for us?" "To be sure he will, but wait till he gets home, and gets his dinner first." "'Mickey,' give me the fiddle case, won't you?" "Aisy, boys, aisy, my fiddle hasn't been well lately and can't bear to be carried by any one barrin' myself."

When "Mickey" was playing for a dance merry banter was always in order, and, blind though he was, his remarks on the performance of the dancers were so apt and humorous that he caused no end of merriment.

"Ah, Jack, you could do it wanst, and can still. You have a kick in you yet." "Why, 'Mickey,' I seen dancing in my time," the old man would reply, his brow relaxed by a remnant of his former pride, "but you see the breath isn't what it used to be wid me when I could dance the 'Baltiorum Jig' on the bottom of a ten-gallon cask. Sure I thought my dancing days were over."

"Bedad, an' you war matched, anyhow," rejoined the fiddler; "Molchy carried as light a heel as ever you did; sorra woman of her years I ever seen could 'cut the buckle' wid her. You would know the tune on her feet still. Come now, sit down, Jack, till I give you your ould favorite, the 'Cannie Sugach.'"

But it was in the dance house that "Mickey" was in all his glory, scattering his jokes about, and so correct and well trained was his ear that he could frequently name the young man who danced by the peculiarity of his step.

"Ah, ha! 'Paddy' Brien, you're there; I'd know the sound of your smoothin' irons anywhere. Is it thrue, 'Paddy,' that you wor sint down to Errigle Keerogue to kill the clocks for 'Dan' McMahon? But nabocklesh! 'Paddy,' what'll you have?"

"Is that Grace Reilly on the flure? Faix, avourneen, you can do it; divil o' your likes I *see* anywhere. I'll lay my fiddle to a penny trump that you could

366

dance your own namesake, 'The Colleen dhas dhoun,' the [bonnie brown girl] upon a spider's cobweb widout breakin' it. Don't be in a hurry, Grace dear, to tie 'the knot; I'll wait for you."

Poor "Mickey" was always playing jokes on the boys, such as asking them to bring him a candle, or getting them to lead him out on account of the night being dark or something equally absurd for a man who was stone blind. He was a professional fiddler when Carleton made his acquaintance about the year 1805, and, if alive, was an old man when immortalized by the great novelist.

JOHN MOOREHEAD

The subject of this sketch, who flourished in the latter half of the eighteenth century, was a native of the County of Armagh. His father, like "Piper" Jackson and "Parson" Stirling, was a violinist and piper of distinction, one of his pupils on the latter instrument being William Kennedy, a noted blind piper of Tanderagee, in the same county.

More famous than his father, John Moorehead won renown as a violinist and composer, and a place among the musical celebrities of the kingdom. It is recorded that he was violinist at the Worcester Festival of 1794, and afterwards played the viola in the orchestra of Sadler's Wells Theatre, London, in which his brother Alexander was leader. In 1798 he was violinist of Covent Garden Theatre and composed music for the above named and other theatres.

The adage that genius is akin to insanity has been well exemplified in this family, for both brothers became insane in middle life. Alexander died in a lunatic asylum at Liverpool in 1803, and John committed suicide by hanging a year later.

Among the latter's musical compositions, according to British Musical Biography, was "Speed the Plough," a famous country dance, written in 1799, whose sparkling strains have retained their popularity undiminished to the present day. Though regarded as an English tune from the fact of its being first heard in English theatres, it is decidedly Irish in character, and much as we have been disposed to include it in the *Dance Music of Ireland,* its alleged English origin effectively repressed the desire.

This delightful folktune germinated in the brain of an Irishman after all, and we are no longer barred from claiming it as our own.

PATRICK COUGHLAN

A native of Crossmalina, County Mayo, had a great reputation as a traditional fiddler in that part of the country. He must have been born about the beginning of the nineteenth century, for he was apparently beyond the scriptural age of seventy years when John McFadden knew him in his boyhood. He played with a free, sweeping bow and, notwithstanding his advanced years, this fine old musician—a type now, alas, very rare—maintained himself in comfort at the local dances and "patrons," which in those days dispelled the monotony of peasant life in poor, persecuted Ireland.

PETER KENNEDY

A worthy successor to Hugh O'Bierne, the famous fiddler of Ballinamore, County Leitrim, elsewhere alluded to, was Peter Kennedy, a farmer who lived a few miles out of town. Born about 1830, he is said to have had no superior in his day in the county, and we can well believe it, judging from the settings of his tunes which we have heard members of his family in Chicago play so delightfully.

Perhaps nothing better illustrates the fascinating influence of his music than the following: In the year 1895, Mr. John Gillan of Chicago embarked for a European trip, accompanied by his wife and son, Rev. John Gillan. While visiting the old home in the adjacent county of Longford Mr. Gillan heard of Mr. Kennedy's great reputation as a fiddler. Ever and always enthusiastic about the music of his native land, he made up his mind to call and not miss such an opportunity. So charmed was he by Mr. Kennedy's performance that he decided to remain in that vicinity instead of proceeding with his family to Rome, according to the original programme. Under their father's training, four of his children—Thomas, Frances, James, and Ellen became fine fiddlers. From personal knowledge we can testify that

JAMES KENNEDY

was a sweet, expressive fiddler, and, as far as time and tone are concerned, he left nothing to be desired. Almost as interesting as his music was the tuning and testing of his instrument. The combination of chords which he brought out in varied and rapid succession before attempting a tune convinced one that his teacher was a master of his art.

A farmer's son, born in the early sixties of the last century, he came to America to better his fortune, but did not follow music as a profession. Many of his tunes hitherto unpublished—and he never played a poor one—were noted down and printed in O'Neill's *Music of Ireland* and *The Dance Music of Ireland*. Of course those tunes, as well as others obtained from his sister Ellen, were learned from their father. A trip to the old home in the winter of 1912 revealed a deplorable state of affairs as far as music was concerned. There were neither fiddlers nor fiddles of any consequence. The spirit of emulation was dead, and not a fiddle of the Perry, or other valuable make, was left in the community. They had been quietly picked up for a few pounds each by speculators.

Since the disintegration of the Irish Music Club some years ago James Kennedy, now a park policeman, seldom swings the bow.

HUGH O'BIERNE

Away back in the early years of the nineteenh century there flourished a famous fiddler of the above name at Ballinamore, County Leitrim. Evidently overlooked by Dr. Petrie, he was encountered by William Forde, the noted Cork musician and collector of Irish airs in his travels. The meeting was turned to good account, for the latter availed himself of the stores of knowledge and musical skill which the generous minstrel placed at his service.

Speaking of the latter, when the Feis Ceoil authorities selected some of his contributions for publication, Dr. P. W. Joyce said: "O'Bierne belonged to a type of country musician to be found sixty or eighty years ago all over Ireland, full of love and enthusiasm for Irish music. But the type has all but vanished, for although there are still musicians, professional and amateur, thinly scattered throughout the country, they have, generally speaking, neither the skill nor the taste nor the knowledge of their predecessors."

John Salts

Among the many famous fiddlers who flourished around the middle of the nineteenth century in the southern part of County Leitrim and the contiguous territory of the County Roscommon, John Salts was deservedly prominent. He was not only a fine musician but an expert dancer, and, being a man of attractive personality, his popularity knew no limitation in that part of the country.

No less renowned as a fiddle player was his teacher

"Mudin" Chalk

whose profession was in a sense the result of necessity. In his infancy a hungry sow strolled into the house in search of provender and finding the baby sprawling on the floor, chewed off the fingers of the right hand before his mother could rescue him. Thus bereft of fingers, the bow had to be strapped on to his maimed hand and, notwithstanding this handicap, Chalk became famous for his music and execution.

The nickname *"Mudin"* (pronounced Moodheen) which eclipsed completely his Christian name, means in the Irish language "little hand without fingers." It will be remembered that the Irish have at all times been noted for the aptness of their descriptive nicknames and topography.

Bryan Sweeney

A professional blind fiddler, hailing from Esker, near Mohill, County Leitrim, was said to be unexcelled in his day, according to Mr. Peter Kennedy of Ballinamore, a celebrated player himself. He owned a valuable Perry fiddle for which he was offered a hundred pounds. The poor blind minstrel a year or so later stumbled and fell on the instrument and smashed it beyond repair.

Michael Rooney

A professional fiddler of Ballina, County Mayo, bore a great reputation for skill and execution in his circuit in that and the adjoining County of Sligo. He was about 35 years of age when Mr. Gillan heard him in 1850. Rooney enjoyed all his faculties unimpaired.

Another famous fiddler of the same generation known as

"Blind" Kernan

taught a noted fiddle player named Kennedy of Drumlisk, County Longford, and Terence Smith, now of Chicago. Many a pleasant hour Mr. Gillan spent listening to Kernan's music in 1850, when he played at the "Red Cow" tavern, a mile distant from the town of Longford.

Martin Roach

To most persons the mention of Kilrush brings to memory the second largest town in the county of Clare and it may be of interest to state that there are no less than five places so named in the *Topographical Dictionary of Ireland*. The Kilrush in which we are interested in this instance is a parish in the barony of Scarawalsh, County Wexford, the same in which Martin Roach, a fiddler of distinction, was born. Roach was a personal friend and sporting companion of

Samuel Rowsome, the celebrated farmer-piper, and his pupil George Carroll, who was considered to be the best resident piper of Wexford outside of the Rowsome family.

Martin Roach, who died in 1881, is still remembered as a first class traditional fiddle player, and as fine a specimen of Irish manhood as was to be found in that part of the country. Standing six feet two inches in his vamps, of perfect proportions, his handsome appearance and genial disposition went a long way to enhance his popularity as a musician. He had been taught by a poor demented migrant fiddler from Galway named Lynch, nicknamed "The Cove," a soubriquet he delighted in. Eccentric, but harmless, the latter fortified himself with all the accessories of his calling, such as tuning forks and scientific appliances for testing the tension of his fiddle strings, etc. Another of his foibles was the purchase of cheap music books of every conceivable kind, a practice in which he spent the greater part of his scant earnings.

DANIEL SULLIVAN

Everybody in Boston and the adjoining towns, and not a few from other parts of this broad land, knew or heard of "Dan" Sullivan, the great Irish fiddler, who departed this life at the end of June, 1912. Though an octogenarian, he was game to the last. A few days before his death he asked his son and namesake to accompany him on the piano while he played a few of his favorite tunes. Realizing that the end was near, he calmly announced that he would be dead soon, but that there was one man left in Boston who could play Irish music, and that was "Bill" Hanafin, his cherished friend and companion for twenty-three years.

The old minstrel's ancestors were of the Kerry stock, but his father being a traveling tradesman, won the heart of a charming colleen at Millstreet, County of Cork, and it was in that town the subject of our sketch was born. After the family had moved to Tralee, young "Dan" studied music under the Whelans, so renowned in their day, but spent much of his early manhood in the northern part of the county enjoying the company and example of "Mike" Hurley, a celebrated blind fiddler of those days.

While in a reminiscent mood one evening at Boston, the amiable old minstrel told his friend Hanafin how he came to lose the first fiddle he had ever owned. He was on his way one Sunday night to Hurley's house at Derrymore, west of Tralee, after playing all the afternoon for a country dance about three miles on the other side of Tralee. Meeting an ass on the road, and being by that time footsore and weary, he congratulated himself on his luck. The donkey, accustomed to ill usage, submitted patiently enough to "Dan's" getting on its back, but as for traveling—why, that was quite another matter. A liberal application of a branch of thorny furze which the rider managed to secure promptly overcame his reluctance, and he started off at rattling pace. With his fiddle under his arm, "Dan" straightened up proudly at the success of his expedient when the ass stopped as suddenly as a man who had forgotten his ticket, and the jockey continued a few yards further but landed on his head in the middle of the road. When the stellar display faded and "Dan" had partially recovered his senses, he groped around for his fiddle; but, alas! he found not a fiddle but a little bag of kindling wood, splintered beyond repair.

Twenty years of Mr. Sullivan's mature life were passed in London where he acquired some musical knowledge at the hands of a certain major. A brief visit to Ireland preceded his coming to America where he remained to the end of his days the most famous professional Irish fiddler in the eastern states.

No one possessed a greater store of ancient Irish airs for he was born and brought up in the midst of tradition and, true instinctive musician that he was, nothing of genuine worth ever escaped his receptive ear. His style of rendering plaintive melodies was extremely florid and involved, and though commendably liberal with his music generally, his choice selections were treasured for his friends.

Learning in Chicago of Mr. Sullivan's great abilities from "Patsy" Touhey, the noted Irish-American piper, the writer paid him a visit in 1905. Like "Paddy" Coneely, the Galway piper, who, according to Dr. Petrie, was over-anxious to display his skill on quadrilles and polkas, Mr. Sullivan insisted on playing concertos for our edification instead of the old Irish melodies we hungered for. Not only was he a teacher but a maker of violins, and like a child with a new toy he lectured us enthusiastically on the scale and capability of a new pipe chanter that he was just learning to manipulate. He was then 75 years old and, from his point of view, entertained us right royally. Still, were the programme one of our own choosing, the result would have been much more satisfactory.

JEREMIAH BREEN

The subject of this sketch hailed from the parish of Ballyconry between Listowell and Ballybunnian, County Kerry. Having lost his sight early in life, music was his only recourse, and as he had talent in that line he became an excellent fiddle player.

Besides playing at Sunday "patrons" with "Tom" Carthy, the centenarian piper of Ballybunnian, Breen made money teaching his art to farmers' sons and playing at Saturday night dances which were by no means uncommon in those days.

Among his pupils was Michael Kissane, a business man of Chicago, well known as one of the best Irish fiddlers in the city. Altogether Breen may be considered one of the most successful and prosperous of his class in the third quarter of the nineteenth century.

MAURICE CARMODY

In many ways the most noted of Jeremiah Breen's pupils was Maurice Carmody, a prosperous farmer near Listowell, County Kerry.

A perfect Adonis in looks and stature, he was no less fluent on the fiddle than supple as a dancer. His company was coveted and no man was better fitted than he to contribute to or enjoy the pleasures and pastimes of the Munster peasantry. Born in 1862, his love of music and sport found convenient opportunities for their indulgence, and from early youth Carmody was conspicuously identified with all local festivities. Richard Sullivan, an exceptionally clever dancer of the traditional style, was one of his boon companions in former days around Listowell.

DENIS SHEEHAN

Quite noted for his proficiency around the middle of the nineteenth century was Denis Sheehan, a professional fiddler of Abbeyfeale, County Limerick. He taught many pupils in that part of the country and was connected with a flourishing dancing school also.

Michael Hogan

One of the celebrated Hogan family of musicians of Cashel Tipperary; Michael, the second oldest of the five brothers, became a violinist. Although the members of the family who elected to play the Union pipes—the real national instrument—became famous, little is known of those who chose the fiddle as their favorite instrument.

A fiddle player of the first class, according to our best information, Michael Hogan lived and died, and left a family at Thurles. His younger brother

Larry Hogan

who is a traveling fiddler, sustains the family reputation for musical excellence. No further intelligence concerning him is available at this writing, except what may be found in the sketch of his father, Michael Hogan, in the chapter on famous pipers.

Michael McCormick

No fiddle player whose fame has been sounded in the "Land of the West" was so supreme in the art of rendering traditional Irish music, according to his Kings County friends, as Michael McCormick of Tullamore. His playing was the standard of excellence by which all violinists were judged, and to their disadvantage invariably, as the following instance will show:

One evening Sergt. James O'Neill, who noted down from the playing of others much of the music in the O'Neill Collections, was playing some slashing tunes in concert with Bernard Delaney, the celebrated piper, in the latter's parlor. After cutting loose on a few rounds of a particularly captivating reel, the sergeant, with a countenance lighted up with triumph, swung around to the audience as if inviting merited applause. Before the others could utter a word of approval, "Jack" Doolin, not at all enthused over the performance, yelled out "Oh. 'Barney,' you ought to hear McCormick play that. He was the boy that could put the right edge on it."

And so it was in every case. "Did you ever hear McCormick?" has become a byword among the "craft," for according to his "townies," McCormick stood unrivaled. His father James, who taught him, was blind, and though an excellent fiddler was excelled by his son.

Both were professionals and played at the races at Mullingar and other places as well as at the ordinary festivities common to all parts of the country. Michael the "Nonpareil" died in 1909 at the scriptural age of three score and ten years.

Patrick Whelan

A man like Mr. Whelan of Scarawalsh Bailycarney, Ferns, County Wexford, is a priceless acquisition in any community. Sincere, helpful, and talented, his presence is an inspiration, and to his influence may be traced much of the activity of the music revival movement in that part of the country. Passionately devoted to music himself, he has been a missionary among those musically inclined, traveling long distances and unselfishly imparting his musical knowledge without fee or reward, other than the consciousness of well-doing, and the pride which is his due when his proteges and pupils like the De Lacy family band become noted prize winners. He was born near Bree, some five miles southwest of Enniscorthy, County Wexford, in 1862, and learned very early in life to play some airs on the flute from John Breen. He joined the Bree Total Abstinence Fife and Drum Band when organized by Father Scallan in 1879. A year later he bought a fiddle and enrolled as one of James Sinnott's pupils. So clever was young Whelan on the flute that he played at the crossroads dances at Ballyhogue, and being equally precocious on the fiddle he was soon playing in concert with his teacher in public. In fact his progress was so rapid that in a short time he took Sinnott's place in playing for mummers and the subsequent dance when the weather was unfavorable or the teacher was disinclined to travel. But perhaps the reader would like to hear from Mr. Whelan himself.

"I was a born lover of native Irish melody, and as my memory extends over a period of forty years I have been a sorrowful witness of its decay almost to extinction—supplanted by a spiritless substitute scarcely deserving the name of music in any degree of comparison with our own beloved strains. Often have I entertained a kind of sorrowing hope that it would in some unaccountable way be preserved from oblivion to which it was fast being consigned; yet I never expected to see my hopes so fully realized as in the publication of your magnificent collections."

We will have to pass over Mr. Whelan's laudation of the present writer's contributions to the cause as being too personal, and pick up the thread of his correspondence further along. Speaking of O'Neill's *Music of Ireland*: "It is my dearest possession; it never palls, never tires. I read, recite, for it is in itself a language—and rehearse with fiddle or bagpipe or flageolet, day in and day out, only to find I can never indulge the passion to satiety.

"Going through the pages listlessly, my eyes rest upon the first classified reel, 'The Girl Who Broke My Heart'. The act re-awakens the celestial strains of 'Jemmy' Sinnott's fiddle, although the hand that produced them has lain for thirty years in the grave. When I turn to the 'Irish Music Club', or 'Cronin's Favorite Reel', 'Jem' Cash, that prince of Irish pipers, is again in the flesh and I am in his presence, and my eyes with tears are wet. I often peruse the pages so intently and so long that when I close the book I see the characters reproduced upon the wall, and as thoughts will come unbidden I sometimes wonder if any of the great composers caught their inspiration in this way. Anon I find the names of the tunes grouping with additional words and short phrases forming word pictures like the following: 'Big Dan O'Mahony' took the 'Blackthorn Stick' to 'Smash the Windows' of the 'Church of Dromore' because the 'Minister's Daughter' played 'Hide and Go Seek' 'Behind the Haystack' with 'Johnny I Hardly Knew You.'"

Only extracts from Mr. Whelan's interesting but lengthy communications can find space in a work of this nature, but as music revival is our present subject, a glimpse of its practical results will not be amiss.

"'Tom' Mulligan, one of my earliest pupils, a wealthy farmer and fine specimen of Irish manhood, delights in giving lessons at his own house to all likely aspirants, two of whom have attained local distinction by their performances at public and parish concerts. 'Tom' himself always shunned the limelight, although he might be fairly taken as an abridged edition of your Edward Cronin. He was one of the best of reel players. The music broke upon the ear in waves, and with a passionate vehemence as if impatient of being so long pent up in a fiddle. I suppose this comes of the native gift of being able to lay on the accent properly. With a hand firm and strong he drew a volume of tone out of the instrument such as I have not yet heard any to equal, even the best of our 'tramp' fiddlers.

"The repose of his countenance while playing and the absence of muscular motion, save of his forearm and fingers, was truly phenomenal. We now live some ten miles apart, but Mulligan is still to the good, and doing service in his own unostentatious way to the beloved cause of traditional Irish music.

"'Pat' Breen, a schoolmate and companion, although he did not learn to play the fiddle until past 25, became a most versatile fiddler, playing not only jigs, reels, and hornpipes, but all kinds of tunes and melodies. He could read and memorize music by sight or hearing equally well, and then transcribe the same accurately.

"For a farmer of brawny muscle his delicacy of touch was no less wonderful than his faculty for the absolutely correct apportionment of time, even in the very quickest movement. And those were only half his qualifications, for in rendering an accompaniment to a singer or in solo, as an exponent of song air he had no compeer beneath the professional rank. He infused his renderings of national songs, whether vocal or instrumental, with the true soul of music."

Alas, for the attainments and virtues of our most cherished friends! Death, which loves a shining mark and is no respector of persons, beckoned the gifted Breen to eternity in the year 1906.

Mr. Whelan writes interestingly of the Ross and Ormonde families to whom music is an inheritance as well as an acquirement, and of several youthful enthusiasts in making, mending, and playing musical instruments; but, as before stated, the De Lacy family band or "Musical Nine" are his special pride. A glance at the picture of the group will be more instructive than a page of description.

In closing our sketch of this shining exemplar in a cherished cause perhaps an extract from a *postscript* to his latest letter may not be inappropriate.

"P. S. Often when out from home or going on a journey I find diversion in calling to mind the names of tunes in the following or similar manner until I can remember every one in the book.

"The 'One-horned Cow', after browsing in the 'Garden of Daisies' and destroying half the 'Blooming Meadows' the 'Night before Larry was Stretched' whipped the 'Old Plaid Shawl' and 'Jackson's Frieze Coat' from off the 'Tinware Lass' and "Spellan, the Fiddler' when they lay among the 'Turkeys in the Straw'. Not yet subdued, she hooked the 'Ladies Pantalettes' from the 'Yellow Legs' of the 'Maid in the Cherry Tree', ate the 'New Apron' on the 'Dark Girl Dressed in Blue', chewed 'Paddy Hagerty's Leather Breeches' and licked the nap off 'Jerry's Beaver Hat', in which he wore the 'White Cockade' at the 'Siege of Troy' and the 'Battle of Aughrim' and the 'Downfall of Paris'."

Regretfully we must take leave of the versatile Patrick Whelan and leave to conjecture the fate which befell the one-horned bovine guerilla after her career of rapacity and rambunctiousness.

JAMES SINNOTT

No name stands out more prominently among the noted minstrels and musicians of central Wexford in the late generations than that of James Sinnott. Born in the year 1800, at the village of Bree (some ten miles south of Enniscorthy), where his parents kept a general store, young Sinnott's life was dedicated to music. Afflicted with defective vision from birth, he was placed at a very early age under the tuition of a celebrated Irish fiddler named Curran, "whose fame has been forgotten," in the language of Mr. Patrick Whelan, our correspondent, "and whose biography has been left unwritten—a fate shared by many a deserving genius of the Irish race in this and other periods of our national history." "Jemmy" Sinnott was a precocious youngster for it is reported that when but nine years old he fiddled for the entertainment of customers. He readily mastered the rudiments of music and acquired a knowledge of the principles of harmony and composition, and was looked up to as an authority on musical history, especially those features relating to the origin and development of musical instruments.

A man of fine physique—strong and athletic—he was unrivaled in his profession, and being also exemplary in his habits, we can well believe that none could boast of greater popularity in the community. In wit and sarcasm like the bard O'Carolan he was equally keen, but the latter gift was sparingly displayed except under provocation.

One night at a party a youth was presented to him as a musical prodigy by his admiring friends. "Jemmy", with the his sightless orbs directed straight at the embryo Paganini, handed him his fiddle and said abruptly "Oh man anouns! Play something." The young fellow, unprepared for this turn of affairs, blushed to the roots of his hair, but timidly taking the proffered instrument, played a tune as best he could, and returning it, stood modestly awaiting the approbation which he felt his effort deserved.

"And, my boy, what name do you call that tune you were playing?" quizzically inquired the professor.

" 'The Girl I Left Behind Me,' sir," replied the prodigy in the flush of his fancied success.

"Oh, then, that was the girl who had the good luck in store the day you turned your back upon her?" was the crushing remark of his questioner.

The great musician didn't always have the best of it, however.

"Arrah where are you going now, Darby?" he once asked a "gaum" or simpleton.

"No place," was the gruff answer.

"And whereabouts is no place, Darby?" continued Sinnott.

"Shut your eyes and you'll see," was the startling response of the "gaum" to the man of music, thus illustrating the old Irish proverb which reckoned a fool's reply as one of the sharpest things in existence.

As an accompanist to traditional singing, "Jemmy" Sinnott enjoyed a great reputation, for his knowledge of folk songs and the airs to which they were adapted was phenomenal.

As a professional fiddler his circuit did not extend beyond a day's journey, but within the compass of his travels he was a veritable musical missionary. He played at barn dances, social gatherings, weddings, christenings and other festivities, and this mode of life he continued unremittingly up to within one year of his death, which occurred in January, 1884. Though defective in sight from birth, he had not become totally blind until late in life.

With a sweeping bow he phrased the melody or tune according to his fancy—staccato or legato—and in his masterly execution the most simple tune realized unexpected possibilities. The exuberance of graces skillfully interwoven into the texture of the theme left nothing to be desired in the way of traditional embellishment. "The gorgeous coloring imparted to his renderings," says Mr. Whelan, "still dwells in the memory of those who once heard, and refuses to be forgotten even after the lapse of years."

No less famous as a teacher than as a performer, Sinnott is said to have taught more "scholars" than any other man of his class in Ireland. Among his most distinguished pupils were Edward Evoy, Knockstown; Patrick Cummins, Raheenduff; Thomas Canning and John J. Evoy of Adamstown; Peter Moran, a farmer of the parish of Glynn; Thomas Asple, of Galbally, County Councilor, an enthusiastic revivalist; Thomas Asple, his cousin; Patrick O'Brien, District Councilor, Hayestown, Taghmon; Philip Cogley, Galbally; Denis Whelan, of Scarawash, Bree; Christopher Maddock, of Glynn; Moses O'Brien, of Wilkinstown, Taghmon; Paul Roche, Bridgetown; and Thomas Freeman, New Ross. His last pupils were Martin and Patrick Whelan of Scarawalsh, the latter being authority for the leading features in the career of the talented and much esteemed musician.

For the last twenty-five years of his life Sinnott lived as a squatter in a little house to which there were two small gardens attached, and which he enjoyed as a free holding on the top of Raheenahone, Burren mountain. Becoming afflicted with cancer on his lower lip in his eightieth year, he had a presentiment that it had come for his death as both his father and grandfather had died at that age. However, he bravely underwent a surgical operation and survived it four years; and Mr. Whelan assures us that having never before been so long separated from his beloved fiddle, their reunion was a thrilling experience.

No music, ancient or modern, came amiss to Sinnott, and he could cater to any company, "gentle or simple," for his mind was a musical treasury. Great as was his reputation, he magnanimously acknowledged a master—one Patrick Quinn of Enniscorthy, whose brilliant career ended prematurely some sixty years ago. He walked off the quay at Enniscorthy one dark and stormy night, and as the river Slaney was in flood at the time, the incomparable Quinn was drowned.

As the clay fell on the coffin enclosing the mortal remains of "Jemmy" Sinnott on a cold morning in January, 1884, his sorrowing friends and pupils could not help regretting the treasures of melody and music lore which passed away with him beyond recovery.

Thomas Mulligan

Not only is Thomas Mulligan—one of "Jemmy" Sinnott's pupils—a famous fiddler, but he is also engaged in the musical "uplift." He was born in 1869, and is a prosperous farmer at Garrenstacle, Bree, County Wexford. In connection with the Bree Dramatic Class, recently organized, Mulligan became the leader of an orchestra consisting of five fiddles, two concert flutes and a piccolo. Three of his pupils—Joseph O'Donahue, Thomas Mernach, and James Sinnott, with a young prodigy named Patrick Clancy—swing the bow, while the chief manipulator of the flutes is Martin Byrne, a prize winner in his line.

The boys of Wexford, it seems, are still to the forefront in all that pertains to Irish nationality.

Sergt. Bernard Kelly

It is surprising how many fine musicians are to be found among the Irish constabulary who, owing to the peculiar conditions and sentiments heretofore existing in Ireland, were doomed, like the flowers of the forest, to waste their sweetness on the desert air of the barrack room. The Royal Irish Constabulary band of Dublin, by the way, is one of the most noted in the kingdom. In America, where all officers of the law are citizens and voters and reside with their families promiscuously in the community and are rather looked up to than otherwise, members of the police force are not objects of prejudice either in private or public life. Being neither constables nor employes of an unpopular government, the American police are peace officers of the State and Municipality and therefore men of standing in the commonwealth.

At a popular demonstration at Ferns, County Wexford, a few years ago, so many bands from the surrounding country attended that the De Lacy Warpipe band were crowded into the police barrack while processions and functions of a solemn and religious character were being conducted. The presence of the De Lacy band naturally attracted people from the street. Influenced, no doubt, by the musical atmosphere, one constable took down his fiddle—one of extraordinary tonal qualities—and rattled off "The Bush in Bloom," "The Harvest Home" and "The Star of Munster."

So inspiring was the example that Sergt. Kelly, a native of Queen's county, came in and took down his fiddle, which had hung up unused since the death of his wife two years before, and started to play. And play he did in grand style and tone when he warmed up to it.

"Playing by note" he regarded as a matter of minor importance once the tune had been acquired. Unconscious that he was drawing a "full house" as the strains of his melody floated through the open doors into the highway, the Irishman beneath the king's livery broke loose from the trammels of officialdom and he reveled in the delights of traditional melody until he found to his dismay on looking around that he was playing to a spellbound audience, among them being his five subordinates and four or five constables from other stations.

Laying down the fiddle, Sergt. Kelly, in real alarm, shouted to his force "Get out, every one of you! Here you all are and not a man in the town if anything happens." Before he could use his cane they had vanished with alacrity.

As a fiddler of the traditional stamp, the sergeant was a "rouser," and being kindly and forbearing, he enjoyed a popularity by no means common to his calling. Now retired on pension, his keen sense of humor, so noticeable among instinctively musical people, and his tuneful fiddle, will, it is to be hoped, render the sunset years of his life pleasant and enjoyable.

Patrick Dunne

When it became publicly known a dozen years ago that some practical steps had been taken towards the preservation of Irish folk tunes in Chicago, one of the first to communicate with the writer on the subject was Patrick Dunne, a Tipperary farmer, of Kilbraugh, the Commons parish of Ballingarry, not far from Thurles. Not only was his sympathetic encouragement an inspiration, but the pages of manuscript music which he unselfishly forwarded proved that kindred spirits in every hobby can be found the world over and that the vastness of Ireland's musical remains can hardly be overestimated.

Mr. Dunne's musical training on the fiddle was obtained from the Morrises of Ballysloe, and splendid fiddlers they were in the opinion of their famous pupil. Following the footsteps of so many of their class, the whole family— father, four sons and two daughters—emigrated to America in the early seventies, where their profession is not looked upon with disfavor.

We can well imagine what cheer and jollity a man of Mr. Dunne's temperament and talent can promote in any community with his fiddle; and even though burdened with a farmer's responsibilities, he found time to attend Feiseanna at Kilkenny, Waterford and Carrick-on-Suir, and capture first prizes at each of the musical competitions.

Regretfully he admits, while nearing the three score milestone in the highway of life, that the outlook for the revival of Irish music is not all that could be desired, for there is but little incentive and less example to stimulate or foster its study and practice.

WILLIAM HENNESSY

Round about the year 1863 a strikingly handsome young fiddle player named William Hennessy happened along to the parish of Ballingarry, barony of Slievardagh, County Tipperary. He was about thirty years of age, over six feet tall and soldierly in his bearing; but his personal attractions were not a circumstance to the fascination of his music. Like the pipers of old who were said to have been kidnapped by the fairies, Hennessy could not get away from his admirers. So many were anxious to learn from him that he was prevailed on to remain and teach. In the language of our friend, Mr. Patrick Dunne of Kilbraugh, "they made a god of him." Not a few of his pupils made rapid progress and gave promise of future fame, when Hennessy's eyesight began to fail and he was obliged to become an inmate of the Urlingford Union or Infirmary, where he died in 1867.

His parents, a respectable old couple, came to the parish after their son's death. The father, who was a much less distinguished performer than his son, proved a very capable teacher. The associations were too painful, however, and they left after a short stay, presumably for Cork, their native county.

The suspicion that William Hennessy had military training proved correct for it developed that he had served as bandmaster in the army for a time.

THE HIGGINS BROTHERS

of Kilkenny whose parents, long since dead, hailed from Killenaule, County Tipperary, are said to rank among the best in their profession in Leinster, at least in this generation.

MICHAEL HIGGINS

One of the trio is a traveling fiddler of whom no other information is available at this writing.

JAMES HIGGINS

lives in the town of Kilkenny and has an interesting family, all musicians, while

THOMAS HIGGINS

who is reputed to have had few equals, is said to be suffering from the effects of a specialized brand of Irish hospitality.

According to Rev. Dr. Henebry, "Tom" Higgins, a famous fiddler and descendant of fiddlers and musicians, "is the last representative of Irish professionalism in music." Born in Kilkenny and taught by his father, he often played in concert with James Cash of Wicklow, whose performance on the Union pipes proved so fascinating to the fair sex. Higgins had a phenomenal bow hand, and his peculiar emphatic "sweeps" gave his reels an indescribable charm. His reverence never saw anything to equal the pliancy of his wrist and consequent command of the bow.

PATRICK O'LEARY

In all that tends to promote the regeneration of Irish ideals in music and dancing, language and literature, among the "Exiles of Erin" at the Antipodes no one is more persistent, potent, and practical, than Patrick O'Leary of Eastwood, Parkside, Adelaide, South Australia.

Endowed with an attractive personality and gifted with uncommon musical attainments, his correspondence proclaims him a writer of no ordinary ability, and were his lofty sentiments and patriotic ardor shared by any considerable portion of his countrymen, Ireland would not be regarded as it is by some—a spot on the map, or a term in geography.

In every movement designed for the rehabilitation of the old land, Mr. O'Leary's name figures conspicuously as organizer, chairman, and even entertainer; for being a fine violinist of the old school, and playing in concert with his no less talented son Eugene on the piano, their joint performance is a rare musical treat.

Phonograph records of Mr. O'Leary's fiddle-playing which we enjoyed at the home of his brother Owen, and sister, Mrs. Kelsey, in Chicago, justify any eulogy which our words could express.

Though his surname is suggestive of Munster origin, the subject of our sketch hails from Benwilt, Drumgoon, near Cootehill, in the county of Cavan, where he was born in 1851. Race suicide found no favor in those days evidently, for Patrick was the youngest in a family of seven sons and five daughters. Before emigrating to Australia in 1876 he had spent a few uneventful years in the United States. From an humble position in that far off land he has risen to that of head attendant of Mental Hospital, Parkside, Adelaide, an office of responsibility and emolument.

His letters to *The Anglo-Celt* of his native county in the interests of the Gaelic Revival should be an inspiration to the "Old Folks at Home" from an expatriated Irishman.

Speaking of those who engage in the "uplift" in any line of undertaking, he says: "The bravest, best, noblest, and most gifted have been assailed, misrepresented and maligned by those for whom they have struggled, labored and died, and it seems to be their lot to feel the pangs of hostility and ingratitude from quarters whence it was least expected or deserved." This bit of moralizing is but the reflex of a transitory reminiscence, and he passes on to tell of more cheerful things: "I had the pleasure of playing that grand old reel, 'Kiss the Maid Behind the Barrel,' on the City Hall stage on St. Patrick's night, 1905. It was tastefully danced by four strapping young lads and received a flattering ovation. My son accompanied me on the piano and I was delighted it went off so well."

With the death of John Coughlan, they were left without an Irish piper in that part of Australia at least, so the "progressives," with Mr. O'Leary at their head, set about introducing the Warpipes, or its later development, the Brian Boru pipes. An appeal through the press for funds to all lovers of Irish music brought them one hundred and sixty pounds sterling, and nine young men began to learn, not under the instruction of a piper, mind you, (for they had none) but a clarinet player and bandmaster. Eugene O'Leary being the Honorable Secretary to the club, there is no lack of enthusiasm.

Many years ago Mr. O'Leary endeavored to obtain a set of Union pipes—the perfected Irish instrument—from an aged piper named Kelly who used to wander about the country, but his efforts were unsuccessful, as the old minstrel had disappeared and finally died in some institution. At one of the meetings of the Band Committee an old man strolled into the room carrying an old faded and worn bag under his arm, and sat beside Mr. O'Leary. "What have I in the bag, eh? Wisha sure, 'tis only an ould set of Union pipes." His questioner promptly assisted him in dragging forth the ancient instrument, the tones of which had haunted him since boyhood days. "Och sure they're no good to me. I got them from poor ould Kelly before he died, but I can't play 'em at all." For ten shillings Mr. O'Leary gained possession of his long-sought treasure after nearly twenty years of fruitless search. Without reeds and in a state of delapidation the old minstrel's instrument was taken home in triumph but remained out of commission for a long time, there being no one capable of putting it in order, until an Englishman—a Northumbrian piper—happened along one day and undertook the job.

The newcomer had a beautiful instrument on which he could play jigs and hornpipes quite well, and in rendering the border minstrelsy of both England and Scotland his performance left little to be desired.

The big drone of the Northumberland small pipes which Mr. O'Leary describes, was only twelve inches long, the other four drones being smaller in proportion. The tone is sweet and pleasing. They are, in fact, a replica of the Irish Union pipes with the exception of the chanter which has fourteen keys and is permanently stopped at the bottom.

"The Northumbrian pipes go well with the fiddle," Mr. O'Leary continues, "and we are able to play very well together owing to the fact that I had spent some years learning Scotch dance music and melodies.

All movements in pursuit of an object either political, social, or musical, are, of course, much discussed by those interested, and more or less valuable information is obtained, often from unexpected sources and out-of-the-way places. The discovery of an Irish piper through a correspondent in the Murray River country, some seventy or eighty miles back from Adelaide, was a rare find indeed. So Mr. O'Leary lost no time in communicating with the backwoods minstrel, Mr. Critchley by name. Nothing loth, the latter promptly accepted the invitation to come to the city, where suitable arrangements were made to have an Irish night at the "Catholic Club" on his arrival.

To attempt to edit Mr. O'Leary's account of subsequent events, and the tumultuous emotions which thronged his breast, would be little short of sacrilege, so we will let the patriotic exile tell the story himself:

I will now try and explain to you my thoughts, feelings, and emotions on hearing and seeing the Union pipes played after a lapse of forty-one years—from 1869 to 1910.

As the time for the piper's arrival drew near I sauntered to the railway depot to meet him, and as I trudged along, Keegan's beautiful lines,

> One winter's day, long, long ago
> When I was a little fellow,
> A piper wandered to our door
> Grey-headed, blind and yellow,

occurred to my memory, and I mentally recited the verses until I arrived at the depot where I discovered *"Caoch"* awaiting me. I brought him home in triumph, and he drew forth the long wished for Union pipes, and also a set of Brian Boru warpipes which he had ordered from Melbourne some time before. But the

Patrick O'Leary

gay and gaudy warpipes had no charm for me as compared with the ancient, much-worn and loved Union pipes. A mist came over my eyes, an uncontrollable rush of feelings and emotions almost shook my very soul. Delight, sorrow, sad memories of the long ago, the old home, the old scenes, the old barn, poor old Phil Goodman the piper, the innocent gay and light-hearted lads and lasses that were assembled on the last night, forty-one years ago, flashed across my mental vision. I could not speak, I tried to pull myself together while I examined the well loved instrument that had so often filled my boyish heart and soul with delight while vainly trying to quell the torrent that was choking me.

Piper Critchley tuned up and commenced to play while I sat with bowed head listening to the well remembered, soft and pleading strains. I seized my fiddle, tuned up with the chanter, and fixing that glorious book, O'Neill *Music of Ireland,* before me, I bade farewell to Australia.

My spirit took wing and I passed—

> Over islands and continents;
> The wide ocean's main—
> Soon sighted Cape Clear
> On my soul's aeroplane;
> Soon viewed the loved haunts,
> With my heart throbs and tears,
> And caressed the loved ones
> Through the vista of years;
> Saw the shadowy forms,
> Through dim dawn of day,
> Of the dear ones I loved,
> Long since turn'd to clay.

We passed over beauteous Munster to the "Banks of the Ilen" and "Tralibane Bridge," where we paid a heartful homage to the spot that gave you birth.

Soon I renewed my acquaintance with the loves of my youth, the peerless "Miss Monaghan," "Bonnie Kate," "Miss Thornton," "The Dark-haired Lass," and "The Merry Sisters," all fresh, fair, beautiful, and enchanting as when I first heard them. "The Bucks of Oranmore," "Buckley's Fancy," and "The Bush in Bloom," then engaged our fancy until we had "A Cup of Tea" with "Drowsy Maggie" and "The Dublin Lasses" while awaiting "Corney's Coming."

We next visited "Peter Street" and the beautiful "Bank of Ireland," and afterwards dwelt long and lovingly on "The Dublin Reel." On the way to "Mooncoin," we picked up the ever green and always beautiful "Ivy Leaf," after which we enjoyed ourselves "Rolling on the Ryegrass." The piper then invited me to help him "Toss the Feathers." This we did with a vim and then indulged in a long interview with "The Scholar" fresh from "Salamanca," also "Lord Gordon," with his friends, "Col. Fraser" and "Col. McBain," accompanied by the beautiful "Miss Wallace" and the "Fermoy Lasses." To this delightful company we bade a reluctant farewell, toasting their healths in "A Flowing Bowl," and mounting the "New Mailcoach," we arrived in time for "The Fox Chase." After a merry run, our attention was attracted to "The Boyne Hunt," which brought us to the banks of the historic river where we met that beautiful but contentious nymph, who, when interviewed, emphatically declared that she was intensely Irish of the Irish—but she added, "like all good things in Ireland, I was seized by the invader and compelled to serve a vile purpose." I felt the truth of her statement and assured her that the date was already visible to the clearsighted when her dishonorable occupation would be gone, and she would be restored to the honored position that her beauty and charm entitled her to.

During the colloquy I kept my eye on the piper just to see how he'd stand it. He wisely suggested that we had better try and "Kiss the Maid Behind the Barrel," and this labor of love we accomplished with a fervor that left nothing to be desired.

Breathless after this pleasing incident, we engaged in the "Five Mile Chase," and soon arrived at the historic "Rock of Muff," otherwise "The Star of Munster." This wild, beautiful, and thrilling melody was a great favorite in Cavan, and was named after the high plateau-topped rock near Kingscourt, on which an annual Feis is held. We next indulged in a "Trip to the Cottage," and started "Round the World for Sport," incidentally calling on "My Love in America." We lingered longingly in the famous Jackson's everblooming "Flowery Garden" at Creeve, County Monaghan, and being but a few miles from Cootehill, courtesy suggested that we pay our respects to the distracted "Nell Flaherty" on the loss of her beautiful "Drake."

From mirth to sadness is but a step. I realized when my eye caught a glimpse of the Lament for "Capt. O'Kane or the Wounded Hussar." The hero of a hundred fights, from Landon to Oudenarde, who, when old and war-worn, tottered back from the Low Countries to his birthplace to die, and found himself not only a stranger, but an outlawed, disinherited, homeless wanderer in the ancient territory that his fathers ruled as Lords of Limavady. His friend and sympathizer, the illustrious Turlogh O'Carolan, has immortalized his name in strains the most plaintive and touching.

On the old racecourse of Cootehill and within a stone throw of the home of my father, I again met "Jack o'Lattan," the product of the musical genius of the renowned "Piper" Jackson. In all directions could be seen "The Swallow's Tail," as well as the verdant corn and unmown hay waving gently with "The Wind that Shakes the Barley," and crowding thickly round the dance circle were the dimly remembered forms and faces of the dancers of fifty years ago, long since passed into the unknown beyond. Full of sadness, my eyes fell on the "Shan Van Vocht," but a thrill of joy flashed through my brain as I recalled the prophetic utterance of O'Connell, for I know that a race now tread these plains,

> With hot blood in their veins,
> Who will burst her galling chains—

A hand was laid softly on my shoulder: I looked up. It was my good wife, who reminded me that tea had been ready for some time. This recalled me from the past to the present and I found myself back in Australia. A glance at my watch showed that the piper and I had played without intermission from one to six-thirty o'clock that afternoon, so we laid away the fiddle and the pipes and "*The Music of Ireland,*" with mingled emotions of joy, sadness, and regret.

Oh God! how I sighed for one month with the O'Neills, Cronin, McFadden, Dillon, Delaney, Early, Enright, Kennedy, Ennis, Kerwin, etc., of the "Irish Music Club" of Chicago, but alas, fate has decreed that, situated as I am on the opposite side of the globe, the joys of such companionship can never be mine.

Mr. Critchley inherited the pipes from his father, who was an accomplished player. He emigrated from his native Wicklow to Australia in 1849, and played around the diggings at Forest Creek, Ballarat, and Bendigo, in the early fifties, and the pipes certainly looked as if they had many and varied experiences. From long-continued fingering the chanter was deeply indented at the vents. The pipes were old ere their advent in Australia over sixty years ago. As they lay on the table, worn, faded, dingy, and dented, with one drone missing, a second reedless and mute, and a third twisted and bent by the fierce heat and varying temperature of sixty subtropical summers, they reminded me of a once beautiful and world-famous prima donna shorn of her beauty, and glories forgotten, and impoverished, and all but dead.

Oh no; surely there are still devoted lovers left who will worship at the shrine of this beautiful and matchless interpreter of our incomparable Irish music. Surely, oh! surely, that magnificent organization of Ireland's choicest sons and daughters—The Gaelic League—will rescue and restore this famous stricken prima donna, who, neglected, forsaken, and alone, has sought shelter in obscure places to die. Surely they will raise up and place her in the proud position that she should occupy—the Prima Donna of Ireland's Music.

There was a sadness almost tragic in those old and service-worn pipes. Where, Oh! where, are the glad-hearted boys and girls who tripped gracefully and joyously to their strains, seventy, eighty, perchance a hundred, years ago?

God only knows. The unconquerable Michael Dwyer may have danced to their music on the day of his bridal,

> When Mary came in her beauty,
> The loveliest maid of Imael,
> The sweetest flower that blossomed
> In all the wild haunts of the vale.

Well, the piper slept soundly that night, and in the morning early I called him up—not to hear him play "The Wind that Shakes the Barley," but to catch the early morning coach to his distant home on the banks of the lonely and legend-less Murray, where the wild scream of the parrot, the raucous yell of the cocka-too, and the mocking shout of the laughing jackass, are the sole incentives to music.

My dear sir, I feel that I am wearying you with this almost interminable epistle, but you can recognize that when a man is full of a subject he rarely possesses that nice sense of discretion which warns him that it is time to leave off. I feel isolated as there are hardly any Irish musicians in Adelaide, and still fewer to whom I can unfold my thoughts and feelings on a subject so absorbing, so overpowering and, alas, so unsatisfied—always yearning for that which I cannot obtain—the fellowship of genuine Irish musicians.

I remain, dear sir, your most sincere and deeply grateful friend,

April 18, 1911.　　　　　　　　　　　　　　　　Patrick O'Leary.

James Whiteside (The Bard of Bray)

Who in this generation more faithfully typifies the bard of ancient days than James Whiteside of Bray, County Wicklow—scholar, poet, musician, and composer? Nothing, except perhaps a flowing beard, would improve the com-bination. Delicacy forbids us to mention the date of his birth, as he is still a bachelor, though confessedly wedded to art. But a quotation from his delightful correspondence epitomizes that story in language both candid and concise:

Yours truly,

James Whiteside

" The Bard of Bray "

"I am an ex-National Teacher, having retired on pension after forty years' service, so I have plenty of time to devote to my favorite hobby—music. I have been awarded first prize on two occasions: at *Oireachtas,* 1903, and *Feis Ceoil,* 1906, for the best performance of Irish music on the violin; and I also play the Irish harp, Irish pipes, and piano, all of which I have in my room. I am the holder of a certificate for drawing also; so I must solace myself with painting, poetry, and music, never having been lucky enough to get a wife."

Mr. Whiteside being a handsome man, we must leave to conjecture the cause of his celibacy. After all, we may as well admit that the versatile bard was born in 1844, his place of birth being in the County Monaghan.

Did he not openly attribute his good health and exemption from ailments to the effects of total abstinence, we could well surmise his temperance tendencies from the opening lines of several of his original songs, he being the author of no less than two score of them. For instance:

> "Sobriety is making way in the Ireland of today,"
> "Fill the bumper fair, every drop is poison,"
> "Will you walk into my parlor said the spider to the fly?
> 'Tis the prettiest little drunkery that ever you did spy,"
> "O! Join the Abstainers, and you'll be the Gainers."

In his Anti-Emigration Song, what could be more poetic or pathetic than the cry of blended alarm and regret—

> "They are going, they are going, and a mother's tears are flowing"?

One would scarcely expect to find such emotional phraseology as "O! My Colleen's a Darling," "My Darling Rose in Beauty Grows," or "Our Honeymoon It Was in June," in the diction of an incorrigible bachelor like "The Bard of Bray." What could be prettier or more natural than "My Pretty Little Girl, Won't You Come Along with Me?" as a name for a song when its author was but twenty years of age. Perhaps the coquettish little thing didn't respond, and her coldness fatally chilled the tender germs of love in a sensitive heart. Who knows?

Such a galaxy of songs—moral, sentimental, and patriotic—and such a selection of musical compositions, airs, dance tunes, and lullabies, has Mr. Whiteside produced that we know not which to admire most. It is gratifying to know that his genius is appreciated, for his patrons hail from near and far, including Scotland, England, and America.

"It was on the Hill of Howth, I believe, that Saint Patrick preached to the heathen Irish, converting them to Christianity," says a writer in *The People* of Dublin, August 14, 1910; "and it was here also, one Sunday afternoon, that I fell under the spell of an apostle of the temperance movement. A musical apostle he was, dressed in an evening suit, with a tall hat, and his breast bedizened with ribbons green and yellow—decorations and badges of which the meaning was beyond me. But his instrument was a fiddle, and he sang to the tune of it— not standing or sitting, but marching up and down with a swaggering air like a Highland piper. He had a fine, noble, and distinguished presence, had this Hill of Howth fiddler, and might have sat to a painter for the figure of an ancient bard. I only hope those bards of old could finger their strings as effectively as my apostolic friend on the Hill of Howth. Like Richard Wagner, he was the author of his own songs, and the one he was now treating me to was called 'Pat of Enniscorthy,' a very good song indeed, of the rousing, rattling kind, whereof the moral was the awful consequences of drink, and the evils which excessive indulgence in whiskey had entailed on 'Poor Ould Ireland.'"

The bard whose mien and music so won the admiration of the Dublin writer was the subject of our sketch, James Whiteside.

With characteristic graciousness, he has submitted his manuscript collection of Irish music amounting to nearly 200 numbers, to Dr. P. W. Joyce of Dublin, who will include a selection therefrom in his next work.

An edifying *Essay on Irish Music and Dancing, Accompaniments, etc.,* from the facile pen of our bard, we find, much to our regret, too comprehensive for our pages.

THOMAS FITZGERALD

Whether famous, fair, or farcical as performers, a large percentage of Irish minstrels for more than a generation, sad to relate, end their days in the Unions or poorhouses.

One of the last of them was "Tom" Fitzgerald, an exceptionally fine fiddler, who played around Dublin for years, and died in 1909 an inmate of the South Union, when less than fifty years old. Competent authorities claim that he had no equal in the city or vicinity as a traditional performer, yet he never sought honors at the Feis Ceoil competitions.

A native of Tramore, County Waterford, "Tom" Fitzgerald was one of a family of fiddlers, and was taught by one "Jerry" Martin, the most renowned instrumentalist in that part of the country in his day.

In the words of one who heard him play at a Dublin concert or entertainment, "'Tom' Fitzgerald, fiddler, was a revelation of traditional playing. He made the violin speak with the Irish voice."

MRS. BRIDGET KENNY, "THE QUEEN OF IRISH FIDDLERS."

In no country save Ireland, would a violinist of such demonstrated ability as the subject of this sketch remain unappreciated and practically unnoticed, while obliged by necessity to contribute to the support of a large family by playing for a precarious pittance along the highways and byways of Dublin for a generation or more.

The Gaelic Revival brought Mrs. Kenny into the limelight, and after she had outclassed all competitors as a traditional violinist at the annual Feiseanna, winning first prize year after year, she was proclaimed "The Queen of Irish Fiddlers."

This remarkable woman's talents ought to have been regarded as a national asset. Yet it does not appear that any effort was made to take advantage of the opportunities presented by her discovery, by the establishment of a school in which the much-vaunted traditional style of rendering Irish music would be taught and perpetuated.

No. "The Queen of Irish Fiddlers," amid salvos of applause, was handed her first prize with monotonous regularity, and allowed to pass out and resume her daily perambulations as before, along the streets of the Irish capital, to woo the reluctant coin from purses often no less slender than her own.

The musical faculty, not wealth nor station, was her inheritance as the daughter of John McDonough, the premier Irish piper of his day and generation, who passed away in obscurity in his native County of Galway more than half a century ago, when little Bridget was less than two years old.

Mrs. Bridget Kenny

Artistic endowment is bound to find expression, and it is not surprising that this little child of genius should start to "play the fiddle" when but seven years of age. "I'm entirely self-taught, and I'm proud of it," is the way she put it when asked how she came to have such wonderful control of her instrument, "and I've never been beaten in playing jigs, reels, or hornpipes, for the last forty years."

A sister, Mary Anne, and a brother, John McDonough, both now dead, were also fine fiddle players.

"Mrs. Kenny is a very excellent performer, the best I have heard," a writer of discrimination reports. "She has a noticeable peculiarity in 'stopping and bowing' which is very quaint and attractive. About nine years ago I heard her for the first time in a bout of playing which lasted three hours. Three years ago I heard her again, and anything better than her rendering of the 'Flogging Reel' it is impossible to conceive. Her playing of airs pleases me not quite so well, but of course her circumstances precluded her from possessing a first-class instrument."

Born and bred in an atmosphere of music and tradition, it was but natural that Bridget McDonough, the fiddler, glorying in her art and a luxuriance of auburn tresses which "sthreeled" on the ground, would favor the suit of John Kenny, a piper, who laid seige to her heart. United by more ties than one, they have since continued to play in concert for a livelihood.

Mr. Kenny, however, does not confine himself exclusively to the Irish pipes, for he can take a turn with equal facility on the bass viol, fiddle, dulcimer, and tambourine.

Their joint collection of unpublished Irish music has been awarded a prize on three different occasions.

Devotion to art does not appear to have unfavorably affected the size of Mrs. Kenny's family, for we are informed she is the prolific mother of thirteen children. Neither did the artistic temperament on both sides mar the domestic peace of the Kenny home, and, though the goddess of plenty slighted them in the distribution of her favors, have they not wealth in health and the parentage of a house full of rosy-cheeked sons and daughters, several of whom bid fair to rival their mother, "The Queen of Irish Fiddlers," in the world of music.

John Flynn

With a luxuriance of snow-white locks encircling his sturdy shoulders like a mantle, a patriarchal beard dignifying a countenance both noble and placid, a Turveydrop in deportment, a Chesterfield in manners, and towering in stature— no bard of old could be more inspiring and impressive than John Flynn, the Bard of Erin, Wisconsin, whose likeness adorns our pages. Standing six feet three inches in his vamps, and erect in bearing as an Indian, a figure so remarkable could not fail to attract the attention of artists as a rare subject for their brush. Restrained by a modesty by no means characteristic of minstrels or musicians, of whom he is one of the most noteworthy, twice only has he been known to yield to importunities to pose for a picture, the last occasion being at the earnest solicitation of the writer in order to furnish a photo for the present work.

His parents, Timothy Flynn and Mary Wallace Flynn, were born near Mallow, in the County of Cork, Ireland, at the beginning of the nineteenth century, and there was nothing of which Mr. Flynn was more proud than having attended school in his boyhood days with Thomas Davis, the poet-patriot, and John Baptist Purcell, who when but thirty-two years of age became bishop of Cincinnati.

John Flynn

Like President Andrew Jackson, our hero, John Flynn, narrowly escaped being born an Irishman, for his parents had been in Massachusetts but a year or so at the time of his birth at Springfield in 1840.

Having saved some money as foreman of a railroad gang, Mr. Flynn started for the west in 1843 and landed at Milwaukee, it being then little better than an Indian village. He settled on a farm in Erin township, Washington County, where the youngest son, James—also a fiddler—was born, beneath the shadows of Wisconsin's primeval forest. "In very early years we had a fiddle in the house —a cheap affair," writes the subject of our sketch, "and James and I learned to tune it accurately by some means—I hardly remember how. We learned to play a few tunes with patience and perseverance by hearing them sung and lilted by our parents. My father, especially, knew an immense number of jigs, reels, and hornpipes, although he never played on any instrument."

The brothers were subsequently taught from written music by James Lynch, a Tipperary man, who was a fine musician, and they attended the Shamrock School in the town of Erin—the first district school organized in that part of the country.

His father desired that John should enter the University of Wisconsin at Madison, the state capital, but, being accustomed to the handling of tools since boyhood, and having learned the carpenter trade from his uncle, Michael Lynch, John preferred to engage in the building business.

While erecting churches, dwellings, and barns, in the country round about with his brother Denis, his fiddling circuit was equally extensive, and so he always kept in excellent practice and circulating the tunes he had learned from Lynch and his parents.

Seeking a wider field and better opportunities, he established himself in Milwaukee in 1883 and took up building and contracting on a larger scale, the Linden hotel being one of his undertakings.

It was the writer's good fortune to spend some pleasant hours in our friend Mr. Flynn's company in April, 1911, at the home of Capt. M. J. Dunn of the Milwaukee Fire Department. He played the fiddle with great spirit and precision in concert with our host, and Sergt. Early of Chicago on the Union pipes. His performance, which was excellent, was less conspicuous than his modesty and the refinement of his manners. And while gazing in admiration if not awe at this unassuming yet splendid type of man, fluently fiddling the music of his Irish ancestors, though brought up in the backwoods, one could not help speculating as to what distinction might he not have attained had he graduated from the University of Wisconsin as his father had intended, instead of from the carpenter's bench in a pioneer settlement on the outskirts of civilization.

Martin Clancy

It would appear that the race of household musicians is not yet extinct in Ireland. Here and there, from Waterford to Clare, and even in Wexford, pipers and fiddlers became attached to certain families as of yore, but it is evident that the underlying motive is not so much the perpetuation of old customs, as the inborn love of Irish music and sympathy for the musicians.

A fiddler of great repute named Martin Clancy has been brought to notice by our friend Patrick Powell of Tulla, County Clare. For years Clancy has been patronized by Hon. William Halpin of Newmarket-on-Fergus, an ardent revivalist, on account of his exceptional talents. Mr. Halpin's nephew, Frank O'Coffey, now connected with *The Irish-American* of New York City, speaks very highly of Clancy's musical versatility. Now about seventy one years of age, he was born at or near Kilrush. Most famous as a fiddler, he has quite a few pupils, but he also plays the flute, Union pipes, and perhaps one or two other instruments. He is generally regarded in Clare and Limerick as without an equal, especially as an exponent of the traditional style. His rendering of "The Fox Chase," *"Taim im Chodhladh," "Eamonn an Chnuic,"* and other ancient pieces, has gained him much local renown. "Rocking the Cradle," in which he mimics the crying of the baby, is another of his masterpieces.

Unfortunately the jovial Martin has his little eccentricities, like most famous musicians, the most pronounced being his free use of the fiddle to enforce domestic discipline while in his Bacchanalian moods. Though but little of the original instrument remains, as a result of frequent repairs, the temperamental Martin's veneration for it is unfaltering. He talks to it as if it had been endowed with life, and sleeps with it snugly reposing under his pillow.

Patrick Clancy

Great as is the reputation of Martin Clancy as a traditional fiddler on the banks of the broad-bosomed Shannon, it is no disparagement to his fame to say that, as an all-around performer on the violin, he is equaled by his son, Patrick Clancy, of New York City.

The only child of his parents, the latter was born in the sixties at the Limerick side of Thomond Bridge, near the barracks. Inheriting his father's musical talent, he profited also by his training, as the sequel proved. Clancy's orchestra, of which he is the leader, is in much demand at Irish balls and entertainments, and competent authorities assert that as an Irish performer on the violin he is unequaled in that city. The son, too, has his peculiarities. He fills his engagements scrupulously and to the minute—but no more. That is simply business without sentiment. Yet, when the ball is over he will visit some bartender friend and roll out jigs and reels for him until morning.

Edward Cronin

Of more ancient vintage than any of the prominent traditional fiddlers of Chicago at the beginning of the twentieth century, was Mr. Cronin, a native of Limerick Junction, in County Tipperary. He was born about 1838, and when little more than a boy was in great demand to play odd tunes and Long dances for expert dancers because he certainly had talent as well as training. If we mistake not, he was taught by one Ryan, whose insatiable love of music was such that, after playing for a dance all night, he would play for his own pleasure along the road on his way home in the early hours of the morning.

A weaver by trade, Edward Cronin finding no demand for his craft on arriving at Troy, New York, has followed any line of employment available ever since. Blest—or shall we say cursed—with the artistic temperament to excess, this remarkable man enjoyed but a few brief years of appreciation in Chicago subsequent to his chance discovery, although he had been a resident of the city for a long time previously. The proverbial failings of the musical fraternity were in his case intensified by a nature so suspicious and unrelenting that it was his open boast that he never forgot nor forgave an injury. And the worst of it

EDWARD CRONIN

was that the injury was more often fancied than real. Making all due allowance for his many good qualities, enduring friendship was unattainable, and more is the pity, for in the great western metropolis whose Irish population exceeds that of Dublin, Edward Cronin had but one rival as an all-around traditional fiddle player.

From long isolation he had forgotten most of his music, and owning almost as many fiddles as he had tunes, he changed from one to another when the tone did not suit him. Can we wonder at this seeming whim in view of the fact that his work, day after day for many years, had been grinding castings on an emery wheel at the Deering Harvester Works. How he played so well with such coarse and scarred fingers was little short of miraculous. Faultless in time and rhythm, he was liberal and obliging with his music when in the humor, and so well recognized were his abilities in this respect that even after he had severed his connection with the Irish Music Club he was engaged by its officials to play at the annual picnic for the stepdancers.

Mr. Cronin's memory proved a rich mine of traditional Irish melody, but it took years of cultivation and suggestion to rouse his dormant faculties to their limit. As this phase of the subject has been dealt with quite freely in *Irish Folk Music: A Fascinating Hobby,* its repetition here is unnecessary. Visits to his home were fraught with pleasure, especially when he played in concert with two young friends from Troy—Patrick Clancy on the flute and Thomas F. Kiley on the mandolin. Clancy, Mrs. Cronin's nephew, possessed a most wonderful voice, powerful and mellow, and to our unscientific ear the most delightful we had ever heard. On the violin the genial "Tom" Kiley swung the bow with a freedom which many professionals might envy. "The Connemara Fiddle," as we facetiously termed the mandolin, was his favorite instrument, however. In playing Irish dance music he displayed a facility of execution almost inconceivable. To him "The Flogging Reel," a lively, three-part dance tune, with its turns and graces, presented no more difficulties than "Home, Sweet Home."

"Pat" Clancy is now on the eastern vaudeville circuit, and the nimble-fingered "Tom" Kiley is connected with *The Knickerbocker Press* of his native city.

A journey of twelve miles each way was made to Mr. Cronin's house twice a week by the present writer, for two years, with unfailing regularity. Temperament and professional jealousy brought it all to an abrupt end without apparent cause. When in the humor, no man could be more obliging and liberal with his music. His muse needed no stimulation, and he would play on for hours at a time such tunes as memory presented, his features while so engaged remaining as set and impassive as the sphinx. An evening spent in the company of this most accommodating of musicians was an event to be remembered.

This genius, in whose expansive breast two conflicting elements struggled for the mastery was an adept in his peculiar style of free-hand bowing and slurring, but what seemed so easy and natural to him proved almost insuperably difficult to many whom he undertook to teach.

Endowed with exceptional attributes in other directions, he could multiply compound numbers mentally and almost instantaneously, a faculty he possessed all through life; and as a composer of dance music, particularly hornpipes, from any given theme, his versatility was surprising.

Such is Edward Cronin, dowered with strength, health, and conspicuous talents, yet handicapped with one constitutional failing which has been fatal alike to the appreciation and prosperity which much less gifted men enjoy.

Timothy M. Dillon

When it comes to traditional fiddle-playing in its most cultured sense, no one displays such marked individuality as Timothy M. Dillon of the Chicago police force. While not a few others of our acquaintance leave little or nothing to be desired in the way of rhythm, graces, and execution, the plaintive, pleading, haunting tones which Officer Dillon produces on his instrument are indescribably weird and wailing even in his reveling reels.

Many a pleasant hour has the present writer enjoyed listening to this wizard of the violin, and wondering how such peculiarly quaint music was produced. Notwithstanding the luxuriance of his turns, trills, and triplets, we noticed that his finger tips slid slightly from the stops with much frequency, thereby shading the tones in a most expressive way. This style of execution is practiced to a limited extent by capable violinists in playing airs. None but an expert who had acquired the art in early life—and Dillon had—would attempt it in the rapid passages of Irish dance music.

Born in the Parish of Rathea a few miles from Newmarket West, County Limerick, the subject of this sketch commenced the study of the violin in 1855, when but nine years old, under the tuition of Patrick O'Grady, and in a few years was ranked with the best of them. Old customs and usages had not yet been placed under the ban, so that young Dillon's practice in dancing kept pace with his progress in music, and many are the contests he won among the disciples of Terpsichore in his native county before heading for the "land of the free."

A genial, kindly gentleman in public and private life, he has never been afflicted with temperament, and is therefore at peace with the world; able and willing to entertain all comers with music and true Irish hospitality. Not the least interesting incidents in Mr. Dillon's life are those set forth in the opening pages of Chapter XXXI.

John McFadden

Long before meeting this phenomenal fiddler the echo of his praises had reached our ears, and if we chanced to express our appreciation of the playing of others in his class, some one would ask, "Did you ever hear McFadden?" This of course implied that we might save our applause until we heard this traditional star. When the opportunity was presented at the wedding of a friend in 1897, all our expectations were realized but one.

The airy style of his playing, the clear crispness of his tones, and the rhythmic swing of his tunes, left nothing to be desired, yet in the manipulation of his instrument he violated all the laws of professional ethics. His bow hand seemed almost wooden in its stiffness, and the bow itself appeared to be superfluously long, for he seldom used more than half of it.

How he came to acquire such proficiency in execution is to many a matter of surprise, still when we consider the beauty of Chinese and Japanese workmanship, accomplished with the aid of tools crude in comparison with ours, the wonder disappears.

John McFadden, now in the sixties, was born in the townland of Carrowmore, a few miles north of Westport, County Mayo. His father and brother were also fiddlers, and whatever little rudimentary instruction he got was picked up in the family. Written music was a stranger to them, consequently all their tunes were memorized from the whistling and playing of others. It is a notable fact that musicians who learn by ear and play from memory have copious repertories, while those who learn from written or printed music are usually deficient in the memorizing faculty.

The facility with which McFadden learns new tunes is only equaled by his versatility in improvising variations as he plays them. So chronic has the latter practice grown that it is a matter of no little difficulty to reduce his playing to musical notation. The following instance may serve to illustrate this peculiarity:

While visiting Sergt. Early during a theatrical engagement in Chicago in 1911, "Patsy" Touhey, on the writer's suggestion, tried to learn "Hawks' Hornpipe" from McFadden. Phrase by phrase they progressed, Touhey submitting patiently to many minor changes according to "Mac's" fancy, until he thought he had the tune noted correctly. Then he played it, apparently in good style, but not to his preceptor's satisfaction evidently. "Let me show you, 'Patsy,' " says "Mac," in a kindly tone, and swinging his bow again ran the tune over once or twice. "Why, man alive, that's not how you gave it to me at all! You've changed the tune again; I guess we'll let it go this time," exclaimed Touhey, as he started to play something else on his pipes.

Possessing the gift of composition as well as execution, McFadden is the author of many fine dance tunes, composed without the aid of notes or memoranda, depending altogether on his memory for their retention. Like the offsprings of O'Carolan's brain, quite a few of McFadden's jigs and reels were preserved by others who taught them to him over again.

An incorrigible, practical joker, many who admired his music feared his eccentricities in this respect, and, though sacrificing friendship to his whims occasionally, come what may, Democratic or Republican administration of municipal government, John McFadden always had friends numerous and influential enough to keep his name on the payroll of the city of Chicago.

JAMES O'NEILL

Talented, but not temperamental, the amiable James O'Neill was unknown as a musician among his neighbors in Chicago for years. To them he was an industrious rolling-mill man, whose grimy countenance was rarely unlit by a smile. In those years preceding his appointment on the police force in 1891, he had no time for fiddling, for, besides a family of his own to support, he had orphaned brothers and sisters to care for.

Born near Banbridge, County Down, in 1863, he was but a few years old when the family moved to Belfast. When old enough, he went to work in the linen mills with his father. The latter, John O'Neill, an excellent violinist, disliked publicity, but took pains to teach his art to every one of his children. The eldest, James, also studied under "Bill" Ellis, an Englishman of great versatility on the violin.

Coming to America in his eighteenth year, he obtained employment as lineman with the Chicago, Alton and St. Louis Railway, but subsequently obtained more lucrative but much more laborious employment at the Bridgeport Iron Mills, involving twelve hours' continuous work each day including Sunday. With such work, such hours, and such hands, no wonder his fiddle was silent and unstrung, and his musical abilities unsuspected by his neighbors.

Conversing one evening with the genial and generous "Joe" Cant, a renowned Highland piper, the latter remarked to the present writer that James O'Neill was the best player of strathspeys on the fiddle he had ever heard. A musician so distinguished could not be allowed to remain in obscurity, so diligent inquiry led

SERGT. JAMES O'NEILL

to his discovery many miles from Mr. Cant's address, but, wonderful to relate, within a hundred yards or so of the Deering Street Police Station, in which the writer was sergeant at the time!

Yes, James O'Neill could play strathspeys, as "Joe" Cant said, to suit the most fastidious Highlander, for, be it remembered, the music of Belfast is no less Scotchy than its language. But he could do more than that. He possessed a copious repertory of all varieties of Irish melodies, learned from both father and mother, who were of the old native stock, which remained true to the traditions of their race and passed them down to their posterity. Irish fiddlers are by no means few, yet how many who revel in the airy jig and reel can render with due expression those airs and melodies, quaint, plaintive, and even bold, which affect our emotions so deeply. James O'Neill could. "Many a time and oft" has he thrilled his audience at Central Music Hall, and the Exposition Building on the lake front, with the strains of "The Exile of Erin," "Colleen Beag Machree," "Father Quin," and "Planxty Peyton," etc., in the nineties, before the demolition of those structures in the march of progress.

Endowed with the faculty of composing original airs to a degree unsuspected by any but his most intimate friends, he would, when the inspiration seized him, produce in short order melodies of such beauty that we know of several instances in which they have been selected out of hundreds, as studies for pupils, by the professors in our musical colleges.

"Like father like son," he never sought the limelight and never accepted fee or reward for his music at either public or private entertainment. As a humble coal shoveler, a telegraph lineman, a uniformed patrolman, or wearing the insignia and service stripes of a sergeant of police, he was the same modest, smiling, companionable man, whose hospitable home at Brighton Park was for many years the Mecca to which lovers of Irish music directed their footsteps, as described in the pages of *Irish Folk Music: A Fascinating Hobby.*

With astonishing facility he reduced to musical notation any tunes sung, whistled, or played in his hearing, and so discriminating was his ear that duplicates and variants were readily detected.

Whatever musical, antiquarian, or regenerative value the various O'Neill Collections of Irish music may possess, no small share of the credit is due to the tireless zeal and unselfish co-operation of Sergeant James O'Neill.

The impress which his musical talents made in these days was very feelingly voiced by John Ennis, secretary of The Irish Music Club, in an interesting article on "The Revival of Erin's Language and Music in Chicago." Happily the ardent author chose the assonant rhythm of such classics as Father Prout's "Bells of Shandon" and Milliken's "Groves of Blarney," as models in giving rein to his fervid fancy and opening up the very sluices of his soul.

> Oh, my heart was weary, my life was dreary,
> And naught was cheery to my troubled mind:
> My soul was longing as my thoughts came thronging
> Of the sweet old music I left behind.
> Since I left green Erin, I was constant fearin'
> I'd ne'er be hearin' a jig or reel,
> But my longing's ended, life's span extended,
> With bright joys blended—I've found James O'Neill.

Oh, my search is finished, my ills diminished,
   My soul's replenished by his violin;
His sweet renditions send melodious missions
   With strong petitions to my heart within.
With ecstatic pleasure I get full measure
   Of bardic treasure—which is my ideal—
As reminiscent, my moist eyes glisten,
   I sit and listen to James O'Neill.

Those sad creations—the "Lamentations"—
   With sweet vibrations his fiddle sings,
In tones of anguish that rise and languish—
   The wail of vanquished thro' my being rings—
In weird caoining, sobs intervening,
   Their woful meaning he does reveal;
Their plaintive story of battles gory,
   And departed glories told by James O'Neill.

When he plays "Slieve Gallen," "Sweet Innisfallen,"
   "The Boys of Calian," and "The Foggy Dew,"
"The Bells of Shandon," "The Bridge of Bandon,"
   "Sweet Molly Brandon," or "The Colleen Rua,"
His skill impelling, the tears come swelling—
   No power quelling the joys I feel,
And sweet recollection of youth's affection
   Is stirred to action by James O'Neill.

Prof. Patrick Joseph Griffith

Conscious of our inability to do justice to the character of the talented and amiable subject of this sketch, we approach the task so oft deferred with much misgiving. The long hoped for inspiration so essential in this case having business elsewhere, perhaps we could not introduce our friend more appropriately than in the enthusiastic words of John S. Wayland of the Cork Pipers Club: "To spend an hour in Prof. Griffith's company is like a college education." And so it is especially in music, whether it be traditional, classical, or modern, and the best of it all is the fact that his high musical attainments in later life have not affected his admiration for the folk music of his boyhood days at Kilsheelan, near Clonmel, County Tipperary.

To extol the talents of one who occupies a position of such prominence as Director, and Professor of the violin and viola at the Leinster School of Music, Dublin, and many other positions of honor and distinction in the world of music, would add nothing to his fame. Patrick Joseph Griffith has been a resident of Dublin since 1874, when he was but eleven years of age. For three years prior to his migration, a wandering fiddler named John Daly took him in hand and taught him about two hundred tunes, "old Irish, modern Irish, and un-Irish." A prize of three pounds was awarded Prof. Griffith for Daly's manuscript collection of unpublished tunes at a Belfast Feis, it being the best submitted at that meeting.

The professor's preliminary training under Daly no doubt accounts for his appreciation and practice of traditional Irish music in later life, and there can hardly be a doubt that its influence contributed not a little to his success in rendering "The Fox Chase" and other pieces so admirably at Feis Ceoil competitions. He played "The Fox Chase" at the Rotunda in Dublin on May 5, 1910, before a large audience, and was followed by Denis Delaney, who gave his version of the piece on the Union pipes, in a manner not quite so varied and masterly. An epic founded on this incident by the facile pen of Mr. Wayland will be found in the sketch of Delaney's life. Prof. Griffith obligingly went all the way to Cork and repeated his performance at a concert given by the Cork Pipers' Club at Christmas in the same year.

Born and brought up in an atmosphere of tradition, the professor remains unconvinced that an untaught traditional fiddler could give a tune a color and keenness unattainable by the trained hand of an Irishman who appreciates the beauty of Irish melody. Some there be, however, including the writer and some of the professor's friends, who cannot acquiesce in this view unreservedly; for that peculiar undefinable something in the tone and swing of an Irish reel, for instance, is instinctive rather than acquired.

His chief characteristics in his profession are his very elegant tone, his power of reading at sight any piece of music whatever in any key, and his soulful playing of Irish airs. In the last named faculty he is said to be markedly superior to certain well known violinists who figure more conspicuously in the public eye. He double stops more sparingly, but he enters into the spirit of what he is playing, including dance music of which he is a fine performer.

Though a man of liberal physical proportions, his hand is that of a lady and there are not wanting many other indications of a refined ancestry.

In the several relations of son, brother, husband, and neighbor, Prof. P. J. Griffith has been a model, and as for hospitality at his home at Rathmines, his exercise of it shames his guests. In a word, it is a privilege to know him, and what more could be said of any man?

The spectacle of a man of his dimensions crowding John McNeill's chair at No. 140 Capel Street suggested to his friend, Mr. Flanagan, the following lines:

> Large is his bounty and his soul sincere—
> In scraping catgut he spends half his time;
> Horse hair and rosin constitute his gear,
> Sweet his finger, and his tone sublime.
> Some fate unkind set him to play the fiddle,
> That genial, hearty, laughter-loving chap,
> To hold the pipes up what a splendid middle,
> And what a thigh on which to tie the strap;
> Yet to really make a tip-top piper,
> One trait he lacks—denied him from on high;
> Of others' fame and tunes he is no swiper,
> And like the immortal George he cannot lie.

JOHN DALY

to whom Prof. Patrick Joseph Griffith owed his primary training on the violin, was a wandering minstrel whose circuit comprised the Counties of Tipperary, Waterford, and Kilkenny. He is said to have been the son of a prosperous farmer in the County of Cork, but wooing the muses appealed to his fancy with more potency than following the plow.

Prof. P. J. Griffith

For thirty years or more prior to his death, which occurred between 1875 and 1880, this typical minstrel spread the knowledge of Irish music in the southern counties, and it speaks well for his repertory that his manuscript collection of tunes was awarded first prize at a Belfast Feis some years ago, when submitted by his former pupil, Prof. Griffith.

Miss Theresa Halpin

A very clever violinist by all accounts is Miss Halpin, daughter of the late Joseph Halpin of the city of Limerick, a celebrated dancer in his day. Although yet in her teens, she possesses an extensive repertory of old tunes in very good settings. Her name appears among the list of prize winners for unpublished airs at the Dublin Feis Ceoil in 1907.

Edward and James O'Mahony

The born musician is easily told and easily taught. Talent soon betrays itself, and so it was in the case of "Eddie" and "Jimmy" O'Mahony, who were born in the years 1898 and 1900 respectively. They were already widely known as fine fiddle players before reaching their teens.

Their father, James O'Mahony, born in the glen of Aherlow, though now weighing considerably over three hundred pounds, was and is famed as an athlete. He has developed the art of violin making to such a degree that it is on fiddles of their father's make that the young prodigies play.

The boys have appeared at public entertainments quite frequently, and it is said they can rattle off with facility any number in O'Neill's *Dance Music of Ireland*.

Enthusiasm and love of music which run in the family seem to be contagious, for "Will" Condon, who takes a turn at the pipes occasionally, accompanied by a son and daughter, takes a run into town once in a while to have an enjoyable time with the O'Mahonys.

Realizing the promise of their boyhood, Edward and James are adding to their laurels at every competition. We can therefore presage for them an enviable future.

John McGlynn

Another fiddler whose execution at the Dublin Feiseanna has attracted attention is John McGlynn of Waterford. Some years ago Mischa Elman, the famous violinist, while at Dublin, happened in to the annual Feis, and hearing McGlynn play, noted down some of his tunes for future use to be included in an Irish rhapsody he contemplated writing.

Michael Daffy

Much may be expected of Michael Daffy, the blind boy-fiddler from County Clare, to preserve and promote an interest in the traditional music of the "Green Isle." Though barely out of his teens, his fine performance and wealth of memorized native tunes have already won him enviable distinction.

His loss of sight, when but eight or nine years old, was by his friends attributed to supernatural agencies or rather to the malign influence of the fairies. While playing in the fields on their father's farm a few miles from Tulla, Michael and his twin brother Thomas had their eyes poisoned in some unaccountable way. The result was fatal to "Tommy," but Michael survived, though his eyes were

JAMES AND EDWARD O'MAHONY

entirely destroyed. Influential friends sent the dark boy to an institution for the blind at Dublin, where he received his musical education.

The emotions which crowded poor Michael's mind on realizing the extent of his misfortune were voiced in verse in his grandfather's days, by an anonymous poet:

Oh, mother, is it spring once more—
The same bright laughing spring
That used to come in days of yore
With glad and welcome wing?

And is the infant primrose born,
And peerless daisy child,
Beneath the bowed and budding thorn,
All beautiful and wild?

And does the sky break out as blue
Between the April showers,
And smilingly impart its hue
To her young violet flowers?

And is the sun, the blessed sun,
As dazzling in its might,
As glorious now to look upon,
As when I loved his light?

As when, with clear and happy eye,
Beneath that light I strayed,
Or in the noonday brilliancy
Sought out some cooling shade?

And when the spring flowers drop away,
Will summer days come fast,
All rich with bloom—oh, mother, say!—
As when I saw them last?

Will merry children gambol o'er
The meadow by the brook—
Seek out the wild bees' honey store
In some deep hidden nook?

Or where the sparkling waters flow,
Go wandering far away,
To cull the tallest reeds that grow,
And weave them all the day?

And will they climb the tall old trees,
And at the topmost height
Find birds of beauty such as those
That charm my long, long night?

They will! but I shall not be there;
   For me, oh! nevermore
Shall spring put forth her blossoms fair,
   Or summer shed her store!

Yet think not, mother, if I weep,
   'Tis for the seasons' gleam;
Or, if I gladden in my sleep,
   'Tis of such things I dream.

SELENA O'NEILL

"Time, place, and action may with pains be wrought,
   But genius must be born, and never can be bought."

To Selena O'Neill love of music was an instinct, and its cultivation and practice an insatiable passion. Even in her infancy the sound of the fiddle was more potent to assuage her tribulations than the soothing voice of her mother. Heredity to some extent may be responsible for her predilection, because her father, "Tim" O'Neill, a jolly Corkonian, loves his fiddles almost as much as he adores his children.

At an early age Selena commenced her studies at the Chicago Musical College, and before long became distinguished for brilliancy of tone and execution.

Talent has been defined as the capacity of doing anything that depends on application and industry. Of this she had an abundance, but wealth was none of her inheritance. Even so, the difficulties suggested by the poet in the following lines were not permitted to check her progress:

"The lamp of genius, though by nature lit,
If not protected, pruned, and fed with care
Soon dies, or runs to waste with fitful glare."

Still in her teens, and a post-graduate of the famous institution above named, Miss O'Neill continues her studies under Leon Sametini, the celebrated violinist, although having a flourishing class of pupils of her own.

While attending the Nativity Parochial School she took piano lessons from the Sisters, but the wonderful rhythm displayed in her playing of all varieties of Irish dance music to suit the most fastidious, is instinctive and self-acquired.

It has been said that individual and national temperaments will always color the music, art and literature of artists, regardless of influence and environment. In her case, association with traditional Irish musicians had much to do with the development of her admirable style.

Having conspicuously carried off first honors in the violin contest at the Chicago Gaelic Feis in July, 1912, Miss O'Neill was engaged by Donal O'Connor, the League organizer, as one of the attractions at the Philadelphia Feis in February, 1913, her name appearing on the programme with such notables as John McCormick and Misses Marie Narelle, Nora Power, and Rita O'Donoghue.

The published accounts of the Feis, which lasted three nights, paid the western girl many compliments—following are a few:

"Miss O'Neill, an accomplished violinist, who could play any piece of Irish music, sustained the introduction with a rendition that created a furore."

"Of the five medals which glistened on her breast, one was from the Chicago Musical College, and another was the first prize won at the Chicago Feis in 1912."

"An exceptional exponent of traditional Irish music."

"Miss O'Neill's playing struck a sympathetic chord in the audience, and set the feet going all over the building in unison with the dances."

"Few men could produce such a volume of tone from the violin as Miss O'Neill, whose every note, clear and distinct, could be heard in the remotest recess of the auditorium. In playing airs she repeats the melody in chords or double stops, and on the expiration of the final note, she swings without premonitory warning into a slashing dance tune, jig, reel or hornpipe, of which she has a copious repertoire. Although the little prodigy appeared before the curtain repeatedly three nights in succession, her numbers were never the same."

"Miss Selena O'Neill's wonderful playing of Irish airs on the violin took the house by storm, and her accompaniments of the dancing were above praise."

In an extended review of the Philadelphia Feis, the *Irish-American* of New York paid her the following tribute:

"Though a mere child in years and experience, Miss O'Neill possesses personality and imagination. When the last notes of 'The Coolin' drifted out across the footlights and lost themselves among the yearning Irish hearts there, the audience received a sudden shock from the western girl's genius when she struck up the 'Swaggering Jig.'"

The diversified roles which she filled at the Feis were not contemplated in the programme. Not only was she one of the stars engaged for the occasion, but she entered the violin and piano contests and won the highest honors in both. The competing dancers from New York and other cities, preferring the swing and rhythm of her execution to the music provided by the management, Miss O'Neill obligingly responded, playing for them without hesitation, and from memory, every tune called for, including such favorites as "The Top of Cork Road," "The Humors of Bantry," "The Bridal Jig," "Miss Thornton's Reel," "Bonnie Kate," "Chief O'Neill's Favorite" (hornpipe), and also such special dances as "The Job of Journeywork," "The Blackbird," "The Humors of Bandon," and "The Garden of Daisies."

In the piano contest Miss O'Neill had no real rivalry, for she alone of the competitors played Irish dance music, a feat which evidently astonished the audience.

Some there were who could not be convinced that anyone not a "native of the soil" could give to Irish dance music such characteristic expression and swing. No, Selena O'Neill never saw Ireland nor the sky over it, and yet as a wondering admirer said: "She goes at it so wicked—so vicious, that she'd lift you off the

Selena O'Neill

floor." So she would; but remember, it is the spirit and emphasis, no less than the appeal of Irish music, that captivates our senses and preserves it as a lasting, living reality long centuries after the contemporary music of other nations has passed away and interests only the musical antiquary.

Concerning her performance at the Emmet Memorial Hall on June 29, 1913, shortly after acquiring the degree of Bachelor of Music at the Chicago Musical College, the published account says: "Miss Selena O'Neill, the ever popular violinist, kept the audience spellbound with the charm of her magic bow and fairy violin. This young artist has the greatest influence over her audiences, moving them to tears and laughter as the spirit moves her sweet self."

The award of first prize to "The Fairy Fiddler," as she has been called, at the Gaelic Feis at Chicago, August 3 following, was a foregone conclusion. Such was the applause which greeted her performance that on being recalled to the platform by Donal O'Connor, the Gaelic League Organizer, the modest little maiden gave the audience a treat in her rendering of "The Fox Chase," with variations, in which the tallyho, baying of the hounds, and other sounds of the chase were distinctly reproduced. This was the first time, by the way, that this famous, but now almost forgotten piece of descriptive music has been played in public in Chicago, but, sad to say, fame, which has its penalties as well as its pleasures, "doth for the most part congregate more enemies than friends."

We have read somewhere that musical geniuses are phenomena. There is no rule of their creation; there is no promise of their reproduction.

In the prevailing attitude of less gifted rivals, we are reminded of Dean Swift's observation: "When a true genius appears in the world, you may know him by this sign; that the dunces are all in a confederacy against him."

CHAPTER XXVII

THE FLUTE AND ITS PATRONS

No musical instrument· was in such common use among the Irish peasantry as the flute. From the "penny whistle" to the keyed instrument in sections it was always deservedly popular, for unlike the fiddle and the bagpipe it involved no expense beyond the purchase price. Complete in itself, the flute needed but a wetting to be always in tune, and disjointed or whole could be carried about without display or inconvenience. Besides, if not broken by accident or design it would outlive its owner. Soft or shrill, its carrying power was remarkable. Who that has heard the mellow music of either whistle or flute a mile away on a fine evening, will ever forget the experience?

It is not recorded that the flute was known to the ancient Irish, unless the *feadan* or *fideog,* which had a reed mouthpiece, and resembled an Irish chanter, may be so regarded. No doubt it was this instrument the ancient chroniclers had in mind in their occasional mention of "pipe players and pipers." The originial flute or tibia was fashioned out of the shinbone of some animal, and blown at the end. Some were double; each with three finger vents, one tube being longer than the other. Such was the strain in blowing them that in Greece and Rome it was the custom to wear a bandage round the cheeks which braced the mouth.

All nations from the most remote times used some form of pipe or flute. The Roman tibia had but five vents for the fingers. A whistle-flute called in England the Tabor pipe was in general use in that country and France in the twelfth century. It had but two finger holes in front and one behind for the thumb; yet strange to say it "was capable of producing by the aid of harmonic sounds a diatonic scale of one and a half octaves," according to the author of *Old English Instruments of Music.*

In the early years of the seventeenth century, when almost a centenarian, a performer named Hall was still "giving the men light hearts by his pipe, and the women light heels by his tabor." A still shorter form of the three-holed pipe— only four inches long—was brought into special prominence, the aforementioned author says, by the wonderful performances of a blind peasant named Picco, who first played in London in 1856. By the use of the palm or the second finger of the right hand, which was placed on the lower end of the tube, he was able, it was said, to obtain a compass of three octaves!

The flute blown from the side, variously named the transverse flute, the oblique flute, and the cross flute, was known both in India and China from remote antiquity. Its introduction about the tenth century, into Greece, gradually extended all over Europe, but in its progress it does not appear to have come into use in England until late in the fifteenth century. During the eighteenth and nineteenth centuries, it came to be known as the German flute, on account, it is said, of the improvements which German musicians had made in the instrument. Quite likely the use of the flute in Ireland was contemporaneous with its popularity in England, but as the instrument has a literature of its own those desiring to pursue the subject more fully will find ample opportunity to indulge their taste for inquiry.

No one but a born musician, or one who had no other outlet for his musical instinct, was likely to learn to play the flute. The halt, lame, and blind, driven to the practice of music as a profession, invariably chose the Union pipes or fiddle, as the most available instrument to touch the sensibilities of the people. Quite often proficiency on the flute led to practice on the pipes, but while in some respects experience on the flute may be regarded as primary training, the flute player who aspires to renown as a piper had much to unlearn also. The same rule holds good with the Warpipes or Highland pipes, which in theory and execution differ radically both from the flute and the Union pipes.

Music schools for the teaching of Irish music on the Union pipes, fiddle, and flute, were unknown. Every individual who undertook to teach had his own conception of method and proficiency, both in style of execution and version of the music taught. Pupils picked up the peculiarities of their teachers as naturally as they picked up the local accent and idiom, and any deviation from their acquired notions was a subject for criticism.

Without standard schools of instruction, the aspirant for musical knowledge had no alternative but to learn wherever he got the chance, sometimes from a neighbor but more often from the nearest professional piper or fiddler who was willing to teach. In our own case we had the good fortune to be taught the flute by Mr. Timothy Downing, a gentleman farmer of illustrious ancestry living in Tralibane, our townland in West Cork, and one of the chief regrets of our life is having lost by early emigration the opportunity to learn the fiddle also, on which he was a fine free-hand performer. His rousing strains still haunt our memory after a lapse of nearly fifty years.

Be it known that ordinarily professional musicians in Ireland—yea, and beyond its shores also—did not care to encourage possible rivals and competitors. Still more careful were they not to teach all they knew, unless it be to a son or close relative who was to succeed them, and whose glory they expected to share. Some of their choice tunes were treasured as personal reserves to which none had a claim, and not infrequently died with them.

As most Irish fluters were amateurs, or rather non-professionals, few are the imprints which their foosteps have left on the sands of time. We make no mistake, however, in awarding first place to the author of "The Traveler," "The Deserted Village," and "The Vicar of Wakefield."

OLIVER GOLDSMITH

Mingling in the games and pastimes of the peasantry at Pallas, near Ballymahon, County Lorgford, where he was born in 1728, Oliver Goldsmith picked up a knowledge of the flute without any special training as is customary. All through the vicissitudes of his eventful life, he indulged his passion for the music of his native land, even neglecting his studies at Trinity College to practice on his beloved flute.

When he started out in 1755 from Leyden, Holland, on his travels on the Continent, his equipment consisted of "a guinea in his pocket, one shirt to his back, and a flute in his hand," but music is a universal language which appeals to all whose hearts respond to the charms of melody.

Goldsmith, as Boswell said to Johnson years afterward, "*disputed* his passage through Europe." Through Flanders and France to Paris, thence to Geneva and over the Alps into Northern and Central Italy, as far as Florence, he wended his way, most often on foot, working his passage by playing his flute, and making himself popular with the natives of many countries with jocose antics and humorous stories. He partook of the free hospitalities of the monks at the monasteries, slept on straw in humble barns, and when he reached a village would pull out his flute and strike up a lively air, to which the rustics would respond with dances, and in recompense for which he would obtain a modest lodging and something to eat. In his "Traveler" he alludes to those scenes:

> "How often have I led the sportive choir,
> With tuneless pipe, beside the murmuring Loire!
> Where standing elms along the margin grew,
> And freshened from the wave the zephyr flew;
> And haply through my harsh touch faltering still,
> But mocked all tune, and marred the dancer's skill,
> Yet would the village praise my wondrous power,
> And dance forgetful of the noontide hour."

Such was the surfeit of music in Italy that his poor flute was powerless, and so when reduced to extremities he did not disdain to beg. He fought his way back to England again, sometimes engaging in competitive discussions at the universities, the champion of which could claim a free dinner and bed.

The knowledge and experience gained during his year's wanderings furnished the theme of his first immortal poem, "The Traveler." Already famous as a prose writer; on the appearance of this masterpiece Goldsmith was hailed as a poet of the first rank. In the glimpses which we get of his intermittent poverty, and life in cheerless garrets in London, playing his flute for the entertainment of the tattered children of his neighbors was one of his chief pleasures. He died in 1774 and rests in an unmarked grave in the Temple churchyard.

Self-taught and traditional flute players of varying degrees of efficiency flourished and still exist among the Irish in such numbers as to render any attempt at exploiting them out of the question. Not only every parish, but every townland in the four provinces, could boast of one or more, but being so numerous, nothing short of conspicuous excellence would be likely to attract special attention. Even that slight tribute to distinction would soon fade, for flute playing is too arduous for any but the young and robust, while the piper and the fiddler retained their powers and proficiency scarcely diminished, until old age had set its seal on their withered frames.

Seldom does a fluter's fame survive him, and as musicians of that class rarely "took to the road" like the pipers and fiddlers, their fame at best was only local. Brief mention of a few personally known to the writer, and others brought to our attention, will be found in the following pages.

MICHAEL WHITE

After coming to America, John McFadden, the renowned traditional Irish fiddler of Chicago, had the good fortune to fall in with Mr. White, an excellent flutist, at Cleveland, Ohio. The latter, who was born at or near Tralee, County Kerry, was also a fine singer and dancer, and it can well be imagined that the public house which he kept was well patronized by lovers of Irish music.

Many of McFadden's best tunes were derived from White's playing, among them being "The Wicklow Hornpipe," which was first printed in O'Neill's *Music of Ireland*.

JOHN O'NEILL

An unrivaled performer on the flute named John O'Neill was born about 1820 in the eastern part of the parish of Bantry, West Cork, and worked as a farm laborer in that vicinity until senile debility led to his removal to the poorhouse, where he died late in the nineties. He was an "airy" fellow, scarcely less noted as a dancer than as a musician, and he was the life of the country round about for more than a generation.

The most honored guest at any gathering, John O'Neill was never too tired after a day's plowing or mowing to play at any farmhouse festivity in the evening, and wherever he went in those instances, he was sure to take with him a pair of dancing shoes, to be worn when giving an exhibition dance on the kitchen table.

Though fifty years and more have flown on the wings of time, since the present writer listened with rapture to the thrilling tones of John O'Neill's flute, as he came over the hills from Loughbofinne one fine evening after dark, to play at the old homestead at Tralibane, the incident remains to this day indelibly stamped on my memory. Though then too young to be allowed the privilege of "staying up" while the dance lasted, I could at least enjoy the music which kept me awake most of the night.

Favored by nature with physical attractions as well as artistic endowments, this popular hero was an incorrigible bachelor. Apparently insensible to female charms, he never fell a victim to woman's wiles, and he openly proclaimed that he was "disinclined to support any man's daughter."

Without kindred, offspring, or home, in his old age, a much worse fate befell him than undertaking the responsibilities of matrimonial life in earlier years.

DENIS MALONEY

Born in 1844 on a farm near Kilfinane, in the County of Limerick, Denis Maloney was the most distinguished performer on the German flute in a family noted for its fluters. He was taught by his cousin, Denis Casey, of the parish of Emly, into which the Maloneys had migrated, though his musical ambition was not encouraged by his father. 'Twas no longer "respectable" to play the flute or pipes, although the fiddle was tolerated. An exception to his cloth, the amiable and patriotic pastor, Father Paul Haney, an excellent fluter himself, was rather proud of his young parishioner's talent. Many a time did the kindly *sagart* plant "Denny" between his knees to play for company at the rectory. And, by the way— we may as well tell it now—Father Haney himself often played the flute at the weddings he attended, and it never entered the good man's mind that he was endangering the morals or salvation of his flock thereby.

The Maloney family emigrated to America in 1857 and it was the writer's good fortune to form their acquaintance in Chicago in 1875. Besides the subject of our sketch, there were Michael, Thomas, Daniel and Mary, but Denis outranked them all, as well as all other fluters we have heard since that time, although he had no great advantage over the latter two in some of their favorite reels.

How a man with calloused hands and fingers, from long years of labor in the iron mills, could play a flute with such grace and execution has been a matter of no little surprise, under the circumstances. As a performer on the Highland pipes he was almost equally expert in his prime, but now in his sixty-ninth year a finger crippled from the nature of his occupation renders him incapable of performing on either. When required to play in concert with others, Denis Maloney possessed the rare faculty of adopting any version of a tune they favored, regardless of the setting to which he had been previously accustomed.

EDWARD CRONIN

There were "gentlemen fluters" as well as "gentlemen pipers" in Ireland in days gone by and Mr. Cronin, the subject of this sketch, was certainly one of them. Though his hair was flecked with the frosts of advanced years, his heart was young and his spirit was gay. Besides being an excellent performer on the flute he was also a clever poet, prose writer and musical critic and had heard all of the great musicians of his day. Like most men of his musical proclivities, he surrendered eventually to the fascinations of the dulcet tones of the Union pipes, although his practice on that instrument commenced late in life.

Born at "Sweet Adare" in County Limerick, he emigrated to the "Greater Ireland" beyond the broad Atlantic in his youth. After making his fortune in the dry goods business in New York he returned to his native home and being an ardent nationalist soon got in touch with the Gaelic Revival. He loved to associate with such companionable men as Michael Donovan of Skibbereen, "Bob" Thompson, the famous Irish piper, and the members of the Cork Pipers' Club.

While in America Mr. Cronin's experience did not extend beyond the Atlantic states, but of all the pipers he had known in Ireland and those he had met in New York and Massachusetts he awarded the palm to "Patsy" Touhey, whom he described to John S. Wayland, founder and secretary of the Cork Pipers' Club, as "the finest piper on top of the earth."

No one but a gentleman in purse and principles would have bequeathed one hundred pounds to the Gaelic League, and twice that amount to the Sinn Fein Society at the time of his death, which occurred in 1909.

Miss Madge Kirwan, pictured with Mr. Cronin, is a talented violinist of Mount Mellick who frequently played duets with the returned exile.

PATRICK FLEMING

The premier flute player of the northern baronies of the County Wexford and probably of a much wider territory for a generation is Patrick Fleming of Camolin, according to competent authority. This reputation he has maintained in all of the numerous competitions in which he engaged in modern times as well as in the years preceding the Irish Revival, although past fifty years of age. He was born near Craanford, and from his boyhood days evinced a rare intelligence outside of his musical faculties. Commencing on a tin whistle he changed to the flute quite naturally, and soon became celebrated for his phenomenal execution. The peculiar style of his playing has been compared to the warbling of the skylark. Later in life he acquired a knowledge of the violin and the melodeon, and to crown all, his voice is so sweet in its traditional pathos as almost to "coax the birds from the bushes."

To the excellence of his music and the charm of his manners is due the maintenance of the instrument in popular favor in his circuit, while in the southern districts of the county the flute, which at one time was no less favored than the fiddle or the pipes, has fallen into disuse. Fleming's execution was scarcely less remarkable than his repertory. A man of his notable accomplishments could not fail to exercise a stimulating influence in any community, and we are prepared to learn that he had many pupils, including "Pat" O'Shea of Thrule, John Kehoe of Askamore, and Andrew McCann of Newbridge, Camolin,

Miss Kirwan   Edwd. Cronin

an enthusiastic supporter of the Gaelic movement. The latter by the way has taken to the practice of the pipes with good prospects of success, based on his proficiency on the flute.

Nor is that all Fleming has done. By precept and example he has encouraged the cultivation of music on any instrument available. His sister, Mrs. Sarah Ormonde, is a capable performer on the concertina and she in turn has transmitted her taste to her daughter Anne, who has acquired fine command of the fiddle. And thus a musical revival goes merrily onward which if wisely fostered will relieve the erstwhile dreary monotony of peasant life that exercised no inconsequential influence in directing the thoughts of the young people to emigration.

ANDREW McCANN

"A splendid type of Irishman, young, tall, handsome, active, and energetic, and an enthusiastic supporter of the Gaelic movement," is the way our correspondent, Mr. Whelan of Scarawalsh, describes Andrew McCann of Newbridge, Camolin, County Wexford, a flute player of great local fame. His first attempt to woo the muses was on a tin whistle, and the first melody attacked was "St. Patrick's Day." The melodeon being "all the go," he acquired commendable proficiency on that alien instrument, but abandoned its use with the Irish Revival. Patrick Fleming's inimitable performance on the flute furnished new inspiration, and he took up the practice of that favorite. Playing in concert with Fleming led to important results, and McCann not only became an excellent fluter, but a promising piper as well.

Such is "Andy's" zeal and love of music that he makes it a point to hear all the best pipers whenever possible, for as he said to his friend, "I never yet was in musical company but I picked up something useful, and there are a lot of players in the country who only want encouragement."

A level-headed man is Andrew McCann, and how keenly he has diagnosed the difficulty. Not less truly does he observe: "It is almost impossible to find a performer who can play both dance music and slow airs well."

For his rendering of "The Blackbird" in slow vocal time on the flute, he was awarded first prize at the Wicklow Feis in 1906 and was also similarly honored for his performance at Feis Loch Carman, held at New Ross, County Wexford. Such was his progress on the Union pipes with the aid and instruction of the helpful John Rowsome of Ballintore, that in 1909 he won first prize against two other competitors; also first prize on the flute from a field of thirteen, on the same day. As he is but thirty years old, the future has much in store for him.

GEO. A. H. LEECH

From the frequency with which Mr. Leech's name appears on the programmes of San Francisco entertainments, we are safe in assuming that his attainments on the concert flute are of a high order. Besides we have it on reliable authority that his acknowledged musical ability is no greater than his liberality in displaying it.

Born in Dublin in 1873, he grew to manhood on the banks of the sunny Erne in the O'Reilly country in County Cavan, where his father, Rev. Robert Leech, was rector of Drumlane, Belturbet, for thirty years. Inheriting musical talent from his father, who was a musician, historian, and poet, young Leech imbibed a taste for traditional music from "Paddy" McDermott, the first good violinist he had ever heard, and whom he met and played with in New York in later years. Following is his own story:

"In the summer of 1885 a lot of returned Americans near the little town of Milltown, County Cavan, were happily thrown amongst us, and 'Phildy' Monaghan and the clever and ingenious 'Phil' Leddy made their violins ring on the cross roads that whole summer twice a week, and until far into the night. It was such a glorious summer!

"My instructors in dance music were the renowned Patrick Fitzpatrick, violinist of Glasstown, and the witty 'Phil' McKernan, who warbled like a lark on the piccolo in the Milltown band, led by the baton of the musical Fitzpatrick."

Professional jealousy finds no lodgment in the heart of Mr. Leech, for he is quite generous in his characterization of the Irish musicians encountered in the city of the Golden Gate. Hear him: "Some very fine flute players here are 'Pat' Wynn, big 'Tim' Carney, 'Jim' McKenna and 'Jim' Barry. Nor can we forget the sweetest Irish violin player that ever came or will come to the Pacific coast in the person of Prof. William McMahon. A very true player of Irish melodies is Prof. 'Bat' Scanlan, who has many social engagements. In rendering 'The Strawberry Blossom' on the flute, 'Pat' Wynn and 'Billy' McNamara are unsurpassed. The first player on the Union pipes I ever heard was Doonan of Cavan, a lame man who went on crutches. Although handicapped with a poor set of pipes, his skill in manipulating them was really surprising."

It is no more than justice to Mr. Leech to mention that it was through his efforts a photograph and sketch of Mr. Cummings, the noted San Francisco piper, were obtained.

Were there a man as talented, unselfish, and enthusiastic in promoting Irish ideals in every parish in Ireland, there would be no need of perennially bolstering up Gaelic Revivals.

CHAPTER XXVIII

DANCING—A LEGITIMATE AMUSEMENT

In every community there must be pleasures, relaxation, and means of agreeable excitement, according to Dr. Channing in his *Address on Temperance,* early in the nineteenth century; and if innocent ones are not furnished, resort will be had to those which are sinful. Man was made to enjoy as well as to labor, and the state of society should be adapted to this principle of human nature. A gloomy state of society is not well calculated to promote temperance, for the craving for excitement and entertainment—insistent as other human wants—will seek some channel for its gratification.

Public amusements bringing multitudes together to kindle with one emotion, to share the same innocent joy, have a humanizing influence, and among those bonds of society perhaps no one produces so much unmixed pleasure as music.

In another part of his *Address* the lecturer speaks of dancing as an amusement which has been discouraged by many of the best people, because it is associated in their minds with balls and their extravagances. On the contrary, dancing which involves a most healthy exercise should not be proscribed because the body as well as the mind feels its gladdening influence. No amusement seems more to have a foundation in our nature. The animation of youth naturally overflows in harmonious movements. It is an art almost as old as the rock-ribbed hills, and certainly antedates music, sculpture, and painting. Considered in the light of its best characteristics dancing is both ancient and honorable. It has ever been the refined expression of the poetry of the human body in motion. In ancient Greece dancing was an indispensible part of the education of youth. King James the First gave as a reason for permitting specific sports and pastimes, such as May Day games and Morris dances, and so forth, on special occasions, that "if these times be taken away from the meaner sort who labor hard all the week, they will have no recreation at all to refresh their spirits."

To many, dancing appears to be a frivolous waste of time and energy, while others regard it merely as an exhibition of tolerated childishness. To the strait-laced and puritanical, its practice is demoralizing, and it was this attitude which worked such a radical change in the social customs of Ireland in the last half of the nineteenth century. Yet who can question the wisdom of the clergyman who said that "people usually do more harm with their tongues than their toes."

"A Sunday with the peasantry in Ireland was not unlike the same day in France," says John Carr, Esq., who toured Ireland in 1805. "After the hours of devotion a spirit of gaiety shines upon every hour, the bagpipe is heard, and every foot is in motion. The cabin on this day is deserted, and families in order to meet together and enjoy the luxury of a social chat, even in rain and snow, will walk three or four miles to a given spot."

As every Irishman knows, the meeting place almost invariably was some cross-roads, where a piper or fiddler played enlivening music for the youthful dancers, while their elders gossiped in the old familiar way. Those more interested in athletics than in music and dancing, found no lack of that kind of entertainment also. Those national customs were observed until well beyond the middle of the nineteenth century, and no doubt it was the prevalent sentiment of the times that inspired the muse of F. Ambrose Butler in the following verses:

The Summer-sun is laughing down,
　And o'er the heather glancing—
We'll haste away ere close of day
　To join the peasants dancing
Beneath the ivy-clothed trees
　That guard the farmer's dwelling,
And softly shake their leafy bells
　While Music's strains are swelling—
We'll haste away, we'll haste away,
　Along the scented heather;
We'll join the merry peasant band
　And "trip the sod" together.

From silent glen, from mossy moor,
　From cabin lone and dreary,
They come—the friezed and hooded band
　With spirits never weary,
With hearts so light that sorrows ne'er
　Can break their sense of pleasure—
The Irish heart that laughs at care
　Is blessed with brightest treasure.
We'll haste away, we'll haste away,
　Along the scented heather;
We'll join the merry peasant band
　And "trip the sod" together.

The stars will peep amidst the trees,
　Their light with moonbeams blended,
Before the music dies away,
　Before the dance is ended.
And joke and laughter, wild and free,
　Ring round the farmer's dwelling,
And lithesome limbs keep measur'd time
　Where Irish airs are swelling.
We'll haste away, we'll haste away,
　Along the scented heather;
We'll join the merry peasant band
　And "trip the sod" together.

As long as happy Irish hearts
　Are throbbing through the Nation,
As long as Irish exiled sons
　Are found on God's creation,
As long as music's thrilling strains
　Can wake a sweet emotion,
We'll save the customs of our sires,
　At home and o'er the ocean.
We'll haste away, we'll haste away,
　Along the scented heather;
We'll join the merry peasant band
　And "trip the sod" together.

Such pastimes never interfered with religious devotions, for before the reformation only the hours for divine service were held sacred, and the rest of the day could be spent in sports if the people so chose, both in England and Scotland. Well, Dr. Joyce ruefully remarks: "The cross-roads are there still, but there is no longer any music or dancing or singing!" And by the way it reminds us of Goldsmith's lines in *"The Deserted Village:"*

> "These were thy charms, sweet village! sports like these
> With sweet procession taught e'en toil to please;
> These round thy bowers their cheerful influence shed;
> These were thy charms—but all these charms are fled."

In those racy old times when the manners and usages of the Irish were more simple and pastoral than when Carleton penned his famous *Traits and Stories of the Irish Peasantry,* the author says dancing was cultivated as one of the chief amusements of life, and the dancing-master looked upon as a person essentially necessary to the proper enjoyment of our national recreation. Of all the amusements peculiar to our population, dancing was by far the most important, although it was admittedly declining in his day. In Ireland it may be considered as a very just indication of the spirit and character of the people; so much so that it would be extremely difficult to find any test so significant of the Irish heart and its varied impulses, as the dance when contemplated in its most comprehensive spirit. In those days no people danced so well as the Irish, according to Carleton. Music and dancing being in fact as dependent the one on the other as cause and effect, it requires little or no argument to prove that the Irish, who are so sensitively alive to the one, should excel in the other. Nobody, unless one who has seen and also *felt* it, can conceive the inexplicable exhilaration of the heart which a dance communicates to the peasantry of Ireland. Indeed, it may be considered inspiration rather than the enthusiasm which manifests itself in all their actions, for Irish movement is in striking contrast with English dancing, which Emil Reich describes as "the melancholy polishing of the ballroom floor."

The love of dancing appears to be inherent amongst the Irish, and constitutes a striking feature in the national character. Even poverty and its attendant evils, which might be supposed sufficient to depress the most elastic spirit, have not been able to extinguish the love of the peasantry for this amusement, that may be said to form an important part of their education in the first half of the nineteenth century. With them, observes Stirling Coyne, who wrote of the *Scenery and Antiquities of Ireland* in the late thirties, it is a natural expression of gaiety and exuberance of animal spirits—indicative of their ardent temperament; and it is doubtful if a more accurate test could be found to judge the character of a people than their national dances. By a people entertaining a passion for music the dance is never neglected. Dancing may be said to have formed a part of the education of even the poorest classes and the skill acquired from their humble teachers was regularly exhibited at weddings and other festivities.

A racial proclivity so conspicuous could not fail to attract the attention of travelers, who with scarcely an exception were favorably impressed. Take for instance Rev. Dr. Campbell, who made his observations in 1775: "The Irish girls are passionately fond of dancing, and they certainly dance well, for last night I was at a ball and I never enjoyed one more in my life. There is a sweet affability and sparkling vivacity in these girls which is very captivating. We frog-blooded English dance as if the practice were not congenial to us; but here (in Cashel) they moved as if dancing had been the business of their lives. 'The Rock of Cashel' was a tune which seemed to inspire particular animation."

THE ROCKS OF CASHEL
from Aird's Selection of Scotch, English, Irish and Foreign Airs
Vol 4 circa 1793

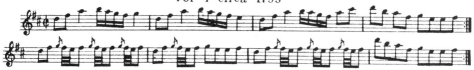

Dr. John Forbes, F. R. S., in his *Memorandums Made in Ireland* in 1852 is no less appreciative of peasant dances and dancing. At Leenane, County Galway, he saw "at the inn door a blind old Irish piper, doing his best to amuse the company with some of the melodies of his country, of which he was certainly no mean exponent.

"After a time the piper began playing jigs; and a dance was immediately gotten up, first by a young woman and an old woman, and then by the young woman and our Galway driver, an active young fellow. He danced zealously and well; but the young woman acquitted herself incomparably. It is but speaking the simple truth in regard to the performance of this young woman to say, that it possessed every charm that an elegant and graceful carriage and the most thorough command over all the varied movements of the dance could give it. If she had not been long and strictly drilled in her vocation, she must have been born with all the aptitudes of orginal genius in this harmonious art. It was really wonderful to see how perfect her execution was on her rough platform, and with her naked feet; though I cannot but think that the nakedness of the feet added not a little to the charm of the whole."

Testimony such as the above from the pen of a "Physician to Her Majesty's Household" could not have been tinged with partiality, yet very different was the impression which piping and dancing made on the English novelist Thackeray while visiting Killarney in 1843. "Anything more lugubrious than the drone of the pipe," he notes in the *Irish Sketch Book*, "or the jig danced to it, or the countenances of the dancers and musicians, I never saw. Round each set of dancers the people formed a ring; the toes went in, and the toes went out; then there came certain mystic figures of hands across and so forth. I never saw less grace or seemingly less enjoyment—no, not even in a quadrille."

None the less for his unappreciative comment, Thackeray's *Sketch* but proves the proneness of the Irish to indulge in the pleasures of the dance on all opportune occasions. Like his celebrated countrymen, Alexander Pope, Charles Lamb, Horace Walpole, and Dr. Johnson, the author of the *Irish Sketch Book* may have had no more ear for music than President Grant. So undiscriminating was the latter's tympanum that when in the field during the Civil War he was always provided with a horse trained to distinguish and respond to bugle calls. The general is said to have acknowledged knowing but two tunes—one was "Yankee Doodle" and the other wasn't.

CHAPTER XXIX

THE DANCING MASTER

HAVING been unduly, perhaps tiresomely, liberal in devoting so many pages to the pipers and fiddlers, it may appear ungenerous to ignore altogether the dancing master—one of the trinity of peasant entertainers. By Shelton Mackenzie he is described as "the light-heeled, light-hearted, jovial, genial fellow who was Master of the Revels in his own particular district."

There used to be as much pride in a village dancing master, he tells us, as in a village schoolmaster in the Munster counties early in the nineteenth century, and the forcible abduction of either, when persuasion and promise had failed, was not an unheard of proceeding. In the language of that charming writer: "To have a first-rate hedge schoolmaster was a credit to any parish. To have engrossed the services of an eminent dancing master was almost a matter of considerable pride and boasting; but to possess both of these treasures was indeed a triumph."

With the Irish peasantry dancing was a passion, hence the necessity for a teacher. On stated evenings during the winter, regardless of the condition of the roads, or the inclemency of the weather, a large company of aspirants for skill, ranging in age from ten to forty years, would assemble in some roomy barn having a smooth hard floor of clay to be instructed in the saltatory art; and once the lessons commenced, the hours passed away on swift pinions, we may be sure.

As Carleton—that versatile delineator of Irish life—has included the dancing master among his character sketches, a quotation from his pen cannot fail to be enlightening:

"Like most persons of the itinerant professions, the old Irish dancing master was generally a bachelor, having no fixed residence, but living from place to place within *his own walk,* beyond which he seldom or never went. The farmers were his patrons, and his visits to their houses always brought a holiday spirit along with them. When he came there was sure to be a dance in the evening after the hours of labor, he himself good-naturedly supplying them with the music. Few indeed were they having the right element in them for the profession, who could not play the fiddle or flute passably well.

"In return for this the 'boys' would get up a little underhand collection for him, amounting probably to half a crown or so, which some one under pretence of taking the snuff-box out of his pocket to get a pinch, would delicately and ingeniously slip into it. On the other hand the dancing master, not to be outdone in kindness, would at the conclusion of the little festivity, desire them to lay down a door, on which he usually danced a few favorite hornpipes to the music of his own fiddle. This performance was the great master-feat of his art, and was looked upon as such by himself as well as by the people.

"Indeed, the old dancing master had some very marked outlines of character peculiar to himself. His dress, for instance, was always far above the fiddler's, and this was the pride of his heart. He also made it a point to wear a Caroline hat whatever may have been its condition, but above all things, his soul within him was set upon a watch, and no one could gratify him more than by asking him before company what o'clock it was. He also contrived to carry an ornamental staff made of ebony, hickory, mahogany, or other rare description of cane, which if possible had a silver head and a silk tassel. This the dancing masters in general seemed to consider as a kind of baton or wand of office, without which they never felt content. But of all the parts of dress used to discriminate them from the fiddler or piper, we must place as standing far above the rest the dancing master's pumps and stockings, for shoes he seldom wore. The utmost limit of their ambition appeared to be such a jaunty neatness as might indicate the extraordinary lightness and activity which were expected from them by the people, in whose opinion the finest stocking, the lightest shoe, and the most symmetrical leg, uniformly denoted the most accomplished teacher."

It does not appear that the profession can boast of any claim to antiquity in the pages of Irish literature—at most not beyond two centuries. That the dancing master flourished quite extensively in the latter half of the eighteenth century is beyond question; the zenith of their glory having been reached in the early part of the nineteenth.

Carleton describes "Buckram-Back," the dancing master, in his character sketch, as "a dapper, light little fellow, with a rich Tipperary brogue." Shelton Mackenzie mentions two in his article on "Irish Dancing Masters"—"Ould Lynch," a County Limerick man, on the confines of "the Kingdom of Kerry," and Hearne, his predecessor at Fermoy, in the County of Cork. Considered in connection with the fact that Thomas O'Kearin and the equally renowned *Tadhg Ruadh* O'Scanlan also hailed from the Counties of Kerry and Limerick, respectively, there seem to be good grounds to sustain the claim that the Munster dancers were unrivaled. In support of this view it may be added that even in our own day in the cosmopolitan city of Chicago, such noted dancers of the old school as Richard Sullivan, Officer Timothy M. Dillon, Sergeants Michael Hartnett and Garret Stack, were born and brought up within a radius of a dozen miles or so of where the Counties of Kerry, Cork, and Limerick come together.

It was O'Kearin, who flourished at the end of the eighteenth century, and O'Scanlan after him, who consolidated Irish step dancing, and reduced it to a system based on precise fundamental movements. Men of genius in their art, both made the Kerry and Limerick schools of dancing famous throughout Ireland.

TADHG RUADH O'SCANLAN

In *A Handbook of Irish Dance,* published in Dublin since the Irish Revival, the authors make complimentary but brief mention of *Tadhg Ruadh* O'Scanlan, the Limerick dancing master, as being a veritable rival of the "Great O'Kearin," of County Kerry. A man so remarkable in the social life of the Irish people in the middle of the nineteenth century deserves better of his country than the mere preservation of his name.

Theigeen Rua O'Scanlan, as our friend Timothy M. Dillon calls him, lived at Glin on the banks of the Shannon, where he had a house and garden free of rent from the Knight of Glin. He was a neat, dapper little man, low-voiced and polite. Though not so "supreme" a dancer as John Kenny of Castlemahon, near Newmarket, he was a far better teacher; in fact, unrivaled in that line.

In those days all the young people had a passion for dancing, an acquirement without which no one's education was complete. Besides the sociability which it promoted, dancing induced freedom of movement and gracefulness of carriage.

Other dancing masters remembered by Mr. Dillon were James Scanlan, James Roche, Paddy King, and Benjamin Sheehy.

So much time and money were devoted to this alluring line of education that it was discountenanced by the clergy, who found the most effective way to put an end to it was to suppress the fiddlers and pipers.

JAMES ANTHONY COX

Around the middle of the nineteenth century there flourished in the County Longford a dancing master known as "Seamin" Anthony Cox. He made some pretentions to an education and was notoriously pedantic in his language. His request for the use of a barn for one of his dances was thus sententiously worded: "My name is Cox, from the rocks of Clooncarn, and will you please be so kind and condescending as to let me have the loan of your barn."

Once he encountered Lord Forbes in one of his hunting trips, Mr. Gillan tells us. To the question: "Did you see a hare cross about here my man?" he replied, with conscious dignity: "Yes, your Lordship, I observed a diminutive quadruped hastily descend the adjacent precipitous declivity." This oratorical response to such a simple question was so unexpected that Lord Forbes naturally asked: "Who are you?" "First, your Lordship," replied "Seamin," with cool assurance, "I'm an artificial rhythmical walker; second, I'm an instructor of youth in the Terpsichorean art; and third—" "You're the devil," interposed his Lordship; "and fourth," continued the dancing master, unabashed, "you're my brother."

Lord Forbes took the banter good-naturedly and presented the egotist with a guinea.

Anthony Cox, "Seamin's" father, was a genius and a "poet," and in fact "Seamin" was no less gifted, so that, like others possessing the faculty of satirical rhyming, the people were afraid of them and careful not to incur their illwill or dislike.

"Paudeen" Fox, an aged relative, requested when dying to have a quart bottle of whiskey and a stout blackthorn stick put in his coffin, promising that "Paudeen" Forbes, ancestor of the present Earl of Granard, wouldn't be alive the next morning.

PROF. PATRICK D. REIDY

Among the surviving dancing masters of the old traditional school, Prof. P. D. Reidy, formerly of Castleisland, County Kerry, but now of London, England, has special claims to distinction. From the fact that his father, who taught him, was one of the "Great O'Kearin's" pupils, it can be said that he is a lineal exponent of O'Kearin's art.

In his boyhood days the future professor was tested in his father's dancing school, and approved by renowned authority. That success determined his choice of a vocation.

The authors of *A Handbook of Irish Dance* are under obligations to Professor Reidy for much valuable information, but he regrets not being given an opportunity to correct the proofs before the work was published.

As with most men who have passed the meridian of life, "there is no time like the old time," and every page of his correspondence breathes a lament for the decadence of Irish ideals. "It is really a miracle that there is any Irish music or dancing in existence," he says. "The parish priests, and sometimes the curates, finished the work of Lord Barrymore. It is like going into a churchyard to visit the villages now, which were formerly alive with music and dancing."

In 1868, he gave an exhibition at Letter House, the residence of Dr. Wren,

Prof P. D. Reidy.

in north Kerry. The Ballybunnian piper, Thomas McCarthy, commonly called "Tom Carty," played the music for him in fine style.

The talented and kindly "Professor of Dancing, London and Castleisland," obligingly forwarded us a MS. book of music and a treatise from his own pen entitled: *Dancing-Theory as It Should Be*. The latter, while decidedly interesting, especially on account of the celebrity of its author, cannot be utilized for the present, however.

In concluding this subject, perhaps a paragraph from an article by J. G. O'Keeffe on "Irish Dances" may not be inappropriate: "Professor Reidy, who has for years past taught the Gaelic League of London, is one of the best Irish traditional dancers living. He comes of a family renowned in Kerry for dance. Mr. W. Murray is the celebrated step dancer who has also taught widely in London. He learned dance in the City of Cork. In the intricacy and variety of steps, as well as in grace and lightness of movement, he has scarcely a rival. Mr. Hugh O'Neill of Limerick City is a famous dancer who has won many prizes at various dancing competitions in Ireland. Mr. James Ward of Tory Island, County Donegal, is one of the best dancers from the north of Ireland."

The Irish dance of the present day is decidedly more rapid than that of a generation ago, and however much we may admire the agility and skill of the many excellent dancers graduated from the Cork Pipers' Club, such as James P. Coleman, the Hennessy brothers, "Paddy" Long, "Tom" Hill, and a dozen others, we must confess that music has the first claim on our affections. If the charm and expression of Irish dance tunes must be sacrificed to meet the requirements of modern stage dancers, neither Irish music, nor Irish step dancing can expect to regain or retain popular favor.

CHAPTER XXX

ANCIENT IRISH DANCES

THE discussion of latter-day dances, such as the jig, reel, and hornpipe, or even the various forms of the *Rinnce Fada* or long-dance, already described at some length in *Irish Folk Music: A Fascinating Hobby*, was not contemplated in this work, yet it may be opportune to mention briefly other peculiar forms of the art which found favor in ancient times, and which are now obsolete, or for the most part forgotten.

The dance belongs to all countries and to all ages. As Mrs. Lilly Grove says, it has come to us through all myths, through all histories, through all religions, in spite of repressive edicts and anathemas, and, though modified by epoch and fashion, it adapts itself to the land of its birth, and has always and everywhere preserved much of its original character.

From the language of some ancient writers, the term dancing seems to imply little more than dancing in a circle with hands joined. As far back as the twelfth century there existed a dance in Ireland termed

FER-CENGAIL

It was of the class known in Germany and France as hopping dances. One person sang the melody, and all joined in the chorus, held each other's hands as the name indicates, and moved in a circle.

CAKE DANCE

This dance is mentioned as a common and popular pastime at least as far back as the seventeenth century. It is not clear that it consisted of any peculiarity other than the object of its institution, which was seemingly to stimulate the dancers' efforts—a toothsome cake being the prize for superior merit. The cake or prize was displayed on the top of a distaff or pole, in full view of all competitors. Not the least interested of those present was the piper, near whose seat was some receptacle—often nothing more than a hollow in the ground—into which contributions were thrown after each dance. The desire of the young swains to appear generous and offhanded in the eyes of the colleens added not a little to the piper's prosperity.

In another form of this popular dance, the cake, decked out in field flowers or else encircled with apples, was awarded to the couple whose endurance outlasted their rivals in the dancing circle.

MAY-DAY DANCES

May-day festivals, as well as others of pagan origin, prevailed in the British Islands even in the late centuries. Maypole dances, common in England, were not unknown in Ireland. It was a favorite pastime on *La Bealtinne* or May Day, when the young men and maidens held hands, and danced in a circle round a tree hung with ribbons or garlands, or round a bonfire, moving in circles from right to left, to the accompaniment of their own voices singing in chorus.

426

Mrs. Anne Plumptre, in her *Narrative of a Residence in Ireland* (in 1815), remarked that dancing parties were "attended by a man and a woman, dressed in ridiculous figures, who are called the *Pickled Herring and his Wife;* they make grimaces and play antics something in the style of a Merry Andrew." Describing a dance she witnessed, Mrs. Plumptre continues: "The men were in number about forty, and, the tree being very tall, they all assisted in carrying it upon their shoulders. By the time they passed my friend's house they were joined by a piper, who was seated across the tree, and thus borne in great state, he playing all the time, while the *Pickled Herring* danced along at the head of the procession." The lady whom they intended to honor was "saluted with loud and repeated shouts." Her permission being obtained for the Long-dance next day, "she was again cheered, and the people resuming their burthen, the piper struck up a merry tune, the *Pickled Herring* resumed his antics, and away they marched with great order and regularity."

No music was found so suitable for Maypole dances among the English as the native bagpipe, as the tones of a fiddle would be almost inaudible in the midst of the general revelry.

Rinnce an Cipin, OR THE STICK DANCE

This was simply a degenerate form of the Sword Dance. Originally the latter was, both in Ireland and England, a duel with naked swords to the music of the bagpipe, as may be seen from the accompanying illustration taken from Knight's *Old England.* In Scotland the "Gillie Callum" was danced over and around two crossed swords, great care being taken not to disturb their position in the exercise.

DROGHEDY MARCH OR DANCING DROGHEDA

Now entirely obsolete, was described at much length by Patrick Kennedy in his *Banks of the Boro.* It was danced by six men or boys, each wielding a stout shillaleh. They kept time to the music with feet, arms, and weapons, and with their bodies swaying right and left. In the progress of the pantomime the movements became more complicated, and assumed the appearance of a rhythmic fencing or battle. This mimic war dance was performed to stately music, such as "Brian Boru's March."

THE COBBLERS' DANCE

Then there was the Cobblers' Dance, in which the performers squatted on their haunches in a position even more cramped than when half-soling a shoe. In this awkward attitude the dancer kicked out with each foot alternately in imitation of the rising step of the double jig. So ludicrous was the performance in its entirety that it never failed to arouse much merriment among the audience.

THE BUTCHERS' MARCH

It requires no great stretch of the imagination to connect this ancient tune with the *Rinnce Fada* which Sylvester O'Halloran, the eminent historian, saw danced by the butchers on May Eve, in his native city of Limerick, away back in the eighteenth century.

In modern times the tune in two strains is danced as a double jig, yet the setting found in O'Farrell's *Pocket Companion for the Irish or Union Pipes,* published in the first decade of the nineteenth century, consists of no less than six.

Old English Sword Dance

THE BUTCHERS' MARCH
from O'Farrell's Pocket Companion for the Irish or Union Pipes
Vol 2. Book 1. Pub. 1810

William Carleton, the novelist, born in 1798, mentions two ancient dances which few living in his time had witnessed. One called the

HORO LHEIG

was performed only at wakes, funerals, and other mournful occasions. It was only in remote parts of the country where the recollection of ancient usages still survived that any elucidation of such obsolete dances could be obtained.

There was another ancient dance executed by one man, not necessarily to the accompaniment of music. It could not, however, be performed without the emblematic aids of a stick and a handkerchief. This dance "was addressed to an individual passion, and was unquestionably one of those symbolic dances that were used in pagan rites."

Cul o Gurradh

An ancient pantomime dance so-called after the place where it was supposed to have originated, was peculiar to the County of Cork. It was performed in reel time by two persons who, in certain passages, simulated an attack and defense with closed fists in rhythmic movement to the music.

Bata na Bplandaighe OR THE PLANTING STICK

In the planting of cabbages or potatoes, a pointed stick with suitable handle on the other end was used to facilitate the work. A pantomime of the process of planting with this instrument is said by Sir William Wilde to have been practiced in the Province of Connacht in olden times. A double jig named "Bryan O'Linn," in the O'Neill collections, is the tune to which it is said to have been performed.

THE PLANTING STICK, OR BRYAN O'LYNN

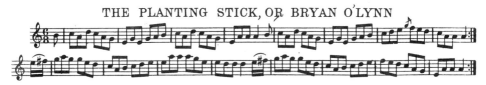

COVER THE BUCKLE

Whether this well known name was originally applied to a tune or a special dance is not easily determined, so conflicting are the references to it by various Irish writers. In "Darby the Blast," a song by Charles Lever, a couplet reads:

"As he plays 'Will I Send for the Priest?'
Or a jig they call 'Cover the Buckle.' "

No room for doubt can be found in that reference. Yet in Hall's *Ireland,* of about the same date, an infatuated swain tells of his charmer Kate Cleary "Covering the buckle, and heel on toe on the flure," opposite his rival.

A respected County Leitrim piper born at the beginning of the last century, named James Quinn, and who had lived in Chicago for many years, played a double jig which he called "Cover the Buckle," or "The Hag and Her Praskeen." This tune is now generally known as "The. Blooming Meadows," a simple version of which by that name is to be found printed without comment in Dr. Joyce's *Ancient Irish Music.*

In a work of such detail as *A Handbook of Irish Dance,* by O'Keeffe and O'Brien, one naturally expects to have the question settled definitely. Not so, however. "Cover the Buckle" is merely included in a list of "Figure" or "Set" dances "usually associated with tunes which are irregular in structure."

We find some solid ground at last in the writings of Shelton Mackenzie, who was born at Mallow, County of Cork, in 1809. In an article on "Irish Dancing Masters," the author describes "that wonderful display of agility known in my time as 'Cover the Buckle'—a name probably derived from the circumstance that the dancing-master, while teaching, always wore large buckles in his shoes, and, by the rapidity of motion with which he would make his 'many twinkling feet' perpetually cross, would seem to 'cover' the appendages in question." While thus exhibiting his skill and agility, the dancing-master was encouraged with such exclamations as "That's the way," "Now for a double cut," "Cover the buckle, ye divel," "Oh, then, 'tis he that handles his feet nately," and so on, until he had literally danced himself off his legs.

Various Special Tunes

Besides the tunes previously named in this chapter, many others have been mentioned in connection with "special" dances, now for the most part if not entirely forgotten. Principal among them are: "The Carpenters' March," two tunes of that name entirely dissimilar in metre and composition being in the Petrie collections; "The Priest in His Boots," "The Lark in the Morning," "The Drogheda Weavers," "The Humors of Limerick," "The Rocky Road to Dublin," "Drops of Brandy," "The Fairy Dance," "The High Caul Cap," "Shuffle and Cut," and "The Canny Sugach"—also known as "The Merry Merchant," and "The Merchant's Daughter."

A rollicking Irish song was sung to this air at least as late as the middle of the nineteenth century, and the agility required to dance it properly was proverbial, for nothing more complimentary could be said of a young man's activity than to remark that "he could dance the 'Canny Sugach.' "

THE MERRY MERCHANT
"Canny Sugach"

And, while we are discussing the subject of "special" tunes of ancient lineage, the occasion seems opportune to present to our readers "The Lark in the Morning," the rarest and certainly not the least interesting of its class, for it possesses marked individuality all its own.

THE LARK IN THE MORNING

This tune was first published in O'Neill's *Music of Ireland,* and the story of its recovery and preservation needs no apology for its presentation here.

James Carbray, a native of Quebec, but now a resident of Chicago, when studying music in his young days picked up some fine tunes from an old Kerry fiddler named Courtney, long settled in Canada. Many years later Mr. Carbray, amiable and accommodating gentleman that he is, recorded them on an Edison phonograph and forwarded the rolls to Sergt. James Early of the Chicago police force. It didn't take John McFadden long to memorize "The Lark in the Morning," and we may be sure it lost nothing of the *blas* or graces at his hands in transmission to Sergt. James O'Neill's notebook, and subsequently in its final setting herewith submitted.

While the display of any form of levity at a wake subjected the Irish to obloquy and ridicule, the Cushion Dance often concluded a country wake in "Merrie" England.

Kissing appeared to have been an essential part of most English dances, a circumstance which probably contributed not a little to their popularity. This custom, according to Mrs. Lilly Grove, author of *Dancing*—a renowned work— still survives in some parts of England, and when the fiddler thinks the young people have had music enough he makes his instrument squeak out two notes which all understand to say "Kiss her." At the end of each strathspey or jig a particular note from the fiddle used to summon the rustic to the agreeable duty of saluting his partner with a kiss, that being his fee or privilege according to established usage.

CHAPTER XXXI

IRISH PIPERS IN LITERATURE AND OTHER STORIES

IDIOSYNCRASIES OF IRISH MUSICIANS

IT was a belief of common acceptance among the people of Ireland in days gone by that inspiration was in some way to be derived from the fairies or other supernatural agencies, the composition of the "Fairy Queen" by Turlogh O'Carolan towards the end of the seventeenth century being a case in point.

The favored beneficiaries of fairy friendship seem to have been the pipers, but others who woo the muses were by no means neglected.

No doubt the superstitious musicians themselves did much to encourage this mysticism. To have dealings with the fairies incurred no loss of prestige. On the contrary, the piper or fiddler lucky enough to be conceded that coveted honor had a decided advantage over his fellows all the remaining days of his life.

How such persons could, with apparent sincerity, tell the most extravagant and improbable stories of their exploits and experiences is beyond comprehension, when we come to consider their normal mentality and behavior in the routine of everyday life.

A dual personality or the theory that those favorites of the fairies and the muses, in the exuberance of their conceit, may have become the victims of self-hypnosis, would account for much that suggests the question of their sanity.

The wonderful tales of enchantment in connection with pipers and the "good people" which find a place in Irish literature, as well as in oral tradition, are peculiar to the Gaelic race, for we find they are or were no less common in the Scottish highlands than in the "Land of Sweet Erin."

Raths and forts, which crown so many hilltops in the Green Isle, are held sacred to the memory of a hoary and mysterious past; and rash indeed would be the one who would desecrate their enclosed area, or mutilate their circular ramparts. As the reputed abodes of the fairies or "good people," they are regarded with awe and even dread by a simple, imaginative peasantry.

In Irish Folk Lore it seems the fairy hosts evinced a decided preference for the music of the Union pipes at their underground entertainments. However that may be, the strains of the violin, when produced by a master hand, in the quaint, traditional style, are no less welcome to mortal ears, nor do they affect the emotions less profoundly than the dulcet tones of the charmed instrument, as the following recital will show:

Timothy M. Dillon, for many years an official of the Department of Police, and an honored member of the once flourishing Irish Music Club of Chicago, was a native of that southwestern angle of Limerick which bounds both Cork and Kerry. The vales and glens in that picturesque and romantic spot were veritable nests of tradition in all that the word implies; and for that reason no one can deny that if we concede any truth in the potency of fairy inspiration, no member of the club could lay better claims to it than Mr. Dillon. When he adjusted his fiddle under his chin and began to play, he was insensible to all surroundings, with upturned face and eyes staring blankly at nothing, it could well be imagined that his performance was affected by some occult influence.

FATAL FASCINATION

"Many a time and oft" has he crossed the Atlantic, but never without his beloved instrument, and it was his never-failing custom to enliven the passage with music every evening. On one of those voyages a rather shy but handsome young lady became noticeably interested in his nightly performance. She listened attentively while feasting her eager, yearning eyes on Mr. Dillon and his instrument. Night after night she sat entranced, almost within reach of his sweeping bow, deliriously happy in his presence, and never left the deck while the voice of the violin vibrated in harmony with her heartstrings. The romanticism of moonlight on the ocean is not proof against the wooing of Morpheus, and for that reason Mr. Dillon's audience gradually grew less one night, until none but the fascinated maiden was left to admire his flow of melody.

Overcome, no doubt, by the charm of delightful strains, the demure damsel drew closer to the object of her adoration and, in a voice which betrayed the intensity of her emotions, whispered: "Oh, to bask in the presence of one's cherished ideal, to listen to the music which thrills the soul, and to enjoy such companionship through life, would be happiness greater than heaven's delights." Now, most men would be jumping with joy under the circumstances, because an avowal of that nature could only have come from a heart overflowing with love. Although her flattery was not distasteful (for Mr. Dillon knew he deserved it), he was proof against her blandishments, so he divulged the fatal fact that much as he would be pleased to reciprocate the young lady's affection, there was one trifling impediment—he was a married man, with a healthy wife and a numerous family awaiting his return to Chicago. With one despairing shriek, the heartbroken maiden plunged over the ship's side before he could prevent her, and disappeared from human sight forever.

There was no witness to this tragedy but the one who was the innocent cause of it. Mr. Dillon being a man of probity, and responsible for the story himself, we may as well accept it with possibly such mental reserve as the circumstances will warrant.

A RIVAL'S CONCEIT COMPLETELY CRUSHED

Mr. Dillon, as we may infer, was a man of unbounded liberality with his music, and nothing afforded him keener pleasure than contributing to the enjoyment of others while entertaining himself. One custom in particular which endeared him to his neighbors was that of fiddling on his front porch for hours at a time, when the weather was favorable. Although commendably modest and unassuming, our artist was by no means unconscious of his talents. Neither was it with any sense of egotism or vainglory that he confided to us the following story:

One morning, after a prolonged spell of jig and reel playing the evening before, his next-door neighbor, Professor Spieler, the violin teacher, paid him an unexpected visit. With the crestfallen demeanor of one whose pride and ambition had been rudely crushed, the professor presented his cherished instrument to the astonished Dillon, saying, with choking voice, "Mine friend and brother Musicker, you must oxcuse me, I have brought you mine instrument. Keep it and play on it. I have no more use for it. Before I heard you I thought I was a musician; but now—I know vat I know, and I know vat I don't know. I never will play no more."

"Drawing the Long Bow"

While the foregoing tales of Mr. Dillon's remarkable experiences may tax our credulity, it cannot be said that he was possessed of an over-developed sense of humor. Neither was there aught in his demeanor which would lead one to question his seriousness. Never boastful, seldom critical, he was not insensible to a little judicious praise, and although always protesting, he never failed to respond to an invitation to play.

At a friend's house one evening he was rolling off a string of reels which he had arranged in a regular sequence, when his host remarked, "What a great lot of tunes you have, Mr. Dillon." "Yes," he replied, modestly, "I have so many that when I start to play I don't know when to stop, as they would keep coming into my head all night." "About how many tunes do you think you have, Mr. Dillon?" the present writer inquired. "Well, I really can't say, Chief, but one night, when I was feeling pretty good, I started in gay and lively. After a while Mr. McFadden put his hand on my shoulder and said, 'You'd better stop now, Tim.' Then he asked me how many tunes did I think I played. I told him I hadn't the least idea. 'Well,' says he, 'I've been keeping tab on you, and you have just played 436 reels, not counting the others.'"

Stories of Pipers, Fiddlers, Etc.

From their peripatetic mode of life, and the circumstance that the nature of their calling brought them almost constantly in touch with cheerful company, pipers, fiddlers, and dancing masters of traditional times acquired an endless fund of anecdotes. Almost all were masters of story telling, and not a few were keen of wit and ready at repartee and rhyming.

Conflicting Interests

Among the latter was a County Leitrim piper, commonly known as "Shaun Bacach" on account of his lameness. Much of his support was derived from playing the pipes at a "patron," near a prominent cross-roads every Sunday afternoon. Whether it was the charm of his music, his pleasant ingratiating manner, or the opportunity for the young people to get better acquainted, or perhaps all combined, that attracted the large attendance, rumors of Shaun's phenomenal prosperity eventually reached the ears of his reverence the pastor.

This happened of course before "patrons" and dancing fell into disfavor. Just out of curiosity, you know, the clergyman happened along one Sunday afternoon and by way of no harm stationed himself where he could keep an eye on the hole in the ground beside the piper's chair. Into this hole, in lieu of some other receptacle, the joyous swains generously pitched a coin or two after each dance.

The pastor soon was convinced that the stories of Shaun's income had not been exaggerated. To his mind, this condition of affairs could not be permitted to continue. It was positively sinful to divert to frivolity so much money needed for more serious purposes; so stepping up to the astonished piper, he told him quietly but firmly that he would have to leave the parish.

"Yerra, Father, what have I done out of the way at all," begged the now alarmed Shaun.

"Well, for one thing," replied his reverence, "you're taking in more money at this 'patron' than my offerings amount to, and there is not enough in the parish for both of us."

"Sure, I'm not to blame for that," protested Shaun. "'Twas your father's fault."

"My father's fault," repeated the pastor in surprise; "how could it be his fault. What had he to do with it, will you tell me?"

"He had everything to do with it, your reverence. He ought to have made a piper out of you instead of a priest!"

Wit and humor will often win where an appeal to reason is doomed to failure. A County Longford version of this story has it that the acute stage of the controversy between the priest and the piper had been reached at a wedding instead of a "patron."

Liberality, no less than hospitality, is a dominant characteristic of the Irish race, and a wedding, particularly of the well-to-do, was sure to be an occasion for the display of this well known trait. The parties on "both sides of the house," in this instance, were determined to be worthy of their people, and "not let it go with anyone" in the way of cleverness and *flaithheamlacht* (flahoolacht). So when a donation was taken up for the pastor, who graced the occasion with his presence, after the ceremony, you may depend on it that the amount was no "small penny."

Without a piper to furnish fine music, of course, the festivities would be incomplete, and so when the "plate was passed around" for Shaun's benefit later on, when all present were in a mellow and generous frame of mind, great was their astonishment to find that the piper's pittance exceeded the pastor's purse! This unexpected denouement was considered an excellent joke by some, but according to my veracious informant, Mr. Gillan, it occasioned his reverence, the *sagart*, no little embarrassment. The interchange of compliments which followed between him and the piper is essentially the same in both cases.

TOM O'SULLIVAN

More remarkable even than the experience of Turlogh McSweeney, "the Donegal Piper," was the manner in which Tom O'Sullivan, "one of the best pipers in Kerry," as his friends termed him, came to acquire his musical skill. When J. G. Kohl, the German traveler, made a tour of Ireland in the early forties of the last century, nothing astounded him so much as the universal belief in the fairies and their potent influence on the affairs of mortals.

"Oh, your honor don't believe our fairy stories," said one of the company who had observed him shaking his head at one of the marvelous tales. "Yet I'll lay a wager there's many a man now abroad to whom the strangest things have happened, and which we must believe, because they are plain, simple, indisputable facts. Now there's 'Tom' O'Sullivan, your honor, there he stands, and 'Tom's' one of the best bagpipe players in Kerry. Well, 'till after he was thirty 'Tom' had never handled a bag of pipes in his life. It happened however, one day, that he was wandering among the hills and lay down to sleep in a place that belonged to the 'good people,' and there are many such places in our country. Now when he was asleep the fairies appeared to him and played him a power of the most beautiful tunes upon the bagpipes, and then laid the bagpipes down by the side of him. Well, when 'Tom' awoke, he felt about in the grass and soon found the pipes, and when he took them up he was able to play off-hand and quite pat every one of the tunes that the fairies had taught him. Now that's a fact, your honor." "Is it so, Tom?" inquired the traveler. "Indeed it is, your honor, and very pretty people they were that taught me. And although it's now thirty years since they gave me the pipes, I have them still, and they play as beautifully now as the first day." "There now, that's a fact, your honor," interposed a listener.

By way of strengthening the evidence to convince the incredulous Mr. Kohl, "Tom" went on and told him of a yet more marvelous adventure of a friend of his, one "Phil" McShane, who had fought in the great battle on the side of the Kerry fairies against the Limerick fairies, and to reward his bravery the victors gave him a cap which, when worn, endowed him with the strength of any other seven men. " 'Phil' has the cap still," continued "Tom," "and when he puts it on there's not a man in the barony will affront him. Now that's another fact, your honor, and when you come to Kerry I'll show you my pipes and my friend 'Phil' will show you his cap."

"I see, sir, you don't believe in 'em," interposed a young woman, meaning of course the fairies or "good people," "and yet it's a wonder you don't. Well, I've seen 'em with my own eyes, dancing on the fairy grounds, and I've heard their music, too, with my own ears, and most beautiful it is. Not long ago, while coming across the bog of Ballinasloe with my husband, both of us well tired, and we laid down to rest by the side of a holy well. My husband fell asleep, but I didn't, and soon I heard the most delightful music. I thought surely there must have been a piper near at hand and stood up to look about me, but as I saw nothing I waked my husband and bid him listen. 'Let us go on,' says he, 'it's the good people that's playing.' Your honor ought to know by this time that there's fairies and plenty of them; yes, and they have pipers and dancers like us Christians, only better, and it isn't lucky for anyone, gentle or simple, to be laughing at 'em ayther."

THADY CONNOR (AND HOW HE GOT HIS PIPES)

"Ye see, yer honors, Thady Connor (who was own brother of Maurice Connor that had the wonderful tune, by the manes of which he married the grand saylady* of Trafraska) was the greatest piper in these parts and taught Mr. Gandsey a power of fine music; and the both of them, as well as Maurice, were stone-blind. Well, Thady's pipes were ould and cracked and had a squeak in 'em that bate the Mullinavat pig all hollow. The gentry were mighty fond of him and many a time said something about the new set they intended to get for him, but they always forgot to remimber their promise, so the dickens a dacent set Thady would ever own, but for the great O'Donoghue that gave 'em to him in the ind, and the way of it was this:

"Thady, like his brother, loved a dhrop—and a big wan—and two dhrops better nor wan. And wan night he went to a wake, but went off airly, on account of a weddin' he had to be at, the morrow morning, a long way off among the Reeks. So to be sure, he was overtaken with a powerful wakeness and an impression about his heart. 'Arrah, what's this?' says he. 'Sure it can't be the licker, and I after drinking no more than a dozen tumblers, though I often took more.' With that he sits down by the roadside and begins to play to keep himself from sinking to sleep. All of a sudden he hears a troop of horsemen riding past him. 'A pretty set of boys ye must be,' says Thady, 'to be out this time o' night,' says he. 'Fitther for ye to be in your dacent beds than gamboling about the counthry. I'll go bail you're all dhrunk,' says he. Well, with that, up comes one of them and says, 'Here's a piper, let's have him with us.' 'Couldn't ye say by yer lave?' says Thady. 'Well then, by yer lave,' says the horseman. 'And that you won't have, seeing I must be at Tim Mahony's wedding by daybreak,' says Thady, 'or I'll lose my good seven thirteens.' So without another word they claps him on a horse's back

---

*Mermaid.

and wan of 'em lays hould of him by the scruff of his neck, and away they rode like the March winds—aye, or faster. After a while they stopped. 'And where am I at all, at all?' inquired Thady. 'Open your eyes and see,' says a voice, and so he did—the dark man that never saw the light till that blessed night; and meelya murther! if there wasn't troops of fine gentlemen and ladies, with swoords and feathers and spurs of goold and lashins of mate and dhrink upon tables, so broad and bright, and everything grand that the world contained since Adam was a gorsoon. 'Ye're welcome to the castle of the great O'Donoghue,' says the voice again. 'I often heard tell of it,' says Thady, nothing daunted, 'and is the prince to the fore?' 'I'm here,' says the prince, himself coming forrid; and a fine portly man he was, sure enough, with a cocked hat and a coat of mail. 'And here's your health, Mr. Connor, and the health of all my descendants great and small,' says he, 'and when they're tired of the sod,' says he, 'they'll know where to get the best entertainment for man and baste, every wan, that ever owned the name,' says he.

"Well, after a while the dance began, and didn't Thady play for the dear life 'Jig Polthogue' and 'Planxty Moriarty' and all the jigs that ever were invented by man or mortal. And the gintlemen and ladies danced with their hearts in their toes.

"'Twas all very well till the ould ancient harper of the O'Donoghues asked for a trial aginst Thady, to see if he wouldn't get louder music out of a handful of cats-guts; and Thady bate him to smithereens. When the consated harper found he was bate, he comes behind Thady, and with an ould knife or skian, rips open the bag, and lets out the wind that makes the music.

"'I'm done for now,' says Thady, as he aims a wallop at the harper's head that sent him reeling along the flure. Then all the company sets up a loud ulla-goane—the dance was over—and tells Thady he might as well go home. 'And who'll pay me for my pipes?' says Thady, who was a cunning boy after all. 'They were as good as new,' says he, 'and they aren't worth minding now.' 'Fair exchange is no robbery,' says the prince, 'and here's a set that will make your fortune, so be off as fast as you can, for the harper is bringing up his faction, and he'll sarve you as he did your pipes.' Well, Thady made a spring to get out of harm's way, and landed in a pool of water which filled his eyes and ears, and he heard a voice after him that he thought was the harper's, only it wasn't, but it was his wife Biddy that was waking him, as she found him asleep under the very hedge where the O'Donoghue horsemen found him earlier in the night.

"And now, plase your honor, nobody misbelieved the story he told the neighbors, because ye see the bran new pipes were to the fore; for there he had 'em under his arm, and sure how would he get 'em if 'twasn't from the great O'Donoghue himself."

DANIEL O'LEARY, THE DUHALLOW PIPER

In the early years of the nineteenth century, when the world-renowned harpers had vanished like snow in spring from the land which their art had glorified, great performers on the melodious Union pipes flourished in goodly numbers. Like the harpers, not a few of them were attached to families of wealth and distinction, regardless of racial origin, while yet others—true minstrels—led a wandering life. They were in fact so much a part of the ordinary institutions of the country that but casual and meagre references, out of all proportion to their numbers, is to be found in Irish literature concerning them, from the early centuries to the present time; and that little which has been preserved to us in print we owe, in a great measure, to travelers and writers in whose veins flow the blood of the invader.

In those days, a traveler rambling through certain wild districts in the north-western part of the County of Cork, by a curious circumstance, had the pleasure of hearing some of the best Irish airs played on the best set of "organ" pipes, by the best piper in Munster—a rare treat, as he says in a communication to the editor of the *Dublin Penny Journal,* in October, 1834.

Seated on the rampart of a rath or fort, he fell to moralizing on the past, and the people who lived and loved and died and left not a trace behind of their identity in the glorious scene before him, where the light and shade of hill and vale were beautifully linked with the evening mist that curled along the banks of the winding Araglin. When he awoke from his reverie, it was too late to reach his destination before dark, so he gladly accepted the invitation of an intelligent herdsman to partake of his hospitality for the night. As a special inducement, he was promised a rare treat of national Irish music, from the chanter of Daniel O'Leary, the first piper of Munster, who luckily had paid them a visit.

When the traveler and his host entered the cozy cabin, right beside the cheer-ful fire sat the piper, a diminutive man, deformed in person, like Willie Wattle's wife, who—

> "Had a hump upon her breast
> The twin of that upon her shoulder."

He had a knowing cast of countenance and a keen, observant eye. After the customary *"Cead mile failthe"* and the ordinary exchange of compliments, O'Leary yoked on his pipes to do the stranger courtesy, and played "Eileen a Roon" and "O'Carolan's Farewell to Music," with exquisite taste and feeling. "I have listened to much music," to quote the traveler's words, "but Jack Pigott's *'Cois na Breedha'* and O'Leary's 'Humors of Glin' are in my estimation the *ne plus ultra* of bagpipe melody."

In the course of the night the hospitable herdsman, seeing how much pleased his guest was with O'Leary's splendid performance, requested the piper to favor him with an account of his adventures with the "good people" at the fort of Doon.

"Ah!" said the piper, "this gentleman has read too much to credit such stories, though in the ancient times people saw strange sights, and seeing was believing." As the traveler loved legendary lore nearly as well as music, he requested the piper to relate his story, which was to the following effect:

One November afternoon, Daniel O'Leary was routed from his bed at his sister's house in the town of Millstreet. He had retired to take a nap, for he had been engaged during the preceding night at the "Wallis Arms" playing for a party of gentlemen that dined there, and had scarcely fetched half a dozen snores when his repose was interrupted. It was a message from the squire of Kilmeen, com-manding his attendance at the Castle. He had a grand party, and though a fiddler or two were in requisition, Miss Julia Twomey, one of the young ladies invited, could abide no other music than O'Leary's. In fact, the estimation in which a "dinner" or wedding was held in Duhallow was regulated by the circumstances of that piper's absence or attendance there. Though our friend Daniel had no relish for the interruption of his much needed rest, he had too much respect for the squire to disregard his wishes.

After treating the messenger, he was about to mount the fine horse which the squire had sent for him, when a blue-eyed *thuckeen* from Knocknagrue, "an ould acquaintance" of O'Leary's, passed by, and he directed the squire's man to walk the horse slowly on before them, while he whispered a word or two to Nancy Walsh.

They entered the public house at the cross-road, and were so agreeably entertained with each other's company, over a glass of punch, that it was dark night before they parted. At length, after taking a parting kiss, the piper pursued his way, in the hope of soon overtaking the man with the horse; but when he reached Finown, no servant lingered .for him on the bank of the rapid water. Having made his way, with some difficulty, over the high stepping stones, he set forward with accelerated. speed, in the hope of overtaking him before he reached Blackwater Bridge, for where the broad river rushes through the glen and sweeps the tall rock at "Justice's Castle" the scene is wild and ·lonely, and the neighborhood of that ancient building had, time out of mind, been deemed a favorite haunt of the *"good people."*

As he approached the bridge, the moon was rising, and our friend O'Leary halted to hear if possible the friendly tramp of the horse's hoofs. 'Twas all in vain. He heard no sound, save the distant voice of the watchdog, and no object met his eyes by the ivied towers of the castle, surmounting the fir trees that crowned the rock, and flung their giant shadows athwart the stream beneath the pale moonbeams, that danced like things of life upon the water.

Though the Duhallow piper was "purty well, I thank ye," yet the punch he quaffed in Nancy Walsh's company could not make him scorn the dangers that superstition taught him to expect in this fairy haunt. Knowing the power of music on those occasions, he yoked on his pipes, intending to raise a sacred melody as a guard against the influence of any evil thing that might hover round his path; but owing to some unaccountable irregularity of idea, after many vain attempts, he could bring no other tune out of the chanter than O'Carolan's "Receipt for Drinking Whiskey."

This beautiful air rose sweetly on the night wind, as he journeyed along, and when the tune was nearly concluded, he thought he could distinguish the tramp of horses. He ceased his strain, thinking it was the servant that came trotting in the distance behind; but soon perceived the sound was multiplied by a hundred hoofs along the road. He could now descry the dim figures of horsemen as they approached nearer and, supposing that he had fallen in with a party of *Rockites,* he withdrew a short distance from the road to the shelter of a furze bush. As the long procession moved onward, he thought he could distinguish among the horsemen the shape of persons whom he had known to be long. dead, and who, he thought, were resting in their quiet graves. But his. surprise was considerably increased to behold his friend "Tom" Tierney, who conversed with him, alive and well, that very evening in Millstreet, in the last rank that ended the cavalcade, and to complete his astonishment, the horse on which "Tom" rode was drowned in a bog hole, to O'Leary's certain knowledge, about a fortnight before.

From these circumstances, the piper was now convinced that these horsemen were the *slua shee* or fairy host. "Tom" wore his usual broad-brimmed beaver, that saved his complexion from the summer's sun, for he always shone as a rustic dandy of the first water. The moon which emerged that moment from behind a cloud gleamed on the large gold ring that circled his forefinger, and which "Tom" on all occasions took no small pains to display, for it descended to him through a long line of ancestry from the sister of *Dhonal Caum,* whose descendent he was.

"A virrah dheelish! is it dhramin' I am, or are my eyes desaving me all out?" says the astonished piper. "'Tom' Tierney, if it's yourself that's there, wouldn't you spake to the son of your own blood relation and not lave him to die with the cowld without the benefit of the clargy by the roadside?" "Ayeh! it's a bad day I wouldn't do more nor that," says "Tom," spurring his horse into the ditch to enable the piper to mount behind him with facility, and at that moment a peal of laughter ran through the whole troop. Had the explorer of an ancient catacomb heard the dead of a thousand years bid him welcome to their silent mansions, he could not have experienced greater fear than did O'Leary, when this wild burst of unnatural mirth rose from the ranks of the strange cavalcade upon his mortal ear.

After mounting, his fear was further increased to find that neither the horse nor the rider had the solidity of frame common to mere matter; in short, they seemed to form an indefinable something between the shadow and substance of bodies.

When they came to the cross-road that led to the squire's, the horsemen pursued the opposite direction; and when the piper either attempted to alight or expostulate with his friend "Tom," he found both his limbs and tongue equally incapable of motion. They halted at the fort of Doon, near the river Araglin, where rose a stately building, the brilliant lights of which put to shame the lustre of the stars and the clear full moon.

In the great hall appeared a splendid company of both sexes, listening to the music of the full orchestra, where sat musicians bearing instruments with which the piper was wholly unacquainted; and bards in white robes, whose long beards flowed across their tall harps. An elderly man, bearing a long white wand, announced "Daniel O'Leary, the Duhallow Piper," and immediately three distinct rounds of cheering rose from the crowded assembly, till the fairy castle shook to the sound.

When the applause had subsided, a beautiful lady rose from her seat, and snatching a certain stringed instrument, sang to the music of its chords the following strain, addressed to the astounded piper:

> Thy welcome, O'Leary, be joyous and high;
> As this dwelling of fairy can echo reply,
> The clarseach and crotal and loud bara-boo
> Shall sound not a note till we've music from you.

> The bara-boo's wildness is meet for the fray,
> The crotal's soft mildness for festival gay,
> The clarseach is meeter for bower and hall;
> But thy chanter sounds sweeter, far sweeter than all.

> When thy fingers are flying the chanter along,
> And the keys are replying in wildness of song;
> The bagpipes are speaking such magical strain,
> As minstrels are seeking to rival in vain.

> Shall bards of this dwelling admire each sweet tune,
> As thy war-notes are swelling that erst were their own;
> Shall beauties of brightness, and chieftains of might,
> To thy brisk lay of lightness dance lightly tonight?

O'er harper and poet we'll place thy high seat;
O'Leary, we owe it to piper so sweet;
And fairies are braiding (such favorite art thou),
Fresh laurel unfading, to circle thy brow.

Thy welcome, O'Leary, be joyous and high;
As the dwelling of fairy can echo reply;
The clarseach and crotal and loud bara-boo
Shall sound not a note till we've music from you.

Then a seat that glittered like a throne was prepared for the delighted O'Leary, and a band of beautiful damsels, with laughing blue eyes, placed a garland of shining laurel 'round his head. The other performers were completely mute during the rest of the night. Fair ladies poured out the red wine and pressed the entranced piper to quaff the inspiring beverage. Every tune elicited fresh applause; and when the dancing ended the lords and ladies all declared that their hearts bounded lighter and their feet beat truer time to O'Leary's music than ever before.

At length, oppressed with wine, and intoxicated with the incense of applause, the piper sunk into profound repose. When he awoke in the morning he found himself reclining at the same bush to whose shelter he had retired to let the horsemen pass; the pipes were yoked and his left hand still grasped the chanter.

He at first conceived that the scenes of the preceding night, which began to assume a definite shape in his memory, were but the dream of imagination, heated by music, whiskey-punch and his conversation with Nancy Walsh; until he found the unfading wreath yet circling his brow. This wreath of laurel he had preserved and still exhibits as his fairy meed of musical excellence.

Such was the adventure of Daniel O'Leary; and the traveler from whose account of it we have liberally availed ourselves concludes: "Many are the opinions afloat concerning the truth of this narrative, but let skeptics examine, as I have done, this curious wreath of laurel, and consider its complicated braiding, and the piper's unimpeachable veracity in all other respects, before they presume to try this singular story by the test of their philosophy."

THE PIPER AND THE PUCA

(Translated from the Irish by Dr. Douglas Hyde)

In the old times there was a half fool living in Dunmore, in the County Galway, and although he was excessively fond of music, he was unable to learn more than one tune, and that was the "Black Rogue." He used to get a good deal of money from the gentlemen, for they used to get sport out of him.

One night the piper was coming home from a house where there had been a dance, and he half drunk, when he came to a little bridge that was up by his mother's house, he squeezed the pipes on, and began playing the "Black Rogue."

The Puca came behind him, and flung him on his own back. There were long horns on the Puca, and the piper got a good grip of them, and then he said: "Destruction on you, you nasty beast, let me home. I have a ten-penny piece in my pocket for my mother, and she wants snuff."

"Never mind your mother," said the Puca, "but keep your hold. If you fall, you will break your neck and your pipes."

Then the Puca said to him, "Play up for me the 'Shan Van Vocht.'"

"I don't know it," said the piper.

"Never mind whether you do or you don't," said the Puca. "Play up and I'll make you know."

The piper put wind in his bag, and he played such music as made himself wonder.

"Upon my word, you're a fine music master," says the piper then; "but tell me where you're for bringing me."

"There's a great feast in the house of the Banshee, on the top of Croagh Patric, tonight," says the Puca, "and I'm for bringing you there to play music and, take my word, you'll get the price for your trouble."

"By my word, you'll save me a journey, then," says the piper, "for Father William put a journey to Croagh Patric on me, because I stole the white gander from him last Martinmas."

The Puca rushed him across hills and bogs and rough places, till he brought him to the top of Croagh Patric. Then the Puca struck three blows with his foot, and a great door opened, and they passed in together into a fine room.

The piper saw a golden table in the middle of the room, and hundreds of old women sitting around it. The old women rose up and said:

"A hundred thousand welcomes to you, you Puca of November. Who is this you have with you?"

"The best piper in Ireland," says the Puca.

One of the old women struck a blow on the ground, and a door opened in the side of the wall, and what should the piper see coming out, but the white gander which he had stolen from Father William.

"By my conscience, then," says the piper, "myself and my mother ate every taste of that gander, only one wing, and I gave that to Moy-rua (Red Mary), and it's she told the priest I stole his gander."

The gander cleaned the table, and carried it away, and the Puca said: "Play up music for these ladies."

The piper played up, and the old women began dancing, and they were dancing until they were tired.

Then the Puca said to "Pay the piper," and every old woman drew out a gold piece, and gave it to him.

"By the tooth of Patric," said he, "I'm as rich as the son of a lord."

"Come with me," says the Puca, "and I'll bring you home."

They went out then, and just as he was going to ride on the Puca, the gander came up to him, and gave him a new set of pipes. The Puca was not long until he brought him to Dunmore, and he threw the piper off at the little bridge, and then he told him to go home, and said to him, "You have two things now that you never had before—you have sense and music."

The piper went home, and he knocked at his mother's door, saying, "Let me in; I'm rich as a lord, and I'm the best piper in Ireland."

"You're drunk," said the mother.

"No, indeed," says the piper, "I haven't drunk a drop."

The mother let him in, and he gave her the gold pieces, and "Wait now," says he, "till you hear the music I'll play."

He buckled on the pipes, but instead of music, there came a sound as if all the geese and ganders in Ireland were screeching together. He awakened the neighbors, and they were all mocking him, until he put on the old pipes, and then he played melodious music for them; and after that, he told them all he had gone through that night.

The next morning when his mother went to look at the gold pieces, there was nothing there but the leaves of a plant.

The piper went to the priest, and told him his story, but the priest would not believe a word from him, until he put the pipes on him, and then the screeching of the ganders and geese began.

"Leave my sight, you thief," says the priest.

But nothing would do the piper till he would put the old pipes on him to show the priest that his story was true.

He buckled on the old pipes and he played melodious music, and from that day till the day of his death, there was never a piper in the County Galway as good as he was.

"Donogh an Asal"

Many long years ago there lived in an obscure Galway village a piper nicknamed *"Donogh an Asal,"* on account of the ass or donkey which served him as a beast of burden in various capacities. Of course he was poor, like all of his tribe, but that did not deter a handsome young colleen from taking a liking to him in preference to many eligible young men of the parish, presumably on account of his musical talent—a not uncommon failing of her sex.

We all know what to expect from early marriages in Ireland, so we can understand that the poor piper had no easy time of it, providing for an increasing family, as he had no other means of supporting them than by his humble profession. Much as the peasantry all around admired and enjoyed his music, their own poverty kept a check on their generosity.

'Twas with Donogh's family as with many others. The eldest kept going away one by one, as the youngest arrived, and the time came when even the last one—a boy—made up his mind to leave home like his brothers and sisters and seek employment among strangers.

With all her children whom she nursed and tended with a mother's self-sacrificing care, gone from her, it is little wonder that anxiety and grief soon undermined the health of Donogh's wife, who did not long survive the departure of the last of her flock. The poor piper's condition was now pitiable indeed, with his faithful and beloved wife dead in the house, and not a child of their's in the country to attend the wake or funeral of their mother.

All Donogh possessed in the world besides his pipes and a few kippens of furniture was the donkey and cart, used mostly to haul home a crate of turf from the bog; and the poor beast, it must be admitted, was almost as tired of the world as his owner. The attendance at the wake was very disappointing to the bereaved piper, although, like all his race, he left nothing possible to him undone "to bury her dacent like her people before her."

Barely enough men to convey the coffin to the donkey cart came to the house on the morning of the funeral. The idea of having a hearse could not be entertained at all; but this he didn't mind, if only the attendance came up to his expectations, for indeed a kind mother and a good neighbor deserved that much respect anyway.

A MUSICAL FUNERAL

As the funeral was just about ready to move, a most unexpected thing happened. Prompted by desperation, arising from his grief and humiliation, *"Donogh an Asal"* ran into the house for his pipes, mounted the cart, took his seat on the coffin, and buckling on his instrument, struck up a lamentation as weird and affecting as the ullagoane of the most renowned *caoiner* in the country.

The wailing of the pipes, besides affording the grief-stricken widower a means of giving vent to his feelings, naturally attracted every one within hearing. By the time they had reached the graveyard (which was over three miles from the house), with the piper still seated on the coffin playing with an elation of spirit superinduced by the constantly increasing attendance, the funeral turned out to be the largest which ever entered the gates of a graveyard in that part of the country. Such is the power of music.

DENNY BYRNE THE PIPER

The remarkable adventures of a piper in the tragic days of the Insurrection in '98 were so full of dramatic situations, that song writers and story tellers were by no means slow to avail themselves of such a suitable theme for the display of their talents. The anonymous poetaster whose effusion is entitled "The Cow That Ate the Piper," introduces his hero as "Denny Byrne the Piper." There being no occasion to make it conform to the necessities of rhyme, we may assume that name to be the true one.

Many years later Samuel Lover heard the story related by a gentleman, who told him he was not aware to whom the original story was attributable. The result was "Paddy the Piper," a rather lengthy tale in the Irish vernacular which was included in his *Legends and Stories of Ireland*. A synopsis of the story in our own diction, though a little foreign to the scope of this chapter, may be excusable, as it is characteristic and undoubtedly founded on facts, which are presented in all versions with but little variation.

THE STORY

In the days of the Insurrection in 1798 many a fine fellow's precious life was cut short by raison of the martial law. A fellow couldn't go out in the evening, good or bad, and when the day's work was done, divil a one dare go out to meet a friend or a colleen at a dance. No, they must shut themselves up, and not raise a latch or pull a bolt until daylight in the morning.

Following is how the song writer depicts the horrors of his time:

"In the year '98 when our troubles were great,
  And 'twas treason to be a Milesian,
The black-whiskered set we will never forget,
  Though history tells us they were Hessian.
In this troublesome time, oh! 'twas a great crime,
  And murder never was riper,
At the side of Glenshee not an acre from me
  There lived one 'Denny' Byrne, a piper.

"Neither wedding nor wake would be worth a shake,
  Where 'Denny' was not first invited;
At squeezing the bags or emptying the kags,
  He astonished as well as delighted;
In these times, poor 'Denny' could not earn a penny,
  Martial law had him stung like a viper;
They kept him within, till the bones and the skin
  Were grinning through the rags of the piper."

While the praties were boiling for supper and the family was sitting around the fireplace, a knock came to one "Tim" Kennedy's door, not far from Rathangan in the County Kildare. They were much alarmed, thinking it was the sojers who saw a light through a crack in the door. But as the woman of the house had taken the precaution to hang a petticoat over it, and an apron to hide the keyhole, it couldn't be them. Another knock, and yet another, convinced the old man that it was no use to pretend they were already in bed, so he ordered his son Shemus to "see who was in it."

"Who's there?" inquired Shemus timidly.

"It's me," came the answer.

"And who are you?"

"A friend," replied the voice outside.

"Baithershin; who are you at all?" persisted Shemus.

"Ah sure, I'm 'Denny the Piper.' I want to get in."

'Twas no use to ask. The risk in opening the door was too great, although 'twas a hanging matter for the piper to be caught out in the night in those times. His pleading for admittance was in vain, but the hospitality of the cowshed was offered him for the night and finally accepted.

After sleeping in the straw under the manger for some hours, "Denny" woke up refreshed, and mistaking the moonlight for dawn, he started off across the fields, so as to be early at the fair; for being a first-rate piper, he hoped to earn a good penny that day. In rattling off "Jenny Banged the Weaver" he had no equal, and to hear him play "The Hare in the Corn," you'd think you'd hear the very dogs and the horsemen in the chase.

As before stated, "Denny" Byrne was taking every short cut on his way, with the green bag under his arm, and while pushing his way through an intervening hedge, what should he do but run plump up against a corpse hanging from the branch of a tree.

"Oh, good morning to you," exclaimed "Denny," as soon as he could catch his breath. "Faith, you took a start out of me anyhow." This politeness was lost on the gentleman, for such he was, evidently. His apparel indicated rank, and the elegant boots which encased the dangling limbs fascinated the piper's covetous eye, particularly as his own footgear had seen their best days.

"Pon me sowl, then, but you have a beautiful pair of boots on you," says he, "and it's what I'm thinking you won't have any great use for 'em anymore, and sure 'tis a shame for the likes of me—the best piper in the county and the next one to it—to be thrampin' in a pair of ould brogues not worth two *thraneens.*" With that "Denny" endeavored to pull the boots off the corpse, but between the swaying of the suspended body, and the stiffness of the feet, the attempt was a failure, and he was about to start off when a desperate idea entered his brain—no less, in fact, than to cut off the man's legs at the knee joints. Repellant as the idea was, the boots were too good to lose, and anyway, it couldn't hurt a dead man. So when he had severed the limbs with the boots on, he tucked them under his other arm, ready for traveling. Just then the moon peeped out from behind a passing cloud, and the coward which at times lurks in all men's natures, took the starch out of my brave "Denny." Rather than run the risk of being treated himself as the corpse had been, seeing that it wasn't yet daylight, he turned back and hastened as fast as he could to "Tim" Kennedy's cowshed; and, hiding the booted legs under the straw, went to sleep again for himself. The song has it:

"Then Denny did run for fear of being hung
  Till he came to 'Tim' Kennedy's cabin;
Says 'Tim' from within, 'I can't let you in,
  You'd be shot if you're caught there a-rappin.'
He went to the shed where the cow was in bed
  With a wisp he began for to wipe her;
They lay down together, on straw 'stead of feathers,
  And the cow fell to licking the piper."

But guess what happened, above all the things in the world? The dickens a long "Denny" Byrne was there until the sojers came in airnest and carried him off with 'em, pipes and all, and you may be sure after what he had done, 'twas little back talk he gave 'em ayther.

When morning came, his father sent Shemus out to the cowshed to call the piper in to his breakfast. He called him by name several times, but getting no answer, he went inside and shouted, " 'Denny,' where are you at all?" Still no answer. Seeing two legs sticking out from under a heap of straw, he added, "Wisha then, 'Denny,' you're fond of a cozy corner, ain't you, but all the same I must disturb your dhrames." With that he grabbed the legs and gave a good pull to frighten him, as he thought, and of course away went Shemus tumbling backwards against the wall. Nearly scared out of his wits, he dropped the legs and ran into the house bawling: "Oh, the unnatheral baste, the murtherin' villan, the thievin' cannable of a cow, to ate poor 'Denny.' Bad cess, to you. How dainty you are that nothin' 'ud sarve you for supper, but to ate the best piper in Ireland." "Arrah, be aisy," said his father. "Oh, bad luck to the lie I tell ye. Divil a bit of him she has left but his two legs." "And d'ye tell me she ate the pipes too?" inquired Mr. Kennedy. "Begor, I believe so," replied the son. "Oh, may the curse of the crows be on her," cried the agonized father; "what a terrible taste she has for music—the *ampalachaun.*"

Although Mrs. Kennedy was as much shocked as anyone, she did not like to hear them cursing a cow, whatever her faults, that had furnished milk for her children; but after what the cow had done, they all agreed that she should be disposed of at once at any price, for not another day could she be allowed to remain on the premises.

Shemus, much against his will, was obliged to tackle the job of driving the man-eating cow to the fair of Rathangan, as his father positively declined the pleasure of her company. He ran no chance of being lonesome, however, as many others had the same destination in view, but that didn't relieve his mind, much oppressed as he was with such an awful secret. "God save you, avic," said a jobber sweetly to him on the road. "God save you kindly," responded Shemus. "That's a fine baste you're dhrivin'," continued the jobber. "Is it to the fair you're going?" Shemus, of course, told him it was, but when asked what he expected for her, he got out of it by saying, "Sure, no one can tell what a baste will bring until they get to the fair and see what price is going."

An Irish jobber on the lookout for a bargain seldom fails to return to the attack, and this one was no exception. He badgered poor Shemus, until in sheer desperation he offered to take "four pounds for the cow and no less." As she was worth twice that amount, at least, the jobber, thinking there must be something wrong with her, remarked, "Maybe she's gone off her milk in regard that she doesn't feed well." "Och, by this and by that," protested Shemus, "in regard to feeding there's not the likes of her in Ireland, so make your mind aisy on that score, and if you like her for the money, you may have her."

This liberal offer, however, did not satisfy the cautious jobber, so he sauntered away saying, "Oh, well, I'm not in a hurry, so I'll wait to see how they are going at the fair."

At length they came to Rathangan, with its crowds, and its stands of ginger-bread and cakes and apples and gooseberries, and its games of pitch and toss, merry-go-rounds and tents, with eating and drinking in 'em, and the fiddlers play-ing for the bare life, to get everybody in humor for spending money. On this occasion the merriment and attractions had but little interest for Shemus, his only anxiety being to get rid of the ravenous cow as soon as possible, for, poor fellow, he felt like a criminal while she was on his hands.

As he pushed his way further into the middle of the fair, what should he hear at the door of a tent but a piper tearing away at "Tatter Jack Walsh." The old cow was evidently not insensible to the music, for cocking her ears, she started towards it. "Oh murther, boys, hould her, hould her!" shouted Shemus. "She ate one piper already, the vagabone, and bad scran to her, she wants another now!" "Is it a cow to ate a piper?" exclaimed some one. "Divil a word of a lie in it, for I seen his corpse myself, and nothin' left but the two legs," admitted Shemus, "and it's folly to be strivin' to hide it, for I see she'll never lave off, as poor 'Denny' Byrne knows to his cost, Lord be marciful to him."

"Who's that taking my name in vain?" said a voice in the crowd, and with that, shoving the throng one side, who in the world should appear but "Denny" Byrne himself! Shemus, now terror-stricken, on sight of him, jumped behind some of the boys for protection, for he thought sure 'twas "Denny's" ghost. Hardly able to speak from fright, he told them all that occurred on the evening before, and how he found only the piper's legs fresh and bloody in the straw in the morning.

When he heard the story "Denny" came near splitting his sides from laugh-ing, but as soon as he could get over it, he up and told 'em how it all happened, and maybe there wasn't fun made of Shemus and his cow after that, and it cost him a full gallon of spirits to square himself and drink long life to "Denny" Byrne and the slandered cow.

After being acquitted of the heinous crime of which she had been accused, the cow was driven home again, of course, and many's the quiet day she enjoyed after that on "Tim" Kennedy's farm.

But the longest life must come to an end. *Drimin dhu dheelish* eventually died, and her hide, after due process of tanning, was made into a showy pair of breeches for her owner, out of respect for her memory.

As was to be expected the breeches "wore like leather" and it was several generations before they were finally discarded. Yet though it was a very becom-ing and durable garment it possessed another remarkable and at times embarrass-ing peculiarity. Regardless of who chanced to wear them, that pair of breeches commenced twitching and jigging in the seat, the minute a piper struck up a tune within hearing, and never would keep still while there was a note in the chanter.

RORY OGE, THE KILLALOE PIPER

While speculating as to the probable site of the palace of Brian Boru at Kin-cora, and calling up in her fancy a long array of "chiefs and ladies bright," listen-ing to the harp of the old minstrel, Mrs. S. C. Hall, who traveled extensively in

Ireland early in the second quarter of the nineteenth century, tells in her writings how she was startled by the tones of the Irish bagpipes coming from Killaloe, nearly a mile distant.

It was a fair day in that ancient town, and after walking along with a gathering crowd she entered a tent from which the music proceeded and was introduced to the piper, familiarly known as "Rory Oge."

"We found him," she says, "very chatty and communicative, as we have found others of his class, and mourning over 'ould times,' as pathetically as did his great prototype, Mac Liag, over the downfall of Kincora. He was particularly wrathful upon two or three points—the decay of mountain stills, the decline of dancing, the departure of all spirit out of the hearts of 'the boys,' and above all the introduction of brass bands." The amiable traveler found him so interesting and entertaining that she has immortalized him in her works.

"Rory Oge" or Young Rory, as he was always called, was as enthusiastic and yet *knowing* a piper as ever "blew music out of an empty bag." He was a large portly man with a bald high brow, framed in a quantity of greyish flaxen hair; his nose had a peculiar twist and his mouth was full of ready laughter.

Though blind from birth, he always jested about this infirmity, and he was in great request all over the country, being even a better piper than his father, "Red Rory." The latter never attempted other than the old established Irish tunes, while "Rory Oge" the son, who had visited Dublin and once heard Catalani sing, assumed the airs of a connoisseur and extolled his country's music in a scientific way.

When he played some of the heart-moving Irish planxties, at the commencement of the movement he would endeavor to look grave and dignified; but before he was half through, his entire face expanded with merriment, and he would give "a whoop" with voice and fingers as it was concluded that manifested his genuine enthusiasm. Once in his life he had visited Dublin, expressly for the purpose of hearing Catalani, and when he was in the mood, to hear the recital of his interview with the "Queen of Song" was a source of much pleasure to his audience.

"You see," he would commence, "I thought it was my duty to hear what sort of a voice she had; and on my way to the great city, in the cool of the evening, I sat myself and my litle boy by the side of two strames—the 'Meeting of the Waters' they call it—and it wasn't long till a thrush began to sing in a rowan tree on the opposite bank, and then another, and then a blackbird would give his tally-ho! of a whistle high and above all the rest, and so they went on singing for ever so long. Then two or three would stop, and one great songster would have it all his own way for a while, and then when they would all start together a great flood of bird music would gush out again."

"In the midst of it all the little *gorsoon* fell asleep, and I felt the tears come down my face just within thinking of the beautiful music the Almighty puts into the throats of them fluttering birds, and wondering if the furrin' lady could bate the thrush in the rowan tree.

"In the afternoon of the next day, I was in Dublin, but not a bit of her was to tune up, till the night after; so I had to hould my patience another day. Why, God bless ye, the Dublineers were going just as mad about her singing as they are now about them nasty, braying brass bands, that has no more of the rale music in 'em than a drove of donkeys.

"Well dears, I'll not be thinking of 'em now putting me past my patience, only just come to the furriner, and more's the pity she was one; so as I said, thinking as I was a born musicianer, and all my family for hundreds of years before me, I thought for the honor of the country I'd call upon her, for in troth I was just fairly ashamed of the fellows that were around her, from all I heard, giving her no iday of the rale music, only playing night after night at the theatre 'St. Patrick's Day,' as if there was ne'er another saint in the calendar, nor e'er another tune in the counthry.

"Well, I got my pipes claned, and my little guide boy a bran' new shoot of clothes, and, to be sure, meself was in the first fashion; and the lace ruffles round my wrists, that my father wore when he rattled the 'Connachtman's Rambles' to the House of Commons there in College Green, and so I sent up my card, and, by the same token, it was on the back of the ten o' diamonds I had it wrote; I knew the card by the ten punches of a nail 'Jimmy' Bulger put in it, for I always had great divarshun with the cards, through the invention of 'Jimmy'—rest his soul!—giving me eyes, as I may say, in the tips of my fingers; and I got the man to write on it 'Rory Oge, the piper of all Ireland and His Majesty, would be proud to *insense* Madame Catherlany into the beauties of Irish music.' Ye see, the honor of ould Ireland's melodies put heart into me, and I just went upstairs as bould as a rint agent, and before she could say a word I recited four varses of my own poethry that I composed on her.

"Oh, bedad! girls, you may wink and laugh; but I'll tell you what—that's what she didn't do, but she welcomed me in her broken English and was as kind as a born Irish. 'Oh! Mr. Rori Ogeri, I'm so glad to see you,' and a whole lot more nate compliments she paid me, and asked me to play her an Irish jig.

"So, before commencing, I just said a few words, by the way, to let her see that I wasn't a mere bog-throtting piper at all, but wan that could play anything from Handel to Peter Purcell, or any of the Parley voos; and, betwixt and between them all, there isn't a better air in any of their roratoryes than a march my own father played one day that restored an ould colonel officer to the use of his limbs—there was the power of music for you; and maybe she didn't think so, and maybe she wasn't delighted!

"Well, though I was consated enough to be proud at introjuicing to her my own family's music, *'twas the music of my counthry my heart bate to tache her;* and so on afther a while I led on from wan fine ould ancient air to another—the glorious melodies of Ireland. Oh, but the wonder of the Irish music—do you see me now—is that its sweetness is never feeble, and its strength is never rude; it's just a holy and wonderful thing, like the songs of the birds.

"Ah, then, jewel, Oge! maybe she didn't drink them down. 'Stop!' she'd say, and then she'd tune them over, every note as clear and pure as the silver bell the fairies (God bless us) do be ringing of a midsummer night under the green hills; and then she'd say, 'Play another,' and in the midst of it all would have my little guide into the room and trated us like a queen (and that's what she was) to fine ould wine. With that she says, 'Now you've played for me, and I'll sing for you,' and—she—did—sing! And now you'll think this hard to believe, but it's true—*she put me out of consate with the pipes!* she did, bedad! and it was as good as a week before I could bring myself to tatther a note out of 'em, though I left myself a beggar going to hear her sing."

In concluding her sketch, Mrs. Hall adds: "We left Rory in despair at the state of national music, and full of dread that, owing to the heresy of brass bands, he would be the last of the pipers."

Remmy Carroll, the Fermoy Piper

Strange, is it not, that nearly all the pipers who have found a place in Irish literature hailed from the southern provinces. Perhaps they possessed other qualifications of an attractive nature which gained for them more attention than persons of this class in other parts of Ireland.

Such, at least, was the case with Remmy Carroll of Fermoy, whose "father before him" was a piper. Standing six feet two in his vamps, a perfect Adonis in shape and beauty, he could outwalk, outrun, and outleap any man in the parish or barony, or the next barony to it for that matter. No wonder such a man, having the additional charm of being a splendid performer on the plaintive pipes, was such a favorite among the fair colleens of Clongibbons, and, regardless of the shabby attire, could "cut out" at pleasure farmers' sons and thriving shop-keepers. Shelton Mackenzie tells us that "Carroll's performance could almost excite the very chairs, tables, and three-legged stools to dance."

Like a true minstrel of the olden time, he was an independent citizen of the world, without a permanent abode, for every door was open to him, from "Teddy" Mulcahy's humble *bohaun* to Bartley O'Mahony's two-story slated house on a three-hundred-acre farm on the banks of the Blackwater.

His daughter, Mary, was an Irish beauty and no mistake—dark hair, fair skin, and violet eyes, and an heiress at that, having been left 500 pounds by a maiden aunt. With all her "fortune" and good fortune, she had neither pride nor conceit, although being the greatest matrimonial catch in the country. Of course, Remmy Carroll, like all the young men, loved her, but knew enough to "suffer in silence."

One Sunday, while returning from Mass, Mary and her cousin took the route along the river and across the fields on their way home. In attempting to jump across a small, deep stream, Mary was precipitated into the water. It was just the piper's luck to be near enough to hear the scream as she fell, to save her from drowning.

Mackenzie devotes pages of "fine writing" to the details of this incident and its resulting emotions, upon which our theme will not permit us to dwell, except to state that from that day the current of Remmy's life seemed changed.

In many respects he was above the generality of his class, for he had a tolerably good education, and not without a certain manly grace of manner. It must be understood that he was still a professional piper, but it was noticeable that his newly acquired habits of economy enabled him to dress quite tastily—in fact, to appear as a regular country beau.

"It is not now I'd be waiting to thank you, man alive," said Mr. O'Mahony to him, one Sunday after Mass, "but Mary never let me know the danger she'd been in till this blessed morning, when her cousin, Nancy Doyle, told me about the ins and outs of the accident. But I do thank you, Remmy, and 'twill go hard with me if I can't find a better way of showing it than by words, which are only breath as one may say."

Then the rich farmer familiarly slapped the piper on the back and insisted that he should accompany them and have dinner.

Everyone knows what effect walking home with Mary had on Remmy's smoldering love, and his frequent visits thereafter to see the "man of the house" never even roused a suspicion in the latter's mind that there could be anything but formal friendship and gratitude between two socially so far apart.

How to reward the piper for his heroic act in saving the rich man's daughter was a problem which O'Mahony solved by announcing that Mary should learn music and appointing Remmy to instruct her. But as he could play only upon one instrument, and that hardly suitable for a young lady, upon due consideration, the father decided to become the musical pupil himself.

At his age his progress was naturally slow, but that didn't matter as long as a legitimate way had been found to put money in Remmy Carroll's pocket, for that worthy would not take it under any other condition.

However, if the pupil did not make good use of his time the teacher did, and before the end of the first quarter Mary had half confessed to her own heart with what aptitude she had taken lessons in the art of love.

Nancy Doyle, her cousin, enjoyed the flirtation as being "fine fun," but it came to a climax one day as they were walking in the meadows.

Poor Remmy declared his love, not with any hope of its being reciprocated, but because he had to tell it or burst. Being unable to endure hopeless love any longer, he told her he was going away. With fine, ambiguous phrases, Mary endeavored to convey the idea that the case was not so hopeless, but, overpowered as her lover was by emotion, he did not seem to understand.

"It's no use trying to banish you from my mind. I've put a penance on myself for daring to think of you, and it's all no use. I try to forget you in the day, but I can't, and when I sleep at night you come into my dreams. Wherever I am, or whatever I do, you are beside me with a kind, sweet smile. It's all no use—I will go for a soldier, and if I am killed in battle, as I hope I may be, they will find your name written on my heart."

Who can blame Mary if she confessed her love under the circumstances. "Remmy! dear Remmy, you must not leave me. If you go my heart goes with you, for I like you better than the richest lord in the land with his own weight of gold and jewels on his back."

We will leave to the imagination of the reader how they parted. Mary went home, her heart torn by conflicting emotions, while Remmy Carroll returned to Fermoy, not knowing whether he stood on his head or his heels.

After resting at his friend Pat Minahan's house for a few hours they set out about dusk for a farmer's house, where there was to be a wedding that night, for Remmy and his pipes were almost as indispensable as the priest or the bridegroom.

His mind was so preoccupied with the thought of Mary O'Mahony, the pearl of his heart, that Minahan's stories of fairies and enchantment fell on dead ears until they reached their destination, where the celebrated piper received the very warmest of welcome.

To describe the "carryings on" at an Irish wedding would be superfluous to the majority of Irish readers, for the festivities are as much alike as one pea is the twin of another—"a sort of mirthful madness," as Mackenzie terms it.

In compliance with the custom at all wedding feasts, where whiskey-punch was as plenty as tea at an old maids' evening party, our piper drank a man's share of the beverage of which it is boasted that "there's not a headache in a hogshead of it." Yet he had not exceeded the bounds of sobriety. His friend Minahan, who had indulged a little more freely, insisted on going home to Fermoy, although he had been proffered a bed in the barn.

So Carroll and Minahan left the house together, linked arm in arm, for the latter was a little wobbly in his gait. The next day Minahan was found lying fast asleep with a soft stone for a pillow, near the footpath at the base of Corran Thierna, but of the piper there was not a trace, as if the earth had swallowed him. His pipes were found on the ground near Minahan, and uninjured.

The whole district was alarmed, for the piper was very popular, so in the course of a few days Father "Tom" Barry, the parish priest, called on Minahan for an explanation.

Grief for the loss of his friend so affected the latter that, between that and the potheen he drank to drown it, Father Barry found him in bed. "Oh! them fairies! them thieves of fairies!" was all the reply he could make to his reverence when half aroused.

When he came to his senses, of which he had never a superfluity, and after he limbered his tongue with a "wetting," he spun out a most weird and wonderful yarn about what befel himself and the piper when they came to the fairy ring on their way home.

Fairy music filled their ears, and a thousand lights suddenly glanced up from the said ring, like an illumination for some great victory. "Then came a thousand dawney fairies, who began dancing jigs as if there were springs in their heels, intermingling backwards and forwards, to and fro. At last one of them came out of the ring and, making a leg and a bow as genteel as ould Lynch, the dancing master, said: 'Mr. Carroll,' says he, 'would you be so kind and condescending and so darn'd disobliging as to oblige us and disoblige yerself and to give us a 'chune'? 'Tis we'd like to foot it a step or two, 'for,' says he, ''tis ourselves have often heard of your beautiful playing.' Then the little mite of a fairy fixed his eyes upon Remmy, and that I mightn't ever if they didn't shine in his head like two coals of red fire, or a cat's eye under a blanket.

"Remmy told them modest enough that he was no player for the likes of them. Ah! they'd take no excuse, so, with their fine *soothering* talk and fixing a stone for a seat for him, he struck up 'Garryowen' in a way that would lift you off the floor. The way St. Vitus danced wasn't a patch to the way they went at it.

"There was nothing slack or deficient about the way Remmy let them have it, until one of the 'faymale' fairies slipped undher his elbow and suggested, 'Maybe, Mr. Carroll, you'd be dhry?' The piper, seeing she was 'purty,' smiled sweetly, but the question being repeated, he said he had been to a wedding and wasn't particularly dry, but he'd drink a good husband to her, soon, and many of them."

Well, to make a long story short, Remmy drank out of the little morsel of a glass she gave him, something that was stronger than holy water. She kissed the glass as he took it, and as he appeared so much refreshed, Minahan, thinking some of the same cordial would be good for his own complaint, he called out to Remmy to save a drop for him. The words were hardly out of his mouth when —whoop! away they vanished, just as Remmy threw his pipes to Minahan by way of a keepsake and dashed down through the earth with the rest of them!

"But, Minahan," said Father Barry, "you certainly don't mean to pass off this wild story for fact?"

"But I do, your Reverence," said Minahan, rather testily, "and that's all I know about it."

Slowly but surely does the tide of time carry year after year into the eternity of the past. Bartley O'Mahony met with a fatal accident; his daughter Mary, yet unmarried, mourned for her mysteriously missing sweetheart, whose disappearance for six long years was a subject for much speculation and the theme of many a tale.

Yet he returned, brawny and bearded, knowing nothing of what transpired during his absence, and when he disclosed his identity his loyal and constant

Mary received him with open arms and, as in the conventional love stories, they were married and lived happy ever after.

The true story of Remmy Carroll's disappearance was scarcely less thrilling than Minahan's supernatural tragedy.

It may be remembered that Remmy had acted as escort to Minahan on their return from that wedding at which the piper had officiated professionally. He had found much difficulty in piloting his companion along the high road from Rathcormac to Fermoy, and when they reached the mountain path Minahan insisted on throwing himself upon the heathy sward, where in a few minutes he was fast asleep. The piper, having seen him safe that far, didn't like to leave him, so he sat down beside him. After a time he, too, very naturally became drowsy, and as a precaution against accident he placed his pipes on the ground some little distance from them and lay down to sleep.

His slumber must have been profound, for on awaking, to his amazement he found himself on a baggage cart, with his head reposing on the lap of a soldier's wife for a pillow, while her husband occupied the driver's seat. No explanations were offered until they reached Glanmire, when the sergeant in charge informed him that he was a duly enlisted recruit in his majesty's service. His remonstrance was useless, for there was the "shilling" in his pocket, the silent but indisputable evidence that he had, all unbeknown to himself, become attached to the military service of "His Most Gracious Majesty, King George the Third."

His remonstrances, denials, and appeals to the officer in command were all in vain, and, as he was carefully watched, escape was impossible.

After the regiment had embarked for the Peninsula, the fierce sergeant told as a good joke how he came to be enlisted.

While the regiment was passing along by the foot of the mountain (Corran Thierna), one of the officers who rode above the highway had noticed Remmy and Minahan asleep, and, marking what an able soldier the former would make, he was picked up bodily and placed in one of the baggage carts without awakening him.

It was long before an opportunity was given him to write, and being afraid that a letter addressed to his heart's idol, Mary O'Mahony, might fall into other hands and betray him, he did write to Minahan. The letter, if ever posted, never reached its destination, and thus for more than six years he was lost to the world at home.

What can't be cured must be endured, so our hero philosophically followed the trade of a soldier, conducted himself admirably, and was promoted to the rank of sergeant.

He lost an arm at the battle of Waterloo. With a respectable pension and a handsome gratuity for the loss of a limb, and what he had already saved up, Remmy Carroll returned to Ireland in good circumstances.

Bronzed and bewhiskered as he was, Mary did not penetrate the disguise, but she was loyal to his memory and had remained unmarried. The wedding followed in due course, and was sure enough a notable event at Carrigbrack, but Minahan's character for "truth and veracity" fell very much into disrepute thereafter in that part of the country.

PHIL CONNER, THE PETRIFIED PIPER

The fairy ring at the foot of Corran Thierna, it appears, was responsible for other mishaps, one of which at least terminated more disastrously than that which befel Remmy Carroll, according to that veracious chronicler Pat Minahan.

As those two worthies were passing along the soft path at the mountain base one night, the piper suddenly stopped—"There's music somewhere about here," said he.

"Maybe 'tis only a singin' in your head," observed Minahan. "I've known such things, 'specially if one had been takin' a dhrop exthra."

"Hush!" said Remmy, "I hear it again as distinctly as I ever heard the sound of my own pipes. There it is again."

Minahan paused and listened. "Sure enough, then, there's music in the air. Oh! Remmy Carroll, 'tis you are the lucky boy, for this must be fairy music, and 'tis said that whoever hears it as you did is surely born to good luck."

"Never mind the luck," said Remmy, laughing, "there's the fairy ring above there, and I'll be bound that's the place it comes from."

"Maybe it does, and maybe it doesn't," replied Minahan. "If you plase, I'd rayther move on, for it is getting dark. 'Twas somewhere about here that Phil Connor the piper had a thrial of skill with the fairies, and they turned him into stone, pipes and all. Didn't you ever hear of it?"

Remmy said he didn't, and if he did he wouldn't believe it.

"Oh, then," continued his companion, emphasizing his remarks with a nod, " 'tis all as true as that you are alive this minute. I heard my mother tell it, and she got it from a cousin, who had the story from good authority.

"Phil Conner was a piper, and a mighty fine player entirely. As he was coming home from a wedding at Rathcormac one fine moonlight night, who should come right forninst him on this very same mountain but a whole troop of fairies, singin' and skippin' and discoorsin' like Christians. So they up and axed him as civil as you plase if he would favor them with a planxty on his pipes.

"Now, lettin' alone that Phil was as courageous as a dog at his own dure, and wouldn't mind facin' even an angry woman, not to mention a lot of weeny hop-o'-my-thumb fairies, he never had the heart to say no when he was civilly axed to do anything.

"So Phil said he'd oblige them and welcome. With that he struck up that fine, lively, ould chune, the 'Fox-hunters' Jig,' and, sure as I'm telling you, no wan could play it better in them days.

"Yerra, the moment the fairies heard it, they all began to caper and dance backward and forward, to and fro, like midges of an evening in summer.

"At last Phil stopped suddenly, and they gother round him, to find out what was the matter. The piper towld them 'twas dying with the druth he was, and that he must have something to wet his whistle.

" 'To be sure!' said a knowledgeable ould fairy, 'that's only raisonable. Bring the gorsoon a drink of something good.' So they handed Phil a fairy finger full of a drink that had a mighty pleasant smell, and they filled a hare-bell cup of the same for the ould fairy who it seems was the king. 'Here's to you,' says he, 'there's not a headache in a hogshead of it, and not a gauger's rod has ever come near it, I warrant ye, and 'twas made in Araglin of mountain barley.'

"Well, with that he drank to Phil, and Phil raised the little weeny measure to his lips, and, though it wasn't more than the size of a thimble, he drank at least a half pint out of it, and yet that I mightn't if 'twasn't as full as ever.

"Arrah! man, it gave the piper the bouldness of a lion, that it did, and nothing would do the *omadhaun* but challenge the whole box and dice of 'em to equal him playing the pipes.

"Some of them who were tinderhearted advised him to keep quiet and not to try. But the more they persuaded, the more he insisted.

"At long last out of patience, the fairies' piper came forward and took up the challenge.

"So at it they went, Phil Conner and the fairy piper, playing against each other until the cock in the nearest house crew, when the whole gang vanished into a cave in the hillside and whipped my brave Phil along with them, pipes and all.

"But that wasn't all of it. They were so downright mad because their musicianer couldn't get the best of Phil, they changed him into a stone statue, which remains in the cave to this day.

"And that's what happened to Phil Conner in the end for offending the 'good people.'"

PIPERS IN CHURCH

When Col. Charles McCarthy, the senior representative for Bandon, County of Cork, in King James the Second's parliament, seized that unfriendly town one Sunday morning early in 1690, a strong force took possession of Ballymodan and Kilbrogan churches. The soldiery which occupied the latter was accompanied by three warpipers.

One of them, according to Bennett, the historian of Bandon, impiously sat on the communion-table, where he struck up "The King Shall Enjoy His Own Again" in triumphant style, beating a tattoo by way of accompaniment upon the leaf of the table with his long hairy legs, and with just as much composure as if he were seated upon the edge of a bank and was playing a lament for the boys at the wake of some mutual friend.

Another fellow, squatted on the circular bench in front of the rail with his hat jauntily set on the side of his head and his eyes brimful of humor and fun, and played "Lillibullero" and the "Humors of Bandon." The latter tune he seemed much to relish, dwelling upon some of the notes in a style peculiarly grotesque.

But the third, we are told, was the most amusing of the lot. He took up his station in front of the pulpit, and signified by squeezing the bag of his instrument what he thought of the discourse. If he had heard anything that pleased him, he'd make the pipes utter three or four jocular squeaks, musically intimating his satisfaction; if otherwise, he'd lower his tubes and give out a deep, melancholy groan of disapprobation.

The ultra-comic nature of the scene, which might have produced much merriment at any other time and place, naturally enough met with but scant encouragement under the circumstances.

Upon Colonel McCarthy's appearance the pipers were ordered out of the church while the fortunes of war were being given effect within.

One of the pipers was subsequently arrested and brought before old John Nash, commonly called "Shaun Dearg," but before the non-commissioned officer in whose custody he was had time to narrate even half the details connected with the arrest, the unfortunate man was on his way to the gallows.

In his history of the County of Cork, published about the year 1750, Dr. Smith says of Bandon: "There was not in this town a popish inhabitant, nor would the townsmen suffer one to dwell in it, nor a piper to play in the place, that being the music used formerly by the Irish in their wars."

This proscription of course has reference to the Warpipes, which were similar to the Highland or Scottish pipes of the time, and from which had been developed the Irish Union pipes, one of the most melodious of musical instruments.

That its softness of tone and extended compass did not overcome the deep-rooted prejudice against pipe music in general is certain, for it is recorded that a wandering Union piper who strayed into this inhospitable town in later years, unaware of the hostility of the inhabitants, had his instrument smashed over his head, and he was glad to escape with his life.

PATRICK BRALLAGHAN

It would appear that every piper christened in honor of Ireland's patron saint came to be called "Paddy the Piper," so fond are the Irish people of alliterative nicknames. Such was the case with the hero of this story.

He was a very remarkable old fellow, according to David O'Callanan, to whom we are indebted for an account of him. He was born blind, so there was no remembrance of the beauties of the visible world to trouble his merry spirit. But his want of sight did not prevent his fingers from finding the stops, or the back of his palm from locating the brass keys on the regulators of his famous Union pipes.

A wondrously merry fellow was he. No frown ever beclouded his brow, but the laugh was constantly ringing on his lips. Fat, roundfaced, baldheaded, every inch of him seemed to dimple with fun, and his face was a study in drollery whenever he was playing his rollicking jigs or reels.

His blindness only served to sharpen his other faculties. His sense of hearing was singularly keen, and his touch so extremely fine that, incredible as it may seem, he had learned by touch to discriminate the colors of any material, hard or soft.

Yet another wonderful faculty he possessed and which he unconsciously demonstrated before wondering witnesses on several occasions. Warned by instinct or intuition, like the bats in their flight, he never collided with an obstruction in his pathway, but hesitated when within a few feet of a wall or other impassable barriers, and made his way safely around it or away from it.

It is stated that once in a fit of bravado "Paddy" walked from one end to the other of Six-Mile-Bridge, in the County of Cork—a feat which O'Callanan says sickened him, for had the piper stumbled or made a misstep he would have fallen a depth of eighty feet into the stony bed of the shallow, brawling stream below. A swift and tireless walker, he never took a guide with him wherever he went. "Sure," he'd say, "don't I know every foot of the road through Munster and Leinster? What do I want to be bothered with a guide."

Brallaghan was really a splendid performer on his remarkable instrument. Sometimes it seemed as if he could make it speak; and when he played some such noble melody as the "Coolin" or the "Dear Irish Boy" or "Billy Byrne's Lament," a strange light appeared to spread over his face, and he looked like one inspired. But you should have heard him play "The Fox Hunt"; that was a treat! While he played he would go on to tell you what the meaning of this singular piece of music was—compounded of musical scraps of different centuries. "We're mounting now," he'd say, "and now ye see we're going gently along to keep the horse's wind fresh. Listen how the dogs are yelping, eager for the fun. And now— oh! bedad! they've unearthed him, and he's off. Listen to the horns, how they roar, Tally-ho! Tally-ho! Tally-ho-o-o! There they go like divils. Och! 'Tis all up with poor Reynard—here's our lament for the death of poor modhereen-rua." Then he played a strange old dirge-like tune, but recovering his jollity he continues, referring to the hunting party: "Tut, tut, they're tackling the mate and drink already, and they're going to dance and want me to play for 'em. Here goes!' and straightway he rattled up that lively slip-dance tune known as "The Fox-Hunters' Jig."

Another musical piece which Brallaghan played with wondrous effect was "Ollistrum's March," a wild and weird composition so called after Alexander* McDonnell of the Isles, brother of Colkitto, who followed the fortunes of the Stuarts into Ireland. This tune, which has almost a literature of its own, will be found discussed more fully in another chapter.

Brallaghan we are told attended the great annual horse-fair of Kilruddery, but he never played in any of your common tents—not he; 'twould be beneath him. He was always installed in the largest tent in the best location at the edge of the fair ground where the gentry came to buy good hunters and the government functionaries picked up troop-horses. With the dignity of an Irish bard of the olden time, the blind piper, changing his music from grave to gay according to fancy or request, delighted all who heard him, and you may be sure his pockets were not empty the next day.

Mr. O'Callanan, more interested in describing the blind piper's courtship, leaves us without many important details of his life, so we must be content with the knowledge that his suit was successful and that he married Nancy Murray, a beautiful girl born blind like himself, who declared, "I'd rather sit by you and hear you play that heavenly music than be courted by the earl himself."

Although "Paddy" (as he preferred being called) was on the shady side of fifty, and Nancy, whom he had nursed as a baby on his knee, was less than half his age, they were linked by love as well as by wedlock, and maybe there wasn't hilarity and dancing when he struck up "Haste to the Wedding" when they came back from the chapel.

But this was many a long day ago. "Paddy" and his loving Nancy now sleep under the green Irish sod, and their daughter is married to a rich farmer in one of the western states; while their son is a prosperous barrister in Australia, who still keeps his father's Union pipes, and they say plays on them himself once in a while, in memory of old times.

The Silent Piper

By a peculiar combination of circumstances not a piper or fiddler was available to play at the wedding of "Mickey" Donovan's daughter "Biddy" to "Morty" Maguire, away back in the year 1840, when by unexpected good luck, who should come along but a strange piper. He was a thin, spare, plaintive-looking, undersized man, much bent by age or sorrow, or perhaps by a mingling of both. Being stone blind, he was led by a pretty, sunny-haired little maiden not yet in her teens. His opportune appearance was hailed with delight by every member of the family, busy though they were preparing for the next day's nuptials, for he carried his welcome with him in the bagpipes under his arm.

"What can you play sir, if you plase?" questioned the pretty bride-to-be.

"'Haste to the Wedding,' or whatever you plase, miss," answered the little girl, half shyly.

"And why can't your father answer for himself?" inquired "Biddy."

"If you plase, miss, it's a vow that's on him for a raison he has," replied the child, "and so I'm his speech as well as his eyes myself, miss."

---

*In Irish Alastair; corrupted into Ollistrum.

"Oh, indeed!" "Poor man!" "See that now!" "A vow!" "Oh musha, but sin is a shockin' thing!" were the exclamations that followed.

" 'Tis no sin of his own," observed the child; "only one he took upon himself, for one he loved."

The Irish are a very inquisitive people, and though "Biddy" had too much delicacy to urge the little girl to betray the piper's secret, the other members of the family were in no way restrained by any such consideration.

After the strangers had been warmed and fed, and every one who could dance had "taken a turn on the flure" to the melodious piping of the old man, artful questioning elicited from the child the information that the blind piper was her father, and that her mother when dying "left a vow on him." He had never spoken since. She did not care to say where they came from, and she could not tell where they were going to.

Kelly, the local piper whose instrument was out of commission, was obliged to confess on the wedding day that he wasn't fit to "hould a candle" to the "silent piper," and everybody declared they had never heard such beautiful music. One or two very old people hinted that all was not right, for they had heard pipers and pipers in their youth, but such music as the newcomer played had never been heard before.

The fame of the "silent piper" reached the houses of the gentry, all who heard him were charmed by his wonderful performance. Liberal offers were made to the blind man if he would settle in the neighborhood; a cottage and garden would be given him, and all his wants supplied.

In reply he only shook his head and sighed and the little maid with tears in her eyes observed: "We have but a short time to stop now, as father seldom stayed more than a week in any one place."

"Obligations" or "vows" were not uncommon among the Irish peasantry, but no one had ever heard of an instance like this. The little daughter by her winning ways had achieved as much popularity as her father, and there were very few who had not bestowed some gift or token of remembrance on both. However, the best of friends must part, so to signalize his leaving the old man played "O'Carolan's Lament" until he drew tears from the eyes of many of his audience.

Many years afterwards, while visiting the ancient and picturesque town of Kinsale, Mrs. S. C. Hall, from whose writings this story has been abstracted, heard the sound of a bagpipe, and followed it to be nearer the player. Had a spectre risen from the earth she could not have been more astonished, for there after a lapse of nearly twenty years sat the "silent piper" with the very same blooming child at his knee!

He played again the bold brave notes of "Brian Boru's March," and the women stamped their feet to the tune and hoisted their little ones in the air, and when he finished they gave so loud a cheer that it animated the old man to an encore of the national march, and all the time the famous author was deeply pondering at the marvel of finding the "silent piper" of Bannow, County Wexford, after a lapse of so many years in the town of Kinsale, County of Cork.

"Eh dear!" said the old man when questioned; "do I mind Bannow? To be sure I do; God be with it!"

"And you?" to the girl half doubtingly.

"I never was there nor in the City of Cork either, ma'am," she answered, while the well-remembered bead necklace glittered in the sun, and the very same blue ribbon seemed to confine her fair hair.

"Ah, my dear lady," pleasantly interposed the old piper, "that was her mother,

God bless ye! her own mother, my daughter Kathleen, who is the mother of a family now," and while the good lady was smiling at her own absurdity the original Kathleen made her appearance—a stout gleeful-looking woman with a mild bland laugh, but with twins in her arms, and twins at her side.

Certainly the realities of life sadly upset the imagination. How our mental pictures are shattered.

"Sure I have all the little keepsakes and tokens I got still," she said with pride, "and the tears do be coming in my eyes when I think of them, and the penance my poor father took on himself that time; he's half childish now and would be so entirely but for the music, and that is what mainly keeps up his interest in life."

TIM CALLAGHAN

Whatever may be thought of the oft-told tale of the piper, whose repertory consisted of but two tunes, and who in a commendable spirit of accommodation, when asked to play, inquired "Which will ye have first?" we feel no diffidence in presenting a sketch of Tim Callaghan, the inimitable Union piper who made a fair living by diplomatically ringing the changes on three tunes within the limits of the baronies of Forth and Bargie, County Wexford.

As the *Irish Penny Journal,* which enjoyed a brief existence of less than one year some seventy years ago, is now decidedly scarce, and a volume inaccessible to most readers, we may be pardoned for quoting freely from its pages in telling the story of this *rara avis.*

According to his own account, Tim "sarved seven long years wid as fine a piper as ever put a bag ondher his arm or a chanter on his knee." After the end of those years of assiduous study and practice, he began to enchant his countrymen with music, master of a splendid set of pipes and three whole tunes, barring a few odd turns here and there which he considered of little consequence—a golden store in his opinion.

"Ah then, Tim," said Miss Edgeworth, when she was perfectly acquainted with himself and his musical merits, "what a pity that with your fine taste, and your superior set of pipes, you didn't try to conquer the half a dozen at least."

"Och musha!" quoth Tim, looking sulky and annoyed, "that same question has been put to me by dozens, and I hate to hear it! It was only yesterday a lady ast me that same. 'Arrah, ma'am,' says I, 'did you ever play a thune on the pipes in yer life?' 'Never indeed,' says she, looking ashamed of her ignorance. 'Because if you did,' says I again, 'you'd soon say, "Bright was yerself, Tim Callaghan, to get over the three thunes dacintly widout axing people to do what's unpossible,"' and now I appale to you, miss; what's the use of boddherin' people's brains wid six or seven when three does my business just as well?"

As in duty bound Miss Edgeworth admitted that his argument was unanswerable, and thenceforward they were the best of friends.

Grateful for the lady's patience and forbearance, he excruciatingly mangled the three unfortunate "thunes" for her special edification.

This complacent performer was a tall, stout, lazy-looking fellow with a pug nose and sleepy eyes; dragging his feet along like clogs; dawdling along the highways or lounging about a public house. Yet withal Tim Callaghan was a polite fellow, and these three tunes were expressly chosen and learned to win the favor of all denominations of Christian men.

Thus the "Boyne Water" was the propitiatory sacrifice at the Protestant's door, "Patrick's Day" at that of the Roman Catholic, and when he was not sure of the creed of the party he wished to conciliate, such as Quakers, Methodists, Seekers and Jumpers, he gave them "God Save the King," his third tune.

For many years he was content to give those favorite airs in their original simplicity, but some wicked wight, probably a gentleman piper, had at last persuaded him that his melodies would be altogether irresistible if he would introduce some ornamental variations—"such as his own fine taste would suggest."

Poor Tim, unaccustomed to flattery and not suspecting the sincerity of his advisor, caught at the bright idea, and conquering his natural and acquired laziness, made the attempt. When he thought he had mastered the new difficulties, he played them for a friend, who was so amused at the "varry-a-shins" that he couldn't muster up courage to tell the "composer" candidly what he thought of them.

When Tim arrived at a gentleman's door his usual plan was to commence with the suitable serenade, and drone away until given the few pence expected. If detained too long, and his music (God save the mark) was unheeded, he became furious and rattled off that one of his three tunes which he supposed would be most disagreeable—"Patrick's Day" for an Orangeman, and the "Boyne Water" for a Catholic.

In such cases Tim threw his whole soul into his performance to emphasize his feelings.

Should he be asked for any favorite or fashionable air—and you might as well ask him to repeat a passage of Homer in the original Greek—his invariable reply was, "I haven't that, but I'll give yez one as good." Then one of the trio follows, of course, and if the impertinent seeker for novelties, in his ignorance of the piper's limitations, persists in demanding more than is to be had, he is cut short, especially if not of superior rank, with, "Yerra, how bad ye are for sortins! Yer masther would be contint wid what I gave ye, and thankful into the bargain."

Imagine if you can the ecstacy of the company in the house of a friend at a retired country place on hearing the inspiring tones of the Union pipes when *anything* in the "shape of music" would have been welcome.

The very servants even were delighted, and begged that the piper be brought into the house and entertained. Their request was granted and Tim, who needed no pressing, was soon planted in the hall.

At a glance he saw that the man of the house was a minister, and of course the "Boyne," as he called it for brevity, was played very sportively and accurately with the exception of a few notes that he omitted as troublesome and unnecessary, or as the servants supposed, in consequence of the cold in his fingers. So they escorted him to the kitchen and seated him before a blazing fire.

"Now he'll play in airnest," said they joyfully as one and all gathered round him in expectation of a real musical treat.

Being now in the lower regions among the inferior gentry, and willing to please all orders and conditions, our piper began to consider whether to repeat the "Boyne" or commence the all-enlivening "Patrick's Day."

"What religion is the sarvints of?" he asked a little cowboy who was gaping with wonder at the grand ornaments of the pipes.

"They're of all soarts, sur," whispered "Tommy" in reply, and reddening all over at the great man's notice.

"All soarts," muttered Tim significantly. For a mixed audience nothing would be more appropriate and concilating than "God Save the King," an air which he played with much strength of arm and conscious pride.

The butler listened a while with the sapient air of a judge. "You're a capital performer, piper," said he at length patronizingly, with a hand on each hip, "and that's a fine piece of *Hannibal's* compersition, but it isn't shutable for all occasions, and a livelier air would agree with our temperaments much better. Change it to something new."

Tucking his apron aside he gallantly took the rosy tips of the housemaid's fingers and led her out, while the gardener as politely handed forth the cook.

The piper looked sullen and still continued the English anthem, as if he knew what he was about and didn't need any advice. The butler's dignity was plainly hurt.

"Railley, we are very loyal people hereabouts," he observed with a supercilious smile, "but at this particular moment we don't want to join in a prayer for our savern's welfare! Stop that solemcholy thing, man alive, and give us one of Jackson's jigs."

"Out of fashion," quoth Tim sullenly, "but I'll give yez one as good," and "Patrick's Day" set them all in motion for a quarter of an hour.

"Oh! we're quite tired of that," at length exclaimed the housemaid. "Do, piper, give us a *walse* or a *chodhreel*. Do you play 'Tanty-polpitty?' 'Jim' Sidebottom used to dance it beautiful with me."

"What do yez call it?" asked Tim rather sneeringly.

"Tanty-polpitty," replied the damsel, drawing herself up with an air fit to freeze him.

"Phew!" returned the musician contemptuously, "that's out of fashion entirely, but I'll give yez one as good," and so the "Boyne" followed, neither faster nor slower than marching time, just as he had been taught it, to the no small annoyance of the dancers.

Jig after jig, and reel after reel, were named and demanded, but to all and each came the same response: "I haven't that, but I'll give yez one as good," so the "King," the "Boyne" and the "Day" followed each other in due succession.

Could anything be more provoking? Four active, eager votaries of Terpsichore anxiously awaiting appropriate dance music of their country from a professional piper. There stood the dancers looking beseechingly at him and there sat the piper staring helplessly at them, wondering what the deuce they waited for, quite satisfied that they had got all which could reasonably be expected of him.

"An' have ye nothin' else in yer bag?" demanded the butler, at last entirely out of patience.

"Arrah, how bad yez are for sortins," retorted the piper. "Yer masther would be contint wid what I gave yez, and thankful into the bargain."

"By Jupiter Ammons!" exclaimed he of the white apron, "this bates all the playin' I ever heard in my life. Arrah, do you ever attind the nobility's concerts? Ha-ha-ha!"

"'Pon my voracity," cried the smiling housemaid, "I'm greatly afeerd he'd get more kicks than ha'pence if he did. Ha-ha-ha!"

"And good enough for him," added the gardener; "a fella that has but three half thunes in the world and nayther of 'em right. Arrah, what's yer name, avic?"

"What's that to you?" growled the piper.

"Oh, nothin', but I thought you might be the piper that played before Moses. Ha-ha-ha!"

> "Oh, the world may wag
> Since he got the green bag
> With me right faladiddy I de o."

sang the cook as she returned to her avocation, but the butler, as master of the ceremonies, showed his disappointment and displeasure in a summary ejection of the unhappy minstrel from the comforts of the fire and the shelter of the house altogether.

PLAYING FOR THE QUALITY

We cannot afford to dismiss from our consideration so abruptly a character so provokingly absurd as the inimitable Tim Callaghan. The profession, if so it may be designated, from the days of the harpers to the present writing abounded with quaint whimsical and even grotesque characters, yet our minstrel possessed a peculiar individuality for which history presents no prototype.

Subsequent to the incident before mentioned, a lady had assembled a number of young persons to a seaside dance one evening, but alas! ere the hour of meeting arrived news came that the fiddler she expected was taken ill, and could not possibly be on hand.

What was to be done? Nothing!

When the guests arrived and learned of their host's predicament the gentlemen inspite of themselves looked terrifically glum, as well they might with a dull evening in prospect. Little did they anticipate the treat in store for them.

The bright countenances of the ladies, God bless them, were also clouded with dismay, though as usual, sweet creatures, they tried to look captivating under all visitations.

In this dilemma one of the beaux suddenly recollected that he had seen a piper sauntering into the village that evening, and he thought it was quite likely he would put up for the night at one of the public houses. Hope instantly illuminated all faces and a messenger was forthwith despatched for the man of music.

"What sort of a person is your piper?" inquired Miss Edgeworth.

"A tall, stout, rather drowsy-looking fellow," answered the gentleman who had seen him coming.

Unmistakably that was the description of our friend, the *only* Tim Callaghan. The question naturally arose, "Was he a good performer?"

Another person present besides the young lady who knew honest Timothy and his ways, with admirable composure answered that he must decline trumpeting the praise of any one because "Whoever enters thus announced appears to disadvantage."

Therefore we leave Tim Callaghan's musical merit to speak for itself. No evasion could be better than this, and the effect Tim produced was correspondingly indescribable.

While the messenger was away in search of our piper, we may as well relate an anecdote of another servant—and a rustic one too, at that—sent on a similar errand.

John's master had friends spending the evening with him, so he desired his servant to procure a musician for the young folks for love or money. In about half an hour, John returned after a fruitless search, and instead of saying in the usual style that he could not find one, he flung open the drawing room door and announced his ill success in the following impromptu:

> "I searched the city's circumference round,
> And not a musician is there to be found;
> I fear for music you'll be at a loss,
> For the fiddler has taken the road to Ross."

The city, by the way, was a village of some half dozen houses. So much for John—and now for Tim Callaghan.

When the identical Tim made his appearance he was placed in high state at the head of the room, with a degree of attention and respect commensurate with his importance. The very sight of him and the thought of his consummate assurance in attempting to play for dancing was irresistibly funny to one who was aware of his incapacity, but all outward symptoms of these were suppressed while eyes and ears were on the alert in expectation of what was to follow.

A bumper of his favorite punch was prepared for him, and while sipping it he cast an anxious and scrutinizing glance on the company, thinking how he should adjust his three tunes to their preferences. He had little time for speculation however, for a quadrille was immediately formed and he was called on to play!

The sapient belles and beaux never dreamt that a modern piper might not be able to play quadrilles. There stood the eight *elegantes* ringleted, perfumed, white-gloved and refined, and there sat Tim Callaghan in all his native surly stupidity, dreadfully puzzled, humming and hawing and droning away, undecided as to which of his own tunes he should play first, and heedless of their request.

The situation was ludicrous, and laughter could hardly be suppressed.

"A quadrille, piper! the first of Montague's," called out the leading gentleman.

"E-ah," said Tim, opening his sleepy eyes, surprised into some little animation.

"The first of Montague's set of quadrilles," repeated the beau.

"Och! Montycute's is out of fashion, but I'll give yez one as good," and the company being mixed, and of whose opinions he could not be sure, the set of dandies were astounded with "God Save the King" in most execrable style.

All stared and most laughed heartily, but what was of more consequence to Tim, his arm was fiercely seized, and thereby abruptly stopped short in saving the King, followed by an angry demand, "Can't you play any quadrilles?"—a dozen of them and some few waltzes being named to him. He had never heard of them in all his days, so what could the poor minstrel do but give the "Boyne."

At this instant some one called the lady of the house; the name seemed to be a Catholic one. A sudden ray of joy shot through his frame to his fingers, and from them to his pipes, and the "Boyne" promptly changed to "Patrick's Day."

A kind of a jigging quadrille was danced by the least fastidious and best humored of the party, while a dandy from London and his perfumed partner retired to their seats with looks and gestures of disgust, quite unnoticed by Tim Callaghan, who bore himself with all the dignity of a household bard in the olden time, in his element playing his own favorite tunes, and the "quolity," if you please, actually dancing to his music. It was a great day for the house of Callaghan and no mistake.

Well, as there seemed nothing better to be had, "Patrick's Day" continued in requisition, now as a quadrille, and again as a country dance, by all who preferred motion to sitting still before and after supper, till at last every one was weary of it, and so they all agreed to take their chances on the "Boyne" and endeavor to move about to it as best they could.

Even the piper had played himself tired of the "Day," so after having quaffed his fourth tumbler of punch he appeared to be rather inclined for a doze than a renewal of his melodies. But it was not to be, for the worthy host, good gay cheerful old man, roused him. "For pity's sake, piper," said he, "try to give us something that we can foot it to. I was not in the right mood for dancing till now. If you be an Irishman, look at the pretty girl who is to be my partner at the next dance, and perhaps her eyes may inspire even you, you drowsy fellow, with momentary animation, and perform a miracle on your instrument!"

Short as this address was, and gaily as it was uttered, it had no other effect than to increase Tim's drowsiness, but a lively shaking roused him temporarily.

"What do yez want " growled he at length. "What the divil do yez want?" looking as if he would say;

> "Now my weary eyes I close,
> Leave me to my sweet repose."

"Music! music!" said the host, laughing, "any sort of music, any sort of noise," and he took his place among the dancers.

Poor Tim mechanically fumbled at the pipes, while the gentlemen busied themselves in procuring partners.

"Begin, piper!" called out the host.

"Out of fashion," muttered Tim in broken, half-finished sentences, "but— I'—give—yez—one—as—good!"

A long loud reverberating snore made good his promise of music anyway, but they couldn't dance to it, although Tim's music for some time previously wasn't much better.

It would be futile to attempt to describe the confusion which followed. Some laughed, some frowned, while yet others had recourse to smelling salts and perfumed handkerchiefs.

When the excitement and laughter subsided and when all considered that their unrivaled musician had been sufficiently refreshed by slumber, he was once more aroused to receive his well-earned reward. The "man of the house," curious to know more of this parody of a piper, asked,

"Pray what is your name?"

"E-ah—why, Tim Callaghan, to be sure."

"Ah! Tim Callaghan. I shall certainly remember the name. I suppose, Tim, you are quite celebrated."

"E-ah?"

"I suppose you are very well known," repeated the host.

"Why, those that knows me wanst, knows me again."

"I do believe so! I think I shall know you, at all events. Who taught you to play the pipes?"

"One Tim Hartigan of the County Clare, sur."

"Had he much trouble in teaching you?"

"He trubble! I knows nothin' of his trubble, but faix, I well remember my own! There's lumps in me head to this very day from the unmarciful cracks he used to give it when I went asthray."

"Ha! ha! ha! Poor fellow! Farewell, Tim Callaghan! Pleasant be your path through life, and may your fame spread throughout the thirty-two counties of Green Erin, till you die surfeited with glory."

"Faith, I'd rayther be surfeited wid a good dinner," was Tim's unsentimental reply, as he passed out, in no wise flattered by his host's fine language.

For a couple of years Tim was lost sight of, and Miss Edgeworth began to fear he had vanished from the earth altogether "without leaving a copy." When lo! his orbit led in that direction again, and what was more, he was accompanied by a strapping wife, and a young Timotheus at his heels—a perfect replica of his father, nose, sleepy eyes, shovel feet and all, and subsisting, nay flourishing, on three tunes and their "varry-a-shins."

CHAPTER XXXII

MISCELLANEA

Traditions and Anecdotes of the Bagpipes

There is at Rome a sculpture, in *basso relievo*, representing a piper playing on an instrument resembling the Highland bagpipe. The Greeks, unwilling as they were to surrender to others the merit of useful inventions, acknowledged that to the Barbarians—i. e., the Celts—they owed much of their music, and many of its instruments. The Romans, who no doubt borrowed the bagpipe from the Greeks, used it as a martial instrument among their infantry. It is represented on several coins, marbles, etc.; but, from rudeness of execution, or decay of the materials, it is difficult to ascertain its exact form. On the reverse of a coin of the Emperor Nero, who thought himself an admirable performer on it, and who publicly displayed his abilities, the bagpipe is represented. An ancient figure, supposed to be playing on it, has been represented and particularly described by Signor Macari, of Cortona, and it is engraved in Walker's *History of the Irish Bards;* but it does not, in my opinion, appear to be a piper. A small bronze figure, found at Richborough, in Kent, and conjectured to have been an ornament of house furniture, is not much more distinct. Mr. King, who has engraved three views of it, and others believe it to represent a bagpiper, to which it has certainly more resemblance than to a person drinking out of a leathern bottle, writes a correspondent in 1877 to *Frank Leslie's Popular Monthly.*

The bagpipe, of a rude and discordant construction, is in use throughout the East; and that it continues the popular instrument of the Italian peasant is well known. In Italy it is the medium through which the good Catholics show their devotion to the Virgin Mother, who received their adoration in the lengthened strains of the sonorous Piva. It is a singular but faithful tradition of the Church that the shepherds who first saw the infant Jesus in the barn expressed their gladness by playing on their bagpipes. That this is probable and natural will not be denied; but the illuminator of a Dutch missal, in the library of King's College, Old Aberdeen, surely indulged his fancy when he represented one of the appearing angels likewise playing a salute on this curious instrument. The Italian shepherds religiously adhere to the laudable practice of their ancestors; and in visiting Rome and other places to celebrate the advent of our Saviour, they carry the pipes along with them, and their favorite tune is "The Sicilian Mariners," often sung in Protestant churches.

It is the popular opinion that the Virgin Mary is very fond of and is an excellent judge of music. I received this information on Christmas morning, when I was looking at two Calabrian pipers, doing their utmost to please her and the infant in her arms. They played for a full hour to one of their images, which stands at the corner of a street. All the other statues of the Virgin which are placed in the streets are serenaded in the same manner every Christmas morning. On my inquiring into the meaning of that ceremony, I was told the above-mentioned circumstance of her character, which, though you have always thought highly probable, perhaps you never before knew for certain. My informer was a pilgrim, who stood

465

listening with great devotion to the pipers. He told me, at the same time, that the Virgin's taste was too refined to have much satisfaction in the performance of these poor Calabrians, which was chiefly intended for the infant; and he desired me to remark, that the tunes were plain, simple, and such as might naturally be supposed agreeable to the ear of a child of his time of life.

How many anecdotes might be given of the effects of this instrument on the hardy sons of Caledonia! In the war in India, a piper in Lord M'Leod's regiment, seeing the British army giving way before superior numbers, played, in his best style, the well-known *"Cogadh na Sith"* (War or Peace), which filled the Highlanders with such spirit that, immediately rallying, they cut through their enemies. For this fortunate circumstance, Sir Eyre Coote, filled with admiration, and appreciating the value of such music, presented the regiment with fifty pounds to buy a stand of pipes. At the battle of Quebec, in 1760, the troops were retreating in disorder, and the general complained to a field-officer in Fraser's regiment of the bad conduct of his corps. "Sir," said the officer, with a degree of warmth, "you did very wrong in forbidding the pipers to play; nothing inspirits the Highlanders so much; even now they would be of some use."

"Let them blow, in God's name, then!" said the general; and the order was given, the pipers with alacrity sounded the *Cruinneachadh* (Gathering), on which the Gaels formed in the rear, and bravely returned to the charge.

George Clark, now piper to the Highland Society of London, was piper to the Seventy-first regiment at the battle of Vimeira, where he was wounded in the leg by a musket ball as he boldly advanced. Finding himself disabled, he sat down on the ground, and putting his pipes in order, called out, "Weel, lads, I am sorry I can gae nae farther wi' you, but deil hae my saul if ye shall want music," and struck up a favorite warlike air, with the utmost unconcern for anything but the unspeakable delight of sending his comrades to battle with the animating sound of the pibroch.

It is a popular tradition that the enemy anxiously level at the pipers, aware of the power of their music; and a story is related of one who, at the battle of Waterloo, received a shot in the bag before he had time to make a fair beginning, which so roused his Highland blood that, dashing his pipes on the ground, he drew his broadsword, and wreaked his vengeance on his foes with the fury of a lion, until his career was stopped by death from numerous wounds. It is related of the pipe-major of the Ninety-second on the same occasion, that, placing himself on an eminence where the shot was flying like hail, regardless of his danger, he proudly sounded the battle-air to animate his noble companions. On one occasion during the Peninsular War, the same regiment came suddenly on the French army, and the intimation of their approach was as suddenly given by the pipers bursting out their "gathering." The effect was instantaneous; the enemy fled, and the Highlanders pursued.

ON THE PRESENT DAY CONDITION OF IRISH MUSIC BROUGHT ABOUT BY THE
RECENT IRISH REVIVAL

By M. Flanagan, Dublin, June 1912

In any weighty undertaking, it behooves the promoters to compare their losses with their gains; to review what has been done and what left undone; also to ascertain whether anything that has been done had been better left undone—in other words, the directors of the concern must, from time to time, "take stock," pushing their inquiries into every department of the trade. Some twenty years ago there was a mighty ferment of Irish sentiment, bringing in its train a desire to promote or resuscitate everything distinctively Irish—language, music, amusements, customs, etc. The time seems opportune now to "take stock" of Irish music.

According to a distinguished authority, speaking at the Rotunda, Dublin, exactly two years ago, Irish harp playing is lost—utterly, irretrievably lost; therefore, the only distinctively Irish instrument remaining is the bagpipe.

In the year 1897 a few patriotic spirits, including Dr. Annie Patterson, organized a Musical Festival (Feis Ceoil), and the first celebration took place at Ballsbridge. There, Irish bagpipe playing occupied an honorable place; the pipe competition became a feature at each succeeding annual function, but the palmy days of bagpipe playing at the Feis Ceoil are apparently past; there were only four competitors at the last Feis. Other considerations apart, it is entirely to the honor of the Feis Ceoil Association that they have hitherto kept out the "Irish War Pipe." For the benefit of the uninitiated it may be well to state what is meant by the "Brian Boru" or "Irish War Pipe."

About the year 1889, certain officers of the British army, having a predilection for Irish music, determined to make an effort to introduce the bagpipes as a "marching" instrument into their own corps. In this course, the gentlemen concerned had doubtless before their minds the example of the Scottish Highland regiments. At any rate, they interviewed the late Mr. John Hingston, T. C. D., at that time the leading authority on matters pertaining to the pipes. As a consequence, an inferior imitation of the great Highland pipe was introduced into the Leinster Regiment (Old Royal Canadian); also into the Old Eightyninth. The inferiority of this instrument consists in the fact that it has only one tenor drone, which is in a great measure overpowered by the bass drone, a distinctively Scottish adjunct to the old Irish war pipe. The advanced Gaels of the period perceived the suitability of the new instrument for marching purposes; it was in a way distinct from the Highland pipe; it was more easily blown, and it was cheaper; and thus the prototype of the "Brian Boru war pipe" is to be found in the "obnoxious British army."

The distinction of popularizing this "Saxon" instrument among Gaelic Leagues belongs to Mr. John S. Wayland, of Cork, who adopted it in the year 1898. That the "Brian Boru war pipe" is essentially the same as the Scotch pipe appears from the fact that a Scotchman, when available, determines the relative merits of competing bands of "Brian Boru war pipers." The situation altogether has its due proportion of humor.

In 1910, Mr. Edward Martyn, a patriotic, wealthy Irish gentleman, purchased a fifty-pound cup, to be competed for by bands of Irish war pipers. Mr. Martyn has very strong views as to Irishmen who enlist in the "British army"; he has even gone so far as to say that such men deserve to be flogged. His fellow members in the Kildare Street Club resented this pronouncement to the extent of voting him out of the club, and Mr. Martyn very pluckily fought a successful legal battle for the recovery of his rights. Very good. Mr. Martyn donates a cup for the encouragement of Irish music. Mr. Rose, of Pitlochrie, N. B., is the judge of the contest. The winning pipers have five sets of Scotch pipes over their shoulders, and the drummer is a soldier discharged from the "hated Saxon army."

According to Mr. Wayland, of Cork, there are at this moment twenty-four bands of war pipes in this island, and five pipers on an average being allowed to each band; we have a total of six score sets of Scotch pipes introduced into Ireland since the year 1898. On the other side, it will be said that of late years there has developed a fine liberal, international spirit. "One in name and in fame are the sea-divided Gaels; what is Irish is Scotch and what is Scotch is Irish." Very true, but it would be nearer the mark to say that what is Irish is Scotch and what is Scotch is Scotch. Have six score sets of Irish pipes been introduced into Scotland since 1898? Have six sets? If Herculean efforts are not made to stem the Scottish invasion, within twenty years an orator may stand up at the Rotunda and assure his hearers that the Irish bagpipe is lost—"utterly, irretrievably lost."

The Irish bagpipe, blown by means of bellows, and having a chanter which may be closed on the thigh, is an instrument unrivalled for playing the dance music of Ireland, and (in the hands of a capable performer) also unrivalled for playing old Irish airs. The few, very few, now living who heard the late Canon Goodman play a bagpipe obligato, to his own singing in Irish, will admit the force of this statement. But it takes years of hard practice to make a proficient player; much easier is it to don the kilt, and, with a repertoire of half a' dozen tunes, to march as one of a band at the head of an admiring crowd.

In the summer of 1887, it was the good fortune of the writer to spend two hours with a genuine Irish piper, Martin Kenneavy, and the venue was Gibney's public house, Knockmaroon Hill, Phoenix Park. Kenneavy traveled in company with a most excellent dancer named Lynch. Where today in Ireland could such a piper and such a dancer be found? Instead we shall have, D. V., at Jones' Road on the 30th inst., a competition among twenty bands of pipers playing an inferior make of Scotch pipes, and, as usual, Mr. Rose of Pitlochrie is billed to adjudicate.

It may be well to insert here a few remarks made by Dr. Duncan Fraser, an enthusiastic admirer of the Scotch pipes. This gentleman says that the big or bass drone is no improvement for practising purposes; that he himself falls back in holiday time on the two-drone pipe, because it is easier to play and easier to dance to; that to modernize the instrument would mean its decay; that the great Highland pipe is the proper accompaniment on the battle field, and was never intended as an accompaniment to song. Further, that no one would dispute Murray's assertion that the bagpipe is unfitted as an accompaniment to the human voice; and the doctor thus winds up: "It is only in the drawing room instrument like the bellows pipe of England and France that you can look for and expect to find in the bagpipe a fitting accompaniment to the human voice." And the drawing room instrument we are at the present moment endeavoring to annihilate!

If Ireland's normal condition were one of warfare, if our climate consisted of perpetual summer, and there were no long, dreary, winter evenings, one could understand the disposition to get rid of the in-door, in favor of the out-door instrument. But here we are, as it is hoped, on the threshold of a peaceful adjustment of the difficulty between the two countries. Home Rule here, Home Rule there. The vicissitudes of the seasons will not be much changed, and the fine old Irish bagpipe, the outcome of years of study and elaboration, must go down before the kilt and a hybrid Scotch pipe first used in the British army!

A SATANIC PIPER

A curious tradition prevalent in a little village in Somersetshire, England, respecting the origin of four groups of stones which formed when complete two circles, serves to remind us that Ireland and the Scottish Highlands had no monopoly of legendary tales in which pipers were the leading characters.

Many hundred years ago on a Saturday evening (so the story runs) a newly married couple, with their relatives and friends, met on the spot now covered by those ruins to celebrate their nuptials. Here they feasted and danced right merrily until the bell in the church tower tolled the hour of midnight, when the piper—a pious man—refused to play any longer. This was much against the inclinations of the guests, and so exasperated the bride, who was fond of dancing, that she swore an oath that she would not be balked of her enjoyment by a beggarly piper, but would find a substitute if she went to the lower regions to get one.

She had scarcely uttered the words when a venerable old man with a long beard made his appearance, and having listened to their request, proffered his services, which were gladly accepted.

The suave old gentleman, who was no other than the arch-fiend himself, took the seat vacated by the godly piper, buckled on his burnished instrument, and commenced playing a slow and solemn air. This wasn't the music his audience wanted—far from it—and they were by no means timid about telling him so. Accordingly he changed the tune into one more lively and rapid.

The company now began to dance, but soon found themselves whirling round the demon piper so fast and furiously that they were more than anxious to rest. But when they attempted to retire they found to their consternation that they were revolving with increased velocity round their diabolical musician, who had resumed his original shape. Their cries for mercy were unheeded until the first glimmering of day warned the fiend that he must depart.

With such rapidity had they moved that the gay and sportive assembly were now reduced to a ghastly troop of skeletons. "I leave you," said the fiend, "a monument of my power and your wickedness to the end of time." He then promptly vanished. The villagers on rising in the morning found the meadows strewn with large pieces of stone and the pious piper lying under a hedge, half dead with fright, having been a witness to the whole transaction.

Similar legends are also in existence in various other parts of Britain, particularly in the west of Cornwall.

FAIRY TUNES

In days of old the fairies were ever busy with the musicians, even the most humble.

Mr. Patrick Whelan, of Scarawalsh, County Wexford, who is an Admirable Crichton in his way—tells of a jocular old wood ranger he knew in his school days who had a large stock of popular tunes which he used to jig and play upon a jewsharp he always carried with him. Among them was one he claimed to have received from some supernatural agency. It came about as follows:

In consideration of his services as estate bailiff he enjoyed free of rent a small farm, the dwelling being situated on the brow of a hill overlooking a lonely valley. As he was retiring one fine calm night about eleven o'clock, the mellow tones of a flute were wafted on the summer air through the open window upon his delighted ear. At first he thought his sense of hearing was at fault, but on coming closer to the opening to listen all doubt disappeared, for sure enough there was "music in the glen" and no mistake. What struck him most was, the tune—a fine lively Irish jig played in dancing time—was a stranger to him, and he was quite certain he had not heard it anywhere before. The strains were well sustained as he listened in rapt attention intent on memorizing it. But who would be playing a flute so late at night in a lonesome glen so far from any human habitation except his own? Were the fairies holding revel and "dancing on the green," a not unlikely contingency, for after all was it not in the vicinity of three raths and the giant's grave, all upon Mrs. Walsh's farm, just across the big river and opposite his own door? Determined to solve the mystery he stepped out into the open fields and proceeded quietly in the direction from whence the music proceeded. Like the rainbow, the mysterious musician eluded him. Gradually it seemed to the wood ranger the music pervaded the atmosphere indefinitely. Brave as he was, his nerves failed him in this instance, so he concluded there was "no place like home" after all. No sooner had he determined on retracing his steps, and before he had time to turn around, the spirit musician to his consternation had apparently taken up his position right behind him. As the perplexed bailiff advanced on his way homeward the fairy fluter preceded him with unflagging persistence, and playing with seemingly increased vigor, as if to embarrass his progress. The "turn of the night" fortunately brought immediate relief, for on the first clarion crow of the crested cock on the roost, as he approached the house, the music ceased with startling abruptness, and he entered his home almost in a state of collapse.

To his dying day the woodranger vouched for the truth of this story in all its mystifying details, and in corroboration of his claims, pointed to the fact that none of the local musicians knew the tune, neither had "Jemmy" Sinnott, the famous fiddler, ever before heard it, so where else could it have come from if not from the faries?

The King of Oude, an Admirer of Irish Music

Among the most liberal contributors to the fund raised in 1819 by the Marquis of Hastings and other distinguished Irishmen in India, for the maintenance of the Belfast Harp Society, was the King of Oude, who desired that an Irish harper and piper be sent for to be attached to his court.

At that time Arthur O'Neill was advanced in years, and no other harper who was sufficiently artistic to uphold the credit of the country could be found except O'Neill's pupil, V. Rainey, and he was much needed at home.

A capable piper whose name is not recorded was sent his majesty however, but his reception at Calcutta was so lavishly hospitable, and he took so kindly to arrack, the native liquor, that while playing "O'Carolan's Receipt" on the state barge the king had sent to convey him up the river Hoogly, he fell overboard and was drowned.

The Poor Old Fiddler

One beautiful summer day there was a great festival in the large park at Vienna. This park is called by the people the Prater. It was almost covered by the crowds of people. Among the number was an old musician. He had once been a soldier, but his pension was not enough to live on. He had a good, faithful dog along with him which lay at his feet and held an old hat in his mouth, so that passers-by might cast coins in it for the poor old man.

On the day of the festival which has been mentioned, the dog sat before him, with the old hat. Many people went by and heard the old musician playing, but they didn't throw much in. He looked sad enough as he saw the multitudes pass in their strength and youth and beauty, but whenever they laughed it was like a dagger to his soul, for he knew on that very evening he would have to go to bed supperless, hungry as he was, and lie on a straw couch in a little garret room. He placed his old violin by his side, and leaned against an old tree. Not far off stood a gentleman in fine clothes who had a kind heart. He listened to the old musician, and when he saw that no one gave him anything, his heart was touched with sympathy. He finally went to the dog, and looking into the hat saw only two little copper coins in it. He then said to the old musician:

"My good friend, why don't you play longer?"

"Oh," replied the old man, "my dear sir, I cannot; my poor arm is so tired that I cannot hold the bow; beside, I have had no dinner, and have little prospect of supper."

The kind gentleman gave him a piece of gold, and said:

"I'll pay you if you will loan me your violin for one hour."

"Very well; you can do what you will," said the owner.

The gentleman took the fiddle and bow, and said to the old man: "Now, my mate, you take the money and I will play. I am quite sure people will give us something." The strange gentleman began to play, and every note was like a pearl. By and by the people began to drop money into the hat, and it soon became so heavy that he could not hold it any longer.

"Empty your hat, old man," said the people, "and we will fill it again for you."

He pulled out an old handkerchief and wrapped the money in it, and put it in his violin bag.

The stranger kept on playing, first one tune and then another—even children seemed carried away with rapture. At last he played that splendid song, "God Bless the Emperor Francis!" All hats and caps flew off their heads, for the people loved their emperor. The song finally came to an end. The hour was ended, and the musician handed back the violin to the old man.

"Thank you," said he. "May God bless you!" and he disappeared in the crowd.

"Who is he? Who is he?" said the people. "Where does he come from?"

A certain person sitting in one of the coaches said:

"I know him. It is Alexander Boucher, the distinguished violinist. It is just like him. He saw that old man needed help, and he determined to help him in the best way he could."

The people then gave three cheers for Boucher, and put more money in the old man's hat. When he went home that evening he was richer than he had ever been before.

Mark Twain on the Accordeon

Mark was, as many other young men are at some period of their lives, anxious to learn music. He tried first one instrument, then another, till finally he settled down to the accordeon. On that soul-stirring article of music he learnt to play that melodious and popular air, "Auld Lang Syne." For about a week he continued to torture his unwilling hearers, when, being of an ingenious turn of mind, he endeavored to improve upon the original melody by adding some variations of his own. But who has ever seen a real genius succeed yet? Just as Mark had finished his only tune, and wound up with an admirable flourish, the landlady rushed into his room. Said she:

"Do you know any other tune but that, Mr. Twain?" I told her meekly that I did not. "Well, then," said she, "stick to it just as it is; don't put any variations in it; because it is rough enough on the boarders the way it is now."

The upshot was, that its "roughness" was soon made manifest, for half the boarders left, and the other half would have left had not the landlady discharged Mark. Then, like the wandering Jew, Mr. Twain went from house to house.

None would undertake to keep him after one night's music; so, at last, in sheer desperation, he went to board at an Italian lady's—Mrs. Murphy by name. He says:

"The first time I struck up the variations, a haggard, care-worn, cadaverous old man walked into my room and stood beaming upon me a smile of ineffable happiness. Then he placed his hand upon my head, and looking devoutly aloft, he said with feeling unction: 'God bless you, young man! God bless you! for you have done that for me which is beyond all praise. For years I have suffered from an incurable disease, and knowing my doom was sealed, and that I must die, I have striven with all my power to resign myself to my fate, but in vain—the love of life was too strong within me. But heaven bless you, my benefactor! for since I heard you play that tune and those variations, I do not want to live any longer—I am entirely resigned—I am willing to die—in fact, I am anxious to die.' And then the old man fell upon my neck and wept a flood of happy tears. I was surprised at these things, but I could not help giving the old gentleman a parting blast, in the way of some peculiarly lacerating variations, as he went out of the door. They doubled him up like a jack-knife, and the next time he left his bed of pain and suffering, he was all right, in a metallic coffin."

At last Mark gave up his penchant for the accordeon, and from that day gave amateur musicians a wide berth.

PLAYING THE PIANO

The poet of the *Breakfast Table* gives this vivid description of the manner in which a girl of the period makes ready to play and plays her grand piano: "It was a young woman, with as many white muslin flounces round her as the planet Saturn has rings, that did it. She gave the music-stool a twirl or two and fluffed down on it like a whirl of soapsuds in a hand basin. Then she pushed up her cuffs as if she was going to fight for the champion's belt. Then she worked her wrists and her hands, to limber 'em, I suppose, and spread out her fingers till they looked as though they would pretty much cover the key-board, from the growling end to the little squeaky one. Then those two hands of hers made a jump at the keys as if they were a couple of tigers coming down on a flock of black and white sheep, and the piano gave a great howl as though its tail had been trod on. Dead stop—so still you could hear your hair growing. Then another jump, and another howl, as if the piano had two tails and you had trod on both of 'em at once, and a grand clatter and scramble and strings of jumps, up and down, back and forward, one hand over the other, like a stampede of rats and mice more than like anything I call music."

THE NEW WOMAN

She warbled the soprano with dramatic sensibility
    And dallied with the organ when the organist was sick;
She got up for variety a brand-new church society
    And spoke with great facility about the new church brick.

She shed great tears of sorrow for the heathen immorality,
    And organized a system that would open up their eyes;
In culinary charity she won great popularity
    And showed her personality in lecturing on pies.

For real unvarnished culture she betrayed a great propensity;
  Her Tuesday talks were famous and her Friday glimmers great;
She grasped at electricity with mental elasticity
  And lectured with intensity about the marriage state.

But with the calm assurance of her wonderful capacity,
  She wouldn't wash the dishes, but she'd talk all day on rocks;
And while she dwelt on density or space and its immensity
  With such refined audacity, her mother darned the socks!
                                                    —*Spare Moments.*

To a Piano

Oh, friend whom glad or grave we seek—
  Heaven-holding shrine!
I ope thee, touch thee, hear thee speak,
  And peace is mine.
No fairy casket full of bliss
  Out values thee;
Love only wakened with a kiss
  More sweet than thee.

To thee when our full hearts o'erflow
  In griefs or joys,
Unspeakable emotions owe
  A fitting voice.
Mirth flies to thee, and love's unrest,
  And memory dear,
And sorrow with his tightened breast,
  Comes for a tear.

The Whistler

Let fretful souls proclaim him "pest,"
  His simple minstrelsy decry;
Yet in his note, though ill-expressed,
  Sings some deep-toned melody.

Dreaming his dream, his thoughts afar,
  Are not on spoils or treason bent;
His peace no threats of vengeance mar,
  He chirps a lay of sweet content.

Hail, warbler! pipe your wordless song!
  Mauger its lack of finished art;
His lips are mute who plots to wrong—
  No evil passions vex your heart.

CHAPTER XXXIII

IRISH REVIVALS

WHAT hope and cheer and pleasurable anticipations does not the glorious word Revival inspire in the breasts of all whose hearts beat true and loyal to the traditions and aspirations of their race.

But, after all, when we come to reflect on its significance dispassionately, the disquieting thought obtrudes on our consciousness that an Irish Revival is but the antidote which patriotic optimists administer periodically to the body politic to check the progress of national decadence.

The story of the Harp Revival Meetings held at Granard, County Longford, in the years 1781, 1782, and 1783, instituted and financed by the patriotic James Dungan, a former townsman engaged in commerce at Copenhagen, has been told in a former work—*Irish Folk Music: A Fascinating Hobby.* Private jealousies among the harpers themselves, and the unendurable truculence of their friends so disheartened the generous exiled Dungan, who came all the way from Denmark to attend the third annual meeting, that he did not attempt thereafter a renewal of those interesting assemblies.

The spirit of revival did not long remain dormant, however, for in 1791 a movement was launched by some influential, music-loving residents of Belfast with the same object in view. The circular which they issued inviting subscriptions pathetically announces that: "They are solicitous to preserve from oblivion the few fragments which have been permitted to remain as monuments of the refined taste and genius of their ancestors." The call met with favor and liberal response. Ten harpers attended, prizes were awarded, and all competitors were lavishly entertained by Dr. McDonnell, the prime mover in the Belfast Harp Festival, which took place in July, 1792.

The Belfast meeting was momentous, not so much in what it effected towards the revival of harp music, as in what was accomplished during the opportunity presented for the preservation of the ancient melodies of the nation. Edward Bunting, the talented young musician, who took down in musical notation the airs played by the harpers assembled on that occasion, laid the foundation on which Moore's epoch-making *Irish Melodies* and many subsequent works were based.

The Harp School established by the Belfast Harp Society in 1807 fell far short of realizing the expectations of its promoters, though conducted by the celebrated Arthur O'Neill; and still less were the results of consequence achieved by the Dublin Harp Society, originated and subsidized by the generous John Bernard Trotter about the same time.

Patriotic desires, though seemingly dead, are but smoldering, and sometimes burst into flame unexpectedly. Liberal contributions from a coterie of Irish noblemen in India, galvanized the moribund Belfast Harp Society into renewed activity in 1819, and it continued in existence as long as the funds lasted, which was nearly a score of years.

The final stand against obliteration was made at Drogheda in 1842. The patriotic zeal of a Dominican priest, Rev. T. V. Burke, of that ancient city, originated a new Harp Society that maintained with varying success a school for harp students, which flickered out after an existence of but little more than five years. It had at one time a class of sixteen pupils, and at its first concert, held in 1844, seven harpers, mostly blind, played together.

Commenting on this and other organized efforts for the preservation of harp music, Kohl, the German scholar, who toured Ireland in 1844, says: "The supposition that the old national art of the bards was really reviving again might be very erroneous, for such sudden and artificial revivals of obsolete customs and amusements are seldom lasting, and are more often only the momentary flickerings of the flame before its utter extinction, then the real indications of reviving health." Prophetic words. All of which goes to show that Revival movements in every age, though born of the highest motives, and conducted with zeal and unselfishness, have but slight prospects of success when obliged to contend with public lethargy.

The same chronic apathy rendered ineffective the sporadic attempts of reviving an interest in Irish literature. For instance, the incomparable *Dublin Penny Journal,* for a time edited by the illustrious George Petrie, survived but a brief four years—June 20, 1832, to June 25, 1836.

A second venture, *The Irish Penny Journal,* whose first number appeared July 4, 1840, fared even worse, for its publication was discontinued after June 26, 1841. The reasons assigned for its short life by the editor, Philip Dixon Hardy, are plainly stated in his valedictory, of which the following is an extract: "However humbling it may be to the national feeling of most of our Irish readers, the fact must be acknowledged that the sale of the *Journal* in London alone has exceeded that in the four provinces of Ireland, not including Dublin; and that in other cities on the other side of the Channel it has been nearly equal to half the Irish provincial sale." Comment is unnecessary.

Another bid for patronage was submitted to the people in 1861 by James Duffy, the Dublin publisher. *The Illustrated Dublin Journal, A Miscellany of Amusement and Popular Information by the Most Eminent Writers,* breathed its last eight months and ten days after its birth!

How pertinent today is the remark of Philip Dixon Hardy in 1836, when editor of *The Dublin Penny Journal:* "That there is very considerable talent in the country there is no doubt; what we want is a little more patronage and public spirit."

Yes; the Irish have talent. They also have a reputation for generosity and liberality excelled by none, yet, strange to say, a deep-rooted aversion to spending money on music or literature, especially their own, is one of the incongruities of their character.

Need it be said that a demand will create the supply. That fact is no more evident than the certainty that a supply for which there is neither demand nor appreciation will disappear.

Contrast the unenviable condition of the impecunious minstrels and musicians of the nineteenth century, most of them wandering about the country dependent on the generosity of a people struggling for a livelihood themselves, with the status of the bards—historians, poets, and harpers—of more ancient days, who had estates settled on them, so that they might not be disturbed by cares or worldly troubles in the practice of their professions. What's the answer? Appreciation and patronage.

Had the intention been to obliterate Irish music in the nineteenth century, no more successful means could have been devised. It would seem as if the seventh of Buddha's commandments, "Thou shalt not dance, sing, or play music, or see it done," had been added to the Decalogue. Yet had the proponents foreseen the results which to a certain extent may be traced to the arbitrary suppression of the time-honored customs and amusements of the people, and which the Gaelic League is now attempting to revive, it is highly improbable that they would resort to such drastic measures to correct a minor evil, if indeed anything connected with peasant pastimes can be viewed with serious concern.

The ravages of persecution and famine could have been repaired in time, had music and national customs been fostered instead of proscribed. Were it necessary or politic at this late day to discuss in extenso this delicate feature of the subject, testimony in abundance is at hand to sustain an affirmative argument. The sole purpose of adverting to it at all is to express the conviction that should the same hostile influences continue to exert their sway, the most persistent efforts of Irish Revivalists will be labor in vain.

Much as traditional Irish musicians affect to deplore the musical degeneracy of the day, few of the fraternity can be held blameless in the premises. Often the victims of misdirected hospitality, pipers and fiddlers were more sinned against than sinning, but who can cure or endure their professional egotism and jealousies?

"Generally speaking, musicians are the most intolerant of men to one another, the most captious, the best humored when flattered, and the worst tempered at all other times," according to Madden, author of *The Infirmities of Genius*. It does not appear that their idiosyncrasies have changed appreciably since the above was printed in 1833. "Musicians live happy lives, enjoying their own music and criticising that of others," writes a late reviewer, "and they are easily tolerated, except when they have temperament; and temperament, in plain English, means artistic swelled head."

To revive a lost art is a task of extreme difficulty, and as far as musical instruments are concerned, we know of but one successful instance in modern times. The Balalaika, a three-stringed instrument of the guitar family, having a triangular body, prohibited in Russia since the introduction of Christianity in the eleventh century, has been restored to use and popularity by the individual efforts of M. W. W. Andreeff. After twenty years of study and labor, and the expenditure of his fortune, he had the satisfaction of seeing Balalaika Orchestras established throughout the Russian Empire, and his successful American tour in 1911 was the crowning glory of his career.

The restoration of the mellow-toned Irish Union pipes involves no such difficulties as confronted the Russian Revivalist, for he had neither instruments nor performers to begin with, while the Irish have both.

The present Revival gives much more promise of success than its predecessors, for the movement is national and less specialized in its scope.

Accepting the decree that the piano has permanently supplanted the harp in popular favor, the promoters have wisely directed their energies in other channels. The tendency to revert to the use of the obsolete and primitive warpipes can hardly be regarded as a step in the right direction. Whatever advantages it may possess as an outdoor or military instrument, is more than offset by its impossibility elsewhere, and the fact that but little Irish music worth while can be performed on an instrument of such limited compass.

An able correspondent from Dublin writes, "The Gaelic League, with its adjuncts, 'Feis' and 'Oireachtas,' ostensibly started with the object of reviving Irish music. If I am not much mistaken, that organization is destined to give the deathblow to the sweet-toned or Irish pipes. When very young I learned that

Frank O'Coffey.
Warpiper in Costume

there was no royal road to Euclid, but there seems to be a royal road to Irish piping. A fellow has only got to get a set of warpipes, hang a kilt around his middle, and throw a bedgown over his shoulders, and he becomes an Irish piper. For this very undesirable consummation may be held responsible three visionaries ranging from Belfast to Cork, with I am sure the best intentions, but still visionaries. The great distinction between the Irish, and the Scotch or warpipes, is that one is a musical instrument and the other is not."

The old race of Union pipers is fast passing away, and lamentably few are they who aspire to succeed them. The warpipe craze apparently has not yet reached its zenith, but if its popularity is to stand the test of time, its music and system of execution must be standardized like the Scotch, and not left to individual whim or capacity. This can best be done by the engagement of competent Scotch instructors who, as a result of the accumulated skill of generations, have attained the acme of execution and efficiency on their picturesque instrument.

The present writer's selection as judge of the pipers' competition at the annual picnic of the United Scottish Societies of Chicago for many successive years, and on other occasions, will, we trust, be accepted as credentials sufficient to justify our unsolicited intrusion. And, by the way, the moment seems opportune to mention that seven Highland pipers—one a young lady in tartans— obligingly came forward to add to the attractions of the "Feis" instituted by Donal O'Connor in August, 1912, at Gaelic Park, Chicago. Furthermore, their splendid performance and their cheerful acceptance of the judicial decision, even though the prizes were awarded to non-residents, when contrasted with the perverseness and truculence of others, made a deep impression on the vast assemblage.

As to those of the rising generation upon whom rest our hopes for the future of national Irish music, little can be said so early in their career. Brief sketches of the most prominent brought to light by the Irish Revival will be found in our pages.

Among the scattered children of the Gael the number seriously interested in the study of Irish music is insignificant. The Irish Music Club of Chicago, once so prosperous, is no longer in existence. A similar organization in Boston can scarcely be said to realize the expectations of its promoters, and a so-called Irish Pipers' Club of San Francisco was disbanded suddenly by the earthquake. Dissensions and jealousies are still doing their deadly work as of yore, but the Revival spirit is by no means dead in Chicago.

Remnants of the Irish Music Club with their musical offspring have enjoyable meetings occasionally at private homes, and the world seems brighter.

> When whispering strains do softly steal
> With creeping passion through the heart,
> And when at every touch we feel
> Our pulses beat and bear a part.

Pipers, fiddlers, fluters, aye and light-fingered pianists, pass many pleasant evenings in this commendable way, and not one of them is dependent on music for a livelihood.

A few hours spent in such congenial company as "the trembling notes ascend the sky," delightful though they be, bring afresh to our memory Philip Dixon Hardy's words, uttered three-fourths of a century ago, concerning the abundance of Irish talent undeveloped for lack of patronage and public spirit.

When the concert is over we awake from our dream to be plunged in despair,

IRISH MUSIC CLUB, CHICAGO.

Father W. K Dollard.   Ed. Cronin.   Rogers F O'Neill.   Francis O'Neill   Timothy Dillon.   John McFadden.   Michael Kissane.   James Kennedy.
John McElligott.   M G. Enright.   John Duffy   John Ennis.   Chas. O'Gallagher.   Wm. McCormick   Michael Dunlap.   Thos. Dunphy.   Father J. K. Feilding
John Conners.   Barney Delaney.   John K. Beatty.   Tom Ennis   James Early   James Cahill.   Adam Tobin.
Garrett J. Stack.   James Kerwin.

479

like the despondent lover. Aside from the few who love it instinctively, and practice it for their own pleasure, there is all too little inducement to study Irish music.

A score of years ago pipers, fiddlers, and singers, filled a large part of every Irish programme, and they were invariably treated with due consideration; and it is more than likely they would be at least as much in evidence on Irish platforms in more recent times, were they satisfied with conventional compliments for their services. Irish music has come to be regarded as merely an accessory to the success of some money-making entertainment, independent of all appreciation of its ethical value.

Of course every one knows that musicians are born, not made, but we don't seem to realize that it takes about one thousand dollars' worth of music lessons to disclose the fact as a rule.

In new and growing communities, church extension absorbs not a little of the energies of the Irish race, and the majority of their organizations also have religious affiliations. Consequently their entertainments, with few exceptions, are gotten up in the interest of charity or church building, hence paid talent is not in favor. Pleasure clubs engage bands or orchestras to play at their balls because nothing but the latest in steps and music will satisfy the members, and if an Irish tune is played at all, it is a hackneyed one included in a set of quadrilles.

Where then is the Irish musician to obtain patronage? If neglected by our own people, what can we reasonably expect from others?

The most accomplished Irish musician must inevitably drop out of sight, unless willing to respond to calls in any part of the city to "play a few tunes" without expectation of fee or reward, other than applause and good wishes.

Under such circumstances, of which we have many instances in mind, what motive except pure love of it can those musically inclined have, to spend time and money in learning to play Irish music from which they can seldom hope to derive any pecuniary advantage.

It can not be said that the Irish no longer possess the talent for music so pronounced in former centuries, for the most conspicuous in the art in the British Kingdom are of that race, and who more renowned in his line in America than Patrick Sarsfield Gilmore, the leader and bandmaster? In our own day Victor Herbert is nobly sustaining the traditions of his forefathers.

While discussing this branch of the subject, we feel justified in mentioning that the best in what may be regarded as American folk music is the product of Irish brains. "Dixie's Land," the national air of the Confederates, was composed to order in 1859 for Bryant's Minstrels by Dan D. Emmett, and such classics as "The Old Folks at Home," or "The Suwanee River," "My Old Kentucky Home," "Old Black Joe," and dozens of others, were the productions of Stephen Collins Foster.

According to a recent writer in a musical magazine, Irish melody is the invaluable or necessary material for the conscious and cultured artist to work upon, for he finds in it some of the very soul of his native land, the very throbs of the hearts of his people. It is the basis of new life for effete and wornout schools of art-music.

Regarded with indifference by the nation which should cherish it as a precious heritage, the beauties of Irish music have attracted the cupidity of a host of composers in this generation, who find it prolific in melodic themes. Perhaps, if subjected to the treatment accorded the bard Cherylus, accompanying Alexander the Great in his campaigns, who received a piece of gold for every good verse and a

Irish Pipers' Club
San Francisco

Top Row, Left to Right.
Owen Maguire   Patrick O'Malley,   W. P. Dorsey
Middle Row.
Joseph Kelly,   George Mulraney,   James Barry,   William Maguire,
Patrick Ratigan,   Percy Lonergan
Lower Row.
Patrick Madden, Thos. Maguire, P.E. McCormack, Wm. McMahan, Jas. Smith.

481

blow for every bad one, composers would be more cautious in their scramble for popularity in modern days.

We may as well be honest with ourselves and give up the delusion that much of value can be accomplished without united effort and personal sacrifice. Commercialism of the day has apparently stunted the nobler impulses of our natures, as far as music is concerned. Instead of securing the best talent available for Irish gatherings, committees on entertainments not infrequently engage the lowest bidder (which of course means the poorest performer) if free service can not be obtained. Quite obviously the result is not calculated to advance the interests of Irish music. Neither is the practice of staging on public platforms the merest amateurs to gratify the vanity of parents and friends. Such puerile exhibitions more often excite pity than admiration; besides it must be remembered that nothing short of excellence will inspire emulation and imitation.

If Irish music is to regain its lost prestige—and its fruition is not beyond the range of possibilities—the attitude of chronic apathy must come speedily to an end. Something more effective than holiday oratory, glorifying "our music, our language, and our literature" in set phrases and ready-made monotonous resolutions, is essential and imperative.

The verbosity and vapidity of some speakers at Irish gatherings remind us of:

> The statesman who throws his shoulders back and straightens out his tie,
> And says, "My friends, unless it rains it surely will be dry";
> And when the thought into our brains has percolated through,
> We simple people nod our heads, and loudly cry "How true!"

Puritanism is not in the Irish blood, neither will it thrive in an Irish atmosphere even under coercive measures. "Let us be ourselves," as the distinguished Dr. Petrie said to the people of Galway. Difficulties will disappear, and the problem will solve itself when we make the study of Irish music worth while, and that will be when we show our appreciation by paying for it liberally on all occasions. The demand will create the supply as with other commodities. If the laborer is worthy of his hire, as the Scripture says, why make an exception of the Irish musician? When the Irish people, lay and clerical, abandon the conventional custom of imposing on the generosity of musicians of their race and creed, and treat them with the consideration and liberality so characteristic of their ancestors, as recorded in history; then, and not till then, will the long-hoped-for Revival of Irish music become a living, lasting reality.

It must be admitted that of late years music is not a profitable profession, except to the few possessed of exceptional talents. The following poem by Wallace Whitlock, though written in a humorous vein, voices a recognized truth, which all lovers of music must deplore:

Play for Pay

> The eldest was John; he elected
>   To play the trombone in the band.
> He said it had been much neglected,
>   And this would enhance the demand.

IRISH CAILINI   GAELIC REVIVAL

Mazie McCarthy,   May McCarthy,
PRIZE DANCER, PIPER   UNION PIPER.
AND DRUMMER.
Alice Dunne,
PRIZE DANCER.

So John learned the trombone and started
  A worthy position to seek—
The last that was heard of his case 'twas averred
  He was earning eight dollars a week.

The second was Joe; he predicted
  The bassoon would come to its own.
So Joe his poor family afflicted
  With horrible sounds like a groan.
Then off for the West he departed,
  To show to the world his technique—
He wrote from Seattle: "They treat us like cattle:
  I'm getting six dollars a week!"

The third son was Frank; he debated
  The pros and the cons quite a while,
But chose the oboe, much elated,
  And learned, too, to play in fine style.
Then, eager for fame and for fortune,
  Forth fared he, with high mantling cheek—
This word came from Bangor: "Pray, pardon my anger,
  I'm making five dollars a week!"

The last son was Tom; though the latest
  To make his appearance on earth,
Of all he was most up-to-datest,
  And showed, too, he knew his own worth.
"No trombones or bassoons or oboes!"
  He thundered, "Away with them all!"
And Tom now makes yearly ten thousand or nearly,
  For he is the one who *PLAYS BALL*.

CONCLUSION

While discussing a business proposition with the manager of the largest publishing house in Chicago a few years ago, he inquired if the subject intended for publication was treated from the viewpoint of an enthusiast, or an unprejudiced writer, and whether the work was of general interest, or appealed only to a limited class. When informed that the author was an enthusiast, and that but few except those of the Irish race would be particularly interested in the theme, he discouraged the undertaking on the ground that the Irish were by no means liberal patrons of literature.

Undismayed by the fact that experience has vindicated the wisdom of the manager's judgment, some impulse akin to instinct impelled the present writer to persist even though his prolixity tends to invite the shafts of censure, from which so few concerned in Irish musical matters have been exempt, however painstaking and conscientious their efforts. And criticism, by the way, cannot always be relied on as an evidence of superior knowledge on the part of the critic, as the following instance will show:

A very youthful and entirely unknown composer read some verses by the renowned Tom Moore which he liked very much. Forthwith the buzz of inspira-

LAY OF THE LAST MINSTREL

tion circulated through his brain, and the next thing he knew he had evolved a tune which went right prettily with the words of the Irish poet. Much elated, the young composer took the product of his muse to a publisher of popular songs and sang it to him. The latter shook his head and oracularly declared: "The music is all right, but the words are bum!"

Although the beauties of Irish melody were made known to the world by the genius of Moore, he has been a target for fault-finders to the present day. Bunting abuses both Moore and Stevenson for tampering with the ancient melodies. Petrie, a personal friend, scarifies Bunting, and is himself in turn, with Walker and Dr. Ledwich, called to account for certain shortcomings by his old associate, Prof. Eugene O'Curry, while Sullivan condemns the whole lot, or damns them with faint praise.

In an article which appeared in *The Weekly Freeman* of March 11, 1911, Grattan Flood says: "It has been proved by many leading musicians that the settings of the Irish Melodies in Stanford's book are wilfully corrupt," yet Alfred Perceval Graves told his audience, in a lecture delivered at Alexandra College, March 12, 1912, that "they owed a great debt to Sir Charles Villiers Stanford for the exquisite way he had arranged those Irish airs and for giving them more beautiful harmonies than Stevenson clothed them with, and having to a large extent restored the native beauty from which they had been divested by Stevenson and Moore.

In the foregoing, enough has been said to afford food for thought, beneficial to those who are prone to be either captious or dogmatic in their conception of correct musical standards, for when such musical celebrities as the above mentioned disagree, who is competent to decide?

> " 'Tis with our judgments as our watches, none
> Go just alike, yet each believes his own."

The most devoted enthusiast in the Irish Revival propaganda has his days of despondency, when, wearied by years of unresponsive endeavor, like the fagged railway manager,

> "He wants to let go
> And drop the whole thing—
> The worries, the frets,
> The sorrows and sins—
> Just to let himself down
> On the bed or the ground—
> Anywhere, so it's down,
> And let himself go."

And, though there were times when a note of Irish music would thrill the writer's soul with the wild, earnest power of harmony and bring back the life to him if he had been dead a month, now he's as tired as the official quoted,

> "Who wants to forget,
> And don't want to think
> Of what's gone or is coming—
> Just to let down his nerves,
> Just to smooth out his brain,
> Just to rest. And that's all.
> Oh, he just wants to let go."

Yet when, in our tribulations, the paralysis of discouragement disposes us to seek relief in the allurements of retirement and the quiet life, free from care, annoyance, and disparagement, we may find some consolation in the reflection that,

If nobody's noticed you, you must be small;
If nobody's slighted you, you must be tall;
If nobody's bowed to you, you must be low;
If nobody's kissed you, you're ugly, we know.

If nobody's envied you, you're a poor elf;
If nobody's flattered you, you've flattered yourself;
If nobody's cheated you, you are a knave;
If nobody's hated you, you are a slave.

If nobody's called you a fool to your face,
Somebody's sneered to your back in its place;
If nobody's called you a tyrant or scold,
Somebody thinks you of spiritless mold.

If nobody knows of your faults but a friend,
Nobody will miss them at the world's end;
If nobody clings to your purse like a fawn,
Nobody'll run like a hound when it's gone.

If nobody's eaten his bread from your store,
Nobody'll call you a miserly bore;
If nobody's slandered you—here is our pen,
Sign yourself "Nobody," quick as you can.

FINIS

CONTENTS

489